YO-AAL-821

CALIFORNIA CRIMINAL DISCOVERY

FOURTH EDITION
2013 CUMULATIVE SUPPLEMENT

L. Douglas Pipes

William E. Gagen, Jr.

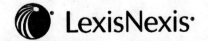

QUESTIONS ABOUT THIS PUBLICATION?

For questions about the **Editorial Content** appearing in these volumes or reprint permission, please call:

Deborah A. Rose at .... (800) 424-0651 ext. 3316
Email: .... deborah.rose2@lexisnexis.com
Jeffrey Canning, Esq. at .... (800) 526-4902 ext. 3341
Email: .... jeffrey.canning@lexisnexis.com

For assistance with replacement pages, shipments, billing or other customer service matters, please call:

Customer Services Department at .... (800) 833-9844
Outside the United States and Canada, please call .... (518) 487-3000
Fax Number .... (518) 487-3584
For information on other Matthew Bender publications, please call
Your account manager or .... (800) 223-1940
Outside the United States and Canada, please call .... (518) 487-3000

Library of Congress Card Number: 2007042868
ISBN: 978-1422-42122-2 (Print)
ISBN: 978-1-5791-1186-1 (eBook)

Cite as:

L. Douglas Pipes, William E. Gagen, Jr., California Criminal Discovery, Sec. No. (Matthew Bender)

Example:

L. Douglas Pipes, William E. Gagen, Jr., California Criminal Discovery, § 1:1 (Matthew Bender)

Editorial Offices
121 Chanlon Rd., New Providence, NJ 07974 (908) 464-6800
201 Mission St., San Francisco, CA 94105-1831 (415) 908-3200
www.lexisnexis.com

MATTHEW◆BENDER

(2013S-Pub.68615)

AUTHORS' PREFACE

In this supplement we discuss the statutory changes and appellate decisions affecting discovery in criminal cases in California state courts that have been published since we finished writing the Fourth Edition text in September of 2007. In some instances these appellate decisions add important new perspectives to the subject of discovery in criminal cases in California courts. Other decisions simply reinforce accepted discovery principles.

However, as in past supplements to the first three editions of this text, we have attempted to make this supplement to the Fourth Edition more than simply an updating of the subjects covered in the main text published in January of 2008. We have added to this supplement discussions of a number of topics which were not specifically addressed in the main text. We have chosen these new subjects based on our determination that they are among the most litigated current discovery questions. We recognize that these new subjects are the focus of contention, and that reasonable minds can differ over their resolution. While we make every effort to present a balanced analysis of these subjects, we feel that it is important for us to reach conclusions as to which point of view appears to present the better argument.

Accordingly, we take positions on these subjects in the hope that our legal analysis will stimulate constructive litigation and help produce sound appellate opinions. Our objective in expanding the scope of the text is to provide a more complete resource for judges and attorneys who must litigate and resolve discovery questions in criminal cases.

As a final note, in coordination with the publisher, we have followed the citation format we utilized in the main text of the Fourth Edition to more closely match the citation format used in California's courts. While Rule 3.1113(c) of the California Rules of Court requires citations to include only the official report volume, page number, and the year of decision, the citations in this text conform to the publisher's case citation format used in its other publications, in computer-assisted research, and in Auto-Cite.

January 2012

L. Douglas Pipes
William E. Gagen, Jr.

TABLE OF CONTENTS

CHAPTER 1	**CONSTITUTIONAL UNDERPINNINGS OF CRIMINAL DISCOVERY—*BRADY* EXCULPATORY EVIDENCE**

Table of Contents

Table of Contents

Table of Contents

Table of Contents

Table of Contents

Table of Contents

Table of Contents

Table of Contents

Table of Contents

Table of Contents

Table of Contents

CHAPTER 3   CRIMINAL DISCOVERY STATUTE—DISCLOSURE BY PROSECUTOR

Table of Contents

Table of Contents

CHAPTER 4   **CRIMINAL DISCOVERY STATUTE—RECIPROCAL DISCLOSURE BY DEFENDANT**

Table of Contents

Table of Contents

Table of Contents

Table of Contents

Table of Contents

CHAPTER 9   THIRD-PARTY DISCOVERY

Table of Contents

CHAPTER 10   PEACE OFFICER PERSONNEL RECORDS

Table of Contents

CHAPTER 1

CONSTITUTIONAL UNDERPINNINGS OF CRIMINAL DISCOVERY-*BRADY* EXCULPATORY EVIDENCE

PART I. OVERVIEW

§ 1:1   The *Brady* rule—in general

More recently, see *Henry v. Ryan* (2013, CA9 Ariz.) 720 F.3d 1073.

Note that Fed. R. Crim. P. 16 grants criminal defendants a broad right to discovery, requiring disclosure of all documents material to preparing the defense. Fed. R. Crim. P. 16(a)(1)(E)(i). Rule 16 is thus broader than the *Brady* decision. Information that is not exculpatory or impeaching may still be relevant to developing a possible defense. Even inculpatory evidence may be relevant. A defendant who knows that the government has evidence that renders his planned defense useless can alter his trial strategy. Or he can seek a plea agreement instead of going to trial. As the United States Supreme Court has noted, criminal justice today is for the most part a system of pleas, not a system of trials. *United States v. Muniz-Jaquez* (2013, CA9 Cal.) 718 F.3d 1180.

Further, California's criminal discovery statutes do not violate the Due Process Clause by failing to require the prosecutor to disclose all exculpatory evidence as mandated by the U.S. Supreme Court in *Brady v. Maryland*. The criminal discovery statutes cannot not violate due process because the new statutes do not affect the defendant's constitutional rights under *Brady*. The prosecutor's duties of disclosure under the Due Process Clause are wholly independent of any statutory scheme of reciprocal discovery. The due process requirements are self-executing and need no statutory support to be effective. The prosecutor is obligated to disclose such evidence voluntarily. No statute can limit the foregoing due process rights of criminal defendants, and the criminal discovery statutes do not attempt to do so. On the contrary, the criminal discovery statutes contemplates disclosure outside the statutory scheme pursuant to constitutional requirements as enunciated in *Brady*. *People v. Gutierrez* (2013) 214 Cal. App. 4th 343, 153 Cal. Rptr. 3d 832.

See also Jensen v. Hernandez (E.D. Cal. 2012) 864 F. Supp. 2d 869, holding, *inter alia*, that due process requires that the prosecution disclose exculpatory evidence within its possession. There are three components of a

Brady violation: the evidence at issue must be favorable to the accused, either because it is exculpatory, or because it is impeaching; the evidence must have been suppressed by the State, either willfully or inadvertently; and prejudice must have ensued. A failure to preserve evidence violates a defendant's right to due process if the unavailable evidence possessed exculpatory value that was apparent before the evidence was destroyed, and is of such a nature that the defendant would be unable to obtain comparable evidence by other reasonably available means. A defendant must also demonstrate that the police acted in bad faith in failing to preserve the potentially useful evidence. The presence or absence of bad faith turns on the government's knowledge of the apparent exculpatory value of the evidence at the time it was lost or destroyed. The mere failure to preserve evidence which could have been subjected to tests which might have exonerated the defendant does not constitute a due process violation.

To prove a *Brady* violation, a habeas petitioner must show (1) that the evidence at issue is favorable to him because it is exculpatory or impeaching; (2) that it was suppressed by the state, either willfully or inadvertently; and (3) that it was material. *Henry v. Ryan* (2013, CA9 Ariz.) 720 F.3d 1073. *See also United States v. Rodriguez* (June 24, 2013, CA9 Cal.) 2013 U.S. App. LEXIS 12918, holding, *inter alia*, in order to establish a *Brady* violation, a defendant must show: (1) that the information was favorable; (2) that the government suppressed it; and (3) prejudice. *See also Dinius v. Perdock* (N.D. Cal. May 24, 2012) 2012 U.S. Dist. LEXIS 72722.

A *Brady* claim fails due to a lack of government suppression where the government provides the defense with the means of obtaining exculpatory evidence. *United States v. Rodriguez* (June 24, 2013, CA9 Cal.) 2013 U.S. App. LEXIS 12918.

The "disclosure of *Brady* and *Jencks* Act material is not a suggestion, but a constitutional and statutory obligation." *United States v. Duval* (2007, CA1 MA) 496 F.3d 64, 73.

§ 1:1.1 The *Brady* rule and ABA Standards for Criminal Justice

Rule 3.8 of the ABA Model Rules of Professional Conduct provides that "[t]he prosecutor in a criminal case shall: . . . (d) make timely disclosure to the defense of all evidence or information known to the prosecutor that tends to negate the guilt of the accused or mitigates the offense." The ABA Standards impose a higher level of responsibility upon the prosecutor than is imposed by the Constitution as articulated in the *Brady* rule. *Johnson v. Bell* (2008, CA6 TN) 525 F.3d 466, 475, n.3.

Ethical standards such as the ABA Model Rules that impose standards upon the conduct of prosecutors provide that the prosecutor's duty to disclose material exculpatory evidence to the defense continues after trial. *In re Lawley* (2008) 42 Cal.4th 1231, 1246, 74 Cal.Rptr.3d 92, 179 P.3d 891.

The ABA Model Rules of Professional Conduct and the Model Code of

Professional Responsibility have "no legal force of their own," and have not been adopted in California. *General Dynamics Corp. v. Superior Court* (1994) 7 Cal.4th 1164, 1190, n.6, 32 Cal.Rptr.2d 1, 876 P.2d 487. Because they have not been adopted in California, and because they have no legal force of their own, the "ABA Model Rules of Professional Conduct . . . do not establish ethical standards in California . . . ." *State Comp. Ins. Fund v. WPS, Inc.* (1999) 70 Cal.App.4th 644, 655–656, 82 Cal.Rptr.2d 799.

With the approval of the California Supreme Court, the Board of Governors of the State Bar has the power to "formulate and enforce rules of professional conduct for all members of the bar in the State." Business and Professions Code section 6076. When approved by the Supreme Court, these Rules of Professional Conduct "are binding upon all members of the State Bar," and their willful breach can subject an attorney to discipline by the State Bar and the California Supreme Court. Business and Professions Code section 6077.

California has adopted Rules of Professional Conduct for attorneys. These rules "are intended not only to establish ethical standards for members of the bar [citation omitted], but are also designed to protect the public. [citations omitted]." *Ames v. State Bar* (1973) 8 Cal.3d 910, 917, 106 Cal.Rptr. 489, 506 P.2d 625.

A California attorney is subject to State Bar and Supreme Court discipline for a willful violation of the California Rules of Professional Conduct, the State Bar Act [Business and Professions Code section 6000 et *seq.*], and California judicial opinions. *In re Edward S.* (2009) 173 Cal.App.4th 387, 412, 92 Cal.Rptr.3d 725. In the absence of an applicable California Rule of Professional Conduct, California statute, or opinion of a California appellate court, a California attorney is not subject to discipline in California for violating an ABA Model Rule of Professional Conduct, an ABA ethical standard, or an ABA formal opinion. *State Comp. Ins. Fund v. WPS, Inc.* (1999) 70 Cal.App.4th 644, 656, 82 Cal.Rptr.2d 799.

The California Supreme Court has occasionally looked to the principles underlying the ABA counterparts to California's Rules of Professional Conduct. *Flatt v. Superior Court* (1994) 9 Cal.4th 275, 282, 36 Cal.Rptr.2d 537, 885 P.2d 950. *See People v. Gonzalez* (1990) 51 Cal.3d 1179, 1261, 275 Cal.Rptr. 729, 800 P.2d 1159, where the Supreme Court cited Rule 3.8(d) of the ABA Model Rules of Prof. Conduct; *People v. Garcia* (1993) 17 Cal.App.4th 1169, 1179, 22 Cal.Rptr.2d 545; and *Goldberg v. Warner/ Chappell Music, Inc.* (2005) 125 Cal.App.4th 752, 765, 23 Cal.Rptr.3d 116.

ABA standards do have an appropriate role in determining the ethical duties of California attorneys. The role of ABA standards is to provide guideposts to the application of California Rules of Professional Conduct. *Higdon v. Superior Court* (1991) 227 Cal.App.3d 1667, 1680, 278 Cal.Rptr. 588. Rule 1-100(A) of the California Rules of Professional Conduct expressly provides that "[e]thics opinions and rules and standards promulgated by other jurisdictions and bar associations may also be considered." Thus, where there is no conflict with the public policy of California, the ABA Model Rules of Professional Conduct can serve as a collateral source for guidance on proper professional conduct in California. *People v. Donaldson* (2001) 93 Cal.App.4th 916, 928, 113 Cal.Rptr.2d 548. State Bar Rules of Professional Conduct, in conjunction with American Bar Association's Standards, "provide guidelines for determining the prevailing norms of practice . . . ." *In re Alvernaz* (1992) 2 Cal.4th 924, 937, 8 Cal.Rptr.2d 713, 830 P.2d 747.

But it is ultimately the California Rules of Professional Conduct, California state statutes, and California judicial opinions that establish enforceable ethical standards for California attorneys.

See Sections 1:97–1:97.4 in this supplement for a complete discussion of prosecutors' ethical disclosure duties.

§ 1:1.2   The *Brady* rule and new-trial motion standards

The *Brady* standards are not identical with the standards a defendant must meet in order to obtain a new trial, even when the defendant moves for a new trial on the basis of one or more *Brady* violations. For a discussion of the difference between *Brady's* three components and the four elements of a successful new-trial motion, see *United States v. Connolly* (2007, CA1 MA) 504 F.3d 206, 212–213. Proof of a *Brady* violation does not automatically entitle a defendant to a new trial. 504 F.3d at 213.

The difference in the two standards—a new trial based upon newly discovered evidence and a new trial based upon a *Brady* violation—is that a "somewhat less formidable standard applies" to a new trial motion "premised on the belated disclosure of evidence that should have been made available to [the defendant] in accordance with the imperatives of *Brady*." The *Brady* standard for a new trial replaces two of the requirements of the standard for a new trial based on newly-discovered evidence. These two requirements are proof that the evidence is material and the evidence, if available upon retrial, would likely result in an acquittal. The *Brady* rule replaces these two requirements with a unitary requirement that the defendant prove that there is a reasonable probability that had the evidence been disclosed to the defendant, the result of the proceeding would have been different. *United States v. Mathur* (2010, CA1 MA) 624 F.3d 498, 503–504.

§ 1:1.3   The *Brady* rule and failure to investigate

The *Brady* rule does not impose a duty upon the prosecution to discover exculpatory information or evidence that is not in the possession of the prosecution team and of which the prosecution is not aware. *United States v. Heppner* (2008, CA8 MN) 519 F.3d 744, 750. Thus, neither the prosecutor nor the investigating agency commits a *Brady* violation by failing to investigate or failing to collect potentially exculpatory evidence or information. The government only has a *Brady* obligation to disclose exculpatory information in its "possession." *United States v. Venegas-Reynoso* (May 17, 2013, CA9 Ariz.) 2013 U.S. App. LEXIS 9954.

§ 1:2   Prosecutor's good or bad faith

A violation of the prosecutor's *Brady* duty to disclose material exculpatory evidence is not dependent upon bad faith by the prosecutor or any member of the "prosecution team." "It matters little whether the government suppresses the evidence out of oversight or guile." *United States v. White* (2007, CA6 OH) 492 F.3d 380, 409.

§ 1:4   Prosecutor as responsible party for *Brady* compliance

The prosecutor's role as the responsible party for *Brady* compliance is an important principle of the *Brady* rule.

"The government is primarily responsible for deciding what evidence it must disclose to the defendant under Brady. [citation omitted] And at least where a defendant has made only a general request for Brady material, the government's decision about disclosure is ordinarily final—unless it emerges later that exculpatory evidence was not disclosed." *United States v. Prochilo* (2011, CA1 MA) 629 F.3d 264, 268.

§ 1:4.1   Prosecutor—not the investigating agency

The government only has a *Brady* obligation to disclose exculpatory information in its "possession." *United States v. Venegas-Reynoso* (May 17, 2013, CA9 Ariz.) 2013 U.S. App. LEXIS 9954. *But see Gantt v. City of Los Angeles* (2013, CA9 Cal.) 717 F.3d 702, holding, *inter alia*, that the *Brady* requirement to disclose material exculpatory and impeachment evidence to the defense applies equally to prosecutors and officers.

In the face of efforts by some prosecutors to absolve themselves of responsible for failure of the government to disclose *Brady* evidence to criminal defendants, by claiming that the investigating officers had failed to disclose or provide that evidence to them, the courts remain firm that the prosecution's *Brady* duty rests squarely on the shoulders of the prosecuting attorney, and not the investigating agency or its officers. *Moldowan v. City of Warren* (2009, CA6 MI) 578 F.3d 351, 377 ["To the extent that *Brady* imposes an obligation on the state to disclose exculpatory evidence to the defense, courts consistently have determined that this duty falls squarely on the prosecutor, not the police."].

While acknowledging that investigating officers sometimes fail to inform the prosecutor of everything they know, "the Supreme Court has placed the responsibility to manage the state's disclosure obligations solely on the prosecutor . . . ." 578 F.3d at 377.

The prosecutor's duty to disclose material exculpatory evidence to a criminal defendant is a duty that is held by the "state or government as a whole . . . ." *Steidl v. Fermon* (2007, CA7 IL) 494 F.3d 623, 630;

Youngblood v. West Virginia (2006) 547 U.S. 867, 869–870, 126 S.Ct. 2188, 165 L.Ed.2d 269.

For this reason "a defendant may base a *Brady* claim on a government investigator's failure to disclose evidence material to guilt or punishment, even when the prosecutor personally did not know of that evidence." *United States v. Velarde* (2007, CA10 NM) 485 F.3d 553, 559. "*Brady's* protections also extend to actions of other law enforcement officers such as investigating officers." *White v. McKinley* (2008, CA8 MO) 514 F.3d 807, 815.

The prosecutor's *Brady* duty is to disclose material exculpatory evidence to the defendant and/or his or her attorney. The investigating officer's *Brady* duty is to disclose such evidence to the prosecutor. Law enforcement officers "must turn over potentially exculpatory evidence when they turn over investigative files to the prosecution." *Harris v. Kuba* (2007, CA7 IL) 486 F.3d 1010, 1014. Investigating officers "satisfy their obligations under *Brady* when they turn exculpatory and impeachment evidence over to the prosecutor . . . ." *McMillian v. Johnson* (1996, CA11 AL) 88 F.3d 1554, 1567; *Steidl v. Fermon*, 494 F.3d 623.

Accordingly, it appears that civil actions against investigating officers for failure to disclose material exculpatory evidence to prosecutors are becoming a more frequent consequence of *Brady* violations. The rationale for allowing such actions is that "[r]equiring culpable officers to pay damages to the victims of their actions, however, holds out promise of both deterring and remediating violations of the Constitution." *Newsome v. McCabe* (2001, CA7 IL) 256 F.3d 747, 752 [cited in Section 1:88.6.3 of the text]; *Harris v. Kuba*, 486 F.3d at 1014.

§ 1:4.1.1   Constitutional disclosure duty of investigating agency

Although the *Brady* duty is the exclusive province of the prosecutor, and the prosecutor may not delegate that responsibility to the investigating agency, the investigating officers play an important role in enabling the prosecutor to fulfill the prosecution's *Brady* obligations. The federal circuit courts generally agree that the investigating officers have a constitutionally based duty to disclose to the prosecuting attorney exculpatory evidence which they uncover or develop in their investigations, in order to enable the prosecutor to comply with *Brady* obligations.

See, e.g., Moldowan v. City of Warren (2009, CA6 MI) 578 F.3d 351, 377–378; *Brady v. Dill* (1999, CA1 MA) 187 F.3d 104, 114; *Walker v. City of New York* (1992, CA2 NY) 974 F.2d 293, 298; *Gibson v. Superintendent of N.J. Dep't of Law & Pub. Safety* (2005, CA3 NJ) 411 F.3d 427, 443; *Jean v. Collins* (2000, CA4 NC) 221 F.3d 656, 662, n.3; *Steidl v. Fermon* (2007, CA7 IL) 494 F.3d 623, 631; *Harris v. Kuba* (2007, CA7 IL) 486 F.3d 1010, 1014; *Tennison v. City and County of San Francisco* (2009, CA9 CA) 570 F.3d 1078, 1087; *McMillian v. Johnson* (1996, CA11 AL) 88 F.3d 1554, 1567.

In *Carvajal v. Dominguez* (2008, CA7 IL) 542 F.3d 561, the Seventh Circuit Court of Appeals summarized the constitutional disclosure duty of the investigating agency in these words: "While most commonly viewed as a prosecutor's duty to disclose to the defense, the duty extends to the police and requires that they similarly turn over exculpatory/impeaching evidence to the prosecutor, thereby triggering the prosecutor's disclosure obligation." 542 F.3d at 566.

In *Moldowan v. City of Warren* (2009, CA6 MI) 578 F.3d 351, the Sixth Circuit Court of Appeals engaged in a similar analysis. The Court held that "[b]ecause prosecutors rely so heavily on the police and other law enforcement authorities, the obligations imposed under *Brady* would be largely ineffective if those other members of the prosecution team had no responsibility to inform the prosecutor about evidence that undermined the state's preferred theory of the crime. As a practical matter then, *Brady's* ultimate concern for ensuring that criminal defendants receive a 'fundamentally fair' trial . . . demands that '*Brady's* protections also extend to actions of other law enforcement officers such as investigating officers.' [citation omitted]" 378 F.3d at 378. The Court concluded that the police "also are bound by the government's constitutional obligation to 'ensure that a miscarriage of justice does not occur.' [citation omitted]" 378 F.3d at 379.

For a more complete discussion of the parameters of the investigating officer's duty to disclose exculpatory evidence to the prosecutor, and the means by which an investigating officer might comply with this duty, see Sections 1:97 through 1:97.4 in this supplement.

§ 1:4.2 Prosecutor—not the courts

In *United States v. Dabney* (2007, CA7 IL) 498 F.3d 455, 459, the Seventh Circuit Court of Appeals rejected a defendant's argument on appeal that his rights under *Brady* were violated when the district court failed to further investigate complaints pending against testifying prosecution officer witnesses. The Court stated: "[T]he district court was under no independent duty to further probe or investigate the pending complaints against the officers that were identified by the government." In order to justify a judicial determination whether material possessed by the prosecution contains *Brady* evidence "the defendant must make some showing that the materials in question could contain favorable, material evidence. . . . [T]he defendant should be able to articulate with some specificity what evidence he hopes to find in the requested materials, why he thinks the materials contain this evidence, and finally, why this evidence would be both favorable to him and material." *United States v. Prochilo* (2011, CA1 MA) 629 F.3d 264, 268, 269.

However, when the court or the probation department, which is an arm of the court, is in possession of potentially exculpatory evidence, such as might be found in the pre-sentence report of a co-defendant, the court does have a *Brady*-type duty to examine that evidence in order to release material exculpatory or impeachment evidence contained therein to the defendant, even though "*Brady* does not apply in the traditional sense because the Government did not have possession of [the] exculpatory information that it should have disclosed to the defense." *United States v. Ogba* (2008, CA5 TX) 526 F.3d 214, 222, n.11.

For a discussion of the non-membership status of courts and probation offices in the prosecution team, see Sections 1:70.14 and 1:70.15 of the text and this supplement.

§ 1:4.3   Prosecutor—not the defendant's attorney

Because the responsibility for disclosing *Brady* evidence is the sole duty of the prosecutor, the defendant is not entitled to conduct an inspection of reports and records in the possession of the prosecution in an effort to find exculpatory evidence contained therein. "*Brady* did not create a broad rule of discovery in criminal cases." *United States v. Prochilo* (2011, CA1 MA) 629 F.3d 264, 269. A discovery order that shifts from the government to the defendant the primary authority to make an assessment whether evidence the government possesses must be disclosed under *Brady* unlawfully endorses a broad rule of discovery in criminal cases that is not authorized by *Brady*. *United States v. Prochilo, supra,* 629 F.3d at 270.

Nor is the defendant entitled to inspect confidential reports or records possessed by the court in order to search for exculpatory evidence. *People v. Martinez* (2009) 47 Cal.4th 399, 450, 97 Cal.Rptr.3d 732, 213 P.3d 77 [Defendant is not entitled to inspect the undisclosed portion of a juvenile file of the alleged victim to search for exculpatory or impeaching evidence]. Thus, "even at trial the defense is not entitled to review confidential documents to determine which are material for its purposes; rather, as occurred in the present case, it is the trial court's duty to review the documents and to determine which, if any, are material and should be disclosed." 47 Cal.4th at 453. "The court's function is to review the confidential records that the juvenile court declined to disclose, in order to determine whether they were material and should have been disclosed." 47 Cal.4th at 453.

The fact that the responsibility for disclosing *Brady* evidence belongs to the prosecutor means that the defendant's attorney may reasonably rely upon the prosecutor to disclose exculpatory evidence as required by *Brady*. *Christenson v. Ault* (2010, CA8 IA) 598 F.3d 990.

§ 1:5   Independence from discovery statutes

The prosecutor's *Brady* duties are independent of any requirements for disclosure of exculpatory evidence placed upon the prosecutor by a statute such as the Criminal Discovery Statute.

§ 1:5.1   Independence of *Brady* rule from prosecutor's ethical disclosure duties

A prosecutor can have ethical discovery obligations arising from the prosecutor's position as the attorney representing the government. These ethical discovery obligations are independent and separate from the *Brady* duty to ensure that a criminal defendant is not denied a fair trial by a failure to disclose material exculpatory evidence to that defendant.

Thus, in *United States v. Price* (2009, CA9 OR) 566 F.3d 900, the Ninth Circuit Court of Appeals explained that a prosecutor's duty to provide discovery to a criminal defendant is broader than the prosecutor's duty to disclose material exculpatory evidence under *Brady*.

An example of a possible ethical discovery obligation that is independent and different from the prosecutor's *Brady* duties is a prosecutor's postjudgment ethical duty to disclose exculpatory evidence that is discovered after the defendant has been sentenced and judgment imposed.

The importance of the distinction between a prosecutor's discovery duty that is constitutionally based and a discovery obligation that is part of the prosecutor's ethical duties lies in the potential consequences of a violation of the duty. Violation of a constitutionally based discovery duty—one that denies a defendant due process of law—exposes a judgment of conviction to being overturned. Violation of a prosecutor's ethical discovery duty does not necessarily have constitutional or case consequences, but the violation might expose the prosecutor to disciplinary action by the State Bar and the California Supreme Court.

For a more complete discussion and analysis of a prosecutor's postjudgment discovery duties, see Sections 1:94 and 1:94.1 in the text and this supplement.

See also Sections 1.7.1, 1:17.5, 1:97.1, and 1:97.3 of this supplement and their discussion of the question whether a prosecutor has an ethical duty to disclose that a material prosecution witness has died or is otherwise unable to testify at trial.

PART II. EVIDENCE REQUIREMENT

§ 1:7 Evidence, not rumor or speculation

A *Brady* suppression occurs when the government fails to turn over even evidence that is known only to police investigators and not to the prosecutor. To state a claim under *Brady*, the plaintiff must allege that (1) the withheld evidence was favorable either because it was exculpatory or could be used to impeach, (2) the evidence was suppressed by the government, and (3) the nondisclosure prejudiced the plaintiff. *Gantt v. City of Los Angeles* (2013, CA9 Cal.) 717 F.3d 702.

Whether evidence is admissible has no bearing on the prosecution's duty to disclose the evidence to the defense under *Brady*. *Mills v. Cal. Dep't of Corr.* (S.D. Cal. Mar. 5, 2012) 2012 U.S. Dist. LEXIS 28887.

The first task in evaluating a claim of *Brady* error is to determine whether favorable evidence exists. The burden to establish the existence of favorable evidence rests on the party asserting its existence, usually the defendant. "A *Brady* claim fails if the existence of favorable evidence is merely suspected. That the evidence exists must be established by the defendant." *United States v. Erickson* (2009, CA10 UT) 561 F.3d 1150, 1163. " 'Although it hardly bears mention, an implicit prerequisite of any Brady claim is that favorable, material evidence actually exists.' [citation omitted]" *United States v. Alverio-Melendez* (2011, CA1 PR) 640 F.3d 412, 424. The prosecution does not commit a *Brady* violation by failing to disclose evidence that does not exist or that has not been created. *United States v. Alverio-Melendez, supra,* 640 F.3d at 424.

Speculation by the defendant that a government file might contain *Brady* material does not justify an *in camera* inspection of that file by the court. "A due process standard which is satisfied by mere speculation would convert *Brady* into a discovery device." *United States v. Bowie* (2010, CA8 MN) 618 F.3d 802, 818.

In *D'Ambrosio v. Bagley* (2008, CA6 OH) 527 F.3d 489, a federal habeas petitioner amended his petition to add a *Brady* claim. The district court held that the prosecution had suppressed material exculpatory evidence and granted the habeas petition. The warden appealed the grant of the habeas petition, arguing for the first time on appeal that the prisoner had failed to exhaust his *Brady* claim in the state courts before raising it in the federal courts. After holding that the warden had expressly waived the exhaustion requirement in the district court proceeding, the Court of Appeals discussed the merits of the *Brady* claim.

The prosecution had suppressed unrecorded conclusions of two of the investigating detectives that that the victim had not been murdered where his body was found. The warden argued in the Court of Appeals that these opinions were not *Brady* evidence; D'Ambrosio argued to the contrary. The Court of Appeals concluded that it need not decide the issue, because the remaining suppressed evidence was material and supported the district court's order.

However, in reaching that conclusion the Court of Appeals opined that characterizing the detective's comments as opinions would not resolve the question whether those opinions were *Brady* evidence. The Court reasoned:

> "It cannot be the law that every stray thought of a police detective about a case must be imputed to the State, such that the prosecutor has a duty to disclose that information . . . On the other hand . . . a police detective's opinion might be so concrete and well-known to other government agents working on a case that the prosecutor's failure to learn the opinion and disclose it to the defense could rise to the level of a *Brady* violation." 527 F.3d at 499.

Similarly, speculation that materials in the government's files constitute exculpatory evidence does not constitute evidence that the prosecution has committed *Brady* error in failing to disclose those materials. In *United States v. Guzman-Padilla* (2009, CA9 CA) 573 F.3d 865, the Ninth Circuit Court of Appeals rejected the defendant's contention that the government violated his due process rights by refusing to disclose the Border Patrol's written policy on the use of controlled tire deflation devices. The Court of Appeals observed that the defendant "failed to identify any basis in the record for his suggestion that [the border patrol agent's] actions were inconsistent with a written policy." 573 F.3d at 890. Accordingly, the defendant's mere speculation about materials possessed by the government does not require a trial court to allow the defendant an opportunity to inspect those files. 573 F.3d at 890. *Accord, United States v. Mincoff* (2009, CA9 CA) 574 F.3d 1186, 1199.

A defendant who wishes to inspect government files must make "a plausible showing" that the files will produce material evidence. *United States v. Williams* (2009, CA10 OK) 576 F.3d 1149. A defendant who is unable to make a showing that is more than bald assertions or speculation as to what the requested information would show does not meet *Brady's* requirement that the defendant show that "the requested evidence would be 'favorable to the accused.' [citation omitted]" *United States v. Caro* (2010, CA4 VA) 597 F.3d 608, 619; *United States v. Wilson* (2010, CA DC) 605 F.3d 985, 1005.

§ 1:7.1 Evidence, not absence of evidence, as *Brady* requirement

The absence of evidence does not ordinarily constitute *Brady* material. "The failure to create exculpatory evidence does not constitute a Brady violation." *United States v. Alverio-Melendez* (2011, CA1 PR) 640 F.3d 412, 424. Thus, the failure of the government to do a fingerprint analysis of latent fingerprints does not itself constitute a *Brady* violation. *United States v. Alverio-Melendez, supra,* 640 F.3d at 424.

A question not addressed by California courts is whether the death or other known trial unavailability of an important prosecution witness must be disclosed by the prosecutor pursuant to the *Brady* rule. There appear to be very few cases dealing with this subject in other jurisdictions. Those cases have arisen in the New York state courts.

In *People v. Jones* (N.Y. 1978) 375 N.E.2d 41, a prosecutor accepted a guilty plea without disclosing that the primary eyewitness against the defendant had died several days earlier. The defendant moved to withdraw his guilty plea when learning of the witness's death, arguing that the death of the witness should have been disclosed because it was exculpatory evidence under *Brady*. In rejecting this argument, the New York State Court of Appeal concluded that "[t]he circumstance that the testimony of the complaining witness was no longer available to the prosecution was not evidence." 375 N.E.2d at 43.

In *People v. Roldan* (1984) 124 Misc.2d 279, 476 N.Y.S.2d 447, the prosecutor agreed to accept a defendant's guilty plea to attempted assault without disclosing that the complaining witness was unwilling to cooperate in the prosecution of the case. When the defendant discovered that the complaining witness would not have testified at trial, the defendant moved to set aside the guilty plea. Relying upon *People v. Jones, supra*, the trial court denied the defendant's request, holding that "[i]f it is the law of the state . . . that a district attorney is not obliged to reveal that a principal witness has died before a plea of guilty is taken, it must follow that even if the assistant district attorney knew that the complainant-witness would not cooperate in the prosecution of the case, he had no duty to reveal that information to the defendant . . . ." 124 Misc.2d at 280–281.

Thus, because the absence of a witness is not evidence, we conclude that the *Brady* rule does not compel a prosecutor to disclose that fact to the defendant.

However, as in postjudgment disclosures (see Sections 1:94 and 1:94.1 of the text and this supplement), the prosecutor might have an ethical duty to disclose the death or unavailability of a material prosecution witness. Such was the holding of the court in *Matter of Wayne M.* (1983) 121 Misc.2d 346, 467 N.Y.S.2d 798, which grounded its conclusion upon Disciplinary Rule 7-103(B) of the New York State Code of Professional Responsibility. Disciplinary Rule 7 provided that "[a] public prosecutor or other government lawyer in criminal litigation shall make timely disclosure . . . of the existence of evidence, known to the prosecutor or other government lawyer, that tends to negate the guilt of the accused, mitigate the degree of the offense, or reduce the punishment." The Court concluded that "[t]his ethical injunction includes a situation such as the one at bar in which a complainant is unavailable." 121 Misc.2d at 347.

California has no comparable rule of professional responsibility. Rule 5-220 of the California Rules of Professional Conduct provides that "[a] member shall not suppress any evidence that the member or the member's client has a legal obligation to reveal or to produce." Rule 5-220 begs the question whether the prosecutor has an ethical duty to disclose the death of a material prosecution witness, because it is dependent upon the very issue—a legal obligation to reveal or to produce—which is the object of this determination. Rule 5-220 does not impose an ethical duty upon a prosecutor to disclose evidence unless the prosecutor otherwise has a legal obligation to reveal or to produce that evidence.

However, it is conceivable that a rule of professional responsibility which requires a prosecutor to refrain from prosecuting a charge that the prosecutor knows is not supported by probable cause could provide the ethical basis for disclosure. Rule 3.8 of the American Bar Association Model Rules of Professional Conduct provides that the "prosecutor in a criminal case shall: (a) refrain from prosecuting a charge that the prosecutor knows is not supported by probable cause."

The ABA Model Rules of Professional Conduct and the Model Code of Professional Responsibility have "no legal force of their own" and have not been adopted in California. *General Dynamics Corp. v. Superior Court* (1994) 7 Cal.4th 1164, 1190, n.6, 32 Cal.Rptr.2d 1, 876 P.2d 487. Because they have not been adopted in California, and because they have no legal force of their own, the "ABA Model Rules of Professional Conduct . . . do not establish ethical standards in California . . . ." *State Comp. Ins. Fund v. WPS, Inc.* (1999) 70 Cal.App.4th 644, 655–656, 82 Cal.Rptr.2d 799.

With the approval of the California Supreme Court, the Board of Governors of the State Bar has the power to "formulate and enforce rules of professional conduct for all members of the bar in the State." Business and Professions Code section 6076. When approved by the Supreme Court, these Rules of Professional Conduct "are binding upon all members of the State Bar," and their willful breach can subject an attorney to discipline by the State Bar and the California Supreme Court. Business and Professions Code section 6077.

California has adopted Rules of Professional Conduct for attorneys. These rules "are intended not only to establish ethical standards for members of the bar [citation omitted], but are also designed to protect the public. [citations omitted]." *Ames v. State Bar* (1973) 8 Cal.3d 910, 917, 106 Cal.Rptr. 489, 506 P.2d 625.

A California attorney is subject to State Bar and Supreme Court discipline for a willful violation of the California Rules of Professional Conduct, the State Bar Act [Business and Professions Code section 6000 et *seq.*], and California judicial opinions. *In re Edward S.* (2009) 173 Cal.App.4th 387, 412, 92 Cal.Rptr.3d 725. In the absence of an applicable California Rule of Professional Conduct, California statute, or opinion of a California appellate court, a California attorney is not subject to discipline in California for violating an ABA Model Rule of Professional Conduct, an ABA ethical standard, or an ABA formal opinion. *State Comp. Ins. Fund v. WPS, Inc.* (1999) 70 Cal.App.4th 644, 656, 82 Cal.Rptr.2d 799.

The California Supreme Court has occasionally looked to the principles underlying the ABA counterparts to California's Rules of Professional Conduct. *Flatt v. Superior Court* (1994) 9 Cal.4th 275, 282, 36 Cal.Rptr.2d 537, 885 P.2d 950. *See People v. Gonzalez* (1990) 51 Cal.3d 1179, 1261, 275 Cal.Rptr. 729, 800 P.2d 1159, where the Supreme Court cited Rule 3.8(d) of the ABA Model Rules of Prof. Conduct; *People v. Garcia* (1993) 17 Cal.App.4th 1169, 1179, 22 Cal.Rptr.2d 545; and *Goldberg v. Warner/ Chappell Music, Inc.* (2005) 125 Cal.App.4th 752, 765, 23 Cal.Rptr.3d 116.

ABA standards do have an appropriate role in determining the ethical duties of California attorneys. The role of ABA standards is to provide guideposts to the application of California Rules of Professional Conduct. *Higdon v. Superior Court* (1991) 227 Cal.App.3d 1667, 1680, 278 Cal.Rptr. 588. Rule 1-100(A) of the California Rules of Professional Conduct expressly provides that "[e]thics opinions and rules and standards promulgated by other jurisdictions and bar associations may also be considered." Thus, where there is no conflict with the public policy of California, the ABA Model Rules of Professional Conduct can serve as a collateral source for guidance on proper professional conduct in California. *People v. Donaldson* (2001) 93 Cal.App.4th 916, 928, 113 Cal.Rptr.2d 548. State Bar Rules of Professional Conduct, in conjunction with American Bar Association's Standards, "provide guidelines for determining the prevailing norms of practice . . . ." *In re Alvernaz* (1992) 2 Cal.4th 924, 937, 8 Cal.Rptr.2d 713, 830 P.2d 747.

But it is ultimately the California Rules of Professional Conduct, California state statutes, and California judicial opinions that establish enforceable ethical standards for California attorneys.

As previously noted, Rule 3.8 of the American Bar Association Model Rules of Professional Conduct provides that the "prosecutor in a criminal case shall: (a) refrain from prosecuting a charge that the prosecutor knows is not supported by probable cause." Rule 5-110 of the California Rules of Professional Conduct appears to be a counterpart to ABA Rule 3.8. Rule 5-110 provides that "[a] member in government service shall not institute or cause to be instituted criminal charges when the member knows or should know that the charges are not supported by probable cause. If, after the institution of criminal charges, the member in government service having responsibility for prosecuting the charges becomes aware that those charges are not supported by probable cause, the member shall promptly so advise the court in which the criminal matter is pending."

Although no California case has so held, an argument could be made that the death of a material prosecution witness which prevents the prosecutor from being able to prove a charge at trial obviates probable cause in support of that criminal charge. Under this approach, undermining the probable cause in support of the criminal charge would trigger the prosecutor's ethical duty to disclose the witness's death to the court. Any such ethical duty under Rule 5-110 to disclose the death of a prosecution witness would almost certainly be limited to the death of a material prosecution witness without whom the prosecutor would be unable to obtain a conviction at trial. An ethical duty would not require disclosure of the death of a prosecution witness whose unavailability would not prevent the prosecution from going forward to trial.

Therefore, although the prosecutor does not have a constitutionally based duty under *Brady* to disclose the death or other unavailability of a material prosecution witness, the prosecutor could have an ethical duty to make such a disclosure under Rule 5-110 of the California Rules or Professional Conduct. Whether the death or other permanent unavailability of a material prosecution witness obviates probable cause in support of a charge has not been addressed by California courts.

Practice Tip for Prosecution: Although you are not obligated by the *Brady* rule to disclose to the defendant the death or other unavailability of a material prosecution witness, you might have an ethical duty under the California Rules of Professional Conduct to make such a disclosure. Prosecutors concerned about their professional reputations and desirous of avoiding the possibility of a State Bar disciplinary action are well advised to disclose the death or other permanent unavailability of a material prosecution witness whose absence undermines the prosecution's ability to obtain a conviction of the charge.

Without clear decisional or other authority that would compel or support it, we are not willing to extend the reasoning behind a possible ethical requirement to disclose the death or other permanent unavailability of a material prosecution witness to other evidentiary problems which prosecutors face. Thus, we are not prepared to conclude that a prosecutor's inability to locate a material witness, a witness's reluctance to cooperate, or a witness's temporary absence from the jurisdiction, become ethically disclosable facts.

See People v. West (2003 Cal.App. Unpub. Lexis 10997), in which the Court of Appeal in an unpublished decision held that "[t]he fact that a prosecution witness fails to show up for a required court appearance does not necessarily mean the witness will be unavailable at the time of a defendant's trial. The witness could be found by the authorities or voluntarily reappear at any point in time, in which case knowledge of the failure to appear is no longer useful to the defendant. The prosecution has no duty to disclose its potential case to the defendant. [citation omitted] Similarly, the prosecution's duty to disclose exculpatory evidence does not extend to disclosure of difficulties that may arise in the securing of witnesses to present its case."

Although *People v. West* as an unpublished opinion is not citable and may not be relied upon by a party or a court, *California Rules of Court*, Rule 8.1115 (2009), its reasoning may be considered by counsel in the litigation of discovery questions.

Practice Tip for Prosecution: Although Rule 5-110 requires that a charge be supported by "probable cause," California prosecutors are required to adhere to a higher filing standard. The general filing standard to be followed by California prosecutors is that a prosecutor may file a criminal charge when four requirements are satisfied. These four requirements are: (1) there has been a complete investigation and thorough consideration of all pertinent data; (2) there is legally sufficient, admissible evidence of a corpus delicti; (3) there is legally sufficient, admissible evidence of the accused's identity as the perpetrator of the crime; and (4) the prosecutor has considered the probability of conviction by an objective fact-finder hearing the admissible evidence. *Professionalism, A Sourcebook of Ethics*

15

and Civil Liability Principles for Prosecutors, California District Attorneys Association, Chap. III, page 18 (2001); *Uniform Crime Charging Standards*, California District Attorneys Association, p. 6 (1996).

The quantity and quality of evidence required for the charging of a crime is that the evidence "should be of such convincing force that it would warrant conviction of the crime charged by a reasonable and objective fact-finder after hearing all the evidence available to the prosecutor at the time of charging and after hearing the most plausible, reasonably foreseeable defense that could be raised under the evidence presented to the prosecutor." *Professionalism, A Sourcebook of Ethics and Civil Liability Principles for Prosecutors*, California District Attorneys Association, Chap. III, page 18 (2001); *Uniform Crime Charging Standards*, California District Attorneys Association, p. 12 (1996). California appellate courts have recognized these principles as establishing the standards for crime charging in California. *See Davis v. Municipal Court* (1988) 46 Cal.3d 64, 82, n.9, 249 Cal.Rptr. 300, 757 P.2d 11; *People v. Robinson* (1995) 31 Cal.App.4th 494, 499, n.5, 37 Cal.Rptr.2d 183; and *Youngblood v. Gates* (1988) 200 Cal.App.3d 1302, 1345, n.11, 246 Cal.Rptr. 775.

§ 1:7.2   Evidence includes oral evidence

The application of the *Brady* rule to *evidence* includes evidence that is oral and that has not been reduced to writing or recorded. *Tennison v. City and County of San Francisco* (2009, CA9 CA) 570 F.3d 1078, 1091, n.6. Thus, the prosecution may not avoid a claim of *Brady* error by arguing that the failure to take notes of an oral statement does not constitute a *Brady* violation, because the *Brady* violation does not consist of the officer's failure to take notes, but the failure to disclose oral material evidence.

This distinction is not a new one, as oral statements not reduced to notes or a written report have previously been held to constitute *Brady* evidence, the nondisclosure of which violated the prosecution's duty to disclose material exculpatory evidence. See the discussion in Sections 1:24.1 and 1:72.2 of the text of *Paradis v. Arave* (2001, CA9 ID) 240 F.3d 1169, and *United States v. Hanna* (1995, CA9 CA) 55 F.3d 1456.

§ 1:8   Evidence, not prosecutor work product

As discussed in the text, a prosecutor's core work product—the prosecutor's opinions, mental impressions, and theories—is not *Brady* evidence that the prosecutor must disclose to the defense.

In *United States v. Coker* (2008, CA6 TN) 514 F.3d 562, a defendant convicted of committing an illegal conflict of interest in violation of federal law appealed on the ground that the government had committed misconduct by suppressing exculpatory evidence. One of the items of evidence was that the government believed federal sentencing guidelines might permit the defendant to reduce the amount of the loss for which she was held accountable based on taxes paid by a co-defendant. The Court of Appeals rejected the defendant's *Brady* argument, concluding that the government's belief was "not a 'fact,' but a potential legal argument. *Brady* obligates the government to disclose '*evidence* favorable to the accused.' [citation to *Brady* omitted] It does not obligate the government to give the defendant legal theories." 514 F.3d at 570.

In *Lopez v. Ryan* (2011, CA9 AZ) 630 F.3d 1198, a defendant convicted in Arizona state court of first-degree murder and sentenced to death filed a federal habeas petition, claiming, inter alia, that a handwritten note written by an unknown author and discovered in a police file that opined that there was insufficient evidence to support a conviction of the defendant of a sexual assault that was independent from the murder charge constituted exculpatory evidence, and the failure to disclose it was *Brady* error. The note stated that the alleged victim of the sexual assault was not credible. The defendant was never charged with the sexual assault.

The Ninth Circuit Court of Appeals held that "the legal opinions contained in the note do not constitute *Brady* material required to be provided to Lopez." 630 F.3d at 1210. *See also United States v. Reed* (2011, CA8 SD) 641 F.3d 992 [government's dismissal of numerous charges against the defendant and its successful motion to preclude the defendant from referring to the dismissed charges does not constitute suppression of evidence within the meaning of the *Brady* rule].

§ 1:9   Irrelevant evidence

The prosecutor's failure to disclose irrelevant evidence does not violate the *Brady* rule. *See, United States v. Mejia* (2010, CA1 RI) 600 F.3d 12, 20; and *Rhoades v. Henry (Michelbacher)* (2010, CA9 ID) 598 F.3d 495, 502–503.

In *Wilson v. Parker* (2008, CA6 KY) 515 F.3d 682, a defendant convicted of kidnapping, rape, and capital murder, and sentenced to death, claimed in a federal habeas petition that he was denied a fair trial. The defendant claimed that the prosecutor knowingly withheld information about a sexual relationship between his co-defendant, who testified against him, and a state court judge who did not preside at his trial. The Court of Appeals found that there was no proof that the other judge had intervened on the co-defendant's behalf, or that the co-defendant had used her relationship to win favorable treatment from the prosecutor or her trial judge. The Court concluded that the relationship between the co-defendant and the other judge was "irrelevant to any bias [the testifying co-defendant] may have had in her testimony that [the habeas petitioner] had been the one who killed the victim." The Court held that the evidence of the co-defendant/witness's sexual affair was not *Brady* evidence, because it was irrelevant. 515 F.3d at 702.

In *United States v. Olofson* (2009, CA7 WI) 563 F.3d 652, a defendant charged in federal court with illegal possession of a machinegun made a motion to compel the disclosure of correspondence from the ATF to the manufacturer of his AR-15 concerning the use of M-16 parts in early models of the AR-15 rifle. The defendant claimed that this evidence was exculpatory, because it was relevant to his knowledge of whether his AR-15 was a machine gun. The district court denied the discovery request on the grounds that the evidence was not exculpatory. On appeal from his conviction, the Seventh Circuit Court of Appeals affirmed the district court's ruling, holding that the ATF letter "has no bearing on Olofson's knowledge of whether his AR-15 was a machinegun." 563 F.3d at 662.

In *United States v. Guzman-Padilla* (2009, CA9 CA) 573 F.3d 865, the Ninth Circuit Court of Appeals concluded that even if a border patrol agent's actions were inconsistent with Border Patrol policy on the use of controlled tire deflation devices, the written policy on the use of controlled tire deflation devices would not have been material (relevant) to the determination by the district court in ruling upon the defendant's motion to suppress evidence seized as a result of the use of controlled tire deflation devices. Thus, the prosecution's failure to disclose that policy did not constitute withholding of evidence favorable to the defendant. 573 F.3d at 869.

Where a defendant is charged with multiple criminal counts, whether evidence is relevant for purposes of the *Brady* rule must be assessed on a count-by-count basis, and whether *Brady* error is committed for failure to disclose evidence must likewise be evaluated count by count. *United States v. Johnson* (2010, CA DC) 592 F.3d 164, 171.

The government's failure to disclose evidence that has no bearing on the defendant's participation in the charged crimes and which, therefore, provides no information relevant to the offense that the defendant was convicted of committing does not constitute a *Brady* violation. Such evidence "is neither exculpatory nor material." *United States v. Wilson* (2010, CA4 MD) 624 F.3d 640, 661. *See also Henness v. Bagley* (2011, CA6 OH) 644 F.3d 308 [The prosecution's failure to disclose a witness statement that a named third person had been involved in a homicide did not constitute *Brady* error without some evidence that the homicide was the same one charged against the defendant.].

Likewise, evidence that does no more than impeach a prosecution witness who does not testify lacks relevance. *United States v. King* (2011, CA4 NC) 628 F.3d 693, 703. However, prosecutors must be careful to determine whether such evidence is relevant for some purpose other than impeachment of a potential prosecution witness. Evidence that would impeach a potential prosecution witness might also support the defendant's defense against the charges; in that situation, the evidence does not lack relevance simply because the witness does not testify and thereby cannot be impeached. *United States v. King, supra*, 628 F.3d at 704.

However, evidence that "speaks to the acts that the jury might have relied on in reaching its verdicts" is not irrelevant evidence, and the prosecution may not escape culpability for its nondisclosure on a claim that the evidence is irrelevant. *United States v. Kohring* (2011, CA9 AK) 637 F.3d 895 902–903.

§ 1:10   Inculpatory evidence

The principle that the *Brady* rule applies to exculpatory, not inculpatory, evidence finds application in a variety of contexts. The *Brady* rule does not require the prosecution to disclose its trial witnesses prior to trial. The due-process basis of *Brady* is that the prosecution must disclose its material or potentially exculpatory evidence prior to the conclusion of the trial. *United States v. Altman* (2007, CA8 IA) 507 F.3d 678, 680; *United States v. Boyce* (2009, CA8 MO) 564 F.3d 911, 918 ["The mere identity of witnesses is not exculpatory and is not covered by *Brady*."].

Evidence that is "exceedingly damaging" to a defendant which a prosecutor has discovered while interviewing a witness prior to trial is not favorable to the defendant, and the prosecutor's failure to disclose that evidence to the defendant prior to the testimony of the witness at trial does not constitute a *Brady* violation. *People v. Verdugo* (2010) 50 Cal.4th 263, 280–281, 113 Cal.Rptr.3d 803, 236 P.3d 1035. Evidence that is not favorable to the defendant is not *Brady* evidence, and the prosecution's failure to disclose that evidence does not become a *Brady* violation. 50 Cal.4th 263.

Nor does the *Brady* rule require the prosecution to disclose the results of its pre-trial reanalysis of physical evidence when that reanalysis increases the strength of inculpatory evidence against the defendant. Although a defendant has a due process right to fair notice of the charges against him, the right to fair notice is not implicated by the prosecution's trial preparation work that strengthens the prosecution's case against the defendant. "The right to fair notice, however, falls short of imposing a constitutional duty on the state to disclose incriminating evidence . . . ." *Wooten v. Thaler* (2010, CA5 TX) 598 F.3d 215, 219.

Thus, in a case in which the prosecution conducted a pretrial DNA re-analysis of its physical evidence, resulting in a strengthening of the DNA evidence against the defendant, the failure of the prosecution to disclose the results of the re-analysis did not violate the prosecutors' *Brady* duties. *Wooten v. Thaler* (2010, CA5 TX) 598 F.3d 215. The Fifth Circuit Court of Appeals in *Wooten* observed that because *Brady* did not create a general constitutional right to discovery, there is no "constitutionally-footed duty to disclose evidence made stronger by state investigative efforts that continue after the defendant's arrest, subsequent to any plea negotiation, or during trial." 598 F.3d at 219.

The *Wooten* court concluded that as long as the prosecution does not deliberately mislead the defense, the prosecution does not violate *Brady* by failing to disclose that it has exercised its right to analyze and reanalyze

DNA evidence to ensure its reliability, and that the results of its efforts have made the evidence against the defendant even stronger. "When the actual physical evidence is in full view, there is no constitutional demand that the prosecution warrant any analyses of that evidence as final—as the best and last attempts." 598 F.3d at 221.

And evidence which is unfavorable to the defendant because it negates an innocent explanation for the charged criminal event is not exculpatory evidence, the suppression of which violates the *Brady* rule. Thus, where a police report eliminated an innocent explanation for the death of a small child, that evidence helped to incriminate, not exculpate, the defendant charged with the child's murder. The withholding of that evidence was not a *Brady* violation. *Pudelski v. Wilson* (2009, CA6 OH) 576 F.3d 595, 613.

Evidence which the prosecutor develops during a trial that supports the testimony of a prosecution witness does not become exculpatory under *Brady* simply because had the defendant's attorney known of that evidence prior to trial, he or she would have used a different strategy in cross-examining that witness. In *United States v. Hernandez* (2007, CA1 MA) 490 F.3d 81, the prosecution discovered during trial that telephone records linked to the defendant's cell telephone and that had been produced in discovery, contained codes that could be used to identify the general location of the cell phone when it was used. This evidence would support the testimony of a prosecution witness who alleged that a meeting with the defendant had taken place in New York City on the date of that call.

The defendant objected to the introduction of the evidence regarding the telephone codes, claiming that the late disclosure of the evidence constituted a *Brady* violation. The defendant argued that had he known of the evidence supporting the testimony of the co-conspirator government witness, he would have used a different strategy in cross-examining that witness. The Court of Appeals rejected the defendant's argument on appeal, holding that because the evidence was not exculpatory or impeaching, but was inculpatory, the evidence was not *Brady* evidence. 490 F.3d at 84.

When evidence could be used to impeach a prosecution witness with a prior inconsistent statement, but the impeaching statement would inculpate the defendant to a greater degree in the charged crime than the witness's trial testimony, such evidence is not *Brady* evidence. *United States v. Sweets* (2007, CA4 MD) 526 F.3d 122, 131.

And when evidence used by the prosecution at trial—such as photographs of the defendant's home where illegal drugs were seized—is simply inculpatory and not also exculpatory, the failure of the prosecution to disclose that evidence before using it at trial is not a *Brady* violation, because inculpatory evidence does not trigger *Brady* protections. *United States v. Garcia* (2009, CA5 TX) 567 F.3d 721, 735. *Accord, United States v. Knowles* (2010, CA6 TN) 623 F.3d 381, 388 [physical evidence that corroborates a prosecution witness's inculpatory testimony and which does not impeach any prosecution witness's testimony, is also inculpatory evidence and its suppression does not constitute a *Brady* violation]; and *United States v. Neal* (2010, CA7 IL) 611 F.3d 399, 401 ["The principle of *Brady v. Maryland* (citation omitted) requires the disclosure of exculpatory evidence, not inculpatory evidence."].

§ 1:11   Evidence both exculpatory and inculpatory

Prosecutors confronted with evidence that is both exculpatory and inculpatory should be careful to distinguish the favorableness determination of such evidence from the materiality determination of that evidence. It is appropriate to consider the overall import of evidence which is both exculpatory and inculpatory when determining whether such evidence is **material** exculpatory evidence. When such evidence is more damaging than it is helpful to the defendant, the failure to disclose that evidence does not constitute a *Brady* violation. *See Edwards v. Ayers* (2008, CA9 OR) 542 F.3d 759, 770, 771. But that evidence is nevertheless favorable to the defendant within the meaning of the *Brady* rule, even though the evidence is both exculpatory and inculpatory.

See, however, *Hammond v. Hall* (2009, CA11 GA) 586 F.3d 1289, 1315, where the Eleventh Circuit Court of Appeals observed that "[b]ecause the effect of [a witness's] statements would have been as harmful as helpful to the defense, we have some question whether they can accurately be described as favorable."

That is why a determination whether the failure to disclose evidence must begin with a favorability analysis, but it must not end with that analysis. When evidence, *in isolation*, can be considered "favorable" to the defendant, whether the failure to disclose that evidence is a *Brady* violation must also consider whether the use of that evidence by the defendant in trial would entitle the prosecution to counter the facially favorable evidence with rebuttal evidence that would be damaging to the defendant. *See, e.g., People v. Verdugo* (2010) 50 Cal.4th 263, 285, 113 Cal.Rptr.3d 803, 236 P.3d 1035.

§ 1:12   Neutral evidence

Evidence that neither identifies nor excludes the defendant as the perpetrator of the charged crime is not evidence that is favorable to the defendant. *Gary v. Hall* (2009, CA11 FL) 558 F.3d 1229, 1257. *See also, United States v. Brown* (2010, CA3 PA) 595 F.3d 498, 513.

However, in *Simmons v. Beard* (2009, CA3 PA) 590 F.3d 223, the Third Circuit Court of Appeals opined that evidence that is otherwise facially neutral can, under some circumstances, be considered favorable to the defendant. In *Simmons* a defendant was convicted in Pennsylvania state court of the robbery and murder of an elderly woman and was sentenced to death. The prosecution introduced evidence against the defendant at trial of a potential sexual assault alleged to have been committed by the defendant against a second woman.

The defendant filed a habeas corpus petition in federal court, alleging, *inter alia*, that the prosecution had withheld an inconclusive lab report—one that did not identify nor did it eliminate him as the perpetrator—regarding the uncharged assault on the second woman, and thus committed *Brady* error. The district court granted the habeas petition, and the Court of Appeals affirmed the judgment of the district court.

Although the Court of Appeals characterized the defendant's *Brady* argument concerning the withholding of the inconclusive lab report as *Simmons'* weakest claim, the Court offered a different *Brady* perspective on evidence commonly viewed as neutral. The Court stated: "Such 'negative' or 'inconclusive' results, however, may be exculpatory even where they do not provide definitive evidence on a particular issue." Citing and quoting the opinion of the Fourth Circuit Court of Appeals in *Patler v. Slayton* (1974, CA4 VA) 503 F.2d 472, 479, the *Simmons* Court concluded that "neutral forensic evidence 'may, because of its neutrality, tend to be favorable to the accused. While it does not by any means establish his absence from the scene of the crime, it does demonstrate that a number of factors which could link the defendant to the crime do not.' [503 F.2d at 479]." The *Simmons* court concluded that "we must at least consider the potential effect of this evidence on the jury's verdict in combination with the other *Brady* material." 590 F.3d at 236–237.

The prosecution is not obligated by *Brady* to disclose evidence that is not exculpatory as a matter of law. Thus, in *United States v. Inzunza* (2011, CA9 CA) 638 F.3d 1006, the failure of the prosecution to disclose statements made by a non-testifying potential witness and co-defendant which characterized payments to the defendant as "campaign contributions" did not constitute a *Brady* violation, because those statements were not exculpatory as a matter of law. 638 F.3d at 1021.

§ 1:13 Immaterial evidence

To establish materiality under *Brady*, a habeas petitioner must show that the state's nondisclosure was so serious that there is a reasonable probability that the suppressed evidence would have produced a different verdict. *Henry v. Ryan* (2013, CA9 Ariz.) 720 F.3d 1073.

But see Mills v. Cal. Dep't of Corr. (S.D. Cal. Mar. 5, 2012) 2012 U.S. Dist. LEXIS 28887, holding, *inter alia*, that whether evidence is admissible has no bearing on the prosecution's duty to disclose the evidence to the defense under *Brady*.

In the context of a *Brady* claim, a finding of prejudice requires that the conduct have some impact on the outcome of the proceeding, i.e., a reasonable probability that the result of the proceeding would have been different or that it so infected the trial with unfairness as to make the resulting conviction a denial of due process. *United States v. Rodriguez* (June 24, 2013, CA9 Cal.) 2013 U.S. App. LEXIS 12918.

It continues to be the rule that immaterial evidence is not *Brady* evidence, and the *Brady* rule does not obligate the prosecution to disclose immaterial evidence, "unless it is apparent that it might lead to the discovery of material evidence." *Price v. Thurmer* (2008, CA7 WI) 514 F.3d 729, 731. By adding the proviso that immaterial evidence can become *Brady* evidence when it appears that it might lead to material exculpatory evidence, the Court of Appeals in *Thurmer* recognized an important principle that also applies to inadmissible evidence [see Section 1:14 of the text for a discussion of inadmissible evidence]. This important principle is that immaterial evidence can become *Brady* evidence when there is an indication that the non-discloseable evidence could lead to *Brady* evidence. Under this standard, the trail leading from otherwise immaterial evidence to *Brady* evidence must be apparent before the prosecution is under a constitutional duty to disclose that immaterial evidence.

There is an important distinction between the prosecution's failure to disclose information or evidence and a *Brady* violation. Although a *Brady* violation includes a failure by the prosecution to disclose favorable evidence to the defendant, "there is never a real '*Brady* violation' unless the nondisclosure was so serious that there is a reasonable probability that the suppressed evidence would have produced a different verdict." *Matthew v. Johnson* (2000, CA5 TX) 201 F.3d 353, 362, n.12.

The California Supreme Court has held that the term "*Brady* violation" is sometimes used to refer to any breach of the broad obligation to disclose exculpatory evidence—that is, to any suppression of so-called "*Brady* material"—although, strictly speaking, there is never a real "*Brady* violation" unless the nondisclosure was so serious that there is a reasonable probability that the suppressed evidence would have produced a different verdict. Favorable evidence is material when it could reasonably be taken to put the whole case in such a different light as to undermine confidence in the verdict. The question is whether, deprived of the information withheld by the prosecution, the defendant received a trial resulting in a verdict worthy of confidence. In deciding whether evidence not disclosed to the defense was material under these standards, a reviewing court considers how the nondisclosure affected the defense investigation and trial strategy. A determination that the prosecution violated its *Brady* disclosure obligations requires reversal without any need for additional harmless error analysis. *In re Bacigalupo* (2012) 55 Cal. 4th 312, 145 Cal. Rptr. 3d 832, 283 P.3d 613.

§ 1:14 Evidence to which *Brady* rule does not apply—inadmissible evidence

But see Mills v. Cal. Dep't of Corr. (S.D. Cal. Mar. 5, 2012) 2012 U.S. Dist. LEXIS 28887, holding, *inter alia*, that whether evidence is admissible has no bearing on the prosecution's duty to disclose the evidence to the defense under *Brady*.

The holding of the Supreme Court in *Wood v. Bartholomew* (1995) 516

U.S. 1, 5–6, 116 S.Ct. 7, 133 L.Ed.2d 1, that "evidence that is inadmissible at trial is not 'evidence' at all, for *Brady* purposes," did not create a "per se rejection of inadmissible evidence as a basis for a *Brady* claim." *People v. Hoyos* (2007) 41 Cal.4th 872, 919, n.28, 63 Cal.Rptr.3d 1, 162 P.3d 528. "*Wood* did not establish that inadmissible evidence can never be material for purposes of a *Brady* claim . . . ." *In re Miranda* (2008) 43 Cal.4th 541, 576, 76 Cal.Rptr.3d 172, 182 P.3d 513.

See, however, the language of the Ninth Circuit Court of Appeals in *Smith v. Baldwin* (2007, CA9 OR) 510 F.3d 1127, 1148 ["Because they are inadmissible in Oregon courts, the results of [a prosecution witness's] polygraph examination do not qualify as 'evidence' for *Brady* purposes, let alone 'material evidence.' [citing *Wood*]." See also the language of the Sixth Circuit Court of Appeals in *Doan v. Carter* (2008, CA6 OH) 548 F.3d 449, 463 ["With respect to results of the voice stress analysis, it cannot be said that this evidence has impeachment value, because under Ohio law, the results cannot not [sic] be used, not even for impeachment purposes, unless both sides agree to their use."].

The federal circuit courts commonly state the rule that "only admissible evidence can be material, for only admissible evidence could possibly lead to a different result." *United States v. Salem* (2009, CA7 WI) 578 F.3d 682, 686; *United States v. Wilson* (2010, CA DC) 605 F.3d 985, 1005; *Ferguson v. Sec'y for the Dep't of Corr.* (2009, CA11 FL) 580 F.3d 1183, 1207.

However, in *United States v. Johnson* (2010, CA DC) 592 F.3d 164, 171, the District of Columbia Circuit Court of Appeals observed that "there is some question in the circuits about whether, in order to make out a *Brady* violation, the undisclosed information must constitute admissible evidence." The Court noted that several circuits have held that "if the suppressed evidence, although itself inadmissible, 'would have led directly to material admissible evidence' the defendant has a viable *Brady* claim. [citation omitted]." 592 F.3d at 171.

Where evidence is admissible in the discretion of the trial court, which may exercise that discretion to exclude evidence, the fact that the trial court might exclude otherwise favorable evidence does not obviate its character as evidence favorable to the defendant within the meaning of the *Brady* rule. *United States v. Price* (2009, CA9 OR) 566 F.3d 900, 912.

The Ninth Circuit Court of Appeals summarized this principle in *United States v. Kohring* (2011, CA9 AK) 637 F.3d 895, 907, as follows: "[I]n order for the newly-discovered information to be material under *Brady/Giglio*, the information must be either admissible, lead to information that will be admissible, or capable of being used for impeachment."

PART III. FAVORABLENESS REQUIREMENT

§ 1:15 Favorableness—in general

Evidence is favorable to the accused under *Brady* if it has either exculpatory or impeachment value. The prosecution must disclose materials that are potentially exculpatory or impeaching. *United States v. Olsen* (2013, CA9 Wash.) 704 F.3d 1172. Further, materials from ongoing investigations are favorable under *Brady*. Indeed, information bearing adversely on the credibility of a prosecution witness is favorable under *Brady* regardless of whether it was part of any investigation at all. *Id.*

Because evidence must be favorable to the defendant in order to constitute *Brady* evidence, evidence that is not demonstrably favorable does not come within the scope of the *Brady* rule. In *United States v. Sanchez-Florez* (2008, CA8 IA) 533 F.3d 938, the prosecution's fingerprint specialist who checked drug packaging materials in an effort to identify fingerprints on them resigned from his position when it was discovered that the examiner had failed to perform all of the required fingerprint tests on that packaging and had falsified information on print examinations that he had performed in other cases.

The prosecutor learned of these facts after the defendant had been convicted at a jury trial, and the day thereafter disclosed these facts to the defendant's attorney. The fingerprint examiner had not identified the defendant's fingerprints on any of the packaging. The prosecutor returned the materials to the crime lab to be retested for prints. The second fingerprint examination again resulted in a finding that no fingerprints of the defendant were identified on the packaging materials.

The defendant made a new-trial motion, claiming that the information about the fingerprint specialist, who never testified at trial, was exculpatory, because the defendant could have used that evidence to attack the validity of the evidence actually presented against the defendant at trial. After making detailed factual findings, the district court denied the new trial motion. The Eighth Circuit Court of Appeals affirmed the defendant's conviction. After concluding that no witness claimed that the drugs belonged to the defendant, the Court decided that "the information regarding [the fingerprint examiner] was not exculpatory or otherwise favorable" and that "[e]vidence of [the fingerprint examiner's] mishandling of fingerprint cases is not a *Brady* violation." 533 F.3d at 941.

However, evidence that is inconclusive or tenuous might not be deemed to be evidence favorable to the defendant. In *Muhammad v. Kelly* (2009, CA4 VA) 575 F.3d 359, in which the defendant was convicted of several sniper murders committed in the Washington, D.C. area, the prosecution failed to disclose an FBI criminal analysis done during the investigation of the shootings that indicated that the sniper was likely acting alone. At trial a prosecution sniper expert testified that it was his opinion that a sniper team carried out the shootings. The defendant filed a federal habeas petition challenging his convictions and judgment.

The defendant in federal district court habeas proceedings argued that he could have used the FBI profile to undermine the trial testimony of the prosecution sniper expert, and thus the suppression of that report had deprived him of favorable evidence. The Fourth Circuit Court of Appeals rejected the defendant's argument, noting that the FBI profile did not definitely conclude that the killings were the work of a single sniper, was based on probabilities, and should not be considered all inclusive. The Court of Appeals concluded that "[g]iven the inconclusive language in the report, it cannot be considered exculpatory . . . ." 575 F.3d at 367–368.

The prosecution is not excused from disclosing evidence that the defendant did not commit the charged crime, simply because the prosecution possesses evidence that the defendant is guilty of that crime. Evidence that is favorable to the defendant because it tends to negate the prosecution's inculpatory evidence does not lose its character as *Brady* evidence in the face of inculpatory evidence to the contrary. *See United States v. Rittweger* (2008, CA2 NY) 524 F.3d 171, 181. This means that the " 'favorable tendency' of a given piece of evidence should be assessed without regard to the 'weight of the evidence' as a whole." *Walker v. Kelly* (2009, CA4 VA) 589 F.3d 127, 140.

However, a *Brady* claim may not be based upon a claim of the existence of favorable evidence that is merely suspected. "That such evidence exists must be established by the defendant." *United States v. Erickson* (2009, CA10 UT) 561 F.3d 1150, 1163. "Mere speculation" about materials possessed by the prosecution does not satisfy the favorability component of the *Brady* rule. *United States v. Mincoff* (2009, CA9 CA) 574 F.3d 1186, 1199–1200.

What the defendant must make is a "plausible showing" that government files contain evidence material to the defense, *United States v. Williams* (2009, CA10 OK) 576 F.3d 1149, 1163, or a "colorable claim" that the withheld materials hold evidence favorable to the defendant. *United States v. Guzman-Padilla* (2009, CA9 CA) 573 F.3d 865, 869.

Ultimately, evidence that does not bear on the defendant's participation in the charged crimes, which provides no information relevant to the offense for which the defendant is charged or has been convicted, and which does not contradict the prosecution's evidence introduced to prove the defendant's criminal culpability in the charged crimes is not evidence that is favorable to the defendant. *United States v. Wilson* (2010, CA4 MD) 624 F.3d 640, 661.

§ 1:16   Relevance as component of favorableness

The prosecution's failure to disclose evidence that is not relevant to the offense that the defendant is charged with committing or has been convicted of committing does not constitute a *Brady* violation, because that evidence is not exculpatory. *United States v. Wilson* (2010, CA4 MD) 624 F.3d 640, 661.

§ 1:17 Evidence directly opposing guilt—generally

Evidence directly opposes a defendant's guilt when that evidence severely undermines the testimony of an important prosecution witness, thereby negating the prosecution's evidence that the defendant is guilty of the charged crime.

In *Montgomery v. Bagley* (2009, CA6 OH) 581 F.3d 440, the defendant was convicted of murder and sentenced to death. In habeas corpus proceedings the federal district court granted the defendant a new trial, because the prosecution had failed to disclose to the defendant a police report written prior to trial that reported that several witnesses had seen one of the defendant's purported victims alive four days after the prosecution alleged that the defendant had murdered her. The government appealed the district court order granting the new trial.

The Court of Appeals affirmed the district court order. The Court of Appeals concluded that the suppressed police report was favorable to the defendant, because evidence that several persons had seen the victim alive long after the prosecution contended that the defendant had killed her would have undercut the testimony of the prosecution's star witness that the defendant was the triggerman in both of the murders for which he was charged and convicted.

The withheld evidence that directly opposed the defendant's guilt constituted evidence favorable to the defendant.

§ 1:17.1 Evidence negating element of crime

In *People v. Uribe* (2008) 162 Cal.App.4th 1457, 76 Cal.Rptr.3d 829, the defendant was convicted of two counts of aggravated sexual assault on his granddaughter, who was a minor. The minor child was examined by a physician assistant, who performed what is known as a sexual assault response team (SART) examination. The SART examination was videotaped, and the existence of the videotape was not disclosed to the defendant, who learned of the videotape after his conviction at trial.

One of the contested issues at trial was whether the victim had been sexually assaulted. Expert testimony on that issue was presented by the prosecution and the defense. After learning of the videotape, the defendant made a motion for a new trial, arguing that he had been denied *Brady* evidence—evidence from the videotape that showed that the victim had not been sexually assaulted. The trial court denied the new-trial motion.

The Court of Appeal reversed the conviction and remanded the case to the trial court for a new trial. The Court concluded that the declaration of the defendant's expert in support of the new-trial motion "established that the SART video was favorable both because it offered potential evidence impeaching a prosecution expert's testimony, and was supportive of the opinions of defendant's expert. We have little difficulty concluding from the record presented here that the SART video constituted 'favorable' evidence under *Brady*." 162 Cal.App.4th at 1475.

The SART videotape was favorable evidence, because it tended to negate an element of the crime for which the defendant was charged.

In *United States v. Kohring* (2011, CA9 AK) 637 F.3d 895, 907, previously undisclosed evidence that tended to cast doubt on the amounts of money allegedly paid to a defendant charged with public corruption, as well as whether the payments were made at all, was found by the Ninth Circuit Court of Appeals to be favorable to the defendant within the meaning of the *Brady* rule, because such evidence tended to negate an element of the crimes for which the defendant was charged.

Evidence negating the defendant's criminal intent in committing the acts charged against him is evidence favorable to the defendant, even when that evidence consists of information offered as a proffer by the attorney of a witness who is seeking favorable treatment for that client witness.

In *United States v. Triumph Capital Group, Inc.* (2008, CA2 CT) 544 F.3d 149, the attorney for a suspect in a racketeering case charging a variety of federal offenses approached the investigating officer on behalf of the suspect. The attorney provided the officer with the client's account of his criminal activity in an effort to convince the government to offer the client a cooperation agreement. The proffer implicated some of the suspects and was exculpatory of one of the suspects, Charles Spadoni. The statements of the witness contained in the proffer were directly relevant to the intent element of the consulting contract bribe charges.

The proffer was memorialized in notes of the meeting taken by one of the government investigators. The proffer notes were not disclosed to the defendants, who were convicted after a trial at which the witness whose attorney had provided the proffer testified. The Second Circuit Court of Appeals reversed the conviction of the defendant Spadoni, concluding that the suppression of the proffer notes "deprived Spadoni of exculpatory evidence going to the core of [the government's] case against him." 544 F.3d at 162.

§ 1:17.2 Evidence negating identity of defendant as crime perpetrator

Physical evidence linking a third person to the charged crime is evidence favorable to the defendant, because that evidence tends to negate the identity of the defendant as the perpetrator of the crime.

In *Trammell v. McKune* (2007, CA10 KS) 485 F.3d 546, a defendant charged in state court with several felonies arising out his alleged stealing of a service station tow truck and using it to steal another vehicle, defended against these charges on the ground that another man, whose identity was known, committed the crime and framed him. The prosecution failed to disclose physical evidence linking the third party to the tow truck theft. The defendant was convicted of the charges.

Six weeks after his conviction the prosecution realized that it had failed to disclose the exculpatory physical evidence to the defense and disclosed that evidence to the defendant's attorneys. The ensuing defense motion for a new trial was denied, and the denial was affirmed on appeal in the Kansas appellate courts.

The defendant petitioned for habeas corpus relief in the federal district court, arguing that he had been denied a fair trial arising out of the prosecution's suppression of exculpatory evidence under *Brady*. The district court agreed with the defendant's argument that the Kansas courts had misapplied the *Brady* rule in affirming his conviction, but denied his habeas petition.

The Tenth Circuit Court of Appeals granted the habeas petition, vacated the convictions, and remanded the case to the Kansas courts for a new trial. The Court of Appeals rejected the prosecution's arguments and explained how the physical evidence could have been utilized as favorable evidence at the trial. The Court stated: "The [towing] receipts [found in the third person's motel room] directly link Cross [the third person] to the stolen truck, and defense counsel could have used the evidence to support his theory of the case—that Cross is the one who stole the tow truck, which is how the box of tow truck receipts got into his motel room." 485 F.3d at 551.

The two truck receipts were evidence tending to negate the identity of the defendant as the perpetrator of the charged crimes, and were thus evidence favorable to the defendant within the meaning of the *Brady* rule.

Thus, evidence that helps a defendant establish that someone else committed the crime for which the defendant is charged is favorable to the defendant. In *United States v. Stever* (2010, CA9 OR) 603 F.3d 747, the defendant was charged in federal court with manufacturing marijuana plants and marijuana. The defendant moved for an order requiring the government to disclose reports describing the operation of Mexican drug trafficking organizations in the area where he lived. The district court refused to order disclosure, concluding that whoever else might be responsible for the growing of the marijuana would not be relevant to assessing the likelihood that the defendant was involved.

The Ninth Circuit Court of Appeals reversed the defendant's conviction, holding that the district court had erred in denying disclosure of the reports on the Mexican drug trafficking organizations. The Court of Appeals observed that the trial court was presented with evidence that Mexican drug trafficking organizations (DTOs) grow marijuana on large tracts of public and private land in Eastern Oregon without the knowledge of the owners, and that these DTOs "are secretive and familial and so are unlikely to have involved a local Caucasian in their operations."

The Court reasoned that evidence that tended to show that a Mexican DTO planted the marijuana would "make it more probable that Stever was not involved, as there would then be an alternative explanation for the grow that would not entail the consent, much less the participation, of any of the Stevers . . . Evidence that makes it more likely that a Mexican DTO—any Mexican DTO—was responsible for this operation makes it less likely that [the defendant] was." 603 F.3d at 753.

Evidence need not point to a third party in order to be favorable to the defendant as evidence negating the defendant's identity as the perpetrator of the crime. Such evidence might simply weaken the prosecution's evidence of the defendant's identity as the perpetrator.

In *Montgomery v. Bagley* (2009, CA6 OH) 581 F.3d 440, the defendant was convicted of murder and sentenced to death. On habeas corpus proceedings the federal district court granted the defendant a new trial, because the prosecution had failed to disclose to the defendant a police report written prior to trial that reported that several witnesses had seen one of the defendant's purported victims alive four days after the prosecution alleged that the defendant had murdered her. The government appealed the district court order granting the new trial.

The Court of Appeals affirmed the district court order. The Court of Appeals concluded that the suppressed police report was favorable to the defendant, because evidence that several persons had seen the victim alive long after the prosecution contended that the defendant had killed her would have undercut the testimony of the prosecution's star witness that the defendant was the triggerman in both of the murders for which he was charged and convicted.

The withheld evidence that directly opposed the defendant's guilt constituted evidence favorable to the defendant.

In *United States v. King* (2011, CA4 NC) 628 F.3d 693, the Fourth Circuit Court of Appeals held that evidence of the relationship between the defendant and his roommate was relevant, "because it would cast a question on . . . whose drugs were in the apartment." 628 F.3d at 704.

The Sixth Circuit Court of Appeals reached a similar result with similar reasoning in *In re Siggers* (2010, CA6 MI) 615 F.3d 477, 480 ["[T]he evidence is exculpatory because it centers on witness statements that would help Siggers establish that someone else committed the murder."], and *Sykes v. Anderson* (2010, CA6 MI) 625 F.3d 294, 320 ["[T]he letter raised serious questions about whether Holmes was even the individual who had wagered the amount of money indicated on the Casino's marketing records, which, if she were not, would have undermined the prosecution's entire theory of the case."].

Moreover, evidence need not directly contradict the prosecution's evidence in order for that evidence to be deemed favorable to the defendant. Even where undisclosed evidence does not directly contradict the testimony of the prosecution's witnesses, it can be considered *Brady* material when the withheld evidence places the prosecution's evidence in a different light. *United States v. Johnson* (2010, CA DC) 592 F.3d 164, 172.

Evidence can be favorable to the defendant when it negates the identity of the defendant as the crime perpetrator in the context of the penalty phase of a capital murder trial.

In *In re Miranda* (2008) 43 Cal.4th 541, 76 Cal.Rptr.3d 172, 182 P.3d 513, the petitioner had been convicted of capital murder. In the penalty phase of the trial the prosecution presented the testimony of a man named Joe Saucedo who testified that the petitioner had killed another man two weeks before the capital crime. Saucedo was the prosecution's "star penalty phase witness." 43 Cal.4th at 575. The petitioner had pled guilty to the prior crime as a second degree murder. The facts of the prior murder were used by the prosecution as evidence in aggravation in the penalty phase of the capital murder trial to argue for a death sentence. The petitioner was sentenced to death for the second murder.

At the time of the capital murder trial the prosecution possessed a letter written by another inmate in the Los Angeles County jail in which the inmate wrote that Saucedo had told him that he (Saucedo), not the defendant, had personally killed the victim in the prior murder. The letter also related that Saucedo claimed he had destroyed evidence relating to the prior murder and that he had developed a false alibi to deflect suspicion from himself for that murder. The prosecution did not disclose that letter to the petitioner.

The petitioner filed a habeas petition in the California state courts. The Supreme Court appointed a referee to conduct an evidentiary hearing on the petitioner's *Brady* violation claims. The referee found that the prosecution had possessed numerous pieces of evidence in addition to the letter from the jail inmate that Saucedo had killed the victim in the prior murder and that this evidence was credible.

The Supreme Court granted the habeas petition and set aside the petitioner's death sentence. The Court concluded that the letter from the jail inmate was favorable to the petitioner, because it constituted evidence that was inconsistent with Saucedo's trial testimony that inculpated the petitioner and rebutted the prosecution's evidence that the petitioner had killed the victim in the prior murder. 43 Cal.4th at 575–576.

The evidence pointing to Saucedo as the actual killer in the prior murder thus constituted evidence negating the identity of the defendant as the actual killer in the charged prior murder.

However, even though a "bald assertion that someone else confessed to [committing the charged crime] can be favorable to the defense . . . a

31

demonstrably false confession . . . probably is not." *Hammond v. Hall* (2009, CA11 GA) 586 F.3d 1289, 1318.

§ 1:17.4   Evidence must negate defendant's guilt without inferences

One federal circuit court, the Seventh Circuit Court of Appeals, has enunciated a principle that in order for evidence to be favorable as exculpating the defendant, the evidence must be favorable without the need to draw inferences to reach that conclusion. *See, e.g., Harris v. Kuba* (2007, CA7 IL) 486 F.3d 1010, 1016; and *Carvajal v. Dominguez* (2008, CA7 IL) 542 F.3d 561, 568. Whether other federal circuit courts or California courts will adopt this test of exculpatory evidence is not yet known.

§ 1:17.5   Death or other loss of material prosecution witness as negating defendant's guilt

A question not addressed by California appellate courts is whether the death or other known trial unavailability of an important prosecution witness must be disclosed by the prosecutor pursuant to the *Brady* rule. There appear to be very few cases dealing with this subject in other jurisdictions. Those cases have arisen in the New York state courts.

In *People v. Jones* (N.Y. 1978) 375 N.E.2d 41, a prosecutor accepted a guilty plea without disclosing that the primary eyewitness against the defendant had died several days earlier. The defendant moved to withdraw his guilty plea when learning of the witness's death, arguing that the death should have been disclosed because it was exculpatory evidence under *Brady*. In rejecting this argument, the New York State Court of Appeal concluded that "[t]he circumstance that the testimony of the complaining witness was no longer available to the prosecution was not evidence." 375 N.E.2d at 43.

In *People v. Roldan* (1984) 124 Misc.2d 279, 476 N.Y.S.2d 447, the prosecutor agreed to accept a defendant's guilty plea to attempted assault without disclosing to the defendant that the complaining witness was unwilling to cooperate in the prosecution of the case. When the defendant discovered that the complaining witness would not have testified at trial, the defendant moved to set aside the guilty plea. Relying upon *People v. Jones, supra*, the trial court denied the defendant's request, holding that "[i]f it is the law of the state . . . that a district attorney is not obliged to reveal that a principal witness has died before a plea of guilty is taken, it must follow that even if the assistant district attorney knew that the complainant-witness would not cooperate in the prosecution of the case, he had no duty to reveal that information to the defendant . . . ." 124 Misc.2d at 280–281.

Thus, because the absence of a witness is not evidence, the *Brady* rule does not compel a prosecutor to disclose that fact to the defendant.

However, as in postjudgment disclosures (see Sections 1:94 and 1:94.1 of the text and this supplement), the prosecutor might have an ethical duty to disclose the death or other known unavailability of a material prosecution witness. Such was the holding of the court in *Matter of Wayne M.* (1983) 121 Misc.2d 346, 467 N.Y.S.2d 798, which grounded its conclusion upon Disciplinary Rule 7-103(B) of New York State's Code of Professional Responsibility. Disciplinary Rule 7 provided that "[a] public prosecutor or other government lawyer in criminal litigation shall make timely disclosure . . . of the existence of evidence, known to the prosecutor or other government lawyer, that tends to negate the guilt of the accused, mitigate the degree of the offense, or reduce the punishment." The Court concluded that "[t]his ethical injunction includes a situation such as the one at bar in which a complainant is unavailable." 121 Misc.2d at 347.

California has no comparable rule of professional responsibility. Rule 5-220 of the California Rules of Professional Conduct provides that "[a] member shall not suppress any evidence that the member or the member's client has a legal obligation to reveal or to produce." Rule 5-220 begs the question whether the prosecutor has an ethical duty to disclose the death of a material prosecution witness, because it is dependent upon the very issue—a legal obligation to reveal or to produce—which is the object of this determination. Rule 5-220 does not impose an ethical duty upon a prosecutor to disclose evidence unless the prosecutor otherwise has a legal obligation to reveal or to produce that evidence.

However, it is conceivable that a rule of professional responsibility which requires a prosecutor to refrain from prosecuting a charge that the prosecutor knows is not supported by probable cause could provide the ethical basis for disclosure. Rule 3.8 of the American Bar Association Model Rules of Professional Conduct provides that the "prosecutor in a criminal case shall: (a) refrain from prosecuting a charge that the prosecutor knows is not supported by probable cause."

The ABA Model Rules of Professional Conduct and the Model Code of Professional Responsibility have "no legal force of their own" and have not been adopted in California. *General Dynamics Corp. v. Superior Court* (1994) 7 Cal.4th 1164, 1190, n.6, 32 Cal.Rptr.2d 1, 876 P.2d 487. Because they have not been adopted in California, and because they have no legal force of their own, the "ABA Model Rules of Professional Conduct . . . do not establish ethical standards in California . . . ." *State Comp. Ins. Fund v. WPS, Inc.* (1999) 70 Cal.App.4th 644, 655–656, 82 Cal.Rptr.2d 799.

With the approval of the California Supreme Court, the Board of Governors of the State Bar has the power to "formulate and enforce rules of professional conduct for all members of the bar in the State." Business and Professions Code section 6076. When approved by the Supreme Court, these Rules of Professional Conduct "are binding upon all members of the State Bar," and their willful breach can subject an attorney to discipline by the State Bar and the California Supreme Court. Business and Professions Code section 6077.

California has adopted Rules of Professional Conduct for attorneys. These rules "are intended not only to establish ethical standards for members of the bar [citation omitted], but are also designed to protect the public. [citations omitted]." *Ames v. State Bar* (1973) 8 Cal.3d 910, 917, 106 Cal.Rptr. 489, 506 P.2d 625.

A California attorney is subject to State Bar and Supreme Court discipline for a willful violation of the California Rules of Professional Conduct, the State Bar Act [Business and Professions Code section 6000 et seq.], and California judicial opinions. *In re Edward S.* (2009) 173 Cal.App.4th 387, 412, 92 Cal.Rptr.3d 725. In the absence of an applicable California Rule of Professional Conduct, California statute, or opinion of a California appellate court, a California attorney is not subject to discipline in California for violating an ABA Model Rule of Professional Conduct, an ABA ethical standard, or an ABA formal opinion. *State Comp. Ins. Fund v. WPS, Inc.* (1999) 70 Cal.App.4th 644, 656, 82 Cal.Rptr.2d 799.

The California Supreme Court has occasionally looked to the principles underlying the ABA counterparts to California's Rules of Professional Conduct. *Flatt v. Superior Court* (1994) 9 Cal.4th 275, 282, 36 Cal.Rptr.2d 537, 885 P.2d 950. *See People v. Gonzalez* (1990) 51 Cal.3d 1179, 1261, 275 Cal.Rptr. 729, 800 P.2d 1159, where the Supreme Court cited Rule 3.8(d) of the ABA Model Rules of Prof. Conduct; *People v. Garcia* (1993) 17 Cal.App.4th 1169, 1179, 22 Cal.Rptr.2d 545; and *Goldberg v. Warner/ Chappell Music, Inc.* (2005) 125 Cal.App.4th 752, 765, 23 Cal.Rptr.3d 116.

ABA standards do have an appropriate role in determining the ethical duties of California attorneys. The role of ABA standards is to provide guideposts to the application of California Rules of Professional Conduct. *Higdon v. Superior Court* (1991) 227 Cal.App.3d 1667, 1680, 278 Cal.Rptr. 588. Rule 1-100(A) of the California Rules of Professional Conduct expressly provides that "[e]thics opinions and rules and standards promulgated by other jurisdictions and bar associations may also be considered." Thus, where there is no conflict with the public policy of California, the ABA Model Rules of Professional Conduct can serve as a collateral source for guidance on proper professional conduct in California. *People v. Donaldson* (2001) 93 Cal.App.4th 916, 928, 113 Cal.Rptr.2d 548. State Bar Rules of Professional Conduct, in conjunction with American Bar Association's Standards, "provide guidelines for determining the prevailing norms of practice . . . ." *In re Alvernaz* (1992) 2 Cal.4th 924, 937, 8 Cal.Rptr.2d 713, 830 P.2d 747.

But it is ultimately the California Rules of Professional Conduct, California state statutes, and California judicial opinions that establish enforceable ethical standards for California attorneys.

As previously noted, Rule 3.8 of the American Bar Association Model Rules of Professional Conduct provides that the "prosecutor in a criminal case shall: (a) refrain from prosecuting a charge that the prosecutor knows is not supported by probable cause." Rule 5-110 of the California Rules of Professional Conduct appears to be a counterpart to ABA Rule 3.8. Rule 5-110 provides that "[a] member in government service shall not institute or cause to be instituted criminal charges when the member knows or should know that the charges are not supported by probable cause. If, after the institution of criminal charges, the member in government service having responsibility for prosecuting the charges becomes aware that those charges are not supported by probable cause, the member shall promptly so advise the court in which the criminal matter is pending."

Although no California case has so held, an argument could be made that the death of a material prosecution witness which prevents the prosecutor from being able to prove a charge at trial obviates probable cause in support of that criminal charge. Under this approach, undermining the probable cause in support of the criminal charge would trigger the prosecutor's ethical duty to disclose the witness's death to the court. Any such ethical duty under Rule 5-110 to disclose the death of a prosecution witness would almost certainly be limited to the death of a material prosecution witness without whom the prosecutor would be unable to obtain a conviction at trial. An ethical duty would not require disclosure of the death of a prosecution witness whose unavailability would not prevent the prosecution from going forward to trial.

Therefore, although the prosecutor does not have a constitutionally based duty under *Brady* to disclose the death or other unavailability of a material prosecution witness, the prosecutor could have an ethical duty to make such a disclosure under Rule 5-110 of the California Rules or Professional Conduct. Whether the death or other permanent unavailability of a material prosecution witness obviates probable cause in support of a charge has not been addressed by California courts.

Practice Tip for Prosecution: Although you are not obligated by the *Brady* rule to disclose to the defendant the death or other unavailability of a material prosecution witness, you might have an ethical duty under the California Rules of Professional Conduct to make such a disclosure. Prosecutors concerned about their professional reputations and desirous of avoiding the possibility of a State Bar disciplinary action are well advised to disclose the death or other permanent unavailability of a material prosecution witness whose absence from the case undermines the prosecution's ability to obtain a conviction of the charge.

Without clear decisional or other authority that would compel or support it, we are not willing to extend the reasoning behind a possible prosecutor's ethical requirement to disclose the death or other permanent unavailability of a material prosecution witness to other evidentiary problems which prosecutors face. Thus, we are not prepared to conclude that a prosecutor's inability to locate a material witness, a witness's reluctance to cooperate, or a witness's temporary absence from the jurisdiction, become ethically disclosable facts.

See People v. West (2003 Cal.App. Unpub. Lexis 10997), in which the Court of Appeal in an unpublished decision held that "[t]he fact that a prosecution witness fails to show up for a required court appearance does not necessarily mean the witness will be unavailable at the time of a defendant's trial. The witness could be found by the authorities or voluntarily reappear at any point in time, in which case knowledge of the failure to appear is no longer useful to the defendant. The prosecution has no duty to disclose its potential case to the defendant. [citation omitted] Similarly, the prosecution's duty to disclose exculpatory evidence does not extend to disclosure of difficulties that may arise in the securing of witnesses to present its case."

Although *People v. West* as an unpublished opinion is not citable and may not be relied upon by a party or a court, *California Rules of Court*, Rule 8.1115 (2009), its reasoning may be considered by counsel in the litigation of discovery questions.

Practice Tip for Prosecution: Although Rule 5-110 requires that a charge be supported by "probable cause," California prosecutors are required to adhere to a higher filing standard. The general filing standard to be followed by California prosecutors is that a prosecutor may file a criminal charge when four requirements are satisfied. These four requirements are: (1) there has been a complete investigation and thorough consideration of all pertinent data; (2) there is legally sufficient, admissible evidence of a corpus delicti; (3) there is legally sufficient, admissible evidence of the accused's identity as the perpetrator of the crime; and (4) the prosecutor has considered the probability of conviction by an objective fact-finder hearing the admissible evidence. *Professionalism, A Sourcebook of Ethics and Civil Liability Principles for Prosecutors*, California District Attorneys Association, Chap. III, page 18 (2001); *Uniform Crime Charging Standards*, California District Attorneys Association, p. 6 (1996).

The quantity and quality of evidence required for the charging of a crime is that the evidence "should be of such convincing force that it would warrant conviction of the crime charged by a reasonable and objective fact-finder after hearing all the evidence available to the prosecutor at the time of charging and after hearing the most plausible, reasonably foreseeable defense that could be raised under the evidence presented to the prosecutor." *Professionalism, A Sourcebook of Ethics and Civil Liability Principles for Prosecutors*, California District Attorneys Association, Chap. III, page 18 (2001); *Uniform Crime Charging Standards*, California District Attorneys Association, p. 12 (1996). California appellate courts have recognized these principles as establishing the standards for crime charging in California. *See Davis v. Municipal Court* (1988) 46 Cal.3d 64, 82, n.9, 249 Cal.Rptr. 300, 757 P.2d 11; *People v.*

Robinson (1995) 31 Cal.App.4th 494, 499, n.5, 37 Cal.Rptr.2d 183; and *Youngblood v. Gates* (1988) 200 Cal.App.3d, 1302 n.11, 246 Cal.Rptr. 775.

§ 1:18 Evidence indirectly opposing guilt [third-party culpability]

Whether and under what conditions evidence that indirectly points to the culpability of someone other than the defendant—a third party—is favorable to the defendant continues to spark conflict in criminal prosecutions. While the focus of our analysis is upon the question whether such evidence is favorable to the defendant within the meaning of the *Brady* rule, most of the reported appellate decisions involve the question whether trial courts have erred in declining to admit such evidence in trial.

Although the question of discoverability is not co-extensive with the question of its admissibility, decisional authority on the admissibility of third-party culpability evidence does help understand whether and under what conditions such evidence is favorable to the defendant for purposes of the *Brady* rule. If third-party culpability evidence is not *admissible*, then it might be logically argued that such evidence is not *favorable* to a defendant.

The basic rule regarding evidence of third-party culpability is this: "Evidence that raises a reasonable doubt as to a defendant's guilt, including evidence tending to show that another person committed the crime, is relevant." *People v. Brady* (2010) 50 Cal.4th 547, 558, 113 Cal.Rptr.3d 458, 236 P.3d 312. To be relevant, third-party culpability evidence "must link this third person to the actual commission of the crime." *People v. Brady, supra,* 50 Cal.4th at 558.

In *Williams v. Ryan* (2010, CA9 AZ) 623 F.3d 1258, the Ninth Circuit Court of Appeals analyzed why "Third-Party Perpetrator" evidence that has been withheld by the prosecution causes a *Brady* violation. The Court stated: "[N]ew evidence suggesting an alternate perpetrator is 'classic *Brady* material.' [citations omitted] Not only are the [suppressed letters found in the prosecutor's office years after the defendant's trial] inconsistent with the State's theory at trial—that Williams was the only individual responsible for [the victim's] murder—but they also point to an alternative suspect who may himself have been responsible for the brutal crime." 623 F.3d at 1265.

The Court of Appeals continued: "Fields is at least a plausible alternative suspect: he had a history of violence against women and lied about being in jail at the time of the murder. [Two potential witnesses named in the letters who later wrote declarations about their observations] both saw Fields disposing of bloody clothing around the time of the murder and a short walk away from where police discovered [the victim's] abandoned car. . . . There was also little physical evidence connecting Williams to the crime. This lends materiality to new evidence that someone else was involved—and possibly solely responsible." 623 F.3d at 1265–1266.

The Court of Appeals concluded that "the government may not, consistent with *Brady*, suppress information that another person committed the crime for which the defendant is on trial." 623 F.3d at 1266.

When determining whether evidence of third-party culpability rises to the level of exculpatory evidence within the meaning of the *Brady* rule, it is not necessary for the court to determine that the "suppressed evidence establishes the guilt of a third party beyond a reasonable doubt or exonerates [the defendant]. [citation omitted] The critical question is whether the suppressed *Brady* material could have provided material evidence that may have changed the result." *Williams v. Ryan, supra,* 623 F.3d at 1266.

In order for third-party culpability evidence to be favorable to the defendant, and thus admissible at trial, " 'there must be evidence' of a 'connection between the other perpetrators and the crime, not mere speculation on the part of the defendant.' [citation omitted]." *United States v. Lighty* (2010, CA4 MD) 616 F.3d 321, 358.

§ 1:18.1   Third-party culpability evidence—links to charged crime

In *People v. McWhorter* (2009) 47 Cal.4th 318, 367, 97 Cal.Rptr.3d 412, 212 P.3d 692, the California Supreme Court reiterated its oft-stated standard for admissibility of third-party culpability evidence. "[T]o be admissible, evidence of the culpability of a third party offered by a defendant to demonstrate that a reasonable doubt exists concerning his or her guilt, must link the third person either directly or circumstantially to the actual perpetration of the crime."

In *People v. Samaniego* (2009) 172 Cal.App.4th 1148, 91 Cal.Rptr.3d 874, two defendants convicted of murder argued on appeal that the trial court erred in excluding evidence that a third person had committed the murder. The Court of Appeal rejected the defendants' contention, concluding that there was no evidence that the third party was present at the scene of the shooting at the time the shooting occurred, and no other evidence that the third party was involved in the murder in any fashion. 172 Cal.App.4th at 1175.

In order for third-party culpability evidence to be favorable to the defendant, and thus admissible at trial, " 'there must be evidence' of a 'connection between the other perpetrators and the crime, not mere speculation on the part of the defendant.' [citation omitted]." *United States v. Lighty* (2010, CA4 MD) 616 F.3d 321, 358.

§ 1:18.1.1   Third-party motive and opportunity evidence

Evidence of the motive of a third party to commit the charged crime, together with evidence of the third-party's opportunity to commit the crime, must be more than speculative. *People v. McWhorter* (2009) 47 Cal.4th 318, 372, 97 Cal.Rptr.3d 412, 212 P.3d 692. "[E]vidence that another person had a motive or opportunity to commit the crime, without more, is irrelevant because it does not raise a reasonable doubt about a defendant's guilt; to be relevant, the evidence must link this third person to the actual commission of the crime." *People v. Brady* (2010) 50 Cal.4th 547, 558, 113 Cal.Rptr.3d 458, 236 P.3d 312.

Moreover, when a defendant's third-party culpability evidence consists of a third-party's "mere evidence of a propensity for violence" to prove the identity of the perpetrator, such evidence of a criminal disposition or a history of violence "does not amount to direct or circumstantial evidence linking the third person to the actual perpetration of the crime." 47 Cal.4th at 372, 373.

To be admissible as third-party culpability evidence, there must be a link or a significant nexus between the third party and the crime. *Miller v. Brunsman* (2010, CA6 OH) 599 F.3d 517, 524; *Webb v. Mitchell* (2009, CA6 OH) 586 F.3d 383, 391.

§ 1:18.1.2 Third-party police suspect evidence

Evidence of Other Suspects

See *United States v. Gorbea Del-Valle* (2009, CA1 P.R.) 566 F.3d 31, in which the First Circuit Court of Appeals rejected the defendant's contention that the government committed *Brady* error in failing to disclose evidence that one of the investigating agents attempted to investigate another man with the same name as one of the defendants in the prosecution.

Neither the fact that the investigating officer nor the prosecutor had suspicions that a third party was involved in the commission of the crime constitute admissible third-party culpability evidence, especially when those suspicions are based upon the same evidence that underlies everyone else's suspicions in the case. *Hammond v. Hall* (2009, CA11 GA) 586 F.3d 1289, 1308. Perforce, the *suspicions* of the investigating officer or the prosecutor do not constitute evidence favorable to a defendant.

§ 1:18.1.5 Third-party culpability evidence—unidentified third party

Third-party culpability evidence "that does not identify a possible suspect is properly excluded." *People v. Brady* (2010) 50 Cal.4th 547, 559, 113 Cal.Rptr.3d 458, 236 P.3d 312. Thus, in *Brady* the California Supreme Court upheld a trial court's exclusion of an unsigned letter sent to the police in which the author of the letter claimed responsibility for the murder of the police officer for which the defendant was convicted. 50 Cal.4th at 559.

§ 1:18.2 Third-party culpability evidence—links to uncharged crimes

In *People v. DePriest* (2007) 42 Cal.4th 1, 43–44, 63 Cal.Rptr.3d 896, 163 P.3d 896, the California Supreme Court summarized and applied the principles of the admissibility of third-party culpability evidence. In *De-Priest* the defendant, who was charged with and ultimately convicted of capital murder and other crimes, sought to introduce evidence in support of his theory that the crime was committed by a third person named Denny who gave the defendant a ride in a vehicle that matched the victim's vehicle, a white Toyota MR2, and who then gave the defendant the murder weapon and some of the victim's property. The victim had last been seen in Garden Grove near her place of employment.

The evidence the defendant wanted to introduce was that on the night of the murder a man named Oscar Mink, who lived in a gated community in Lake Arrowhead, located some 75 miles to the north of Garden Grove, heard a loud argument between two male voices and then saw a white Toyota MR2 drive away from the scene. The defendant proposed to introduce evidence that Garden Grove Detective Glenn Overley, who was investigating the victim's murder, went to Lake Arrowhead to interview a woman named Bianca St. James about her relationship with the defendant, and that Ms. St. James and Mr. Mink lived near one another in gated communities. The defendant proposed to use this evidence to support the defense theory that the third party (Denny) was the murderer, not the defendant.

The trial court sustained the prosecutor's objection to the proposed defense evidence. The Supreme Court upheld the trial court's ruling. The Supreme Court first reviewed the applicable principles of the limits upon third-party culpability evidence. "Evidence that another person had 'motive or opportunity' to commit the charged crime, or had some 'remote' connection to the victim or crime scene, is not sufficient to raise the requisite reasonable doubt . . . third party culpability evidence is relevant and admissible only if it succeeds in 'linking the third person to the actual perpetration of the crime.' [citations omitted]." 42 Cal.4th at 43. The Court then applied those principles.

> "[T]he trial court properly found that Detective Overley's testimony raised no reasonable doubt as to defendant's guilt. When defendant called Overley as a witness, testimony by [three defense witnesses] had suggested, *at most*, that two men were in [the victim's] car, and that defendant might have been one of them. Overley's proffered testimony arguably corroborated these inferences by suggesting that defendant's friend Bianca lived near Mink in Lake Arrowhead, and that defendant was hunting for Bianca's house when Mink saw the car. However, even assuming defendant established that he was in Lake Arrowhead with a third party in the murder victim's car, such fact is not inconsistent with defendant killing, sexually assaulting, and robbing [the victim] earlier that night. In other words, Overley's proffered testimony did not tend to link anyone other than defendant to 'actual perpetration' of the charged crime." 42 Cal.4th at 43–44. [italics in original]

Thus, even if third-party culpability evidence corroborates some of the defense evidence or theory that a third person committed the crime, unless that evidence links someone other than the defendant to the **actual perpetration** of the charged crime, it is not admissible.

In *United States v. Jernigan* (2007, CA9 AZ) 492 F.3d 1050, a female defendant was convicted in federal district court of bank robbery and sentenced to prison. While in prison the defendant learned that after she had been apprehended and was in custody pending trial, two other banks in the area were robbed by a woman whose description matched the defendant's and whose modus operandi was similar to the robbery for which she had been convicted. The defendant's motion for a new trial was denied and she appealed the denial, arguing that "the government had failed to meet its *Brady* obligations by not disclosing the existence of a phenotypically similar bank robber who had been robbing banks in the same area after [her] incarceration." 492 F.3d at 1053.

In the Ninth Circuit Court of Appeals the government conceded that the evidence of an additional female bank robber matching the defendant's description was favorable to the defendant. 492 F.3d at 1053. After finding that the government had suppressed the evidence of the other bank robber, and that the suppressed evidence was material within the meaning of the *Brady* rule, the Court of Appeals reversed the denial of the defendant's new-trial motion and remanded the case to the district court.

The link of a third party to crimes for which the defendant was not charged became evidence favorable to the defendant when the description of that third party matched the defendant's description, the modus operandi in the charged and the two uncharged crimes was similar, and the defendant could not have committed the uncharged crimes, because she was in custody when they were committed.

In *Harris v. Kuba* (2007, CA7 IL) 486 F.3d 1010, the Court of Appeals reached a contrary result on evidence similar to that in *Jernigan*. Harris was convicted at trial of armed robbery and attempted murder arising out of a gasoline station robbery and was sentenced to 50 years in prison. After 20 years Harris was pardoned based on a finding by the governor of Illinois that Harris was factually innocent. Harris then filed a civil action against the officers who had investigated and arrested him. Harris's action was based on a claim that the officers violated his due-process rights by failing to disclose three pieces of exculpatory evidence to the prosecutors prior to his trial.

The three pieces of unrevealed evidence were: (1) that the defendant had an alibi for a shooting/murder that occurred three weeks after the charged robbery; (2) that a witness had identified the defendant in that subsequent shooting/murder; and (3) a third person had confessed to the subsequent shooting/murder. The link between the charged robbery and the uncharged shooting/murder was that the same firearm was used in both crimes.

The Seventh Circuit Court of Appeals rejected the defendant's *Brady* argument, concluding, without much explanation, that the fact that the same firearm was used at both robberies did not help the defendant, and the facts that a third person had confessed to the uncharged crime and that the defendant had an alibi for the evening of the uncharged crime were "not relevant to the Caseyville Shell Station shooting," the uncharged robbery, because they did not directly bear on the defendant's guilt for the charged gas station shooting. The Court concluded that the evidence claimed to have been suppressed was not favorable to the defendant's defense. 486 F.3d at 1016. The Court of Appeals did not discuss whether the suppressed evidence could have been favorable to the defendant as evidence indirectly opposing his guilt.

§ 1:19   Evidence supporting affirmative defense

The Tenth Circuit Court of Appeals has joined the Ninth Circuit opinion in *United States v. Ross* (2004, CA9 CA) 372 F.3d 1097, discussed in the text, in holding that evidence supporting an affirmative defense can meet the favorableness criteria of the *Brady* rule.

In *United States v. Ford* (2008, CA10 CO) 550 F.3d 975, a defendant convicted of illegally possessing or selling a machinegun made a new-trial motion, arguing that the government withheld e-mails sent to the defendant by an informant to whom the defendant sold a machine gun. The defendant claimed that these e-mails were exculpatory, because they would have provided documentary support for the defendant's claim that he was entrapped when he sold the automatic weapon to the informant. The trial court denied the new-trial motion.

On appeal the defendant again argued that the government's *Brady* violation entitled him to a new trial. Although the Court of Appeals ultimately rejected the defendant's argument on the ground that the suppressed evidence did not meet the materiality element of the Brady rule, the Court of Appeals concluded that the e-mails bolstered Ford's entrapment defense by supporting his argument that the informant's persistence was the reason the defendant committed the crime. 550 F.3d at 983.

In *Sandoval v. Ulibarri* (2008, CA10 NM) 548 F.3d 902, a defendant convicted of aggravated battery and shooting at an automobile filed a federal habeas petition challenging his convictions. His petition was denied by the district court, and the defendant appealed the petition's denial. The defendant-petitioner argued in his appeal that the prosecution committed *Brady* error by failing to disclose the victim's medical records, which the defendant-petitioner claimed would have supported his defense that the victim was holding a firearm at the time he suffered a gunshot wound to the hand.

The Court of Appeals rejected the *Brady* claim on the grounds that there was no evidence to support the defendant-petitioner's claim and that the claim was simply speculative. Although the Court of Appeals concluded that the medical report on the victim's injury constituted material exculpatory evidence, the Court appears to have accepted the premise that evidence supporting an affirmative defense of self-defense would have met the favorableness component of the *Brady* rule.

Although the Court of Appeals was not presented with, and accordingly did not decide, the question, the Seventh Circuit Court of Appeals appears to have accepted the notion that evidence supporting an affirmative defense can be favorable to a defendant within the meaning of the *Brady* rule. *See*, *United States v.* Daniel (2009, CA7 IN) 576 F.3d 772, where the court rejected the defendant's argument that by failing to disclose the real names of two persons posing as minor girls who participated in internet chat room conversations with the defendant, the government impeded the defendant's ability to mount an entrapment defense to the charged crime of knowingly persuading, inducing, enticing, or coercing a person under the age of 18 to engage in criminal sexual activity. The Court of Appeals rejected the defendant's *Brady* argument without questioning whether the defendant was entitled to disclosure of favorable evidence for purposes of presenting the entrapment affirmative defense.

In *United States v. Prochilo* (2011, CA1 MA) 629 F.3d 264, the First Circuit Court of Appeals observed that *Brady* "requires the government to disclose all favorable and material evidence in its possession to the defendant; this includes any evidence indicating that the witness had improperly induced Prochilo or others to commit crimes." 629 F.3d at 269.

§ 1:21 Evidence supporting defense motion

The Ninth Circuit Court of Appeals continues to consider claims of *Brady* error arising from the prosecution's alleged failure to disclose exculpatory evidence that is relevant to a pretrial motion to suppress evidence as properly alleging a violation of being within the scope of a prosecutor's *Brady* duties. *See United States v. Brobst* (2009, CA9 MT) 558 F.3d 982, 994–995.

Some prosecutors have questioned whether the Ninth Circuit Court of Appeals has correctly determined that the *Brady* rule applies to evidence that would assist a defendant in litigating a motion which, if granted, would reduce the defendant's guilt or punishment exposure. These prosecutors point out that the *Brady* right to disclosure of exculpatory evidence is a trial-related right, whereas motions to suppress evidence and other such motions, the effect of which can reduce the charges and evidence against a defendant, are pretrial in their nature. These prosecutors also contend that pretrial motions to suppress evidence determine law enforcement miscon-duct, whereas trials determine guilt or innocence.

The first of these arguments—that *Brady* is a trial-related right, and motions to suppress evidence and other motions that reduce the charges and evidence against the defendant are ordinarily pretrial in nature—is an excellent argument that militates against holding that a prosecutor's *Brady* duties are triggered at pretrial motions.

However, the second of these arguments—that pretrial motions do not determine a defendant's guilt or innocence—appears to have less merit. The prosecutor's *Brady* duty to disclose exculpatory evidence extends to a whole body of evidence that is favorable to the defendant only because that evidence impeaches the credibility of material prosecution witnesses. Evidence that impeaches the credibility of material prosecution witnesses is *Brady* evidence, because its disclosure has the potential for reducing the force or strength of the prosecution's evidence against the defendant, and that result thereby reduces the defendant's exposure to conviction and/or punishment.

The granting of a defendant's pretrial motion that weakens the prosecution's case or reduces the defendant's punishment exposure is of the same character and has the same impact as evidence that impeaches a material prosecution witness. By weakening the prosecution's case, evidence that impeaches a material prosecution witness and evidence that supports a defense motion thereby reduce a defendant's exposure to conviction and/or punishment. It makes little sense to hold that one of these types of evidence—evidence impeaching a material prosecution witness—is within the scope of the prosecutor's *Brady* duty while the other—evidence supporting a defense motion, the granting of which would weaken the prosecution's evidence or reduce the defendant's punishment exposure—is not covered by the *Brady* rule.

In *Magallan v. Superior Court* (2011) 192 Cal.App.4th 1444, 121 Cal.Rptr.3d 841, the Sixth District Court of Appeal held that a magistrate has the power to order the prosecution to disclose evidence prior to a preliminary examination that could be used by a defendant to present a motion to suppress evidence at the preliminary examination. The Court of Appeal grounded its decision on an analysis of the California Criminal Discovery Statute and the statutes allowing a defendant to make a suppression motion at a preliminary examination, and did not consider whether the *Brady* rule requires disclosure of favorable, material evidence that would enable the defendant to make a suppression motion. However, the Court did conclude that an additional basis for holding that a magistrate has the power to order disclosure of evidence prior to the preliminary examination that would help a defendant litigate a motion to suppress evidence at the preliminary examination is that the defendant has been granted a statutory right to make a suppression motion at the preliminary hearing. Having been granted that right, the Court concluded, "the defendant must have a fair opportunity to litigate the claim." 192 Cal.App.4th at 1462, n.8. The Court thus held that a defendant's right to due process of law under the California Constitution would support mandatory disclosure of evidence that would assist a defendant to prevail in a motion to suppress evidence.

A more complete analysis of *Magallan v. Superior Court, supra*, as it relates to the authority of a magistrate to order discovery, is found in Section 2:12.1 of this supplement.

§ 1:21.1　Evidence of a "wall" traffic stop

"Walls" are a law enforcement investigative technique used in a variety of situations. In one situation a "wall" is used to shield confidential information about a vehicle or its occupant that is stopped on probable cause or a reasonable suspicion of criminal activity by or about an occupant of that vehicle.

A "wall stop" involving a vehicle has been described in several unpublished state and federal opinions. In *People v. Sanchez* (2008 Cal.App. Unpub. LEXIS 5737), an officer assigned to a High Intensity Drug Trafficking Area Team described a "wall stop" as a tool in which officers investigating a subject contact patrol officers in the area and request the officers follow the subject and "find their own probable cause [to stop the vehicle]." In *United States v. Pedraza-Bucio*, (2009 U.S. Dist. LEXIS 35367), the United States District Court for the District of Utah, quoting a commentator, stated that " '[t]he term 'wall stop' is based on the theory that there is a wall between the stopping officers and the investigators who give the tip to the stopping officers. Essentially, the investigators have 'handed off' the information to the stopping officers.' " Wallenstine, *Street Legal: A Guide to Pre-trial Criminal Procedure for Police, Prosecutors, and Defenders* 61 (2007).

In a second situation a "wall" is used to shield controlled drug buys which form probable cause for a suspect's arrest or search, but which are not themselves charged as criminal offenses against the suspect.

In a third situation a "wall" is used to prevent the disclosure of non-exculpatory information about other suspects that has been provided in a proffer by a cooperating suspect who is seeking a more favorable disposition for himself.

All three of these scenarios can become the subject of a defense motion, such as a motion to suppress evidence or a motion to disclose the identity of a confidential informant. The question confronting prosecutors and courts in these situations is whether the defendant is entitled to disclosure of information contained behind the "wall" that either would materially undermine probable cause to stop, arrest, or search, or in some other way is materially exculpatory to the defendant.

Because prosecution efforts to protect confidential information behind "walls" and defense efforts to pierce the walls to gain access to that protected information are simply another aspect of the struggle over defense efforts to force disclosure of confidential informants and their information, the subject of "walls" is discussed in Sections 7:35.1 and 7:35.2 of this supplement.

§ 1:22 Evidence mitigating punishment

The opinion of the California Supreme Court in *In re Miranda* (2008) 43 Cal.4th 541, 76 Cal.Rptr.3d 172, 182 P.3d 513, has expanded the list of cases in which evidence mitigating punishment has been found to constitute favorable evidence within the meaning of the *Brady* rule. In *Miranda* the petitioner had been convicted of capital murder. In the penalty phase of the trial the prosecution presented the testimony of a man named Joe Saucedo who testified that the petitioner had killed another man two weeks before the capital crime. Saucedo was the prosecution's "star penalty phase witness." 43 Cal.4th at 575. The petitioner had pled guilty to the prior crime as a second degree murder. The facts of the prior murder were used by the prosecution as evidence in aggravation in the penalty phase of the capital murder trial to argue for a death sentence. The petitioner was sentenced to death for the second murder.

At the time of the capital murder trial the prosecution possessed a letter written by another inmate in the Los Angeles County jail in which the inmate wrote that Saucedo had told him that he (Saucedo), not the defendant, had personally killed the victim in the prior murder. The letter also related that Saucedo claimed he had destroyed evidence relating to the prior murder and that he had developed a false alibi to deflect suspicion from himself for that murder. The prosecution did not disclose that letter to the petitioner.

The petitioner filed a habeas petition in the California state courts. The Supreme Court appointed a referee to conduct an evidentiary hearing on the petitioner's *Brady* violation claims. The referee found that the prosecution had possessed numerous pieces of evidence in addition to the letter from the jail inmate that Saucedo had killed the victim in the prior murder and that this evidence was credible.

The Supreme Court granted the habeas petition and set aside the petitioner's death sentence. The Court concluded that the letter from the jail inmate was favorable to the petitioner, because it constituted evidence that was inconsistent with Saucedo's trial testimony that inculpated the petitioner and rebutted the prosecution's evidence that the petitioner had killed the victim in the prior murder. 43 Cal.4th at 575–576.

The evidence pointing to Saucedo as the actual killer in the prior murder thus constituted evidence mitigating the punishment of the petitioner—and as such was evidence favorable to the defendant in his criminal case within the meaning of the *Brady* rule.

In *Cone v. Bell* (2009) 556 U.S. 449, 129 S. Ct. 1769, 173 L. Ed. 2d 701, the United States Supreme Court held that evidence of a defendant's heavy drug use, and of his bizarre conduct and appearance at the time of a murder for which he was convicted in state court and sentenced to death, was evidence mitigating the defendant's punishment, and the suppression of that evidence violated the *Brady* rule.

Cone v. Bell has a tortured procedural history in the state courts of Tennessee and in the federal courts. Following denial of his direct appeal of the conviction and judgment of death, the defendant, Gary Cone, filed a series of petitions for postconviction relief. Almost all of his petitions were denied. However, Mr. Cone was finally able to use the State of Tennessee's Public Records Act to access the prosecutor's file in his murder prosecution.

In that file he located a number of documents which had never been disclosed to him or his attorneys. These documents included statements from witnesses who had seen the defendant several days before and several days after the murders. The witnesses described Cone's appearance as "wild eyed," and his behavior as "real weird." One witness wrote that Cone had appeared "drunk or high." Also in the prosecutor's file was a police report of the defendant's arrest on the murder charge in which the arresting officer wrote that Cone looked around "in a frenzied manner" and walked in an "agitated manner." Finally, the documents included multiple police bulletins that described Cone as a drug user.

Cone finally obtained a hearing in the United States Supreme Court on the merits of his *Brady* claim. The Supreme Court held that the suppression of evidence that Cone was impaired by his drug use around the time his crimes were committed deprived him of a fair trial on the question of whether he should have been sentenced to death, or whether his drug use, which might have resulted from honorable military service, was sufficiently serious to justify a decision by the jury that he should instead have been sentenced to prison for life.

The conclusion that the *Brady* rule applies to evidence that would be material to the defendant's sentence or punishment is not open to serious question. *See, e.g., United States v. King* (2011, CA4 NC) 628 F.3d 693, 704 ["King has made a plausible showing that Bilal's grand jury testimony contained evidence material to his sentence."]; *Basden v. Lee* (2002, CA4 NC) 290 F.3d 602, 611 [*Brady* applies to evidence material to sentencing.].

Evidence mitigating punishment can be favorable when that evidence reduces the culpability of the defendant's conduct. In *Jells v. Mitchell* (2008, CA6 OH) 538 F.3d 478, the habeas petitioner was convicted of the murder of a woman and sentenced to death. The trial evidence supported a conclusion that the petitioner had randomly kidnapped the murder victim as a total stranger and then killed her. After exhausting his appellate and state habeas corpus remedies, the petitioner filed a federal habeas petition. In his federal habeas petition the petitioner argued that the government had suppressed numerous items of evidence showing that he and his victim were acquainted and that she had voluntarily accompanied him on the night of her murder. Thus, the petitioner argued, disclosure of this suppressed evidence would have negated the aggravating factor of a stranger kidnapping which caused the trial court to sentence him to death. The district court denied the habeas petition.

The Sixth Circuit Court of Appeals reversed the denial of the habeas petition and directed that the death sentence be vacated unless the state held a new penalty-phase trial. The Court concluded that "the withheld *Brady* information refutes the prosecution's weak presentation of evidence regarding whether a kidnapping occurred." 538 F.3d at 508.

Evidence can mitigate punishment, and thus be favorable evidence under the *Brady* rule, when that evidence could be used by the defendant to argue for a reduced punishment in a capital murder prosecution, by creating a residual doubt of the defendant's guilt of the charge.

In *Montgomery v. Bagley* (2009, CA6 OH) 581 F.3d 440, the defendant was convicted of murder and sentenced to death. On habeas corpus proceedings the federal district court granted the defendant a new trial, because the prosecution had failed to disclose to the defendant a police report written prior to trial that reported that several witnesses had seen one of the defendant's purported victims alive four days after the prosecution alleged that the defendant had murdered her. The government appealed the district court order granting the new trial.

The Court of Appeals affirmed the district court order. The Court of Appeals concluded that the suppressed police report was favorable to the defendant, because evidence that several persons had seen the victim alive long after the prosecution contended that the defendant had killed her would have undercut the testimony of the prosecution's star witness that the defendant was the triggerman in both of the murders for which he was charged and convicted.

The withheld evidence that directly opposed the defendant's guilt constituted evidence favorable to the defendant, because such evidence could have caused one juror to have a doubt about the defendant's guilt or the nature of his participation in the crime, and thus could have caused such a juror to decline to vote for a death sentence under a "residual doubt" instruction. 581 F.3d at 449.

However, the failure of the prosecution to disclose its list of witnesses that are to be called to testify in a sentencing hearing does not constitute the withholding of evidence favorable to the defendant. "The mere identity of witnesses is not exculpatory and is not covered by *Brady*." *United States v. Boyce* (2009, CA8 MO) 564 F.3d 911, 918.

§ 1:23　Evidence impeaching prosecution witness credibility—generally

The failure of the prosecution to disclose impeachment evidence against a prosecution witness can be *Brady* error only when that prosecution witness actually testifies. *United States v. Johnson* (2008, CA DC) 519 F.3d 478, 489. If the prosecution witness does not testify, the prosecution's failure to disclose impeaching evidence regarding that witness is not material to the outcome of the hearing.

In *Mosley v. City of Chicago* (2010, CA7 IL) 614 F.3d 391, a defendant acquitted of a charge of beating a man to death claimed as part of his civil suit against the City of Chicago that the officers who investigated the homicide withheld evidence that one of the possible witnesses to the beating was "drunk as hell" on that night and did not have an independent recollection of the incident. Mosley claimed that this was impeachment evidence that should have been disclosed. The Seventh Circuit Court of Appeals rejected Mosley's argument, "because the state did not call [that witness] at trial and therefore the state had no obligation to turn over evidence that could impeach his testimony." 614 F.3d at 399.

§ 1:23.3   Evidence impeaching defense witness

The prosecution has no *Brady* duty to disclose to the defendant evidence that the prosecution intends to use to impeach a defense witness.

In *United States v. Johnson* (2009, CA6 MI) 581 F.3d 320, the defendant was charged with bank robbery and conspiracy to commit bank robbery. The defendant called a witness to testify that at the time of the robbery the defendant was using crutches and wearing a bandage for a foot injury, implying that he could not have been the robber. The prosecutor then informed the court and counsel that the government intended to impeach the defense witness by asking the witness questions about his own involvement in the robbery. After being appointed counsel, the defense witness invoked his right to remain silent, and the court struck the testimony of the witness and instructed the jury to disregard that testimony.

After being convicted the defendant claimed on appeal that the government had violated *Brady* by failing to disclose the evidence impeaching the defense witness prior to that witness's testimony. The Court of Appeals rejected the defendant's *Brady* argument, concluding that "the Government did not violate *Brady* by not informing the defense of the evidence it planned to use to impeach [the defense witness] until after [that witness's] direct examination. The evidence in question was not favorable to Johnson; rather, it called a defense witness's credibility into question." 581 F.3d at 331.

See also United States v. Faulkenberry (2010, CA6 OH) 614 F.3d 573, in which the Sixth Circuit Court of Appeals held that the government did not violate the defendant's due process right to a fundamentally fair trial by failing to produce reports prepared by the FBI of its interviews of a government informant who later became a defense witness, and by then using those interview reports to impeach the informant witness's testimony. 614 F.3d at 590.

§ 1:24   Inconsistent or conflicting statements—generally

It is sometimes difficult to determine from a police report of an interview of a witness what language in the report constitutes the statement of the witness and what language constitutes a note of the interviewer that does not contain words spoken by the witness.

In *Jennings v. McDonough* (2007, CA11 FL) 490 F.3d 1230, the prosecutor in a capital murder case interviewed an inmate who had told law enforcement authorities about the defendant's confession to the charged crime. The prosecutor's written note of the interview contained a description of the order in which the inmate and another inmate had come forward to report the defendant's confession. The defendant on appeal contended that this note, which was not disclosed to the defendant at or prior to his trial, constituted *Brady* evidence, because it could have been used to impeach the inmate's testimony as to the order in which the witnesses had reported the defendant's confession to authorities.

The Florida Supreme Court rejected the defendant's interpretation of the note, concluding that the inscription was the prosecutor's "parenthetical note to himself, not something conveyed to him by the witness." 490 F.3d at 1239–1240. The defendant filed a habeas petition in the federal courts. The district court denied the habeas petition, and the Eleventh Circuit Court of Appeals affirmed the district court's denial of the petition. The Court of Appeals concluded that "[t]he parenthetical note of [the prosecutor] appears to be an error on the part of [the prosecutor]" which was "based solely on his review of previously disclosed case reports." 490 F.3d at 1240. The prosecutor's note, therefore, did not constitute a statement of the inmate witness that conflicted with his trial testimony.

In order for a statement by a prosecution witness to be inconsistent or to conflict with the witness's testimony, the statement must be actually inconsistent or conflicting. In *Mosley v. City of Chicago* (2010, CA7 IL) 614 F.3d 391, a plaintiff in a federal civil rights action appealed from a grant of summary judgment in favor of the defendants. On appeal the plaintiff contended that during his criminal prosecution for beating a man to death, a charge for which he was acquitted, the government unlawfully failed to disclose a witness's statement that conflicted with his trial testimony. The Court of Appeals concluded that the suppressed witness's statement did not conflict with his trial testimony in which the witness said that he saw Mosley with the group that attacked the victim but did not see or could not remember seeing Mosley participate in the attack. Thus, the withheld statement was not favorable to Mosley. 614 F.3d at 398.

§ 1:24.1   Statements that conflict with each other

In *In re Miranda* (2008) 43 Cal.4th 541, 76 Cal.Rptr.3d 172, 182 P.3d 513, the petitioner had been convicted of capital murder. In the penalty phase of the trial the prosecution presented the testimony of a man named Joe Saucedo who testified that the petitioner had killed another man two weeks before the capital crime. Saucedo was the prosecution's "star penalty phase witness." 43 Cal.4th at 575. The petitioner had pled guilty to the prior crime as a second degree murder. The facts of the prior murder were used by the prosecution as evidence in aggravation in the penalty phase of the capital murder trial to argue for a death sentence. The petitioner was sentenced to death for the second murder.

At the time of the capital murder trial the prosecution possessed a letter written by another inmate in the Los Angeles County jail in which the inmate wrote that Saucedo had told him that he (Saucedo), not the defendant, had personally killed the victim in the prior murder. The letter also related that

Saucedo claimed he had destroyed evidence relating to the prior murder and that he had developed a false alibi to deflect suspicion from himself for that murder. The prosecution did not disclose that letter to the petitioner.

The petitioner filed a habeas petition in the California state courts. The Supreme Court appointed a referee to conduct an evidentiary hearing on the petitioner's *Brady* violation claims. The referee found that the prosecution had possessed numerous pieces of evidence in addition to the letter from the jail inmate that Saucedo had killed the victim in the prior murder and that this evidence was credible.

The Supreme Court granted the habeas petition and set aside the petitioner's death sentence. The Court concluded that the letter from the jail inmate was favorable to the petitioner, because it constituted evidence that was inconsistent with Saucedo's trial testimony that inculpated the petitioner as the actual killer in the prior murder. 43 Cal.4th at 575–576.

Conflicting statements of a witness can constitute favorable evidence impeaching that witness, even when one of the conflicting statements is memorialized in a proffer made by the attorney for that witness while seeking favorable treatment for the witness.

In *United States v. Triumph Capital Group, Inc.* (2008, CA2 CT) 544 F.3d 149, the attorney for a suspect in a racketeering case charging a variety of federal offenses approached the investigating officer on behalf of the suspect and provided the officer with the client's account of his criminal activity in an effort to convince the government to offer the client a cooperation agreement. The proffer implicated some of the suspects and was exculpatory of one of the suspects, Charles Spadoni. The statements of the witness contained in the proffer were directly relevant to the intent element of the consulting contract bribe charges.

The proffer was memorialized in notes of the meeting taken by one of the government investigators. The proffered statement of the witness conflicted with later statements made by that witness and the witness's trial testimony. The proffer notes were not disclosed to the defendants, who were convicted after a trial at which the witness whose attorney had provided the proffer testified. The Second Circuit Court of Appeals reversed the conviction of the defendant Spadoni, concluding that the suppression of the proffer notes "deprived Spadoni of exculpatory evidence going to the core of [the government's] case against him," and that Spadoni "could have used the proffer notes . . . also to impeach [the witness's] credibility." 544 F.3d at 162.

Moreover, a prior conflicting statement might be contained in a presentence report of the government witness. *See, e.g., United States v. Garcia* (2009, CA8 MO) 562 F.3d 947, 952–953; and *United States v. Shyres* (1990, CA8 MO) 898 F.2d 647, 656.

A prior statement of a witness might conflict with another statement by that witness by virtue of the absence of content in one statement that is included in the other statement. *See, e.g., United States v. Andrews* (2008, CA DC) 532 F.3d 900, 905–906.

§ 1:24.4 Conflicting statements as to memory of events

A withheld witness statement does not conflict with a prosecution witness's testimony when the witness states in both his or her statement and his or her testimony that he or she does not remember an event. *See Mosley v. City of Chicago* (2010, CA7 IL) 614 F.3d 391, 398. A claimed failure to recollect an event is a conflicting statement only when the witness has also stated or testified to details about that event.

§ 1:24.6 Minor inconsistent statements

Where the inconsistency between an undisclosed witness statement and the testimony of that witness is minor or not directly in conflict, that undisclosed evidence does not constitute evidence favorable to the defendant within the meaning of the *Brady* rule.

In *Mize v. Hall* (2008, CA11 GA) 532 F.3d 1184, a death-sentenced prisoner in Georgia filed a federal habeas petition alleging, among other arguments, that he had been denied *Brady* evidence when the notes of the interview of an important prosecution witness had not been disclosed to him. The petition claimed that the notes of the interview differed from the testimony of the witness in this respect: the notes reflect that the witness claimed that just before the shooting of the victim she heard "someone" in the woods where the shooting took place say, "If you cannot do it I can." The witness's testimony was that the petitioner made this statement. The federal district court denied the habeas petition.

The Eleventh Circuit Court of Appeals affirmed the denial of the petition, concluding that although "the prosecutor should have turned over the notes," the impeachment value of the notes was minor, and the word "someone" did not directly conflict with the word "Mize."

§ 1:24.9 Statements of witness's attorney

When making a determination whether a statement constitutes an inconsistent witness statement, it is necessary to know that the statement was made by the witness and not by some other person on behalf of the witness.

In *United States v. Whitehill* (2008, CA8 MO) 532 F.3d 746, a number of defendants convicted of participating in a telemarketing scheme that defrauded would-be credit card purchasers argued on appeal that the prosecution committed *Brady* error in not disclosing prior to trial a letter written by the attorney for one of the prosecution witnesses. The letter stated that the witness believed that there was no evidentiary basis for charging three of the defendants with fraud. The witness later disavowed his attorney's statements.

The Eighth Circuit Court of Appeals concluded that the suppression of the letter did not violate the *Brady* rule, because it did not contain evidence that could have been used to impeach the prosecution witness. The Court stated that the "letter was written by [the witness's] lawyer and did contain opinions [the witness] refuted. Thus, it could not have been used to impeach [the witness] and there was no duty under *Brady* to disclose the letter." 532 F.3d at 753.

In contrast to *Whitehill*, proffered testimony of a potential government witness submitted to the government by the attorney for the witness can constitute evidence favorable to the defendant when that proffered testimony conflicts with later statements or testimony of the witness.

In *United States v. Triumph Capital Group, Inc.* (2008, CA2 CT) 544 F.3d 149, the attorney for a suspect in a racketeering case charging a variety of federal offenses approached the investigating officer on behalf of the suspect and provided the officer with the client's account of his criminal activity in an effort to convince the government to offer the client a cooperation agreement. The proffer implicated some of the suspects and was exculpatory of one of the suspects, Charles Spadoni. The statements of the witness contained in the proffer were directly relevant to the intent element of the consulting contract bribe charges.

The proffer was memorialized in notes of the meeting taken by one of the government investigators. The proffered statement of the witness conflicted with later statements made by that witness and the witness's trial testimony. The proffer notes were not disclosed to the defendants, who were convicted after a trial at which the witness whose attorney had provided the proffer testified. The Second Circuit Court of Appeals reversed the conviction of the defendant Spadoni, concluding that the suppression of the proffer notes "deprived Spadoni of exculpatory evidence going to the core of [the government's] case against him," and that Spadoni "could have used the proffer notes . . . also to impeach [the witness's] credibility." 544 F.3d at 162.

§ 1:25   False reports—generally

In order for a report of a prosecution witness to constitute evidence favorable to the defendant as a false report made by that witness, the prior report or complaint must have actually been untrue or false. If the prosecution witness's "prior complaint was in fact true, it would have no relevance for impeachment whatsoever." *People v. Waldie* (2009) 173 Cal.App.4th 358, 363–364, 92 Cal.Rptr.3d 688.

§ 1:25.2   Similar/Identical false reports by victim

In *United States v. Velarde* (2007, CA10 NM) 485 F.3d 553, a defendant convicted in federal district court of sexually abusing a minor within Indian country learned after his conviction that the minor had reportedly made similar accusations against her school teacher and vice principal that were false. These similar accusations had been reported to law enforcement authorities but had not been disclosed to the defendant. The defendant filed a new-trial motion, claiming that the failure to disclose these false reports to him violated his due process rights under *Brady*. The district court denied the new-trial motion.

The Tenth Circuit Court of Appeals vacated the district court's order denying the new-trial motion. The Court held that the district court erred in holding that the suppressed evidence regarding the supposedly false accusation was not material. The Court concluded that the trial court should have determined whether the prosecution suppressed the information about the child's accusations and should have allowed discovery to determine the nature and veracity of the accusations. The Court of Appeals remanded the case to the district court to conduct a hearing to determine whether it would have been an abuse of discretion to preclude the defense from cross-examining the child victim about the prior false accusations. The Court decided that if the trial court would have abused its discretion in precluding the defendant from such cross-examination, "it is a *Brady* violation for the government to withhold from the defense the information on which it would conduct such a cross-examination." 485 F.3d at 563.

§ 1:25.3   False reports protecting another person

A false report by a prosecution witness that is evidence favorable to a defendant is not limited to a false accusatory report by the witness. A false report by a witness that protects another person can also constitute a false report that impeaches that witness's testimony.

In *United States v. Oruche* (2007, CA DC) 484 F.3d 590, the prosecution failed to disclose the grand jury testimony of a prosecution witness who was the defendant's girlfriend. In that testimony the girlfriend admitted that she had lied to police to protect her boyfriend nine years prior to the defendant's trial. The Court of Appeals determined that this constituted evidence favorable to the defendant. "Defense counsel could have used this evidence to support a claim that [the girlfriend] was a liar who would say whatever suited her purposes in the moment, even when speaking with authority figures about a matter of grave importance." 484 F.3d at 599.

§ 1:25.4   False statements under oath

An aggravated form of false reports as evidence favorable to a defendant is false statements by a prosecution witness while under oath.

In *Simmons v. Beard* (2009, CA3 PA) 590 F.3d 223, a defendant was charged in Pennsylvania state court with the robbery and murder of an elderly woman. The prosecution introduced evidence against the defendant at trial of a potential sexual assault alleged to have been committed by the defendant against a second woman. That second woman testified against the defendant, who was convicted and sentenced to death.

Following his conviction the defendant filed a habeas corpus petition in federal court, alleging, *inter alia*, that the prosecution had withheld evidence that the second woman misrepresented her criminal history when signing a form under penalty of perjury in order to purchase a handgun. The Court of Appeals, in affirming the district court's order granting the defendant's habeas corpus petition, observed that this fact could have been used by the defendant to impeach her testimony. The Court quoted the opinion of the District of Columbia Circuit Court of Appeals in *United States v. Cuffie* (1996, CA DC) 80 F.3d 514, 517–518, that a prior perjurious statement is an "infirmity . . . that is almost unique in its detrimental effect on a witness' credibility."

A particularly egregious false statement under oath is one in which the witness testified falsely against another person resulting in that person's conviction. *Brooks v. Tennessee* (2010, CA6 TN) 626 F.3d 878, 892.

§ 1:26 Inaccurate statements—generally

§ 1:26.1 Inaccurate statements undermining witness's expertise or competence

In the context of a *Brady* claim, a finding of prejudice requires that the conduct have some impact on the outcome of the proceeding—i.e., a reasonable probability that the result of the proceeding would have been different or that it so infected the trial with unfairness as to make the resulting conviction a denial of due process. *United States v. Rodriguez* (June 24, 2013, CA9 Cal.) 2013 U.S. App. LEXIS 12918.

§ 1:27 Inability to recall

The inability of a witness to recall events is different from a witness's claim that he or she knew nothing about the subject matter of questioning. *See United States v. Amato* (2008, CA2 NY) 540 F.3d 153 [Court of Appeals deduced that the witness's statement that he did not recall might have been used to some extent to impeach the witness's testimony, but the testimony would have been a very minor issue. 540 F.3d at 163.].

Evidence that a prosecution witness has experienced difficulty with remembering important facts and details of key events about which the witness is to testify is evidence that is favorable to the defendant. *United States v. Kohring* (2011, CA9 AK) 637 F.3d 895, 906, 907. Evidence of poor mental and emotional health bears on a witness's credibility and constitutes impeachment evidence relating to that witness. *United States v. Kohring, supra,* 637 F.3d at 910.

§ 1:28 Evidence contradicting statements or reports

Evidence that contracts the statements or reports of statements of a prosecution witness is favorable to the defendant.

§ 1:28.1 Contradictory evidence as favorable to defendant

In *People v. Uribe* (2008) 162 Cal.App.4th 1457, 76 Cal.Rptr.3d 829, the defendant was convicted of two counts of aggravated sexual assault on his granddaughter, who was a minor. The minor child was examined by a physician assistant, who performed what is known as a sexual assault response team (SART) examination. The SART examination was video-taped, and the existence of the videotape was not disclosed to the defendant, who learned of the videotape after his conviction at trial.

One of the contested issues at trial was whether the victim had been sexually assaulted. Expert testimony on that issue was presented by the prosecution and the defense. After learning of the videotape the defendant made a motion for a new trial, arguing that he had been denied *Brady* evidence—evidence from the videotape that showed that the victim had not been sexually assaulted. The trial court denied the new trial motion.

The Court of Appeal reversed the conviction and remanded the case to the trial court for a new trial. The Court concluded that the declaration of the defendant's expert in support of the new-trial motion "established that the SART video was favorable both because it offered potential evidence impeaching a prosecution expert's testimony, and was supportive of the opinions of defendant's expert. We have little difficulty concluding from the record presented here that the SART video constituted 'favorable' evidence under *Brady*." 162 Cal.App.4th at 1475.

The SART videotape was favorable evidence, because it contained evidence contradicting the prosecution's expert witness's testimony.

In *Montgomery v. Bagley* (2009, CA6 OH) 581 F.3d 440, the defendant was convicted of murder and sentenced to death. In habeas corpus proceedings the federal district court granted the defendant a new trial, because the prosecution had failed to disclose to the defendant a police report written prior to trial that reported that several witnesses had seen one of the defendant's purported victims alive four days after the prosecution alleged that the defendant had murdered her. The government appealed the district court order granting the new trial.

The Court of Appeals affirmed the district court order. The Court of Appeals concluded that the suppressed police report was favorable to the defendant, because evidence that several persons had seen the victim alive long after the prosecution contended that the defendant had killed her would have undercut the testimony of the prosecution's star witness that the defendant was the triggerman in both of the murders for which he was charged and convicted.

The withheld evidence that contradicted prosecution evidence thereby constituted evidence favorable to the defendant.

When evidence possessed by the prosecution directly contradicts the testimony of a prosecution witness, that evidence is favorable to the defendant. *See Sykes v. Anderson* (2010, CA6 MI) 625 F.3d 294, 320.

In the face of a claim that evidence that had not been disclosed to the defendant constituted a statement that conflicted with the testimony of the author of the withheld evidence, the withheld evidence must be viewed in the context of other evidence introduced at trial. When the withheld evidence viewed in context is not inconsistent with the testimony of the author of that withheld evidence, the withheld evidence is not favorable to the defendant. And the failure to disclose that evidence does not constitute a *Brady* violation. *United States v. Hill* (2011, CA11 FL) 643 F.3d 807, 844, 845.

§ 1:29 Promises, offers, benefits, and inducements

There is no magic in the word "promise" in the context of the *Brady* rule. Although a promise of benefit offered to a prosecution witness is evidence favorable to a defendant, a "promise" is often not the crucial undisclosed evidence at issue. "Although *Giglio* and *Napue* use the term 'promise' in referring to covered-up deals, they establish that the crux of a Fourteenth Amendment violation is deception. A promise is unnecessary. Where, as here, the witness's credibility 'was . . . an important issue in the case . . . evidence of *any understanding or agreement as to a future prosecution* would be relevant to his credibility and the jury was entitled to know of it.' [citation omitted]" *Tassin v. Cain* (2008, CA5 LA) 517 F.3d 770, 778 [italics in original].

§ 1:29.1 Explicit promises, offers, and inducements

Cases in which the prosecution has made undisclosed explicit promises to or deals with prosecution witnesses continue to confront the courts, although it appears that the cases involving these explicit promises and deals were tried many years ago and have only recently resulted in published opinions after percolating through state and/or federal habeas proceedings. *See, e.g., In re Miranda* (2008) 43 Cal.4th 541, 577–580, 76 Cal.Rptr.3d 172, 182 P.3d 513 [prosecution made undisclosed explicit agreement with a whole cadre of important prosecution witnesses in a capital murder case, and dismissed and reduced pending charges against those witnesses in exchange for their testimony].

The principle that an explicit promise, offer, or inducement made to a prosecution witness constitutes evidence favorable to the defendant is not restricted to such promises that are contained in "formal plea bargains, immunity deals or other notarized commitments," but it also applies to less formal, unwritten, or tacit agreements "so long as the prosecution offers the witness a benefit in exchange for his cooperation." *Harris v. Lafler* (2009, CA6 MI) 553 F.3d 1028, 1034.

While normally the words used by the prosecution agent to the witness are judged by their objective content, the Sixth Circuit Court of Appeals held in *Doan v. Carter* (2008, CA6 OH) 548 F.3d 449, that the statement of a prosecutor to two government witnesses that the State of Ohio would not prosecute them if they implicated Mr. Doan in the murder, and that "they would not be charged" unless they lied to the investigating officers, was not really a promise within the meaning of the *Brady* rule. The Court stated that the prosecutor did not make a promise to the witnesses that they would not be prosecuted in exchange for their providing testimony. Instead, the Court stated that the prosecutor "merely admonished Lori and Watkins that they needed to be truthful," 548 F.3d at 461, and concluded that this was not evidence that the prosecution had to disclose under *Brady*. The Court's construction of the words spoken to the two witnesses appears to be a strained one.

When, however, an important prosecution witness who functioned as a professional informant for law enforcement personally negotiated a reduction in the sentence for his own pending criminal cases, that explicit promise and benefit constituted favorable evidence for the defendant against whom the witness testified. The favorable nature of the reduced sentence deal for the informant-witness is especially compelling when the witness has negotiated a more favorable deal for himself than his attorney had previously negotiated. *Maxwell v. Roe* (2010, CA9 CA) 628 F.3d 486, 509–510. "[T]he details of Storch's plea negotiations would have helped to establish Storch's sophistication and directly contradicted the naivete he professed at trial. The fact that Storch had worked a deal with [the prosecution] without his public defender would have been the only evidence—other than the evidence of Storch's informant past, which was also suppressed—of Storch's informant sophistication." 628 F.3d at 510.

The making of explicit promises to prosecution witnesses to induce their testimony appears to be most commonly encountered when the prosecution witnesses are informants. *See, e.g., Jackson v. Brown* (2008, CA9 CA) 513 F.3d 1057.

Explicit promises made to a prosecution witness constitute evidence favorable to the defendant even when the benefits of those promises do not flow directly to the prosecution witness, but enure to the benefit of the witness's family. *LaCaze v. Warden La. Corr. Inst. for Women* (2011, CA5 LA) 645 F.3d 728, 735.

§ 1:29.2   Implied or implicit promises, offers, and inducements

Although "[t]he existence of a less formal, unwritten or tacit agreement is also subject to *Brady* disclosure mandate," there must be some evidence that the prosecution and the prosecution witness have reached a mutual understanding, which can be an unspoken one. A mutual understanding "would qualify as favorable impeachment material under *Brady*." *Bell v. Bell* (2008, CA6 TN) 512 F.3d 223, 233. *Accord, Ragheed Akrawi v. Booker* (2009, CA6 MI) 572 F.3d 252, 262 [" '[t]he existence of a less formal, unwritten or tacit agreement is also subject to *Brady's* disclosure mandate.' " [citations omitted] '*Brady* is not limited to formal plea bargains, immunity deals or other notarized commitments. It applies to 'less formal, unwritten, or tacit agreement[s],' so long as the prosecution offers the witness a benefit in exchange for his cooperation, ... so long in other words as the evidence is 'favorable to the accused.' " [citation omitted]]

However, a witness's expectation of future benefits does not necessarily mean that a tacit agreement subject to a *Brady* disclosure duty existed. A witness's expectation does not amount to an agreement with the prosecution. *Bell v. Bell*, 512 F.3d at 233. However, a witness's expectation of and efforts to get benefits in return for testifying for the prosecution can constitute evidence favorable to a defendant independent of any tacit agreement. See Sections 1:29.11 and 1:29.13 of the text.

Nor does the conferring of assistance to a prosecution witness following that witness's testimony require a court to infer a preexisting deal between the prosecution and the witness that is subject to disclosure under *Brady*, particularly where the prosecutor who conferred the benefit had no knowledge about the case in which the witness testified. 512 F.3d at 233–234.

§ 1:29.3 Secret promises, offers, and inducements

One federal circuit court has held that a benefit conferred on a government witness—a request that other jurisdictions not arrest the witness on outstanding warrants—was not a *Brady* secret promise, because the witness was unaware of the request. Thus, stated the Court, "the prosecution could not have made the request in exchange for [the witness's] testimony." *Doan v. Carter* (2008, CA6 OH) 548 F.3d 449, 460.

The fact that a prosecution witness does not know of even the existence of a deal, much less its details, might be the key difference from the cases discussed in the text in which the prosecution made a deal for benefits with the witness's attorney, the witness knew of the deal, but the witness did not know any details of that deal.

§ 1:29.4 Ambiguous promises, offers, and inducements

ERRATA: The citation of *Boone v. Paderick* on page 80 of the text is incorrect. The correct citation is *Boone v. Paderick* (1976, CA4 VA) 541 F.2d 447.

§ 1:29.4.1 Contingent promises, offers, and inducements

Closely akin to ambiguous promises, offers, and inducements are "contingent" promises, offers, and inducements. A contingent promise, offer, or inducement is one that holds out the possibility that the witness will receive a benefit that is dependent upon the achievement of a result that satisfies the prosecution. "Th[e] possibility of a reward gave [the witnesses] a direct, personal stake in respondent's conviction. The fact that the *stake was not guaranteed through a promise or binding contract*, but was expressly contingent on the Government's satisfaction with the end result, *served only to strengthen any incentive to testify falsely* in order to secure a conviction." *Tassin v. Cain* (2008, CA5 LA) 517 F.3d 770, 778. [italics in original]

§ 1:29.5 Promises, inducements, and benefits in prior cases

However, *Brady v. Maryland* does not impose an obligation to necessarily produce the entire file of a confidential informant. *United States v. Bermudez-Chavez* (Apr. 12, 2012, CA9 Ariz.) 2012 U.S. App. LEXIS 6739.

Evidence of a prosecution witness's experience as an informant in prior cases is evidence that can be favorable to the defendant. In *Maxwell v. Roe* (2010, CA9 CA) 628 F.3d 486, the prosecution used as a witness Sidney Storch, a man with a long record of informant activities, to testify against a defendant charged in the "Skid Row Stabber" killings in Los Angeles. The prosecution did not disclose to the defendant the long experience of Mr. Storch as an informant. The defendant was convicted of two counts of first-degree murder and sentenced to life in prison without the possibility of parole.

The defendant then filed a federal habeas petition, which was denied. On appeal from the denial of his habeas petition, Maxwell argued that the prosecution had violated its *Brady* duty by withholding material information concerning Storch's prior informant history. The Ninth Circuit Court of Appeals held that the withheld information "could have been used to discredit Storch had it been revealed at the time of trial," and that this information "would have provided additional evidence that Storch was a sophisticated informant with developed connections and relationships within the LAPD." 628 F.3d at 511. The Court concluded that had the prosecution disclosed Storch's prior informant history, the defense could have investigated Storch more carefully and learned that he was "an experienced informant with a history of lying." 628 F.3d at 512. All of this evidence was favorable to Maxwell within the meaning of the *Brady* rule.

§ 1:29.6   Status benefits

Evidence that a prosecution witness has a long history of serving as a police informant, receiving compensation for his or her work as an informant, is evidence that can be used to impeach the credibility of the informant, and is thus evidence favorable to the defendant. *See, Eulloqui v. Superior Court* (2010) 181 Cal.App.4th 1055, 1068, 105 Cal.Rptr.3d 248; *Wilson v. Beard* (2009, CA3 PA) 589 F.3d 651, 662; and *Robinson v. Mills* (2010, CA6 TN) 592 F.3d 730, 737.

Evidence of a prosecution witness's experience as an informant in prior cases is evidence that can be favorable to the defendant. In *Maxwell v. Roe* (2010, CA9 CA) 628 F.3d 486, the prosecution used as a witness Sidney Storch, a man with a long record of informant activities, to testify against a defendant charged in the "Skid Row Stabber" killings in Los Angeles. The prosecution did not disclose to the defendant the long experience of Mr. Storch as an informant. The defendant was convicted of two counts of first-degree murder and sentenced to life in prison without the possibility of parole.

The defendant then filed a federal habeas petition, which was denied. On appeal from the denial of his habeas petition, Maxwell argued that the prosecution had violated its *Brady* duty by withholding material information concerning Storch's prior informant history. The Ninth Circuit Court of Appeals held that the withheld information "could have been used to discredit Storch had it been revealed at the time of trial," and that this information "would have provided additional evidence that Storch was a sophisticated informant with developed connections and relationships within the LAPD." 628 F.3d at 511. The Court concluded that had the prosecution disclosed Storch's prior informant history, the defense could have investigated Storch more carefully and learned that he was "an experienced informant with a history of lying." 628 F.3d at 512. All of this evidence was favorable to Maxwell within the meaning of the *Brady* rule.

§ 1:29.7 Benefits without explicit promise or agreement

While a benefit conferred upon a prosecution witness need not result from an explicit promise or agreement in order to constitute evidence that can impeach the testimony of that witness, it appears that (1) there must be a benefit to the prosecution witness, and (2) that any benefit must exchanged for the testimony of the witness. Thus, in *Lamarca v. Sec'y, Dep't of Corr.* (2009, CA11 FL) 568 F.3d 929, 941, the presence of one of Lamarca's prosecutors at the sentencing in another case of a prosecution witness against Lamarca, was not evidence impeaching that witness and was not required to be disclosed to Lamarca, without evidence that the prosecutor's presence produced a benefit for that witness. Likewise, where there is no evidence that a benefit received by a prosecution witness, such as a delay in sentencing in the witness's own case, was in exchange for the witness's testimony, the benefit is not evidence that impeaches the witness's testimony and is thus not favorable to the defendant. *See Lamarca v. Sec'y, Dep't of Corr.* (2009, CA11 FL) 568 F.3d 929 [Defendant failed to establish that the delay in sentencing a second government witness until after the defendant's trial was "in exchange for his testimony." 568 F.3d at 941.].

In *Ragheed Arkawi v. Booker* (2009, CA6 MI) 572 F.3d 252, 263, the Sixth Circuit Court of Appeals concluded that "the mere fact of favorable treatment received by a witness following cooperation is also insufficient to substantiate the existence of an agreement. '[I]t is not the case that, if the government chooses to provide assistance to a witness following trial, a court must necessarily infer a preexisting deal subject to disclosure under *Brady*.' [citation omitted] 'The government is free to reward witnesses for their cooperation with favorable treatment in pending criminal cases without disclosing to the defendant its intention to do so, *provided* that it does not promise anything to the witness prior to the testimony.' [citation omitted] (*emphasis* in original)."

When, however, the government bestows benefits upon a prosecution witness, it can be difficult to dispel the conclusion that the benefits were provided in return for the witness's cooperation or otherwise motivated the witness to provide testimony to help the government in its prosecution of the defendant.

In *Simmons v. Beard* (2009, CA3 PA) 590 F.3d 223, a defendant was charged in Pennsylvania state court with the robbery and murder of an elderly woman. The prosecution introduced evidence against the defendant at trial of a potential sexual assault alleged to have been committed by the defendant against a second woman. That second woman testified against the defendant, who was convicted and sentenced to death.

Following his conviction the defendant filed a habeas corpus petition in federal court, alleging, *inter alia*, that the prosecution had withheld evidence that the second woman misrepresented her criminal history when signing a form under penalty of perjury in order to purchase a handgun—she failed to disclose that she had been convicted of felony burglary, a conviction that rendered her ineligible to purchase a firearm.

The prosecution also failed to disclose that the prosecution witness was charged with violating the Pennsylvania Uniform Firearms Act, which bars a convicted felon from purchasing a firearm. The charge was dropped, however, after the Simmons' investigating officer and prosecutor arranged for the witness to voluntarily surrender her gun to the police in exchange for the dismissal of the charge against her.

The Third Circuit Court of Appeals concluded that evidence of the help given to the prosecution witness was favorable to the defendant, even if the witness had provided law enforcement with the highly inculpatory evidence to which she testified at trial prior to receiving any benefits for her cooperation. The Court stated that "the chronology of events is irrelevant, since the defense could just as well have argued either that [the witness] came up with the [inculpatory] statements with the intent of leveraging them for help from the investigators, or that she was pressured into making those statements by the investigators armed with knowledge of her predicament." 590 F.3d at 236.

In *United States v. Salem* (2009, CA7 WI) 578 F.3d 682, the government failed to disclose to a defendant charged in federal district court with witness intimidation offenses that a principal witness against him had not been charged for a lying-in-wait gang-related homicide in which law enforcement authorities had evidence of the witness's participation. The defendant's motion for a new trial was denied, and he appealed.

The Seventh Circuit Court of Appeals vacated the denial of Salem's new-trial motion, concluding that suppressed evidence of the witness's non-prosecution for a homicide was evidence favorable to Salem. The Court stated that "[p]roof of bias or motive to lie is admissible impeachment evidence," that "courts routinely admit evidence suggesting a witness curried favor with the government in exchange for his testimony as proof of bias or motive to testify falsely." 578 F.3d at 686. The Court concluded:

"The plea agreement [of another suspect in the homicide] alone suggests that Lopez [the witness] was a participant in the lying-in-wait murder . . . even without a note from the U.S. Attorney or the local D.A. expressly outlining a no-charges-for-testimony quid pro quo, such evidence could be admissible to show [the witness's] motive to testify against Salem." 578 F.3d at 687.

An informal "tit-for-tat" arrangement between the prosecution and a prosecution witness "could be enough to show bias, even without evidence of an actual agreement between him and the government." *United States v. Salem* (2011, CA7 WI) 643 F.3d 221, 228.

§ 1:29.8 Prosecution leniency in other cases

Courts appear to reach different results when confronting cases in which prosecution witnesses who themselves are facing criminal charges receive favorable treatment following their testifying as prosecution witnesses. Some courts are inclined to conclude that such post-testifying benefits are evidence of tacit or explicit deals. Others are reluctant to reach that result.

"[I]t is not the case that, if the government chooses to provide assistance to a witness following a trial, a court must necessarily infer a preexisting deal subject to disclosure under *Brady*. 'The government is free to reward witnesses for their cooperation with favorable in pending criminal cases without disclosing to the defendant its intention to do so, *provided* that it does not promise anything to the witnesses prior to their testimony.' [citation omitted] To conclude otherwise would place prosecutors in the untenable position of being obligated to disclose information prior to trial that may not be available to them or to forgo the award of favorable treatment to a participating witness for fear that they will be accused of withholding evidence of an agreement." *Bell v. Bell* (2008, CA6 TN) 512 F.3d 223, 234. [italics in original]; *see also, Matthews v. Ishee* (2007, CA6 OH) 486 F.3d 883, 896.

§ 1:29.10 Federal witness protection program as benefit

The idea that evidence that a prosecution witness has been promised or received federal witness protection in return for the witness's testimony constitutes evidence favorable to the defendant is not without dispute. In *United States v. Davis* (2010, CA5 LA) 609 F.3d 663, the Fifth Circuit Court of Appeals, in rejecting the defendant's claim of a *Brady* violation from the government's failure to disclose an agreement to provide a government witness with witness protection, observed that "[t]he information about the witness protection was not favorable to [the defendant] because the jury may have assumed that [the witness] needed protection from Davis, who allegedly had [the murder victim] killed for filing a complaint against him." 609 F.3d at 696.

§ 1:29.11   Unrelated post-testimony benefits

Evidence that a prosecution witness has received post-testimony benefits in another criminal case in another jurisdiction does not constitute evidence of benefits, offers, or inducements that may be used to impeach the testimony of that prosecution witness, unless there is evidence to connect the benefits in one jurisdiction to the witness's testimony in the other jurisdiction.

Thus, in *Parker v. Allen* (2009, CA11 AL) 565 F.3d 1258, the Eleventh Circuit Court of Appeals held that the prosecution did not commit *Brady* error in failing to disclose to a defendant that a prosecution witness had been released from custody into a Supervised Intensive Restitution Program (SIR) in a different jurisdiction. The Court of Appeals held that there was no evidence the defendant's prosecutor knew anything about the witness's release, and no evidence connected the witness's release to his testimony against the defendant. The Court characterized the witness's release and his testimony against the defendant as a "coincidence of facts" that had no relationship to each other. 565 F.3d at 1277–1278.

§ 1:29.12   Witness's efforts to obtain benefits for testifying

The fact that a prosecution witness had discussed a plea agreement with the government in the witness's own criminal case does not necessarily mean that the witness made efforts to obtain benefits for his or her testimony. *See, e.g., United States v. Davis* (2010, CA5 LA) 609 F.3d 663, 696.

§ 1:29.13   Witness's hope of receiving benefits

The Fifth Circuit Court of Appeals has held that a witness's mere "hope or expectation" of beneficial treatment in return for cooperating with the prosecution might not be sufficient to cross the threshold into *Brady* disclosure duties. *Tassin v. Cain* (2008, CA5 LA) 517 F.3d 770, 779.

The Sixth Circuit Court of Appeals expressed this concept in more firm terms, concluding that "the mere fact that a witness desires or expects favorable treatment in return for his testimony is insufficient; there must be some assurance or promise from the prosecution that gives rise to a *mutual* understanding or tacit *agreement.* [citation omitted]" *Ragheed Akrawi v. Booker* (2009, CA6 MI) 572 F.3d 252, 263. [italics in original]

§ 1:29.20   Negotiations with non-testifying co-defendants

A prosecutor occasionally will enter into negotiations with a co-defendant in order to enable the prosecutor to call the co-defendant to testify against the defendant as a prosecution witness. Unless such negotiations result in an agreement and the co-defendant actually testifies against the defendant, the fact of the negotiations does not become evidence favorable to the defendant. In *United States v. Inzunza* (2009, CA9 CA) 580 F.3d 894, several defendants were indicted in federal court on charges of honest services fraud, conspiracy to commit honest services fraud, and extortion. The prosecution entered into negotiations with one of the defendants to testify as a government witness. The negotiations did not result in testimony from the co-defendant.

The defendant was convicted. On appeal the defendant argued that the government's failure to disclose its negotiations with the co-defendant constituted *Brady* error. The Ninth Circuit Court of Appeals rejected the defendant's argument, stating: "There is no merit to [the defendant's] claim that the government made an impermissible 'side deal' with [the co-defendant], which, if known to the jury, might have cast doubt on the government's credibility. [The defendant] cites no authority for his argument that evidence of negotiations with non-testifying co-defendants, without more, is exculpatory. *Brady* is simply not implicated." 580 F.3d at 907.

§ 1:30 False testimony

If a prosecutor willfully suppresses favorable evidence by either ensuring that a witness perjure himself or herself, or by pressuring a witness do so, the conduct of the witness in providing false testimony that the prosecutor does not disclose to the defendant constitutes a suppression of favorable evidence within the meaning of the *Brady* rule and is also a violation of the Due Process Clause by the prosecution's knowing use of perjured testimony. *In re McDonald* (2008, CA6 OH) 514 F.3d 539, 545–546, n.5.

Evidence that the prosecutor has sponsored perjured testimony to conceal suppression of evidence has been described as "*Brady* plus prosecutorial misconduct." "A false-testimony claim is cognizable in habeas because the 'deliberate deception of a court and jurors by the presentation of known false evidence is incompatible with rudimentary demands of justice.' [citations omitted]" *Ragheed Akrawi v. Booker* (2009, CA6 MI) 572 F.3d 252, 265. To be evidence favorable to the defendant, the false testimony "must be 'indisputably false rather than 'merely misleading.' " 572 F.3d at 265.

Evidence of prosecutor-sponsored perjured testimony is not only evidence favorable to the defendant within the meaning of the *Brady* rule, but is also an independent violation of a defendant's due process rights. "A false-testimony claim is cognizable in habeas because the 'deliberate deception of a court and jurors by the presentation of known false evidence is incompatible with rudimentary demands of justice.' [citations omitted] To prevail on such a claim, Akrawi must show '(1) that the prosecution presented false testimony (2) that the prosecution knew was false, and (3) that was material.' [citation omitted]" 572 F.3d at 265.

A perjured statement or testimony by a prosecution witness is impeachment evidence of that witness that is uniquely favorable to the defendant, because it constitutes an "infirmity that is almost unique in its detrimental effect on a witness' credibility." *United States v. Cuffie* (1996, CA DC) 80 F.3d 514, 517–518; *Simmons v. Beard* (2009, CA3 PA) 590 F.3d 223, 236.

§ 1:30.1   Disclosing false testimony generally

In *Campbell v. Superior Court* (2008) 159 Cal.App.4th 635, 71 Cal.Rptr.3d 594, the petitioner was charged with first degree murder with special circumstances and requested a mental retardation hearing. The trial court found that the petitioner was not mentally retarded, thus permitting the prosecution to seek the death penalty. A lay witness at the mental retardation hearing testified that he had mentored the petitioner while the petitioner was a high school student and that petitioner appeared to him to be of normal intelligence. That witness apparently realized while testifying that the man he had tutored was not the petitioner with the same name.

After completing his testimony the witness informed a prosecution investigator of his error. The investigator reassured the witness, but the report of that conversation that was supplied to the defense did not include any reference to the witness's mistake and the investigator's reassurance. When the petitioner's attorneys later discovered the false testimony, the petitioner filed a motion to reopen the mental retardation hearing. The trial court declined to reopen the motion on jurisdictional grounds. The petitioner then filed a motion in the Court of Appeal for permission to file a supplemental petition for writ of mandate or prohibition based upon the discovery of the witness's erroneous or false testimony.

The Court of Appeal granted the request to file a supplemental petition. Quoting from opinions of the United States and California Supreme Courts, the Court of Appeal stated:

> " 'Allowing false testimony to go unchallenged impairs the integrity of the factfinding objective of a trial [citation omitted], because such testimony hinders or blocks the disclosure of the truth to the trier of fact [citations omitted].' 'A criminal judgment obtained through use of false evidence violates due process, whether the prosecution solicits the false evidence or simply allows it to go uncorrected when it appears.' [citations omitted] 'Under well-established principles of due process, the prosecution cannot present evidence it knows is false and must correct any falsity of which it is aware in the evidence it presents, even if the false evidence was not intentionally submitted.' [citation omitted]." 159 Cal.App.4th at 652.

§ 1:30.2   Actual falsity required

"[I]n the context of *Giglio*, the statement must actually be false (as opposed to the suggestion of falsehood) in order to qualify as perjured testimony." *United States v. Svete* (2008, CA11 FL) 521 F.3d 1302, 1313. *Accord, Hein v. Sullivan* (2010, CA9 CA) 601 F.3d 897, 911, n.11.

In the same manner that a false report must be actually false in order for that report to constitute evidence impeaching the testimony of a prosecution witness (see Section 1:25 of the text and this supplement), the testimony of a prosecution witness must actually be false in order for that testimony to be used to impeach a prosecution witness. *Rosencrantz v. Lafler* (2009, CA6 MI) 568 F.3d 577, 583. Although the standard might be limited to claims that a prosecutor has knowingly presented false or perjured testimony, the Sixth Circuit Court of Appeals in *Rosencrantz v. Lafler* held that the testimony asserted to be false must be "indisputably false." 568 F.3d at 384, 385.

In *United States v. Mejia* (2010, CA DC) 597 F.3d 1329, a prosecution witness denied knowing that any federal judge had made a finding that he was not entirely truthful or that a judge had doubted his truthfulness. Even though a court had made a finding regarding the witness's credibility in another case, the Court of Appeals held that the testimony of the witness that he had no direct knowledge of that finding was not actually false. The Court concluded that "in context, [the witness] testified truthfully as to his lack of personal knowledge." 597 F.3d at 1339.

The Ninth Circuit Court of Appeals, in listing the requirements to establish a *Napue* violation, stated: "To succeed on a *Napue* claim, a defendant 'must show that (1) the testimony (or evidence) [presented by the prosecution] was actually false, . . .' [citation omitted]." *Hayes v. Ayers* (2011, CA9 CA) 632 F.3d 500, 520.

However, evidence that is technically accurate can be presented in such a manner that it misleads the trier of fact. In that situation "accurate testimony could be delivered in a sufficiently misleading context to make the evidence false for *Napue* purposes." *Towery v. Schriro* (2010, CA9 AZ) 641 F.3d 300, 309. *Accord, United States v. Vozzella* (1997, CA2 NY) 124 F.3d 389, 390.

§ 1:30.3 Minor inaccuracies as false testimony

The inconsistent testimony of a prosecution witness does not necessarily become false testimony, especially when the inconsistent testimony is immediately apparent and the testimony appears to be confused. Such testimony "is not the kind of undisclosed false statement that creates a due process concern." *United States v. Boyce* (2009, CA8 MO) 564 F.3d 911, 917.

Because "perjury requires willful intent to provide false testimony, rather than confusion or mistake," 564 F.3d at 917, *United States v. Thomas* (1996, CA8 IA) 93 F.3d 479, 489. Thus, "mere inconsistency is not necessarily equated with perjury and every contradiction may not be material." *United States v. Nelson* (1992, CA8 IA) 970 F.2d 439, 443.

§ 1:30.4 Conflict with other testimony as false testimony

Convicted federal defendants frequently argue that their convictions were obtained by the use of false or perjured testimony. The federal circuit courts have established a number of principles to determine whether prosecution testimony is false. These principles include the following: "[T]he mere presence of conflicts in witness testimony is insufficient to establish perjury." *United States v. Coplen* (2009, CA8 IA) 565 F.3d 1094, 1096.

Inconsistencies in the testimony of prosecution witnesses do not establish that any of their testimony was false. *United States v. Hunter* (2009, CA6 OH) 558 F.3d 495, 505; *Brooks v. Tennessee* (2010, CA6 TN) 626 F.3d 878, 895; *Coe v. Bell* (1998, CA6 TN) 161 F.3d 320, 343.

A prosecution witness's vacillation in his or her testimony does not establish that the witness has given "indisputably false" testimony. *Rosencrantz v. Lafler* (2009, CA6 MI) 568 F.3d 577, 585. And differences in witnesses' recollections do not establish that the witnesses have provided perjured or false testimony. *United States v. Josephberg* (2009, CA2 NY) 562 F.3d 478, 494. Inconsistencies in a witness's testimony commonly have "innocent provenance such as confusion, mistake, or faulty memory." 562 F.3d at 495.

§ 1:30.6   Prosecutor's duty to investigate false testimony

The existence of a prosecutor's duty to investigate false testimony is closely tied to the imputation to the prosecution of any false prosecution testimony that the prosecution knew "or should have known" was false. "If the prosecutor has a duty to investigate and disclose favorable evidence known only to the police, he 'should know' when a witness testifies falsely about such evidence. Accordingly, we agree with the California Supreme Court's conclusion that 'the prosecution should have known of the false and misleading nature of the informants' testimony,' and therefore 'the prosecution was under a constitutional obligation to correct that testimony.' [citing *In re Jackson*, 3 Cal.4th 578, 597]" *Jackson v. Brown* (2008, CA9 CA) 513 F.3d 1057, 1075.

§ 1:30.8   Disclosing false testimony regarding promises, offers, inducements, and benefits

Evidence that a prosecution witness has falsely denied receiving promises of benefits for testifying for the prosecution is favorable to the defendant, and the prosecution has a *Brady* duty to correct such false testimony. *Jackson v. Brown* (2008, CA9 CA) 513 F.3d 1057.

§ 1:30.10   Creating false incriminatory evidence

The deliberate or knowing creation of misleading and/or false inculpatory evidence, combined with the suppression of exculpatory evidence, by a member of the prosecution team violates a defendant's due process rights. *Brown v. Miller* (2008, CA5 LA) 519 F.3d 231.

§ 1:31   Felony convictions

Felony convictions of a prosecution witness constitute evidence favorable to the defendant.

§ 1:31.6   Disclosing guilty plea of co-defendant prosecution witness

In *United States v. Carson* (2009, CA6 MI) 560 F.3d 566, a number of police officers were prosecuted for an assault of an arrestee and a subsequent conspiracy to cover up that assault. One of the police officers negotiated a plea agreement, pled guilty, and then testified against the other officers. The prosecutor referenced the officer witness's guilty plea in his argument, and the co-defendants argued on appeal that the prosecutor erred in making such a reference.

The Sixth Circuit Court of Appeals rejected the argument, holding that the prosecutor properly used the officer witness's guilty plea to encourage the jury to consider that plea in evaluating the credibility of the officer-witness. 560 F.3d at 574.

It necessarily follows that since a guilty plea of a co-defendant who becomes a prosecution witness may be used by the prosecution to support the credibility of the witness, it may be used by the defendants to attack the credibility of that witness. Therefore, such evidence could be favorable to the defendant within the meaning of the *Brady* rule.

§ 1:32   Misconduct involving moral turpitude

In *United States v. Price* (2009, CA9 OR) 566 F.3d 900, the prosecution failed to disclose evidence of its prime witness's prior arrests, conduct, and convictions in a federal prosecution of a defendant charged with being a felon in possession of a firearm. The defendant was convicted, and his motion for a new trial based upon claimed *Brady* violations was denied. On appeal the defendant repeated his *Brady* argument, and the government replied that the prosecutor believed that he was required to disclose only evidence of the witness's criminal convictions.

The Ninth Circuit Court of Appeals rejected the government's argument, citing its opinion in *Carriger v. Stewart* (1997, CA9 AZ) 132 F.3d 463, 480, that " '[I]t is the state's obligation to turn over *all* information bearing on [a government] witness's credibility. This must include the witness's criminal *record*, including prison records, and any information therein which bears on credibility.' " [italics in original] The Court of Appeals predicated its holding upon Federal Rule of Evidence 608(b), which permits impeachment of a witness by specific acts that have not resulted in a criminal conviction. The Court of Appeals also characterized the withholding of the evidence of the witness's criminal record as a *Brady* violation. 566 F.3d at 912–913. The Court reversed the defendant's conviction and remanded the case to the district court for further proceedings.

§ 1:32.1   Moral turpitude misconduct as impeaching evidence

Evidence that a prosecution witness has attempted to suborn perjurious testimony from a minor with whom the witness had engaged in sexual misconduct is evidence that is favorable to the defendant against whom the prosecution witness is expected to testify. Evidence of an attempt to suborn perjury "would have been highly probative of his 'character for truthfulness.' " *United States v. Kohring* (2011, CA9 AK) 637 F.3d 895, 904.

§ 1:32.3   Misdemeanor convictions involving moral turpitude misconduct

While misdemeanor convictions involving moral turpitude are inadmissible to impeach a witness, disclosure of such convictions can enable a defendant to develop the criminal conduct of the witness underlying those convictions to enable the defendant to impeach a prosecution witness with moral turpitude misconduct. *People v. Chatman* (2006) 38 Cal.4th 344, 373, 42 Cal.Rptr.3d 621, 133 P.3d 534 ["Misdemeanor convictions themselves are not admissible for impeachment, although evidence of the underlying *conduct* may be admissible subject to the court's exercise of discretion."]; *accord, People v. Cadogan* (2009) 173 Cal.App.4th 1502, 1514, 93 Cal.Rptr.3d 881.

In *People v. Clark* (2011) 52 Cal.4th 856, 982, 131 Cal.Rptr.3d 225, 261 P.3d 243, the California Supreme Court stated that although information that a prosecution witness's misdemeanor welfare fraud conviction "was favorable to defendant as impeachment evidence, it was not material."

§ 1:32.4   Misdemeanor moral turpitude misconduct

Conduct of a prosecution witness that involves moral turpitude may be used by the defendant to impeach that prosecution witness even though the conduct resulted in or could have resulted in only a misdemeanor conviction. *People v. Chatman* (2006) 38 Cal.4th 344, 373, 42 Cal.Rptr.3d 621, 133 P.3d 534 ["Misdemeanor convictions themselves are not admissible for impeachment, although evidence of the underlying *conduct* may be admissible subject to the court's exercise of discretion."]; *People v. Cadogan* (2009) 173 Cal.App.4th 1502, 1514, 93 Cal.Rptr.3d 881.

§ 1:32.5   Non-criminal moral turpitude misconduct

In *United States v. Robinson* (2010, CA4 SC) 627 F.3d 941, the week following the defendant's trial it was learned that several narcotics officers who had worked on Robinson's case and testified as prosecution witnesses in Robinson's trial had committed misconduct. The officers' agency conducted an investigation of this misconduct—which included misuse of county funds, improper disposition of drugs purchased by an informant, and improper use of evidence seized in criminal cases—which resulted in the termination or resignation of four officers who had worked on Robinson's case and testified against him. None of the misconduct related to Robinson's case.

After he learned of the dismissed officers' misconduct, Robinson moved for a new trial, which the trial court granted as to convictions to which the narcotics division was connected. Robinson appealed his convictions, arguing that he deserved a new trial on all charges, not just the now-dismissed ones. The Fourth Circuit Court of Appeals declined to reverse the trial court's denial of a new trial on the non-dismissed counts. In reaching this decision, the Court of Appeals observed that the evidence of the officers' misconduct "is offered to cast doubt on the testimony of the dismissed officers and the evidence they helped to collect, about as textbook an example of impeachment evidence as there could be." 627 F.3d at 949.

In *People v. Clark* (2011) 52 Cal.4th 856, 131 Cal.Rptr.3d 225, 261 P.3d 243, the California Supreme Court held that the trial court had properly allowed the prosecutor to impeach a defendant charged with the murder of his wife with evidence of his sexual infidelity toward her, where the defendant had introduced evidence that he had a common law marriage to his wife, that he loved her, and that he had a good relationship with her. 52 Cal.4th at 934–935. The Court observed that the evidence of the defendant's infidelity toward his wife "had some tendency in reason . . . to call his credibility into question." 52 Cal.4th at 935. In reaching this conclusion the Supreme Court cited with approval the holding of the Court of Appeal in *People v. Houston* (2005) 130 Cal.App.4th 279, 307, 29 Cal.Rptr.3d 818.

§ 1:33 Misdemeanor convictions involving moral turpitude

The statement in the text that "[m]isdemeanor convictions of prosecution witnesses are probably now admissible to impeach the credibility of prosecution witnesses, as long as those convictions are for crimes involving moral turpitude," is not yet the law (and might never become the law) in California. In *People v. Chatman* (2006) 38 Cal.4th 344, 373, 42 Cal.Rptr.3d 621, 133 P.3d 534, the California Supreme Court stated that "[m]isdemeanor convictions themselves are not admissible for impeachment, although evidence of the underlying *conduct* may be admissible subject to the court's exercise of discretion."

In *People v. Cadogan* (2009) 173 Cal.App.4th 1502, 1514, 93 Cal.Rptr.3d 881, the Court of Appeal quoted *Chatman* with approval and held that a trial court erred in allowing the prosecutor to impeach the defendant with his misdemeanor convictions. The Court of Appeal, however, found that the defendant's appeal on this issue was noncognizable, because the defendant had not made a timely objection in the trial court to the use of his prior convictions as impeachment evidence. 173 Cal.App.4th at 1515.

§ 1:34 Pending charges

The principle that pending charges against a prosecution witness may constitute evidence favorable to the defendant is not confined to pending *criminal* charges. This principle also extends to pending *administrative* or *disciplinary* charges.

In *United States v. Banks* (2008, CA7 IL) 546 F.3d 507, the prosecution presented the testimony of a forensic chemist in the prosecution of a defendant for four drug-related crimes. Following the defendant's conviction, it was revealed for the first time to the prosecutor and the defendant that at the time of her testimony, the chemist was under investigation for professional misconduct arising from her misuse of a government-issued credit card. The district court held that the suppression of this evidence constituted a *Brady* violation and granted the defendant a new trial. The government appealed the grant of the new trial.

The Seventh Circuit Court of Appeals affirmed the district court's judgment granting the new trial. The Court of Appeals treated the pending disciplinary action against the prosecution witness as if it were the same for *Brady* impeachment purposes as a pending criminal prosecution. The Court observed that "it is plausible that [the witness] felt pressure to testify favorably to the Government because of her pending disciplinary action." 546 F.3d at 513.

§ 1:34.1   Pending investigation of officer

Evidence that a prosecution witness knows that he or she is under investigation for suspected wrongful conduct is favorable to the defendant.

In *United States v. Wilson* (2010, CA DC) 605 F.3d 985, the prosecution failed to disclose until the middle of trial that an undercover officer who testified against five defendants charged with numerous drug charges was herself under investigation by the internal affairs division of her agency and had been suspended by the agency for alleged conduct that was redacted from the opinion of the Court of Appeals. The Court of Appeals concluded that the undisclosed information for which she was under investigation "would have been admissible . . . to show motive and bias," and that the favorability of this evidence to the defendant was not changed simply because the investigation was by her own agency, instead of by the prosecutor's office. 605 F.3d at 1006–1007. The Court of Appeals held that the district court had erred in failing to order the government to disclose the admissible impeachment evidence to the defense during the trial.

It is the prosecution officer witness that must be under investigation in order for that fact to be favorable evidence to the defendant. The fact that the officer's supervisor was under investigation for suspected wrongful or unlawful conduct does not constitute evidence favorable to a defendant where the supervisor played no significant role in the investigation of the crimes for which the defendant is charged. *United States v. De La Paz-Rentas* (2010, CA1 PR) 613 F.3d 18, 27.

§ 1:37   Untruthful reputation of prosecution witness

The untruthful reputation of a prosecution witness constitutes evidence favorable to a criminal defendant. This untruthful reputation can occur in a variety of contexts.

§ 1:37.1   Polygraph results—generally

The categorical exclusion from evidence of polygraph results in California courts provided by Evidence Code section 351.1 is not unconstitutional, and the exclusion extends to the penalty phase of a capital case. People v. Richardson (2008) 43 Cal. 4th 959, 1032–1033, 77 Cal.Rptr.3d 163, 183 P.3d 1146.

§ 1:37.4   Instances of untruthfulness

The question occasionally arises whether judicial credibility determinations are admissible to impeach the testimony of a witness. Such determinations might be evidence favorable to a defendant within the meaning of the *Brady* rule. In *United States v. Jeanpierre* (2011, CA8 MN) 636 F.3d 416, the Eighth Circuit Court of Appeals observed that "[a] majority of our sister circuits to consider the issue have held 'that judicial findings of facts are hearsay, inadmissible to prove the truth of the findings unless a specific hearsay exception exists.' " 636 F.3d at 423. The *Jeanpierre* Court cited three sister circuit opinions, *United States v. Sine* (2007, CA9 CA) 493 F.3d 1021, 1036; *Herrick v. Garvey* (2002, CA10 WY) 298 F.3d 1184, 1191–1192; and *United States v. Jones* (1994, CA11 GA) 29 F.3d 1549, 1554, in support of this proposition, and one contrary circuit court opinion, *United States v. Dawson* (2006, CA7 IL) 434 F.3d 956, 959.

Even though a judicial credibility determination regarding a prosecution witness might itself be inadmissible to impeach that witness, the determination might lead the defendant to admissible evidence to impeach the prosecution witness, and, therefore, it should be considered as evidence favorable to the defendant within the meaning of the *Brady* rule.

In *People v. Clark* (2011) 52 Cal.4th 856, 131 Cal.Rptr.3d 225, 261 P.3d 243, the California Supreme Court held that the trial court had properly allowed the prosecutor to impeach a defendant charged with the murder of his wife with evidence of his sexual infidelity toward her, where the defendant had introduced evidence that he had a common law marriage to his wife, that he loved her, and that he had a good relationship with her. 52 Cal.4th at 934–935. The Court observed that the evidence of the defendant's infidelity toward his wife "had some tendency in reason . . . to call his credibility into question." 52 Cal.4th at 935. In reaching this conclusion the Supreme Court cited with approval the holding of the Court of Appeal in *People v. Houston* (2005) 130 Cal.App.4th 279, 307, 29 Cal.Rptr.3d 818.

§ 1:37.5   Judicial findings of a witness's lack of credibility

The question occasionally arises whether judicial credibility determinations are admissible to impeach the testimony of a witness. Such determinations might be evidence favorable to a defendant within the meaning of the *Brady* rule. In *United States v. Jeanpierre* (2011, CA8 MN) 636 F.3d 416, the Eighth Circuit Court of Appeals observed that "[a] majority of our sister circuits to consider the issue have held 'that judicial findings of facts are hearsay, inadmissible to prove the truth of the findings unless a specific hearsay exception exists.' " 636 F.3d at 423. The *Jeanpierre* Court cited three sister circuit opinions, *United States v. Sine* (2007, CA9 CA) 493 F.3d 1021, 1036; *Herrick v. Garvey* (2002, CA10 WY) 298 F.3d 1184, 1191–1192; and *United States v. Jones* (1994, CA11 GA) 29 F.3d 1549, 1554, in support of this proposition, and one contrary circuit court opinion, *United States v. Dawson* (2006, CA7 IL) 434 F.3d 956, 959.

Even though a judicial credibility determination regarding a prosecution witness might itself be inadmissible to impeach that witness, the determination might lead the defendant to admissible evidence to impeach the prosecution witness, and, therefore, it should be considered as evidence favorable to the defendant within the meaning of the *Brady* rule.

§ 1:38   Incompetence/impairment of prosecution witness

Evidence that a prosecution witness is or has been incompetent as a witness or has been or is impaired in his or her ability to perceive, recall, or testify is evidence that is favorable to the defendant. The incompetence or impairment can occur in a variety of contexts.

§ 1:38.1   Impairment of prosecution witness [alcohol or drug use]

Evidence that a prosecution witness has used drugs or been under the influence of drugs is favorable to the defendant. In *United States v. Robinson* (2009, CA10 KS) 583 F.3d 1265, investigating officers used a confidential informant to purchase a firearm from a person that the informant identified as the defendant. The officers did not observe the firearm purchase, which occurred outside of their view inside a house.

The defendant moved that the trial court order disclosure of mental health records of the confidential informant. The trial court declined to order disclosure. After conviction the defendant argued on appeal that the denial of the informant's mental health records violated his right to due process of law. Those records apparently included evidence of illegal drug use by the informant, evidence relating to the informant's mental health condition, and evidence of the informant's use of prescription medications at the time of trial.

The Tenth Circuit Court of Appeals concluded that the denial of defendant's request for disclosure of these records was error. The Court observed that the "medical records reveal evidence of illegal drug use by the CI that is far more extensive than the jury was led to believe." The Court stated that evidence of the CI's extensive illegal drug use, which continued even through the investigation of the defendant up to the defendant's trial, directly contradicted the informant's testimony that he had only "a little bit" of a drug problem, and it also was evidence that the informant violated his cooperation agreement, which prohibited him from engaging in criminal activity, including illegal drug use. The Court concluded that the jury could have decided that an informant willing to repeatedly breach the terms of his informant agreement might also be willing to testify falsely. 583 F.3d at 1271–1272.

The Court of Appeals concluded that evidence of the informant's illegal drug use also bore on his capacity as a witness, both at the time of the alleged firearm sale and at the time of his testimony. 583 F.3d at 1272.

The informant's medical records also showed that the informant had been prescribed a number of medications when he was discharged from the hospital shortly before the defendant's trial and that he was using these medications at the time of the trial. The Court of Appeals concluded that evidence of the informant's legal drug use had potential to affect his ability to perceive the underlying events surrounding his testimony, to color his testimony, and to affect his ability to testify lucidly. The Court held that a witness's use of drugs may be used to attack a witness's ability to perceive and to testify. 583 F.3d at 1272–1273.

In *Wilson v. Beard* (2009, CA3 PA) 589 F.3d 651, an eyewitness to a shooting in a bar identified the defendant as the shooter. The eyewitness testified at the defendant's trial; the defendant was convicted of murder and sentenced to death.

The prosecution did not disclose to the defendant that the eyewitness had a history of mental health problems and psychiatric interventions, including an emergency room visit the day after he testified in the defendant's trial. The witness's mental health records revealed that the witness had been taking Haldol, a psychotropic drug used to control psychoses or schizophrenia, during the relevant time period. The records also showed that the witness was a heavy drug and alcohol user, that he mixed street drugs, alcohol and prescription medications, and that he was intoxicated at the time he witnessed the shooting.

The district court granted the defendant's habeas petition and vacated the conviction and judgment. The government appealed the district court's order. The Third Circuit Court of Appeals affirmed the district court's judgment, finding, *inter alia*, that "[t]here can be no dispute that all of this information would have been favorable to Wilson" and could have been used to impeach the prosecution witness. 589 F.3d at 662.

The Court of Appeals in *Wilson* reached a similar conclusion regarding a second prosecution eyewitness to the shooting, finding that the second eyewitness's memory problems, combined with his drug and alcohol abuse, were "clearly relevant to his credibility as a witness." 589 F.3d at 666.

§ 1:38.3   Mental and emotional instability of prosecution witness

Evidence of poor mental and emotional health bears on a witness's credibility and constitutes impeachment evidence relating to that witness. *United States v. Kohring* (2011, CA9 AK) 637 F.3d 895, 906, 910.

In *Brooks v. Tennessee* (2010, CA6 TN) 626 F.3d 878, the defendant (who was a habeas petitioner) contended, and the government agreed, that evidence of a prosecution witness's chronic mental illnesses that had been withheld by the government was favorable to the defendant as impeachment material that could have been used to discredit the witness's testimony about the defendant's putative jailhouse confession. 626 F.3d at 891.

§ 1:39   Rehearsed or coerced testimony of prosecution witness

Evidence that a prosecution witness's testimony has been rehearsed or coerced is favorable to the defendant, because such evidence can be used to impeach the credibility of that witness.

§ 1:39.1   Rehearsed testimony

It is a dangerous practice for a prosecutor to provide a summary of a witness's expected testimony to that witness, because such a summary can be viewed as a script for the witness to rehearse. Evidence that a prosecution witness has rehearsed his or her testimony can be favorable to the defendant.

In *Pederson v. Fabian* (2007, CA7 MN) 491 F.3d 816, the defendant was convicted of aiding and abetting a first degree murder committed in the course of a burglary and was sentenced to life in prison. Following his conviction the defendant obtained a copy of what he called a "script" that the prosecution had provided to an important witness against him to assist that witness in his testimony. The prosecution had not disclosed this "script" to the defense. The "script" was a summary prepared by one of the prosecutors describing portions of the witness's police statement and his grand jury testimony. A note was attached to the summary that admonished the witness to read the summary and be very familiar with the information contained in it.

The Minnesota Supreme Court rejected the defendant's contention on appeal that the prosecution's failure to disclose the summary constituted *Brady* error. The Supreme Court agreed that the summary was evidence affecting the witness's credibility, but found that since the witness's testimony at trial went beyond the summary, the summary was not strong evidence of scripted testimony and was thus not material evidence within the meaning of the *Brady* rule.

Pederson then filed a federal habeas corpus petition which made the same *Brady* argument he had made in state court. The district court rejected his *Brady* argument. On appeal the Eighth Circuit Court of Appeals upheld the trial court's denial of the habeas petition on the grounds that it was not material evidence within the meaning of *Brady*. However, the Court of Appeals found that the summary of the witness's testimony was favorable to the defendant. The Court stated:

> "Here, as correctly found by the Minnesota Supreme Court, the summary is favorable to the accused in that it speaks to the credibility of an important witness for the state. Had the defense been able to inform the jury that [the witness] studied a summary prepared by the prosecutors, and had the defense been able to show the summary to the jury, the jurors may have viewed [the witness] as less credible than they otherwise deemed him to be." 491 F.3d at 826.

Practice Tip for Prosecution: You should be very careful how you prepare your witnesses to testify. It is generally considered that providing the witness with a copy of the police report containing the substance of an interview of a witness or the statements of the witness is not an ethical violation. The same comments would also apply to providing a witness with a transcript of his or her prior testimony to read prior to calling the witness to testify. The reason that allowing the witness to review these documents is not a violation of ethical practice is that the witness would be entitled to review these documents to "refresh his or her memory" in order to be able to answer questions during the testimony. Such documents are generally allowed to be used for the purpose of refreshing a witness's recollection.

While a witness may refer to any document (including a telephone directory), as long as that document refreshes his or her recollection, a summary prepared by the prosecutor or investigating officer specifically for the purpose of refreshing the witness's recollection bears too many earmarks of a "script" that tells the witness what to say while testifying. The other feature of a summary specifically created to prepare a witness to testify is that, unlike police reports and transcripts of prior testimony, the defendant, as in the *Pederson* case discussed above, does not ordinarily have a copy of the summary. A summary that has been specifically prepared to prepare a prosecution witness to testify has the earmarks of a script, and scripted testimony of a prosecution witness reduces that witness's credibility.

Practice Tip for Defendant: You are entitled to know what documents and information have been shown or provided to a prosecution witness prior to his or her testimony. You should specifically request disclosure of any such document and information concerning the circumstances under which the document was shown or provided to the witness.

§ 1:39.2   Coerced testimony

Evidence that a prosecution witness has been coerced into cooperating with law enforcement and/or into testifying against the defendant can be used to impeach the testimony of that witness, and is thus evidence favorable to the defendant.

In *Simmons v. Beard* (2009, CA3 PA) 590 F.3d 223, the defendant was prosecuted for the murder and robbery of an elderly woman in her home. One of the principal witnesses against the defendant was the defendant's girlfriend, who changed her initial story about the whereabouts of the defendant on the night of an attack on a second elderly woman, an event that the prosecution used to help convict the defendant of the murder. The prosecution did not disclose that prior to her testimony the investigating detective pressured the girlfriend to consent to electronic surveillance of her conversations with the defendant by suggesting to the witness that there was evidence tying her to the murder.

Following his conviction of murder and robbery, the defendant filed a habeas petition in the federal district court, arguing, *inter alia,* that the prosecution had committed *Brady* error in failing to disclose the evidence of the coercion of the girlfriend. The district court granted the habeas petition, and the Court of Appeals affirmed the district court's order. The Court of Appeals observed that had the information been disclosed, "the defense would have taken advantage of the opportunity to offer a competing explanation: that [the girlfriend] implicated Simmons in the Cobaugh assault because of a fear that otherwise she herself might face criminal liability." 590 F.3d at 235. The Court concluded that the "the fact that [the girlfriend] seemed willing to condemn her boyfriend without any outside incentive to do so may very well have reinforced the damning nature of her testimony. The information about the threats against [the girlfriend] was essential to explain why she might testify against Simmons even if he was not in fact guilty." 590 F.3d at 235.

See also, United States v. Scheer (1999, CA11 FL) 168 F.3d 445 [prosecutor's attempt to intimidate a prosecution witness by threatening to return him to prison was material *Brady* information, because it could have been used to impeach the witness at trial.].

A defendant who claims that a prosecution witness was coerced into lying or subjected to pressure to provide inculpatory evidence against the defendant has the burden to prove such a claim. Where there is "no evidence that [the investigating officers] coerced [the witness] to lie or were otherwise withholding exculpatory evidence on this point from the defense," a *Brady* claim is not established. *Holland v. City of Chicago* (2011, CA7 IL) 643 F.3d 248, 256.

§ 1:39.3 Prosecution meeting with witness

While evidence that a prosecution witness has been programmed or coerced to give testimony adverse to the defendant can be used to impeach that prosecution witness, and is thus favorable to the defendant, evidence that the prosecution witness has met with the prosecutor or another prosecution team official prior to his or her testimony has little impeachment value. It is questionable whether such evidence is favorable to the defendant. *See, e.g., Banks v. Thaler* (2009, CA5 TX) 583 F.3d 295, 322. " '[T]here is absolutely nothing improper about the prosecutor's having interviewed [a prosecution witness] prior to trial . . . This is in keeping with one of the most basic and well-known rules of trial advocacy: 'Never ask a question for which you do not know the answer'." "[T]here is little, if any, impeachment value to a mere showing that [the witness] has met with prosecutors prior to trial . . . such a meeting was expected; moreover, it was completely proper under Texas law . . . ." 583 F.3d at 323.

§ 1:41 Bias of prosecution witness toward defendant—generally

Evidence that a prosecution witness has a "bias or motive to lie is admissible impeachment evidence." *United States v. Salem* (2009, CA7 WI) 578 F.3d 682, 686.

§ 1:41.2 Personal bias

A personal bias of a prosecution witness can take many forms. One such bias is a personal bias in favor of the prosecution by virtue of a personal or intimate relationship with the prosecutor, a member of the prosecution's staff, the investigating officer, or a member of the investigating agency's staff.

In *In re McDonald* (2008, CA6 OH) 514 F.3d 539, a key prosecution witness developed an intimate sexual relationship with the prosecutor which the witness later asserted was coerced and non-consensual. That relationship was not disclosed to the defendant. The defendant was convicted of the charges and sentenced to prison. The defendant petitioned for habeas corpus relief, alleging that the prosecution's failure to disclose this relationship violated *Brady*. The Sixth Circuit Court of Appeals concluded that the evidence of the witness's intimate relationship with the prosecutor was evidence favorable to the defendant within the meaning of the *Brady* rule. The Court stated: "Also, the state clearly failed to inform McDonald of any relationship between Harris, a testifying witness, and the prosecutor. Both of these pieces of information were clearly favorable to McDonald." 514 F.3d at 545.

Practice Tip for Prosecution: You should NEVER develop a relationship with a prosecution witness that goes beyond the kind of professional rapport necessary to gain the witness's confidence and trust. Allowing a sexual relationship to develop with a witness is simply non-professional conduct that you should avoid at all costs. If you discover that one of your witnesses has a pre-existing personal relationship (familial or otherwise) with a member of your office or with a member of the investigating agency, you should call that relationship to the attention of your supervisor and should disclose that relationship to the defendant close in time to when you discover it.

§ 1:41.3 Economic bias

Evidence that a witness has a possible economic bias can take many forms. Evidence of an economic bias is favorable to the defendant within the meaning of the *Brady* rule.

Economic bias can arise from an agreement with an expert witness to compensate that witness for his or her time or work. Thus, the prosecution's fee agreement with an expert witness is evidence favorable to the defendant, because such an agreement can be used by the defendant to impeach the expert witness's motive to tell the truth. *United States v. Valencia* (2010, CA5 TX) 600 F.3d 389, 418–419.

Economic bias can also arise from an economic arrangement with a witness during the investigation of a crime. A typical economic arrangement that creates an economic bias arises when a law enforcement agency pays a confidential informant for his or her work as an informant. *Robinson v. Mills*

(2010, CA6 TN) 592 F.3d 730, 737–738.

§ 1:41.4   Bias in favor of prosecution

The bias of a prosecution witness need not be a bias directed *against* or *toward* the defendant in order for that bias to constitute evidence favorable to the defendant. The bias can be bias in *favor* of the *prosecution*. The term 'bias' describes "the relationship between a party and a witness which might lead the witness to slant, unconsciously or otherwise, his testimony in favor of or against a party." *United States v. Abel* (1984) 469 U.S. 45, 52, 105 S.Ct. 465, 83 L.Ed.2d 450. Bias is, therefore, " 'not limited to personal animosity against a defendant or pecuniary gain.' [citation omitted]" *Robinson v. Mills* (2010, CA6 TN) 592 F.3d 730, 737.

Evidence that a prosecution witness has curried favor with the government in exchange for his or her testimony is routinely admitted by trial courts "as proof of bias or motive to testify falsely." *United States v. Salem* (2009, CA7 WI) 578 F.3d 682, 686.

Thus, in *United States v. Salem* (2009, CA7 WI) 578 F.3d 682, the Seventh Circuit Court of Appeals concluded that evidence that a prosecution witness who was a suspect in an uncharged murder had never been charged for his suspected participation in that murder "could be admissible to demonstrate [the witness's] incentive to lie to avoid a murder charge." 578 F.3d at 686.

Evidence that a prosecution witness has a pro-prosecution bias does not depend upon the witness's expectation of a benefit from the prosecution or the government in return for his assistance. In *Wilson v. Beard* (2009, CA3 PA) 589 F.3d 651, evidence that a prosecution eyewitness to a charged murder had a history and an "ingrained psychological need" to impersonate a police officer, to help the police, and to associate himself with and attach himself to police activities, caused the Court of Appeals to conclude that such evidence was favorable to the defendant as evidence that the witness was biased in favor of law enforcement within the favorability component of the *Brady* rule. 589 F.3d at 665.

§ 1:42   Prosecutor's knowing presentation of false/perjured testimony

Evidence of prosecutor-sponsored perjured testimony is not only evidence favorable to the defendant within the meaning of the *Brady* rule, but it is also an independent violation of a defendant's due process rights. "A false-testimony claim is cognizable in habeas because the 'deliberate deception of a court and jurors by the presentation of known false evidence is incompatible with rudimentary demands of justice.' [citations omitted] To prevail on such a claim, Akrawi must show '(1) that the prosecution presented false testimony (2) that the prosecution knew was false, and (3) that was material.' [citation omitted]" *Ragheed Akrawi v. Booker* (2009, CA6 MI) 572 F.3d 252, 265.

The defendant can satisfy the second required showing of a due process violation—the knowledge element—by establishing that the prosecution should have known that the testimony was actually false. *Towery v. Schriro* (2010, CA9 AZ) 641 F.3d 300, 308. However, in order to establish that the prosecution should have known that prosecution testimony was false, it must be shown that the prosecution had knowledge of underlying facts from which a reasonable prosecutor would have known that the testimony was false. 641 F.3d at 309.

The principle that the prosecutor denies a defendant due process of law by the knowing presentation of false or perjured testimony does not require that the prosecutor know that the prosecution testimony is false at the time the testimony is given, if the prosecutor later learns of the falsity. A prosecutor denies a defendant due process of law when the prosecutor fails to correct what he or she subsequently learns was materially false testimony. *United States v. McNair* (2010, CA11 AL) 605 F.3d 1152, 1208. "[T]he prosecution's duty to disclose false testimony should not be 'narrowly and technically limited to those situations where the prosecutor knows that the witness is guilty of the crime of perjury.' [citation omitted] Rather, 'when it should be obvious to the Government that the witness' answer, although made in good faith, is untrue,' it has an obligation to correct that testimony." *United States v. Stadtmauer* (2010, CA3 NJ) 620 F.3d 238, 268.

The knowing presentation of false or perjured testimony need not directly relate to the defendant's guilt; it may also relate to the witness's credibility. "A conviction obtained using knowingly perjured testimony violates due process, even if the witness's perjured testimony goes only to his credibility as a witness and not to the defendant's guilt." *United States v. Houston* (2011, CA9 CA) 648 F.3d 806, 814.

§ 1:42.1 Correcting false/perjurious testimony not solicited by prosecutor

The principle that the prosecutor denies a defendant due process of law by the knowing presentation of false or perjured testimony does not require that the prosecutor know that the prosecution testimony is false at the time the testimony is given, if the prosecutor later learns of the falsity. A prosecutor denies a defendant due process of law when the prosecutor fails to correct what he or she subsequently learns was materially false testimony. *United States v. McNair* (2010, CA11 AL) 605 F.3d 1152, 1208. "[T]he prosecution's duty to disclose false testimony should not be 'narrowly and technically limited to those situations where the prosecutor knows that the witness is guilty of the crime of perjury.' [citation omitted] Rather, 'when it should be obvious to the Government that the witness' answer, although made in good faith, is untrue,' it has an obligation to correct that testimony." *United States v. Stadtmauer* (2010, CA3 NJ) 620 F.3d 238, 268.

When the government does not know, and has no way of knowing, that a prosecution witness's testimony is false, the government "could not, and [is] not required to correct a supposed misstatement that it did not know was false." *Hayes v. Ayers* (2011, CA9 CA) 632 F.3d 500, 521.

§ 1:42.2 Prosecutor's knowing and unknowing presentation of false/perjured testimony contrasted

In *United States v. Agurs* (1976) 427 U.S. 97, 103, 96 S.Ct. 2392, 49 L.Ed.2d 342, the United States Supreme Court identified the test for determining whether a conviction has been gained through the use of false testimony as whether "the prosecution knew, or should have known, of the perjury." In *Agurs*, however, "there was no allegation that the prosecutor should have known of any false statements. 427 U.S. at 104. Thus, in *Drake I*, we identified the 'should have known' language in *Agurs* as dicta." *Drake v. Portuondo* (2009, CA2 NY) 563 F.3d 230, 240.

Even though the principle that the failure to investigate the testimony of a prosecution witness that the prosecutor has reason to believe might be false constitutes *Napue* error was not clearly established as of the time of the trial of Robie Drake, there is little question that such a failure today violates the prosecutor's duty to correct false or perjured testimony as announced by the United States Supreme Court in *Napue v. Illinois* (1959) 360 U.S. 264, 269, 79 S.Ct. 1173, 3 L.Ed.2d 1217.

The critical factor in establishing the due process violation of a knowing use of perjured testimony is that the prosecutor must know or have reason to know that the testimony is false or perjured at the time the testimony is offered. *Perkins v. Russo* (2009, CA1 MA) 586 F.3d 115, 119–120; *United States v. Boyce* (2009, CA8 MO) 564 F.3d 911, 917.

See the discussion in Section 1:42.8 of the text and this supplement.

The Ninth Circuit Court of Appeals appears to have extended the knowing due process violation for use of false or perjured testimony to situations in which the prosecution unwittingly presented false or perjured testimony. *See Maxwell v. Roe* (2010, CA9 CA) 628 F.3d 486, 506–508 [We "conclude that . . . to permit a conviction based on uncorrected false material evidence to stand is a violation of a defendant's due process rights under the Fourteenth Amendment." 628 F.3d at 507]; and *Killian v. Poole* (2002, CA9 CA) 282 F.3d 1204, 1206–1208. The Court of Appeals held that to permit a conviction to stand on the basis of perjured evidence violates a defendant's due process of law, irrespective of whether the prosecutor knew that the witness had given false testimony. The Court stated in *Killian v. Poole, supra*, that "a government's assurances that false evidence was presented in good faith are little comfort to a criminal defendant wrongly convicted on the basis of such evidence. A conviction based in part on false evidence, even false evidence presented in good faith, hardly comports with fundamental fairness." 282 F.3d at 1209.

§ 1:42.3 Knowing use of false/perjured testimony as a *Brady* violation

The knowing and undisclosed use of perjured testimony by a prosecution witness is a violation of due process of law on its own accord and can also constitute a *Brady* violation.

In *In re McDonald* (2008, CA6 OH) 514 F.3d 539, a key prosecution witness developed an intimate sexual relationship with the prosecutor which the witness later asserted was coerced and non-consensual. The witness also alleged that the non-consensual relationship with the prosecutor caused her to perjure herself by failing to give potential alibi testimony for the defendant. The witness's relationship with the prosecutor was not disclosed to the defendant. The defendant was convicted of the charges and sentenced to prison.

The defendant petitioned for habeas corpus relief, alleging that the prosecution's failure to disclose this relationship violated *Brady*. The Sixth Circuit Court of Appeals concluded that the evidence of the witness's undisclosed intimate relationship with the prosecutor was evidence favorable to the defendant within the meaning of the *Brady* rule and also constituted knowing use of perjured testimony. The Court stated: "Also, the state clearly failed to inform McDonald of any relationship between Harris, a testifying witness, and the prosecutor. Both of these pieces of information were clearly favorable to McDonald." 514 F.3d at 545. "[T]he alleged conduct might also have violated the Due Process Clause by constituting a knowing use of perjured testimony. However, as the new evidence presented by McDonald is sufficient to make out a *Brady* claim, we need not consider how many permutations of due process violations we can conjure up based upon the same set of facts." 514 F.3d at 546, n.5.

In *Rosencrantz v. Lafler* (2009, CA6 MI) 568 F.3d 577, the Sixth Circuit Court of Appeals characterized a habeas petitioner's *Brady/Giglio* argument that the prosecutor in his prosecution knowingly presented false evidence and also failed to disclose evidence favorable to the accused as "a specific type of *Brady* violation: one where the prosecutor failed to correct false testimony that he knew, or should have known, to be false (a 'knowing-presentation-of-false-testimony claim')." 568 F.3d at 583.

Evidence of prosecutor-sponsored perjured testimony is not only evidence favorable to the defendant within the meaning of the *Brady* rule, but is also an independent violation of a defendant's due process rights. Evidence that the prosecutor has sponsored perjured testimony to conceal suppression of evidence has been described as "*Brady* plus prosecutorial misconduct." *Ragheed Akrawi v. Booker* (2009, CA6 MI) 572 F.3d 252, 265.

§ 1:42.4 Limitations on rule against knowing presentation of false/perjured testimony

The constitutional prohibition against a prosecutor's knowing presentation of perjured or false evidence is not without limitations. These limitations include inconsistent testimony, conflicts in testimony, the prosecutor's doubts about testimony, and the results of the witness's testimony in other trials.

§ 1:42.4.1   Witness with inconsistent testimony

Convicted federal defendants frequently argue that their convictions were obtained by the use of false or perjured testimony. The federal circuit courts have established a number of principles to determine whether prosecution testimony is false. These principles include the following: "[T]he mere presence of conflicts in witness testimony is insufficient to establish perjury." *United States v. Coplen* (2009, CA8 IA) 565 F.3d 1094, 1096. Inconsistencies in the testimony of prosecution witnesses do not establish that any of their testimony was false. *United States v. Hunter* (2009, CA6 OH) 558 F.3d 495, 505. A prosecution witness's vacillation in his or her testimony does not establish that the witness has given "indisputably false" testimony. *Rosencrantz v. Lafler* (2009, CA6 MI) 568 F.3d 577, 585. And differences in witnesses' recollections do not establish that the witnesses have provided perjured or false testimony. *United States v. Josephberg* (2009, CA2 NY) 562 F.3d 478, 494. Inconsistencies in a witness's testimony commonly have "innocent provenance such as confusion, mistake, or faulty memory." 562 F.3d at 495. *Accord, Brooks v. Tennessee* (2010, CA6 TN) 626 F.3d 878, 895. " 'Merely inconsistent statements do not establish use of false testimony' [citation omitted]." *United States v. Moore* (2011, CA8 NE) 639 F.3d 443, 446.

§ 1:42.4.3   Conflicts in witness testimony

The fact that there are conflicts in the testimony of prosecution witnesses does not establish that any of the witnesses have committed perjury. "[T]he mere presence of conflicts in witness testimony is insufficient to establish perjury." *United States v. Coplen* (2009, CA8 IA) 565 F.3d 1094, 1097.

§ 1:42.4.4   Results of other trials in which witnesses testified

In *United States v. Coplen* (2009, CA8 IA) 565 F.3d 1094, a defendant convicted of conspiracy to distribute cocaine and sentenced to life in prison as a career offender appealed the denial of his motion for a new trial. In his appeal he argued that many of the prosecution witnesses in his trial had also testified for the prosecution in related cases in which juries had acquitted the defendants. Coplen argued that these acquittals, in conjunction with alleged inconsistencies in some of the testimony, established that the witnesses had committed perjury in his trial.

The Eighth Circuit Court of Appeals rejected the defendant's argument, holding that acquittals in other trials were not relevant to Coplen's case and failed to demonstrate perjury or the government's knowing use of fabricated testimony.

§ 1:42.4.5   Prosecutor corroboration of witness

When a prosecutor seeks out and finds evidence to support and corroborate the testimony of a prosecution witness alleged to have given false testimony, the prosecutor has satisfied his or her duty to discover and investigate false or perjured testimony. *See, e.g., United States v. Inzunza* (2011, CA9 CA) 638 F.3d 1006, 1021.

§ 1:42.4.6 Actual falsity requirement

In the same way that evidence of a prior false statement by a witness offered to impeach that witness requires that the prior statement be actually false, a claimed due process violation predicated on a witness's material false testimony requires that the witness's false testimony was actually false. *Brooks v. Tennessee* (2010, CA6 TN) 626 F.3d 878, 894–895; *Hayes v. Ayers* (2011, CA9 CA) 632 F.3d 500, 520. The person asserting the falsity of a statement or testimony has the burden to prove that claim. *United States v. Houston* (2011, CA9 CA) 648 F.3d 806, 814.

§ 1:42.7 Burden to prove knowing presentation of false/perjured testimony

A defendant who claims that the prosecution has knowingly presented false testimony has the burden to prove that the evidence was indisputably false, and that the prosecution knew the evidence was false. *Rosencrantz v. Lafler* (2009, CA6 MI) 568 F.3d 577, 584; *United States v. Josephberg* (2009, CA2 NY) 562 F.3d 478, 494; *Boyd v. Allen* (2010, CA11 AL) 592 F.3d 1274, 1308. The person asserting the falsity of a statement or testimony has the burden to prove that claim. *United States v. Houston* (2011, CA9 CA) 648 F.3d 806, 814.

§ 1:42.8 Prosecutor's duty to discover/investigate false/perjured testimony

The Ninth Circuit Court of Appeals continues to hold that a prosecutor who suspects that a prosecution witness has committed perjury " 'must at least investigate' further, consistent with his 'duty to correct what he knows [or suspects] to be false and elicit the truth.' [citations omitted]." *United States v. Price* (2009, CA9 OR) 566 F.3d 900, 910.

The prosecutor's duty to investigate false or perjured testimony requires the prosecutor to investigate obvious leads. But a defendant who claims that the government failed in this duty must be able to identify what else the government should have done that the government did not do to investigate the alleged false or perjured testimony. *United States v. Houston* (2011, CA9 CA) 648 F.3d 806, 815.

When a prosecutor seeks out and finds evidence to support and corroborate the testimony of a prosecution witness alleged to have given false testimony, the prosecutor has satisfied his or her duty to discover and investigate false or perjured testimony. *See, e.g., United States v. Inzunza* (2011, CA9 CA) 638 F.3d 1006, 1021.

§ 1:42.9   False testimony vs. perjured testimony

The prosecutor's duty to correct false testimony of a prosecution witness does not depend upon that testimony's constituting perjurious testimony. There is constitutional error if a prosecutor knows that a witness has testified falsely and fails to correct that falsity. "The question of whether the witness's 'untruthfulness . . . constituted perjury' makes no 'material difference' where the issue is a conviction 'on tainted testimony.' [citations omitted]." *Drake v. Portuondo* (2009, CA2 NY) 553 F.3d 230, 242, n.7.

§ 1:42.9.1   Perjured testimony defined

The terms "perjured" testimony and "false" testimony are not coterminous. *United States v. Dunnigan* (1993) 507 U.S. 87, 94, 113 S.Ct. 1111, 122 L.Ed.2d 445 [A witness does not commit perjury if his or her false testimony is the "result of confusion, mistake, or faulty memory."]. " 'One commits perjury if, while under oath, he or she gives false testimony concerning a material matter with a willful intent to provide false testimony, rather than as a result of confusion, mistake, or faulty memory.' [citation omitted]." *United States v. Lathrop* (2011, CA7 WI) 634 F.3d 931, 940; *accord United States v. McNair* (2011, CA11 AL) 605 F.3d 1152, 1208. A statement or testimony that is the product of confusion and which does not rise to the level of willful deceit is not a perjured statement or testimony. *United States v. Lathrop, supra,* 634 F.3d at 939. Thus, a statement can be false without being perjured.

§ 1:42.10   Harmless error of knowing presentation of perjured testimony

Even when the court finds that a prosecutor has knowingly presented or failed to correct perjured testimony of a prosecution witness, the court may still conclude that the constitutional error of such conduct is harmless under the United States Constitution. *Rosencrantz v. Lafler* (2009, CA6 MI) 568 F.3d 577, 588–589.

However, the harmless error test which might apply to the knowing presentation of perjured testimony does not apply to *Brady* error. *Douglas v. Workman* (2009, CA10 OK) 560 F.3d 1156, 1173. See Section 1:46 of the text.

PART IV.   MATERIALITY REQUIREMENT

§ 1:43   Materiality requirement—in general

To be material under *Brady*, evidence must be admissible as evidence or capable of being used to impeach a government witness. *Henry v. Ryan* (2013, CA9 Ariz.) 720 F.3d 1073. *See also United States v. Olsen* (2013, CA9 Ariz.) 704 F.3d 1172, holding, *inter alia*, that even if evidence favorable to the defendant has been suppressed or not disclosed by the prosecution, there is no true *Brady* violation unless that information is material. Evidence has been found to be material when there is a reasonable probability that, had the evidence been disclosed to the defense, the result of the proceeding would have been different. A reasonable probability is one that is sufficient to undermine confidence in the outcome of the trial. The question is not whether the defendant would more likely than not have received a different verdict with the evidence, but whether in its absence he received a fair trial, understood as a trial resulting in a verdict worthy of confidence. Reversal of a conviction or sentence is required only upon a showing that the favorable evidence could reasonably be taken to put the whole case in such a different light as to undermine confidence in the verdict. This necessarily is a retrospective test, evaluating the strength of the evidence after trial has concluded. *See also United States v. Harkonen* (Mar. 4, 2013, CA9 Cal.) 2013 U.S. App. LEXIS 4472, holding, *inter alis*, that the government's withholding of evidence causes prejudice for purposes of a *Brady* claim if the evidence withheld undermines confidence in the outcome of the trial.

§ 1:46   No harmless error test

Once suppressed favorable evidence has been determined to be material, the court need not consider whether the suppression of that evidence was harmless error. "This is because a reasonable probability of a different result in the proceeding 'necessarily entails the conclusion that the suppression must have had substantial and injurious effect or influence in determining the jury's verdict.' [citation omitted]" *Douglas v. Workman* (2009, CA10 OK) 560 F.3d 1156, 1173.

§ 1:47   Cumulative effect of suppression

In the context of a *Brady* claim, a finding of prejudice requires that the conduct have some impact on the outcome of the proceeding—i.e., a reasonable probability that the result of the proceeding would have been different or that it so infected the trial with unfairness as to make the resulting conviction a denial of due process. *United States v. Rodriguez* (June 24, 2013, CA9 Cal.) 2013 U.S. App. LEXIS 12918.

The assessment of the cumulative effect of suppression is not simply a numerical comparison of the number of *Brady* violations committed by the prosecution when compared to the number of disclosures of material exculpatory evidence. Nor does the *Brady* materiality assessment simply consider the numbers of prosecution witnesses to which the suppressed *Brady* evidence relates. The standard for measuring the cumulative effect of suppression evaluates both the "quantity and exculpatory persuasiveness of the suppressed evidence." *Johnson v. Bell* (2008, CA6 TN) 525 F.3d 466, 478.

In a series of opinions the Eleventh Circuit Court of Appeals has explained its approach to assessing the cumulative effect of the prosecution's suppression of evidence in order to determine whether the suppressed evidence is material.

The first step in the process is for the court to examine and size up each piece of suppressed evidence standing alone. *Hammond v. Hall* (2009, CA11 GA) 586 F.3d 1289, 1313; *Smith v. Sec'y, Dep't of Corr.* (2009, CA11 FL) 572 F.3d 1327, 1346. This step in the process of determining the materiality of suppressed evidence is derived from the opinion of the United States Supreme Court in *Kyles v. Whitley* (1995) 514 U.S. 419, 433, 115 S.Ct. 1555, 1565, 131 L.Ed.2d 490, in which the Supreme Court stated: "We evaluate the tendency and force of the undisclosed evidence item by item; there is no other way. We evaluate its cumulative effect for purposes of materiality separately and at the end of the discussion." The first step in an examination of the materiality of each piece of suppressed evidence must be taken prior to the second step of a collective materiality examination. *United States v. Kohring* (2011, CA9 AK) 637 F.3d 895, 903. " 'Indeed, the only way to evaluate the cumulative effect is to first examine each piece standing alone.' [citation omitted]" *Allen v. Sec'y, Fla. Dep't of Corr.* (2010, CA11 FL) 611 F.3d 740, 749.

The second step in the process is for the court to aggregate all of the suppressed evidence and determine the cumulative impact of the suppressed evidence as a whole. *Hammond v. Hall* (2009, CA11 GA) 586 F.3d 1289, 1313. This second step is necessary, because the "sum of the parts almost invariably will be greater than any individual part." *Smith v. Sec'y, Dep't of Corr.* (2009, CA11 FL) 572 F.3d 1327, 1347. The suppressed evidence favorable to the defendant must also be added to the evidence favorable to the defendant that was presented at the trial. 572 F.3d at 1347.

The third step in the process is for the court to weigh the exculpatory evidence (which includes the suppressed favorable evidence plus the favorable evidence presented at trial) against the totality of the inculpatory evidence presented at the trial. This step requires not only the addition of the suppressed favorable evidence to the favorable evidence presented at trial, but it also requires the court to subtract the undisclosed impeachment evidence from the weight of the prosecution's inculpatory evidence. "[T]he force and effect of all of the undisclosed exculpatory evidence is added to the weight of the evidence on the defense side, while the force and effect of all the undisclosed impeachment evidence is subtracted from the weight of the evidence on the prosecution's side." 572 F.3d at 1347.

The fourth and final step is for the court to determine whether what is left on both sides of the scale, after adjustments for the suppressed evidence, creates a reasonable probability that a jury presented with that evidence would have acquitted the defendant. 572 F.3d at 1347. Stated another way, the question the court must resolve is this: "whether we can be confident that the jury's verdict would have been the same." *Hammond v. Hall* (2009, CA11 GA) 586 F.3d 1289, 1313.

See, Ward v. Hall (2010, CA11 GA) 592 F.3d 1144, 1187, n.28, for an abbreviated summary of this four-step process.

This analytical process means, of course, that "the stronger the evidence of guilt to begin with, the more favorable to the defense the undisclosed evidence will have to be to create a reasonable probability that a jury would have acquitted had the evidence been disclosed." *Smith v. Sec'y, Dep't of Corr.* (2009, CA11 FL) 572 F.3d 1327, 1347.

One potential wrinkle in this analysis is not discussed by the Eleventh Circuit Court of Appeals' opinions. The wrinkle is this: what should the court do in its cumulation of suppressed favorable evidence with *Brady* claims that have already been decided.

However, in *Banks v. Thaler* (2009, CA5 TX) 583 F.3d 295, a case arising out of the Supreme Court's decision in *Branks v. Dretke* (2004) 540 U.S. 668, 124 S.Ct. 1256, 157 L.Ed.2d 1166, discussed in the text, the Fifth Circuit Court of Appeals held that the cumulative materiality determination does not consider *Brady* claims of which the court has already disposed. "Already-disposed-of habeas claims are not properly before us, and may *not* be considered in our assessment of the Cook transcript's materiality." 583 F.3d at 312.

It is too early to know whether other federal circuit courts or the California Supreme Court will agree with this approach to evaluating the materiality of withheld evidence.

It should go without saying, but one Court of Appeals found it necessary to opine the obvious—that when the government suppressed only one piece of favorable evidence, the second step in the materiality analysis is superfluous. "[If] one of the [suppressed] reports was favorable to the defense in some useful way, cumulative materiality consideration would still be beside the point unless another report was favorable as well. Adding nothing to any weight does not increase that weight." *Allen v. Sec'y, Fla. Dep't of Corr.* (2010, CA11 FL) 611 F.3d 740, 747.

§ 1:48 Basic definition of materiality—reasonable probability of different result

In *Bower v. Quarterman* (2007, CA5 TX) 497 F.3d 459, 477, the Fifth Circuit Court of Appeals penned a clear statement of the materiality standard in these words: "[W]e have held that '[t]he materiality of *Brady* evidence depends almost entirely on the value of the evidence relative to the other evidence mustered by the State.' [citations omitted]."

Although the number of exculpatory items suppressed by the prosecution plays a role in determining the prejudicial effect of the suppression, the ultimate standard for determining the materiality of that suppressed evidence is the probative force of the suppressed evidence, not the number of items of suppressed evidence. *See Mark v. Ault* (2007, CA8 IA) 498 F.3d 775, 786 [prosecution's suppression of 24 items of exculpatory evidence held not material "in light of the strong circumstantial evidence connecting Mark to the murders, the 'net effect of' the minimally exculpatory evidence cannot 'reasonably be taken to put the whole case in such a different light as to undermine confidence in the verdict.' "].

Cases which determine whether a habeas petitioner has defaulted his right to bring a *Brady* challenge in federal courts often turn on the issue of prejudice. "Procedural default analysis on the issue of prejudice mirrors *Brady* materiality analysis . . . so in determining whether [the habeas petitioner] has procedurally defaulted his *Brady* claim, we will follow the Supreme Court's example and proceed under a *Brady* materiality analysis." *Fautenberry v. Mitchell* (2008, CA6 OH) 515 F.3d 614, 629. In the context of a *Brady* claim, a finding of prejudice requires that the conduct have some impact on the outcome of the proceeding—i.e., a reasonable probability that the result of the proceeding would have been different or that it so infected the trial with unfairness as to make the resulting conviction a denial of due process. *United States v. Rodriguez* (June 24, 2013, CA9 Cal.) 2013 U.S. App. LEXIS 12918.

Two components of the *materiality standard*—whether the suppressed favorable evidence undermines "confidence in the verdict" and whether such evidence creates a "reasonable probability of a different result"—are in fact synonymous and constitute different ways of expressing the same concept. *Simmons v. Beard* (2009, CA3 PA) 590 F.3d 223, 234, n.6. "A 'probability' reaches the level of 'reasonable' when it is high enough to 'undermine confidence in the verdict.' [citation omitted]" *United States v. Johnson* (2010, CA DC) 592 F.3d 164, 170.

This standard of a reasonable probability of a different result does not require that the suppressed favorable evidence conclusively establish the defendant's innocence—only a reasonable probability that the new evidence would lead to a different result. *Goudy v. Basinger* (2010, CA7 IN) 604 F.3d 394, 400. The probability of a different result standard is not an " 'actual probability that the result would have differed'; it may be 'a merely theoretical (but still reasonable) probability.' [citation omitted]" *United States v. Mathur* (2010, CA1 MA) 624 F.3d 498, 504.

Moreover, the court must not speculate whether the defendant's attorney would have uncovered the favorable evidence had that evidence been disclosed. "The question under Brady is whether 'disclosure of the suppressed evidence to *competent* counsel would have made a different result reasonably probable.' [citations omitted]" *Wilson v. Beard* (2009, CA3 PA) 589 F.3d 651, 664.

The reason underlying the requirement that the defendant must prove a reasonable probability of a different result as an element of a *Brady* violation is that such a standard "accord[s] with the purpose of *Brady*. At its core, *Brady* seeks to ensure a fair trial, a trial whose verdict is reliable." *Smith v. Almada* (2010, CA9 CA) 623 F.3d 1078, 1087.

§ 1:48.2 Materiality as distinct from favorableness

As assessment of the *materiality* of a given piece of evidence should be made without regard to the *favorableness* of the evidence, and the "favorable tendency of a given piece of evidence should be assessed without regard to the "weight of the evidence" as a whole." *Kyles v. Whitley* (1995) 514 U.S. 419, 451, 115 S.Ct. 1555, 1565, 131 L.Ed.2d 490; *Walker v. Kelly* (2009, CA4 VA) 589 F.3d 127, 140.

§ 1:48.3 Materiality and prejudice—reasonable probability of different result is prejudice materiality, not relevance materiality

In the context of a *Brady* claim, a finding of prejudice requires that the conduct have some impact on the outcome of the proceeding—i.e., a reasonable probability that the result of the proceeding would have been different or that it so infected the trial with unfairness as to make the resulting conviction a denial of due process. *United States v. Rodriguez* (June 24, 2013, CA9 Cal.) 2013 U.S. App. LEXIS 12918.

The relationship between materiality and prejudice in the *Brady* rule is simply stated: " 'Demonstrating prejudice requires the defendant to show that the suppressed favorable evidence at issue is material.' [citations omitted]." *Johnson v. Bell* (2008, CA6 TN) 525 F.3d 466, 475, n.4.

In *United States v. Price* (2009, CA9 OR) 566 F.3d 900, 911, the Ninth Circuit Court of Appeals quoted with approval its statement in *Benn v. Lambert* (2002, CA9 WA) 283 F.3d 1040, 1053, n.9, that " '[t]he terms 'material' and 'prejudicial' are used interchangeably in *Brady* cases. Evidence is not 'material' unless it is 'prejudicial,' and not 'prejudicial' unless it is 'material.' Thus for *Brady* purposes, the two terms have come to have the same meaning." *United States v. Kohring* (2011, CA9 AK) 637 F.3d 895, 902; *Brooks v. Tennessee* (2010, CA6 TN) 626 F.3d 878, 892.

§ 1:48.4 Reasonable probability and undermining confidence in the verdict

Two components of the *materiality standard*—whether the suppressed favorable evidence undermines "confidence in the verdict" and whether such evidence creates a "reasonable probability of a different result"—are in fact synonymous and constitute different ways of expressing the same concept. *Simmons v. Beard* (2009, CA3 PA) 590 F.3d 223, 234, n.6. "A 'probability' reaches the level of 'reasonable' when it is high enough to 'undermine confidence in the verdict.' [citation omitted]" *United States v. Johnson* (2010, CA DC) 592 F.3d 164, 170.

§ 1:48.5 Reasonable probability of different result applied

The United States Supreme Court has clarified what it meant by a "reasonable probability of a different result" as meaning that had the suppressed evidence been disclosed "there is a reasonable probability that the withheld evidence would have altered at least one juror's assessment" in the case. *Cone v. Bell* (2009) 556 U.S. 449, 129 S.Ct. 1769, 1773, 173 L.Ed.2d 701; *accord, United States v. Price* (2009, CA9 OR) 566 F.3d 900, 914.

§ 1:48.6   Reasonable probability of different result for an acquitted defendant

An interesting question that has been raised in a number of federal cases is whether a defendant who is ultimately acquitted can maintain a *Brady* claim as the basis of a federal civil rights action against members of the prosecution team.

In *Smith v. Almada* (2010, CA9 CA) 623 F.3d 1078, the Ninth Circuit Court of Appeals declined to recognize a *Brady* claim as the basis of a civil plaintiff's cause of action against the officers who investigated his case. The Court of Appeals concluded that "an acquitted defendant fails to establish a *Brady* violation because he cannot show 'that the favorable evidence could reasonably be taken to put the whole case in such a different light as to *undermine confidence in the verdict.*' [citations omitted]" 623 F.3d at 1086 [italics in original]. The Court of Appeals cited three sister federal circuit holdings that agreed— *Morgan v. Gertz* (1999, CA10 CO) 166 F.3d 1307, 1310; *Flores v. Satz* (1998, CA11 FL) 137 F.3d 1275, 1278; and *McCune v. Grand Rapids* (1988, CA6 MI) 842 F.2d 903, 907—and concluded that "[t]hese decisions accord with the purpose of *Brady*. At its core, *Brady* seeks to ensure a fair trial, a trial whose verdict is reliable." 623 F.3d at 1086, 1087.

The *Smith* court further reasoned that "extending *Brady* to cases without a conviction would render the materiality standard unworkable . . . [and] would open the door to a potentially unlimited number of such claims for decisions at every stage of the criminal process." 623 F.3d at 1087, 1088. The Court concluded: "In sum, allowing *Brady*-based § 1983 claims absent a conviction is not compelled by our circuit's case law, conflicts with other circuits' case law and the central purpose of *Brady*, would render *Brady's* materiality standard unworkable, and lacks a limiting principle." 623 F.3d at 1088.

§ 1:49   Materiality as component of *Brady* duty and *Brady* error

There is some decisional support for the principle that the prosecutor has a broad duty to disclose exculpatory evidence that is greater than whether a violation of the *Brady* rule occurs when the prosecution fails to perform that duty.

In *Bell v. Bell* (2008, CA6 TN) 512 F.3d 223, 235, n.7, the Sixth Circuit Court of Appeals stated:

> "[T]he government's withholding of evidence does not necessarily mean that it has suppressed the evidence for purposes of ascertaining whether a *Brady* violation has occurred. And whether a *Brady*

violation is ultimately found is not determinative of the extent of the prosecutor's broad duty to disclose exculpatory evidence . . . . In this opinion we use the term '*Brady* violation' in the strict sense of the term. Thus, saying that a particular nondisclosure was not a *Brady* violation in no way suggests that the prosecutor did not have a duty to disclose the information."

There is language in *Strickler v. Greene* (1999) 527 U.S. 263, 281–282, 119 S.Ct. 1936, 144 L.Ed.2d 286, that can be used to support this argument. In *Strickler* the Supreme Court stated:

"This special status [of the prosecutor as the representative of the government] explains both the basis for the prosecution's broad duty of disclosure and our conclusion that not every violation of that duty necessarily establishes that the outcome was unjust."

In *United States v. Price* (2009, CA9 OR) 566 F.3d 900, the Ninth Circuit Court of Appeals echoed the opinion of the Sixth Circuit Court of Appeals in *Bell*, when the Court quoted with approval the analysis of two district courts that "the 'materiality' standard usually associated with *Brady* . . . should not be applied to pretrial discovery of exculpatory materials . . . . [J]ust because a prosecutor's failure to disclose evidence does not violate a defendant's due process rights does not mean that the failure to disclose is proper . . . . [T]he absence of prejudice to the defendant does not condone the prosecutor's suppression of exculpatory evidence [*ex ante*] . . . . [Rather,] the proper test for pretrial disclosure of exculpatory evidence should be an evaluation of whether the evidence is favorable to the defense . . . ." 566 F.3d at 913.

The language of the Supreme Court in *Strickler* could be read to mean that the prosecutor's duty to disclose material exculpatory evidence is broader than the violation of due process that could occur when that duty is not performed. Resolution of this apparent conflict between this language in *Strickler* and the Court's holding in *United States v. Agurs* (1976) 427 U.S. 97, 108–109, 96 S.Ct. 2392, 49 L.Ed.2d 342, that the standard of the prosecutor's duty to disclose material exculpatory evidence under *Brady* is the same before trial and on appellate review, awaits another day.

§ 1:50   Reasonable probability of different result and immaterial evidence

When suppressed favorable evidence impeaching a prosecution witness is relatively minor when compared to a "mountain of inculpatory evidence" against the defendant, and when compared to other impeachment evidence already introduced regarding that prosecution witness, the suppressed impeaching evidence is not likely to be deemed material for purposes of the *Brady* rule. Thus, in *Hammond v. Hall* (2009, CA11 GA) 586 F.3d 1289, the Eleventh Circuit Court of Appeals concluded that suppressed impeachment evidence about a prosecution witness that "[e]veryone knew . . . was bad

. . . would have been raindrops in the waterfall of evil surrounding [that witness]." 586 F.3d at 1321.

In *Whisenhant v. Allen* (2009, CA11 AL) 556 F.3d 1198, the prosecution did not disclose FBI profile reports generated to assist law enforcement in finding the unknown killer of a murder victim to a defendant charged with the murder of a different victim. The prosecution also failed to disclose the statement of a co-worker of the defendant's that described the defendant's conduct as "weird" and inappropriate. The defendant was convicted of murder and sentenced to death. Following exhaustion of his appellate remedies, the defendant filed a federal habeas petition in which he argued that the prosecution had committed *Brady* error in failing to disclose these items. The district court denied the habeas petition, and Whisenhant appealed.

The Eleventh Circuit Court of Appeals rejected the claim of *Brady* error, concluding that the suppressed evidence was not material, because its "marginal value" at the penalty trial would not have put the whole case in such a different light that it would have undermined confidence in the verdict. The Court concluded that the undisclosed information was immaterial evidence.

Suppressed favorable evidence impeaching a prosecution witness is immaterial for *Brady* purposes when the prosecution witness played only a "bit part" in the investigation of the crimes for which the defendant is prosecuted. *United States v. Robinson* (2010, CA4 SC) 627 F.3d 941, 950.

§ 1:51   Reasonable probability of different result and inadmissible evidence

In order for suppressed evidence to constitute material evidence within the meaning of the *Brady* rule, that evidence or evidence acquired through that information must either be admissible or capable of being used to impeach a prosecution witness. *United States v. Kohring* (2011, CA9 AK) 637 F.3d 895, 903. Evidence that is almost entirely inadmissible cannot normally be shown to be material favorable evidence within the meaning of *Brady* and *Giglio. United States v. Tate* (2011, CA8 MN) 633 F.3d 624, 630.

§ 1:53   Reasonable probability of different result and discovery violation

Discovery rulings are reviewed for abuse of discretion, looking to whether the district court reaches a result that is illogical or implausible. *United States v. Muniz-Jaquez* (2013, CA9 Cal.) 718 F.3d 1180. But see the Ninth Circuit case out of Washington holding that a district court's *Brady* determinations and all other questions of law are reviewed de novo. *United States v. Olsen* (2013, CA9 Wash.) 704 F.3d 1172.

§ 1:54   Factors impacting reasonable probability of different result

When considering whether suppressed favorable evidence is material, a court must conduct a balanced evaluation of the nature and strength of the suppressed evidence and the evidence presented by both sides at trial. *Toliver v. McCaughtry* (2008, CA7 WI) 539 F.3d 766, 780–781.

§ 1:54.1   Importance of prosecution witness/evidence

"The materiality of undisclosed information which could have served to impeach a government witness is affected by the importance of the witness's testimony." *United States v. Spinelli* (2008, CA2 NY) 551 F.3d 159, 165.

Where the suppressed impeachment evidence relates to a prosecution witness whose testimony is merely confirmatory of the testimony of a co-conspirator who provided the main evidence linking the defendant to the crime, the suppressed evidence is not material. *United States v. Spinelli, supra*, at 165. *Accord, Beuke v. Houk* (2008, CA6 OH) 537 F.3d 618, 635–636.

However, where suppressed impeachment evidence relates to the "key witness for the prosecution," whose testimony provided the only eyewitness evidence directly linking the defendant to the shooting, and when "the prosecution's case hinges on the testimony" of that witness, the suppressed evidence is material. *Harris v. Lafler* (2009, CA6 MI) 553 F.3d 1028, 1033–1034. *See also Douglas v. Workman* (2009, CA10 OK) 560 F.3d 1156, 1174 ["[W]e have upheld the materiality of nonduplicative impeachment evidence where the witness provided the sole evidence linking the petitioner to the crime."].

In *United States v. Gabrion* (2011, CA6 MI) 648 F.3d 307, the government failed to disclose a report concluding that a Michigan county prosecutor who testified briefly on peripheral issues in the guilt phase of the defendant's death penalty murder trial had violated federal regulations by making public comments about the defendant's case several weeks after the defendant's initial indictment. The report suggested that the prosecutor, who lost her federal appointment due to the public statements, might have had a vendetta against the defendant. After his conviction the defendant argued on appeal that the government had violated *Brady* by failing to disclose this report.

The Court of Appeals rejected the defendant's *Brady* argument, concluding that because the prosecutor had testified only as to peripheral and uncontested facts, the impeaching report was not material. 648 F.3d at 337.

§ 1:54.2   Uniqueness/replaceability of prosecution witness

When the prosecution has suppressed evidence impeaching a prosecution witness, a determination whether that suppressed evidence was material so as to constitute a *Brady* violation must take into account whether the prosecution could have proved its case without the impeachable witness, or whether there were other witnesses that the prosecution could have called to testify in lieu of the impeachable witness. "When the government has other qualified witnesses to prove its case, we cannot assume that it 'would have foolishly charged ahead, blindly offering [the compromised witness] and exposing itself to his inevitable demolition on cross.' [citation omitted] In such cases, nondisclosure would not be material in *Brady* terms." *United States v. Johnson* (2008, CA DC) 519 F.3d 478, 489.

§ 1:54.3   Relevance of the favorable evidence

"The materiality of undisclosed information which could have served to impeach a government witness is affected by . . . the importance of the disclosed information to the impeachment of the witness." *United States v. Spinelli* (2008, CA2 NY) 551 F.3d 159, 165.

In *United States v. Boyce* (2009, CA8 MO) 564 F.3d 911, the government did not disclose the criminal records of three prosecution witnesses who testified against the defendant at a sentencing hearing. On appeal the defendant contended that this failure constituted *Brady* error. The Eighth Circuit Court of Appeals rejected the defendant's argument, finding that the suppressed evidence had little relevant value. The Court observed that "[t]he government did not present the witnesses as law abiding citizens, but rather as participants in the local cocaine trade which significantly reduced the impeachment value of their conviction records." 564 F.3d at 918.

Where evidence of third-party culpability in a murder prosecution is weak and speculative, and where the disclosure of that evidence would not have created a reasonable probability of a different result, the undisclosed evidence is not material. *Moseley v. Branker* (2008, CA4 NC) 550 F.3d 312, 324.

The prosecution's failure to disclose evidence which might impeach a prosecution witness does not meet the materiality requirement of *Brady*, where that impeachment evidence pertains only to the details of collateral matters. *Hamilton v. Ayers* (2009, CA9 CA) 583 F.3d 1100, 1112.

The withholding of evidence on unrelated crimes that do not have any connection to the crimes charged against the defendant does not constitute a *Brady* violation, because that undisclosed evidence is not material (relevant) to the charged crime. *Smith v. Almada* (2011, CA9 CA) 640 F.3d 931, 938–940.

When, however, the prosecution withholds evidence that would "speak[] to the acts that the jury might [rely] upon in reaching its verdicts," that evidence is relevant, and the withholding constitutes suppression of evidence favorable to the defendant. *United States v. Kohring* (2011, CA9 AK) 637 F.3d 895, 902.

§ 1:54.4   Overall strength of the prosecution's case

The materiality of undisclosed exculpatory evidence " 'depends almost entirely on the value of the evidence relative to the other evidence mustered by the [government].' [citations omitted]." *United States v. Mauskar* (2009,

CA5 TX) 557 F.3d 219, 231. "Whether impeachment evidence is material depends on a number of factors, most importantly the strength of the case against the defendant." *United States v. Lewis* (2009, CA7 IN) 567 F.3d 322, 328.

Thus, in assessing the materiality of suppressed favorable evidence, the courts consider the strength of the prosecution's evidence introduced at trial. Where the courts determine that the prosecution's evidence against the defendant was strong, suppressed favorable evidence is commonly considered to lack materiality. *See, e.g., Moseley v. Branker* (2008, CA4 NC) 550 F.3d 312, 322–324; *Beuke v. Houk* (2008, CA6 OH) 537 F.3d 618, 635–636; *Powell v. Quarterman* (2008, CA5 TX) 536 F.3d 325, 340.

The federal Courts of Appeals appear to focus strongly on the overall strength of the prosecution's evidence when determining whether suppressed favorable evidence is material. See, e.g., *Hammond v. Hall* (2009, CA11 GA) 586 F.3d 1289, 1317; *Schad v. Ryan* (2010, CA9 AZ) 595 F.3d 907, 916; *Hamilton v. Ayers* (2009, CA9 CA) 583 F.3d 1100, 1112.

The strength of the prosecution's evidence against the defendant might be the most important factor in determining whether undisclosed exculpatory or impeachment evidence is material. *Schad v. Ryan* (2010, CA9 AZ) 595 F.3d 907, 916 ["Finally, **and most important**, the circumstantial evidence demonstrating [the defendant's] guilt was powerful . . . ." [emphasis added]].

In cases in which the appellate courts have determined that the overall strength of the prosecution's evidence was sufficient to overcome a claim that withheld favorable evidence was material, the courts have described the prosecution's evidence as "ample" and "strong," *United States v. Pettiford* (2010, CA DC) 627 F.3d 1223, 1229; a "mountain of incriminating evidence against the defendant," *United States v. Mathur* (2010, CA1 MA) 624 F.3d 498, 505; "strong physical evidence . . . linking [the defendant] to the February 2003 fire," *Smith v. Almada* (2011, CA9 CA) 640 F.3d 931, 939; and "simply overwhelming," *United States v. Gabrion* (2011, CA6 MI) 648 F.3d 307, 337; *United States v. Robinson* (2010, CA4 SC) 627 F.3d 941, 950.

No matter the phraseology used by the court, the standard is the same—when the prosecution's evidence against the defendant is strong and convincing, the force of suppressed favorable evidence must also be strong in order for that evidence to be considered "material" within the meaning of the *Brady* rule.

In evaluating the strength of the prosecution's evidence to determine whether suppressed evidence was "material," the only incriminating evidence that may be considered is that evidence that was in existence at the time of the defendant's trial. Evidence that was discovered or created at a later time may not be weighed. *See Apanovitch v. Bobby* (2011, CA6 OH) 648 F.3d 434. In *Apanovitch v. Bobby, supra,* a defendant convicted of murder and sentenced to death filed a habeas petition in federal court in which he contended that the government had suppressed favorable evidence in violation of *Brady*. Almost eight years after the crime and the defendant's conviction the prosecution team located the semen evidence that had been recovered from the victim at the scene of the murder. The semen evidence was subjected to DNA testing, the results of which proved highly incriminatory of the defendant.

When the defendant's *Brady* argument was considered by the district court, the district court included the DNA results in the weighing of the prosecution's evidence. The district court concluded that the evidence of the defendant's identity as the killer was strong, relying upon the DNA evidence found (or created) years after the trial had concluded. The Sixth Circuit Court of Appeals held that in considering the DNA evidence the habeas court erred. The Court stated:

> The results of a DNA test performed two decades after the trial has concluded shed no light on the question of whether there is a probability that the jury in 1984 would have reached a different result had the *Brady* evidence not been withheld by the prosecution. New, non-*Brady*, evidence is enlightening as to whether a petitioner is—seen as of now—actually innocent. However, it is *not* enlightening as to the probability that a petitioner would have—at trial—been acquitted based on the evidence that was presented to the jury and on the evidence that was withheld from the defense, which is the *Brady* inquiry. 648 F.3d at 437.

§ 1:54.5   Corroboration of the impeachable prosecution witness

Suppressed impeachment evidence regarding a prosecution witness is not material when the prosecution's evidence strongly corroborates the impeachable witness. *United States v. Hall* (2009, CA1 ME) 557 F.3d 15, 19; *Walker v. Kelly* (2009, CA4 VA) 589 F.3d 127, 143; *Johnson v. Mitchell* (2009, CA6 OH) 585 F.3d 923; *Hammond v. Hall* (2009, CA11 GA) 586 F.3d 1289, 1320. The reason why corroboration of the testimony of a prosecution witness about whom impeachment material has been suppressed is important is that corroborating evidence diminishes the impeachment potential of the suppressed evidence. *United States v. Mathur* (2010, CA1 MA) 624 F.3d 498, 505.

In *United States v. Robinson* (2010, CA4 SC) 627 F.3d 941, the Fourth Circuit Court of Appeals concluded that the impeaching evidence in that case of misconduct by the investigating officers "pales in comparison with that suppressed in cases where *Brady's* materiality requirement was actually met. . . . [N]umerous other law enforcement officers and more than a dozen co-defendants or cooperating witnesses corroborated each other's testimony and the physical evidence demonstrating Robinson's crimes. . . . Evidence regarding a few officers' unrelated misconduct could do little to damage the extensive physical and testimonial foundation of the case." 627 F.3d at 952–953.

The importance for *Brady* purposes of strong corroboration of an impeachable witness's testimony is made clear by the general rule espoused by the courts. "[W]hen the testimony of the witness who might have been impeached by the undisclosed evidence is strongly corroborated by additional evidence supporting a guilty verdict, the undisclosed evidence generally is not found to be material." *United States v. Sipe* (2004, CA5 TX) 388 F.3d 471, 478; quoted with approval, *United States v. Davis* (2010, CA5 LA) 609 F.3d 663, 697. *See also People v. Clark* (2011) 52 Cal.4th 856, 982, 131 Cal.Rptr.3d 225, 261 P.3d 243 ["Given that other witnesses provided testimony similar to that of Mrs. Farkas, and the strong evidence of defendant's guilt, we conclude there is no reasonable probability that the outcome of trial would have been different had the defense impeached Mrs. Farkas with her misdemeanor welfare fraud conviction. The prosecutor's failure to disclose this information to the defense did not violate defendant's right to due process."].

However, when the prosecution's remaining evidence only "somewhat corroborate[s]" an impeachable prosecution witness, and where that witness is the "only eyewitness to the shooting and there was no other direct evidence connecting [the defendant] to the crime," suppressed impeachment evidence regarding that witness is material. *Douglas v. Workman* (2009, CA10 OK) 560 F.3d 1156, 1174.

And when the prosecution fails to disclose impeachment evidence regarding a critical prosecution witness without whose testimony the government's case would fail, the fact that the witness's testimony is corroborated "to some extent" is not sufficient to negate the conclusion that the undisclosed impeachment evidence is material. *United States v. Salem* (2009, CA7 WI) 578 F.3d 682, 688.

§ 1:54.6 Self-validation of the prosecution evidence

Evidence is not "self-validating" simply because it is corroborating evidence. Self-validating evidence is corroborated evidence that the witness could not have known unless it were true [such as when a prosecution witness testifies to statements about the crime allegedly made by the defendant which the prosecution witness could not have otherwise known other than by hearing the statements from the defendant]. But the simple fact of corroboration by other prosecution evidence does not turn a prosecution witness's testimony into self-validated evidence. *Douglas v. Workman* (2009, CA10 OK) 560 F.3d 1156, 1175.

§ 1:54.7 Uniqueness or cumulativeness of the favorable evidence

The *quality* of suppressed impeachment evidence is important to a determination whether that evidence was material. "[E]vidence insignificantly impacting the degree of impeachment may not be sufficient to meet the *Kyles* materiality standard, while evidence significantly enhancing the quality of the impeachment evidence usually will." *Douglas v. Workman* (2009, CA10 OK) 560 F.3d 1156, 1174. Thus, when suppressed evidence "is merely cumulative of *equally impeaching evidence* introduced at trial, so that it would not have materially increased the jury's likelihood of discrediting the witness, it is not material." *United States v. Spinelli* (2008, CA2 NY) 551 F.3d 159, 165 [italics added].

Suppressed impeaching evidence is especially likely to be material if it " 'would have provided the defense with a new and different ground of impeachment.' [citation omitted]" *United States v. Price* (2009, CA9 OR) 566 F.3d 900, 914.

In determining whether suppressed cumulative impeachment evidence is material, the court may also consider whether the impeaching evidence also has inculpatory value. Thus, in *Doan v. Carter* (2008, CA6 OH) 548 F.3d 449, the Sixth Circuit Court of Appeals concluded that numerous items of undisclosed favorable evidence were not material evidence, reasoning that "[c]onsidering the fact that the witnesses to which the undisclosed evidence pertained had already been impeached by the defense, and that much of the evidence was just as inculpatory as exculpatory, the cumulative effect of the evidence indicates that the undisclosed evidence was not material." 548 F.3d at 463.

§ 1:54.7.1　Cumulative favorable evidence

Undisclosed impeachment evidence regarding a prosecution witness is not material when that evidence virtually duplicates impeaching evidence already known to the defendant and/or used to impeach the witness's testimony. Thus, in *United States v. Bailey* (2007, CA7 IL) 510 F.3d 726, 736, the Court of Appeals held that the district court did not err in declining to order disclosure of the tax records of a government informant witness after the witness admitted that he had not paid taxes on his informant income. The court concluded that "[i]t is thus hard to see what benefit Bailey would have obtained by the tax records. The impeaching bell had been rung; the tax records would not have amplified the toll." 510 F.3d at 736–737. Suppressed material that offers no new factual evidence to impeach a prosecution witness is not likely to be "material," because it is simply cumulative. *Lopez v. Ryan* (2011, CA9 AZ) 630 F.3d 1198, 1210. Duplicative impeachment evidence is normally immaterial. *United States v. Inzunza* (2011, CA9 CA) 638 F.3d 1006, 1021.

Even when the undisclosed impeaching evidence regarding a prosecution witness does not duplicate the known impeaching evidence on that witness, when the suppressed impeaching evidence is of the same type as impeaching evidence already known to the defendant and used in the trial, the suppressed evidence is ordinarily cumulative and not material. *See United States v. Svete* (2008, CA11 FL) 521 F.3d 1302, 1315.

To be cumulative, and thus not material, suppressed impeaching evidence regarding a prosecution witness "must be 'the same kind of evidence' as that introduced in trial. [citation omitted]" Where the "withheld evidence was simply another illustration of [the witness's] untruthfulness rather than evidence 'almost unique in its detrimental effect' on [the witness's] credibility," such evidence is cumulative and not material. *United States v. Brodie* (2008, CA DC) 524 F.3d 259, 269.

In *Schad v. Ryan* (2010, CA9 AZ) 595 F.3d 907, the prosecution failed to disclose letters written by a prosecutor and a detective to California authorities on behalf of a prosecution witness who was facing a pending, unrelated criminal case. However, the prosecution had disclosed and the defense had used at trial other evidence of the witness's lengthy criminal history that included the fact that the witness was currently serving a sentence for theft and had asked for and received a letter from the detective to California authorities in return for his help in the Schad investigation.

In response to the defendant's argument that the withholding of the two letters constituted a *Brady* violation, the Ninth Circuit Court of Appeals found that through the impeaching evidence the defense already had and used, "the defense established [the witness] had a motivation to testify falsely. The letters themselves would have provided some documentation of his motivation, but would not have provided a new or further motivation." 595 F.3d at 914–915. The Court concluded that the suppressed letters provided no independent basis for impeaching the witness with a new and different form of impeachment. Rather, "the undisclosed evidence related to the same motives to lie as evidence already known to and utilized by the defense." 595 F.3d at 915.

Where the defense is able to impeach a prosecution witness with the same kind of evidence as the evidence that the prosecution has suppressed, or where the defense is able to impeach that witness with even more damaging evidence than the suppressed evidence [for example, with evidence of perjury and other lies told by the witness], the suppressed evidence is not material. *United States v. Hemphill* (2008, CA DC) 514 F.3d 1350, 1360. *See also, Parker v. Allen* (2009, CA11 AL) 565 F.3d 1258, 1277–1278 [additional suppressed convictions of witness cumulative of convictions used by defendant to impeach witness].

Likewise, when suppressed impeachment evidence differs from evidence available to and used by the defendant at trial only in the manner in which it was preserved, the evidence is not material. *See United States v. Collins* (2009, CA9 CA) 551 F.3d 914, 923–925 [nondisclosed audiotape recording not material when a prosecution witness who had listened to the recording testified to its contents at trial].

The materiality of undisclosed evidence that is favorable to the defendant because it would assist in the defendant's defense against the charges is subject to the same cumulative evidence determination as applies to evidence impeaching prosecution witnesses—if suppressed evidence that is favorable because it would assist in a defendant's defense, but that evidence is cumulative of other evidence actually presented at trial, the undisclosed evidence is not material. *See Irick v. Bell* (2009, CA6 TN) 565 F.3d 315, 322–323.

Undisclosed favorable evidence that is cumulative to favorable evidence already known and available to the defendant is deemed to be insignificant and thus immaterial. *Hamilton v. Ayers* (2009, CA9 CA) 583 F.3d 1100, 1112; *United States v. Inzunza* (2009, CA9 CA) 580 F.3d 894, 907; *Davis v. Booker* (2009, CA6 MI) 589 F.3d 302, 309. The reason is simple. "Cumulative impeachment evidence is generally not material because the marginal effect of additional impeachment is relatively small and unlikely to result in a different outcome." *United States v. Emor* (2009, CA DC) 573 F.3d 778, 782.

Where undisclosed impeachment evidence "merely furnishes an additional basis on which to challenge a witness whose credibility has already been shown to be questionable or is subject to extensive attack by reason of other evidence, the undisclosed evidence may properly be viewed as cumulative, and hence not material" *United States v. Persico* (2011, CA2 NY) 645 F.3d 85, 111. This is particularly true when the undisclosed impeachment evidence consists of yet another instance of criminal conduct by a prosecution witness who has already been exposed as someone ready to lie to evade harsh punishment. "[A]dding more icing to the impeachment cake would not improve the likelihood that the jury would swallow it." *United States v. Salem* (2011, CA7 WI) 643 F.3d 221, 227.

And some federal circuit court opinions even extend the cumulative impeachment doctrine to undisclosed impeachment regarding a prosecution witness who has already been effectively impeached at trial. *See, e.g., Brooks v. Tennessee* (2010, CA6 TN) 626 F.3d 878, 894 ["Evidence of his history of mental illness would have provided additional reasons not to credit [the] testimony [of a prosecution witness], but would have been cumulative to the evidence already in the record."].

Even more unlikely to be material is suppressed favorable evidence that is of far lesser consequences than disclosed favorable evidence. Thus, in *Hamilton v. Ayers* (2009, CA9 CA) 583 F.3d 1100, the Ninth Circuit Court of Appeals held that the prosecution had not committed *Brady* error by withholding evidence from a defendant charged with a capital murder that it had facilitated the release on bond of a co-defendant also charged with the same murder who had agreed to be a prosecution witness. The prosecution entered into a plea agreement with the co-defendant witness in which the co-defendant pled guilty to second degree murder with a sentence of 16 years in prison. The plea agreement was disclosed to the defendant.

The Court of Appeals held that the prosecution's failure to disclose the release on bond of the witness co-defendant pending the trial of the defendant did not constitute the suppression of material evidence. The Court concluded that "given that [the witness] faced the death penalty in the absence of his plea agreement, the prosecution's facilitation of [the witness's] release on bond during the trial appears insignificant." 583 F.3d at 1111.

In *Heishman v. Ayers* (2010, CA9 CA) 621 F.3d 1030, the Ninth Circuit Court of Appeals commented that withheld evidence that a prosecution witness had received payment for transportation, meals, and lodging to facilitate the witness's testimony "is petty in comparison to [the witness's] receipt of immunity," impeachment that had been disclosed, and thus the withheld evidence was not material. 621 F.3d at 1035.

§ 1:54.7.2 Unique/highly damaging favorable evidence

A number of federal circuit courts have been more accepting of the argument that suppressed impeaching evidence regarding a prosecution witness that is different in kind or effect than the impeaching evidence available to the defendant at trial is material within the meaning of the *Brady* rule. *See, e.g., United States v. Kohring* (2011, CA9 AK) 637 F.3d 895, 904 ["The fact that [the prosecution witness] might have had a motive to testify against Kohring in order to gain leniency as to his corruption charges does not mean that evidence of a different bias or motive would be cumulative. . . . Indeed, evidence of [the witness's] sexual misconduct with a minor would have shed light on the magnitude of [the witness's] incentive to cooperate with authorities and would have revealed that he had much more at stake than was already known to the jury."]; *Maxwell v. Roe* (2010, CA9 CA) 628 F.3d 486, 512 ["[T]he withheld impeachment evidence . . . would have created substantial doubt as to [the witness's] credibility for different reasons. The withheld evidence went to [the witness's] sophistication and motivation in his capacity as a prosecution informant and not, like the other evidence produced at trial, to his general propensity for dishonesty."].

The Third Circuit Court of Appeals has observed that "it is patently unreasonable to presume—without explanation—that whenever a witness is impeached in one manner, any other impeachment becomes immaterial. . . . [U]ndisclosed *Brady* material that would have provided a different avenue of impeachment is material, even where the witness is otherwise impeached. . . . Here, the withheld information provided a *unique* basis on which to impeach—specifically, a basis that shredded [the witness's] credibility on the one point on which the jury could have inferred that he had any credibility." *Lambert v. Beard* (2011, CA3 PA) 633 F.3d 126, 134. The Court further observed that other federal courts of appeals have concurred with this approach, citing *United States v. Torres* (2009, CA10 NM) 569 F.3d 1277, 1284; *Horton v. Mayle* (2005, CA9 CA) 408 F.3d 570, 580; and *Reutter v. Solem* (1989, CA8 SD) 888 F.2d 578, 581. *Lambert v. Beard, supra*, 633 F.3d at 135.

Where the undisclosed evidence "would have opened an entirely new line of impeachment," that evidence is material. *Lambert v. Beard, supra,* 633 F.3d at 135.

In determining whether undisclosed impeachment of a prosecution witness constitutes suppression of material evidence, the proper standard is not to decide "which of two competing sources of bias a court, in hindsight, determines the jury would have considered more important. Rather, the inquiry is whether an undisclosed source of bias—even if it is not the only source or even the 'main source'—could reasonably be taken to put the whole case in a different light." *LaCaze v. Warden La. Corr. Inst. for Women* (2011, CA5 LA) 645 F.3d 728, 736.

It is true that cause and prejudice may sometimes be established on the merits of a *Brady* claim itself, with cause and prejudice corresponding respectively to the suppression and materiality elements of a *Brady* claim. It is not the case, however, that a defendant is excused from failing to raise a *Brady* claim in state court every time he can prove that material was suppressed by the state and may materially affect the verdict. Rather, the state's suppression establishes cause only when it is the reason for his failure to develop facts in state court proceedings. *Henry v. Ryan* (2013, CA9 Ariz.) 720 F.3d 1073.

§ 1:54.8   Extent of conflict with prosecution evidence

When suppressed favorable evidence would conflict with only a small part of the prosecution's evidence, the withheld evidence is less likely to be material within the meaning of the *Brady* rule.

In *Apanovitch v. Bobby* (2011, CA6 OH) 648 F.3d 434, a defendant convicted of capital murder and sentenced to death contended in a federal habeas petition that the prosecution had withheld four pieces of favorable evidence from him in violation of *Brady*. The Sixth Circuit Court of Appeals rejected Apanovitch's argument, saying: "[A]lthough the evidence introduced against Apanovitch at trial was not overwhelming, the exculpatory evidence at issue would have been of little or no value to him. Although the state's conduct cannot be justified, the evidence that it withheld would have enabled Apanovitch to dispute only the very weakest of the prosecution's evidence and only slightly expand upon theories of innocence that, despite the state's conduct, he was still able to present to the jury. Accordingly, the state's wrongdoing, while deserving of scorn, does not 'put the whole case in such a different light as to undermine confidence in the verdict' [citation omitted]." 648 F.3d at 438.

§ 1:54.9   Evidence opening door to unfavorable prosecution evidence

When nondisclosed favorable evidence that could be used to impeach a prosecution witness would "open the door" to unfavorable evidence against the defendant, the undisclosed evidence might not be material. *See Edwards v. Ayers* (2008, CA9 CA) 542 F.3d 759 [prosecution witness's undisclosed prison file not material when that file "contained extremely damaging information that on the whole was far more likely to aggravate Edwards' crime in the eyes of the jury." 542 F.3d at 770].

In *People v. Verdugo* (2010) 50 Cal.4th 263, 285, 113 Cal.Rptr.3d 803, 236 P.3d 1035, the defendant was charged with and ultimately convicted of two counts of first-degree murder and was sentenced to death. The sister-in-law of the defendant provided help to law enforcement officers investigating the murders and then provided incriminating evidence against the defendant as a prosecution witness. When the witness's family learned of the woman's assistance to the prosecution, she was threatened by members of the defendant's family. The prosecution then assisted her in relocating to a new home and paid some of her rent. The prosecution did not disclose its relocation assistance to the witness until the trial had been concluded.

The defendant argued on automatic appeal of his convictions and judgment of death to the California Supreme Court that the prosecution's suppression of its relocation assistance to the witness violated *Brady*. The Supreme Court rejected the defendant's argument. The Court concluded:

"[E]ven assuming some of the information (such as the financial assistance [the witness] received), in isolation, could be considered favorable to defendant, there is no 'reasonable probability its disclosure would have altered the trial result.' [citation omitted] If the defense had attempted to present this evidence at trial in an effort to undermine [the witness's] credibility, the prosecution would have been entitled to present evidence explaining the reasons for [the witness's] relocation, which were that a member of the Verdugo family had threatened her, that she was fearful that defendant would have her killed unless she moved, and that defendant had ties to a criminal street gang. This rebuttal evidence would have effectively countered the defense assertion that [the witness] was benefiting from her cooperation with the prosecution. In fact, [the witness's] willingness to testify against defendant despite justifiable concerns about her safety arguably would have enhanced her credibility." 50 Cal.4th at 285.

§ 1:54.10 Evidence not providing legal or factual defense

Undisclosed favorable evidence is not material when the disclosure and use of that evidence would not have provided the defendant with a legal or factual defense against the charges.

In *Irick v. Bell* (2009, CA6 TN) 565 F.3d 315, the prosecution failed to disclose a statement of a witness who had seen the defendant drinking beer and talking to himself the night of the murder for which the defendant was convicted. Following his conviction and the exhaustion of his appellate remedies, the defendant filed a federal habeas corpus petition, arguing that the nondisclosure of the statement violated *Brady*. The district court denied the petition.

On his appeal from the denial of his habeas petition, the defendant argued that he could have used the undisclosed statement to negate the mental intent necessary for his felony murder conviction. The Sixth Circuit Court of Appeals rejected the defendant's argument, concluding that even if the suppressed statement could have established that the defendant was intoxicated on the night of the murder, "it could not have negated his intent to commit aggravated rape, and thus could not have undermined his felony murder conviction," 565 F.3d at 322, and that the suppressed evidence was not inconsistent with the witness's trial testimony that the defendant was angry, able to talk coherently, and walk without stumbling. 565 F.3d at 323.

The Fifth Circuit Court of Appeals reached a similar conclusion in *United States v. Severns* (2009, CA5 TX) 559 F.3d 274. In *Severns* the defendant was charged and convicted of arson of his business. The issue at trial was whether the fire was intentionally set. The defendant contended that the fire started accidentally and that the fire spread from exploding aerosol cans. Following the defendant's conviction, an ATF training video was found that showed aerosol cans exploding in a house fire and starting a blaze in an area other than the point of origin. The defendant's motion for a new trial based on a claim of *Brady* error in the failure to disclose the video prior to trial was denied by the district court.

On appeal to the Fifth Circuit Court of Appeals the defendant argued that the nondisclosure of the video constituted *Brady* error. The Court of Appeals rejected the defendant's *Brady* argument, reasoning that the defendant had not presented any evidence or even a logical theory as to how exploding aerosol cans "could have surmounted physical obstacles between one point of the fire's origin and the other two." 559 F.3d at 280. The Court concluded that there was no reasonable likelihood that the jury's decision after a new trial would be different, because the disclosure of the suppressed evidence would not have provided the defendant with a factual defense.

And in *United States v. Pulliam* (2009, CA8 MO) 566 F.3d 784, the Eighth Circuit Court of Appeals held that undisclosed evidence that would have supported a defense that the traffic stop of the defendant had been pretextual was not material evidence, because "[t]he subjective intent of an officer is rarely relevant to the propriety of a traffic stop." 566 F.3d at 787. Because the officer had an objectively lawful reason for stopping the defendant's vehicle, the Court concluded that disclosure of the suppressed impeachment evidence of the officer's intent "would have had little or no impact." *Id.*

Likewise, in *United States v. Daniel* (2009, CA7 IN) 576 F.3d 772, the defendant was charged and convicted of knowingly persuading, inducing, enticing, or coercing a minor under the age of 18 to engage in criminal sexual activity, arising out of a sting operation in which the defendant exchanged communications through an on-line chat room with a police officer thinking that he was communicating with a minor girl.

The government did not disclose, because the government itself did not know, that the defendant's on-line "chats" with two other apparent minor girls were actually conversations with other police officers working in the same sting operation. When this information was disclosed to the defendant, the defendant claimed *Brady* error, arguing that the suppression denied him the use of this evidence to prove that he was entrapped on the changed crime.

The Seventh Circuit Court of Appeals held the suppressed information was not material, because it would not have advanced the defendant's entrapment argument. The Court observed that the defendant's "chats" with the other two "girls" occurred after the defendant had initiated the chats with the police officer for which he was charged and convicted. The Court concluded that "[s]ubsequent chats with police officers do not show that the government induced the illegal conduct with Amanda [the on-line name of the first officer]." 576 F.3d at 775.

Because the suppressed evidence would not have supported or constituted an affirmative defense, that evidence was not material within the meaning of the *Brady* rule.

Accord United States v. Inzunza (2011, CA9 CA) 638 F.3d 1006, 1021 [Undisclosed statements of non-testifying potential witness that payments to a public official were "campaign contributions" were not exculpatory as a matter of law, and were thus not material under *Brady*.].

§ 1:54.11 Favorable trial outcome for defendant

In a civil action pursuant to 42 U.S.C. section 1983 for intentional deprivation of civil rights, evidence that had been suppressed in a criminal trial of the civil plaintiff that resulted in the civil plaintiff' acquittal did not prejudice the plaintiff by denying him a fair trial. The suppressed evidence, therefore, was not material within the meaning of the *Brady* rule, because its disclosure would not have produced a different verdict. *See Bielanski v. County of Kane* (2008, CA7 IL) 550 F.3d 632, 644; *Carvajal v. Dominguez* (2008, CA7 IL) 542 F.3d 561, 570; *Morgan v. Gertz* (1999, CA10 CO) 166 F.3d 1307, 1310; *Flores v. Satz* (1998, CA11 FL) 137 F.3d 1275, 1278; *McCune v. City of Grand Rapids* (1988, CA6 MI) 842 F.2d 903, 907. *Contra, Haupt v. Dillard* (1994, CA9 NV) 17 F.3d 285, 287–288.

§ 1:54.12 Independence of suppressed benefit from witness's testimony

In *Libberton v. Ryan* (2009, CA9 AZ) 583 F.3d 1147, the defendant was charged with first-degree murder, robbery, theft, and kidnapping. A co-participant in the murder, who was a minor, struck a plea agreement with the prosecution and pled guilty in juvenile court. The minor then testified as a prosecution witness in the defendant's trial pursuant to an oral agreement which the prosecution did not disclose to the defendant. The defendant was convicted and sentenced to death.

The defendant filed a habeas petition in the federal courts. The district court denied the habeas petition, and the defendant appealed the denial of his petition to the Court of Appeals. The defendant argued in his appeal that the prosecution had committed *Brady* error in failing to disclose the terms of the oral agreement between the prosecution and the co-participant minor witness. The Ninth Circuit Court of Appeals affirmed the denial of the habeas petition as to the defendant's conviction, but reversed the judgment of the district court with respect to the defendant's sentencing. With respect to the defendant's *Brady* argument, the Court of Appeals held that the undisclosed agreement with the witness was not material. The Court reasoned that because the minor witness had already given a deeply incriminating statement before the deal was consummated that corroborated his trial testimony, the witness's trial testimony was not the product of his agreement to testify, but was the product of his prior incriminating statement. Therefore, even if the jury had known of the agreement, "it is unlikely that the jury would have reached a different conclusion as to [the defendant's] guilt . . . ." 583 F.3d at 1163–1164.

§ 1:55   Favorable evidence held to be material

In *Trammell v. McKune* (2007, CA10 KS) 485 F.3d 546, a defendant charged in state court with several felonies arising out his alleged stealing of a service station tow truck and using it to steal another vehicle, defended against these charges on the ground that another man, whose identity was known, committed the crime and framed him. The prosecution failed to disclose physical evidence linking the third party to the tow truck theft. The defendant was convicted of the charges.

Six weeks after his conviction the prosecution, realizing that it had failed to disclose the exculpatory physical evidence to the defense, then disclosed that evidence to the defendant's attorneys. The ensuing defense motion for a new trial was denied, and the denial was affirmed on appeal in the Kansas appellate courts.

The defendant petitioned for habeas corpus relief in the federal district court, arguing that he had been denied a fair trial arising out of the prosecution's suppression of exculpatory evidence under *Brady*. The district court agreed with the defendant's argument that the Kansas courts had misapplied the *Brady* rule in affirming his conviction, but denied his habeas petition.

The Tenth Circuit Court of Appeals granted the habeas petition, vacated the convictions, and remanded the case to the Kansas courts for a new trial. The Court of Appeals rejected the prosecution's arguments and explained how the physical evidence could have been utilized as favorable evidence at the trial. The Court stated: "The [towing] receipts [found in the third person's motel room] directly link Cross [the third person] to the stolen truck, and defense counsel could have used the evidence to support his theory of the case—that Cross is the one who stole the tow truck, which is how the box of tow truck receipts got into his motel room." 485 F.3d at 551.

Even though three eyewitnesses had identified the defendant as the truck thief, and the Court of Appeals admitted that it was "not certain that timely disclosure of the [suppressed physical evidence] would have resulted in a different result," the standard of materiality is whether the " 'evidentiary suppression undermines confidence in the outcome of the trial.' [citation omitted]" 485 F.3d at 552. The Court of Appeals concluded that the suppressed physical evidence was material under *Brady* and denied the habeas petitioner due process of law.

In *Toliver v. McCaughtry* (2008, CA7 WI) 539 F.3d 766, the defendant was charged in state court with being a party to a murder. He was convicted of the charge and ultimately filed a habeas petition in the federal courts. In his habeas petition the defendant argued that prior to trial a man sent a letter to the prosecutor relating statements that a codefendant had acted alone in the murder and that the defendant had attempted to stop the killing. The prosecutor did not disclose this letter to the defendant. The district court denied the habeas petition, and the defendant appealed.

The Seventh Circuit Court of Appeals concluded that the suppressed evidence would have bolstered the defendant's defense that he did not intend that the victim be killed and had tried to dissuade the killer. The Court of Appeals determined that the district court failed to " 'carefully assess [] what purposes the suppressed evidence might have served and how that evidence might have affected the jury's consideration of the evidence that was introduced.' " 539 F.3d at 782. The Court concluded that the disputed evidence "might well have created a reasonable doubt as to whether Mr. Toliver, despite his prominence that night, intentionally aided and abetted in the murder of Rogers or attempted to prevent it." 539 F.3d at 782.

In *United States v. Price* (2009, CA9 OR) 566 F.3d 900, the Ninth Circuit Court of Appeals held that evidence of the criminal record and history of a prosecution witness who testified that she saw a gun in the defendant's waistband 15 minutes before his arrest was material when that evidence was the only direct evidence of the defendant's guilt of being a felon in possession of a firearm. The Court reasoned that the defendant was denied evidence of the prosecution witness's dishonest and fraudulent conduct, the disclosure of which would have likely produced a different result in the trial. 566 F.3d at 913–914.

In *Mahler v. Kaylo* (2008, CA5 LA) 537 F.3d 494, the prosecution failed to disclose three eyewitness statements in a prosecution of the defendant for manslaughter that occurred in a physical altercation. The witness statements related that the victim and the defendant's brother were wrestling at the time the defendant shot the victim. The question whether the struggle was ongoing at the time of the shooting was at the heart of the defense to the charge. The prosecution evidence contended that the struggle had ended and the victim had turned away from the defendant when he shot the victim.

Because the suppressed statements would have supported the defendant's assertion that the struggle was still ongoing at the time of the shooting, the Court of Appeals held that they constituted material evidence, the suppression of which denied the defendant a fair trial.

In *United States v. Aviles-Colon* (2008, CA1 P.R.) 536 F.3d 1, the defendant Carrion was convicted of conspiracy to distribute illegal drugs and possession of firearms. The government's allegation and evidence was that the defendant conspired with other named co-conspirators to commit the offenses. After his conviction the defendant learned of DEA reports detailing a drug war among the defendants. The defendant's motion for a new trial based on a claim that the government had committed *Brady* error was denied, and the defendant appealed.

The First Circuit Court of Appeals vacated the defendant's convictions, finding that the evidence suppressed by the DEA—reports of the drug wars among the defendants—was material, and its suppression violated the *Brady* rule. The Court concluded: "The DEA reports, which described ongoing hostility between Carrion and Galiany prior to and during the period of the alleged conspiracy, undermine the testimony of the key witnesses in the government's case against Carrion. Under these circumstances, the DEA reports establish a reasonable probability that the results of Carrion's trial would have been different if the DEA reports had been disclosed." 536 F.3d at 21.

In *Douglas v. Workman* (2009, CA10 OK) 560 F.3d 1156, the prosecution failed to disclose a deal made with a witness who identified the defendant and his co-defendant as the gunmen in a murder for which the defendants were sentenced to death. The prosecution witness provided the only direct evidence linking the defendants to the murder and was the "linchpin to a conviction." 560 F.3d at 1174. The Court of Appeals held that the evidence of a deal made by the government with the witness constituted material evidence, and its suppression violated the *Brady* rule. The Court concluded: "Because impeachment of the witness who held the key to the successful prosecution of Mr. Powell was denied to the defense, the district court correctly concluded that the State's *Brady* violations were material." 560 F.3d at 1175.

Courts seem to be more inclined to hold that suppressed favorable evidence is material when the prosecution has suppressed multiple pieces of favorable evidence and the Court thereby considers the cumulative effect of suppression, the prosecution's evidence supporting conviction is either weak or chiefly based upon witnesses to which suppressed impeachment evidence relates, and the prosecution witnesses to which the suppressed favorable evidence relates are critical to the prosecution's case. *See, e.g., Simmons v. Beard* (2009, CA3 PA) 590 F.3d 223, 238; *United States v. Torres* (2009, CA10 NM) 589 F.3d 1277, 1280, 1282–1284; *Valdivinos v. McGrath* (2010, CA9 CA) 598 F.3d 568, 577–580.

§ 1:56 Materiality and defendant's guilty plea

Where the prosecution has suppressed favorable evidence in a case in which the defendant entered a guilty plea, the standard of materiality is determined by deciding whether "there is a reasonable probability that, but for the non-disclosure of evidence, '[the defendant] would not have [entered his plea] and would have insisted on going to trial.' [citation omitted.]" *Fautenberry v. Mitchell* (2008, CA6 OH) 515 F.3d 614, 629. *Accord, Smith v. Baldwin* (2007, CA9 OR) 510 F.3d 1127, 1148.

§ 1:57 Materiality and defense trial strategy/preparation

Courts continue to emphasize that "the impact of undisclosed evidence on [a defendant's] trial preparations is irrelevant to materiality under *Brady*; only the effect on the trial's outcome matters." *Wilson v. Parker* (2008, CA6 KY) 515 F.3d 682, 702.

In *United States v. Aleman* (2008, CA8 MN) 548 F.3d 1158, a defendant convicted of conspiring to distribute methamphetamine learned after the close of the government's case at trial of a statement made by a witness who decided to waive his Fifth Amendment rights and testify. The statement incriminated the defendant as the source of drugs provided to the witness. The defendant was convicted and appealed. On appeal the defendant argued that the prosecution had committed *Brady* error in failing to disclose the witness's statement prior to trial. The government replied that because the witness's statement was not exculpatory or favorable to the defendant, withholding that statement did not constitute a *Brady* violation.

The defendant rejoined that even though incriminatory, the witness's statement would have assisted his defense, because the witness's statement referred to other persons whom the defendant could have investigated or called as witnesses. The Eighth Circuit Court of Appeals rejected the defendant's argument, concluding that "*Brady* does not cover evidence that would merely help a defendant prepare for trial but is otherwise immaterial to the issues of guilt or punishment." 548 F.3d at 1164.

The California Supreme Court, however, has twice cited *United States v. Bagley* (1985) 473 U.S. 667, 682–683, 105 S.Ct. 3375, 87 L.Ed.2d 481, and *In re Brown* (1998) 17 Cal.4th 873, 887, 72 Cal.Rptr.2d 698, 952 P.2d 715, in stating that "[m]ateriality includes consideration of the effect of the nondisclosure on defense investigations and trial strategies." *People v. Verdugo* (2010) 50 Cal.4th 263, 279, 113 Cal.Rptr.3d 803, 236 P.3d 1035; and *People v. Zambrano* (2007) 41 Cal.4th 1082, 1132–1133, 63 Cal.Rptr.3d 297, 163 P.3d 4, overruled on other grounds, *People v. Doolin* (2007) 45 Cal. 4th 390, 87 Cal.Rptr.3d 209, 198 P.3d 11.

However, in the very same paragraph in which the Supreme Court made this pronouncement, the Court also stated that "[e]vidence is material if there is a reasonable probability its disclosure would have altered the *trial result.*" *People v. Verdugo, supra,* 50 Cal.4th at 279; *People v. Zambrano, supra,* 41

Cal.4th at 1132–1133. [italics added] It is possible to reconcile these two apparently conflicting statements by construing them to mean that the effect of nondisclosure of the favorable evidence upon defense investigations and trial strategies must be considered, but that the ultimate question focuses upon the result at trial—whether there is a reasonable probability that the result at trial would have been different had the suppressed evidence been disclosed. Considering the effect of nondisclosure on defense investigations and trial strategies is, therefore, only one factor in making the ultimate determination of the effect of nondisclosure upon the trial, result.

§ 1:59   Materiality as affected by verification of evidence

A determination of the materiality of facially favorable evidence is impacted by a determination whether that evidence can be verified or whether that evidence is untrustworthy and unsubstantiated.

§ 1:59.2   Prosecutor's personal views regarding accuracy/truthfulness of evidence

The question whether the prosecutor is either entitled or even required to consider the *reliability* or the *verification* of evidence that is facially favorable to the defendant before making a determination whether the evidence must as a matter of constitutional compulsion be disclosed to the defendant continues to be a subject of debate.

On the one hand, several federal and state appellate opinions exhort prosecutors to disclose favorable evidence in their possession without their exercising discretionary decision-making whether that evidence is reliable or trustworthy. *See, e.g., United States v. Alvarez* (1996, CA9 CA) 86 F.3d 901, 905.

On the other hand, since the materiality of facially favorable evidence is an essential component of the *Brady* duty of disclosure, and the duty of making *Brady* disclosure determinations rests squarely on the shoulders of the prosecutor, it seems anomalous to conclude that the prosecutor should not be free to act in compliance with this duty. Thus, several federal Courts of Appeals have held that "[t]he failure to disclose untrustworthy and unsubstantiated allegations against a government witness is not a *Brady* violation." *United States v. Souffront* (2003, CA7 IL) 338 F.3d 809, 823; *United States v. Locascio* (1993, CA2 NY) 6 F.3d 924, 948–950.

These conflicting authorities are hard to reconcile.

Practice Tip for Prosecution: As the United States Supreme Court has repeatedly admonished, prosecutors should not "tack[ ] too close to the wind" when making *Brady* determinations. *See Kyles v. Whitley* (1995) 514 U.S. 419, 439, 115 S.Ct. 1555, 131 L.Ed.2d 490. We caution prosecutors that playing "materiality games" is rarely productive of good prosecutorial ethics and can lead to serious appellate issues and potential disciplinary actions by the State Bar against the prosecutor.

§ 1:60   Burden to prove materiality

The burden to prove that suppressed favorable evidence is material rests on the shoulders of the defendant or other party asserting a *Brady* violation. *Douglas v. Workman* (2009, CA10 OK) 560 F.3d 1156, 1173; *United States v. Erickson* (2009, CA10 UT) 561 F.3d 1150, 1163; *United States v. Severns* (2009, CA5 TX) 559 F.3d 274, 278.

§ 1:61   Materiality standard on use of perjured testimony

The standard for determining whether perjured testimony is "material" within the meaning of the *Napue* rule—*Napue v. Illinois* (1959) 360 U.S. 264, 79 S.Ct. 1173, 3 L.Ed.2d 1217—is significantly different from the standard for determining whether suppressed evidence is "material" for purposes of the *Brady* rule. A *Napue* violation is material when there is any reasonable likelihood that the false testimony could have affected the judgment of the jury; in contrast, a *Brady* violation is material to a jury's verdict when there is a reasonable probability that the result of the proceeding would have been different but for the violation. Where the prosecution has violated its constitutional obligations under both *Napue* and *Brady*, an appellate court first considers the *Napue* violations collectively and ask whether there is any reasonable likelihood that the false testimony could have affected the judgment of the jury. If so, habeas relief must be granted. However, if the *Napue* errors are not material standing alone, the appellate court considers all of the *Napue* and *Brady* violations collectively and asks whether there is a reasonable probability that, but for the errors, the result of the proceeding would have been different. At both stages, the appellate court must ask whether the defendant received a trial resulting in a verdict worthy of confidence. *Phillips v. Ornoski* (2012, CA9 Cal.) 673 F.3d 1168.

§ 1:61.1   Materiality standard for knowing presentation of false testimony

"[W]hen a prosecutor knowingly uses perjured testimony, 'a conviction . . . is fundamentally unfair, and must be set aside if there is any reasonable likelihood that the false testimony could have affected the judgment of the jury.' [citations omitted]" *Perkins v. Russo* (2009, CA1 MA) 586 F.3d 115, 119.

There is a reason why the courts have established a more defendant-friendly standard of materiality when the prosecution knowingly uses perjured testimony than when the prosecution suppresses favorable evidence. "This distinction between *Brady* materiality and *Napue* materiality seems to reflect a sentiment that the prosecution's knowing use of perjured testimony will be more likely to affect our confidence in the jury's decision, and hence more likely to violate due process, than will a failure to disclose evidence favorable to the defendant. It likely also acknowledges that every *Napue* claim has an implicit accompanying *Brady* claim: Whenever the prosecution knowingly uses false testimony, it has a *Brady* obligation to disclose that witness's perjury to the defense." *Jackson v. Brown* (2008, CA9 CA) 513 F.3d 1057, 1076, n.12.

The standard of materiality applicable to a prosecutor's knowing presentation of perjured testimony "is less exacting than in the case of a prosecutor's failure to perform *Brady* or *Giglio* obligations. If the prosecution knew of the perjury, then the conviction must be vacated 'if there is any reasonable likelihood that the false testimony could have affected the judgment of the jury.' [citations omitted]" *United States v. Spinelli* (2008, CA2 NY) 551 F.3d 159, 166.

However, even though the test of materiality is facially different in cases where the prosecution has knowingly presented or allowed false or perjured testimony to stand uncorrected from cases in which the prosecution has suppressed favorable evidence, the test of materiality might actually be the same in its practical application. In *Douglas v. Workman* (2009, CA10 OK) 560 F.3d 1156, 1174, the Tenth Circuit Court of Appeals observed that because the harmless error standard is applicable to knowing presentation of false or perjured evidence, and such a standard does not apply to the suppression of material favorable evidence, the lesser materiality standard applicable to knowing presentation of false or perjured evidence might be the same in practice as the *Brady* rule standard of materiality. The Court analyzed:

> "[A]ssuming the *Giglio* 'reasonable likelihood' standard is in fact less demanding than the *Kyles* 'reasonable probability' standard, a petitioner who succeeds under that standard will still have to meet the harmless error standard of *Brecht v. Abrahamson*, 507 U.S. 619, 113 S.Ct. 1710, 123 L.Ed.2d 353 (1993), which the Supreme Court has held is met by the *Kyles* test. [citation omitted] Thus, for all practical purposes the two standards ultimately mandate the same inquiry. [citation omitted]" 560 F.3d at 1174.

The court's determination whether the prosecution's knowing use of perjured testimony is material—whether there is any reasonable likelihood that the false testimony could have affected the judgment of the jury—involves a fact-specific analysis. When the false testimony is given by a critical prosecution witness, and the prosecution's other incriminating evidence is either weak or limited, the courts are likely to conclude that there is a reasonable likelihood that the false testimony could have affected the judgment of the jury. *See, e.g., Maxwell v. Roe* (2010, CA9 CA) 628 F.3d 486, 506–508.

When, however, the false testimony was provided by a witness whose testimony, although important, was not necessary to establish the defendant's guilt, and the prosecution evidence of the defendant's guilt was otherwise weighty or persuasive, the courts have concluded that there was no reasonable likelihood that the false testimony could have affected the jury's judgment. *See, e.g., Griffin v. Pierce* (2010, CA7 IL) 622 F.3d 831, 841–843; *Brooks v. Tennessee* (2010, CA6 TN) 626 F.3d 878, 894–896.

§ 1:61.3 Materiality standard for combination of *Brady* and *Napue* errors in same case

Because the materiality standard for the prosecution's knowing use of perjured testimony in violation of *Napue v. Illinois* (1959) 360 U.S. 264, 79 S.Ct. 1273, 3 L.Ed.2d 1317, is different from the materiality standard for the prosecution's suppression of favorable evidence in violation of *Brady v. Maryland* (1963) 373 U.S. 83, 83 S.Ct. 1194, 10 L.Ed.2d 215, it becomes more analytically difficult to assess materiality in a case in which there are possibly both *Napue* and *Brady* errors.

In *Jackson v. Brown* (2008, CA9 Cal.) 513 F.3d 1057, the Ninth Circuit Court of Appeals confronted this problem and came up with this resolution:

> "The *Napue* and *Brady* errors cannot all be collectively analyzed under *Napue's* 'reasonable likelihood' standard, as that would overweight the *Brady* violations. On the other hand they cannot be considered in two separate groups, as that would fail to capture their combined effect on our confidence in the jury's decision. To resolve this conflict, we first consider the *Napue* violations collectively and ask whether there is 'any reasonable likelihood that the false testimony *could* have affected the judgment of the jury.' [citation omitted] (emphasis added). If so, habeas relief must be granted. However, if the *Napue* errors are not material standing alone, we consider all of the *Napue* and *Brady* violations collectively and ask whether 'there is a reasonable probability that, but for counsel's unprofessional errors, the result of the proceeding *would* have been different.' [citations omitted]." 513 F.3d at 1076.

The Ninth Circuit Court of Appeals reaffirmed its analytical model for collectively assessing the materiality of *Brady* and *Napue* claims in *Hamilton v. Ayers* (2009, CA9 CA) 583 F.3d 1100, 1110, n.3.

PART V. DISCLOSURE REQUIREMENT

§ 1:62 Disclosure requirement—four elements of disclosure/suppression

In order for a *Brady* violation to have occurred, the favorable evidence at issue must have been suppressed by the prosecution and suppression may be either intentional or inadvertent. An innocent failure to disclose favorable evidence constitutes suppression even where there is no allegation that the prosecutor acted willfully, maliciously, or in anything but good faith—sins of omission are equally within *Brady's* scope. *Brady* has no good faith or inadvertence defense. *United States v. Olsen* (2013, CA9 Wash.) 704 F.3d 1172.

The three elements of a claim for a *Brady* violation are that the evidence at issue must be favorable to the accused, either because it is exculpatory, or because it is impeaching; that evidence must have been suppressed by the State, either willfully or inadvertently; and prejudice must have ensued. *United States v. Olsen* (2013, CA9 Wash.) 704 F.3d 1172. As stated, *supra*, the prosecutor must be in possession of the evidence. *But see Gantt v. City of Los Angeles* (2013, CA9 Cal.) 717 F.3d 702, holding, *inter alia*, that the *Brady* requirement to disclose material exculpatory and impeachment evidence to the defense applies equally to prosecutors and officers.

§ 1:63   First Element of evidence suppression—possession of favorable evidence

The first element of a suppression of evidence favorable to a criminal defendant is that the prosecution team must possess that favorable evidence. At the heart of this first element of a suppression of exculpatory evidence is the requirement that such evidence actually exists. *United States v. Warshak* (2010, CA6 OH) 631 F.3d 266, 295, 299 ["[I]t would not be prejudicial if the defendants were denied the chance to excavate in a mine that contained no ore."].

§ 1:63.1   Actual possession

The government only has a *Brady* obligation to disclose exculpatory information in its "possession." *United States v. Venegas-Reynoso* (May 17, 2013, CA9 Ariz.) 2013 U.S. App. LEXIS 9954. *But see Gantt v. City of Los Angeles* (2013, CA9 Cal.) 717 F.3d 702, holding, *inter alia*, that the *Brady* requirement to disclose material exculpatory and impeachment evidence to the defense applies equally to prosecutors and officers.

§ 1:63.3   Burden to prove possession

The party making a *Brady* claim, usually the defendant, "bears the initial burden of producing some evidence to support an inference that the government possessed or knew about material favorable to the defense and failed to disclose it." *United States v. Price* (2009, CA9 OR) 566 F.3d 900, 910. A defendant who claims that the prosecution possesses *Brady* evidence or that the prosecution has committed a *Brady* violation by failing to disclose such evidence has the burden to establish that the prosecution possesses or possessed such evidence. There can be no "suppression" of exculpatory evidence that the prosecution team does not possess. *United States v. Naranjo* (2011, CA11 FL) 634 F.3d 1198, 1211–1212. *Accord United States v. Celestin* (2010, CA1 MA) 612 F.3d 14, 22.

§ 1:64   "Prosecution team"—defined

See Gantt v. City of Los Angeles (2013, CA9 Cal.) 717 F.3d 702, holding, *inter alia*, that the *Brady* requirement to disclose material exculpatory and impeachment evidence to the defense applies equally to prosecutors and officers.

Determining whether the prosecution possesses evidence favorable to the defendant requires an understanding of the nature and scope of the "prosecution team."

§ 1:64.1 "Prosecution team"—prosecutor's office

The office of the prosecuting attorney is an integral member of the prosecution team. The reason for this principle is easily understood when it is remembered that all prosecutions conducted by deputy or assistant prosecutors in California are conducted in the name and under the statutory authority of the elected or appointed prosecuting attorney—the district attorney or the city attorney.

The California Legislature has by statute established the office of the District Attorney as a county officer. Government Code section 24000(a). The Legislature has designated the District Attorney as the "public prosecutor," upon whom is imposed the duty to initiate and conduct all prosecutions of all public offenses on behalf of the People. Government Code section 26500. In carrying out his or her duties as the public prosecutor, the District Attorney represents the People of the State of California in whose sovereign name the case is presented. Government Code section 100; *Dix v. Superior Court* (1991) 53 Cal.3d 442, 451, 279 Cal.Rptr. 834, 807 P.2d 1063.

The District Attorney as the public prosecutor is "vested with the power to conduct on behalf of the People all prosecutions for public offenses within the county." *People v. Eubanks* (1996) 14 Cal.4th 580, 589, 59 Cal.Rptr.2d 200, 927 P.2d 310.

Because the elected or appointed public prosecutor would be unable to personally handle all of the criminal prosecutions brought in his or her jurisdiction, the public prosecutor may appoint deputy prosecutors to assist him or her. Government Code section 7 provides that "[w]henever a power is granted to, or a duty is imposed upon, a public officer, the power may be exercised or the duty may be performed by a deputy of the officer or by a person authorized, pursuant to law, by the officer, unless this code expressly provides otherwise." Government Code section 1194 provides that "[w]hen not otherwise provided for, each deputy possesses the powers and may perform the duties attached by law to the office of his principal."

The power to appoint deputy or assistant prosecutors belongs to the District Attorney, who alone has the power to "appoint as many deputies as are necessary for the prompt and faithful discharge of the duties of his office." Government Code section 24101. *Hicks v. Board of Supervisors* (1977) 69 Cal.App.3d 228, 241, 138 Cal.Rptr. 101.

Appointed deputy prosecutors act in the name and under the authority of the public prosecutor. "Under Government Code section 24101, the district attorney may appoint deputies as necessary for the prompt and faithful discharge of the district attorney's duties." Fort Emory Cove Boatowners Assn v. Cowett (1990) 221 Cal.App.3d 508, 514, 270 Cal.Rptr. 527; *accord,*

Miller v. Filter (2007) 150 Cal.App.4th 652, 661, 58 Cal.Rptr.3d 671.

In this respect the deputy prosecutors appointed by the District Attorney have the same status as deputy clerks appointed by the County Clerk and deputy sheriffs appointed by the Sheriff. *See, Romero v. County of Santa Clara* (1970) 3 Cal.App.3d 700, 703, 83 Cal.Rptr. 758 ["the clerk of the superior court is the county clerk . . . authorized to act by deputies (Gov. Code, sec. 24101) . . . ."]; and *People v. Woods* (1970) 7 Cal.App.3d 382, 387, 86 Cal.Rptr. 508 ["The sheriff is designated in the general statutes (Sec. 24000 Gov. Code) as a county officer and 'may appoint as many deputies as are necessary for the prompt and faithful discharge of the duties of his office.' [citation omitted] As to the extent of the power exercisable by a deputy sheriff, both the general statutes and decisional law establish that he possesses all of the powers and may perform all of the duties attached by law to the office of sheriff."].

It therefore naturally follows that because all prosecutions are conducted under the authority and in the name of the public prosecutor, the prosecutor's office is a member of the prosecution team.

This does not necessarily mean, however, that every deputy or assistant prosecutor is a member of the prosecution team in every prosecution conducted by the prosecutor's office. We discuss this potentially limiting concept in the following section of this supplement, section 1:64.1.1.

§ 1:64.1.1　Individual deputy or assistant prosecutors as members of the prosecution team

The question whether every prosecutor in the office of the prosecuting attorney is a member of the prosecution team in every criminal prosecution handled by that office is a thorny one. Neither the United States Supreme Court nor the California Supreme Court have explicitly addressed the question whether a prosecutor is deemed to possess exculpatory information known to another prosecutor in the same prosecuting agency, when the prosecutor who possesses the exculpatory information has had no involvement in the prosecution of the defendant. In fact, the California Supreme Court has specifically declined to decide that question when impeaching evidence regarding a prosecution witness in a criminal prosecution was possessed by the welfare fraud unit in the district attorney's office. *See People v. Clark* (2011) 52 Cal.4th 856, 982, 131 Cal.Rptr.3d 225, 261 P.3d 243 ["To the extent there is any question whether the welfare fraud unit in the district attorney's office, which possessed the information regarding [the prosecution witness's] conviction, is part of the prosecution team for *Brady* purposes, we need not decide that issue."].

A morass of potentially conflicting language in federal and state courts has served to give mixed signals on this question to prosecutors and courts alike. Some of this language and holdings support an expansive definition of the scope of the prosecution team within the office of the prosecuting attorney.

Other language and holdings support giving a more restrictive definition of the scope of the team.

Authorities supporting expansive prosecution team composition

Some attorneys believe that the language of the United States Supreme Court in *Giglio v. United States* (1972) 405 U.S. 150, 154, 92 S.Ct. 763, 31 L.Ed.2d 104, that "[t]he prosecutor's office is an entity and as such it is the spokesman for the Government," is a sufficiently broad statement that it should be read as a holding that because the prosecuting agency as an entity is a member of the prosecution team, all of the prosecutors who work for that entity are also members of the prosecution team in every criminal prosecution handled by that agency. The thrust of this position is that holding that the entire prosecution entity is part of the prosecution team necessarily entails holding that its component parts—its individual prosecutors—are also members of the team.

This statement from *Giglio* has been quoted with approval by the California Supreme Court in *In re Brown* (1998) 17 Cal.4th 873, 879, 72 Cal.Rptr.2d 698, 952 P.2d 715, and by the California Fourth District Court of Appeal in *People v. Kasim* (1997) 56 Cal.App.4th 1360, 1385–1386, 66 Cal.Rptr.2d 494.

State courts in Maryland, Pennsylvania, and Texas have directly addressed this question, concluding that exculpatory information known to one prosecutor is deemed as a matter of law to be known by all other prosecutors in the same office. *See, State v. Williams* (2006) 392 Md. 194, 206, 896 A.2d 973, 980 (Maryland Court of Appeals); *Diallo v. State* (2010) 413 Md. 678, 707, 994 A.2d 820, 837 (Maryland Court of Appeals); *Commonwealth v. Wallace* (1983) 500 Pa. 270, 276, 455 A.2d 1187, 1190 (Pennsylvania Supreme Court); and *Hall v. State* (2009) 283 S.W.3d 137, 170 (Texas Court of Appeals). The argument that a prosecutor is deemed to know exculpatory information known by other prosecutors in his or her same office is argued forcefully in *State v. Williams*, 392 Md. 194.

In addition to these state courts, the District of Columbia Circuit Court of Appeals reached a similar conclusion in *In re Sealed Case No. 99-3096* (1999, CA DC) 185 F.3d 887, 896, in rejecting the government's argument that exculpatory evidence contained in a separate case file in a different prosecution unit—the one handling prosecutions in the District of Columbia Superior Court—in the United States Attorney's Office for the District of Columbia was not possessed by the prosecution team in the federal court prosecution of the defendant. The Court of Appeals, citing *Giglio*, held that a witness cooperation agreement negotiated in other cases by other prosecutors of the U.S. Attorney's Office is deemed to be known to all prosecutors of that office, stating:

> "Nor does it matter that agreements in other cases may have involved other prosecutors. The United States Attorney's Office for

the District of Columbia prosecutes cases in both the federal District Court and the local Superior Court, and the prosecutor is responsible (at a minimum) for all *Brady* information in the possession of that office." 185 F.3d at 896.

There is also some language in California appellate opinions suggesting that the prosecution team in a criminal case in California consists of the entire prosecution staff of a prosecutor's office.

In *People v. Superior Court (Barrett)* (2000) 80 Cal.App.4th 1305, 1315, 96 Cal.Rptr.2d 264, the Court of Appeal stated that "[a] prosecutor has a duty to search for and disclose exculpatory evidence if the evidence is possessed by a *person or agency* that has been used by the prosecutor or the investigating agency to assist the prosecution or the investigating agency in its work. The important determinant is whether the *person or agency* has been 'acting on the government's behalf' [citation omitted]." [italics added].

This statement in *Barrett* has been quoted with approval by a number of Courts of Appeal. *See, e.g., People v. Jordan* (2003) 108 Cal.App.4th 349, 133 Cal.Rptr.2d 434, in which the California Court of Appeal, in concluding that that the prosecution does not have a *Brady*-based duty to disclose complaints of police misconduct made by other defendants in other trials, noted that the prosecution team "includes both investigative and prosecutorial agencies and personnel . . . [and] [t]he important determination is whether the person or agency has been 'acting on the government's behalf . . . .' " 108 Cal.App.4th at 358; *Abatti v. Superior Court* (2003) 112 Cal.App.4th 39, 53, 4 Cal.Rptr.3d 767; and *People v. Uribe* (2008) 162 Cal.App.4th 1457, 1476, 76 Cal.Rptr.3d 829.

Therefore, there is decisional authority supporting the argument that the prosecution team for *Brady* purpose includes all prosecutors in the office of the prosecuting attorney.

Authorities supporting restrictive prosecution team composition

There is also decisional authority which can be cited to support the argument that only those prosecutors who have assisted in the prosecution of the case on the government's behalf are members of the prosecution team.

The argument that only those prosecutors who have had a participatory connection to a prosecution are members of the prosecution team in that case is based upon a more restrictive reading of *Giglio v. United States* (1972) 405 U.S. 150, 154, 92 S.Ct. 763, 31 L.Ed.2d 104.

Giglio v. United States was a case in which two deputy prosecutors had handled Giglio's prosecution. The first prosecutor orally promised a witness a benefit in return for the witness's cooperation in testifying against *Giglio*. The case was then re-assigned to a second prosecutor, and the first prosecutor failed to inform the second prosecutor of the promise made to the witness and made no notation in the prosecution's case file about the agreement with the witness. The Supreme Court ultimately concluded in *Giglio* that the second prosecutor had constructive knowledge of the promise made by the first prosecutor in the same case, and held that the failure of the second prosecutor to disclose the promise to the defendant constituted a *Brady* violation. Thus, *Giglio* represented an early application of the rule later enunciated by the Supreme Court in *Kyles v. Whitley* (1995) 514 U.S. 419, 437, 115 S.Ct. 1555, 131 L.Ed.2d 490, that "the individual prosecutor has a duty to learn of any favorable evidence known to the *others acting on the government's behalf in the case*, including the police." [italics added]

Giglio did not involve the failure by the trial prosecutor to disclose to the defendant exculpatory or impeaching evidence possessed by another prosecutor who had no connection to or involvement in Giglio's prosecution. Because the facts in *Giglio* did not entail an uninvolved prosecutor with knowledge of exculpatory evidence, the Supreme Court did not have reason to consider in *Giglio* whether an uninvolved prosecutor with exculpatory knowledge is a member of the prosecution team.

This analysis means that the language from *Giglio* that the "prosecutor's office is an entity" might not support the broad argument that the prosecution team in a criminal case includes all prosecutors in the same office, even those who have had no connection to or involvement in that criminal prosecution. Rather, this language might be limited to supporting only the conclusion reached in *Giglio* that a prosecutor's responsibility for *Brady* compliance extends to all exculpatory evidence and information known to all other persons in the prosecutor's office who have acted on the government's behalf in that case.

There is a principle of stare decisis followed by the California Supreme Court that "[t]he language of an opinion must be construed with reference to the facts presented by the case, and the positive authority of a decision is coextensive only with such facts." *Brown* v. *Kelly Broadcasting Co.* (1989) 48 Cal.3d 711, 734–735, 257 Cal.Rptr. 708, 771 P.2d 406. The California Supreme Court has reiterated this principle in numerous opinions. *See, Elsner v. Uveges* (2004) 34 Cal.4th 915, 933, 22 Cal.Rptr.3d 530, 102 P.3d 915 ["The holding of a case is coextensive with its particular facts."]; *People v. Mendoza* (2000) 23 Cal.4th 896, 922, 98 Cal.Rptr.2d 431, 4 P.3d 265; and *PLCM Group, Inc. v. Drexler* (2000) 22 Cal.4th 1084, 1097, 95 Cal.Rptr.2d 198, 997 P.2d 511.

What this principle means is that "[a] decision 'is not authority for everything said in the . . . opinion,' " *People v. Mendoza* (2000) 23 Cal.4th 896, 915, and a statement of a legal principle announced in the opinion must be construed in light of the underlying facts of the case to which the statement relates. The language of an opinion "is to be understood in accordance with the facts and issues before the court. An opinion is not authority for propositions not considered." *Chevron U.S.A., Inc. v. Workers'*

Comp. Appeals Bd. (1999) 19 Cal.4th 1182, 1195, 81 Cal.Rptr.2d 521, 969 P.2d 613.

Following this principle of *stare decisis* means that in light of its factual scenario, the statement by the United States Supreme Court in *Giglio* that a "prosecutor's office is an entity, and as such it is the spokesman for the Government," supports only a more restrictive definition of the scope of the prosecution team. That restrictive definition would include in the prosecution team only those prosecutors who have acted on the government's behalf in that case.

The opinions from sister jurisdictions that hold that the prosecution team includes all prosecutors in the office of the prosecuting attorney seem to suffer from the same problem that can be deemed to afflict a broad definition of the holding in *Giglio*. In reaching the conclusion that exculpatory information known to one prosecutor is deemed to be known by all other prosecutors in the same office, sister jurisdiction opinions have relied upon the same "prosecutor's office is an entity" language from *Giglio*. For the reasons already discussed, that reliance might be misplaced.

Moreover, opinions of sister courts in other jurisdictions do not have binding precedential impact in California state courts. *Miller v. Filter* (2007) 150 Cal.App.4th 652, 667, 58 Cal.Rptr.3d 671. The same is true of decisions of the lower federal courts which, when interpreting federal law, are persuasive, but not binding on California state courts. *Raven v. Deukmejian* (1990) 52 Cal.3d 336, 352, 276 Cal.Rptr. 326, 801 P.2d 1077; *People v. Bradley* (1969) 1 Cal.3d 80, 86, 81 Cal.Rptr. 457, 460 P.2d 129. Accordingly, California courts are not required to follow decisions from other jurisdictions.

In the absence of explicit California authority to the contrary, opinions from other jurisdictions can have persuasive value. *San Jose Crane & Rigging v. Lexington Ins. Co.* (1991) 227 Cal.App.3d 1314, 1321, 278 Cal.Rptr. 301. In deciding whether decisions from sister jurisdictions are persuasive California courts evaluate the reasoning and analysis of the opinion from a sister jurisdiction and determine whether the opinion of the sister jurisdiction conflicts with existing California appellate authority.

Adopting the broader definition of the prosecution team which these sister jurisdictions have adopted goes beyond the definition of the prosecution team announced by the Supreme Court in *Kyles v. Whitley* (1995) 514 U.S. 419, 437, 115 S.Ct. 1555, 131 L.Ed.2d 490. In *Kyles v. Whitley* the Supreme Court decided that "the individual prosecutor has a duty to learn of any favorable evidence known to the *others acting on the government's behalf in the case*, including the police." [italics added] The Supreme Court reiterated this statement in two places in its opinion in *Strickler v. Greene* (1999) 527 U.S. 263, 275, n.12, 281, 119 S.Ct. 1936, 144 L.Ed.2d 286.

This quoted language from *Kyles v. Whitley* has been followed by the

California Supreme Court and California Courts of Appeal. *See, Barnett v. Superior Court* (2010) 50 Cal.4th 890, 902, 114 Cal.Rptr.3d 576,237 P.3d 980; *In re Brown* (1998) 17 Cal.4th 873, 878, n.3, 72 Cal.Rptr.2d 698, 952 P.2d 715; *City of Los Angeles v. Superior Court* (2001) 29 Cal.4th 1, 8, 124 Cal.Rptr.2d 202, 52 P.3d 129; and *People v. Uribe* (2008) 162 Cal.App.4th 1457, 1475, 76 Cal.Rptr.3d 829.

The italicized language in *Kyles v. Whitley*—*"others acting on the government's behalf in the case"* can be argued to have defined the scope of the membership of the prosecuting attorney in the prosecution team. There are two important components of the *Kyles* language that could be used to fix an outward limit on the scope of the team.

The first component of the *Kyles* language is that membership in the prosecution team is based upon **actions** by prosecuting attorneys ("others acting on the government's behalf"), instead of being based upon their **status** as prosecutors. The second component of the *Kyles* language is that membership in the prosecution team is dependent upon actions "in the case." The fact that all prosecutors in a prosecuting attorney's office routinely act on the government's behalf does not meet the *Kyles* language; membership in the prosecution team in a particular criminal prosecution requires that the prosecutor have acted "in the case." If this language in *Kyles v. Whitley* is deemed to fix the outward limit of the scope of the prosecution team, both of these components must be satisfied in order for a particular prosecutor to be included in the prosecution team in a particular case.

A conservative construction of the "prosecutor's office is an entity" language of *Giglio* and the *"others acting on the government's behalf in the case"* language of *Kyles v. Whitley* to mean that the prosecution team extends to others who have acted on the government's behalf in the case, but goes no further, would thereby define and fix the scope of the prosecutor's office in the prosecution team—that only prosecutors with a participatory connection to a defendant's case are part of that team, and that prosecutors with no such participatory connection would not have acted on the government's behalf in the case, and would not be part of the prosecution team.

A more liberal construction of that language would require that the prosecution team extend to others who have acted on the government's behalf in the case as a minimum requirement, but leave open the question whether the prosecution team extended further. A more liberal construction of the language from *Kyles v. Whitley* would thus not fix a maximum scope of the prosecutor's office in the prosecution team.

However, California appellate courts appear to have adopted a conservative standard for determining the membership in the prosecution of individuals employed by an entity which is indisputably part of the prosecution team. In two opinions the California Supreme Court held, albeit in different contexts than when describing a prosecutor's discovery obligations, that the prosecution team consists of only those prosecutors and law enforcement officers who have been involved in the investigation or prosecution of the case.

In *People v. Ervine* (2009) 47 Cal.4th 745, 768, and n.11, 102 Cal.Rptr.3d 786, 220 P.3d 820, the California Supreme Court held, in a different context, that "misconduct by a government agent who has no involvement in the investigation or prosecution of the criminal charge against the defendant cannot automatically be imputed to the prosecution team for purposes of the Sixth Amendment." The Court appears to have limited the scope of the prosecution team to "anyone [who has been or is] involved in either the investigation or prosecution of [the] case."

In *People v. Jacinto* (2010) 49 Cal.4th 263, 270, 109 Cal.Rptr.3d 610, 231 P.3d 341, the California Supreme Court similarly limited the membership in the prosecution team of employees of the agency that has investigated the criminal charges against the defendant. The Court held that the prosecution team had not been involved in destroying defense evidence by releasing a prisoner from the county jail to federal authorities who deported the prisoner. The Court based its decision on the Court's determination that officers in the sheriff's investigating unit were part of the prosecution team, but sheriff's deputies whose jobs were limited to the sheriff's jail security and administration were not part of that team.

The majority in *People v. Jacinto* reached this conclusion in the face of a concurring opinion by Justice Kennard that urged the Court to not reach the question whether individual members of the sheriff's department could be excluded from the prosecution team, when the sheriff's department itself was the investigating agency and thereby a member of the team. Justice Kennard observed that "[t]his is a difficult issue that, in light of the majority's correct conclusion pertaining to the federal immigration detainer, need not be addressed in this case. Whether the prosecution team includes the investigating law enforcement agency itself or only some of its personnel and, if so, which personnel under what circumstances, are substantial questions" which Justice Kennard urged the Court not to reach in *Jacinto*. 49 Cal.4th at 275–276 (Kennard, J., concurring).

In *People v. Jordan* (2003) 108 Cal.App.4th 349, 133 Cal.Rptr.2d 434, the Court of Appeal implicitly limited the prosecution team to those prosecutors who had actually participated in the prosecution of a case, for the purpose of deciding who in the prosecutor's office is deemed by the *Brady* rule to possess exculpatory or impeaching evidence. *People v. Jordan* appears to support the conclusion that prosecutors who have had no participatory connection to the investigation or prosecution of a defendant's case are not members of the prosecution team.

In *Jordan* a defendant charged with possession of cocaine base for sale argued that the prosecution had a *Brady*-based duty to disclose complaints of police misconduct made by other defendants in other trials. The trial court rejected his argument; so did the Court of Appeal.

The Court of Appeal observed that a "prosecutor's duty under *Brady* to disclose material exculpatory evidence applies to evidence the prosecutor, or the prosecution team, knowingly possesses or has the right to possess. The prosecution team includes both investigative and prosecutorial agencies and personnel. [citations omitted] The prosecution must disclose evidence that is actually or constructively in its possession or accessible to it. [citation omitted] The important determination is whether the person or agency has been 'acting on the government's behalf' [citing *Kyles v. Whitley*] or 'assisting the government's case' [citing *In re Brown*]." 108 Cal.App. 4th at 358.

The Court of Appeal concluded that the defendant's proposed rule would violate the constitutional principles that there is no general constitutional right to discovery in a criminal case, and the prosecution has no general duty to seek out, obtain, and disclose all evidence that might be beneficial to the defense. The defendant's argument "would require the People to catalog the testimony of every witness called by the defense at every criminal trial in the county, cull from that testimony complaints about peace officers and disclose these complaints to the defense whenever the People called the peace officer as a witness at another trial. Even in a computer age, such a task is daunting, especially in a major metropolitan area." 108 Cal.App.4th at 361–362.

The Court further noted that "a rule requiring disclosure of defense complaints made at unrelated criminal trials would transform the prosecution into a '*Brady* vessel' of information that had to be disclosed every time the People called a peace officer witness. [citation omitted] Thus, the fact the People may have been a party to every criminal case prosecuted in the county does not give rise to a duty to collect evidence for the defense." 108 Cal.App.4th at 362.

If the standards announced in *People v. Ervine, People v. Jacinto*, and *People v. Jordan*, are deemed to fix the limit of the scope of the prosecuting attorney's office in the prosecution team, then prosecutors in the office of the prosecuting attorney who have had no participatory connection to the investigation or prosecution of the defendant's case would not be members of the prosecution team in that case.

A recent opinion of the California Court of Appeal might suggest that even when an entity becomes part of the prosecution team, membership of individuals in that team might be smaller than the entire personnel of the entity.

In *People v. Uribe* (2008) 162 Cal.App.4th 1457, 76 Cal.Rptr.3d 829, the Court of Appeal held that two physicians at a medical center who performed a sexual assault examination of a child sexual assault victim at the request of law enforcement authorities were members of the prosecution team. After quoting the "person or agency" language from *People v. Superior Court (Barrett)* (2000) 80 Cal.App.4th 1305, 1315, 96 Cal.Rptr.2d 264, discussed earlier in this section, 162 Cal.App.4th at 1476, the Court of Appeal concluded that the Center at Valley Medical (the agency) was a member of the prosecution team, because it had acted on the government's behalf and assisted the government. But then the Court determined that "the personnel in the Center at Valley Medical responsible for conducting SART exams— namely, Ritter and Dr. Kerns—were part of the "prosecution team" for *Brady* purposes." 162 Cal.App.4th at 1481.

What could be significant is what the Court did not say—that the entire medical staff of the medical center was part of the prosecution team. It is difficult to tell whether the Court of Appeal was holding simply that the two named physicians were members of the prosecution team (because that was the issue presented to the Court), or that only the two physicians, to the exclusion of other personnel of the medical center, were members of the team.

Federal and state courts have not imposed an "all or nothing" requirement for membership in the prosecution team in a criminal case. Construing the membership of the prosecutor's office in the prosecution team to include only those prosecutors who have had a participatory connection to the case, and excluding those who haven't, would be consistent with, or at least a logical extension of, the partial prosecution team membership doctrine developed for determining the scope of the investigating agency's membership in the prosecution team. *People v. Superior Court (Barrett)* (2000) 80 Cal.App.4th 1305, 1317–1318, 96 Cal.Rptr.2d 264; and *United States v. Pellulo* (2005, CA3 NJ) 399 F.3d 197. See Sections 1:68 through 1:68.3 of the text for a discussion of the partial prosecution team membership doctrine.

We wonder if there is any principled basis for distinguishing the prosecutor's office from the investigating agency for purposes of determining the standards by which individual prosecutors and investigators are deemed to be in the prosecution team and which prosecutors and investigators are excluded from the team.

Conceptual and practical difficulties in a conservative determination of the prosecution team

A conservative standard for defining the scope of the prosecution team by fixing its membership at those prosecutors who have had a participatory involvement in assisting the government in the case would inevitably encounter difficulties. Drawing a line between those prosecutors who have had a participatory involvement in a case and those who have not could be difficult. For example, would a prosecutor who makes a brief appearance on behalf of a prosecutor colleague in order to continue a case thereby become part of the prosecution team in that case? Would a prosecutor who litigates a motion to suppress evidence in a case, but who is otherwise unfamiliar with other aspects of the case, be considered part of the prosecution team in that case?

It is conceivable that difficulties of application could cause the courts to adopt a "bright-line" rule—that all prosecutors in the office of the prosecuting attorney are part of the prosecution team in every criminal case prosecuted by that office.

Moreover, the courts might recoil at the idea that a prosecutor in the office of the prosecuting attorney could lawfully suppress exculpatory evidence that he or she knows is relevant to a prosecution, simply because that prosecutor has not been involved in that prosecution and, therefore, is not part of the prosecution team in that case. This concern might cause the courts to conclude that membership of individual prosecutors in the prosecution team must include not only those prosecutors who have had a participatory involvement in the case, but also those prosecutors in the office of the prosecuting attorney who know or reasonably should know that there is a pending prosecution for which they possess exculpatory information or evidence.

Defining the prosecution team to include uninvolved prosecutors simply because these other prosecutors have knowledge of exculpatory information regarding that case could announce a new definition of the prosecution team. No court of which we are aware has announced a "knowledge standard" by which an individual prosecutor becomes a member of the prosecution team in a case simply because that prosecutor knows of exculpatory information regarding that case, but otherwise has no participatory involvement in the case and does nothing to assist the government's prosecution of the case.

We are not sure how much weight to attach to this absence of an explicit "knowledge standard" holding. The absence of explicit decisional authority on this issue could easily be the result of a general understanding that the prosecution team includes every prosecutor in the office of the prosecuting attorney, thus obviating the need for a holding that an individual prosecutor becomes a member of the prosecution team in a case by virtue of knowing exculpatory information regarding that case, but without any participatory involvement in the case and without any action to assist the government's prosecution of the case.

A knowledge of exculpatory evidence standard as a basis for including a prosecutor in the prosecution team would be consistent with the general principle of *Brady* discovery that exculpatory evidence is possessed by the prosecution team if that evidence is "reasonably accessible" to the team.

Moreover, a more liberal standard for determining membership in the prosecution team would itself create conceptual and practical difficulties. It can be argued that it is unfair, impractical, and verging on irrationality to determine that a prosecutor is deemed to know about exculpatory evidence possessed by another prosecutor who has no connection to the case, who does not know that the exculpatory evidence is relevant to that case, and/or who could not reasonably know that the information has exculpatory value. Lest this argument seem to be an over-statement when applied to a small or moderate sized prosecutor's office, it has some force when applied to a large prosecutor's office in a large jurisdiction.

The Los Angeles District Attorney's Office consists of 44 separate branch offices staffed by more than 1,100 prosecutors. To construe the Due Process Clause of the United States Constitution to require that every one of these prosecutors must know the exculpatory evidence that is known to more than 1,000 colleagues scattered across a large geographical metropolitan area would set a constitutional standard that might be impossible to meet, even with the establishment of a *Brady* information management system. Even conceding that prosecutors as representatives of the government have special duties and standards of conduct that do not apply to other attorneys, prosecutors are still ordinary human beings. It is fair to ask the question whether the United States Constitution sets constitutional standards for prosecutors that ordinary people are unable to meet.

The issues as to the scope of the prosecutor's office in the prosecution team, and whether exculpatory information known to one prosecutor is deemed to be known by all other prosecutors in the same office, raise difficult and complicated questions. The arguments on both sides of these issues are compelling. While we do not pretend to know the answers to these questions, we believe that it behooves courts and criminal case litigants to understand these issues and be prepared to deal with them. It is certain that these questions are ripe for extensive further litigation.

§ 1:64.3   District Attorney investigator personnel records

Many prosecutor's offices have hired peace officers to serve as investigators. These investigators retain their peace officer status when they serve as district attorney investigators, but unlike police or other law enforcement officers, district attorney investigators are employed by and work for the elected prosecutor. These DA investigators work criminal cases in an investigative capacity, and they sometimes become material witnesses in their cases. The employing District Attorney commonly keeps personnel records on these investigators. These personnel records can contain derogatory or other information that could be used to impeach the investigators when they testify in criminal cases.

Difficult questions are presented when a defendant's attorney seeks disclosure of unfavorable information from the personnel records of a DA investigator who is a material witness in a criminal case. On the one hand, the employing District Attorney is in actual and legal possession of these personnel records, in the same manner that the chief of police or sheriff is in actual and legal possession of personnel records of peace officers employed by investigative agencies other than the prosecutor's office. Thus, the District Attorney has lawful access to these personnel records and the right to review those records as the investigator's employer.

On the other hand, the DA investigator as a peace officer has the right to confidentiality in his or her personnel records, and part of that confidentiality protects the right of privacy in those personnel records as against the prosecutor. See Chapter 10 of the text for a discussion of the confidential nature of peace officer personnel records. Thus, the District Attorney faces a conflict between the role as the investigating officer's employer and the role as the prosecuting attorney in a criminal case. The question is clearly presented: Is the District Attorney deemed to possess and know the contents of the personnel records of DA investigators within the meaning of both the *Brady* rule and the *Pitchess* statutes and the body of cases developed under those statutes?

The District Attorney is the public prosecutor charged with the duty of initiating and conducting all prosecutions of public offenses on behalf of the People of the State of California. Government Code section 26500. The District Attorney's duty to prosecute includes the duty to investigate and gather evidence relating to criminal offenses, since investigation of crimes is inseparable from prosecution. Government Code section 25303; *Hicks v. Board of Supervisors* (1977) 69 Cal.App.3d 228, 241, 138 Cal.Rptr. 101; *Los Angeles City Ethics Com. v. Superior Court* (1992) 8 Cal.App.4th 1287, 1302, 11 Cal.Rptr.2d 150.

The District Attorney thus has statutory authority to investigate crime occurring in his or her jurisdiction. Government Code section 26500. Investigators employed by the District Attorney to perform that investigative function have the status of peace officers. Penal Code section 830.1, subdivision (a). Thus, the personnel records of these investigators are protected by the statutes which generally protect peace officer personnel records.

As an employer of peace officers, the District Attorney is charged with the statutory responsibility of protecting the confidentiality of those personnel records. As the employer, the District Attorney has the right to review and inspect those records. As a practical matter, the District Attorney either knows about unfavorable information and evidence in the personnel records of his or her employees or is charged with constructive knowledge of those records. As the employer, the District Attorney has the duty to protect these personnel records from unauthorized disclosure.

However, as the public prosecutor, the District Attorney has a constitutionally based duty to disclose material exculpatory evidence possessed by any member of the prosecution team, which includes the prosecutor's office. This conundrum presents the District Attorney with a dilemma—which of these duties must he or she follow? If the District Attorney unlawfully discloses evidence and information from the personnel record of a district attorney investigator, the District Attorney and the County are exposed to potential civil liability for that unauthorized disclosure of those records. On the other hand, if the District Attorney fails to disclose *Brady* evidence contained in the personnel record, the District Attorney endangers the integrity of his or her office's prosecutions and convictions.

There are no reported California opinions on this subject. The best analysis we can provide is that when the District Attorney is a member of the prosecution team as both the public prosecutor and as an investigating agency, the office of the District Attorney is a dual partial member of the prosecution team. To the extent that the office of the District Attorney is the public prosecutor, all of the records and personnel of the prosecution component of the District Attorney's office are part of the prosecution team. To the extent that the office of the District Attorney is an investigating agency, the investigating personnel and the records of their investigative work are also part of the prosecution team. But to the extent that the District Attorney performs an administrative function of keeping personnel records, those records of a DA investigator who is a prosecution witness, like the personnel records of a peace officer employed by a separate investigative agency, are not possessed by or part of the prosecution team.

For a more complete discussion of the partial prosecution team membership concept, see Section 1:68 through Section 1:68.3 of the text. For practical suggestions on how the District Attorney can and should attempt to reconcile these apparently conflicting duties, see the Practice Tip for Prosecution at the end of this section, and also see Section 10:19 through Section 10:30 of Chapter 10 of the text.

Practice Tip for Prosecution: When you are aware that your office has or might have *Brady* evidence in the personnel records of a district attorney investigator who is a prosecution witness in a case you are handling, we recommend that you bring a prosecutor's *Pitchess* motion in which you request the court to conduct an *in camera* inspection of those personnel records to determine if they contain exculpatory or impeaching evidence that should be disclosed to the defendant. You should request that the elected District Attorney, or someone delegated by the District Attorney to perform this task, file a declaration with the court under seal. This declaration, which should set forth the good-cause justification for an *in camera* inspection by the court of the personnel records in question, should not be shared with or disclosed to the defendant and the prosecutor assigned to the case. The prosecutor assigned to the case should file an unsealed declaration with the *Pitchess* motion that establishes the materiality of the investigator's testimony, so that the court in conducting an *in camera* inspection of the investigator's personnel records will be able to determine whether exculpatory or impeaching information in those records is relevant to an issue in the case and should be disclosed to the defendant.

§ 1:65   "Prosecution team"—investigating agencies

Investigating officers and their employing agencies become members of the prosecution team to the extent that they have been "acting on the government's behalf." *Strickler v. Greene* (1999) 527 U.S. 263, 280, 119 S.Ct. 1936, 144 L.Ed.2d 286. Investigating officers are "acting on the government's behalf" when they have "work[ed] for the prosecution" in investigating the case against the defendant. *United States v. Bender* (2002, CA1 ME) 304 F.3d 161,164.

§ 1:65.1 Investigating agencies and Penal Code section 1054.9

Discovery rulings are reviewed for abuse of discretion, looking to whether the district court reaches a result that is illogical or implausible. *United States v. Muniz-Jaquez* (2013, CA9 Cal.) 718 F.3d 1180.

§ 1:65.3 Joint investigation/prosecution and pooled resources

Investigating agencies become members of the prosecution team in a case when those agencies pool their resources in an investigation, share information gained by the investigation, cooperate extensively in investigating, or conduct a joint investigation. However, in order for the investigating agency and the prosecutor in a criminal case to be charged with constructive possession of exculpatory evidence possessed by a non-investigating agency, there must be evidence to establish pooled investigative resources, a cooperative investigation, or a joint investigation between the investigating agency and the non-investigating agency. *Owen v. Sec'y for the Dep't of Corr.* (2009, CA11 FL) 568 F.3d 894, 921.

Where investigators working for different agencies conduct separate investigations and do not collaborate in their investigative activities, knowledge that one agency obtains is not imputed for *Brady* purposes to the other agency, and evidence gained by one agency is not deemed to be possessed by the other agency for *Brady* purposes. *United States v. Naranjo* (2011, CA11 FL) 634 F.3d 1198, 1211–1212 ["Knowledge of information that state investigators obtain is not imputed for *Brady* purposes to federal investigators who conduct a separate investigation when the separate investigative teams do not collaborate extensively."].

§ 1:65.4 Joint criminal and civil investigation

When law enforcement authorities combine their criminal investigations with civil investigations, thereby forming a strong, cooperative relationship in the investigation, the prosecution team consists of both the criminal and civil investigators, and the prosecution team is deemed to possess all evidence favorable to the defendant that is pocessed by both groups of investigators within the meaning of the *Brady* rule. Thus, in *United States v. Reyes* (2009, CA9 CA) 577 F.3d 1069, in a case in which the United States Attorney's Office and the FBI in conducting a criminal investigation cooperated as a team with civil investigators for the Securities and Exchange Commission, the prosecution team was charged with possession of any evidence unearthed by the civil investigators for the SEC. "The prosecution is legally charged with responsibility for information uncovered in its civil investigations and may be required to disclose it in criminal cases that it prosecutes." 577 F.3d at 1078.

§ 1:65.5　Parallel criminal and civil investigations

When parallel criminal and civil investigations take place in separate governmental agencies, unless the criminal investigators have worked jointly with the civil investigators, evidence obtained by the civil investigators and not possessed by the criminal investigators is not deemed to be possessed by the prosecution team. *See, e.g., United States v. Faulkenberry* (2010, CA6 OH) 614 F.3d 573, 589.

§ 1:65.6　Individual investigating officers as members of the prosecution team

Questions have been raised as to whether individual members of the investigating agency are members of the "prosecution team" whose knowledge is thereby imputed constructively to the prosecutor. This question is similar to the one discussed in § 1:64.1.1—whether individual deputy or assistant prosecutors are part of the prosecution team simply by virtue of their employment by the prosecuting agency.

In *United States v. Robinson* (2010, CA4 SC) 627 F.3d 941, it was learned post-trial that a number of the narcotics officers who had worked on the defendant's case had engaged in actions of misconduct unrelated to the officers' investigation of the defendant's case. These actions of misconduct were known only to the individual officers, and were not known to the prosecutors handling the defendant's case until after the trial. The officers were ultimately disciplined and several were fired.

On appeal the defendant argued that the prosecution had committed *Brady* error in failing to disclose these acts of misconduct, depriving him of the ability to impeach the officers' testimony at trial with these acts of misconduct. The defendant reasoned that "the knowledge of some of those who are part of the investigative team is imputed to prosecutors regardless of prosecutors' actual awareness." 627 F.3d at 951. The defendant concluded that "[b]ecause the dismissed officers obviously knew about their own misconduct and because they were working on the government's behalf . . . the prosecution violated its duty to disclose those improprieties even though no prosecutor actually knew about them." 627 F.3d at 951–952.

The Court rejected the defendant's argument. "Whatever the proper scope of *Brady's* imputed knowledge doctrine, it cannot be this broad. . . . [The defendant's] view . . . would also impose unacceptable burdens on prosecutors and the police. Courts have routinely refused to extend *Brady's* constructive knowledge doctrine where doing so would cut against the agency principles underlying imputed knowledge and would require prosecutors to do full interviews and background checks on everyone who touched the case. . . . And with good reason: it is one thing to require prosecutors to inquire about whether police have turned up exculpatory or impeachment evidence during their investigation. It is quite another to require them, on pain of a possible retrial, to conduct disciplinary inquiries into the general conduct of every officer working the case." 627 F.3d at 952.

The Court concluded that "where no one other than the officers themselves had any idea of any impropriety, and where the misconduct evidence was unrelated to [the defendant's] own investigation—the principle of imputed knowledge cannot be said to apply." 627 F.3d at 952.

§ 1:66 "Prosecution team"—assisting agencies

Agencies that have assisted either the investigating agency or the office of the prosecuting attorney thereby become members of the prosecution team in the case in they provide assistance.

§ 1:66.1 Crime laboratories

In *Brown v. Miller* (2008, CA5 LA) 519 F.3d 231, a former convict sued a state crime lab technician under the federal Civil Rights Act, 42 U.S.C. sec. 1983. The civil action alleged that the technician had created a misleading and materially inaccurate inculpatory serology report and had concealed, suppressed, or destroyed the results of additional tests whose results would have exonerated the convict of rape. Although the Fifth Circuit Court of Appeals affirmed the district court's dismissal of the action, the Court observed that the district court did not err in denying the qualified immunity defense to the technician. The Court reasoned: "A police officer's deliberate concealment of exculpatory evidence violates [a defendant's right to a fair trial], and can give rise to liability under sec. 1983 . . . the law was sufficiently clear in 1984 that a state crime lab technician would have known that suppression of exculpatory blood test results would violate a defendant's rights." 519 F.3d at 237–238.

§ 1:66.2 Victim-witness counselors

Commonwealth v. Liang (2001) 434 Mass. 131, 747 N.E.2d 112, was cited with approval by the New Mexico Supreme Court in *Brandenburg v. Blackmer* (2005) 137 N.M. 258, 110 P.3d 66. In *Brandenburg* the prosecutor cited *Liang* for the proposition that the victim-witness counselor is part of the prosecution team in an effort to shield discovery from the defense by claiming that it was the protected work product of the prosecution. The New Mexico Supreme Court held that a victim advocate employed by the district attorney's office is part of the prosecution team, and the rules of attorney-client confidentiality and disclosure by the State apply, because victim advocates perform many tasks similar to those of other members of the prosecution team.

The question has been raised whether California Penal Code section 679.04 causes a victim-witness counselor to become a part of the prosecution team, even without any direct employment relationship with the prosecutor's office. Section 679.04 requires notice to a sexual assault victim by a prosecution or law enforcement agency of the victim's right to have a victim advocate or support person at any interview or contact by law enforcement or prosecution authorities or by a criminal defense attorney. A victim advocate includes a sexual assault counselor as defined in Evidence Code section 1035.2 and an advocate working with a qualifying victim-witness center.

The legislative history of Section 679.04 does not appear to support the conclusion that the involvement of a victim advocate or counselor brings that advocate or counselor within the "prosecution team." From the time of its original enactment in 1996 through its latest amendment in 2006, Penal Code section 679.04 has been a statute intended to protect the sexual assault victim from improper interview procedures and tactics by law enforcement and improper prosecutorial questioning. Rather than bringing victim advocates and counselors into the prosecution team, Section 679.04 appears to treat those advocates and counselors as a shield against the prosecution team. See, e.g., the Assembly Public Safety Committee analysis of AB 807, which amended Section 679.04 [Stats. 1997 ch. 846].

§ 1:66.4   Prosecution expert witness

In *Avila v. Quarterman* (2009, CA5 TX) 560 F.3d 299, the Fifth Circuit Court of Appeals reached a decision that agreed with the Second Circuit Court of Appeals in *United States v. Skelly* (2006, CA2 NY) 442 F.3d 94, and *United States v. Stewart* (2006, CA2 NY) 433 F.3d 273—that a witness who testifies as an expert witness for the prosecution does not thereby automatically become a member of the prosecution team, and information favorable to the defendant known to that witness, but not to the prosecution, is not constructively imputed to the prosecution team.

In *Avila* the defendant was convicted of the murder of a 19-month-old child, after the child was left alone with the defendant by the child's mother. The child was taken to a hospital with abdominal injuries which caused his death. A pathologist in his capacity as a physician at the hospital prepared a pathology report regarding the child's injuries. Although the prosecution at first intended to call the pathologist to testify at trial, the prosecution ultimately used other expert witness testimony. The defendant was convicted of capital murder and sentenced to death.

Following his conviction the defendant learned that the pathologist had formed an opinion that the child had suffered only one blow causing his injuries. This opinion was contrary to the prosecution's expert witness evidence that the child suffered three stomps or kicks. The defendant contended that the expert's opinion constituted favorable evidence for him, because it could have enabled him to contend that his conduct resulted from a sudden loss of control, not a conscious desire to kill the child. The state court hearing the defendant's habeas corpus petition found that the prosecution did not know of the pathologist's opinion and rejected the defendant's argument that the nondisclosure of the pathologist's opinion constituted *Brady* error.

In his federal habeas petition the defendant contended that the prosecution's lack of knowledge of the pathologist's opinion did not negate *Brady* error, because the pathologist was part of the prosecution team, and the pathologist's opinion was constructively imputed to the prosecutor. Thus, the prosecutor's failure to disclose the pathologist's opinion violated *Brady*. The district court granted the habeas petition on this basis, and the government cross-appealed. The Fifth Circuit Court of Appeals reversed the order of the district court, holding that the government had not committed *Brady* error. The Court of Appeals concluded that the pathologist did not become part of the prosecution team—that his role was only that of a pathologist prepared to testify as an expert percipient witness for the prosecution. Because he did not become part of the prosecution team, the Court of Appeals concluded that knowledge of the pathologist's opinion was not constructively imputed to the prosecution. 560 F.3d at 306–309.

§ 1:66.6 Sexual Assault Response Team (SART)

A governmentally created team whose function is to examine victims of alleged sexual assault in order to gain evidence to be used in a criminal prosecution of the perpetrator of the assault becomes part of the prosecution team which may not suppress or fail to disclose material exculpatory evidence to the defendant.

In *People v. Uribe* (2008) 162 Cal.App.4th 1457, 76 Cal.Rptr.3d 829, the defendant was convicted of two counts of aggravated sexual assault on his granddaughter, who was a minor. The minor child was examined by a physician assistant, who performed what is known as a sexual assault response team (SART) examination. The SART examination was videotaped, and the existence of the videotape was not disclosed to the defendant, who learned of the videotape after his conviction at trial.

One of the contested issues at trial was whether the victim had been sexually assaulted. Expert testimony on that issue was presented by the prosecution and the defense. After learning of the videotape the defendant made a motion for a new trial, arguing that he had been denied *Brady* evidence—evidence from the videotape that showed that the victim had not been sexually assaulted. The trial court denied the new trial motion.

The Court of Appeal reversed the conviction and remanded the case to the trial court for a new trial. The Court concluded that the declaration of the defendant's expert in support of the new-trial motion "established that the SART video was favorable both because it offered potential evidence impeaching a prosecution expert's testimony, and was supportive of the opinions of defendant's expert. We have little difficulty concluding from the record presented here that the SART video constituted 'favorable' evidence under *Brady*." 162 Cal.App.4th at 1475.

The SART videotape was favorable evidence, because it tended to negate an element of the crime for which the defendant was charged and it constituted evidence that contradicted the prosecution's expert witness. Because the favorable evidence was generated and held by an agency that was assisting the prosecution in the criminal action against the defendant, the suppression of the evidence was attributable to the prosecution.

The Court of Appeal rejected the prosecution's argument that the SART examination was non-investigative. "A major purpose of the examination was to determine whether the allegation [of the sexual assault] could be corroborated with physical findings. [The physician assistant who conducted the examination] collected and preserved physical evidence, consistent with statutory protocol . . . [and the physician assistant] provided a copy of the forensic report to the police." 162 Cal.App.4th at 1479.

The Court of Appeal rejected the argument that the SART examination constituted private treatment of the victim. The Court stated that the examination was initiated by a law enforcement referral in the investigation of criminal conduct. Law enforcement was given quick access to the medical report that was generated by the SART examination. Photographs taken during the examination were also used for an investigative purpose, so it did not matter that the source material for the photographs was also used for a non-investigative purpose. 162 Cal.App.4th at 1480–1481.

The Court concluded that because the SART team acted on the government's behalf and assisted the government's case, the SART team and its personnel were part of the prosecution team for *Brady* purposes. 162 Cal.App.4th at 1481.

§ 1:68 "Prosecution team"—partial agency membership in team

The concept that an agency can be a member of the prosecution team when carrying out one function and outside the scope of that team when carrying out another function is critically important to a determination of the prosecution's responsibilities for disclosing material evidence favorable to a defendant.

§ 1:68.2 Authority supporting partial agency membership

The California Supreme Court has joined the California Courts of Appeal and the federal courts of appeals in recognizing that a law enforcement agency which has multiple and separate functions is a member of the prosecution team when it functions as an investigative agency, but remains outside the team in its incarceration capacity. In this situation the law enforcement agency has a partial membership in the prosecution team.

In *People v. Jacinto* (2010) 49 Cal.4th 263, 109 Cal.Rptr.3d 610, 231 P.3d 341, the Sheriff of Sonoma County investigated a stabbing that had occurred in a restaurant. The defendant was charged with attempted murder and assault with a deadly weapon. One of the witnesses to the stabbing was an illegal alien who was later incarcerated in the county jail on an unrelated domestic violence charge. An investigator hired by the defense interviewed the incarcerated witness and determined that he could give testimony that would be favorable to the defendant. The sheriff's jail staff later released the witness to federal authorities for deportation at the request of the Immigration and Naturalization Service. As a consequence, that witness was not available for the defense to utilize in trial.

The defendant moved to dismiss the charges on the grounds that the deportation deprived him of his rights under the Due Process Clause and the Compulsory Process Clause. The trial court granted the motion and the prosecution appealed. The Court of Appeal reversed the dismissal of the charges, and the defendant petitioned for review in the California Supreme Court.

The California Supreme Court affirmed the order of the Court of Appeal reversing the dismissal of the charges. The Supreme Court concluded that the deportation of the witness was not the result of prosecutorial misconduct. 49 Cal.4th at 270. The Court reasoned that since it was not the prosecutor who caused or facilitated the deportation of the defense witness, the deportation would be chargeable to the prosecution only if the sheriff's jail officials were part of the prosecution team.

The Court concluded that the sheriff's jail officials were not part of the prosecution team, even though the sheriff's criminal investigators handled the investigation of the charges against the defendant, and even though those criminal investigators were part of the prosecution team. The Court stated: "[F]ormal identity between sheriff's deputies operating and providing protective services in the jail and detectives in the law enforcement division investigating crimes does not automatically render the deputies assigned to the jail members of the prosecution team. Absent some additional showing of affirmative prosecutorial involvement in [the witness's] removal, we cannot hold the prosecutor legally responsible merely because a sheriff's deputy working at the jail was involved." The Supreme Court quoted with approval the words of the Court of Appeal that " '[t]he sheriff's department was no more than the custodian of witness Esparza. In this case, it was not part of the prosecutorial investigative team . . . [and] the action of the sheriff's department or county jail personnel may not be attributed to the prosecution.' " 49 Cal.4th at 270–271.

In reaching this holding the California Supreme Court ratified the *partial agency membership doctrine* to determine the prosecution team for purposes of the *Brady* rule.

§ 1:68.4   Partial membership by sheriff—as investigating agency and as jailor

When criminal investigators working for the sheriff of a county conduct a criminal investigation, the criminal investigative division of the sheriff's office is part of the prosecution team. But sheriff's employees working in the sheriff's county jail do not thereby become members of the prosecution team.

In *People v. Jacinto* (2010) 49 Cal.4th 263, 109 Cal.Rptr.3d 610, 231 P.3d 341, the sheriff of Sonoma County investigated a stabbing that had occurred in a restaurant. The defendant was charged with attempted murder and assault with a deadly weapon. One of the witnesses to the stabbing was an illegal alien who was later incarcerated in the county jail on an unrelated domestic violence charge. An investigator hired by the defense interviewed the incarcerated witness and determined that he could give testimony that would be favorable to the defendant. The sheriff's jail staff later released the witness to federal authorities for deportation at the request of the Immigration and Naturalization Service. As a consequence, that witness was not available for the defense to utilize in trial.

The defendant moved to dismiss the charges on the grounds that the deportation deprived him of his rights under the Due Process Clause and the Compulsory Process Clause. The trial court granted the motion and the prosecution appealed. The Court of Appeal reversed the dismissal of the charges, and the defendant petitioned for review in the California Supreme Court.

The California Supreme Court affirmed the order of the Court of Appeal reversing the dismissal of the charges. The Supreme Court concluded that the deportation of the witness was not the result of prosecutorial misconduct 49 Cal.4th at 270. The Court reasoned that since it was not the prosecutor who caused or facilitated the deportation of the defense witness, the deportation would be chargeable to the prosecution only if the sheriff's jail officials were part of the prosecution team.

The Court concluded that the sheriff's jail officials were not part of the prosecution team, even though the sheriff's criminal investigators handled the investigation of the charges against the defendant, and even though those criminal investigators were part of the prosecution team. The Court stated: "[F]ormal identity between sheriff's deputies operating and providing protective services in the jail and detectives in the law enforcement division investigating crimes does not automatically render the deputies assigned to the jail members of the prosecution team. Absent some additional showing of affirmative prosecutorial involvement in [the witness's] removal, we cannot hold the prosecutor legally responsible merely because a sheriff's deputy working at the jail was involved." The Supreme Court quoted with approval the words of the Court of Appeal that " '[t]he sheriff's department was no more than the custodian of witness Esparza. In this case, it was not part of the prosecutorial investigative team . . . [and] the action of the sheriff's department or county jail personnel may not be attributed to the prosecution.' " 49 Cal.4th at 270–271.

In reaching this holding the California Supreme Court ratified the *partial agency membership doctrine* to determine the prosecution team for purposes of the *Brady* rule. The fact that the criminal investigative branch of the sheriff's office becomes part of the prosecution team by virtue of their work investigating a criminal offense does not cause other employees in separate branches of the Sheriff's Office—such as county jail officials—to thereby become members of the prosecution team.

§1:70 "Prosecution team" nonmembers—generally

Nonmembers of the prosecution team consist of any person or entity which is not part of the investigation or prosecution of the case. The persons and entities which are not part of the prosecution team are widespread and varied.

§1:70.1 Victims and citizen witnesses

Because victims and citizen witnesses are not members of the prosecution team, evidence and information possessed by these persons is not constructively imputed to the prosecution team.

In *Johnson v. Norris* (2008, CA8 AR) 537 F.3d 840, the defendant was charged with murder. The daughter of the murder victim identified the defendant as the killer. The defendant's petition to the trial court for an order granting him access to the daughter's psychotherapy records was denied on the grounds that the prosecution did not have access to those records. The defendant was convicted and sentenced to death. After exhausting his appellate remedies the defendant filed a habeas corpus petition in the federal courts. In his petition the defendant argued that the denial of access to the daughter's psychotherapy records constituted a *Brady* violation, because it prevented him from using those records to impeach the daughter during her testimony.

The Eighth Circuit Court of Appeals rejected the defendant's argument, holding that the record did "not refute the state court's determination that the prosecution had no access to records of [the daughter's] psychotherapy treatment." 537 F.3d at 847. Implicit in the Court's decision is a determination that the daughter as an ordinary prosecution witness was not a member of the prosecution team, and her knowledge and psychotherapy records were not constructively imputed to the prosecution for purposes of the *Brady* rule.

Likewise, in *United States v. Sarras* (2009, CA11 FL) 575 F.3d 1191, a defendant charged in federal court with sexually abusing his minor stepdaughter moved the court for an order requiring the government to produce the computers and camera belonging to the alleged victim and her mother. The district court denied the motion, and the defendant was convicted. On appeal the defendant argued that the trial court erred in denying his discovery motion. The Eleventh Circuit Court of Appeals rejected the defendant's argument, holding that because the items were in the possession and control of the minor victim and her mother, these items were not possessed by the prosecution team. The Court ruled that the victim and her mother were third parties to the criminal prosecution, not members of the prosecution team. 575 F.3d at 1214–1215.

§ 1:70.2   Non-investigating prosecution expert witnesses

In *Avila v. Quarterman* (2009, CA5 TX) 560 F.3d 299, the Fifth Circuit Court of Appeals reached a decision that agreed with the Second Circuit Court of Appeals in *United States v. Skelly* (2006, CA2 NY) 442 F.3d 94, and *United States v. Stewart* (2006, CA2 NY) 433 F.3d 273—that a witness who testifies as an expert witness for the prosecution does not thereby automatically become a member of the prosecution team, and information favorable to the defendant known to that witness, but not to the prosecution, is not constructively imputed to the prosecution team.

In *Avila* the defendant was convicted of the murder of a 19-month-old child, after the child was left alone with the defendant by the child's mother. The child was taken to a hospital with abdominal injuries which caused his death. A pathologist in his capacity as a physician at the hospital prepared a pathology report regarding the child's injuries. Although the prosecution at first intended to call the pathologist to testify at trial, the prosecution ultimately used other expert witness testimony. The defendant was convicted of capital murder and sentenced to death.

Following his conviction the defendant learned that the pathologist had formed an opinion that the child had suffered only one blow causing his injuries. This opinion was contrary to the prosecution's expert witness evidence that the child suffered three stomps or kicks. The defendant contended that the expert's opinion constituted favorable evidence for him, because it could have enabled him to contend that his conduct resulted from a sudden loss of control, not a conscious desire to kill the child. The state court hearing the defendant's habeas corpus petition found that the prosecution did not know of the pathologist's opinion and rejected the defendant's argument that the nondisclosure of the pathologist's opinion constituted *Brady* error.

In his federal habeas petition the defendant contended that the prosecution's lack of knowledge of the pathologist's opinion did not negate *Brady* error, because the pathologist was part of the prosecution team, and the pathologist's opinion was constructively imputed to the prosecutor. Thus, the prosecutor's failure to disclose the pathologist's opinion violated *Brady*. The district court granted the habeas petition on this basis, and the government cross-appealed. The Fifth Circuit Court of Appeals reversed the order of the district court, holding that the government had not committed *Brady* error. The Court of Appeals concluded that the pathologist did not become part of the prosecution team—that his role was only that of a pathologist prepared to testify as an expert witness for the prosecution. Because he did not become part of the prosecution team, the Court of Appeals concluded that knowledge of the pathologist's opinion is not imputed to the prosecution. 560 F.3d at 306–309.

§ 1:70.3   Attorney for crime victim or witness

In *Murdoch v. Castro* (2010, CA9 CA) 609 F.3d 983, a prosecution witness and participant in a murder apparently wrote a letter to his attorney in which he claimed that the defendant was not involved in the murder and that he (the witness) had been coerced into implicating the defendant. The prosecutor informed the court and the defendant of this information when the prosecutor learned of it. The defendant's efforts to gain access to the letter in state court were rejected by the trial judge, who ruled in the face of an assertion by the witness's attorney of the attorney-client privilege that the letter was a protected attorney-client communication. The defendant was convicted of murder and sentenced to life in prison without the possibility of parole.

After exhausting his appellate remedies and state court habeas proceedings, the defendant filed a habeas petition in the federal courts in which he argued, *inter alia*, that the trial court had erred in ruling on his discovery request. Following the district court's denial of his habeas petition, the defendant appealed to the Court of Appeals. The Ninth Circuit Court of Appeals *en banc* rejected the defendant's argument regarding his denied access to the witness's letter, holding that since the attorney-client privilege protects only the communications between the attorney and the client, and not the subject matter of those communications, the defendant remained free to question the witness at trial regarding the matters contained in the letter. The Court of Appeals did not address the question whether its ruling would have been different had the letter been possessed by the prosecution team, as opposed to its possession by the attorney for a witness, a third party to the criminal prosecution.

§ 1:70.5   Non-investigating law enforcement agencies

It is becoming increasingly clear that under California law agencies which have not participated in the investigation or prosecution of a defendant are not considered to be part of the prosecution team.

§ 1:70.5.1   Non-investigating law enforcement agencies and the *Brady* rule

Possession by a law enforcement agency that does not participate in the criminal prosecution at issue is not attributed to the investigating agency, because the non-participating law enforcement agency is not a member of the prosecution team in that case.

In *Owen v. Sec'y for the Dep't of Corr.* (2009, CA11 FL) 568 F.3d 894, the defendant was convicted of the murder and sexual battery of a woman in her home and sentenced to death. After the defendant had exhausted his direct appeals, he ultimately filed a habeas corpus petition in the federal court. His habeas petition alleged, *inter alia*, that the prosecution had committed *Brady* error in failing to disclose to him the notes made by a therapist from therapy sessions conducted upon the defendant pursuant to a court order in a prior case in Michigan. The defendant alleged he was informed that the FBI had gained possession of the notes, and that by failing to disclose those notes to him, the state agency prosecuting his murder case deprived him of favorable evidence he could have used to defend against the charge. The district court denied the habeas petition, and the defendant appealed.

The Eleventh Circuit Court of Appeals rejected the defendant's *Brady* argument on the basis that the defendant failed to establish that the state of Florida authorities possessed the therapist's notes. The Court observed:

> "[The petitioner] never demonstrated that the State had the notes, or that the State and the FBI had sufficiently pooled their resources such that the information in the FBI's possession could be imputed to the State . . . . Indeed, we have unearthed nothing in the record that suggests either that the FBI had substantial involvement in the [murder case], or that the State ever had access to, or knowledge of, [the therapist's] notes." 568 F.3d at 921.

As a non-member of the prosecution team in Owen's murder prosecution, any exculpatory evidence possessed by the FBI was therefore not attributed to the prosecution team in his case.

In *People v. Ervine* (2009) 47 Cal.4th 745, 102 Cal.Rptr.3d 786, 220 P.3d 820, the defendant was charged in Lassen County with the murder of a peace officer and the attempted murder of three other peace officers. The defendant's motion for a change of venue was granted and the case was moved to Sacramento County.

While the defendant was incarcerated in the Sacramento County jail pending trial, Sacramento County sheriff's deputies searched the defendant's jail cell and read his legal papers. The defendant's resulting motion to dismiss the charges against him was denied, in the face of evidence that neither the investigating agency nor the prosecutor had known of this conduct by the jail personnel, nor had they received any information from the Sacramento County deputies who had read the defendant's papers.

The defendant was convicted of murder and attempted murder of peace officers and sentenced to death. On automatic appeal to the California Supreme Court, the defendant contended that the prosecution had committed misconduct by reading his legal mail, and that the trial court had erred in denying his motion to dismiss. The California Supreme Court rejected the defendant's argument.

Citing and quoting from its opinion in *In re Steele* (2004) 32 Cal.4th 682, 10 Cal.Rptr.3d 536, 85 P.3d 444, the Supreme Court observed that it had already ruled that " 'information possessed by an agency that has no connection to the investigation or prosecution of the criminal charge against the defendant is not possessed by the prosecution team.' [citation omitted]" 47 Cal.4th at 768. The Court held that "misconduct by a government agent who has no involvement in the investigation or prosecution of the criminal charge against the defendant cannot automatically be imputed to the prosecution team for purposes of the Sixth Amendment." 47 Cal.4th at 768.

Because there was "no evidence that anyone involved with either the investigation or prosecution of his case participated in or was even aware of the misconduct by the Sacramento County Sheriff's Department," the defendant's Sixth Amendment rights had not been violated by the prosecution. 47 Cal.4th at 768. The Sacramento County Sheriff's office, which had no part in the investigation or prosecution of the defendant's case, was not a member of the prosecution team in his case.

§ 1:70.5.2 Non-investigating law enforcement agencies and the Criminal Discovery Statute

In *Barnett v. Superior Court* (2010) 50 Cal.4th 890, 114 Cal.Rptr.3d 576, 237 P.3d 980, the California Supreme Court reaffirmed its holding in *In re Steele* (2004) 32 Cal.4th 682, 696, 10 Cal.Rptr.3d 536, 85 P.3d 444, that law enforcement agencies which have not participated in the investigation of the criminal charges against the defendant are not part of the prosecution team within the meaning of Penal Code section 1054.9. In *Barnett* the Court stated: "Reading all of these provisions [section 1054.1, section 1054.5, and section 1054.9] together, we concluded [in *Steele*] that the pretrial discovery obligations and section 1054.9's discovery rights 'do not extend to materials possessed by law enforcement agencies that were not involved in investigating or preparing the case against the defendant.' [citation omitted]" 50 Cal. 4th at 902.

See the discussion in Section 3:19.7 of this supplement [Information possessed by law enforcement agency not acting on the government's behalf in the case].

§ 1:70.5.5 Independent investigating agencies

An independent and separate governmental agency that conducts its own investigation is not part of the prosecution team, unless that agency's investigators have worked jointly with the agency conducting the criminal investigation of the defendant, and evidence obtained by the independent investigating agency and not also possessed by the criminal investigators is not deemed to be possessed by the prosecution team. *See, e.g., United States v. Faulkenberry* (2010, CA6 OH) 614 F.3d 573, 589.

§ 1:70.7 Private business entities

In *United States v. Sarras* (2009, CA11 FL) 575 F.3d 1191, a defendant charged in federal court with sexually abusing his minor step-daughter moved the court for an order requiring the government to disclose medical records of tests performed upon the alleged victim. The district court denied the motion, and the defendant was convicted. On appeal the defendant argued that the trial court erred in denying his discovery motion. The Eleventh Circuit Court of Appeals rejected the defendant's argument, holding that because the items were in the possession and control of the Kid's House of Seminole County, none of these records were possessed by the prosecution team. The Court ruled that the defendant should have followed subpoena duces tecum procedures for obtaining records from third parties to the criminal prosecution, because the private business entity which possessed the victim's records was not a member of the prosecution team. 575 F.3d at 1214–1215.

In *United States v. Gray* (2011, CA7 IN) 648 F.3d 562, a defendant convicted of Medicaid fraud and conspiracy to defraud the United States government claimed on appeal that the prosecution had suppressed exculpatory evidence in violation of *Brady*. The evidence in issue was information supplied to the government by EDS, a private company hired by the State of Indiana to process and pay Medicaid claims. The critical data was not in the file that the government had initially received from EDS, but was extracted from EDS's database during the defendant's trial at the government's request and then supplied to the defendant. The defendant argued that the government's failure to direct EDS to extract this data from its database prior to trial constituted a suppression of exculpatory evidence.

The Court of Appeals rejected the defendant's argument. The Court reasoned that "EDS was not a part of the prosecutorial team. . . . It was not a private detective agency hired by the state agency to assist state and federal prosecutors in prosecuting Medicaid fraud. Medicaid fraud investigators were part of the prosecutorial team, but EDS was not. Because it does the billing for Indiana Medicaid, the company has records that can be useful as evidence in fraud prosecutions. But the defense had the same access to those records as the prosecutors did, and so there was no *suppression* of evidence. [citations omitted]" 648 F.3d at 566–567. The Court of Appeals then concluded: "To charge prosecutors with knowledge of exculpatory evidence buried in the computer databases of institutions that collect and store vast amounts of digitized data would be an unreasonable extension of the *Brady* rule. The courts, rightly in our view, have refused to make it." 648 F.3d at 566–567.

§ 1:70.11   County hospitals and medical clinics

A governmentally created team whose function is to examine victims of alleged sexual assault in order to gain evidence to be used in a criminal prosecution of the perpetrator of the assault becomes part of the prosecution team which may not suppress or fail to disclose material exculpatory evidence to the defendant. For this purpose it does not matter that the facility in which the examination is performed is a county hospital or a private hospital.

In *People v. Uribe* (2008) 162 Cal.App.4th 1457, 76 Cal.Rptr.3d 829, the defendant was convicted of two counts of aggravated sexual assault on his granddaughter, who was a minor. The minor child was examined by a physician assistant, who performed what is known as a sexual assault response team (SART) examination. The SART examination was video-taped, and the existence of the videotape was not disclosed to the defendant, who learned of the videotape after his conviction at trial.

One of the contested issues at trial was whether the victim had been sexually assaulted. Expert testimony on that issue was presented by the prosecution and the defense. After learning of the videotape, the defendant made a motion for a new trial, arguing that he had been denied *Brady* evidence—evidence from the videotape that showed that the victim had not been sexually assaulted. The trial court denied the new trial motion.

The Court of Appeal reversed the conviction and remanded the case to the trial court for a new trial. The Court concluded that the declaration of the defendant's expert in support of the new-trial motion "established that the SART video was favorable both because it offered potential evidence impeaching a prosecution expert's testimony, and was supportive of the opinions of defendant's expert. We have little difficulty concluding from the record presented here that the SART video constituted 'favorable' evidence under *Brady*." 162 Cal.App.4th at 1475.

The SART videotape was favorable evidence, because it tended to negate an element of the crime for which the defendant was charged, and because it constituted evidence that contradicted the prosecution's expert witness. Because the favorable evidence was generated and held by an agency that was assisting the prosecution in the criminal action against the defendant, the suppression of the evidence was attributable to the prosecution.

The Court of Appeal rejected the conclusion of the trial court that under the authority of *People v. Webb* (1993) 6 Cal.4th 494, 24 Cal.Rptr.2d 779, 862 P.2d 779, the SART examination was not possessed by the prosecution team, because it was possessed by a county hospital or clinic. The Court of Appeal observed that in *Webb* the hospital records were not generated or obtained by the prosecution in the course of a criminal investigation, and the prosecution had no greater access to those records than the defendant. 162 Cal.App.4th at 1480. The Court of Appeal noted that the sexual assault examination of the child "was initiated through a referral by the police in their investigation of a report of criminal conduct. And the prosecution had greater access to the records generated from the exam than defendant since [the physician assistant], in compliance with the law [citations omitted], forwarded the report to law enforcement." 162 Cal.App.4th at 1480–1481.

The Court of Appeal concluded that "when it performed [the victim's] SART exam, including the collection of data necessary for the report, the Center at Valley Medical was, in fact, 'acting on the government's behalf or assisting the government's case. [citation omitted]' In this instance, the personnel in the Center at Valley Medical responsible for conducting SART exams . . . were part of the 'prosecuting team' for Brady purposes." 162 Cal.App.4th at 1481.

§ 1:70.12   Government agencies unassociated with prosecution or investigation of case

In *United States v. Redcorn* (2008, CA10 OK) 528 F.3d 727, the defendants were convicted in federal district court of embezzlement from a health care benefit program. Two months after their conviction the Oklahoma Insurance Department, which is a state agency, provided the defendants with more than 500 pages of documents that the Department had not previously produced in response to a defense subpoena. The defendants' motion for a new trial because of newly discovered evidence was denied.

On appeal the defendants claimed that the prosecution had violated its *Brady* duty by failing to disclose the documents held by the Insurance Department, an argument the defendants had not made in the district court. The Tenth Circuit Court of Appeals rejected the newly raised *Brady* argument. The Court found that the documents had never been disclosed to the government and were not in the government's possession. The Court concluded: "We find nothing in the cases to show that federal prosecutors may be held responsible for the omissions of a state regulatory agency—an arm of a different government altogether—and nothing in the record of this case to indicate that the U.S. Attorney's Office and the OID had a working relationship close enough to trigger such a rule if it existed." 528 F.3d at 744.

§ 1:70.14   Courts

Although courts are not part of the "prosecution team," when the court or the probation department, which is an arm of the court, possesses potentially exculpatory evidence, such as might be found in the pre-sentence report of a co-defendant, or in the transcript of an *in camera* hearing involving the court and a prosecution witness, the court has a *Brady*–type duty to examine that evidence in order to release material exculpatory or impeachment evidence contained therein to the defendant. "*Brady* does not apply in the traditional sense because the Government did not have possession of [the] exculpatory information that it should have disclosed to the defense." *United States v. Ogba* (2008, CA5 TX) 526 F.3d 214, 222, n.11. *See United States v. Jackson* (1992, CA5 TX) 978 F.2d 903, 909 [pre-sentence reports possessed by the court treated as if they were possessed by the prosecution and subject to the *Brady* rule].

Although the prosecution team does not include the courts, when a defendant identifies potential exculpatory evidence in the presentence report of a prosecution witness and requests disclosure of that evidence, the court may and should conduct an *in-camera* review of that report to determine if it contains evidence that, if possessed by the prosecution team, would constitute *Brady* or *Giglio* evidence. *See United States v. Garcia* (2009, CA8 SD) 562 F.3d 947, 952–953.

§ 1:70.15   Probation offices

Although probation offices are not normally treated as if they were part of the "prosecution team," when the court or the probation department, which is an arm of the court, possesses potentially exculpatory evidence, such as might be found in the pre-sentence report of a co-defendant, the court has a *Brady*-type duty to examine that evidence in order to release exculpatory or impeachment evidence contained therein to the defendant. "*Brady* does not apply in the traditional sense because the Government did not have possession of [the] exculpatory information that it should have disclosed to the defense." *United States v. Ogba* (2008, CA5 TX) 526 F.3d 214, 222, n.11. *See United States v. Jackson* (1992, CA5 TX) 978 F.2d 903, 909 [pre-sentence reports possessed by the court treated as if they were possessed by the prosecution and subject to the *Brady* rule].

Although probation offices, like the courts for which they are an arm, are not a member of the prosecution team, when a defendant identifies potential exculpatory evidence in the presentence report of a prosecution witness—a report that is normally possessed by the probation office and the court—and requests disclosure of that evidence, the court may and should conduct an *in-camera* review of that report to determine if it contains evidence that, if possessed by the prosecution team, would constitute *Brady* or *Giglio* evidence. *See United States v. Garcia* (2009, CA8 SD) 562 F.3d 947, 952–953.

A criminal defendant does not have a due process right to disclosure of a probation officer's recommended sentence or action, as long as any factual information in the recommendation that the court relies upon in its sentencing of the defendant is disclosed. *United States v. Whitlock* (2011, CA9 ID) 639 F.3d 935, 940–941. *See also United States v. Baldrich* (2006, CA9 CA) 471 F.3d 1110, 1113–1114.

A probation officer who receives information from a government witness in the process of preparing a pre-sentence report is not a member of the prosecution team, and knowledge of allegedly exculpatory evidence learned by that probation officer in preparing that report is not attributed to the prosecutor or the prosecution team without some evidence that the prosecutor or some agent working for the prosecutor had this information before or during the defendant's trial. *United States v. Rivera-Rodriguez* (2010, CA1 PR) 617 F.3d 581, 595.

California Penal Code section 1203.05(a) provides that when a new criminal charge is filed against a defendant, probation reports of the defendant filed in connection with prior cases of that defendant are open to the public for inspection until 60 days after judgment is pronounced or probation is granted in the new case, whichever is earlier.

§ 1:70.17 Foreign governments

A foreign government which has not joined investigative or prosecution forces with the prosecution team is not part of the prosecution team, and that government's possession of favorable information or evidence is not attributed to the prosecution team.

In *United States v. Reyeros* (2008, CA3 NJ) 537 F.3d 270, the defendants were prosecuted in federal court for offenses related to a conspiracy to import cocaine into the United States. One of the defendants was extradited from Columbia to face these charges. That defendant demanded the prosecution obtain and disclose documents he had filed with Columbian authorities opposing his extradition. The defendant argued that even if the prosecution did not actually possess these documents, the prosecution constructively possessed them, because Columbia had cooperated with the United States in their investigation of the defendant. The district court denied the defendant's request, and he was convicted.

On appeal the Third Circuit Court of Appeals rejected the defendant's argument that the denial of his request for the documents from Columbia violated the *Brady* rule. The Court applied the analysis it had previously developed in *United States v. Risha* (2006, CA3 PA) 445 F.3d 298, to hold that the prosecution team did not include the Columbian government. In determining that there was no cross-jurisdictional constructive possession of the documents possessed by the Columbian government, the Court of Appeals concluded that the Columbian government had not intermingled its forces with the United States prosecuting authorities, had not been part of the American prosecution team, had not engaged in a joint prosecution effort with the American prosecution team, and had not shared any investigative resources with the American prosecution team. Finally, the Court reasoned that the record suggested that the prosecution team did not have access to the documents in the court file of that defendant on his extradition proceedings in Columbia.

§ 1:70.17.1   Indian reservations

Indian nations were "separate sovereigns pre-existing the Constitution . . . ." *Santa Clara Pueblo v. Martinez* (1978) 436 U.S. 49, 56, 98 S.Ct. 1670, 56 L.Ed.2d 106. Accordingly, Indian tribes "have historically been regarded as unconstrained by those constitutional provisions framed specifically as limitations on federal or state authority." *Santa Clara Pueblo v. Martinez, supra,* 436 U.S. at 56.

Although the United States Constitution is the supreme law of the land, it is part of the laws of the United States, and binds Indian nations "only where it expressly binds them, or is made binding by treaty or some act of Congress." *Native American Church v. Navajo Tribal Council* (1969, CA10 NM) 272 F.2d 131, 134–135. Indian nations are "domestic dependent nations," *Cherokee Nation v. Georgia* (1831) 30 U.S. (5 Pet.) 1, 17, 8 L.Ed. 25, and are under the protection of the United States government. An Indian tribe is much like a state or political entity within the United States.

The United States Congress "has plenary authority to limit, modify or eliminate the powers of local self-government which the tribes otherwise possess." *Santa Clara Pueblo v. Martinez, supra,* 436 U.S. at 56. Article I, section 8 of the United States Constitution gives Congress the power to regulate commerce with Indian tribes. *United States v. Antelope* (1977) 430 U.S. 641, 97 S.Ct. 1395, 51 L.Ed.2d 701. *See generally, People v. Ramirez* (2007) 148 Cal.App.4th 1464, 1469–1470, 56 Cal.Rptr.3d 631.

Indian reservations are treated as independent territory to the extent that Congress has not granted state jurisdiction over offenses committed by or against Indians in "Indian country."

In 1953 Congress enacted Public Law 280. Public Law 280 gave six states—Alaska, California, Minnesota, Nebraska, Oregon and Wisconsin—criminal jurisdiction over tribal members and other people on Indian reservations. The heart of Public Law 280 is found in 18 U.S.C. sec. 1162. Subdivision (a) of Section 1162 provides that:

"[e]ach of the States or Territories listed in the following table shall have jurisdiction over offenses committed by or against Indians in the areas of Indian country listed opposite the name of the State or Territory to the same extent that such State or Territory has jurisdiction over offenses committed elsewhere within the State or Territory, and the criminal laws of such State or Territory shall have the same force and effect within such Indian country as they have elsewhere within the State or Territory."

Section 1162 granted state jurisdiction over criminal offenses to Alaska, California, Minnesota, Nebraska, Oregon, and Wisconsin. Three of these states, California, Nebraska, and Wisconsin, have jurisdiction over criminal offenses in all Indian country within their state. The other three have jurisdiction over all Indian country, except for named reservations for which federal jurisdiction is reserved. *Anderson v. Gladden* (1961, CA9 OR) 293 F.2d 463.

The grant of state jurisdiction extends to and includes Indian reservations which were created after Section 1162 was enacted in 1953. *United States v. Hoodie* (1978, CA9 OR) 588 F.2d 292. The grant of state jurisdiction does not give these six states exclusive jurisdiction over offenses that arise under federal laws having general application. *United States v. Anderson* (2004, CA9 CA) 391 F.3d 1083.

The Ninth Circuit Court of Appeals held in *Bishop Paiute Tribe v. County of Inyo* (2002, CA9 CA) 291 F.3d 549, *vacated on other grounds and remanded, Inyo County v. Paiute-Shoshone Indians of the Bishop Cmty. Of the Bishop Colony* (2003) 538 U.S. 701, 123 S.Ct. 1887, 155 L.Ed.2d 933, that Section 1162 granted jurisdiction to the State of California over criminal *offenses* committed by or against Indians in Indian country in California, but did not confer state jurisdiction over the Indian *tribes* themselves. 291 F.3d at 556–557. Thus, concluded the Ninth Circuit, the tribes themselves retained their sovereign immunity, which includes immunity from the processes of California state courts. 291 F.3d at 557. Therefore, held the Ninth Circuit, California state courts may not issue a warrant to search and seize the records and property of an Indian tribe in California. 291 F.3d at 557–560.

Indian tribes retain attributes of sovereignty over their members and their land, and that sovereignty is dependent upon and subordinate to only the United States Government, not a state government. *California v. Cabazon Band of Mission Indians* (1987) 480 U.S. 202, 207, 107 S.Ct. 1083, 94 L.Ed.2d 244. Indian tribes retain their sovereign power to operate a tribal law enforcement agency on and within an Indian reservation to enforce laws regarding crimes committed on that reservation. *Cabazon Band of Mission Indians v. Smith* (1998, C.D. CA) 34 F.Supp.2d 1195; *reversed on other grounds, Cabazon Band of Mission Indians v. Smith* (2004, CA9 CA) 388 F.3d 691.

Except when an Indian tribe participates in the investigation of a criminal act prosecuted in state court, Indian tribes in California are treated as independent sovereign powers for purposes of determining the possession component of the *Brady* rule and membership in the prosecution team. The exception to Indian tribe sovereignty is important. Indian tribes are allowed to establish tribal police forces with the power to enforce tribal criminal law against Indians on their reservations and to detain and turn over to state or local authorities non-Indians who commit suspected offenses on an Indian reservation. *United States v. Terry* (2005, CA8 SD) 400 F.3d 575, 579–580; *Ortiz-Barraza v. United States* (1975, CA9 AZ) 512 F.2d 1176, 1180. When a tribal law enforcement agency participates in the investigation of a crime that is prosecuted in state court, the tribal law enforcement agency becomes a part of the prosecution team. As the attorney for the prosecution team, the prosecutor is accountable for evidence and information possessed by and known to the tribal police force as an investigating agency.

Moreover, although the provisions of the United States Constitution do not apply to Indian nations or their governments, Indian tribal authorities are subject to the Indian Civil Rights Act (25 USC sec. 1302) enacted by Congress in 1968. Section 1302 provides, in pertinent part, that "[n]o Indian tribe in exercising powers of self-government shall . . . (8) . . . deprive any person of liberty or property without due process of law." Due process under the Indian Civil Rights Act is the same as due process in the United States Constitution. *Red Fox v. Red Fox* (1977, CA9 OR) 564 F.2d 361, 364.

While we have not found any cases involving this subject, we believe that generally-accepted principles regulating discovery of and by the prosecution team apply. Thus, although the Indian tribe is an independent sovereign, the state court has the power to hold the prosecutor accountable for the evidence held by and information known to the tribal police force as the investigating agency, in the same way that the prosecutor is accountable for evidence and information held by and known to any non-tribal law enforcement investigating agency that becomes part of the prosecution team in a criminal prosecution. In order to avoid problems that could impede the prosecutor's compliance with constitutional and statutory discovery duties, the prosecutor should implement discovery protocols and agreements with an Indian tribe when agreeing to file a criminal case in which an Indian tribe has served as an investigating agency. See Practice Tip for Prosecution below.

Practice Tip for Prosecution: While the sovereign authority of an Indian tribe can enable that tribe to decline to submit to the discovery obligations imposed upon the prosecution team, prosecutors can take steps to avoid an obstinate attitude and conduct toward the prosecution's discovery obligations by a tribal investigating agency. The prosecution should obtain a discovery cooperation agreement from the tribe when initially agreeing to file a criminal complaint in state court for a criminal act committed on or against an Indian reservation. The discovery cooperation agreement should include provisions in which the tribe agrees to provide supplemental discovery as requested by the prosecutor, material exculpatory evidence within the meaning of the *Brady* rule, and cooperation in producing tribal members who are necessary witnesses for both the prosecution and the defense in the criminal case.

The prosecutor can help ensure that a tribe will live up to a discovery cooperation agreement by dismissing cases where the tribe fails to cooperate in discovery, and by declining to file future criminal cases occurring on Indian land of a tribe which has a history of failing to provide discovery cooperation and compliance.

§ 1:70.18 Defendant's habeas counsel

Evidence that has been obtained by the habeas counsel of the defendant, and which has never been part of the files of the prosecution team, is not evidence possessed by the prosecution team. The defendant's habeas counsel is never part of the prosecution team. *See Valdovinos v. McGrath* (2010, CA9 CA) 598 F.3d 568, 577.

§ 1:71 Second element of evidence suppression—knowledge requirement

Knowledge as an element of a *Brady* suppression of evidence is an important component of the *Brady* rule.

§ 1:71.2 Constructive knowledge

The prosecution is deemed to have constructive knowledge of *Brady* evidence possessed by the investigating agency, even though the prosecutor does not actually know of that exculpatory evidence. The prosecution's constructive knowledge of such evidence arises from the prosecutor's duty to investigate and disclose favorable evidence possessed by members of the prosecution team. Because of that duty, the prosecutor *should know* of the exculpatory evidence, which constitutes constructive knowledge of that evidence. *Jackson v. Brown* (2008, CA9 CA) 513 F.3d 1057, 1074, 1075; *Harris v. Lafler* (2009, CA6 MI) 553 F.3d 1028, 1033. The prosecutor's knowledge is not gauged by what the prosecutor personally knew. The knowledge for which the prosecutor is charged is "the relevant information in the possession of *any* of its agents involved in [the defendant's] prosecution; not just what the prosecutor himself personally knew." *United States v. Price* (2009, CA9 OR) 566 F.3d 900, 908.

Although "[i]t is well settled that 'if a member of the prosecution team has knowledge of *Brady* material, such knowledge is imputed to the prosecutors, [citations omitted]," *Avila v. Quarterman* (2009, CA5 TX) 560 F.3d 299, 307, the person with actual knowledge must be a member of the prosecution team. Knowledge of exculpatory evidence by a non-member of the prosecution team is not imputed to the prosecutor. *Avila v. Quarterman, supra,* 560 F.3d at 309; *United States v. Reyeros* (2008, CA3 NJ) 537 F.3d 270.

This imputed knowledge doctrine is not without limits. Questions have been raised as to whether individual members of the investigating agency are members of the "prosecution team" whose knowledge is thereby imputed constructively to the prosecutor. This question is similar to the one discussed in § 1:64.1.1—whether individual deputy or assistant prosecutors are part of the prosecution team simply by virtue of their employment by the prosecuting agency.

In *United States v. Robinson* (2010, CA4 SC) 627 F.3d 941, it was learned post-trial that a number of the narcotics officers who had worked on the defendant's case had engaged in actions of misconduct unrelated to the officers' investigation of the defendant's case. These actions of misconduct were known only to the individual officers, and were not known to the prosecutors handling the defendant's case until after the trial. The officers were ultimately disciplined and several were fired.

On appeal the defendant argued that the prosecution had committed *Brady* error in failing to disclose these acts of misconduct, depriving him of the ability to impeach the officers' testimony at trial with these acts of misconduct. The defendant reasoned that "the knowledge of some of those who are part of the investigative team is imputed to prosecutors regardless of prosecutors' actual awareness." 627 F.3d at 951. The defendant concluded that "[b]ecause the dismissed officers obviously knew about their own misconduct and because they were working on the government's behalf . . . the prosecution violated its duty to disclose those improprieties even though no prosecutor actually knew about them." 627 F.3d at 951–952.

The Court rejected the defendant's argument. "Whatever the proper scope of *Brady's* imputed knowledge doctrine, it cannot be this broad. . . . [The defendant's] view . . . would also impose unacceptable burdens on prosecutors and the police. Courts have routinely refused to extend *Brady's* constructive knowledge doctrine where doing so would cut against the agency principles underlying imputed knowledge and would require prosecutors to do full interviews and background checks on everyone who touched the case. . . . And with good reason: it is one thing to require prosecutors to inquire about whether police have turned up exculpatory or impeachment evidence during their investigation. It is quite another to require them, on pain of a possible retrial, to conduct disciplinary inquiries into the general conduct of every officer working the case." 627 F.3d at 952.

The Court concluded that "where no one other than the officers themselves had any idea of any impropriety, and where the misconduct evidence was unrelated to [the defendant's] own investigation—the principle of imputed knowledge cannot be said to apply." 627 F.3d at 952.

The Seventh Circuit Court of Appeals reached a similar result when considering to what extent the prosecution is charged with constructive knowledge of exculpatory evidence possessed by a private business entity.

In *United States v. Gray* (2011, CA7 IN) 648 F.3d 562, a defendant convicted of Medicaid fraud and conspiracy to defraud the United States government claimed on appeal that the prosecution had suppressed exculpatory evidence in violation of *Brady*. The evidence in issue was information supplied to the government by EDS, a private company hired by the State of Indiana to process and pay Medicaid claims. The critical data was not in the file that the government had initially received from EDS, but was extracted from EDS's database during the defendant's trial at the government's request and then supplied to the defendant. The defendant argued that the government's failure to direct EDS to extract this data from its database prior to trial constituted a suppression of exculpatory evidence.

The Court of Appeals rejected the defendant's argument. The Court reasoned that "EDS was not a part of the prosecutorial team. . . . It was not a private detective agency hired by the state agency to assist state and federal prosecutors in prosecuting Medicaid fraud. Medicaid fraud investigators were part of the prosecutorial team, but EDS was not. Because it does the billing for Indiana Medicaid, the company has records that can be useful as evidence in fraud prosecutions. But the defense had the same access to those records as the prosecutors did, and so there was no *suppression* of evidence [citations omitted]" 648 F.3d at 566–567. The Court of Appeals then concluded: "To charge prosecutors with knowledge of exculpatory evidence buried in the computer databases of institutions that collect and store vast amounts of digitized data would be an unreasonable extension of the *Brady* rule. The courts, rightly in our view, have refused to make it." 648 F.3d at 566–567.

§ 1:71.3 Burden to prove knowledge

The party making a *Brady* claim, usually the defendant, "bears the initial burden of producing some evidence to support an inference that the government possessed or knew about material favorable to the defense and failed to disclose it." *United States v. Price* (2009, CA9 OR) 566 F.3d 900, 910.

§ 1:72   Prosecutor's duty to search and inquire—generally

The prosecutor has the duty to search for and inquire about exculpatory evidence within the prosecution team, and no duty to search for and inquire about exculpatory evidence outside the prosecution team. Thus, the duty to search is necessarily dependent upon a determination whether a person or entity is or is not a member of the prosecution team.

§ 1:72.1   Duty to search prosecutor's office records

The prosecutor's duty to search prosecutor's office records for *Brady* evidence is defined by the determination of the extent to which the prosecutor's office and the staff of that office are members of the prosecution team. See the discussion of this subject in Sections 1:64.1 and 1:64.1.1 in this supplement.

§ 1:72.2   Duty to search investigating agency records

The prosecutor has a duty to search the records of the investigating agency in order to determine whether those records include evidence favorable to the defendant. This duty is particularly apropos when the prosecutor has requested the investigating detective to perform work relating to potential impeachment evidence on prosecution witnesses. *United States v. Price* (2009, CA9 OR) 566 F.3d 900, 910–911 ["[T]he government has failed to demonstrate that the prosecutor satisfied his constitutional duty to learn the results of Anderson's investigation. Certainly, where the prosecutor states either that he cannot remember or does not know what information his agents relayed to him, the government's burden is not met." 566 F.3d at 910].

§ 1:72.4   Duty to search foreign government records

A foreign government which has not joined investigative or prosecution forces with the prosecution team is not part of the prosecution team. That government's possession of favorable information or evidence is not attributed to the prosecution team, and the prosecution has no duty to search the records of that foreign government for *Brady* evidence.

In *United States v. Reyeros* (2008, CA3 NJ) 537 F.3d 270, the defendants were prosecuted in federal court for offenses related to a conspiracy to import cocaine into the United States. One of the defendants was extradited from Columbia to face these charges. That defendant demanded the prosecution obtain and disclose documents he had filed with Columbian authorities opposing his extradition. The defendant argued that even if the prosecution did not actually possess these documents, the prosecution constructively possessed them, because Columbia had cooperated with the United States in their investigation of the defendant. The district court denied the defendant's request, and he was convicted.

On appeal the Third Circuit Court of Appeals rejected the defendant's argument that the denial of his request for the documents from Columbia violated the *Brady* rule. The Court applied the analysis it had previously developed in *United States v. Risha* (2006, CA3 PA) 445 F.3d 298, to hold that the prosecution team did not include the Columbian government. In determining that there was no cross-jurisdictional constructive possession of the documents possessed by the Columbian government, the Court of Appeals concluded that the Columbian government had not intermingled its forces with the United States prosecuting authorities, had not been part of the American prosecution team, had not engaged in a joint prosecution effort with the American prosecution team, and had not shared any investigative resources with the American prosecution team. The Court reasoned that the record suggested that the prosecution team did not have access to the documents in the court file of that defendant on his extradition proceedings in Columbia.

The Court concluded that there was no *Brady* violation, because not only did the prosecution not possess the records of the defendant's extradition from Columbia to the United States, but the prosecution did not have a duty to examine and obtain those records. 537 F.3d at 285.

A similar analysis governs a claim that the prosecution has a duty to search the records and information of Indian tribes. For a discussion of the status of Indian tribes as independent sovereign governments, see Section 1:70.17.1 of this supplement.

§ 1:72.6   Duty to search assisting agency/person's records

The prosecutor's duty to search the records of an agency or person assisting the investigation or prosecution of the case to determine whether those records contain exculpatory evidence arises in a number of contexts.

§ 1:72.6.1   Crime laboratories

A crime lab technician who is part of the prosecution team in a criminal prosecution is subject to suit under the federal civil rights act [42 U.S.C. section 1983] for violating the due process rights of a defendant by failing to disclose exculpatory evidence to the prosecutor, in violation of the *Brady* rule. *Brown v. Miller* (2008, CA5 LA) 519 F.3d 231, 238.

§ 1:72.6.2   Victim-witness counselors

Commonwealth v. Liang (2001) 434 Mass. 131, 747 N.E.2d 112, was cited with approval by the New Mexico Supreme Court in *Brandenburg v. Blackmer* (2005) 137 N.M. 258, 110 P.3d 66. In *Brandenburg* the prosecutor cited *Liang* for the proposition that the victim-witness counselor is part of the prosecution team in an effort to shield discovery from the defense by claiming that it was the protected work product of the prosecution. The New Mexico Supreme Court held that a victim advocate employed by the district attorney's office is part of the "prosecution team," and the rules of attorney-client confidentiality and disclosure by the State apply, because victim advocates perform many tasks similar to those of other members of the "prosecution team."

The question has been raised whether California Penal Code section 679.04 causes a victim-witness counselor to become a part of the "prosecution team," even without any direct employment relationship with the prosecutor's office. Section 679.04 requires notice to a sexual assault victim by a prosecution or law enforcement agency of the victim's right to have a victim advocate or support person at any interview or contact by law enforcement or prosecution authorities or by a criminal defense attorney. A victim advocate includes a sexual assault counselor as defined in Evidence Code section 1035.2 and an advocate working with a qualifying victim-witness center.

The legislative history of Section 679.04 does not appear to support the conclusion that the involvement of a victim advocate or counselor brings that advocate or counselor within the "prosecution team." From the time of its original enactment in 1996 through its latest amendment in 2006, Penal Code section 679.04 has been a statute intended to protect the sexual assault victim from improper interview procedures and tactics by law enforcement and from improper prosecutorial questioning. Rather than bringing victim advocates and counselors into the "prosecution team," Section 679.04 appears to treat those advocates and counselors as a shield against the "prosecution team." *See, e.g.*, the Assembly Public Safety Committee analysis of AB 807, which amended Section 679.04 [Stats. 1997 ch. 846].

§ 1:72.8   Duty to question prosecution witnesses and search their records

The prosecution does not have a duty to question its witnesses in order to determine whether they have opinions about the case, and if they do, whether those opinions would constitute evidence favorable to the defendant.

In *People v. Verdugo* (2010) 50 Cal.4th 263, 285, 113 Cal.Rptr.3d 803, 236 P.3d 1035, the defendant was charged with and ultimately convicted of two counts of first-degree murder and was sentenced to death. The vehicle of one of the victims was found at the scene of the murders. One of the investigating officers observed a whitish color mark on the victim's car. That officer also examined the defendant's vehicle, which was found at a different location. The officer did not include any conclusions regarding the white mark on the victim's vehicle in his report.

The defendant's attorney engaged the officer in an informal conversation outside the courtroom during the trial. During that conversation the defendant's attorney asked the officer about paint transfer on the victim's car and said that the transfer looked white, so it would seem that it came from a white car. The officer replied that in his opinion the transfer could have come from any color car or it could have been a wax or lacquer transfer from the outer or protective coating of the other vehicle that had struck the victim's vehicle. The defendant's vehicle was black.

The defendant's attorney reported this conversation to the trial court, contending that the officer's failure to include his opinion in his report constituted a discovery violation. The trial court found no discovery violation, because the officer was not qualified as a paint expert.

The defendant argued on appeal that the failure of the officer to include his opinion in his report did not alert the defense to the need to find an expert who would have testified that the mark was white paint from a white car, and, therefore, deprived the defense of exculpatory evidence. The Supreme Court rejected the defendant's argument, holding that "the prosecution cannot be faulted for failing to disclose [the officer's] nonexpert opinion about the white mark, because there is no evidence that the prosecution knew [the officer's] opinion." 50 Cal.4th at 288.

The Court concluded that the prosecution had no duty to question the officer concerning his nonexpert opinion regarding a possible paint transfer, and, therefore the prosecution did not commit a *Brady* violation. 50 Cal.4th at 288–289.

§ 1:73 Limits on constructive knowledge and duty to search

The duty of the prosecution to search agencies in the prosecution team does not require the prosecutor to search the entirety of those agencies and their personnel looking for exculpatory evidence. The *Brady* principle that imposes constructive knowledge and possession upon the prosecution does not create an unlimited duty to search within the prosecution team.

§ 1:73.1 Persons outside prosecution team

The *Brady* rule does not require the prosecution to disclose items it does not possess, look for evidence outside the prosecution team of which it has no knowledge, or attempt to obtain evidence from outside the prosecution team which the team does not already possess. *Parker v. Allen* (2009, CA11 AL) 565 F.3d 1258, 1277; *United States v. Sarras* (2009, CA11 FL) 575 F.3d 1191, 1215.

§ 1:73.3 Uninvolved staff

Even though an agency is part of the prosecution team in a criminal prosecution, not all staff of that agency are part of the team. Only those staff that have participated in the investigation or prosecution of the case are part of the team.

For a complete discussion of the limitations of membership in the prosecution team of personnel employed by the prosecuting attorney's office and by the investigating agency, see Sections 1:64.1 and 1:64.1.1 in this supplement.

§ 1:73.5 Unrelated misconduct known only to the miscreant

Whether individual members of the investigating agency are members of the "prosecution team" whose knowledge is thereby imputed constructively to the prosecutor raises an interesting issue. The question is this one: if individual investigating officers of the investigating agency are individually members of the prosecution team for purposes of the *Brady* rule, is the knowledge of these officers about their own personal misconduct unrelated to their investigation of the defendant's case constructively imputed to the prosecution team? This question is similar to the one discussed in § 1:64.1.1—whether individual deputy or assistant prosecutors are part of the prosecution team simply by virtue of their employment by the prosecuting agency.

In *United States v. Robinson* (2010, CA4 SC) 627 F.3d 941, it was learned post-trial that a number of the narcotics officers who had worked on the defendant's case had engaged in actions of misconduct unrelated to the officers' investigation of the defendant's case. These actions of misconduct were known only to the individual officers, and were not known to the prosecutors handling the defendant's case until after the trial. The officers were ultimately disciplined and several were fired.

On appeal the defendant argued that the prosecution had committed *Brady* error in failing to disclose these acts of misconduct, depriving him of the ability to impeach the officers' testimony at trial with these acts of misconduct. The defendant reasoned that "the knowledge of some of those who are part of the investigative team is imputed to prosecutors regardless of prosecutors' actual awareness." 627 F.3d at 951. The defendant concluded that "[b]ecause the dismissed officers obviously knew about their own misconduct and because they were working on the government's behalf . . . the prosecution violated its duty to disclose those improprieties even though no prosecutor actually knew about them." 627 F.3d at 951–952.

The Court rejected the defendant's argument. "Whatever the proper scope of *Brady's* imputed knowledge doctrine, it cannot be this broad. . . . [The defendant's] view . . . would also impose unacceptable burdens on prosecutors and the police. Courts have routinely refused to extend *Brady's* constructive knowledge doctrine where doing so would cut against the agency principles underlying imputed knowledge and would require prosecutors to do full interviews and background checks on everyone who touched the case. . . . And with good reason: it is one thing to require prosecutors to inquire about whether police have turned up exculpatory or impeachment evidence during their investigation. It is quite another to require them, on pain of a possible retrial, to conduct disciplinary inquiries into the general conduct of every officer working the case." 627 F.3d at 952.

The Court concluded that "where no one other than the officers themselves had any idea of any impropriety, and where the misconduct evidence was unrelated to [the defendant's] own investigation—the principle of imputed knowledge cannot be said to apply." 627 F.3d at 952.

§ 1:73.6 Exculpatory evidence in records possessed by defendant

When exculpatory evidence is found in records that are the property of the defendant and that are possessed by the defendant, and the prosecutor does not have actual knowledge of that exculpatory evidence, the prosecutor is not charged with constructive knowledge of that evidence.

In *United States v. Warshak* (2010, CA6 OH) 631 F.3d 266, the defendant was convicted in federal court of various crimes that included fraud and money laundering relating to a business owned by the defendant. The government seized large amounts of the defendant's business records, which the government then disclosed to the defendant in discovery. After his conviction the defendant appealed to the Sixth Circuit Court of Appeals. The defendant argued, *inter alia*, that the government abdicated its *Brady* duties by inundating him in "gargantuan 'haystacks' of discovery that swallowed any 'needles' of exculpatory information." 631 F.3d at 295.

The Sixth Circuit Court of Appeals rejected the defendant's *Brady* arguments. The Court observed that "the overwhelming majority of the discovery at issue was taken directly from [the defendant company's] computers, which means the defendants had ready access to that information. It also means that the defendants had access to the documents 'as they [were] kept in the usual course of business.'" 631 F.3d at 296.

The Ninth Circuit Court of Appeals reached a similar conclusion in *United States v. Pelisamen* (2011, CA9 NMI) 641 F.3d 399. In *Pelisamen* a defendant was convicted of wire fraud, conspiracy to commit wire fraud, money laundering, and conspiracy to commit money laundering for his actions as administrator of a family estate. On appeal the defendant argued that the government had failed to disclose documents showing that the account of the defendant's attorney at the time of how the attorney transferred money to the defendant's successor attorney, was an inaccurate account. The Court of Appeals did not agree with the defendant's argument. The Court stated that "the record indicates that both the government and Defendant's attorney were surprised by the disclosure at trial of the bank records. Nothing in the record suggests that these records were possessed by or known to any agent of the government at any point before [the defendant's first attorney] testified. Rather, it was Defendant who possessed the records and introduced them into evidence at trial." 641 F.3d at 408.

§ 1:76 Third element of evidence suppression—failure to disclose

The Supreme Court has used the term "turn over" to describe that duty in only two of these 19 opinions— *California v. Trombetta, supra,* 467 U.S. at 485, and *Pennsylvania v. Ritchie, supra,* 480 U.S. at 57, and in both of these opinions has also used the term "disclose" to describe that duty. This is clear evidence that the Supreme Court's has used the term "turn over" as a synonym of the word "disclose," and not as an extension of the prosecutor's duty beyond disclosure. It is a mistake, therefore, to attach any significance to the Court's use in two opinions of the term "turn over" beyond a stylistic desire to use different words to describe the same conduct.

Moreover, the Court's opinion in *Brady v. Maryland* (1963) 373 U.S. 83, 87; 83 S.Ct. 1194, 10 L.Ed.2d 215, used the term "suppression" to describe the unconstitutional conduct by the prosecutor giving rise to the *Brady* rule. The Court has since made clear that "suppression of so-called 'Brady material' " is a "breach of the broad obligation to disclose exculpatory evidence." *Strickler v. Greene, supra,* 527 U.S. at 281.

Finally, even the Seventh Circuit Court of Appeals, which has twice loosely used the term "turn over" in describing the prosecutor's *Brady* duty, has correctly identified the prosecutor's duty in those same opinions as a duty to "disclose," thus signifying that the Court's use of the term "turn over" is only a synonym for the word "disclose." *See Carvajal v. Dominguez, supra,* 542 F.3d at 566; and *Harris v. Kuba, supra,* 486 F.3d at 1014–1015.

Therefore, the correct and legally accurate terminology describing the prosecutor's constitutional duty under *Brady* is that the prosecutor must "disclose" materially exculpatory evidence, and the prosecutor violates that duty when the prosecution "suppresses" such evidence by failing to "disclose" it.

The prosecutor's *Brady* duty to disclose material exculpatory evidence might be satisfied by a disclosure of the existence of a written document which contains that material exculpatory evidence. The prosecutor's disclosure duty might not require the prosecutor to disclose the exculpatory content of a document or writing, as long as the prosecutor discloses enough about the existence of the document—its identity and where it is located—to enable the defendant to access the document itself. *See, Hein v. Sullivan* (2010, CA9 CA) 601 F.3d 897, 907.

§ 1:76.2   Failure to disclose vs. failure to identify

"As a general rule, the government is under no duty to direct a defendant to exculpatory evidence within a larger mass of disclosed evidence." *United States v. Skilling* (2009, CA5 TX) 554 F.3d 529, 576. *Accord, United States v. Mulderig* (1997, CA5 LA) 120 F.3d 534, 541; *United States v. Gray* (2011, CA7 IN) 646 F.3d 562, 567 [The government is not required to sift through millions of pages of documents in order to direct the defendant's attention to exculpatory evidence contained therein.]; *United States v. Warshak* (2010, CA6 OH) 631 F.3d 266, 297 ["[D]efendants contend that the government was obliged to sift fastidiously through the evidence—the vast majority of which came from [the defendant's company] itself—in an attempt to locate anything favorable to the defense. This argument comes up empty."].

Nor is the government obligated to identify exculpatory evidence found in records that are equally available to the prosecution and the defendant. Thus, in *United States v. Jackson* (2008, CA7 IN) 546 F.3d 801, the Seventh

Circuit Court of Appeals rejected the defendant's argument that the government suppressed evidence favorable to the defendant when the government utilized part of the defendant's records that tended to incriminate the defendant, but failed to identify or introduce into evidence other parts of the defendant's records that were favorable to her. The Court observed that the defendant, through her attorney, was free to introduce the exculpatory portions of the defendant's bank records. 546 F.3d at 813.

This principle of *Brady*—that the prosecution is not required to identify exculpatory evidence found in records already disclosed or available to the defendant—applies not only to written documents or records, but applies also to recorded words and images. Thus, *Brady* does not require the prosecutor to point out or "single out a particular segment of a videotape . . . ." *Rhoades v. Henry (Baldwin)* (2010, CA9 ID) 596 F.3d 1170, 1182.

The principle that the government is not required by *Brady* to identify *Brady* material in evidence disclosed to the defendant applies to more than just documentary evidence—it applies equally to videotape and audiotape evidence. In *Rhoades v. Henry* (2011, CA9 ID) 638 F.3d 1027, a defendant convicted of kidnapping and capital murder and sentenced to death filed a writ petition in federal court challenging his conviction. In his petition the defendant-petitioner claimed that the state had failed to disclose a recorded witness statement in which the witness described a man leaving the crime scene whose characteristics did not match the defendant's. The statement was contained on a videotape that was disclosed to the defendant, but the defendant's attorney apparently did not find the statement, which followed a 10-minute gap in recordings on the tape. The Ninth Circuit Court of Appeals rejected the defendant's *Brady* argument, concluding that the defendant "points to no authority requiring the prosecution to single out a particular segment of a videotape, and we decline to impose one." 638 F.3d at 1039.

§ 1:76.2.1 Failure to disclose vs. failure to create

The prosecution's duty to disclose exculpatory evidence does not impose on the prosecution a duty to create such evidence. In *United States v. Gray* (2011, CA7 IN) 648 F.3d 562, a defendant convicted of Medicaid fraud and conspiracy to defraud the United States government claimed on appeal that the prosecution had suppressed exculpatory evidence in violation of *Brady*. The evidence in issue was information supplied to the government by EDS, a private company hired by the State of Indiana to process and pay Medicaid claims. The critical data was not in the file that the government had initially received from EDS, but was extracted from EDS's database during the defendant's trial at the government's request and then supplied by the government to the defendant. The defendant argued that the government's failure to direct EDS to extract this data from its database prior to trial constituted a suppression of exculpatory evidence.

The Court of Appeals rejected the defendant's argument. The Court characterized this argument as a "non-starter" and difficult to even understand. Noting that the defendant's argument " 'implies that the state has a duty not merely to disclose but also to create truthful exculpatory evidence,' [citations omitted]," the Court held that " '[t]he failure to create exculpatory evidence does not constitute a *Brady* violation.' [citations omitted]" 648 F.3d at 567.

§ 1:76.3　Failure to disclose vs. making evidence available ["open files policy"]

Questions continue to arise in connection with prosecution "open files policies" and under what conditions such policies satisfy the prosecution's *Brady* duty of disclosure of material, exculpatory evidence.

§ 1:76.3.1　"Open files" policy as disclosure under *Brady* rule and Criminal Discovery Statute

In *United States v. Serfling* (2007, CA7 IL) 504 F.3d 672, a defendant convicted of wire fraud and mail fraud arising out of a scheme to defraud an insurance company appealed his convictions, arguing on appeal that the prosecution had withheld material exculpatory evidence from him in violation of the *Brady* rule.

Prior to trial the defendant had requested the prosecution to disclose any evidence relevant to the desire of the Fifth Third Bank, which owned the property that was the subject of the charged fraud, to sell that property. The defendant sought to prove that the bank intended to shed the property from its portfolio and had conspired with his co-defendant to perpetrate the fraud.

The prosecution informed the defendant that it had obtained 10,000 pages of documents that had been produced during civil litigation involving the bank. The prosecution told the defendant it had not photocopied the documents, but the prosecution would make the documents available for inspection at any time. The defendant never inspected the documents, which included a document that the defendant claimed on appeal was exculpatory evidence.

The Seventh Circuit Court of Appeals rejected the defendant's *Brady* argument, concluding that the government had not suppressed the document. The Court stated: "The government 'suppresses' evidence for purposes of *Brady* if it fails to disclose the evidence in time for the defendant to use it in his defense, and the evidence was not otherwise available to the defendant through the exercise of reasonable diligence. [citation omitted] In this case, the government made the memorandum available for inspection—a fact inconsistent with suppression." 504 F.3d at 678–679.

The Court rejected the defendant's argument that the government's statement that the documents did not appear to be relevant to the trial excused his lack of due diligence in failing to examine the documents. The Court stated: "The uncritical reliance on the government's characterization of the documents as 'not relevant' hardly qualifies as reasonable diligence." 504 F.3d at 679.

See also Brooks v. Tennessee (2010, CA6 TN) 626 F.3d 878, 896 [Where both the prosecution and the defendant had access to the investigative reports during the defendant's trial, and those reports included a government witness's inconsistent statements, the failure of the prosecution to direct the defendant's attention to these inconsistent statements did not constitute a *Brady* violation.]. *Accord, United States v. Serfling* (2007, CA7 IL) 504 F.3d 672, 678 [government made available to defendant documents produced during a civil litigation and provided to the government investigators].

§ 1:76.3.2 "Open files" policy danger for prosecution

The Sixth Circuit Court of Appeals has distinguished the situation in which the prosecutor represents that all exculpatory evidence has been disclosed to the defense, but the prosecution's files contain exculpatory evidence that the defendants had no reason to know about and that the defense could not have discovered without an extensive and possibly fruitless investigation, from the situation in which the prosecutor makes the same representation, but the prosecution's files contain exculpatory evidence about which the defense could learn with the exercise of reasonable diligence.

In *Bell v. Bell* (2008, CA6 TN) 512 F.3d 223, an inmate convicted of murder brought a habeas corpus petition in the federal courts. In his habeas petition the inmate argued that the prosecution had committed a *Brady* violation by failing to disclose the sentencing records of a prosecution witness who testified that the defendant confessed to the murder while the two men were together in custody. The prosecution had informed the petitioner's trial attorney that the prosecution had disclosed all discoverable information to the defense. In his habeas proceeding the inmate contended that because of the prosecutor's representation, the defense was excused from a due diligence duty to find the sentencing records on their own efforts.

The Sixth Circuit Court of Appeals rejected this contention, saying that "the known fact of [the witness's] incarceration strongly suggested that further inquiry was in order, whether or not the prosecutor said he had turned over all the discoverable evidence in his file, and the information was a matter of public record . . . . The absence of reasonable reliance distinguishes this case from *Strickler* and *Banks*." 512 F.3d at 236.

§ 1:76.3.3 "Open files" policy and voluminous files

A prosecutor's "open files" policy does not always eliminate a defendant's argument that the prosecution has suppressed materially exculpatory evidence contained in those files. Where the prosecution's or government's files are voluminous, the defendant might claim that the sheer volume of the open files prevented an effective review of them, and that no amount of diligence, to say nothing of reasonable diligence, could have accomplished the task of reviewing the files for exculpatory evidence.

In *United States v. Skilling* (2009, CA5 TX) 554 F.3d 529, the former chief executive officer (CEO) of Enron Corporation was prosecuted and convicted of a number of criminal offenses arising out of the operations of that company. On appeal from his conviction Skilling argued, *inter alia*, that the government's open files consisted of several hundred million pages of documents, effectively concealing a large quantity of exculpatory evidence, thereby violating the government's *Brady* obligation to disclose exculpatory evidence to him. The defendant argued that the sheer volume of the government's open file prevented him from effectively reviewing the files.

The Fifth Circuit Court of Appeals rejected the defendant's argument. The Court observed that although there is little case law on the question whether a voluminous open file can itself violate *Brady*, the case law focuses on the conduct of the government in addition to allowing open files access. In the case of Mr. Skilling, the

> "government did much more than drop several hundred million pages on Skilling's doorstep. The open file was electronic and searchable. The government produced a set of 'hot documents' that it thought were important to its case or were potentially relevant to Skilling's defense. The government created indices to these and other documents. The government also provided Skilling with access to various databases concerning prior Enron litigation." 554 F.3d at 577.

Skilling contended that despite the steps the government took to assist in his location of exculpatory evidence in the government's files, the government should have scoured its open files in search of exculpatory information to disclose to him. The Court of Appeals rejected the defendant's argument, observing that the government was in no better position to locate potentially exculpatory evidence than was Skilling, and there was no evidence that the government found exculpatory evidence in the files, but failed to disclose it. Moreover, there was no evidence that the government hid exculpatory evidence in the open files, hoping that Skilling would not find it. Finally, the Court observed that if the government's open files contain exculpatory evidence, "the government does not know about it either." 554 F.3d at 577.

The Court recognized that evidence that the government "padded" an open file with "pointless or superfluous information to frustrate a defendant's review of the file might raise serious *Brady* concerns . . . the government may not hide *Brady* material of which it is actually aware in a huge open file in the hope that the defendant will never find it." 554 F.3d at 577. But because the Court found no evidence that the government had created its open files in bad faith, and because the government had taken additional steps beyond simply providing the defendant with open files access to assist the defendant in his use of those files, the prosecution did not commit *Brady* error. 554 F.3d at 577.

In *United States v. Warshak* (2010, CA6 OH) 631 F.3d 266, the defendant was convicted in federal court of various crimes that included fraud and money laundering relating to a business owned by the defendant. The government seized large amounts of the defendant's business records, which the government then disclosed to the defendant in discovery. After his conviction the defendant appealed to the Sixth Circuit Court of Appeals. The defendant argued, *inter alia*, that the government abdicated its *Brady* duties by inundating him in "gargantuan 'haystacks' of discovery that swallowed any 'needles' of exculpatory information." 631 F.3d at 295. The defendant contended that "the government shrugged off its obligations under *Brady* by simply handing over millions of pages of evidence and forcing the defense to find any exculpatory information contained therein. In essence, the defendants contend that the government was obliged to sift fastidiously through the evidence—the vast majority of which came from [the defendant's company] itself—in an attempt to locate anything favorable to the defense." 631 F.3d at 297.

The Sixth Circuit Court of Appeals rejected the defendant's *Brady* arguments. Citing the opinion of the Fifth Circuit Court of Appeals in *Skilling*, the Court determined that there was no proof that the government larded its production of discovery with entirely irrelevant documents; the government did not make access to the documents *unduly* onerous; and there was no indication that the government deliberately concealed exculpatory evidence in the information it disclosed to the defense. 631 F.3d at 297–298.

The Court further declined to accept the defendant's argument that the government's ignorance of the presence of *Brady* evidence in the discovery it disclosed, arising from the government's failure to review all of the evidence it disclosed, established that the government intentionally produced irrelevant discovery or that the government was willfully blind to the importance of the materials it disclosed. 631 F.3d at 298.

§ 1:76.3.4   Open files policy and the duty to deliver ["turn over"] exculpatory evidence

Some have argued that the *Brady* rule obligates the prosecutor to deliver material exculpatory evidence to the defendant, and that an open files policy fails to comport with that duty.

As extensively discussed in Section 1:76 of this supplement, the prosecution's *Brady* duty is a duty to "disclose" material exculpatory evidence to the defendant. The *Brady* duty does not obligate the prosecutor to "deliver" such evidence to the defendant. Because the prosecutor's duty to disclose such evidence can be accomplished without delivering it to the defendant, an open files policy appears to satisfy the prosecutor's constitutional duty to disclose material exculpatory evidence.

§ 1:76.3.5   Investigating agency open files policy for prosecutor access

There appears to be substantial disagreement over the question what duties are placed upon the investigating agency and its officers with regard to exculpatory evidence they uncover in the course of their investigation. This question becomes critical when a civil lawsuit against the investigating agency and officers alleges that the officers failed to disclose exculpatory evidence to the prosecutor, thereby depriving the former defendant of exculpatory evidence to which he was entitled by *Brady*. In this scenario the investigating agency and its officers face a civil judgment against them arising out of their work.

In *Tennison v. City and County of San Francisco* (2009, CA9 CA) 570 F.3d 1078, a civil rights action against the officers who had investigated the plaintiffs for a murder, leading to their conviction and incarceration, the Ninth Circuit Court of Appeals held that the officers failed to fulfill their duty to disclose exculpatory information contained in a witness's oral statement by placing a note summarizing the statement in the investigating agency's homicide file. The Court characterized the officers' conduct as burying the statement in a police department file. 570 F.3d at 1090–1091.

An analysis of the correctness of the holding of the Ninth Circuit Court of Appeals in *Tennison* and a more complete discussion of the constitutional duties of investigating officers to disclose exculpatory evidence to the prosecutor is contained in Sections 1:96 through 1:96.4 of Part X of this chapter [entitled Disclosure Duties of Investigating Officers] in this supplement.

§ 1:76.3.6   Open files policies and digital evidence

The *Brady* principle that a prosecution "open files" policy can be sufficient to satisfy the *Brady* duty of disclosure of material, favorable evidence extends to cases in which the prosecution's "open files" consist of or include evidence contained in a digital format. *See, United States v. Kimoto* (2009, CA7 IL) 588 F.3d 464. As in the case of an open files policy for hard copy written and documentary evidence, an "open files" policy can satisfy the prosecution's *Brady* duty of disclosure of material favorable evidence if no one affiliated with the prosecution team incorrectly represents to the defense that the digital files contain all digital evidence possessed by the prosecution. 588 F.3d at 487.

§ 1:76.3.7   Open files procedures

If a defendant chooses to conduct discovery by examining the open files of the prosecution, the prosecution must enable the defendant to conduct this examination in a setting that protects the defendant's attorney-client privilege and his or her attorney's work product privilege, while at the same time protecting the integrity of the prosecutions' files and evidence. *Schaffer v. Superior Court* (2010) 185 Cal.App.4th 1235, 1245, 111 Cal.Rptr.3d 245.

In *Schaffer v. Superior Court*, the Court of Appeal suggested possible procedures to protect these interests of both parties to a criminal prosecution. "[T]he district attorney could allow the defendant and his counsel to view the items in private or in a discreet location where their conversation would not be overheard by the district attorney's staff but precautions could be made to protect against theft or destruction." 185 Cal.App.4th at 1245.

§ 1:76.4 Failure to disclose defendant's own records

The government is not obligated to identify exculpatory evidence found in the defendant's own records, because such records are equally available to the prosecution and the defendant.

Thus, in *United States v. Jackson* (2008, CA7 IN) 546 F.3d 801, the Seventh Circuit Court of Appeals rejected the defendant's argument that the government suppressed evidence favorable to the defendant when the government utilized part of the defendant's records that tended to incriminate the defendant, but failed to identify or introduce into evidence other parts of the defendant's records that were favorable to her. The Court observed that the defendant, through her attorney, was free to introduce the exculpatory portions of the defendant's bank records. 546 F.3d at 813.

In *United States v. Warshak* (2010, CA6 OH) 631 F.3d 266, the defendant was convicted in federal court of various crimes that included fraud and money laundering relating to business owned by the defendant. The government seized large amounts of the defendant's business records, which the government then disclosed to the defendant in discovery. After his conviction the defendant appealed to the Sixth Circuit Court of Appeals. The defendant argued, *inter alia*, that the government abdicated its *Brady* duties by inundating him in "gargantuan 'haystacks' of discovery that swallowed any 'needles' of exculpatory information." 631 F.3d at 295.

The Sixth Circuit Court of Appeals rejected the defendant's *Brady* arguments. The Court observed that "the overwhelming majority of the discovery at issue was taken directly from [the defendant company's] computers, which means the defendants had ready access to that information. It also means that the defendants had access to the documents 'as they [were] kept in the usual course of business.' " 631 F.3d at 296.

The Ninth Circuit Court of Appeals reached a similar conclusion in *United States v. Pelisamen* (2011, CA9 NMI) 641 F.3d 399. In *Pelisamen* a defendant was convicted of wire fraud, conspiracy to commit wire fraud, money laundering, and conspiracy to commit money laundering for his actions as administrator of a family estate. On appeal the defendant argued that the government had failed to disclose documents showing that the account of the defendant's attorney at the time of how he transferred money to the defendant's successor attorney, was an inaccurate account. The Court of Appeals did not agree with the defendant's argument. The Court stated that "the record clearly indicates that both the government and Defendant's attorney were surprised by the disclosure at trial of the bank records . . . . Nothing in the record suggests that these records were possessed by or known to any agent of the government at any point before [the defendant's first attorney] testified. Rather, it was Defendant who possessed the records and introduced them into evidence at trial." 641 F.3d at 408.

§ 1:76.5   Failure to disclose and uncooperative prosecution witness

The refusal of a prosecution witness to speak with and to provide exculpatory evidence to the defense does not constitute suppression of material exculpatory evidence within the meaning of the *Brady* rule. *United States v. Heppner* (2008, CA8 MN) 519 F.3d 744, 750. "No constitutional violation occurs when a witness chooses of her own volition not to be interviewed by the defense." *United States v. Cheatham* (1990, CA8 MN) 899 F.2d 747, 753.

§ 1:76.6   Failure to disclose and false statement by prosecution witness

A false statement by a prosecution witness to the prosecutor which causes the prosecutor to present the prosecution's case based on that false statement does not constitute a "suppression" of favorable evidence within the meaning of the *Brady* rule.

In *Harris v. Kuba* (2007, CA7 IL) 486 F.3d 1010, the defendant, who was a pardoned prisoner, brought a federal civil rights action [42 U.S. Code sec. 1983] in federal court against two police officers whom he claimed had violated his due process rights by, among other things, not disclosing exculpatory *Brady* evidence prior to his trial. Harris claimed that the officers had lied to the prosecution to preserve his conviction while the defendant's post-trial motions were pending. The district court granted summary judgment to the officers.

On the defendant's appeal from the grant of summary judgment, the defendant argued that the officers' lies to the prosecutor constituted a *Brady* violation, creating section 1983 liability. The Seventh Circuit Court of Appeals rejected the defendant's argument, saying that "*Brady* does not apply. Harris essentially seeks an extension of *Brady* to provide relief if a police officer makes a false statement to a prosecutor by arguing that an officer is 'suppressing' evidence of the truth by making the false statement. This court has already foreclosed this extension . . . . Harri's theory does not constitute a viable claim under *Brady*, the only form of constitutional claim he propounds, and therefore his section 1983 claim is without merit." 486 F.3d at 1017.

The Court cited its prior opinion in *Sornberger v. City of Knoxville* (2006, CA7 IL) 434 F.3d 1006, 1029, in which the Court stated: " 'Nor can *Brady* serve as the basis of a cause of action against the officers for failing to disclose [a coerced confession] to the prosecutor . . . . The Constitution does not require that police testify truthfully; rather, 'the constitutional rule is that the defendant is entitled to a trial that will enable jurors to determine where the truth lies.' "

In an earlier case, *Gauger v. Hendle* (2003, CA7 IL) 349 F.3d 354, 360, overruled in part on other grounds, *Wallace v. City of Chicago* (2006, CA7 IL) 440 F.3d 421, 423, the Court of Appeals stated: "We find the proposed extension of *Brady* [to require the police to render truthful records of interrogations to the prosecutors] difficult even to understand. It implies that the state has a duty not merely to disclose but also to create truthful exculpatory evidence . . . The problem was not that evidence useful to him was being concealed; the problem was that the detectives were giving false evidence. Gauger wants to make every false statement by a prosecution witness the basis for a civil rights suit, on the theory that by failing to correct the statement the prosecution deprived the defendant of *Brady* material, that is, the correction itself."

Thus, the simple fact of false testimony by a prosecution witness does not constitute *Brady* suppression of material exculpatory evidence.

However, if a prosecution witness gives false testimony that covers up material exculpatory evidence, the false testimony by that prosecution witness should constitute suppression of that exculpatory evidence within the meaning of the *Brady* rule. In *Brown v. Miller* (2008, CA5 LA) 519 F.3d 231, a crime lab technician was sued under 42 U.S.C. § 1983 as the result of the creation of a misleading and inaccurate inculpatory serology report that led to the defendant's conviction. The district court denied the technician's motion to dismiss the civil action due to qualified immunity, and the technician appealed. The Fifth Circuit Court of Appeals held that "the deliberate or knowing creation of a misleading and scientifically inaccurate serology report amounts to a violation of a defendant's due process rights" 519 F.3d at 237.

§ 1:76.7   Failure to disclose vs. failure to call witness

The suppression of material exculpatory evidence results from the prosecution's failure to disclose that evidence to the defendant. However, the prosecution does not suppress material exculpatory evidence by failing to call a witness to testify regarding that exculpatory evidence, when the defendant also knows of the exculpatory evidence possessed by the witness and the substance of the witness's expected testimony and is free to call that witness to testify as a defense witness.

In *United States v. Bond* (2009, CA9 CA) 552 F.3d 1092, the government informed a defendant charged with conspiracy to commit and committing mail and wire fraud that the government would call a named witness at trial. The government provided the defendant with interview summaries of the witness and notes from meetings with the witness. The government ultimately did not call the witness to testify, and the defendant did not attempt to subpoena the witness. The defendant was convicted and appealed. In his appeal the defendant argued that the witness's testimony would have been favorable to him, and he claimed that the government suppressed the witness's testimony in violation of *Brady*.

The Ninth Circuit Court of Appeals rejected the defendant's argument, concluding that the government did not conceal the witness or the witness's information, that there was no material that was favorable to the defendant, and the government did not selectively disclose items that mislead the defense. Instead, the Court concluded, the government "provided [the defendant] with the information needed to acquire all trial testimony, and provided him with the essential factual data to determine whether the witness' testimony might be helpful [citation omitted] . . . . We decline to extend *Benn* beyond cases in which the government has affirmatively misled the defendant by a selective disclosure of information." 552 F.3d at 1097.

§ 1:76.8   Failure to disclose vs. loss or destruction of evidence

The prosecution does not violate its *Brady* duty when the prosecution team loses, destroys, or gives to a third party evidence that the defendant claims was exculpatory. A defendant's remedy for loss or destruction of exculpatory evidence is a motion to dismiss pursuant to *California v. Trombetta* (1984) 467 U.S. 479, 104 S.Ct. 2528, 81 L.Ed.2d 413, and *Arizona v. Youngblood* (1988) 488 U.S. 51, 109 S.Ct. 333, 102 L.Ed.2d 281. See Chapter 11 in the text and this supplement.

In *Lewis v. Horn* (2009, CA3 PA) 581 F.3d 92, a defendant convicted of murder in state court and sentenced to death contended in a federal habeas corpus proceeding that the prosecution had committed *Brady* error by delivering the briefcase the defendant was carrying at the time of his arrest to the defendant's fianc,e. The defendant claimed that the briefcase contained a bus ticket that showed that at the time of the murder he was travelling on a bus from Philadelphia to San Diego.

The district court rejected the defendant's *Brady* argument, and the defendant appealed to the Court of Appeals. The Third Circuit Court of Appeals likewise rejected the defendant's argument, holding that the prosecution cannot commit a *Brady* violation by suppressing evidence that it does not possess. The Court concluded that because the prosecution did not possess the bus ticket, the prosecution did not commit *Brady* error. 581 F.3d at 109.

§ 1:76.9   Failure to disclose and presentation at trial

The prosecution does not violate its *Brady* duty by failing to disclose exculpatory evidence prior to trial, if the prosecution presents that evidence at trial.

In *People v. Verdugo* (2010) 50 Cal.4th 263, 113 Cal.Rptr.3d 803, 236 P.3d 1035, the defendant was charged with and ultimately convicted of two counts of first-degree murder and was sentenced to death. The murders were committed following a dispute at a party. Part of the evidence against the defendant consisted of the testimony of a witness that following the party the witness encountered the defendant, who told him in referring to the argument at the party that "the situation had been handled." Even though the defendant contended that the prosecution's failure to disclose this inculpatory evidence constituted a *Brady* violation, and even though the California Supreme Court held that because the evidence was not favorable to the defendant its suppression did not violate the *Brady* rule, the Court further opined that because the prosecution presented this evidence at trial, there was no *Brady* error. 50 Cal.4th at 281.

In *United States v. Persico* (2011, CA2 NY) 645 F.3d 85, a defendant convicted of murder in aid of racketeering, witness tampering, and conspiracy contended that the government suppressed impeachment evidence on a government witness—that a large amount of money found in the vents of her parents' home was not forfeited to the government, and that she was allowed to keep the money and not pay taxes on it. This evidence was brought out during the government's direct examination of the witness. The defendant's contention that because the government had not disclosed this information prior to trial, and that, therefore, there had been no "formal disclosure" of the impeaching evidence," the government had suppressed that evidence, was rejected by the Court of Appeals. 645 F.3d at 112.

§ 1:76.10 Failure to disclose vs. defense failure to utilize

The prosecution's duty under *Brady* is to *disclose* exculpatory evidence; this duty to disclose does not include a duty to ensure that the defendant and his or her attorney will "further develop and utilize that evidence." *United States v. King* (2011, CA4 NC) 628 F.3d 693, 702.

§ 1:76.11 Failure to disclose in defendant's language

The prosecution is not required by *Brady* to provide discovery in the language of the defendant, if that defendant does not speak or read English. In *United States v. Celis* (2010, CA DC) 608 F.3d 818, a defendant convicted of conspiring to import cocaine and to manufacture and distribute cocaine for import appealed her conviction, arguing, *inter alia*, that the trial court erred in failing to order that all discovery documents containing English be translated into Spanish by the government. Describing the defendant's claim as "audacious," the Court of Appeals rejected this appellate argument, saying that there is no support for a claim that the Constitution compels that in every case in which the defendant is not fluent in English, all discovery documents must be translated, in written form, into the defendant's native tongue. The Court of Appeals concluded that a decision to provide written translations in difficult and complicated cases is committed to the district court's discretion. 608 F.3d at 840–841.

§ 1:77 Fourth element of evidence suppression—prejudice

The fourth and final element necessary to constitute a prosecution suppression of material, favorable evidence is that the defendant must have been prejudiced by that failure to disclose.

§ 1:77.1 Defendant unaware of exculpatory evidence—generally

In *Tennison v. City and County of San Francisco* (2009, CA9 CA) 570

F.3d 1078, the defendants were prosecuted and convicted of murder. In the course of the investigation of the murder, one of the investigators spoke over the telephone to a woman who gave the officer information pointing the finger of suspicion at someone other than the defendants. The officer made a note of the telephone conversation and placed it in the investigating agency's homicide file. The note surfaced following the defendant's convictions and sentences to prison.

One of the defendants brought a federal habeas corpus action, which resulted in his being released from custody and the charges dismissed by the district attorney. The defendants then filed a civil rights action against the officers, claiming that the failure to disclose the note of the witness's telephone statement constituted *Brady* error. The officer-defendants countered that the defendants had been aware of this exculpatory evidence from other sources, and, therefore, no *Brady* error had occurred.

The district court denied summary judgment to the officers, and the officers appealed. The Ninth Circuit Court of Appeals rejected the officers' argument and held that the plaintiffs had incomplete and inaccurate information about the witness's statements, and they lacked the extensive statements by the witness to the police. The Court concluded that the information which the defendants had was "not the same as [the witness's] extensive statements to the police." 570 F.3d at 1091.

For a similar holding based on evidence that the defendant was not aware of "essential facts" that would have enabled the defendant to obtain the evidence that was not disclosed by the prosecution team, see *Sykes v. Anderson* (2010, CA6 MI) 625 F.3d 294, 319–320.

§ 1:77.2   Defendant aware of exculpatory evidence

The principle that the *Brady* rule does not apply to evidence that was known to the defendant has its roots in opinions of the United States Supreme Court: *United States v. Agurs* (1976) 427 U.S. 97, 103; 96 S.Ct. 2392, 49 L.Ed.2d 342 [*Brady* claims involve "the discovery, after trial of information which had been known to the prosecution but unknown to the defense."]; and *Kyles v. Whitley* (1995) 514 U.S. 419, 437; 115 S.Ct. 1555, 131 L.Ed.2d 490 ["On the one side, showing that the prosecution knew of an item of favorable evidence unknown to the defense does not amount to a *Brady* violation, without more."].

The Seventh Circuit Court of Appeals continues to take the lead in holding that when the defendant is aware of exculpatory evidence, the failure of the prosecution to disclose that evidence does not constitute a suppression of the evidence. *See Harris v. Kuba* (2007, CA7 IL) 486 F.3d 1010, 1015; *United States v. Mahalick* (2007, CA7 IL) 498 F.3d 475, 478 ["[T]he government cannot be said to have suppressed evidence of what the defendant himself said, 'because the defendant[ ], being part[y] to the conversation, [was] equally aware. *Brady* requires disclosure only of exculpatory material

known to the government *but not to the defendant.*' [citation omitted]."]
[italics in original]

The principle that *Brady* does not require the prosecution to disclose what the defendant already knows is generally accepted among the federal circuit courts. *United States v. Bender* (2002, CA1 ME) 304 F.3d 161, 164; *Leka v. Portuondo* (2001, CA2 NY) 257 F.3d 89, 100; *United States v. Perdomo* (1991, CA3 V.I.) 929 F.2d 967, 973; *Moore v. Quarterman* (2008, CA5 TX) 534 F.3d 454, 462; *United States v. Coker* (2008, CA6 TN) 514 F.3d 562, 570; *Owens v. Guida* (2008, CA6 TN) 549 F.3d 399; *United States v. Gonzales* (1996, CA8 MN) 90 F.3d 1363, 1368; *United States v. Bond* (2009, CA9 CA) 552 F.3d 1092; *United States v. Quintanilla* (1999, CA10 NM) 193 F.3d 1139, 1149; *Jennings v. McDonough* (2007, CA11 FL) 490 F.3d 1230, 1238.

In practical application, this principle means that the prosecution does not commit *Brady* error in failing to disclose a statement of a witness which recounts what the defendant told him. In *Pondexter v. Quarterman* (2008, CA5 TX) 537 F.3d 511, a defendant convicted of capital murder and sentenced to death contended in a federal habeas proceeding that the state had committed *Brady* error in failing to disclose the statement of the defendant's cellmate which recounted that the defendant told him that he knew the victim was dead when he shot her. The Fifth Circuit Court of Appeals rejected the *Brady* argument, concluding that "if [the defendant] made these statements to [his cellmate], [he, Pondexter] was fully aware both of having done so and of [his cellmate's] ability to verify they had been made." 537 F.3d at 526.

In short, "a defendant is not deprived of due process by the government's failure to disclose information if the defendant has obtained the information through other means." *United States v. Erickson* (2009, CA10 UT) 561 F.3d 1150, 1165.

In *United States v. Skilling* (2009, CA5 TX) 554 F.3d 529, the former chief executive officer (CEO) of Enron Corporation was prosecuted and convicted of a number of criminal offenses arising out of the operations of that company. On appeal from his conviction, Skilling argued that the government violated *Brady* by failing to disclose material information regarding the plea agreement of a witness against him. The Fifth Circuit Court of Appeals characterized Skilling's argument as a claim that the government "suppressed the fact that [the witness's] sentence was not irrevocably and inevitably fixed at ten years." 554 F.3d at 575.

The Court of Appeals rejected Skilling's argument. The Court stated that "there was nothing that the government suppressed. Skilling knew, or at least should have known, that a sentencing court could reduce [the witness's] sentence . . . . Skilling also had to know this, and thus the government did not suppress anything." 554 F.3d at 575.

The principle that the *Brady* rule does not apply to evidence that is already known by the defendant, is applied in several different contexts.

The first context is where there is evidence that the allegedly suppressed evidence was actually disclosed to the defendant. *See Valdovinos v. McGrath* (2010, CA9 CA) 598 F.3d 568, 577; *United States v. Warshak* (2010, CA6 OH) 631 F.3d 266, 299.

The second context is where, although there is no evidence that the defendant actually knew of the exculpatory evidence, that evidence was located in a place to which the defendant had access equal to that of the prosecution in order to obtain it. *See Parker v. Allen* (2009, CA11 AL) 565 F.3d 1258, 1277; *United States v. Warshak* (2010, CA6 OH) 631 F.3d 266, 301.

The third context is where the defendant's conduct in trial, such as the questioning of witnesses or the testimony of the defendant, demonstrates that the defendant knew the exculpatory evidence. *See United States v. Ladoucer* (2009, CA8 MN) 573 F.3d 628, 636; *United States v. Are* (2009, CA7 IL) 590 F.3d 499, 510; *Abdur'Rahman v. Colson* (2011, CA6 TN) 649 F.3d 468, 474–475 [withholding of an accomplice's pre-trial statements did not constitute a suppression of *Brady* evidence, because defendant's trial testimony demonstrated that he knew the essential evidence contained in the accomplice's statements].

The fourth context is where the exculpatory evidence itself was part of a conversation in which the defendant participated. *See United States v. Phillips* (2010, CA7 IL) 596 F.3d 414, 418; *Rhoades v. Henry (Michelbacher)* (2010, CA9 ID) 598 F.3d 495, 501; *Rhoades v. Henry (Baldwin)* (2010, CA9 ID) 596 F.3d 1170, 1181.

§ 1:77.3   Duplicative disclosures

The prosecution's failure to provide duplicative disclosures of exculpatory evidence does not violate the *Brady* rule.

In *United States v. Skilling* (2009, CA5 TX) 554 F.3d 529, the former chief executive officer (CEO) of Enron Corporation was prosecuted and convicted of a number of criminal offenses arising out of the operations of that company. On appeal from his conviction, Skilling argued that the government violated *Brady* by failing to disclose material information regarding an important government witness, the former chief financial officer of Enron. Government agents conducted several hundred hours of interviews with this witness and took more than 400 pages of handwritten notes of the interviews. From the interview notes the government compiled two FBI Form 302s that summarized the substance of the interview notes. The government disclosed the 302s to Skilling but refused to provide him with the interview notes or with draft versions of the 302s.

While Skilling's appeal was pending, the Fifth Circuit Court of Appeals ordered the government to turn over the interview notes in their entirety to

Skilling. However, the government informed the Court that the draft 302s had been destroyed.

Skilling argued that the failure of the government to disclose the interview notes and the draft 302s violated *Brady*. The Court of Appeals, based on its own review of the interview notes, concluded that the government had not committed *Brady* error in failing to disclose the interview notes to the defendant. 554 F.3d at 578. The Court held that if the information in the 302s that was disclosed to the defendant duplicated the information in the interview notes, failure to disclose the interview notes did not constitute *Brady* error. 554 F.3d at 579–580.

Skilling then argued that the government's failure to disclose the draft 302s denied him due process of law. The Court of Appeals rejected the defendant's argument. The Court stated that "the draft 302s are merely an intermediary step between what [the witness] said—recorded in the raw notes—and what the government reported [the witness] as saying—recorded in the 302s—any destruction of the draft 302s is immaterial for purposes of *Brady*." 554 F.3d at 577.

In a series of cases arising in Idaho state courts, the Ninth Circuit Court of Appeals similarly held that the prosecution does not violate its *Brady* duty by failing to disclose written reports, the contents of which are duplicative in substance. *See Rhoades v. Henry (Michelbacher)* (2010, CA9 ID) 598 F.3d 495, 502–503; *Rhoades v. Henry (Baldwin)* (2010, CA9 ID) 596 F.3d 1170, 1182.

Likewise, in *United States v. Isaacs* (2010, CA7 IL) 593 F.3d 517, in which the defendant was charged with defrauding customers by fraudulently using unauthorized access devices, the prosecution turned over to the defendant a new version of computer records in the form of compact disks three days before trial. The defendant's argument on appeal of his conviction that the government's conduct violated the prosecution's discovery obligations was rejected by the Seventh Circuit Court of Appeals, which held that the defendant failed to show that there were any material differences in the underlying data contained on those disks from the data previously disclosed by the government.

See also, United States v. Kimoto (2009, CA7 IL) 588 F.3d 464, 489 [prosecution's provision of hard copies of e-mails to defendant satisfied prosecution's duty to disclose e-mails]; *United States v. Warshak* (2010, CA6 OH) 631 F.3d 266, 299 [disclosure of the government's trial exhibits six weeks prior to trial did not constitute a suppression of exculpatory evidence, because the trial exhibits were culled from discovery material already disclosed to the defendant]; and *Rhoades v. Henry* (2011, CA9 ID) 638 F.3d 1027, 1038–1039 [prosecution's failure to disclose officer's written report did not suppress exculpatory evidence contained in that report, because the withheld report did not add any detail not already disclosed in two other officers' reports].

§ 1:77.4 Disclosure at trial

Because the underlying purpose of the *Brady* duty of disclosure is to ensure that a criminal defendant receives a fair trial, the prosecution's failure to provide pre-trial disclosure to the defendant of material, exculpatory evidence is cured by the prosecution's presentation of that evidence at the trial. *People v. Verdugo* (2010) 50 Cal.4th 263, 281, 283, 286, 287, 289, 113 Cal.Rptr.3d 803, 236 P.3d 1035, citing and quoting *People v. Morrison* (2004) 34 Cal.4th 698, 27 Cal.Rptr.3d 682, 101 P.3d 568, discussed in this section in the main text.

Practice Tip for Prosecution: Prosecutors who might be tempted to rely upon the principle of *Brady* that disclosure of material, favorable evidence at trial can serve to expiate the prosecutor's knowing failure to disclose that evidence prior to trial, would do well to remember that the chief trial counsel of the California State Bar does not view an at-trial disclosure of *Brady* evidence that was known to the prosecutor prior to trial as compliance with a prosecutor's ethical duties. At least one California prosecutor was suspended from the practice of law for intentional pre-trial suppression of evidence impeaching a critical prosecution witness, even though the prosecutor was forced to disclose that evidence by the trial court at the time of trial.

§ 1:78 Defendant's "due diligence self-help" obligation

The prosecutor's *Brady* duty to disclose material, favorable evidence does not excuse the defendant's attorney from his or her responsibility to take reasonable steps to learn about exculpatory evidence through his or her own "due diligence self-help" efforts.

In *Owens v. Guida* (2008, CA6 TN) 549 F.3d 399, the defendant was charged with and convicted of murdering her husband. There was evidence known to the defendant that the husband-victim was having an extramarital affair with another woman. At trial the defendant requested the prosecution to disclose all evidence about the victim's marital affairs. Although the investigating officers had seized sexually suggestive cards and love notes exchanged between the husband and his paramour, the investigating agency had returned those items to the victim's girlfriend.

In a federal habeas action filed by the defendant, the defendant contended that the failure of the prosecution to disclose the notes and cards constituted *Brady* error. The district court rejected the defendant's argument and an appeal followed. The Sixth Circuit Court of Appeals rejected the *Brady* argument of the defendant. The Court observed that *"Brady* does not apply when the defendant 'knew or should have known the essential facts permitting him to take advantage of any exculpatory information.' [citation omitted]." 549 F.3d at 417. The Court observed that the defendant "knew of the affair, and if she wanted to present evidence of the affair, she could have testified, produced [an anonymous letter she had received informing her about the affair], or subpoenaed [the victim's girlfriend]." The Court concluded that the defendant " 'knew or should have known the essential facts permitting h[er] to take advantage of any exculpatory information,' and the evidence she wanted was clearly 'available from another source.' [citation omitted]." 549 F.3d at 417.

The failure of the defendant's attorney to take reasonable steps to locate and obtain exculpatory evidence can serve to undermine a defense claim of a *Brady* error. *Parker v. Allen* (2009, CA11 AL) 565 F.3d 1258, 1277.

§ 1:78.1 Reasonable "due diligence self-help" actions

Speaking to known witnesses

A defendant has the obligation to speak to known witnesses to determine their knowledge of the case. In *Jennings v. McDonough* (2007, CA11 FL) 490 F.3d 1230, the defendant was convicted of capital murder. He then filed a habeas corpus petition, arguing, among other contentions, that the prosecution had suppressed a tape-recorded statement from a woman who had driven the defendant to his home and back to a bar earlier on the evening of the murder. The witness had told the investigating officers that she had provided this transportation, because she knew that he had too much to drink and could not drive himself. When she last saw the defendant in the bar, he was very intoxicated. The defendant argued in his habeas proceeding that this evidence would have helped him in the guilt and penalty phases of his murder trial to mitigate his level of culpability and also to mitigate his punishment.

The Fifth Circuit Court of Appeals rejected Jenning's argument. The Court concluded that the tape "was not suppressed for purposes of the *Brady* analysis." The Court adopted the findings of the Florida Supreme Court that the defendant "had knowledge not only of [the witness's] name but also the subject matter of her knowledge about the case" 490 F.3d at 1238. The Court also pointed out that the defense was aware of the statements of two other witnesses that recounted the same events as were contained in the undisclosed witness statement. The Court concluded that the prosecution had not suppressed the tape-recorded statement, because the defendant was "plainly aware of Slocum and thus had within his knowledge information by which he could have ascertained her statement," because the defendant also "was aware of the import and tenor of the Slocum tape from other sources," and because "nothing prevented Jennings himself from talking to Slocum. Thus, there was no suppression of the tape." 490 F.3d at 1238–1239.

Questioning witnesses at trial on relevant subjects

A defendant also has the obligation to question witnesses at trial on subjects that are relevant to the criminal case against the defendant. A defendant who does not conduct such questioning may not complain that the prosecution's failure to reveal exculpatory evidence constitutes "suppression" of that evidence, when defense questioning of trial witnesses would have revealed that evidence. *See, e.g., United States v. Santisteban* (2007, CA8 MO) 501 F.3d 873, 877–878.

Examining notes and worksheets of prosecution expert witnesses

Where the defendant has ready access to the notes and working papers of crime lab experts who examined serologic fluid found at crime scenes and a plaster exemplar of a bite mark discovered on one of the victim's breasts in a murder prosecution, the defendant has the due diligence self-help duty to request the experts to provide him access to those notes and worksheets. The failure of the defendant to make such a request obviates a claim that the evidence contained in those notes and worksheets was suppressed by the prosecution. *Gary v. Hall* (2009, CA11 FL) 558 F.3d 1229, 1254–1256.

Conducting a timely and careful review of reports and records disclosed by the prosecution

The defendant's attorney has a professional responsibility to carefully read and review reports and documents disclosed to the defense by the prosecution to ensure that the defense has obtained copies or at least access to all of the evidence possessed by the prosecution team. This duty includes the duty to review digital information disclosed by the prosecution at an early enough time in the litigation that any misunderstandings or oversights can be corrected and overcome. The defendant's failure to conduct a timely and thorough review of prosecution-disclosed evidence can seriously undermine a defendant's *Brady* claim. *United States v. Kimoto* (2009, CA7 IL) 588 F.3d 464, 488–489.

Reading transcripts

The defendant's attorney is responsible for knowing the content of proceedings in the case, and if the attorney is unable to appear at a proceeding in the case, the attorney must read a transcript of that proceeding in order to know of any oral disclosures of *Brady* evidence at the proceeding from which he or she was absent. *See, e.g., Hein v. Sullivan* (2010, CA9 CA) 601 F.3d 897, 907–908.

Subpoenaing third-party records

The defendant and his or her attorney are responsible for issuing a subpoena duces tecum to obtain exculpatory evidence located in the business records of a third party. *United States v. Celestin* (2010, CA1 MA) 612 F.3d 14, 22 ["Celestin was well aware of his own time and attendance records, and could have subpoenaed them himself in the two-and-a-half years between his indictment and trial."]; *accord, United States v. Todd* (2005, CA7 IL) 424 F.3d 525, 534.

§ 1:78.3   "Due diligence self-help" and public records

And in *United States v. Coplen* (2009, CA8 IA) 565 F.3d 1094, a defendant charged with conspiracy to distribute cocaine learned after he was convicted that several witnesses who had testified against him also testified in trials involving his alleged co-conspirators. The defendant learned that in the other trials, these witnesses testified that several witness had fabricated testimony against the defendant so they could get sentence reductions. The defendant argued that the prosecution's failure to disclose the statements of these prosecution witnesses constituted a *Brady* violation. Two of the witnesses had testified as defense witnesses in a related proceeding that predated the defendant's trial by several months "and their testimony was a matter of public record." 565 F.3d 1097.

The Eighth Circuit Court of Appeals rejected the defendant's *Brady* argument, holding that " '[t]he government does not suppress evidence in violation of *Brady* by failing to disclose evidence to which the defendant had access through other channels.' [citation omitted]" 565 F.3d at 1097.

And where criminal conviction records are "matters of public record" and available to the defendant through defense counsel's own efforts, the government's failure to disclose those records does not constitute a suppression of the criminal records. *Parker v. Allen* (2009, CA11 AL) 565 F.3d 1258, 1277.

§ 1:78.4   "Due diligence self-help" and court records

The Sixth Circuit Court of Appeals has held in several cases that where evidence which would impeach a prosecution witness is contained in court records, and the defendant had knowledge of or an easy ability to learn about the court proceedings involving the prosecution witness, the failure of the prosecution to disclose that impeaching evidence does not constitute *Brady* error.

In *Matthews v. Ishee* (2007, CA6 OH) 486 F.3d 883, a defendant convicted of murder discovered several years after his conviction that one of the key prosecution witnesses against him had received a plea-bargained reduced sentence about two weeks after his conviction. The defendant then attacked his conviction by filing a motion for a new trial. After the trial court granted the defendant a new trial, the Ohio Court of Appeals overturned the new-trial order. The defendant then filed a petition for writ of habeas corpus in federal court. The district court granted the writ, finding that the prosecution's failure to disclose the witness's plea bargain violated *Brady*, and that the defendant was excused for not bringing the new-trial motion prior to discovering the post-trial proceedings involving the witness.

The Sixth Circuit Court of Appeals reversed the district court. The Court observed that the witness's "withdrawal of his original guilty plea, plea to reduced charges, and re-sentencing were all public information. . . . Where, like here, 'the factual basis for a claim' is 'reasonably available to' the petitioner or his counsel from another source, the government is under no duty to supply that information to the defense. [citations omitted] In other words, when the information is readily available to the defense from another source, there simply is nothing for the government to 'disclose.' [citation omitted]" 486 F.3d at 890–891.

In *Bell v. Bell* (2008, CA6 TN) 512 F.3d 223, an inmate convicted of murder brought a habeas corpus petition in the federal courts. In his habeas petition the inmate argued that the prosecution had committed a *Brady* violation by failing to disclose the sentencing records of a prosecution witness who testified that the defendant confessed to the murder while the two men were together in custody. The prosecution had informed the petitioner's trial attorney that the prosecution had disclosed all discoverable information to the defense. In his habeas proceeding the inmate contended that because of the prosecutor's representation, the defense was excused from a due diligence duty to find the sentencing records on their own efforts.

The Sixth Circuit Court of Appeals rejected this contention, saying that "the known fact of [the witness's] incarceration strongly suggested that further inquiry was in order, whether or not the prosecutor said he had turned over all the discoverable evidence in his file, and the information was a matter of public record . . . . The absence of reasonable reliance distinguishes this case from *Strickler* and *Banks*." 512 F.3d at 236.

In *Price v. Thurmer* (2008, CA7 WI) 514 F.3d 729, the defendant was convicted of attempted murder and other crimes and sentenced to 185 years in prison. The jury rejected the defendant's not guilty by reason of insanity defense, primarily because of the testimony of a prosecution psychiatrist. The prosecution did not disclose (and apparently did not know) that its psychiatrist witness had been indicted by the federal government for Medicare fraud. The indictment had been dismissed. After failing in state court collateral proceedings to overturn his conviction, the defendant petitioned for writ of habeas corpus in federal court. The district court denied relief without a hearing.

The Seventh Circuit Court of Appeals upheld the district court, concluding that because the prosecution witness's indictment "was a matter of public record readily accessible to Price's lawyer . . . [citations omitted], the prosecution had no obligation to disclose it to the defense." 514 F.3d at 732.

California statutes provide that a probation report filed with the court "may be inspected or copied . . . [b]y any person, from the date judgment is pronounced or probation granted or, in the case of a report arising out of a previous arrest, from the date the subsequent accusatory pleading is filed, to and including 60 days from the date judgment is pronounced or probation is granted, whichever is earlier," Penal Code section 1203.5, subdivision (a), and that a probation report. "constitute[s] a part of the records of the court and shall at all times be open to the inspection of the court or any person appointed by the court for that purpose . . . ." Penal Code section 1203.7, subdivision (b).

And in *United States v. Coplen* (2009, CA8 IA) 565 F.3d 1094, a defendant charged with conspiracy to distribute cocaine learned after he was convicted that several witnesses who had testified against him also testified in trials involving his alleged co-conspirators. The defendant learned that in the other trials, these witnesses testified that several witness had fabricated testimony against the defendant so they could get sentence reductions. The defendant argued that the prosecution's failure to disclose the statements of these prosecution witnesses constituted a *Brady* violation. Two of the witnesses had testified as defense witnesses in a related proceeding that predated the defendant's trial by several months "and their testimony was a matter of public record." 565 F.3d 1097.

The Eighth Circuit Court of Appeals rejected the defendant's *Brady* argument, holding that " '[t]he government does not suppress evidence in violation of *Brady* by failing to disclose evidence to which the defendant had access through other channels.' [citation omitted]" 565 F.3d at 1097.

Likewise, in *United States v. Ladoucer* (2009, CA8 MN) 573 F.3d 628, the defendant argued on appeal of his conviction of various firearms charges that the prosecution violated its *Brady* disclosure duties by failing to provide him with a transcript of the witness's testimony in an unrelated state case in which the witness testified to things about his past that could have been used in Ladoucer's trial to impeach the witness. The Eighth Circuit Court of Appeals rejected the defendant's *Brady* argument, holding that (1) the defendant was aware of the witness's involvement in the unrelated state case; (2) the transcript of the witness's testimony in the state case was as available to the defendant as it was to the defendant; and (3) the defendant himself could have obtained a copy of the transcript of the witness's testimony. 573 F.3d at 636.

The Court of Appeals concluded that because the defendant could have obtained a copy of the transcript himself, he could not show that the government suppressed evidence. 573 F.3d at 636.

§ 1:78.6 "Due diligence self-help" and misleading prosecution conduct

The "due diligence self-help" doctrine relies upon the absence of misleading conduct by the prosecution. Where the prosecution does not engage in misleading conduct by tactics such as a selective disclosure of favorable evidence, the "due diligence self-help" doctrine operates to negate the element of suppression of favorable evidence in a defendant's *Brady* claim.

In *United States v. Bond* (2009, CA9 CA) 552 F.3d 1092, the government informed a defendant charged with conspiracy to commit and committing mail and wire fraud that the government would call a named witness at trial. The government provided the defendant with interview summaries of the witness and notes from meetings with the witness. The government ultimately did not call the witness to testify, and the defendant did not attempt to subpoena the witness. The defendant was convicted and appealed. In his appeal the defendant argued that the witness's testimony would have been favorable to him, and he claimed that the government suppressed the witness's testimony in violation of *Brady*.

The Ninth Circuit Court of Appeals rejected the defendant's argument, concluding that the government did not conceal the witness or the witness's information, that there was no material that was favorable to the defendant, and that the government did not selectively disclose items that mislead the defense. Instead, the Court concluded, the government "provided [the defendant] with the information needed to acquire all trial testimony, and provided him with the essential factual data to determine whether the witness' testimony might be helpful [citation omitted]. . . . We decline to extend *Benn* beyond cases in which the government has affirmatively misled the defendant by a selective disclosure of information." 552 F.3d at 1097.

§ 1:78.10 "Due diligence self-help" and knowledge of the law

In *United States v. Skilling* (2009, CA5 TX) 554 F.3d 529, the former chief executive officer (CEO) of Enron Corporation was prosecuted and convicted of a number of criminal offenses arising out of the operations of that company. On appeal from his conviction, Skilling argued that the government violated *Brady* by failing to disclose material information regarding the plea agreement of a witness against him. The Fifth Circuit Court of Appeals characterized Skilling's argument as a claim that the government "suppressed the fact that [the witness's] sentence was not irrevocably and inevitably fixed at ten years." 554 F.3d at 575.

When the witness testified as a prosecution witness at Skilling's trial, the government bolstered the witness's credibility by emphasizing that the witness had no reason to lie, because the witness would spend ten years, and no less, in prison. After Skilling had been convicted, however, a judge sentenced the witness to approximately six years. The defendant argued in the Court of Appeals that the government and the witness had an undisclosed side deal regarding the witness's testimony, and the government's failure to disclose the side deal violated *Brady*.

The Court of Appeals rejected Skilling's argument. The Court stated that "there was nothing that the government suppressed. Skilling knew, or at least should have known, that a sentencing court could reduce [the witness's] sentence . . . . Skilling also had to know this, and thus the government did not suppress anything." 554 F.3d at 575. Skilling's misapprehension of the law was not a *Brady* violation by the government.

PART VI. REQUESTING AND PRODUCING EXCULPATORY EVIDENCE

§ 1:79 Voluntary disclosure of exculpatory evidence—in general

In *United States v. Price* (2009, CA9 OR) 566 F.3d 900, the Ninth Circuit

Court of Appeals cited to and quoted from a federal district court opinion that provides advice and counsel to prosecutors "who must regularly decide what material to turn over" in order to comply with their *Brady* duties. Prosecutors are advised to make voluntary disclosure of exculpatory evidence without engaging in "materiality" inquiries. The district court opinion quoted by the Ninth Circuit is *United States v. Acosta* (2004, D. NV) 357 F.Supp.2d 1228, 1239–1240. The language of the district court is as follows:

"[T]he 'materiality' inquiry usually associated with *Brady* . . . should not be applied to pretrial discovery of exculpatory materials . . . . [J]ust because a prosecutor's failure to disclose evidence does not violate a defendant's due process rights does not mean that the failure to disclose is proper . . . . [T]he absence of prejudice to the defendant does not *condone* the prosecutor's suppression of exculpatory evidence [ex ante] . . . . [Rather,] the proper test for pretrial disclosure of exculpatory evidence should be an evaluation of whether the evidence is favorable to the defense, i.e., whether it is evidence that helps bolster the defense case or impeach the prosecutor's witnesses . . . . [I]f doubt exists, it should be resolved in favor of the defendant and full disclosure made . . . . [T]he government [should therefore] disclose all evidence relating to guilt or punishment which might reasonably be considered favorable to the defendant's case, even if the evidence is not admissible so long as it is reasonably likely to lead to admissible evidence." 566 F.3d at 913.

Practice Tip for Prosecution: The advice to prosecutors from the Ninth Circuit Court of Appeals is that prosecutors should disclose favorable evidence possessed by the prosecution team, without subjecting that evidence to a materiality test as a precondition to disclosure. We likewise commend that advice as constituting practical good sense.

§ 1:79.1   Voluntary disclosure of oral exculpatory evidence

The prosecution's constitutional duty to disclose material exculpatory evidence pursuant to *Brady v. Maryland* (1963) 373 U.S. 83, 87, 83 S.Ct. 1194, 10 L.Ed.2d 215, is not avoided because of the failure of the prosecution team to reduce that evidence to a written form.

In *United States v. Rodriguez* (2007, CA2 NY) 496 F.3d 221, the defendant was convicted of drug dealing in a multi-defendant trial. The prosecution's case rested upon the testimony of two cooperating witnesses. At trial one of these witnesses testified that the witness had lied "about everything" in her initial interviews with investigators. After the prosecution stated that no notes had been made of the false statements, the trial court declined to order the prosecution to disclose the oral false statements that had been made by the witness. The trial court did not explain its reason for denying the defense request for disclosure.

The Second Circuit Court of Appeals remanded the case to the district court for that court to determine whether the prosecution's failure to disclose the oral false statements constituted a *Brady* violation. The Court of Appeals, however, opined that "[i]f the district court's reason for declining to compel disclosure was that the statements were not recorded, we do not agree. When the Government is in possession of material information that impeaches its witness or exculpates the defendant, it does not avoid the obligation under *Brady/Giglio* to disclose the information by not writing it down." 496 F.3d at 222.

In *United States v. Duval* (2007, CA1 MA) 496 F.3d 64, 73, the First Circuit Court of Appeals described the investigating officers' practice of keeping scant notes of conversations with a witness that tended to exculpate the prime suspects as "a practice whose propriety is questionable." In *United States v. Houlihan* (1996, CA1 MA) 92 F.3d 1271, 1289, the First Circuit opined: "Eschewing tape recordings and ordering law enforcement agents not to take notes during pretrial interviews is risky business—and not guaranteed to redound either to the sovereign's credit or to its benefit. By adopting a 'what we don't create can't come back to haunt us' approach, prosecutors demean their primary mission: to see that justice is done."

§ 1:82   Prosecutor review of *Brady* evidence—generally

The question whether a prosecutor can comply with his or her *Brady* duties by making judgments about the reliability, accuracy, or truthfulness of facially exculpatory evidence is a difficult one. The issue is this one: may a prosecutor determine that facially exculpatory evidence is unreliable, inaccurate, or untruthful, and then decide that the evidence need not be disclosed as *Brady* evidence. The arguments on both sides of this issue have merit, and the conflicting positions on this question are not easily reconciled.

§ 1:82.2   Prosecutor review of *Brady* evidence—truthfulness of evidence as consideration

On the one hand, the argument that the prosecutor has no legitimate role in evaluating the reliability, accuracy, or truthfulness of facially favorable evidence has powerful decisional support.

The California Supreme Court has accepted the reasoning of the Ninth Circuit Court of Appeals in *United States v. Alvarez* (1996, CA9 CA) 86 F.3d 901, that a prosecutor is not entitled to withhold facially exculpatory evidence from a defendant simply because the prosecutor does not believe that the evidence is exculpatory, or because the prosecutor believes that the evidence would be inadmissible.

In *In re Miranda* (2008) 43 Cal.4th 541, 76 Cal.Rptr.3d 172, 182 P.3d 513, the petitioner had been convicted of capital murder. In the penalty phase of the trial the prosecution presented testimony from one Joe Saucedo that the defendant/habeas petitioner had killed another man two weeks before the capital crime. Saucedo was the prosecution's "star penalty phase witness." 43 Cal.4th at 575. The defendant had pled guilty to the prior crime as a second degree murder. The facts of the prior murder were used by the prosecution as evidence in aggravation in the penalty phase of the capital murder trial to argue for a death sentence. The defendant/petitioner was sentenced to death for the second murder.

At the time of the capital murder trial the prosecution possessed a letter written by another inmate in the Los Angeles County jail that Saucedo had told him that he (Saucedo), not the defendant, had personally killed the victim in the prior murder. The letter also related that Saucedo claimed he had destroyed evidence relating to the prior murder, and that he had developed a false alibi to deflect suspicion from himself for that murder. The prosecution did not disclose that letter to the defendant/petitioner.

The defendant/petitioner filed a habeas petition in the California state courts. The Supreme Court appointed a referee to conduct an evidentiary hearing on the petitioner's *Brady* violation claims. The referee found that the prosecution had possessed numerous pieces of evidence in addition to the letter from the jail inmate that Saucedo had killed the victim in the prior murder and that this evidence was credible.

The Supreme Court granted the habeas petition and set aside the petitioner's death sentence. The Court concluded that the letter from the jail inmate was favorable to the petitioner, because it constituted evidence that was inconsistent with Saucedo's trial testimony that inculpated the petitioner and rebutted the prosecution's evidence that the petitioner had killed the victim in the prior murder. 43 Cal.4th at 575–576.

The Court rejected the argument that the prosecutor had not committed *Brady* error in withholding the letter, because the prosecutor believed that the letter would not be admissible in the defendant's trial. The Court, quoting from the *Alvarez* opinion, stated:

" 'In the end, the trial judge, not the prosecutor, is the arbiter of admissibility, and the prosecutor's *Brady* obligations cannot turn on the prosecutor's view of whether or how defense counsel might employ particular items of evidence at trial.' It is not the role of the prosecutor to decide that facially exculpatory evidence need not be turned over because the prosecutor thinks the information is false. It is 'the criminal trial, as distinct from the prosecutor's private deliberations' that is the 'chosen forum for ascertaining the truth about criminal accusations.' " 43 Cal.4th at 577.

In *United States v. Rittweger* (2008, CA2 NY) 524 F.3d 171, the Second Circuit Court of Appeals rejected the argument that a prosecutor does not commit *Brady* error by withholding exculpatory evidence, because the prosecution had evidence of the defendant's guilt. The Court held that the prosecution is not excused from disclosing evidence that the defendant did not commit the charged crime, simply because the prosecution possesses evidence that the defendant is guilty of that crime. Evidence that is favorable to the defendant because it tends to negate the prosecution's inculpatory evidence does not lose its character as *Brady* evidence in the face of inculpatory evidence to the contrary. 524 F.3d at 181.

In *Tennison v. City and County of San Francisco* (2009, CA9 CA) 570 F.3d 1078, two men brought a federal civil rights action against the officers who had investigated them for murder. The homicide investigation had resulted in the filing of murder charges against the two men. The men were convicted of murder and sentenced to prison, where they remained until freed from custody following their filing of a habeas corpus petition in the federal courts. The two men then filed a civil action against the officers, the prosecutor, and the City and County of San Francisco, alleging, *inter alia*, that the officers had withheld exculpatory evidence from the prosecutor, and that the prosecutor had committed *Brady* violations in failing to disclose that evidence to them. The district court denied the officers' motion for summary judgment, and the defendants in the civil action (the City and County, the investigating officers, and the prosecutor), appealed to the Court of Appeals.

The officers argued in the Court of Appeals that the withheld evidence they had unearthed in their investigation was not all that important. The Ninth Circuit Court of Appeals rejected this argument, concluding that the argument was an effort to dismiss their *Brady* duty by downplaying the importance of the favorable evidence. Quoting from the opinion of the Second Circuit Court of Appeals in *DiSimone v. Phillips* (2006, CA2 NY) 461 F.3d 181, 195, the Court of Appeals stated that "[i]f there were questions about the reliability of the exculpatory information, it was the prerogative of the defendant and his counsel—and not of the prosecution—to exercise judgment in determining whether the defendant should make use of it, because '[t]o allow otherwise would be to appoint the fox as henhouse guard.' [citation omitted]." 570 F.3d at 1094.

On the other hand, since the materiality of facially favorable evidence is an essential component of the *Brady* duty of disclosure, and the duty of making *Brady* disclosure determinations rests squarely on the shoulders of the prosecutor, it seems anomalous to conclude that the prosecutor should not be free to act in accordance with this duty. Thus, several federal Courts of Appeals have held that "[t]he failure to disclose untrustworthy and unsubstantiated allegations against a government witness is not a *Brady* violation." *United States v. Souffront* (2003, CA7 IL) 338 F.3d 809, 823; *United States v. Locascio* (1993, CA2 NY) 6 F.3d 924, 948–950. *See also, United States v. Wilson* (2010, CA DC) 605 F.3d 985, 1005 [bald assertions and unproven allegations are not probative of truthfulness or untruthfulness.].

These conflicting authorities are hard to reconcile. The language from the opinion of the Second Circuit Court of Appeals in *DiSimone v. Phillips* (2006, CA2 NY) 461 F.3d 181, 195, that equates the prosecutor with being the "fox" guarding the *Brady* "henhouse" is particularly galling to prosecutors, because the courts have repeatedly admonished that prosecutors are expected to adhere to high ethical standards of ensuring that all parties to a criminal prosecution, including the criminal defendants being prosecuted, receive fair trials.

Even though more than a few prosecutors have crossed the line of fair advocacy by intentionally disregarding their *Brady* duties, denigrating prosecutors as a group by equating them to sly foxes waiting to rob defendants of their rights to fair trials is itself an unfair characterization.

Practice Tip for Prosecution: As the United States Supreme Court has repeatedly admonished, prosecutors should not "tack[ ] too close to the wind" when making *Brady* determinations. *See Kyles v. Whitley* (1995) 514 U.S. 419, 439, 115 S.Ct. 1555, 131 L.Ed.2d 490. We caution prosecutors that playing "materiality games" is rarely productive of good prosecutorial ethics and can lead to serious appellate issues and potential disciplinary actions by the State Bar against the prosecutor.

Practice Tip for Defendant: Even though it is tempting, and occasionally justified, to treat the prosecutor as an untrustworthy foe who should be presumed to be ready and willing to fail to follow constitutional discovery rules, we recommend that criminal defense attorneys adopt a more professional approach. We recommend that defense attorneys constantly remind prosecutors in their cases of the prosecutors' duties to ensure fair trials for everyone, including the defendant, by voluntarily and willingly disclosing evidence that would assist the defendant in resisting the criminal charges.

Some prosecutors will fail to uphold their high standards of discovery conduct even in the face of admonitions of courts and opposing counsel. Those prosecutors can and should be subjected to different forms of ethics "encouragement." But unless and until an individual prosecutor fails to adhere to his or her constitutional discovery responsibilities, we believe that the better approach for courts and counsel generally is to affirmatively exhort prosecutors to do their jobs with dignity and high ethical standards, rather than to presume and claim that prosecutors want only to "win" convictions, no matter how unfairly obtained those convictions might be.

§ 1:83 Judicial review of *Brady* evidence—generally

The extent to which a court should become involved in reviewing government files and evidence searching for suppressed exculpatory evidence depends upon the court's determination whether the prosecution is complying with its *Brady* duties.

§ 1:83.2 Judicial supervisory role

Where it appears that the prosecution is not fulfilling its duty to disclose material exculpatory evidence to the defendant, the court is obligated to become involved in examining the evidence to determine whether it should be disclosed.

In *United States v. White* (2007, CA7 OH) 492 F.3d 380, defendants convicted of Medicare fraud offenses requested the trial court to hold an evidentiary hearing to determine whether the prosecution had withheld material exculpatory evidence in violation of *Brady*. The trial court declined to hold such a hearing or to examine the allegedly exculpatory evidence.

On appeal the Sixth Circuit Court of Appeals held that the district court had abused its discretion in failing to hold such a hearing. The Court observed that the government had gone to great lengths to deny the defendants access to the requested documents.

The Court criticized the district court's characterization of the defendants' request for a hearing as a "fishing expedition," saying that "the fish swim just below the surface of the pond and, for reasons squarely within the government's control, the waters run cloudy, rendering Defendants unable to discern the nature of the fish. Defendants allege a serious constitutional violation. We will not so easily and off-handedly dismiss Defendants' claim, and the district court abused its discretion in doing so without first peering below the surface." 492 F.3d at 413, n.16.

The Court of Appeals concluded that absent a detailed examination by the district court, the Court of Appeals cannot determine whether the government violated its *Brady* duties, and the failure of the district court to conduct its own examination of the contested materials would "effectively permit the government to ride roughshod over the accused, stripping the accused of both sword and shield." 492 F.3d at 413.

While the defendant has the burden to establish by more than mere speculation or unsupported assertions that the prosecution is failing to carry out its constitutionally-based disclosure duties, if the defendant makes a plausible showing that documents possessed by the government contain materially favorable evidence, the defendant may request the court to conduct an *in camera* review of the government's files and records. Such a review is the "accepted procedure for resolving legitimate doubt about the existence of undisclosed materials and one that balances the defendant's important need for access to potentially relevant material with the Government's valid interest in protecting confidential files and the integrity of pending investigations." *United States v. Jumah* (2010, CA7 IL) 599 F.3d 799, 810.

This procedure has the imprimatur of approval of the United States Supreme Court. *See Pennsylvania v. Ritchie* (1987) 480 U.S. 39, 58, 107 S.Ct. 989, 94 L.Ed.2d 40.

The showing that a defendant must make in order to obtain an *in camera* judicial review of materials possessed by the prosecution to determine whether those materials contain *Brady* evidence that must be disclosed to the defendant was explained by the Fourth Circuit Court of Appeals in *United States v. King* (2011, CA4 NC) 628 F.3d 693.

In *King* the government refused to disclose the grand jury testimony of a prosecution witness unless the defendant obtained a court order to release grand jury testimony. On appeal of his conviction, the defendant argued that the government's refusal violated *Brady*. The Court of Appeals vacated the defendant's conviction and sentence on the charge relating to the witness's grand jury testimony and remanded the case to the district court for that court to conduct an *in camera* inspection of the grand jury testimony.

The Court of Appeals observed that when a defendant does not know, but simply suspects, that evidence possessed by the prosecution contains exculpatory evidence, the defendant " 'is not required . . . to make a particular showing of the exact information sought and how it is material and favorable.' [citation omitted] In such circumstances, a defendant need only 'make some plausible showing' that exculpatory material exists. [citation omitted] Once he has done so, he becomes 'entitled . . . to have the information'—not immediately disclosed to him—but 'submitted to the trial court for *in camera* inspection' to determine if in fact the information is *Brady* material subject to disclosure. [citations omitted] In making the requisite 'plausible showing' of the existence of exculpatory information, a defendant must 'identify the requested confidential material with some degree of specificity.' [citation omitted]" 628 F.3d at 703.

The Court of Appeals concluded that the defendant had made the required "plausible showing" of possible exculpatory information "by identifying the grand jury transcript of one particular witness." This showing "thus identified the information sought with sufficient particularity so as to trigger his right to an *in camera* inspection." 628 F.3d at 703.

In *United States v. Prochilo* (2011, CA1 MA) 629 F.3d 264, the First Circuit Court of Appeals appeared to impose further requirements on a defendant who seeks to meet the plausible showing requirement of *Pennsylvania v. Ritchie, supra.* "This showing cannot consist of mere speculation. [citations omitted] Rather, the defendant should be able to articulate with some specificity what evidence he hopes to find in the requested materials, why he thinks the materials contain this evidence, and finally, why this evidence would be both favorable to him and material." 629 F.3d at 268–269.

§ 1:83.4 Judicial review of *Brady* evidence—satisfying *Brady* rule

In *United States v. De La Paz-Rentas* (2010, CA1 PR) 613 F.3d 18, the First Circuit Court of Appeals appeared to hold that evidence that the government submits to a court for an *in camera* review has not been "suppressed." The Court stated that "[w]hether any information was 'suppressed' is far from clear. . . . Information . . . was submitted by the government for *in camera* review, and the district court then determined that these files did not need to be disclosed." 613 F.3d at 27.

PART VII.   TIMING OF *BRADY* DISCLOSURES

§ 1:84   Timing of *Brady* evidence disclosures—generally

The timing requirements for disclosure of materially favorable evidence are not the same as the statutory timing requirements for prosecution disclosure of exculpatory evidence under the Criminal Discovery Statute. The differences, as discussed in the following sections of the text and this supplement, are important.

A seminal question is whether *Brady* disclosures must be made prior to trial. While the Seventh Circuit Court of Appeals in 2009 stated that "the doctrine of *Brady v. Maryland* [citation omitted] does not require pretrial turnover. It is a disclosure rather than a discovery rule," *Evans v. Circuit Court* (2009, CA7 IL) 569 F.3d 665, 667, it is questionable in the light of *Dist. Attorney's Office for the Third Jud. Dist. v. Osborne* (2009) 557 U.S. 52, 129 S.Ct. 2308, 174 L.Ed.2d 38, whether the statement from *Evans* remains good law. The opinion in *Evans* was filed only five days after the filing of the Supreme Court opinion in *Osborne*, in which the Supreme Court stated: "In [*Brady v. Maryland*], we held that due process requires a prosecutor to disclose material exculpatory evidence to the defendant *before trial*." 129 S.Ct. at 2319. [italics added]

It is possible that the import of this statement from *Osborne* is only that *Brady* evidence must be disclosed *before trial* as distinguished from *after trial*. This was the construction of this statement from *Osborne* given by the Sixth Circuit Court of Appeals in *Montgomery v. Bagley* (2009, CA6 OH) 581 F.3d 440, 442 ["The law under *Brady* follows the common sense proposition that the State must disclose the 'material exculpatory evidence to the defendant before trial' not afterward."].

But this language from *Osborne* calls into question the many federal court opinions that have held that as long as disclosure is made in time for the defendant to make effective use of the favorable evidence in trial, the prosecution may disclose *Brady* evidence at or during trial. These statements from the Circuit Courts of Appeals have continued, however, even after the decision of the Supreme Court in *Osborne*. In *United States v. Houston* (2011, CA9 CA) 648 F.3d 806, 813, the Ninth Circuit Court of Appeals stated that "there is no *Brady* violation so long as the exculpatory or impeaching evidence is disclosed at a time when it still has value." In *Houston* the prosecution disclosed the name of a witness in advance of trial but did not produce the FBI interview notes regarding the witness until the witness was undergoing cross-examination in trial. The Court of Appeals held that the production of the interview notes during the witness's testimony in trial did not violate *Brady*'s disclosure time requirements. The Court concluded that "[a]t this point, the notes still had evidentiary value to the defense because they could be used—and were used—during cross examination." 648 F.3d at 813.

In fact, the Eighth Circuit Court of Appeals stated in *United States v. Jeanpierre* (2011, CA8 MN) 636 F.3d 416, 422: "We have previously held that '*Brady* does not require pretrial disclosure, and due process is satisfied if the information is furnished before it is too late for the defendant to use it at trial.' [citation omitted]" In the face of the defendant's claim in *Jeanpierre* that the government violated *Brady* by providing fingerprint reports to the defendant during trial, the Court of Appeals rejected the claim, observing that the government provided the fingerprint report prior to any testimony being offered at trial, and the defendant used the report in his cross examination of a government witness and in the defense closing argument. 636 F.3d at 423.

And the Court of Appeals of the District of Columbia Circuit held in *United States v. Bailey* (2010, CA DC) 622 F.3d 1, 9, that the government did not violate the *Brady* rule by its disclosure on the last day of trial that the government was unable to locate a traffic ticket that was the basis for the stop and detention of the defendant. The Court of Appeals stated that the "traffic ticket was disclosed at trial in sufficient time for appellant to make effective use of the ticket's absence. . . . [A]ppellant was able to argue the ticket's absence during closing argument to the jury in attacking [the officer's] credibility and, indeed, the government's evidence generally." 622 F.3d at 9.

See also United States v. Struckman (2010, CA9 WA) 611 F.3d 560, 577–578 ["[T]he 'animating purpose of *Brady* is to preserve the fairness of criminal trials.' [citation omitted]."].

§ 1:84.1   Effective use at trial rule

In *United States v. Douglas* (2008, CA2 NY) 525 F.3d 225, the Second Circuit Court of Appeals explained the principle that governs the timing of the disclosure of material exculpatory evidence under the *Brady* rule. In giving this explanation the Court utilized the prejudice/materiality standard that is a component of the basic *Brady* rule: whether there is a reasonable probability that the disclosure of the withheld evidence would have produced a different result at trial. The Court stated:

"*Brady* material that is not 'disclos[ed] in sufficient time to afford the defense an opportunity for use' may be deemed suppressed within the meaning of the *Brady* doctrine. [citation omitted] But as long as a defendant possesses *Brady* evidence in time for its effective use, the government has not deprived the defendant of due process of law simply because it did not produce the evidence sooner. There is no *Brady* violation unless there is a reasonable probability that earlier disclosure of the evidence would have produced a different result at trial." 525 F.3d at 245.

Determining whether late or delayed disclosure of exculpatory evidence is a *Brady* violation is very much a fact-specific exercise that includes a consideration of the amount of exculpatory evidence that is disclosed, the manner in which the exculpatory evidence is organized, and the proximity of the disclosure to the commencement of the trial. In *United States v. Douglas*, although the *Brady* disclosures were made only one day prior to the start of the trial, the total pages disclosed were only 290 pages in length, and they were organized so as to facilitate easy reading and understanding by the defendant. 525 F.3d at 245–246.

See also, United States v. Heppner (2008, CA8 MN) 519 F.3d 744, 750 [Disclosure of FBI investigation into financial transaction of government witness made the day before trial; Court of Appeals found that defendants had the information in time to use it at trial.].

In *United States v. Duval* (2007, CA1 MA) 496 F.3d 64, the First Circuit Court of Appeals concluded that a delayed disclosure of exculpatory evidence that was completed six months prior to the start of the trial left sufficient time for the defendants' attorneys to incorporate the exculpatory information into their defense strategy.

Another factor in determining whether a delayed disclosure of exculpatory evidence violated the *Brady* rule is for the court to examine how the defense was actually able to use the evidence in the trial.

In *United States v. Van Anh* (2008, CA1 RI) 523 F.3d 43, the First Circuit Court of Appeals articulated the delayed disclosure standard as whether "the delay prevented defense counsel from using the disclosed material effectively in preparing and presenting the defendant's case." 523 F.3d at 51. Applying that standard, the Court considered that the withheld exculpatory evidence consisted of the criminal record of the victim and prosecution witness, and that the evidence was disclosed to the defense six days before trial. The Court of Appeals concluded from a review of the trial record that "the record reflects ample use of the disclosed evidence." 523 F.3d at 52. *See also, United States v. Mendez* (2008, CA10 KS) 514 F.3d 1035, 1047 ["Further, the material was actually disclosed to the defense and used during cross-examination."].

In evaluating whether a late disclosure of exculpatory evidence prevented the defendant from making effective use of the evidence at trial, appellate courts consider whether the defendant requested a continuance because of the delayed or late disclosure. It is a general rule that "a defendant who does not request a continuance will not be heard to complain on appeal that he suffered prejudice as a result of late-arriving discovery." *United States v. Sepulveda* (1993, CA1 NH) 15 F.3d 1161, 1178; *United States v. Mangual-*

Garcia (2007, CA1 P.R.) 505 F.3d 1, 5–6.

In *Tennison v. City and County of San Francisco* (2009, CA9 CA) 570 F.3d 1078, two men brought a federal civil rights action against the officers who had investigated them for murder. The homicide investigation had resulted in the filing of murder charges against the two men. The men were convicted of murder at separate trials and sentenced to prison, where they remained until freed from custody following their filing of a habeas corpus petition in the federal courts. The two men then filed a civil action against the officers, the prosecutor, and the City and County of San Francisco, alleging, *inter alia*, that the officers had withheld exculpatory evidence from the prosecutor, and that the prosecutor had committed *Brady* violations in failing to disclose that evidence to them. The district court denied the officers' motion for summary judgment, and the defendants in the civil action (the City and County, the investigating officers, and the prosecutor) appealed to the Court of Appeals.

One of the items of exculpatory evidence that the prosecution had failed to disclose to the defendants was a tape-recorded statement of a third person confessing to the murder. This tape was disclosed to defendant Goff after his judgment sentencing him to prison, and to defendant Tennison during his post-conviction motion for a new trial. The prosecution claimed that Tennison could have made effective use of the tape recording on that motion. The Court of Appeals rejected the officers' argument, noting that "Tennison did not learn about the tape until the second to the last day of the hearing on his motion for a new trial, much too late for the disclosure to be of value to him." 570 F.3d at 1093.

In *Bielanski v. County of Kane* (2008, CA7 IL) 550 F.3d 632, a young woman was accused and ultimately acquitted of sexually abusing a six-year-old neighbor. She then filed a civil action against a number of public officials and entities, alleging that, among other claims, they had denied her due process of law in violation of *Brady* by withholding evidence that would have enabled her to discredit the testimony of the six-year-old victim. The district court held that the withheld evidence would not have destroyed the prosecution's case and would not have caused a pretrial dismissal of the charges. The district court dismissed the complaint.

The woman appealed to the Court of Appeals, which affirmed the judgment of the district court. The Seventh Circuit Court of Appeals concluded that the prosecution's decision to go to trial would not have been affected by the withheld evidence, and earlier disclosure of the evidence would not have caused the prosecution to dismiss the charges prior to trial. The Court observed that the withheld evidence was impeaching, rather than exculpatory, and although it would have weakened the prosecution's case, it was not the type of evidence that would have precluded the trier of fact from convicting her of the charges. Since the woman was ultimately acquitted at trial, the Court concluded that she "did not suffer the harm that *Brady* aims to prevent," and there was no *Brady* violation. 550 F.3d at 645.

For two additional cases in which Courts of Appeals have held that the late disclosure of favorable evidence did not deny the defendant a fair trial and thus did not constitute *Brady* error, see *Powell v. Quarterman* (2008, CA5 TX) 536 F.3d 325, 334–342; and *United States v. Kuehne* (2008, CA6 OH) 547 F.3d 667, 697 [disclosure of tape recording of prosecution witness making statements regarding his supplier of an illegal drug one day before the witness testified did not prevent the defendant from effectively using the tape recording to impeach the witness at trial]. *See also, United States v. Kimoto* (2009, CA7 IL) 588 F.3d 464, 489 [prosecution's in-trial provision of hard paper copies of e-mails to defendant satisfied government's *Brady* duty, as defendant was able to make effective use of the hard paper copies in cross-examining prosecution witness.].

Whether or not *Brady* imposes a duty on prosecutors to make disclosures of materially favorable evidence prior to trial, the standard for determining whether the timing of the prosecutor's disclosure is constitutionally adequate is whether it is reasonably probable that an earlier disclosure would have created a reasonable doubt of guilt. *See United States v. Burke* (2009, CA10 WY) 571 F.3d 1048, 1053, 1054; *United States v. Livingstone* (2009, CA8 MN) 576 F.3d 881, 884; *United States v. Celis* (2010, CA DC) 608 F.3d 818, 835.

The defendant who makes a claim that the delay in disclosing *Brady* evidence prevented his or her attorney from using the disclosed material effectively in preparing and presenting the defendant's case must make a showing that identifies *how* the delayed disclosure prevented the attorney from providing effective representation. *United States v. Rivera Calderon* (2009, CA1 PR) 578 F.3d 78, 93.

§ 1:84.1.1   Effective use at trial rule in habeas proceeding

When the defendant raises a *Brady* contention in the context of a habeas corpus proceeding, the correct point of reference for determining *Brady* materiality is the underlying trial, not the pending habeas proceeding. *Eulloqui v. Superior Court* (2010) 181 Cal.App.4th 1055, 105 Cal.Rptr.3d 248. In *Eulloqui* a habeas petitioner filed a discovery motion seeking access to the personnel records of the police detective who had testified as a prosecution witness at the defendant's trial. The court hearing the habeas petition denied the motion without reviewing the officer's personnel records in an *in camera* proceeding.

The Court of Appeal issued a peremptory writ commanding the trial court to conduct an *in camera* review of the detective's personnel records before ruling on the defendant's motion. In reaching this holding the Court of Appeal emphasized that because the sole concern in *Brady* was the fairness of the defendant's trial, 181 Cal.App.4th at 1065, and because the California Supreme Court has "repeatedly stressed the focus upon the importance of the undisclosed evidence to the trial," 181 Cal.App.4th at 1066, the "the pertinent inquiry for *Brady* materiality regarding the matters sought in petitioner's discovery motion is whether petitioner's *trial* was unfair in the absence of possible evidence from Eagleson's personnel file." 181 Cal.App.4th at 1067–1068 [italics in original].

Accordingly, the Court held that the defendant would not be entitled to discovery of complaints alleging misconduct by the officer that occurred subsequent to the defendant's trial. 181 Cal.App.4th at 1068.

§ 1:84.2   Adverse effect on trial preparation rule

Although a delayed disclosure of material exculpatory evidence can produce a *Brady* violation if the delayed disclosure deprives the defendant of an opportunity to follow up on leads resulting from the disclosed evidence, courts do not assume that the defendant has been deprived of that opportunity absent evidence of that result. *United States v. Douglas* (2008, CA2 NY) 525 F.3d 225, 246.

§ 1:84.4   Effect on pleading decision rule

The *Brady* rule does not consider whether a delayed disclosure of material exculpatory evidence violated *Brady*, if the delayed disclosure thereby caused the defendant to decline to plea bargain the charges. A criminal defendant does not have a constitutional right to plea bargain. *Weatherford v. Bursey* (1977) 429 U.S. 545, 561, 97 S.Ct. 837, 51 L.Ed.2d 30 ["But there is no constitutional right to plea bargain; the prosecutor need not do so if he prefers to go to trial. It is a novel argument that constitutional rights are infringed by trying the defendant rather than accepting his plea of guilty."]; *Wooten v. Thaler* (2010, CA5 TX) 598 F.3d 215, 221–222.

In *United States v. Mathur* (2010, CA1 MA) 624 F.3d 498, a convicted defendant argued on appeal that late disclosure by the prosecution of exculpatory evidence deprived him of the opportunity to negotiate a favorable plea deal by making the government less amenable to a plea bargain. The First Circuit Court of Appeals rejected the defendant's argument, stating: "The animating principle of Brady is the 'avoidance of an unfair trial.' [citation omitted] It is, therefore, universally acknowledged that the right memorialized in *Brady* is a trial right. . . . In urging us to extend *Brady*'s prejudice component to pretrial plea negotiations, the defendant exhorts us to break new ground. He does not cite a single case standing for this novel approach . . . . The *Ruiz* Court evinced a reluctance to extend a *Brady*-like right to the realm of pretrial plea negotiations, . . . *Ruiz* teaches that *Brady* does not protect against the possible prejudice that may ensue from the loss of an opportunity to plea-bargain with complete knowledge of all relevant facts. This makes good sense: when a defendant chooses to admit his guilt, *Brady* concerns subside." 624 F.3d at 506–507.

§ 1:84.5   Effective use for motion rule

A late disclosure of exculpatory evidence can violate a defendant's right to a fair trial when it is disclosed during the defendant's motion for a new trial. In *Tennison v. City and County of San Francisco* (2009, CA9 CA) 570 F.3d 1078, two men brought a federal civil rights action against the officers who had investigated them for murder. The homicide investigation had resulted in the filing of murder charges against the two men. The men were convicted of murder at separate trials and sentenced to prison, where they remained until freed from custody following their filing of a habeas corpus petition in the federal courts. The two men then filed a civil action against the officers, the prosecutor, and the City and County of San Francisco, alleging, *inter alia*, that the officers had withheld exculpatory evidence from the prosecutor, and that the prosecutor had committed *Brady* violations in failing to disclose that evidence to them. The district court denied the officers' motion for summary judgment, and the defendants in the civil action (the City and County, the investigating officers, and the prosecutor) appealed to the Court of Appeals.

One of the items of exculpatory evidence that the prosecution had failed to disclose to the defendants was a tape-recorded statement of a third person confessing to the murder. This tape was disclosed to defendant Tennison during his post-conviction motion for a new trial. The prosecution claimed that Tennison could have made effective use of the tape recording on that motion. The Court of Appeals rejected the officers' argument, noting that "Tennison did not learn about the tape until the second to the last day of the hearing on his motion for a new trial, much too late for the disclosure to be of value to him." 570 F.3d at 1093.

§ 1:84.6   Continuing duty through trial rule

The *Brady* duty to disclose materially exculpatory evidence continues throughout the criminal proceedings against the defendant. *Tennison v. City and County of San Francisco* (2009, CA9 CA) 570 F.3d 1078, 1094. "[T]he duty to disclose [exculpatory] information continues throughout the judicial process. [citation omitted]" *Douglas v. Workman* (2009, CA10 OK) 560 F.3d 1156, 1173. "Although *Brady* claims typically arise from nondisclosure of facts that occurred before trial, they can be based on nondisclosure of favorable evidence (such as impeachment evidence) that is unavailable to the government until trial is underway." *United States v. Headman* (2010, CA10 CO) 594 F.3d 1179, 1183. *Accord, Douglas v. Workman* (2009, CA10 OK) 560 F.3d 1156, 1174.

§ 1:87   Waivers of right to *Brady* evidence

It appears in light of the decision of the United States Supreme Court in *United States v. Ruiz* (2002) 536 U.S. 622, 122 S.Ct. 2450, 153 L.Ed.2d 586, that the issue is clearly decided that the Due Process Clause of the United States Constitution does not require a prosecutor to disclose impeachment evidence about a prosecution witness prior to making a plea agreement with a defendant. *Post v. Bradshaw* (2010, CA6 OH) 621 F.3d 406, 426. But the rule announced in *United States v. Ruiz* that the United States Constitution does not require the prosecution to disclose material impeachment evidence as a precondition to agreeing to a plea agreement, does not excuse the prosecution's failure to disclose material evidence that tends to show the defendant's innocence of the charge.

In *In re Miranda* (2008) 43 Cal.4th 541, 76 Cal.Rptr.3d 172, 182 P.3d 513, the petitioner had been convicted of capital murder. In the penalty phase of the trial the prosecution presented the testimony of a man named Joe Saucedo, who testified that the petitioner had killed another man two weeks before the capital crime. Saucedo was the prosecution's "star penalty phase witness." 43 Cal.4th at 575. The petitioner had pled guilty to the prior crime as a second degree murder. The facts of the prior murder were used by the prosecution as evidence in aggravation in the penalty phase of the capital murder trial to argue for a death sentence. The petitioner was sentenced to death for the second murder.

At the time of the capital murder trial the prosecution possessed a letter written by another inmate in the Los Angeles County jail in which the inmate wrote that Saucedo had told him that he (Saucedo), not the defendant, had personally killed the victim in the prior murder. The letter also related that Saucedo claimed he had destroyed evidence relating to the prior murder and that he had developed a false alibi to deflect suspicion from himself for that murder. The prosecution did not disclose that letter to the petitioner.

The petitioner filed a habeas petition in the California state courts. The Supreme Court appointed a referee to conduct an evidentiary hearing on the petitioner's *Brady* violation claims. The referee found that the prosecution had possessed numerous pieces of evidence in addition to the letter from the jail inmate that Saucedo had killed the victim in the prior murder and that this evidence was credible.

The Supreme Court granted the habeas petition and set aside the petitioner's death sentence. The Court concluded that the letter from the jail inmate was favorable to the petitioner, because it constituted evidence that was inconsistent with Saucedo's trial testimony that inculpated the petitioner and rebutted the prosecution's evidence that the petitioner had killed the victim in the prior murder. 43 Cal.4th at 575–576.

The evidence pointing to Saucedo as the actual killer in the prior murder thus constituted evidence negating the identity of the defendant as the actual killer in the charged prior murder. The California Supreme Court held that *United States v. Ruiz* does not apply to excuse the prosecution's non-disclosure of the material exculpatory evidence. The Court stated:

> "*Ruiz* does not foreclose relief from petitioner's conviction of the
> Hosey murder [the charged prior murder]. *Ruiz* by its terms applies

only to material *impeachment* evidence, and the high court emphasized that the government there had agreed to 'provide any information establishing the factual innocence of the defendant regardless.' [citation omitted] Here, although the undisclosed evidence would indeed have served an impeachment function in petitioner's penalty trial by casting doubt on the veracity of Saucedo's testimony, in the context of the Hosey case the undisclosed evidence also would have tended to exculpate petitioner by showing that another person did the killing." 43 Cal.4th at 582. [italics in original].

The question whether the defendant's guilty plea vitiates the prosecution's failure to disclose evidence of the defendant's factual innocence has not yet been resolved by the United States Supreme Court. However, the federal circuit Courts of Appeals have spoken to this question. *See McCann v. Mangialardi* (2003, CA7 IL) 337 F.3d 782, 787; *Matthew v. Johnson* (2000, CA5 TX) 201 F.3d 353, 361 [nolo contendere plea waived claim that the state violated defendant's constitutional rights by failing to disclose allegedly material exculpatory information]; *Orman v. Cain* (2000, CA5 LA) 228 F.3d 616, 617 ["*Brady* requires a prosecutor to disclose exculpatory evidence for purposes of ensuring a fair trial, a concern that is absent when a defendant waives trial and pleads guilty."]

In *United States v. Moussaoui* (2010, CA4 VA) 591 F.3d 263, the defendant, who was allegedly the 20th hijacker in the September 11, 2001, terrorist attacks on the United States, moved to set aside his guilty plea, alleging that his plea was not voluntarily entered because he was denied disclosure of exculpatory evidence. The district court denied the defendant's motion, and the defendant was sentenced to life in prison without the possibility of release. The defendant appealed to the Court of Appeals.

The Fourth Circuit Court of Appeals, while noting the cases discussing the subject, declined to resolve the question whether the *Brady* rule entitles a defendant to disclosure of factually exculpatory evidence prior to the defendant's entry of a guilty plea, because the Court of Appeals concluded that the defendant's guilty plea was knowingly and voluntarily entered. However, the Court observed that "[t]he *Brady* right, however, is a trial right . . . When a defendant pleads guilty [concerns about the fairness of a trial protected by *Brady*] are almost completely eliminated, because his guilt is admitted." 591 F.3d at 285.

In *Jones v. Cooper* (2002, CA4 NC) 311 F.3d 306, 315, n.5, the Fourth Circuit Court of Appeals held that a defendant who pleads guilty waives his or her right to disclosure of information that is potentially relevant as mitigation evidence in the death-penalty phase of the defendant's trial.

The issue whether pursuant to *Brady* the prosecution must disclose evidence of factual innocence prior to the defendant's entry of a guilty or no contest plea remains unresolved.

PART VIII. CONSEQUENCES OF *BRADY* VIOLATION

§ 1:88 Consequences—in general

A trial court that determines that the prosecuting attorney has committed a *Brady* violation has discretion to determine an appropriate remedy that is restrained only by statutory limitations and constitutional constraints. A *Brady* violation can result in numerous consequences, and none of these consequences are helpful to the prosecution.

§ 1:88.1 Setting aside judgment of conviction

The government's withholding of evidence causes prejudice for purposes of a *Brady* claim if the evidence withheld undermines confidence in the outcome of the trial. *United States v. Harkonen* (Mar. 4, 2013, CA9 Cal.) 2013 U.S. App. LEXIS 4472.

" '[T]he appropriate remedy' for a *Brady/Giglio* violation 'will usually be a new trial.' [citation omitted]." *United States v. Kohring* (2011, CA9 AK) 637 F.3d 895, 913. Because the grant of a new trial requires that first the judgment of conviction be set aside, setting aside the judgment of conviction can be a consequence of a *Brady* violation.

When the government suppresses exculpatory evidence that is material to only one of a number of charges for which the defendant has been convicted, but not to other charges, invalidation of the judgment of conviction as to that charge, but not invalidation of the remaining convictions, is an appropriate remedy. *Silva v. Brown* (2005, CA9 CA) 416 F.3d 980, 990–991. When, however, withheld impeachment evidence regarding a material prosecution witness undermines confidence in verdicts of guilt of multiple counts, the appropriate remedy is for the trial court to set aside the judgments of conviction of those multiple counts. *Breakiron v. Horn* (2011, CA3 PA) 642 F.3d 126, 135.

§ 1:88.1.1 New trial

" '[T]he appropriate remedy' for a *Brady/Giglio* violation 'will usually be a new trial.' [citation omitted]." *United States v. Kohring* (2011, CA9 AK) 637 F.3d 895, 913. Because the grant of a new trial requires that first the judgment of conviction be set aside, setting aside the judgment of conviction and the granting of a new trial are consequences of a *Brady* violation that are normally tied together.

§ 1:88.2 Setting aside guilty plea

Where the trial court determines that the prosecution has committed a *Brady* violation by withholding evidence of the defendant's factual innocence, and the defendant has entered a guilty or a no contest plea, the court has the power to set aside the guilty plea, if the court determines that the withholding of the evidence of factual innocence has resulted in a guilty or no contest plea that is not freely and voluntarily entered. *See United States v. Moussaoui* (2010, CA4 VA) 591 F.3d 263, 285–286.

§ 1:88.6   Civil action for damages

Civil actions for damages have become a common consequence of *Brady* violations. However, the viability of civil actions to redress the harms of *Brady* violations is highly dependent upon the defendants selected as the targets of such actions.

§ 1:88.6.1   Civil action against prosecutor

While a civil action filed by a former criminal defendant against the prosecutor in his or her criminal prosecution is a possible consequence of an intentional *Brady* violation committed by the prosecutor, it appears to be well-established that "prosecutors have absolute immunity from civil liability for the non-disclosure of exculpatory information at trial." *Koubriti v. Convertino* (2010, CA6 MI) 593 F.3d 459, 467.

In *Koubriti*, a defendant charged with the commission of several federal offenses, including conspiracy to provide material support or resources to terrorists, was convicted of these offenses. Then Assistant United States Attorney Richard Convertino was the prosecutor in Mr. Koubriti's prosecution. Following his conviction, it was discovered that the government had failed to disclose numerous items of materially favorable evidence. The district court dismissed the terrorism charge without prejudice and granted a new trial on another count. A grand jury then indicted Convertino for violating several federal statutes arising out of his participation in the withholding of evidence that was materially favorable to Koubriti. That prosecution went to trial, and Convertino was acquitted of all charges.

Koubriti, who was free on bond awaiting trial on the fraud charge for which he had been granted a new trial, then filed a civil action against Convertino. In his civil action Koubriti alleged that Convertino, while acting in an investigative role, withheld exculpatory evidence from or fabricated evidence against Koubriti. Convertino filed a motion to dismiss, arguing, *inter alia*, that he had absolute immunity from civil action arising out of his role as the prosecutor in Koubriti's criminal prosecution. The trial court denied the motion to dismiss as to alleged acts of Convertino that were investigatory in nature, as opposed to prosecutorial in nature. Convertino appealed the denial of his motion to dismiss to the Sixth Circuit Court of Appeals.

The Court of Appeals reversed the district court's denial of the motion to dismiss. The Court held that Convertino enjoyed absolute immunity from civil action for an alleged *Brady* violation. The Court stated: "When Koubriti's claim is characterized as a traditional *Brady* violation, it becomes clear that Convertino is entitled to absolute immunity from civil liability," even when Convertino's conduct is characterized as administrative in nature, as opposed to prosecutorial in nature. 593 F.3d at 470. The Court concluded that calling Convertino's actions "investigative" did not strip Convertino of his absolute immunity. "Convertino's directive was part of his effort to prepare for trial and to control how his witness' testimony would play out at the trial . . . a prosecutor's conduct in his role as an advocate is protected by absolute immunity [citation omitted], even when that conduct is improper." 593 F.3d at 471.

The Court of Appeals declined to reach the question whether Convertino's conduct amounted to a more general due process violation, because that question had not been not briefed in the district court or in the Court of Appeals. 593 F.3d at 471.

The absolute immunity of the prosecutor for intentional suppression of evidence materially favorable to a criminal defendant extends to conduct of the prosecutor occurring post-judgment.

In *Warney v. Monroe County* (2009, CA2 NY) 587 F.3d 113, a defendant convicted of murder sought post-trial DNA testing in connection with a habeas corpus petition that the defendant filed in federal court. The DNA testing was performed by the district attorney's office; that test apparently showed that the defendant was not the person who had committed the murder. The favorable result was not disclosed to the defendant in a timely manner. The defendant filed a civil action against the prosecutor's office and against individual prosecutors in that office arising out of the delayed disclosure of the DNA testing results.

The prosecutors asserted in the district court that they enjoyed absolute immunity for their roles in the post-trial DNA testing and delayed disclosure to the defendant. The district court denied their motion for absolute or qualified immunity, and the prosecutors appealed the denial of the motion to the Second Circuit Court of Appeals.

The Second Circuit Court of Appeals reversed the district court's denial of the prosecutors' motion for immunity, holding that "[b]ecause the testing was undertaken in connection with post-trial proceedings and was therefore integral to the advocacy function . . . prosecutors enjoy absolute immunity under Imbler v. Pachtman [citation omitted]." 587 F.3d 113, 115.

The Court reasoned that "[a]lthough a collateral attack is technically a separate, civil proceeding, a prosecutor defending a post-conviction petition remains the state's advocate in an adversarial proceeding that is an integral part of the criminal justice system." 587 F.3d at 122. The Court determined that the DNA testing, the disclosure of the results, and even the delay in disclosing the results, were "integral to and subsumed in the advocacy functions." 587 F.3d at 123. "The decisions made by the prosecutors in this case—whether to test for potentially inculpatory (or exculpatory) information, how and when to disclose or use that information, and whether to seek to vacate Warney's conviction—were exercises of legal judgment made in the 'judicial phase' of proceedings integral to the criminal justice process." 587 F.3d at 123–124.

Thus, because "the disclosure of evidence to opposing counsel is an advocacy function," the defendants were entitled to absolute immunity for their roles in the delayed disclosure of the DNA testing results. 587 F.3d at 125.

The absolute immunity that protects prosecutors from civil actions against them for alleged *Brady* violations also extends to protect prosecutors from civil actions predicated on claims that as supervisors of a prosecutor who committed intentional *Brady* violations they failed to provide adequate supervision, training, or information-system management that might have prevented the prosecutor's *Brady* violation. *Van de Kamp v. Goldstein* (2009) 555 U.S. 335, 129 S.Ct. 855, 172 L.Ed.2d 706. The Court reasoned that "[t]he management tasks at issue, insofar as they are relevant, concern how and when to make impeachment information available at a trial. They are thereby directly connected with the prosecutor's basic trial advocacy duties." 129 S.Ct. at 863.

The Court determined that absolute immunity extends to a prosecutor's implementation of an information system for impeachment and exculpatory evidence. The Court reasoned that "[t]he critical element of any information system is the information it contains. Deciding what to include and what not to include in an information system is little different from making similar decisions in respect to training. Again, determining the criteria for inclusion or exclusion requires knowledge of the law." 129 S.Ct. at 864. The Court decided that were Goldstein's claim to be allowed to defeat absolute immunity for the supervising attorneys in the prosecutor's office, "a court would have to review the office's legal judgments, not simply about *whether* to have an information system but also about *what* kind of system is appropriate, and whether an appropriate system would have included *Giglio*-related information about one particular kind of trial information. Such decisions—whether made prior to or during a particular trial—are 'intimately associated with the judicial phase of the criminal process.' [citations omitted]" 129 S.Ct. at 864.

§ 1:88.6.2   Civil action against prosecutor's employer

A municipality or other governmental entity may be subject to liability under 42 U.S.C. section 1983 "if the governmental body itself 'subjects' a person to a deprivation of rights or 'causes' a person 'to be subjected' to such deprivation." *Connick v. Thompson* (2011) ___ U.S. ___, 131 S.Ct. 1350, 1359, 179 L.Ed.2d 417. "But, under section 1983, local governments are responsible only for 'their own illegal acts.' [citations omitted] They are not vicariously liable under section 1983 for their employees' actions. [citations omitted]" 131 S.Ct. at 1359.

This means that although a criminal defendant who has been denied due process of law by virtue of the suppression of exculpatory evidence in violation of *Brady* may bring a civil action for damages under 42 U.S.C. § 1983, the plaintiff will be entitled to prevail only if the plaintiff proves that action pursuant to official municipal policy caused the plaintiff's injuries.

What must be established is a deliberate indifference to the rights of persons with whom untrained employees come into contact. "Deliberate indifference" requires proof that a municipal actor disregarded a known or obvious consequence of his or her action. 131 S.Ct. at 1359–1360.

The plaintiff in such an action must ordinarily prove a pattern of similar constitutional [Brady] violations by employees who are untrained in the law of constitutionally mandated disclosure of exculpatory evidence in order to demonstrate deliberate indifference for purposes of establishing failure to train. 131 S.Ct. at 1360. Proving a series of discovery violations that are not similar to the violation which forms the basis of a civil action would not put the governmental agent on notice that specific training was necessary to avoid the constitutional violation. 131 S.Ct. at 1360.

Accordingly, "a district attorney's office may [not] be held liable under section 1983 for failure to train [its prosecutors on the law of Brady] based on a single Brady violation." 131 S.Ct. at 1356.

§ 1:88.6.3   Civil action against investigating agency/officers

Unlike a prosecutor, who has absolute immunity from civil liability for an intentional Brady violation, an investigating officer who fails to disclose materially favorable evidence to the prosecuting attorney can be held civilly liable to the defendant for that conduct. The investigating officer does not have absolute immunity from civil liability.

In Moldowan v. City of Warren (2009, CA6 MI) 578 F.3d 351, the lead detective investigating an alleged sexual assault failed to include an oral exculpatory witness statement in his police report, and then failed to disclose that exculpatory witness statement. The defendant was arrested, prosecuted, and convicted for the assault. After serving a term of incarceration on the conviction, the defendant's conviction was overturned when a key prosecution witness recanted her testimony and new evidence was discovered. In a retrial the defendant was found not guilty. The defendant then filed a federal civil action for intentional deprivation of his civil rights pursuant to 42 U.S. Code section 1983 against numerous defendants, including the lead detective. The defendant claimed that the defendants violated his constitutional rights by withholding the exculpatory witness statement.

The district court denied the detective's motion for summary judgment. On appeal the Sixth Circuit Court of Appeals upheld the district court's denial of summary judgment, concluding that the detective was constitutionally required to disclose the exculpatory evidence to the prosecutor.

The Court of Appeals stated that although the Brady duty "falls squarely on the prosecutor, not the police . . . [t]his well-established rule, however, does not resolve whether the police have a concomitant or derivative duty under the constitution to turn potentially exculpatory material over to the prosecutor." 578 F.3d at 377. The Court reasoned that '[b]ecause prosecutors rely so heavily on the police and other law enforcement authorities, the obligations imposed under *Brady* would be largely ineffective if those other members of the prosecution team had no responsibility to inform the prosecutor about evidence that undermined the state's preferred theory of the crime. As a practical matter then, *Brady's* ultimate concern for ensuring that criminal defendants receive a 'fundamentally fair' trial [citation omitted], demands that '*Brady's* protections also extend to actions of other law enforcement officers such as investigating officers' [citation omitted]." 578 F.3d at 378.

The Court of Appeals continued: "[T]he constitutional principles recognized in *Brady* apply just as equally to similar conduct on the part of police, and thus support our recognizing that the police can commit a constitutional deprivation analogous to that recognized in *Brady* by withholding or suppressing exculpatory material." 578 F.3d at 379. "As far as the Constitution is concerned, a criminal defendant is equally deprived of his or her due process rights when the police rather than the prosecutor suppressed exculpatory evidence because, in either case, the impact on the fundamental fairness of the defendant's trial is the same." 578 F.3d at 379.

The Court noted that "virtually every other circuit has concluded either that the police share in the state's obligations under *Brady*, or that the Constitution imposes on the police obligations analogous to those recognized in *Brady*." 578 F.3d at 381. The Court then concluded that the police bear a " '*Brady*-derived' responsibility to turn over potentially exculpatory evidence to the prosecutor's office. . . ." 578 F.3d at 381.

In *Sykes v. Anderson* (2010, CA6 MI) 625 F.3d 294, 319, the Sixth Circuit Court of Appeals reaffirmed its holding in *Moldowan* that a plaintiff in a civil rights action may bring a due-process claim against a police officer for a *Brady* violation.

§ 1:88.6.4   Civil action against assisting agency

The principle that an investigating officer may be held civilly liable to a criminal defendant from whom the officer has unlawfully suppressed exculpatory evidence also finds application when an employee of an agency that has been brought into the prosecution team to assist either the prosecutor or the investigating agency suppressed exculpatory evidence. In *Brown v. Miller* (2008, CA5 LA) 519 F.3d 231, a crime lab technician was sued under 42 U.S.C. § 1983 as the result of the concealing, suppression, and destruction of lab results that exonerated the defendant. The district court denied the technician's motion to dismiss the civil action due to qualified immunity, and the technician appealed. The Fifth Circuit Court of Appeals held that the "suppression of exculpatory blood test results [by the technician] would violate a defendant's [due process] rights," and the district court's denial of the motion to dismiss the complaint was a correct decision. 519 F.3d at 238.

§ 1:88.7   Continuance of trial

The "appropriate course" for a defendant who discovers that exculpatory evidence has been withheld by the prosecution is to seek a continuance, if the defendant determines that he or she needs "more time to investigate the exculpatory potential of the evidence." *United States v. Kimoto* (2009, CA7 IL) 588 F.3d 464, 489. A defendant who fails to make such a motion might be hard-pressed to later claim convincingly that he or she has been prejudiced by late disclosure that prevented the defense from making effective use of the evidence. 588 F.3d at 489.

See also, *McCann v. Mangialardi* (2003, CA7 IL) 337 F.3d 782, 787.

"The customary remedy for a *Brady* violation that surfaces mid-trial is a continuance and a concomitant opportunity to analyze the new information and, if necessary, recall witnesses." *United States v. Mathur* (2010, CA1 MA) 624 F.3d 498, 506. The remedy of granting a trial continuance is not undermined by a claim that the jury had already formed first impressions. In *Mathur*, the First Circuit Court of Appeals rejoined that "[o]ther courts have rejected conclusory arguments along these same lines. [citations omitted] So do we: the defendant never explains why, in this case, first impressions should be regarded as decisive. Thus, accepting his argument would create an exception that would swallow in a single gulp the general rule requiring parties to ask for continuances." 624 F.3d at 506.

§ 1:88.8   Dismissal

A federal district court may dismiss a charge pursuant to the court's supervisory powers "to implement a remedy for the violation of a recognized statutory or constitutional right; to preserve judicial integrity by ensuring that a conviction rests on appropriate considerations validly before a jury; and to deter future illegal conduct." *United States v. Simpson* (1991, CA9 CA) 927 F.2d 1088, 1090. The power to dismiss pursuant to the federal court's supervisory powers extends to dismissals for discovery violations when the prosecution has engaged in flagrant misconduct. *United States v. Chapman* (2008, CA9 NV) 524 F.3d 1073, 1084–1085.

In *Chapman* the Ninth Circuit Court of Appeals upheld the district court's exercise of discretion in dismissing an indictment of three defendants for concocting a complex securities trading scheme known as a "box job," in which the defendants secretly controlled a corporation's shares and manipulated the stock price through strawmen officers, directors, and shareholders. The district court found that the prosecution acted flagrantly, willfully, and in bad faith in failing to provide discovery of more than 650 pages of discoverable materials to the defense, that the prosecutor had affirmatively misrepresented his conduct to the court, that the defendants would be prejudiced by a new trial, and that no lesser sanction could adequately remedy the harm done. The Court of Appeals upheld the district court's exercise of its supervisory powers and did not consider whether the dismissal was also justified by the government's violation of the defendants' due process rights. *Accord United States v. Struckman* (2010, CA9 WA) 611 F.3d 560, 577–578.

In California state courts the authority for a court to dismiss a charge for a discovery violation is more constrained. Penal Code section 1054.5, subdivision (c), limits the power of courts to dismiss charges for discovery violations. That provision ["The court shall not dismiss a charge pursuant to subdivision (b) unless required to do so by the Constitution of the United States."] constrains trial courts from dismissing charges for a discovery violation unless a dismissal for that violation is mandated by the United States Constitution. *See also United States v. Kohring* (2011, CA9 AK) 637 F.3d 895, 912–913 [Absent evidence that the prosecution acted flagrantly, willfully, and in bad faith, dismissal as a sanction for a discovery violation is unwarranted.].

In *People v. Superior Court (Meraz)* (2008) 163 Cal.App.4th 28, 77 Cal.Rptr.3d 352, the trial court dismissed a special circumstances allegation in a capital murder prosecution, because the prosecution failed to disclose to the defense a field identification card and photographs taken in connection with a traffic stop that occurred in the vicinity of and shortly after the homicide. The trial court stated that it was dismissing the special circumstances allegation to ensure that such untimely disclosures would not occur again. The prosecution petitioned the Court of Appeal for a writ, which was granted.

The Court of Appeal observed that the trial court's authority to dismiss a charge for a discovery violation is restricted to dismissals that are mandated by the United States Constitution. After holding that the dismissal restrictions of Penal Code section 1054.5, subdivision (c), apply to special circumstances allegations as well as to the underlying substantive charges, the Court observed that *Brady* exculpatory evidence is the only substantive discovery which is mandated by the United States Constitution. 163 Cal.App.4th at 50. Accordingly, the Court held that a dismissal for a discovery violation is mandated by the federal constitution only if the discovery violation constituted a denial of a defendant's right to a fair trial ("due process of law") pursuant to *Brady*. Quoting its opinion in *People v. Ashraf* (2007) 151 Cal.App.4th 1205, 1212, 60 Cal.Rptr.3d 624, the Court stated that " '[i]f there was no *Brady* violation, then there was no conceivable basis for concluding the federal Constitution required dismissal.' " 163 Cal.App.4th at 50.

The Court of Appeal found that there was no *Brady* violation in the withholding of the field identification card and accompanying photographs, because the prosecution had disclosed those items to the defense during jury selection, and the Court agreed with the trial court that the evidence was not favorable to the defendant, because witnesses to the killing excluded the vehicle as not being the one used by the shooter. 163 Cal.App.4th at 51. The Court concluded that "[t]here being no *Brady* violation, the trial court erred by impliedly concluding the federal Constitution required dismissal of the special circumstances allegation." 163 Cal.App.4th at 53.

The Court, accordingly, did not reach the question whether dismissal would have been an appropriate remedy had the Court found the prosecution had committed a *Brady* violation. However, the Court, quoting from *Derek L. v. Superior Court* (1982) 137 Cal.App.3d 228, 235, 186 Cal.Rptr. 870, stated that "the sanction of dismissal, imposed as punishment 'is not appropriate, and lesser sanctions must be utilized by the trial court, unless the effect of the prosecution's conduct is such that it deprives the defendant of the right to a fair trial.' [citations omitted]."

This articulated standard—that a dismissal is appropriate when the effect of the prosecutor's conduct is to deprive the defendant of the right to a fair trial—is troublesome. The essence of every *Brady* violation is that the defendant has been deprived of due process of law—the right to a fair trial. Thus, if deprivation of the right to a fair trial justifies dismissal, then conceivably every *Brady* violation should be remedied by a dismissal. That cannot be and is not the standard.

Probably the best articulated standard for determining when a dismissal is required for a *Brady* violation is the suggestion by the United States Supreme Court in *United States v. Russell* (1973) 411 U.S. 423, 431–32, 93 S.Ct. 1637, 36 L.Ed.2d 366, that dismissal could be justified by a "situation in which the conduct of law enforcement agents is so outrageous that due process principles would absolutely bar the government from invoking judicial processes to obtain a conviction . . . ." This standard was cited by the Seventh Circuit Court of Appeals in *United States v. Childs* (2006, CA7 IL) 447 F.3d 541, 545, discussed in the text.

Dismissal as a remedy for a *Brady* violation is justified "only in cases rising 'to the level of flagrant prosecutorial misconduct.' [citation omitted]." *United States v. Williams* (2008, CA9 CA) 547 F.3d 1187, 1202.

In *United States v. Mauskar* (2009, CA5 TX) 557 F.3d 219, the Fifth Circuit Court of Appeals declined to dismiss charges against a defendant whose signature had been forged on documents used by the prosecution in trial, when evidence established that the government had known about the forged signatures for two years and had failed to disclose the forged signatures to the defendant. The Court of Appeals observed that misconduct by the government does not require that an indictment be dismissed absent conduct that is " 'so outrageous' that it violates the principle of 'fundamental fairness' under the due process clause of the Fifth Amendment." 557 F.3d at 232. The Court of Appeals concluded that even the government's knowledge that its evidentiary documents were forged is not so shocking to a universal sense of justice that "the government should have been deprived for all time of the opportunity to prosecute [the defendant]." 557 F.3d at 232.

In evaluating whether the government acted flagrantly, willfully, and in bad faith, the court may consider remedial or corrective action voluntarily taken by the prosecution to rectify the damage of the discovery violation. *United States v. Kohring* (2011, CA9 AK) 637 F.3d 895, 913 n.5.

One factor that should not be a basis for the Court's exercise of its supervisory power to dismiss an indictment for a discovery violation is a desire to release the defendant from "further anguish and uncertainty." *United States v. Kohring, supra,* 637 F.3d at 913 n.5.

§ 1:88.9 Jury Instruction

A trial court may, but is not required to, give a jury instruction to inform the jury of a *Brady* violation by the prosecution. *People v. Sons* (2008) 164 Cal.App.4th 90, 100–102, 78 Cal.Rptr.3d 679; *United States v. Burke* (2009, CA10 WY) 571 F.3d 1048, 1054.

§ 1:88.10 Mistrial

A trial court has the discretion to enter any order or apply any remedy to redress a *Brady* violation by the prosecution, including the ordering of a mistrial where the *Brady* violation is discovered during the trial. *United States v. Burke* (2009, CA10 WY) 571 F.3d 1048, 1054.

§ 1:88.11 Criminal prosecution of prosecutor

Although a prosecutor who commits a *Brady* violation has absolute immunity from civil action arising out of that violation, the prosecutor's absolute immunity from civil action does not afford the prosecutor any protection from a criminal prosecution for an intentional *Brady* violation. This principle was first enunciated by the United States Supreme Court in *Imbler v. Pachtman* (1976) 424 U.S. 409, 428–429, 96 S.Ct. 984, 47 L.Ed.2d 128, in which the Court stated: "We emphasize that the immunity of prosecutors from liability in suits under [42 U.S. Code] sec. 1983 does not leave the public powerless to deter misconduct or to punish that which occurs. This Court has never suggested that the policy considerations which compel civil immunity for certain governmental officials also place them beyond the reach of the criminal law."

In *Warney v. Monroe County* (2009, CA2 NY) 587 F.3d 113, the Second Circuit Court of Appeals, citing and quoting from *Imbler v. Pachtman,* observed that "[a] civil law suit is not a necessary enforcement mechanism for ensuring that prosecutors disclose exculpatory information promptly. Prosecutors remain ethically bound to disclose exculpatory information, and, in extreme cases of intentional suppression, prosecutors may be subject to criminal liability." 587 F.3d at 125.

Indeed, there have been at least two noteworthy criminal prosecutions of prosecutors for intentional *Brady* violations. *See, e.g., Knight v. Chi. Tribune Co.* (2008) 385 Ill.App.3d 347, 895 N.E.2d 1007 [describing Illinois state court criminal prosecution of four police officers and three prosecutors, known as the "Dupage 7," for perjury and obstruction of justice in connection with their handling of a capital murder investigation and prosecution]; and *Koubriti v. Convertino* (2010, CA6 MI) 593 F.3d 459, 463–464 [describing federal criminal prosecution of former Assistant United States Attorney Richard Convertino for numerous alleged violations of federal law based on allegations that Convertino had intentionally suppressed exculpatory evidence in a criminal prosecution of Karim Koubriti].

There are two California criminal statutes that are comparable to the statutes under which the Dupage 7 and Mr. Convertino were prosecuted. These statutes are California Penal Code section 182(a)(5) [conspiracy to pervert or obstruct justice, or the due administration of the laws], and Penal Code section 118 [perjury].

PART IX. PARAMETERS OF CONSTITUTIONALLY MANDATED DISCOVERY

§ 1:90   Inculpatory evidence and the Due Process Clause

The prosecution is generally not obligated by the Due Process Clause of the United States Constitution to disclose inculpatory or incriminatory evidence to the defendant. *Wooten v. Thaler* (2010, CA5 TX) 598 F.3d 215, 219. This fundamental tenet of the *Brady* rule, however, is subject to a possible exception. See Section 1:90.1 following.

§ 1:90.1   Inculpatory evidence ambush

Although disclosure of material exculpatory evidence is the only discovery that is generally accepted as mandated by the Constitution of the United States, there is a hint in federal court jurisprudence that under certain circumstances the prosecution's failure to disclose inculpatory evidence could constitute a violation of the defendant's right to due process of law.

A deliberate withholding by the prosecution of inculpatory evidence with the intent to set a trap for the defendant using that inculpatory evidence could constitute an "inculpatory evidence ambush" that violates the defendant's right to a fair trial. *See United States v. Hernandez* (2007, CA1 MA) 490 F.3d 81, 84; *United States v. Gilbert* (1999, CA1 MA) 181 F.3d 152, 162.

In *Wooten v. Thaler* (2009, CA5 TX) 598 F.3d 215, a defendant convicted of capital murder and sentenced to death, contended in a federal habeas corpus action that at the time of his plea negotiations and trial preparation the prosecution misled him into believing that the DNA evidence against him was not as strong as that evidence turned out to be when the case went to trial, and that the prosecution's delay in showing the full weight of the prosecution's DNA evidence violated his right to due process of law. The district court rejected the defendant's argument.

The Court of Appeals affirmed the district court's denial of the habeas petition. The Court, after observing that *Brady* did not create a constitutional duty for the prosecution to disclose its inculpatory evidence, 598 F.3d at 219, noted that the Supreme Court in *Gray v. Netherland* (1996) 518 U.S. 152, 165–166, 116 S.Ct. 2074, 135 L.Ed.2d 457, remanded a defendant's claim that prosecutors misled his attorney about the evidence the prosecution intended to use at trial. The *Wooten* Court observed that this line of authority "leaves open the possibility that a defendant who is *deliberately* misled as to the full weight and import of the state's evidence might have a cognizable due process claim." 598 F.3d at 220. [italics in original] The *Wooten* Court opined that the Supreme Court in *Gray v. Netherland* "took seriously the notion that due process could be violated if a prosecutor knowingly and affirmatively acts to deceive the defendant by concealing inculpatory evidence." 598 F.3d at 220.

In *Wooten v. Thaler*, however, the Court of Appeals determined that the conduct of the prosecution did not constitute a deliberate misleading of the defendant. The prosecution did nothing more than analyze and reanalyze DNA evidence to make certain that its testing was reliable. The Court held that the prosecution had every right to conduct this testing. "When it is the *analysis* of physical evidence, and not the physical evidence itself that is at issue, requiring a hold on its development would ignore the fact—well-known to prosecution and defense counsel alike—that the physical evidence is still out there, capable of providing additional blood samples for DNA work-ups. We do not apply a snapshot test to evidence. When the actual physical evidence is in full view, there is no constitutional demand that the prosecution warrant any analyses of that evidence as final—as the best and last attempts. As everyone knows, the continuing existence of physical evidence—and late-coming DNA analyses of that evidence—cuts both ways for those accused of crimes." 598 F.3d at 221.

§ 1:91 Inculpatory evidence and the Confrontation And Compulsory Process Clauses

Because the attorney-client privilege is "one of the oldest recognized privileges for confidential communications," *Swidler & Berlin v. United States* (1998) 524 U.S. 399, 403, 118 S.Ct. 2081, 141 L.Ed.2d 379, and because that privilege protects only a communication between an attorney and a client, not the facts that are communicated, the privilege does not prevent a criminal defendant from questioning a witness about the underlying facts. The attorney-client privilege does not infringe upon the defendant's constitutional Right of Confrontation. *Murdoch v. Castro* (2010, CA9 CA) 609 F.3d 983, 995. Thus, a criminal defendant was not denied his Sixth Amendment confrontation rights when the trial court declined to order disclosure of a letter written by a prosecution witness to the witness's attorney in which the witness stated that the defendant was not involved in the crime and that the witness had been coerced into implicating the defendant. *Murdoch v. Castro*, (2010, CA9 CA) 609 F.3d 983.

§ 1:94 Post judgment prosecutor disclosure of favorable evidence—generally

The question whether the prosecutor's *Brady* duty to disclose materially favorable evidence after the defendant has been convicted and judgment has been imposed continues to be a subject of interest.

§ 1:94.1 *Brady* rule post-judgment—generally

Prior to June of 2009 support for the principle that the prosecutor's *Brady* duty to disclose material exculpatory evidence extends to post-trial proceedings had been growing.

In *In re Lawley* (2008) 42 Cal.4th 1231, 1246, 74 Cal.Rptr.3d 92, 179 P.3d 891, the California Supreme Court stated: "Before and during trial, due process requires the prosecution to disclose to the defense evidence that is material and exculpatory. [citations omitted] This obligation continues after trial: '[Even] after a conviction[,] the prosecutor . . . is bound by the ethics of his office to inform the appropriate authority of . . . information that casts doubt upon the correctness of the conviction.' [citations omitted]."

It is perhaps important that the Supreme Court's statement in *Lawley* was made in the context of a postjudgment habeas corpus proceeding in which a court had issued an order to show cause, thus creating a cause and controversy to which the constitutional duty to disclose material exculpatory evidence could attach.

Certainly the prosecution's duty to disclose material exculpatory evidence under *Brady* continues through appeal and authorized postjudgment proceedings for any such evidence of which the prosecution was aware during the defendant's trial.

> "[T]he *Brady* line of cases has clearly established a defendant's right to be informed about exculpatory evidence through the proceedings, including appeals and authorized post-conviction procedures, when that exculpatory evidence was known to the state at the time of the original trial." *Steidl v. Fermon* (2007, CA7 IL) 494 F.3d 623, 625.

The prosecution is not enabled to avoid its *Brady* duty to disclose material exculpatory evidence by successfully suppressing that evidence through the trial and into a postjudgment posture. If the prosecution had a duty to disclose material exculpatory evidence to a defendant during the trial, that duty extends to postjudgment proceedings.

However, in June of 2009 the United States Supreme Court filed its opinion in the case of *District Attorney's Office for Third Judicial Dist. v. Osborne* (2009) 557 U.S. 52, 129 S.Ct. 2308, 174 L.Ed.2d 38. The *Osborne* opinion resolved the question whether a defendant in a criminal case has a *Brady*-based right to disclosure of exculpatory evidence after the conclusion of a criminal case. *Osborne* held that there is no federal constitutional right to obtain postjudgment access to the State's evidence for purposes of DNA testing.

In *Osborne* a state prisoner in Alaska brought a civil rights action in federal court pursuant to 42 U.S. Code section 1983 in which he sought to compel the defendants to allow him postjudgment access to biological evidence that had been used to convict him of kidnapping and sexual assault. The plaintiff wanted to subject that evidence to DNA testing methodology that had been unavailable at the time of his trial and conviction. The district court granted his request and ordered that the habeas defendants provide the petitioner with access to the evidence he sought.

The Ninth Circuit Court of Appeals affirmed the judgment of the district court, holding that the prisoner was entitled to assert in his action the due process right to post-conviction access to potentially exculpatory DNA evidence. The Court of Appeals relied upon the prosecutorial duty to disclose exculpatory evidence recognized in *Pennsylvania v. Ritchie* (1987) 480 U.S. 39, 107 S.Ct. 989, 94 L.Ed.2d 40, and *Brady v. Maryland* (1963) 373 U.S. 83, 83 S.Ct. 1194, 10 L.Ed.2d 215. Based on that authority, the Court of Appeals concluded that "the Due Process Clause also 'extends the government's duty to disclose (or the defendant's right of access) to *post-conviction* proceedings.' " 129 S.Ct. at 2315 [italics in original]. "The court held that these potential claims extended some of the State's *Brady* obligations to the postconviction context." 129 S.Ct. at 2315.

The government petitioned the United States Supreme Court for writ of certiorari. The United States Supreme Court granted the writ of certiorari, reversed the judgment of the Court of Appeals, and remanded the case for further proceedings. In reaching its decision the Supreme Court majority observed that " '[a] criminal defendant proved guilty after a fair trial does not have the same liberty interests as a free man.' [citation omitted]" 129 S.Ct. at 2320. After a conviction the defendant's presumption of innocence disappears. *Id.* A convicted defendant has only a limited interest in post-conviction relief, and that limited interest is not parallel to a trial right. *Brady*, therefore is the "wrong framework" with which to review a case of the defendant seeking postconviction relief. *Id.*

The Supreme Court's opinion in *Osborne* resolves the question whether the *Brady* rule applies to postjudgment proceedings—it does not. Prior authority that is contrary to the Supreme Court's opinion in *Osborne* is no longer good law and should be disregarded. The *Osborne* opinion casts doubt upon recent Court of Appeals holdings that the *Brady* rule applies to new trial and post-conviction proceedings. *See Tennison v. City and County of San Francisco* (2009, CA9 CA) 570 F.3d 1078, 1094, an opinion filed just five days after the *Osborne* opinion was filed. In light of the Supreme Court's decision in *Osborne*, the parameters of a defendant's post-conviction *Brady* rights will have to be determined by the federal and state courts.

Several federal Courts of Appeals have held that the thrust of the *Brady* rule is a defendant's right to a fair trial, and that a defendant who does not proceed to trial is not the victim of a *Brady* violation for the prosecution's failure to disclose exculpatory evidence prior to his or her plea. *See, e.g., Becker v. Kroll* (2007, CA10 UT) 494 F.3d 904, 924 ["Nevertheless, Becker never proceeded to trial, and she cannot therefore rest her section 1983 claims on a *Brady* violation."].

At least one federal circuit court, the First Circuit Court of Appeals, has concluded that *Osborne* resolves the question whether *Brady* is applicable to post-conviction proceedings. In *Tevlin v. Spencer* (2010, CA1 MA) 621 F.3d 59, 70, the Court of Appeals, citing and quoting from *Osborne*, stated:

> "[T]he Supreme Court has explicitly rejected *Brady's* applicability to postconviction proceedings." The Court then concluded that "*Brady* is thus the 'wrong framework' for analyzing Tevlin's due process claim relating to postconviction discovery. Rather, the question is whether Massachusetts postconviction discovery procedures are 'fundamentally inadequate to vindicate the substantive rights provided.' [citation omitted] We hold that they are not." 621 F.3d at 70.

PART X. *"BRADY* INFORMATION MANAGEMENT SYSTEMS" (*"BRADY* BANKS")

§ 1:96 Prosecuting attorney *Brady* information management systems (*"Brady* banks")

In response to substantial public interest arising from news media exposures of unprofessional and sometimes unethical conduct perpetrated by a few law enforcement officers, a number of California district attorneys have implemented information management systems, which have become known and are commonly referred to as "*Brady* banks." "*Brady* banks" are a means by which prosecuting attorneys' offices can collect, store, track, and make available information about law enforcement officers and other persons who are used as prosecution witnesses. This information consists of allegations and evidence of unprofessional and unethical conduct by these witnesses that prosecutors might be required by *Brady* to disclose when these persons are called to testify as prosecution witnesses. Defendants against whom these witnesses testify might be able to use this evidence to impeach their credibility.

Although these information management systems are commonly known by their colloquial name as "*Brady* banks," we shall refer to them as *Brady* information management systems.

The first *Brady* information management system was established by the District Attorney of Los Angeles County on May 13, 2002. Other California jurisdictions have since followed the lead of the Los Angeles County District Attorney's office, although prosecutors' offices in other jurisdictions have utilized different names—such as a "Brady index"—for their record-keeping system. The written procedures and standards employed in the operation of these information management systems vary from jurisdiction to jurisdiction. Not all prosecution offices in California have established a *Brady* information management system.

§ 1:96.1 Constitutional basis of *Brady* Information Management Systems ("Brady banks")

The prosecution community in California has been splintered on the question whether prosecutors' offices should establish *Brady* information management systems. Some prosecutors believe that such systems are constitutionally-required. Other prosecutors believe that while not constitutionally-required, *Brady* information management systems are either necessary or useful tools to assist prosecutors in meeting their *Brady* duties. Still other prosecutors believe that *Brady* information management systems are neither constitutionally-required, nor are they necessary to enable prosecutors to comply with *Brady*, because they are able to meet their *Brady* duties without any kind of formal information management system.

The subjects of whether a prosecuting attorney's office is constitutionally required to establish a *"Brady* bank" or its functional equivalent, or if not constitutionally-required to do so, whether a prosecutor's establishment of a *Brady* information management system is a necessary or useful tool to help prosecutors carry out their *Brady* duties, have not received the careful public written analysis that their seriousness warrants. While we do not claim to know for certain the answers to these questions, we believe that the importance of these subjects and the need for public discussion of them is so great that an effort on our part to provide some guidance is justified.

We will discuss the subject of *Brady* information management systems in three parts: (1) Is a *"Brady* information management system" (a *"Brady* bank") constitutionally-compelled? (2) If not constitutionally-compelled, is a *Brady* information management system a necessary or useful tool to assist prosecutors in meeting their *Brady* duties? And (3) if a *Brady* information management system is established in a prosecutor's office, how should that system be constructed and operated in order to help prosecutors meet their *Brady* duties?

We are aware that our efforts to answer these questions could cause us to tread upon dangerous territory, because there is no decisional authority of which we are aware that holds whether a prosecutor's office must establish a *Brady* information management system. While we are certainly not the first to think about this subject, we are unable to point to prior judicial decisions or similar authorities on the subject.

In fact, when presented with the opportunity to decide whether the United States Constitution requires a prosecutor's office to establish *Brady* information management systems, the United States Supreme Court declined to resolve the question, and simply "assume[d] . . . purely for argument's sake, that *Giglio* imposes certain obligations as to training, supervision, or information-system management." *Van de Kamp v. Goldstein* (2009) 555 U.S. 335, 129 S.Ct. 855, 861, 172 L.Ed.2d 706.

In *Van de Kamp v. Goldstein*, the Supreme Court commented: "We recognize that sometimes it would be easy for a court to determine that an office's decision about an information system was inadequate. Suppose, for example, the office had no system at all." 129 S.Ct. at 864. This statement of the Supreme Court in *Van de Kamp v. Goldstein* might be a tantalizing implication that having no *Brady* information management system at all constitutes constitutionally inadequate performance of a prosecutor's *Brady* duties. On the other hand, because the Supreme Court did not explain its statement in *Van de Kamp v. Goldstein*, it might be a mistake to read too much into the Court's language.

It would also appear to be a mistake to reach a categorical conclusion that a prosecutor who otherwise complies with all of his or her *Brady* duties somehow inadequately performs those duties by failing to establish a *Brady* information management system.

What we believe is fair to say is that the three questions which we have posed above are deserving of serious comment and analysis. Before attempting to address these three questions, we believe that a consideration of lessons learned from important *Brady* opinions of the United States Supreme Court, the California Supreme Court, and the California Courts of Appeal is a useful exercise.

The lesson of *Giglio v. United States*

In *Giglio v. United States* (1972) 405 U.S. 150, 154, 92 S.Ct. 763, 31 L.Ed.2d 104, a prosecutor assigned to handle the prosecution of Giglio made an oral promise to a government witness to induce that witness's testimony. However, the prosecutor did not memorialize that promise in the prosecutors' case file and did not otherwise communicate the promise to a second prosecutor who assumed responsibility for the case. The promise was not disclosed to the defendant.

The United States Supreme Court in *Giglio* held that the second prosecutor's ignorance of the promise to the witness made by the first prosecutor did not absolve the government from a violation of its *Brady* duty to disclose the promise to the defendant. The Court stated: "The prosecutor's office is an entity and as such it is the spokesman for the Government." 405 U.S. at 154.

This statement from *Giglio* has been quoted with approval by the California Supreme Court in *In re Brown* (1998) 17 Cal.4th 873, 879, 72 Cal.Rptr.2d 698, 952 P.2d 715, and by the California Fourth District Court of Appeal in *People v. Kasim* (1997) 56 Cal.App.4th 1360, 1385–1386, 66 Cal.Rptr.2d 494.

The lesson of *Giglio* is the first principle relevant to this inquiry: that every prosecutor who has had a connection to the prosecution of a criminal case is chargeable with the knowledge about the case and its witnesses possessed by every other prosecutor who has had or who has a connection to that case.

The lessons of *Kyles v. Whitley*

The second principle relevant to this inquiry is provided by *Kyles v. Whitley* (1995) 514 U.S. 419, 437, 115 S.Ct. 1555, 131 L.Ed.2d 490. In *Kyles v. Whitley,* a defendant convicted of first degree murder and sentenced to death in a Louisiana state court learned on collateral review of his conviction and judgment that the prosecution had withheld evidence favorable to him. The suppressed evidence included, *inter alia,* (1) contemporaneous eyewitness statements taken by the police following the murder; (2) various statements made to the police by an informant who was not called to testify; and (3) a computer print-out of license numbers of cars parked at the crime scene on the night of the murder which did not list the license number of Kyles's car.

The state trial court denied relief, and the Louisiana Supreme Court denied Kyles's application for discretionary review. The defendant then sought relief in federal habeas, claiming, *inter alia,* that his conviction was obtained in violation of *Brady* v. *Maryland* (1963) 373 U.S. 83, 83 S.Ct. 1194, 10 L.Ed.2d 215. The Federal District Court denied relief, and the Fifth Circuit Court of Appeals affirmed the denial. The United States Supreme Court granted Kyles's petition for writ of certiorari.

In the United States Supreme Court, the State of Louisiana argued that some of the favorable evidence involved in the case had not been disclosed even to the prosecutor until after trial. The State argued that it should not be held accountable for evidence known only to police investigators and not to the prosecutor. The Supreme Court rejected the State of Louisiana's argument. The Court stated:

"In the State's favor it may be said that no one doubts that police investigators sometimes fail to inform a prosecutor of all they know. But neither is there any serious doubt that 'procedures and regulations can be established to carry [the prosecutor's] burden and to insure communication of all relevant information on each case to every lawyer who deals with it.' [quoting *Giglio* v. *United States*]. Since, then, the prosecutor has the means to discharge the government's *Brady* responsibility if he will, any argument for excusing a prosecutor from disclosing what he does not happen to know about boils down to a plea to substitute the police for the prosecutor, and even for the courts themselves, as the final arbiters of the government's obligation to ensure fair trials." 514 U.S. at 438.

The Supreme Court held that "the individual prosecutor has a duty to learn of any favorable evidence known to the *others acting on the government's behalf in the case,* including the police." 514 U.S. at 437. [italics added]

The Supreme Court reiterated this statement in two places in its opinion in an important *Brady* case four years later— *Strickler v. Greene* (1999) 527 U.S. 263, 275, n.12, 281, 119 S.Ct. 1936, 144 L.Ed.2d 286.

The italicized language—*others acting on the government's behalf in the case*—is helpful to a determination of the scope of the prosecution team in the office of the prosecuting attorney. This language means that the prosecution team extends to others in the prosecutor's office or in the investigating agency who have been "acting on the government's behalf in the case." Thus, prosecutors and investigators who have had a participatory connection to a defendant's case have acted on the government's behalf in the case and are members of the prosecution team.

In *Kyles* and in *Strickler*, the United States Supreme Court did not address the question whether prosecutors and investigators with no participatory connection to a criminal case and who have not acted on the government's behalf in that case are or are not members of the prosecution team in that case.

The lessons from California courts

The quoted language from *Kyles v. Whitley*—"the individual prosecutor has a duty to learn of any favorable evidence known to the *others acting on the government's behalf in the case*, including the police"—has been adopted by the California Supreme Court and California Courts of Appeal. *See, In re Brown* (1998) 17 Cal.4th 873, 878, n.3, 72 Cal.Rptr.2d 698, 952 P.2d 715; *City of Los Angeles v. Superior Court* (2001) 29 Cal.4th 1, 8, 124 Cal.Rptr.2d 202, 52 P.3d 129; *People v. Uribe* (2008) 162 Cal.App.4th 1457, 1475, 76 Cal.Rptr.3d 829.

In several recent opinions, the California Supreme Court appears to have construed this language from *Kyles v. Whitley* to mean that the prosecution team consists of prosecutors and law enforcement officers who have been involved in the investigation or prosecution of the case, and does not include prosecutors and law enforcement officers who have had no participatory connection to the case.

In *People v. Ervine* (2009) 47 Cal.4th 745, 768, and n.11, 102 Cal.Rptr.3d 786, 220 P.3d 820, the California Supreme Court held in a different context that "misconduct by a government agent who has no involvement in the investigation or prosecution of the criminal charge against the defendant cannot automatically be imputed to the prosecution team for purposes of the Sixth Amendment." The Court appears to have limited the scope of the prosecution team to "anyone [who has been or is] involved in either the investigation or prosecution of [the] case." 47 Cal.4th at 768.

The California Supreme Court similarly limited the membership in the prosecution team of employees of the agency that has investigated the criminal charges against the defendant to include the officers in the sheriff's investigating unit, but has excluded the sheriff's officers whose function was limited to the sheriff's jail security and administration. *People v. Jacinto* (2010) 49 Cal.4th 263, 270, 109 Cal.Rptr.3d 610, 231 P.3d 341.

The majority in *People v. Jacinto* reached this conclusion in the face of a concurring opinion by Justice Kennard that urged the Court to not reach the question whether individual members of the sheriff's department could be excluded from the prosecution team, when the sheriff's department itself was the investigating agency and thereby a member of the team. Justice Kennard observed that "[t]his is a difficult issue that, in light of the majority's correct conclusion pertaining to the federal immigration detainer, need not be addressed in this case. Whether the prosecution team includes the investigating law enforcement agency itself or only some of its personnel and, if so, which personnel under what circumstances, are substantial questions" which Justice Kennard urged the Court not to reach in *Jacinto*. 49 Cal.4th at 275–276 (Kennard, J., concurring).

People v. Jordan (2003) 108 Cal.App.4th 349, 133 Cal.Rptr.2d 434, appears to provide support for the argument that only prosecutors and investigators who have had a participatory connection to the investigation or prosecution of the defendant's case are members of the prosecution team in that case.

In *Jordan* a defendant charged with possession of cocaine base for sale argued that the prosecution had a *Brady*-based duty to disclose complaints of police misconduct made by other defendants in other trials. The trial court rejected his argument; so did the Court of Appeal.

The Court of Appeal observed that a "prosecutor's duty under *Brady* to disclose material exculpatory evidence applies to evidence the prosecutor, or the prosecution team, knowingly possesses or has the right to possess. The prosecution team includes both investigative and prosecutorial agencies and personnel. [citations omitted] The prosecution must disclose evidence that is actually or constructively in its possession or accessible to it. [citation omitted] The important determination is whether the person or agency has been 'acting on the government's behalf' [citing *Kyles v. Whitley*] or 'assisting the government's case' [citing *In re Brown*]." 108 Cal.App.4th at 358.

The Court of Appeal concluded that the defendant's proposed rule would violate the constitutional principles that there is no general constitutional right to discovery in a criminal case, and the prosecution has no general duty to seek out, obtain, and disclose all evidence that might be beneficial to the defense. The defendant's argument "would require the People to catalog the testimony of every witness called by the defense at every criminal trial in the county, cull from that testimony complaints about peace officers and disclose these complaints to the defense whenever the People called the peace officer as a witness at another trial. Even in a computer age, such a task is daunting, especially in a major metropolitan area." 108 Cal.App.4th at 361–362.

The Court further noted that "a rule requiring disclosure of defense complaints made at unrelated criminal trials would transform the prosecution into a '*Brady* vessel' of information that had to be disclosed every time the People called a peace officer witness. [citation omitted] Thus, the fact the

People may have been a party to every criminal case prosecuted in the county does not give rise to a duty to collect evidence for the defense." 108 Cal.App.4th at 362.

The standards announced in *People v. Ervine, People v. Jacinto*, and *People v. Jordan* seem to lead to the conclusion that prosecutors in the office of the prosecuting attorney and law enforcement officers in the investigating agency who have had no connection to the investigation or prosecution of the defendant's case, are not members of the prosecution team in that case.

Summary of these lessons

The principles announced in the *Brady* opinions discussed above lead us to reach the following three conclusions about the prosecutor's *Brady* duties:

1. The prosecution team is charged by the Due Process Clause of the United States Constitution with knowledge of exculpatory information and evidence possessed by every other member of the prosecution team.

2. The prosecution team's constructive knowledge of materially exculpatory information and evidence possessed by every agency that is a member of the prosecution team in a criminal prosecution extends to the knowledge of materially exculpatory evidence possessed by only those investigating officers and prosecutors who have or have had a participatory connection to the case. In other words, the prosecution is responsible only for knowing that which is known to those investigating officers and prosecutors who have acted on the government's behalf in the case.

3. The prosecution has a duty to discover and learn the materially exculpatory information and evidence known to those investigating officers and prosecutors who have acted on the government's behalf in the case.

Application of These Lessons

We now attempt to apply the lessons of these United States Supreme Court and California state court *Brady* opinions. We have reached two conclusions.

1. *Brady* Information Management System is not constitutionally—compelled.

Our first conclusion, in answer to the question whether a *"Brady* information management system" (a *"Brady* bank") is constitutionally-compelled, is that the Constitution itself does not impose a duty upon a prosecutors' office to establish a *Brady* management information system.

While prosecutors have a clear constitutionally-based due process duty to disclose to the defendant materially favorable evidence in their possession, neither the United States Supreme Court nor any California courts have ever held that a prosecutors' office has a constitutionally-based duty to establish and operate a management information system for exculpatory evidence and information obtained by that office. What is constitutionally-compelled is the duty to disclose such evidence. There is no independent constitutional basis for mandating that a prosecutors' office establish and maintain a system to manage exculpatory evidence and information.

This conclusion, however, is not the end of our inquiry, because it does not answer the question whether establishment of a *Brady* information management system is a necessary incident to the prosecutors' *Brady* duty of disclosure.

2.   *Brady* Information Management System is probably essential to performance of prosecutor's *Brady* duties.

Our second conclusion is that if establishing a *Brady* information management system, or its functional equivalent, is necessary to enable prosecutors to comply with their *Brady* duties, then a prosecutors' office must establish some kind of information management system that enables a prosecutor handling a criminal prosecution to learn about materially exculpatory information and evidence known to all other persons in the prosecution team.

Our basis for reaching this conclusion is *Kyles v. Whitley* (1995) 514 U.S. 419, 115 S.Ct. 1555, 131 L.Ed.2d 490. In *Kyles*, the Supreme Court rejected the argument of the State of Louisiana that the State should not be held accountable for evidence known only to police investigators and not to the prosecutor, saying that "the individual prosecutor has a duty to learn of any favorable evidence known to the *others acting on the government's behalf in the case*, including the police." 514 U.S. at 437. [italics added]

The Supreme Court in *Kyles* concluded that in order for the prosecution to carry out its constitutionally-mandated *Brady* duties, the prosecutor must search for materially favorable evidence possessed by other members of the prosecution team. This duty to search had not been part of the holding of the Supreme Court in *Brady*. Yet, when the Supreme Court determined that the prosecutor's searching the prosecution team for favorable evidence is a necessary component of complying with the prosecutor's *Brady* duties, a duty to search the prosecution team became, in effect, a constitutionally-based duty of the prosecutor.

Likewise, if establishment of a *Brady* information management system is determined to be a necessary component of the prosecutor's compliance with his or her *Brady* duties, then it is quite possible that the courts will hold that the duty to establish a *Brady* information management system becomes, in effect, a constitutionally-based duty. Put in simple terms, if the prosecutor is unable to comply with his or her *Brady* duties without establishing a *Brady* information management system, then the prosecutor must set up such a system.

It is less important to argue over the question whether the duty to establish a *Brady* information management system is phrased as a constitutionally-based duty, or a duty that is integral to the constitutionally-based *Brady* duty to disclose materially-favorable evidence. Rather than quibbling over its name or character, prosecutors should focus on the question whether a *Brady* information management system is necessary or helpful to the prosecutor's compliance with his or her *Brady* duties. The different phraseology used to describe the nature of the duty to establish such a system—whether it is a constitutionally-based duty or whether it is a necessary or helpful component to achieve *Brady* compliance—is simply a semantic distinction without a substantive difference.

In deciding whether a *Brady* information management system must be established, the critical question is whether a prosecutor's office is able to comply with its *Brady* duties without establishing such a system. Resolving this question might be closely tied to the resolution of the question discussed in Section 1:64.1.1 of this supplement whether the prosecution team includes all prosecutors in the office of the prosecuting attorney—whether the prosecutor's *Brady* responsibility extends to all prosecutors in the prosecuting attorney's office, or whether the prosecution team is limited to only those prosecutors who have had a participatory connection to the case.

If as a matter of law the prosecution team in a criminal case includes all prosecutors in the office of the prosecuting attorney, it is difficult to conceive, except for very small prosecuting attorney offices whose prosecutors are in regular and direct contact with each other and each other's cases, how the prosecutor would be able to meet his or her *Brady* duties without the establishment and operation of an office *Brady* information management system.

If all prosecutors in the office are members of the prosecution team, whether a prosecutor's office must establish and operate a formalized *Brady* information management system probably depends on factors such as the size of the prosecutor's office, the number of prosecutors in the office, the size of the office's caseload, the geographical spread of the office, and the manner in which prosecutors in the office are able to communicate with each other. The larger the office, the greater the number of prosecutors in the office, and the more detached that the prosecutors are from each other, the more essential to *Brady* compliance is the establishment of a formalized *Brady* information management system, or a system that is functionally equivalent to the kind of *Brady* information management systems implemented in some of the larger California counties.

On the other hand, if the prosecution team includes only those individual prosecutors who have acted on the government's behalf in the case, and who thereby have had a participatory connection to that case, the establishment of a formalized *Brady* information management system becomes less critical, but still useful. In this situation, prosecutors handling a criminal prosecution would ordinarily have a much smaller universe of other prosecutors for whose knowledge of exculpatory information and evidence they are constructively responsible.

Even with a narrowed scope of an office's prosecutors who are members of the prosecution team in a particular case, the prosecuting attorney handling that case would still be responsible for exculpatory evidence known to or possessed by any other prosecutor who had acted on the government's behalf in the case. This means that every prosecutor's office must have some "system" or protocol to ensure that the fellow prosecutor members of the prosecution team communicate exculpatory evidence or information to the prosecutor assigned to that case.

The "system" or protocol might include such simple components as requiring prosecutors to make and keep detailed case notes in the prosecutor's case file. Such notes would necessarily include details of promises made or benefits provided to prosecution witnesses in that case. However, because mandated *Brady* disclosures include impeaching facts about material prosecution witnesses that are commonly unrelated to the facts of the case being prosecuted, detailed case notes cannot be relied upon to communicate to the assigned prosecutor all evidence and information the disclosure of which will fully satisfy the prosecutor's *Brady* duties. Therefore, even with a narrowed scope of the prosecution team, some kind of *Brady* information management system beyond detailed case notes in the prosecutor's file would seem to be essential.

Moreover, because some *Brady*-mandated disclosures involve sensitive facts and events which should not be generally disclosed, even in the prosecutor's office, recording these facts and events in the prosecutor's case file might cause that information to be known by people who do not have a legitimate reason to know it.

All of this means that unless a prosecutor's office is so small that all of the prosecutors in that office always know everything about each other's cases, and reliably communicate exculpatory evidence and information about their cases to each other, every prosecutor's office must establish and use some kind of formalized *Brady* information management system, or its functional equivalent, to ensure that its prosecutors learn about and disclose materially exculpatory information for which they are charged with constructive knowledge and possession. There must be some formal mechanisms by which materially favorable information and evidence known to the other persons in the investigating agency and prosecutor's office who have acted on the government's behalf in a case is made available or communicated to the prosecutor handling the case for the People.

And even in a small prosecutor's office, reliance upon an *ad hoc* "system" for communicating exculpatory information within the prosecution team that functions on a "hit or miss" basis, might not be sufficient to satisfy the prosecutor's *Brady* duties.

§ 1:96.2 Important components of a prosecution *Brady* Information Management System

The question whether establishing a prosecution *Brady* information management system is a constitutionally-compelled duty or simply a tool to help meet the constitutionally-based duty is not nearly as critical as determining the components of such as system—how the system should be constructed and operated. As in many things in life, the "devil is in the details." *People v. Humphrey* (1996) 13 Cal.4th 1073, 1092, 56 Cal.Rptr.2d 142, 921 P.2d 1.

Prosecutors designing a *Brady* information management system should give serious consideration to the following eight features, which we view as important components of a successful *Brady* information management system.

1. Scope of People Covered by System.

The first feature of a *Brady* information management system is that it should contain exculpatory information or evidence known to the prosecution team about any prosecution witness. While *Brady* banks have been commonly thought to apply only to peace officer witnesses for the prosecution, there is no principled basis for limiting *Brady* banks to peace officer witnesses. A *Brady* information management system should be broad enough to contain material impeachment evidence regarding non peace officer witnesses who are regularly utilized by the prosecution. Thus, *Brady* information management systems should include impeaching evidence and information known to the prosecuting attorney's office about non-law enforcement professionals, such as prosecution expert witnesses, informants, and other cooperating individuals.

We are not prepared to conclude that a *Brady* information management system must or even should include impeaching information or evidence about every prosecution witness, including crime victims and percipient witnesses, whose involvement in the criminal justice process is likely to be a one-time event. But when a person becomes more than a one-time prosecution witness, such as a domestic violence victim in a continuing abusive relationship that produces ongoing criminal prosecutions of the alleged abuser, it could be necessary to include impeaching information about that ordinary citizen witness.

It is thus a mistake to conclude that a *Brady* information management system is only for peace officer prosecution witnesses.

2. Known to Office's Prosecutors.

A second essential feature of a *Brady* information management system is that the existence of the system must be communicated to and known by all prosecutors in the prosecuting attorney's office. The information management system should not be a secret one. If all of the deputy and assistant prosecutors in a prosecuting agency do not know of the "bank," and if the deputy and assistant prosecutors do not know how to access its information, there can be no assurance that the "*Brady* bank" will meet the expectation of *Kyles v. Whitley* "to insure [sic] communication of all relevant information on each case to every lawyer who deals with it." 514 U.S. at 438.

3. Training of Office's Prosecutors.

A third essential feature of a *Brady* information management system is that the office's prosecutors must be trained how and when to use the system and to supplement the system with their own initiatives. A *Brady* information management system that collects and stores essential *Brady* information and evidence is as useless as having no system at all unless the prosecutors are trained to reliably access that system for its information. Moreover, prosecutors should be trained to ask material prosecution witnesses questions such as, "Do you know whether you are in our *Brady* bank?" and "Have you ever been convicted of any crime, including a misdemeanor?"

4. Fail Safe Alert Features.

A fourth essential feature of a *Brady* information management system is that the system should include "fail safe" features that alert a prosecutor to the fact that there is information about a witness in the *Brady* information management system. These alerts can be triggered by witness lists generated at the time a case is filed, and can also be triggered by the issuance of subpoenas for any proceeding in the case.

Some systems include alerts to the prosecutor's office from the employing law enforcement agency when an officer or other employee of that agency has impeaching information or evidence about which the prosecutor's office needs to know. Law enforcement agency alerts are normally the result of a cooperative agreement for exchange of information between the prosecutor's office and the law enforcement agency, and do not normally function unless and until the lawfulness of such alerts has either been litigated or negotiated with the union representing the peace officers and other employees of that law enforcement agency.

5. Public Prosecutor's Knowledge in *Brady* Information Management System.

A fifth essential feature of a *Brady* information management system is that the system should contain all exculpatory evidence and information known to the elected or appointed prosecuting attorney—the public prosecutor.

All prosecutions conducted by deputy or assistant prosecutors in California are conducted in the name and under the statutory authority of the elected or appointed prosecuting attorney-the district attorney or the city attorney.

The District Attorney (or city attorney) is the "public prosecutor," upon whom is imposed the duty to initiate and conduct all prosecutions of all public offenses on behalf of the People. Government Code section 26500. In carrying out his or her duties as the public prosecutor, the District Attorney represents the People of the State of California in whose sovereign name the case is presented. Government Code section 100; *Dix v. Superior Court* (1991) 53 Cal.3d 442, 451, 279 Cal.Rptr. 834, 807 P.2d 1063.

The District Attorney as the public prosecutor is "vested with the power to conduct on behalf of the People all prosecutions for public offenses within the county." *People v. Eubanks* (1996) 14 Cal.4th 580, 589, 59 Cal.Rptr.2d 200, 927 P.2d 310.

Because the elected or appointed public prosecutor cannot physically handle all of the criminal prosecutions brought in his or her jurisdiction, the public prosecutor may appoint deputy prosecutors to assist him or her. Government Code section 7 provides that "[w]henever a power is granted to, or a duty is imposed upon, a public officer, the power may be exercised or the duty may be performed by a deputy of the officer or by a person authorized, pursuant to law, by the officer, unless this code expressly provides otherwise." Government Code section 1194 provides that "[w]hen not otherwise provided for, each deputy possesses the powers and may perform the duties attached by law to the office of his principal."

The power to appoint deputy or assistant prosecutors belongs to the District Attorney, who alone has the power to "appoint as many deputies as are necessary for the prompt and faithful discharge of the duties of his office." Government Code section 24101. *Hicks v. Board of Supervisors* (1977) 69 Cal.App.3d 228, 241, 138 Cal.Rptr. 101.

Appointed deputy prosecutors act in the name and under the authority of the public prosecutor. "Under Government Code section 24101, the district attorney may appoint deputies as necessary for the prompt and faithful discharge of the district attorney's duties." Fort Emory Cove Boatowners Assn. v. Cowett (1990) 221 Cal.App.3d 508, 517, 270 Cal.Rptr. 527; *accord*, *Miller v. Filter* (2007) 150 Cal.App.4th 652, 661, 58 Cal.Rptr.3d 671.

See Section 1:64.1.1 in this supplement for a more complete discussion of the role of the public prosecutor as the prosecuting attorney in every criminal case prosecuted by his or her office.

Because every criminal prosecution is brought in the name and by the authority of the elected or appointed public prosecutor, the public prosecutor is necessarily a member of the prosecution team in every case prosecuted by his or her office. This means that any materially exculpatory evidence or information known to the public prosecutor is deemed as a matter of law to be known to the deputies handling criminal prosecutions on his or her behalf.

For that reason, we believe that a *Brady* information management system should contain all exculpatory evidence and information known to the elected or appointed prosecuting attorney.

6. Scope of Information in System.

A sixth feature of a *Brady* information management system is that the system should contain and disclose to a prosecutor who has a legitimate need to know any information and evidence that the prosecutor might be required by *Brady* to disclose to the defendant.

While there is no constitutional compulsion under *Brady* for a prosecutor to disclose speculation or rumors (See Section 1.7 of the text and this supplement), a number of prosecutors believe that *Brady* does not require the disclosure of an allegation of misconduct by an officer that has not been proven or which has been found to be "not sustained" by the officer's agency. Whether this position is in accord with the requirements of the *Brady* rule is not at all clear.

A number of courts, including the California Supreme Court, have held that it is not the prerogative of the individual prosecutor to decline to disclose favorable evidence to the defendant on the grounds that the prosecutor does not believe that the evidence is trustworthy or reliable. " 'It is not the role of the prosecutor to decide that facially exculpatory evidence need not be turned over because the prosecutor thinks the information is false. It is 'the criminal trial, as distinct from the prosecutor's private deliberations' that is the 'chosen forum for ascertaining the truth about criminal accusations.' [citation omitted]" *In re Miranda* (2008) 43 Cal.4th 541, 577, 76 Cal.Rptr.3d 72, 182 P.3d 513.

The constitutional adequacy of a filtering process by which facially impeaching information or evidence is excluded from a "*Brady* bank," simply because an officer's agency has investigated that information and found it to be untrue, unreliable, or unsustained, is open to question. Information or evidence is "facially impeaching" if that information or evidence is on its face impeaching, without regard to the reliability or trustworthiness of that information or evidence.

If the prosecuting attorney is constitutionally disallowed from making the determination that facially exculpatory evidence is unreliable or untrue and thus need not be disclosed, there appears to be no principled basis for giving that power to someone other than the prosecutor, such as the employer of a law enforcement officer.

In reaching this conclusion, we are cognizant of conflicting authority that can be read to authorize or require prosecutors to evaluate the source of exculpatory evidence when deciding whether that evidence is materially exculpatory evidence.

In *In re Cox* (2004) 30 Cal.4th 974, 135 Cal.Rptr.2d 315, 70 P.3d 313, the California Supreme Court concluded that because allegedly exculpatory evidence-that the charged murders were committed by a cult of which the defendant was the leader, not the perpetrator of the murders—was thoroughly investigated by three different agencies and found to be patently untrue, the prosecution was absolved of any duty to disclose that evidence to the defendant. 30 Cal.4th at 1007–1008. In reaching this conclusion the

Supreme Court was guided by the findings of the referee who heard the testimony of the person who was the source of this evidence, that the witness was the "epitome of noncredibility, testifying in a confused manner and making assertions that could not possibly be true." 30 Cal.4th at 1007.

Similarly, in *People v. Jordan* (2003) 108 Cal.App.4th 349, 133 Cal.Rptr.2d 434, the Court of Appeal rejected a defense contention that a prosecutor's office is required to maintain records of and disclose claims of police officer misconduct made at criminal trials. The Court observed that "a claim of peace officer misconduct, asserted only at an unrelated criminal trial by a defendant trying to avoid criminal liability, [does not] constitute[ ] favorable evidence within the meaning of *Brady*." 108 Cal.App.4th at 362. The Court of Appeal observed that such complaints "do not immediately command respect as trustworthy or indicate actual misconduct on the part of the officer." 108 Cal.App.4th at 362.

In spite of these apparently conflicting authorities, we believe that facially exculpatory or impeaching information or evidence should be entered into the *Brady* information management system, even if that information or evidence is deemed to be insignificant, or has been determined by the law enforcement agency to be unreliable, untrustworthy, or unfounded. Our reason for this belief is that whether evidence constitutes materially favorable evidence for the defendant should be determined on a case-by-case basis by the prosecutor handling that case. What might be immaterial favorable evidence in one case could be material favorable evidence in another case. What might be irrelevant impeachment evidence in one case could be highly relevant impeachment evidence in a different prosecution. Claims regarding an officer that have been determined to be unreliable or untrue when originally reported to the officer's agency might be found to gain credence with further investigation or the passage of time.

Excluding these claims from the *Brady* information management system effectively terminates any possibility that a defendant could use them in his or her defense in a later criminal prosecution. Preserving these claims about a witness enables the trial prosecutor and the court in a later prosecution in which that person is a prosecution witness to make a legal determination whether that information or evidence constitutes materially favorable evidence that must be disclosed to the defendant under the compulsion of *Brady*.

Thus, although the question is far from clear and is subject to legitimate debate, we think that the words of the Supreme Court in *Kyles v. Whitley* that admonish prosecutors to err on the side of disclosure when the issue is a close one, could be construed to mean that a *Brady* information management system should contain and make available to a prosecutor any information and evidence that the prosecutor might be required by *Brady* to disclose to the defendant.

7. Reasonable Accessibility of Information.

The seventh feature of a *Brady* information management system is that the information contained in the system must be reasonably accessible to the prosecutors handling criminal cases, and inaccessible to others who do not have a legitimate need to know the information.

Prosecuting attorney's offices which have established "*Brady* banks" have correctly established procedures to ensure that information in their *Brady* information management systems is not disclosed to persons who do not have a need to know that information. This kind of security surrounding a "*Brady* bank" is necessary, because much of the information and evidence in these "banks" consists of facially derogatory and impeaching information about and claims against peace officers. Were this information about an officer to be disclosed to persons who do not have a legitimate *Brady*-based reason to know the information, the officer's reputation, job-effectiveness, and perhaps his or her employment could easily be damaged. Thus, the sensitive nature of the information in a *Brady* information management system requires that access to the information in that system be carefully monitored and controlled.

However, a prosecutor who has a *Brady*-based reason to know the information contained in the system should be able to access that information and evidence in a reasonably timely manner.

8. Appropriate Uses of Information.

The eighth feature of a *Brady* information management system is that it should provide for appropriate uses of the information contained in the system. There are three potentially appropriate uses of the information: (1) to provide guidance to the prosecuting attorney in deciding whether and how to bring a criminal prosecution; (2) to advise a peace officer's employer when the prosecuting attorney's office decides that the impeaching evidence or information about the officer is such that the prosecuting attorney's office either will decline to bring charges based upon that officer's status as a material witness, or will otherwise require corroboration of the officer's testimony; and (3) to disclose information to the defendant when the person is a material prosecution witness.

The subject of whether it is appropriate for a prosecuting attorney's office to inform a peace officer's employer that it will decline to prosecute cases in which that officer is a material witness has been subject to some litigation. The prosecuting attorney has executive discretion, albeit not unlimited, to decide whether and when to prosecute. The exercise of discretion by the prosecutor that the prosecutor's office will not prosecute a case in which a particular peace officer is a material witness is not subject to judicial review and oversight. *See, e.g., Roe v. City and County of San Francisco* (1997, CA9 CA) 109 F.3d 578.

Summary of Conclusions

The eight recommended components of a prosecution *Brady* information management system discussed above appear to be useful tools to help ensure that a *Brady* information management system fulfills its role of assisting prosecutors to comply with their *Brady* duties. This list of recommended features of a *Brady* information management system should not be viewed as an exhaustive list. There are probably other features of a prosecution *Brady* information management system which we have not discussed, but that could be deemed to be useful to an effective system.

We also caution that our discussion of the importance of prosecution *Brady* information management systems should not be viewed as an invitation or an authorization for civil actions against a prosecuting attorney or agency whose office does not establish such systems. As discussed extensively in Section 1:88.6.1 of this supplement, individual prosecutors (including supervisory prosecutors) would almost certainly have absolute immunity from civil suit arising out of an alleged failure by a prosecutor to comply with *Brady* because of the failure of that prosecutor's office to establish and/or follow a *Brady* information management system. Although it has not been extensively litigated or decided, the same factors that militate against exposure of individual prosecutors to civil liability for *Brady* violations also argue against imposing municipal or governmental liability for such violations.

The subject of whether a county or city could be held liable for a failure of the public prosecutor of that governmental entity to establish a *Brady* information management system that resulted in a *Brady* violation damaging a criminal defendant is a currently contentious one. As of the date of the submission of this supplement, the United States Supreme Court has under consideration in *Connick v. Thompson* (2010) No. 09-571, the question whether imposing failure to train liability on a district attorney's office for a single *Brady* violation contravenes the culpability and causation standards for municipal liability announced in *City of Canton v. Harris* (1989) 489 U.S. 378, 109 S.Ct. 1197, 103 L.Ed.2d 412, and *Bd. of County Comm'rs of Bryan County v. Brown* (1997) 520 U.S. 397, 117 S.Ct. 1382, 137 L.Ed.2d 626. *Connick v. Thompson* was argued on October 6, 2010, and the case is awaiting a decision and the filing of an opinion from the United States Supreme Court.

While it is conceivable that a civil action could be brought against a prosecutor's office alleging that the failure of that office to implement a *Brady* information management system abridged a criminal defendant's due process rights in violation of 42 U.S.C. section 1983, the plaintiff in such an action would be required to prove more than a simple failure of the prosecutor's office to employ a *Brady* information management system. The plaintiff would be required to prove that the lack of a *Brady* information management system constituted deliberate action that was the "moving force" behind the *Brady* violation, that the *Brady* violation damaged the plaintiff, *Bd. of County Comm'rs of Bryan County v. Brown* (1997) 520 U.S. at 399, and that the prosecutor's failure to implement a *Brady* information management system amounted to deliberate indifference by the prosecutor's office to the due process rights of persons prosecuted by that office. *City of Canton v. Harris*, 489 U.S. at 388.

§ 1:96.3　Possible discovery consequences of prosecution *Brady* Information Management Systems

The prosecutor's establishment of a *Brady* information management system might have discovery consequences that have not been anticipated by a prosecutor's office that follows a policy that its prosecution teams consist of only those prosecutors who have acted on the government's behalf in the case. Before establishing a *Brady* information management system and formulating the policies and procedures of that system, these prosecutors who adhere to a conservative definition of the prosecution team should give careful thought to the possible impacts on their operations of a *Brady* information management system. How a *Brady* information management system is designed and the policies regulating that system could have critical impacts on the prosecutor's office.

In the absence of a *Brady* information management system, prosecutors are arguably charged with constructive knowledge and possession of exculpatory and impeachment evidence of only those persons who have acted on the government's behalf in the case. See Sections 1:64.1 and 1:64.1.1 in this supplement.

This conservative view of the scope of the prosecution team means that law enforcement officers in the investigating agency and prosecuting attorneys in the office of the prosecutor who have not participated in or contributed to the investigation or prosecution of the case are not members of the prosecution team, and the prosecutor assigned to that case is not charged with constructive knowledge of everything exculpatory known by these other non-assisting officers and prosecutors.

If a prosecutor's office establishes a *Brady* information management system that requires all of the prosecutors in the office to report *Brady* information and evidence to a central repository or to a designated person, and that information and evidence thereby becomes accessible to every prosecutor in the office with a witness affected by that information and evidence, it is possible that defendants would be able to make a persuasive argument that the prosecution team had been expanded to include every prosecutor in the office.

The resulting substantial enlargement of the prosecution team would create no discovery problem for a prosecutor whose fellow attorneys fully comply with their duty to report exculpatory and impeaching information and evidence. However, the discovery, which often occurs years later in habeas proceedings, that a fellow prosecutor failed to report *Brady* information or evidence to the *Brady* information management system would subject that prosecution to a claim of *Brady* error and a reversal of an important prosecution conviction.

Unless *Brady* and *Giglio* establish that the prosecution team is an office-wide one, the failure of a fellow prosecutor who has not acted on the government's behalf in the case to disclose exculpatory or impeaching information and evidence would have no *Brady* consequences in a prosecutor's office which does not have a formalized *Brady* information management system. But even if *Brady* and *Giglio* do not impose an office-wide prosecution team, the creation of a *Brady* information management system which requires prosecutors to report *Brady* exculpatory and impeachment evidence and information could hand defendants the claim that the information management system itself created an office-wide prosecution team. The creation of an office-wide prosecution team could generate *Brady* duties that the prosecutor would not otherwise face and could thereby facilitate claims of *Brady* error that defendants would not otherwise be able to successfully make.

By requiring its prosecutors to report all officer misconduct to a *Brady* information management system (*Brady* bank), and by also requiring its prosecutors to check the *Brady* information management system for exculpatory and impeaching evidence contained therein, the government might thereby bestow upon a defendant a state-created right that this procedure be followed. If the procedure is not followed—such as when prosecutors fail to report officer misconduct to the information management system—the defendant might be able to persuasively argue that his or her right to procedural due process of law has been violated.

There is precedent supporting the argument that the government's voluntary grant of a right to a criminal defendant obligates the government to comply with that right, and the government's abridgement of that right can constitute a due process violation. Although a criminal defendant does not have a constitutional right to a preliminary hearing, *Bowens v. Superior Court* (1991) 1 Cal.4th 36, 45, 2 Cal.Rptr.2d 376, 820 P.2d 600, when the state enacts a statute granting the right to a preliminary hearing to defendants charged by felony complaint, the state has created a protected liberty interest. Once a protected liberty interest has been created, the due process clause protects that state-created right from arbitrary abrogation by the state. *Wolff v. McDonnell* (1974) 418 U.S. 539, 557, 94 S.Ct. 2963, 41 L.Ed.2d 935.

We call this potential problem to the attention of prosecutors and criminal defense attorneys alike, because we are concerned that there has not been enough consideration of this potential problem.

PART XI. DISCLOSURE DUTIES OF INVESTIGATING OFFICERS

§ 1:97 Disclosure duties—in general

The investigating officers in a criminal case have constitutionally-based duties to disclose evidence favorable to the defendant to the prosecuting attorney.

§ 1:97.1 Disclosure duties of prosecutor on behalf of prosecution team

The duty to comply with *Brady v. Maryland's* disclosure obligations rests on the shoulders of the prosecutor, not the investigating agency or its officers. The prosecutor is charged with this duty on behalf of the entire prosecution team.

The prosecutor's duty to disclose material exculpatory evidence to a criminal defendant is a duty that is held by the "state or government as a whole . . . ." *Steidl v. Fermon* (2007, CA7 IL) 494 F.3d 623, 630; *Youngblood v. West Virginia* (2006) 547 U.S. 867, 869–870, 126 S.Ct. 2188, 165 L.Ed.2d 269.

For this reason "a defendant may base a *Brady* claim on a government investigator's failure to disclose evidence material to guilt or punishment, even when the prosecutor personally did not know of that evidence." *United States v. Velarde* (2007, CA10 NM) 485 F.3d 553, 559. "*Brady's* protections also extend to actions of other law enforcement officers such as investigating officers." *White v. McKinley* (2008, CA8 MO) 514 F.3d 807, 815.

The prosecutor's *Brady* duty is to disclose material exculpatory evidence to the defendant and/or his or her attorney.

§ 1:97.2 Disclosure duties of investigating officers

Although the *Brady* duty to disclose materially exculpatory evidence to the defendant is imposed on the prosecutor and is the exclusive province of the prosecutor, and although the prosecutor may not delegate that responsibility to the investigating agency, the investigating officers and agency, as members of the prosecution team, play an important role in enabling the prosecutor to perform the prosecution's *Brady* duties.

The duty of the investigating agency and its officers is to disclose favorable evidence discovered by the investigating officers to the prosecuting attorney.

The federal circuit courts generally agree that the investigating officers have a constitutionally based duty to disclose to the prosecuting attorney exculpatory evidence which they uncover or develop in their investigations, in order to enable the prosecutor to comply with the prosecution's *Brady* obligations.

The nature of the investigating officers' duty as generally expressed by the federal circuit courts is a duty to "disclose" exculpatory evidence to the prosecutor. *Walker v. City of New York* (1992, CA2 NY) 974 F.2d 293, 298; *Gibson v. Superintendent of N.J. Dep't of Law & Pub. Safety* (2005, CA3 NJ) 411 F.3d 427, 443; *Jean v. Collins* (2000, CA4 NC) 221 F.3d 656, 662, n.3; *Steidl v. Fermon* (2008, CA7 IL) 494 F.3d 623, 630–631; *Villasana v. Wilhoit* (2004, CA8 MO) 368 F.3d 976, 980; *Clemmons v. Armontrout* (2007, CA8 MO) 477 F.3d 962, 966; *White v. McKinley* (2008, CA8 MO) 514 F.3d 807, 815; *Tennison v. City and County of San Francisco* (2009, CA9 CA) 570 F.3d 1078, 1090; *McMillian v. Johnson* (1996, CA11 AL) 88 F.3d 1554, 1567.

The federal circuit courts do not always use the word "disclose" to describe the duty of the investigating officer. Sometimes the circuit courts use the term "reveal" to describe the officer's duty. *See Brady v. Dill* (1999, CA1 MA) 187 F.3d 104, 114. Sometimes the courts use the term "apprise." *Brady v. Dill, supra,* 187 F.3d at 114. Sometimes the courts use the term "inform." *Kelly v. Curtis* (1994, CA11 GA) 21 F.3d 1544, 1552.

Sometimes the courts use the term "turn over" to describe the officer's duty to disclose. *See Harris v. Kuba* (2007, CA7 IL) 486 F.3d 1010, 1014 [Law enforcement officers "must turn over potentially exculpatory evidence when they turn over investigative files to the prosecution."]; *Steidl v. Fermon, supra,* 494 F.3d 623, 631 [Investigating officers "satisfy their obligations under *Brady* when they turn exculpatory and impeachment evidence over to the prosecutor . . . ."].

And sometimes the federal circuit courts use both "disclose" and "turn over" in the same opinion to describe the investigating officer's duty. *See Jean v. Collins, supra,* 221 F.3d 656, 707–712; *McMillian v. Johnson, supra,* 88 F.3d 1554,1567, n.12, and 1568, n.17 and n.18; and *Carvajal v. Dominguez* (2008, CA7 IL) 542 F.3d 561, 566 ["While most commonly viewed as a prosecutor's duty to disclose to the defense, the duty extends to the police and requires that they similarly turn over exculpatory/impeaching evidence to the prosecutor, thereby triggering the prosecutor's disclosure obligation."].

Like the Supreme Court's very occasional use of the term "turn over" to describe the prosecutor's *Brady* duty (see Sec. 1:76 in this supplement), the federal circuit courts' use of that term to describe the investigating officer's duty is simply a stylistic use of a different phrase to describe the investigator's duty to "disclose" exculpatory evidence to the prosecutor. As the courts have used these terms, the duty to "turn over" exculpatory evidence to the prosecutor means the same thing as the duty to "disclose" that evidence to the prosecutor. The term "turn over" is only a synonym of the word "disclose," and not an extension of the investigator's duty beyond the duty of disclosure.

While it is certainly possible that the courts' use of the phrase "turn over" is intended to create a disclosure duty on investigators that is greater than the duty to "disclose" imposed on prosecutors, we have found no evidence of that intent in the reported cases. In fact, the evidence is to the contrary. The United States Supreme Court has imposed upon prosecutors the duty to search the records of the investigating agency for *Brady* evidence possessed by that agency. See Section 1:72.2 in the text and this supplement. It would make no sense to hold that the investigating officers have a constitutionally based duty to physically deliver such evidence to the prosecutor or to affirmatively inform the prosecutor of that evidence when the Court has already placed upon the prosecutor the duty to search the investigating agency for that evidence.

Construing the investigating officer's responsibility as a duty to "disclose" exculpatory evidence to the prosecutor by making that evidence available to the prosecutor, and not hiding or withholding that evidence, is the only construction that makes sense. The prosecutor satisfies his or her duty to "disclose" exculpatory evidence to the defendant when the prosecutor makes that evidence available to the defendant. We see no evidence that the courts have imposed a responsibility on the investigating officer that is greater than the duty imposed on the prosecutor.

In *Moldowan v. City of Warren* (2009, CA6 MI) 578 F.3d 351, the lead detective investigating an alleged sexual assault failed to include an oral exculpatory witness statement in his police report, and then failed to disclose that exculpatory witness statement. The defendant was arrested, prosecuted, and convicted for the assault. After serving a term of incarceration on the conviction, the defendant's conviction was overturned when a key prosecution witness recanted her testimony and new evidence was discovered. In a retrial the defendant was found not guilty. The defendant then filed a federal civil action for intentional deprivation of his civil rights pursuant to 42 U.S. Code section 1983 against numerous defendants, including the lead detective. The defendant claimed that the defendants in the civil action had violated his constitutional rights by withholding the exculpatory witness statement.

The district court denied the detective's motion for summary judgment. On appeal the Sixth Circuit Court of Appeals upheld the district court's denial of summary judgment, concluding that the detective was constitutionally required to disclose the exculpatory evidence to the prosecutor.

The Court of Appeals stated that although the *Brady* duty "falls squarely on the prosecutor, not the police . . . [t]his well-established rule, however, does not resolve whether the police have a concomitant or derivative duty under the constitution to turn potentially exculpatory material over to the prosecutor." 578 F.3d at 377. The Court reasoned that '[b]ecause prosecutors rely so heavily on the police and other law enforcement authorities, the obligations imposed under *Brady* would be largely ineffective if those other members of the prosecution team had no responsibility to inform the prosecutor about evidence that undermined the state's preferred theory of the crime. As a practical matter then, *Brady's* ultimate concern for ensuring that criminal defendants receive a 'fundamentally fair' trial [citation omitted], demands that '*Brady's* protections also extend to actions of other law enforcement officers such as investigating officers' [citation omitted]." 578 F.3d at 378.

The Court of Appeals continued: "[T]he constitutional principles recognized in *Brady* apply just as equally to similar conduct on the part of police, and thus support our recognizing that the police can commit a constitutional deprivation analogous to that recognized in *Brady* by withholding or suppressing exculpatory material." 578 F.3d at 379. "As far as the Constitution is concerned, a criminal defendant is equally deprived of his or her due process rights when the police rather than the prosecutor suppressed exculpatory evidence because, in either case, the impact on the fundamental fairness of the defendant's trial is the same." 578 F.3d at 379.

The Court noted that "virtually every other circuit has concluded either that the police share in the state's obligations under *Brady*, or that the Constitution imposes on the police obligations analogous to those recognized in *Brady*." 578 F.3d at 381. The Court then concluded that the police bear a " '*Brady*-derived' responsibility to turn over potentially exculpatory evidence to the prosecutor's office . . ." 578 F.3d at 381.

The Sixth Circuit Court of Appeals once again affirmed its holding in *Moldowan* in *Sykes v. Anderson* (2010, CA6 MI) 625 F.3d 294: "Traditionally, [the *Brady* duty] applied to prosecution rather than police, but in *Moldowan* we held that 'the due process guarantees recognized in *Brady* also impose an analogous or derivative obligation on the police [to disclose to the prosecutor evidence whose materially exculpatory value should have been 'apparent' to him at the time of his investigation].' [citation omitted] Thus, Elkins had a constitutional right to have favorable evidence disclosed to the prosecution and court." The Court of Appeals thus reaffirmed that a plaintiff in a civil rights action may bring a due-process claim against a police officer for a *Brady* violation.

§ 1:97.3 Actions of investigating officer that constitute disclosure

It seems clear that an investigating officer who personally *delivers* to the prosecutor exculpatory evidence uncovered in the agency's investigation of a case satisfies the officer's duty to *disclose* that evidence to the prosecutor. *Walker v. City of New York* (1992, CA2 NY) 974 F.2d 293, 298; *McMillian v. Johnson* (1995, CA11 AL) 88 F.3d 1554, 1567.

However, the question has arisen whether an investigating officer who simply *makes available* exculpatory evidence to the prosecutor satisfies the officer's duty to *disclose* that evidence to the prosecutor. In *Tennison v. City and County of San Francisco* (2009, CA9 CA) 570 F.3d 1078, officers investigating a gang-related homicide placed information regarding a request for a reward through a secret witness program of the police department and also a note of an inspector's telephone conversation with a potential prosecution witness into the department's homicide file. The potential witness gave the inspectors names of possible suspects other than the two men who were ultimately charged and convicted of the murder and sentenced to prison. The witness also provided a scenario of events surrounding the homicide that differed from the statements of two claimed prosecution eyewitnesses to the crime.

More than 10 years later the two convicted men were freed from custody following a federal habeas corpus action, and the District Attorney declined to prosecute them again. The men then filed a civil action for damages against the governmental entity, the investigating officers, and the prosecutor under 42 U.S.C. section 1983. The defendants moved for summary judgment. The district court granted the defendants partial summary judgment but denied summary judgment on some of the allegations in the complaint. The defendants appealed to the Ninth Circuit Court of Appeals.

The question whether the investigating officers had failed in their duty to disclose the reward request and the note of the witness's statement placed in the police department's homicide file was a point of contention on appeal. The investigators claimed that placing these items in the department's homicide file satisfied their duty to disclose exculpatory information to the prosecutor, because the prosecutor had access to the homicide file.

The Ninth Circuit Court of Appeals rejected the investigating officers' argument. Addressing the question of the note of the witness's statement, the Court said: "Placing the notes regarding Smith's statements in the police file did not fulfill the inspectors' duty to disclose exculpatory information to the prosecutor." The Court said that this evidence "should not have been buried in a file, but should have been made known to the prosecutor." 570 F.3d at 1090.

Addressing the secret witness program reward request, the Court of Appeals stated: "The Inspectors' placement of the request in their file does not satisfy their obligation to disclose evidence to [the prosecutor]. [One of the eyewitnesses named Massina] was their key witness, so any evidence of a reward paid to her should have been made known to the prosecutor." 570 F.3d at 1095.

The Court of Appeals concluded that the investigating officers had failed to comply with their duty to disclose exculpatory evidence to the prosecutor, because placement of that evidence in their investigative file did not satisfy their duty to disclose the evidence.

The opinion of the Court of Appeals in *Tennison* does not make reference to whether placing investigative materials in the police department's homicide file was an accepted procedure that had been agreed upon by the police department and the District Attorney's office for submitting evidence and follow-up investigative reports to the prosecutor after the initial filing of a case.

If the investigating agency and the prosecutor's office had implemented an agreed-upon procedure whereby the investigating officers placed into their investigative file materials they obtained after the initial filing of charges, and the prosecutor under this agreed-upon procedure was provided full and unfettered access to that investigative file, the investigators' conduct in placing the secret witness reward information and the note of the witness's statement into the homicide file pursuant to that procedure would appear to have satisfied their duty to make that evidence available to the prosecutor. *See, e.g., McMillian v. Johnson* (1996, CA11 AL) 88 F.3d 1554, 1568, and *Kelly v. Curtis* (1994, CA11 GA) 21 F.3d 1544 [An investigator who is aware that it is the practice of a state crime lab to send a copy of a crime lab report directly to the prosecutor is not derelict in his duty by failing to personally disclose that report to the prosecution.].

The prosecutor's failure to check that homicide file in accordance with an agreed-upon procedure would not constitute a dereliction of duty by the investigators.

§ 1:97.4 Actions of investigating officer that do not constitute disclosure

An investigating officer does not fulfill the duty to disclose exculpatory evidence or information to the prosecutor when the investigator affirmatively withholds, hides, or conceals that evidence from the prosecutor. *Jones v. City of Chicago* (1988, CA7 IL) 856 F.2d 985, 993; *Newsome v. McCabe* (2001, CA7 IL) 256 F.3d 747, 752; *Villasana v. Wilhoit* (2004, CA8 MO) 368 F.3d 976, 980.

An investigating officer fails to comport with the officer's duties when the officer deliberately supplies misleading information to the prosecutor. *Jones v. City of Chicago, supra*, 856 F.2d at 994.

If an investigating officer becomes aware that the prosecuting attorney is presenting incriminating evidence against a defendant without disclosing to the defendant other evidence possessed by the investigating officer which contradicts the incriminating evidence, the investigating officer must inform the prosecutor of that exculpatory evidence. *Barbee v. Warden, Maryland Penitentiary* (1964, CA4 MD) 331 F.2d 842, 846. However, an investigating officer has no duty to disclose exculpatory evidence to the prosecutor "where [he or] she has reason to believe that the prosecutor is aware of that evidence." *Kelly v. Curtis* (1994, CA11 GA) 21 F.3d 1544, 1552; *McMillian v. Johnson* (1996, CA11 AL) 88 F.3d 1554, 1568.

PART XII. ETHICAL DISCLOSURE DUTIES OF PROSECUTORS

§ 1:98 Prosecutor's ethical disclosure duties—generally

A prosecutor has a basic ethical duty to know his or her disclosure responsibilities under the *Brady* rule and to perform legal research when uncertain about the scope of those obligations. *Connick v. Thompson* (2011) ___ U.S. ___, 131 S.Ct. 1350, 1363, 179 L.Ed.2d 417. In *Bielanski v. County of Kane* (2008, CA7 IL) 550 F.3d 632, 645, the Seventh Circuit Court of Appeals opined: "[P]urposefully withholding exculpatory or impeaching evidence until the last moment would be a risky and ethically questionable practice for government agents to undertake, and we certainly do not condone that approach with our opinion today."

A prosecutor might have ethical disclosure duties that do not rise to the level of a constitutionally mandated disclosure. These duties can be imposed by rules and codes of professional conduct. They differ in their application from a prosecutor's *Brady* duties, because violation of a prosecutor's ethical duties does not normally subject a criminal prosecution to adverse consequences. However, a prosecutor's violation of ethical disclosure duties can impact the prosecutor as a member of the bar.

The prosecutor's ethical duties of disclosure might arise in three contexts: (1) the duty to disclose favorable evidence that does not meet the materiality standards of the *Brady* rule; (2) the duty to disclose events that impact the prosecutor's ability to proceed with a prosecution based upon probable cause; and (3) the duty to disclose exculpatory evidence discovered by the prosecutor after judgment has been imposed upon the defendant.

§ 1:98.1 Prosecutor's ethical duties and State and American Bar Association Standards

Ethical discovery duties of California prosecutors find their sources in California Rules of Professional Responsibility, California statutes, and California appellate opinions. Over the past 40 years the American Bar Association has also published model rules of professional conduct, model codes of professional responsibility, standards of the prosecution function in the criminal justice system, and formal ethics opinions. Questions have arisen about the relationship between California ethics rules and the ABA's rules and opinions, and whether the ABA Rules and Standards are binding on California prosecutors.

The ABA Model Rules of Professional Conduct and the Model Code of Professional Responsibility have "no legal force of their own" and have not been adopted in California. *General Dynamics Corp. v. Superior Court* (1994) 7 Cal.4th 1164, 1190, n.6, 32 Cal.Rptr.2d 1, 876 P.2d 487. Because they have not been adopted in California, and because they have no legal force of their own, the "ABA Model Rules of Professional Conduct . . . do not establish ethical standards in California . . . ." *State Comp. Ins. Fund v. WPS, Inc.* (1999) 70 Cal.App.4th 644, 655–656, 82 Cal.Rptr.2d 799.

With the approval of the California Supreme Court, the Board of Governors of the State Bar has the power to "formulate and enforce rules of professional conduct for all members of the bar in the State." Business and

Professions Code section 6076. When approved by the Supreme Court, these Rules of Professional Conduct "are binding upon all members of the State Bar," and their willful breach can subject an attorney to discipline by the State Bar and the California Supreme Court. Business and Professions Code section 6077.

California has adopted Rules of Professional Conduct for attorneys. These rules "are intended not only to establish ethical standards for members of the bar [citation omitted], but are also designed to protect the public. [citations omitted]." *Ames v. State Bar* (1973) 8 Cal.3d 910, 917, 106 Cal.Rptr. 489, 506 P.2d 625.

A California attorney is subject to State Bar and Supreme Court discipline for a willful violation of the California Rules of Professional Conduct, the State Bar Act [Business and Professions Code section 6000 et seq.], and California judicial opinions. *In re Edward S.* (2009) 173 Cal.App.4th 387, 412, 92 Cal.Rptr.3d 725. In the absence of an applicable California Rule of Professional Conduct, California statute, or opinion of a California appellate court, a California attorney is not subject to discipline in California for violating an ABA Model Rule of Professional Conduct, an ABA ethical standard, or an ABA formal opinion. *State Comp. Ins. Fund v. WPS, Inc.* (1999) 70 Cal.App.4th 644, 656, 82 Cal.Rptr.2d 799.

The California Supreme Court has occasionally looked to the principles underlying the ABA counterparts to California's Rules of Professional Conduct. *Flatt v. Superior Court* (1994) 9 Cal.4th 275, 282, 36 Cal.Rptr.2d 537, 885 P.2d 950. *See People v. Gonzalez* (1990) 51 Cal.3d 1179, 1261, 275 Cal.Rptr. 729, 800 P.2d 1159, where the Supreme Court cited Rule 3.8(d) of the ABA Model Rules of Professional Conduct; *People v. Garcia* (1993) 17 Cal.App.4th 1169, 1179, 22 Cal.Rptr.2d 545; and *Goldberg v. Warner/ Chappell Music, Inc.* (2005) 125 Cal.App.4th 752, 765, 23 Cal.Rptr.3d 116.

In *People ex rel. Clancy v. Superior Court* (1985) 39 Cal.3d 740, 746, 218 Cal.Rptr. 24, 705 P.2d 347, the California Supreme Court cited Ethical Consideration 7-13 of the ABA Standards for Criminal Justice Prosecution Function (1992) in support of the Court's statement that the role of the prosecutor is to seek justice.

ABA standards do have an appropriate role in determining the ethical duties of California attorneys. The role of ABA standards is to provide guideposts to the application of California Rules of Professional Conduct. *Higdon v. Superior Court* (1991) 227 Cal.App.3d 1667, 1680, 278 Cal.Rptr. 588. Rule 1-100(A) of the California Rules of Professional Conduct expressly provides that "[e]thics opinions and rules and standards promulgated by other jurisdictions and bar associations may also be considered." Thus, where there is no conflict with the public policy of California, the ABA Model Rules of Professional Conduct can serve as a collateral source for guidance on proper professional conduct in California. *People v. Donaldson* (2001) 93 Cal.App.4th 916, 928, 113 Cal.Rptr.2d 548. State Bar

Rules of Professional Conduct, in conjunction with American Bar Association's Standards, "provide guidelines for determining the prevailing norms of practice . . . ." *In re Alvernaz* (1992) 2 Cal.4th 924, 937, 8 Cal.Rptr.2d 713, 830 P.2d 747.

But it is ultimately the California Rules of Professional Conduct, California state statutes, and California judicial opinions that establish enforceable ethical standards for California attorneys.

The United States Supreme Court has in several opinions commented that ethical disclosure duties of prosecutors can exceed the prosecutors' constitutionally mandated disclosure duties under *Brady*.

In *Cone v. Bell* (2009) 556 U.S. 449, 129 S.Ct. 1769, 1783, 173 L.Ed.2d 701, n.15, the United States Supreme Court, citing ABA Model Rule 3.8(d), opined that "[a]though the Due Process Clause of the Fourteenth Amendment, as interpreted by Brady, only mandates the disclosure of material evidence, the obligation to disclose evidence favorable to the defense may arise more broadly under a prosecutor's ethical or statutory obligations."

In *Kyles v. Whitley* (1995) 514 U.S. 419, 437, 115 S.Ct. 1555, 131 L.Ed.2d 490, the Supreme Court observed that "the rule in Bagley (and, hence, in Brady) requires less of the prosecution than the ABA Standards for Criminal Justice Prosecution Function and Defense Function 3-3.11(a) (3d ed. 1993)."

Practice Tip for Prosecution: While ABA Model Rule 3.8(d) provides an excellent guideline for California prosecutors when making decisions about the disclosure of exculpatory evidence, and is a standard that we commend to all California prosecutors, the violation of Rule 3.8(d) by a California prosecutor should not in and of itself expose the prosecutor to disciplinary action by the California State Bar or California Supreme Court. Only when the prosecutor's conduct violates the California Rules of Professional Conduct, California statutes, or California decisional authority, is the prosecutor subject to disciplinary action.

§ 1:98.2   Prosecutor's ethical duty to disclose favorable evidence that does not meet *Brady* materiality standards

A prosecutor does not have a constitutionally mandated duty to disclose evidence that is favorable to the defendant when that evidence is not *material*—when it is not reasonably probable that disclosure of that evidence would affect the outcome of the case. See Section 1:48 and following of the text.

However, it is conceivable that a California prosecutor who comes into possession of evidence that is favorable to a defendant, but is not material, might have an ethical duty to disclose that evidence to the defendant. Rule 3.8(d) of the American Bar Association Model Rules of Professional Conduct (2009) provides:

"The prosecutor in a criminal case shall . . . (d) make timely disclosure to the defense of all evidence or information known to the prosecutor that tends to negate the guilt of the accused or mitigates the offense, and, in connection with sentencing, disclose to the defense and to the tribunal all unprivileged mitigating information known to the prosecutor, except when the prosecutor is relieved of this responsibility by a protective order of the tribunal."

Standard 3-3.11(a) [Disclosure of Evidence by the Prosecutor] of the American Bar Association *Standards for Criminal Justice, Prosecution Function* (1992), provides:

"A prosecutor should not intentionally fail to make timely disclosure to the defense, at the earliest feasible opportunity, of the existence of all evidence or information which tends to negate the guilt of the accused or mitigate the offense charged or which would tend to reduce the punishment of the accused."

On July 8, 2009, the American Bar Association Standing Committee on Ethics and Professional Responsibility issued Formal Opinion 09-454 entitled "Prosecutor's Duty to Disclose Evidence and Information Favorable to the Defense." In this opinion the Standing Committee determined that ABA Model Rule 3.8(d) "does not implicitly include the materiality limitation recognized in the constitutional case law . . . ." The opinion concluded that Rule 3.8(d) "requires the disclosure of evidence or information favorable to the defense without regard to the anticipated impact of the evidence or information on a trial's outcome."

The prosecutor would have an ethical disclosure duty under the ABA Standards, if those standards were to apply, that would be broader than the prosecutor's constitutional disclosure duty under *Brady*. For a discussion whether ABA standards, rules, and opinions have any effect or authority over California prosecutors, see Section 1:97.1 of this supplement.

In *Bielanski v. County of Kane* (2008, CA7 IL) 550 F.3d 632, 645, the Seventh Circuit Court of Appeals provided this advice to prosecutors: "*Brady* requires that the government disclose material evidence in time for the defendant to make effective use of it at trial. [citation omitted] Even late disclosure does not constitute a *Brady* violation unless the defendant is unable to make effective use of the evidence. [citations omitted] Under these cases, *Brady* evidence can be handed over on the eve of trial or even during trial so long as the defendant is able to use it to his or her advantage. That said, purposefully withholding exculpatory or impeaching evidence until the last moment would be a risky and ethically questionable practice for government agents to undertake, and we certainly do not condone that approach with our opinion today." *See also Brooks v. Tennessee* (2010, CA6 TN) 626 F.3d 878, 892 ["[T]he *Brady* standard for materiality is less demanding than the ethical obligations imposed on a prosecutor."].

Practice Tip for Prosecution: When making decisions about disclosing exculpatory evidence, prosecutors are well advised to follow the repeated admonitions of the United States Supreme Court that were first articulated in *United States v. Agurs* (1976) 427 U.S. 97, 108, 96 S.Ct. 2392, 49 L.Ed.2d 342 ["[T]he prudent prosecutor will resolve doubtful questions in favor of disclosure."], that were repeated in *Kyles v. Whitley, supra,* 514 U.S. at 439 ["[A] prosecutor anxious about tacking too close to the wind will disclose a favorable piece of evidence. [citation omitted] This is as it should be."], and that were most recently emphasized in *Cone v. Bell, supra,* 129 S.Ct. at 1783, n.15, that "the prudent prosecutor will err on the side of transparency, resolving doubtful questions in favor of disclosure."

§ 1:98.3   Prosecutor's ethical duty to disclose events impacting prosecution's probable cause to prosecute

The death or other known trial unavailability of an important prosecution witness is probably not a fact that must be disclosed by the prosecutor pursuant to the *Brady* rule. See Sections 1:7.1 and 1:17.5 of this supplement. However, the prosecutor might have an ethical duty to disclose the death or other known permanent trial unavailability of a material prosecution witness.

This issue has not been the subject of any California appellate opinion, and there do not appear to be many cases in other jurisdictions dealing with this subject. The few reported cases have arisen in the New York state courts.

While there does not appear to be a *Brady* duty to disclose the death or other unavailability of an important prosecution witness, *People v. Jones* (N.Y. 1978) 375 N.E.2d 41, 43, and *People v. Roldan* (1984) 124 Misc.2d 279, 280–281, 476 N.Y.S.2d 447 (see the discussion in Sections 1:7.1 and 1:17.5 of this supplement), the prosecutor might have an ethical duty to disclose to the defendant the death or other known permanent unavailability of a material prosecution witness.

Such was the holding of the court in *Matter of Wayne M.* (1983) 121 Misc. 2d 346, 467 N.Y.S.2d 798, which grounded its conclusion upon Disciplinary Rule 7-103(B) of New York State's Code of Professional Responsibility. Disciplinary Rule 7 provided that "[a] public prosecutor or other government lawyer in criminal litigation shall make timely disclosure . . . of the existence of evidence, known to the prosecutor or other government lawyer, that tends to negate the guilt of the accused, mitigate the degree of the offense, or reduce the punishment." The Court concluded that "[t]his ethical injunction includes a situation such as the one at bar in which a complainant is unavailable." 121 Misc.2d at 347.

California has no comparable rule of professional responsibility. Rule 5-220 of the California Rules of Professional Conduct provides that "[a] member shall not suppress any evidence that the member or the member's client has a legal obligation to reveal or to produce." Rule 5-220 begs the question whether the prosecutor has an ethical duty to disclose the death of a material prosecution witness, because it is dependent upon the very issue—a legal obligation to reveal or to produce—which is the object of this determination. Rule 5-220 does not impose an ethical duty upon a prosecutor to disclose evidence unless the prosecutor otherwise has a legal obligation to reveal or to produce that evidence.

However, it is conceivable that a rule of professional responsibility which requires a prosecutor to refrain from pursuing a charge that the prosecutor knows is not supported by probable cause might provide the ethical basis for disclosure. Rule 3.8 of the American Bar Association Model Rules of Professional Conduct provides that the "prosecutor in a criminal case shall: (a) refrain from prosecuting a charge that the prosecutor knows is not supported by probable cause."

Rule 5-110 of the California Rules of Professional Conduct appears to be a counterpart to ABA Rule 3.8. Rule 5-110 provides:

"A member in government service shall not institute or cause to be instituted criminal charges when the member knows or should know that the charges are not supported by probable cause. If, after the institution of criminal charges, the member in government service having responsibility for prosecuting the charges becomes aware that those charges are not supported by probable cause, the member shall promptly so advise the court in which the criminal matter is pending."

Although no California case has so held, an argument could be made that the death of a material prosecution witness which prevents the prosecutor from being able to prove a charge at trial obviates probable cause in support of that criminal charge. Under this approach, undermining the probable cause in support of the criminal charge would trigger the prosecutor's ethical duty to disclose the witness's death to the court. Any such ethical duty under Rule 5-110 to disclose the death or other permanent unavailability of a prosecution witness would be limited to the death of a material witness without whom the prosecutor would be unable to obtain a conviction at trial. An ethical duty would not require disclosure of the death of a prosecution witness whose unavailability would not prevent the prosecution from going forward to trial.

Therefore, although the prosecutor does not have a constitutionally based duty under *Brady* to disclose the death or other unavailability of a material prosecution witness, the prosecutor could have an ethical duty to make such a disclosure under Rule 5-110 of the California Rules of Professional Conduct. Whether the death or other permanent unavailability of a material prosecution witness obviates probable cause in support of a charge has not been addressed by California courts.

Practice Tip for Prosecution: Although you are not obligated by the *Brady* rule to disclose to the defendant the death or other unavailability of a material prosecution witness, you might have an ethical duty under the California Rules of Professional Conduct to make such a disclosure. Prosecutors concerned about their professional reputations and desirous of avoiding the possibility of State Bar disciplinary actions are well advised to disclose the death or other permanent unavailability of a material prosecution witness whose absence undermines the prosecution's ability to obtain a conviction of the charge.

Without clear decisional or other authority that would compel or support it, we are not willing to extend the reasoning behind a possible ethical requirement to disclose the death or other permanent unavailability of a material prosecution witness to other evidentiary problems which prosecutors face. Thus, we are not prepared to conclude that a prosecutor's inability to locate a material witness, a witness's reluctance to cooperate, or a witness's temporary absence from the jurisdiction, become ethically disclosable facts.

See People v. West (2003 Cal.App. Unpub. Lexis 10997), in which the Court of Appeals in an unpublished decision held that "[t]he fact that a prosecution witness fails to show up for a required court appearance does not necessarily mean the witness will be unavailable at the time of a defendant's trial. The witness could be found by the authorities or voluntarily reappear at any point in time, in which case knowledge of the failure to appear is no longer useful to the defendant. The prosecution has no duty to disclose its potential case to the defendant. [citation omitted] Similarly, the prosecution's duty to disclose exculpatory evidence does not extend to disclosure of difficulties that may arise in the securing of witnesses to present its case."

Although *People v. West* as an unpublished opinion is not citable and may not be relied upon by a party or a court, *California Rules of Court,* Rule 8.1115 (2009), its reasoning may be considered by counsel in the litigation of discovery questions.

Practice Tip for Prosecution: Although Rule 5-110 requires that a charge be supported by "probable cause," California prosecutors are required to adhere to a higher filing standard. The general filing standard to be followed by California prosecutors is that a prosecutor may file a criminal charge when four requirements are satisfied. These four requirements are: (1) there has been a complete investigation and thorough consideration of all pertinent data; (2) there is legally sufficient, admissible evidence of a corpus delicti; (3) there is legally sufficient, admissible evidence of the accused's identity as the perpetrator of the crime; and (4) the prosecutor has considered the probability of conviction by an objective fact-finder hearing the admissible evidence. *Professionalism, A Sourcebook of Ethics and Civil Liability Principles for Prosecutors,* California District Attorneys Association, Chap. III, page 18 (2001); *Uniform Crime Charging*

Standards, California District Attorneys Association, p. 6 (1996).

The quantity and quality of evidence required for the charging of a crime is that the evidence "should be of such convincing force that it would warrant conviction of the crime charged by a reasonable and objective fact-finder after hearing all the evidence available to the prosecutor at the time of charging and after hearing the most plausible, reasonably foreseeable defense that could be raised under the evidence presented to the prosecutor." *Professionalism, A Sourcebook of Ethics and Civil Liability Principles for Prosecutors*, California District Attorneys Association, Chap. III, page 18 (2001); *Uniform Crime Charging Standards*, California District Attorneys Association, p. 12 (1996). California appellate courts have recognized these principles as establishing the standards for crime charging in California. *See Davis v. Municipal Court* (1988) 46 Cal.3d 64, 82, n.9, 249 Cal.Rptr. 300, 757 P.2d 11; *People v. Robinson* (1995) 31 Cal.App.4th 494, 499, n.5, 37 Cal.Rptr.2d 183 and *Youngblood v. Gates* (1988) 200 Cal.App.3d 1302, 1345, n.11, 246 Cal.Rptr. 775.

§ 1:98.4 Prosecutor's ethical duty to disclose exculpatory evidence discovered post judgment

The prosecutor does not have a constitutional duty based on *Brady* to disclose to a defendant exculpatory evidence discovered by the prosecution following the judgment of conviction of the defendant. See Section 1:94.1 of the text and this supplement, and *District Attorney's Office for Third Judicial Dist. v. Osborne* (2009) 557 U.S. 52, 129 S.Ct. 2308, 174 L.Ed.2d 38.

However, even though a prosecutor does not have a *Brady* duty to disclose exculpatory evidence the prosecutor discovers or about which the prosecutor is informed after judgment has been imposed on the defendant, the prosecutor might have an ethical duty to make such a disclosure.

In *Imbler v. Pachtman* (1976) 424 U.S. 409, 96 S.Ct. 984, 47 L.Ed.2d 128, which was a civil rights action against a prosecutor by a convicted murderer whose conviction had been overturned on habeas corpus, Imbler asserted that the prosecutor had withheld exculpatory evidence at trial. The issue in the civil action was whether the prosecutor was entitled to immunity from civil suit. The Supreme Court held that the prosecutor was immune. The Court then described a duty to disclose exculpatory evidence in these words:

"At trial [the prosecutor's duty to disclose materially exculpatory evidence] is enforced by the requirement of due process, but after a conviction the prosecutor also is bound by the ethics of his office to inform the appropriate authority of after-acquired or other information that casts doubt upon the conviction." 424 U.S. at 427, n.25.

In support of its determination in *Imbler*, the Supreme Court cited Ethical Consideration 7-13 of the American Bar Association's Code of Professional Responsibility and section 3.11 of the American Bar Association Project on

Standards for Criminal Justice, Prosecution and Defense Function (approved draft 1969). 424 U.S. at 427, n.25.

Ethical Consideration 7-13 of the ABA Code of Professional Responsibility provides, in pertinent part:

"With respect to evidence and witnesses, the prosecutor has responsibilities different from those of a lawyer in private practice: the prosecutor should make timely disclosure to the defense of available evidence, known to him, that tends to negate the guilt of the accused, mitigate the degree of the offense, or reduce the punishment."

Section 3.11 of the approved draft of the ABA Project on Standards for Criminal Justice, Prosecution Function, became Standard 3-3.11(a) in the approved ABA *Standards for Criminal Justice Prosecution Function* (1992). Standard 3-3.11(a) states:

"A prosecutor should not intentionally fail to make timely disclosure to the defense, at the earliest feasible opportunity, of the existence of all evidence or information which tends to negate the guilt of the accused or mitigate the offense charged or which would tend to reduce the punishment of the accused."

In *Warney v. Monroe County* (2009, CA2 NY) 587 F.3d 113, the Second Circuit Court of Appeals, in holding that the "disclosure of evidence to opposing counsel is an advocacy function," and that a prosecutor who fails to disclose exculpatory evidence to the defendant has absolute immunity from civil liability for that conduct, concluded that "[p]rosecutors remain ethically bound to disclose exculpatory information . . . The advocacy function of a prosecutor includes seeking exoneration and confessing error to correct an erroneous conviction. Thus, prosecutors are under a continuing ethical obligation to disclose exculpatory information discovered post-conviction. Any narrower conception of a prosecutor's role would be truly alarming." 587 F.3d at 125.

The California Supreme Court has twice cited this statement of the United States Supreme Court in *Imbler v. Pachtman, supra. In re Lawley* (2008) 42 Cal.4th 1231, 1246, 74 Cal.Rptr.3d 92, 179 P.3d 891; *People v. Gonzalez* (1990) 51 Cal.3d 1179, 1261, 275 Cal.Rptr.2d 729, 800 P.2d 1159. And the California Courts of Appeal have also twice cited *Imbler's statement. Curl v. Superior Court* (2006) 140 Cal.App.4th 310, 318, 44 Rptr.3d 320; and *People v. Garcia* (1993) 17 Cal.App.4th 1169, 1179, 22 Cal.Rptr.2d 545. In citing *Imbler* California courts have not explained how these ABA standards have become ethical standards for California prosecutors.

Thus, it is not certain whether a California prosecutor has an enforceable ethical duty to disclose to the defendant exculpatory evidence the prosecutor discovers or about which the prosecutor is informed after judgment has been imposed on the defendant.

In *Friedman v. Rehal* (2010) 618 F.3d 142, a defendant pled guilty to child sex abuse violations and served a term in prison for those convictions. After he had been paroled, the defendant learned of a consensus within the social science community that suggestive memory recovery tactics could create false memories, and that aggressive investigation techniques could induce false reports. He filed a federal habeas petition seeking to set aside his convictions, arguing that exculpatory evidence—evidence that the prosecution team had used hypnosis to stimulate memory recall, and thus possibly induce false memories of abuse—had been withheld from him.

The district court denied the petition for writ of habeas corpus and the defendant appealed the denial. The Second Circuit Court of Appeals rejected the defendant's argument on the basis that the defendant had pled guilty, the withheld evidence was impeachment evidence and not evidence of factual innocence, and under *United States v. Ruiz* (2002) 536 U.S. 622, 122 S.Ct. 2450, 153 L.Ed.2d 586, there was no *Brady* duty to disclose impeachment evidence regarding a prosecution witness prior to the defendant's plea of guilty.

However, the Court of Appeals was troubled by the circumstances of the defendant's conviction and the evidence that the defendant might be a wrongfully convicted person. The Court stated: "The focus on the impediment to legal relief, however, should not obscure the continuing ethical obligation of the District Attorney to seek justice." The Court of Appeals quoted Comment 6B of the New York Rules of Professional Conduct 3.8, which provides: " '[W]hen a prosecutor comes to know of new and material evidence creating a reasonable likelihood that a person was wrongly convicted, the prosecutor should examine the evidence and undertake such further inquiry or investigation as may be necessary to determine whether the conviction was wrongful. The scope of the inquiry will depend on the circumstances. In some cases, the prosecutor may recognize the need to reinvestigate the underlying case; in others, it may be appropriate to await development of the record in collateral proceedings initiated by the defendant. The nature of the inquiry or investigation should be such as to provide a 'reasonable belief' . . . that the conviction should or should not be set aside.' " 618 F.3d at 159.

CHAPTER 2

CALIFORNIA CRIMINAL DISCOVERY STATUTE: DEVELOPMENT AND SCOPE

PART I.   CRIMINAL DISCOVERY STATUTE—OVERVIEW AND HISTORICAL DEVELOPMENT

§ 2:2   Judicially declared discovery rules

If there were any question whether trial court's inherent powers to order discovery in criminal cases had survived the enactment of Proposition 115 in 1990, those doubts were put to rest by the opinion of the California Supreme Court in *Verdin v. Superior Court* (2008) 43 Cal.4th 1096, 1106, 77 Cal.Rptr.3d 287, 183 P.3d 1250.

In *Verdin* the Supreme Court held that the enactment of Penal Code section 1054, subdivision (e), abrogated the inherent power of trial courts to order discovery in criminal cases that is not expressly authorized by the Criminal Discovery Statute, expressly authorized by some other statute, or mandated by the United States Constitution. The Court explicitly rejected the argument made by the prosecution that two of the Supreme Court's own prior opinions and a Court of Appeal opinion supported the inherent power of a trial court to order a psychiatric or mental examination by a prosecution psychiatrist of a defendant who had announced a defense of diminished actuality.

In *People v. McPeters* (1992) 2 Cal.4th 1148, 9 Cal.Rptr.2d 834, 832 P.2d 146, and *People v. Carpenter* (1997) 15 Cal.4th 312, 63 Cal.Rptr.2d 1, 935 P.2d 708, the Supreme Court upheld trial court authority to order a defendant to undergo a mental examination by a prosecution psychiatrist. In *People v. Danis* (1973) 31 Cal.App.3d 782, 107 Cal.Rptr. 675, the Court of Appeal likewise upheld trial court authority to order such a mental examination of a defendant. In rejecting the prosecution's argument that the Court should follow *McPeters, Carpenter,* and *Danis,* because of courts' inherent power to order such discovery, the Court stated:

> "*Danis, McPeters,* and *Carpenter* have not survived the passage of Proposition 115. *Danis* [citation omitted] opined that prosecutorial discovery from a criminal defendant, in the form of a court-ordered mental examination, was permissible even absent an 'authorizing statute,' because the trial court possessed inherent power to order

such discovery. This reasoning is unsupportable following the 1990 enactment of section 1054, subdivision (e), which insists that rules permitting prosecutorial discovery be authorized by the criminal discovery statutes or some other statute, or mandated by the United States Constitution. Although *Danis's result* may have been supportable when decided more than 30 years ago . . . no part of its *reasoning* can have survived the enactment of section 1054, subdivision (e).

"Similarly, the rule announced in *McPeters* [citation omitted] and followed in *Carpenter* [citation omitted] did not survive Proposition 115. Neither decision explained the basis—statutory or otherwise—of their assertion that a criminal defendant who places his mental state in issue thereby creates in the prosecution the right to discovery in the form of a mental examination by a prosecution expert. Because neither *McPeters* nor *Carpenter* rests on a statutory or constitutional basis, both are inconsistent with section 1054, subdivision (e)." 43 Cal.4th at 1106–1107 [italics in original].

This holding in *Verdin* makes it unmistakably clear that following the enactment of the Criminal Discovery Statute as Penal Code section 1054 *et. seq.*, trial courts do not have inherent power to order discovery in criminal cases. Courts' powers to order discovery are conferred by statute and by the United States Constitution. Beyond those explicitly granted powers, courts may not order discovery.

PART II.   PROPOSITION 115: CRIMINAL DISCOVERY STATUTE

§ 2:6   Constitutional and statutory amendments

"The voters' intent in enacting the discovery statutes as part of Proposition 115 was not reciprocity, but the ascertainment of truth, conserving judicial resources, minimizing delays during trial, and protecting victims and witnesses from danger, harassment, and undue delay of proceedings. (Sec. 1054) The reciprocity aspect of the discovery statutes was intended to increase the prosecution's ability to obtain discovery from the defense while providing a system that was sufficiently fair to defendants to conform with due process. [citation omitted] Due process has never been held to require precise equality or symmetry between the prosecutor's and the defendant's abilities and resources to obtain discovery or investigate. Instead, the due process reciprocity requirement is intended to avoid an unfair trial, especially unfair surprise to the defendant." *People v. Appellate Division of Superior Court* (2011) 197 Cal.App.4th 985, 994, 130 Cal.Rptr.3d 116.

§ 2:7   Effective date and retroactive application

In *People v. Richardson* (2008) 43 Cal.4th 959, 77 Cal.Rptr.3d 163, 183 P.3d 1146, the California Supreme Court held that the reciprocal discovery provisions of the Criminal Discovery Statute enacted by Proposition 115 apply to discoverable evidence generated after June 5, 1990, by a defendant whose crime predated the enactment of Penal Code section 1054.3, even though the trial court had erroneously ruled in September of 1990 that the Criminal Discovery Statute did not apply to that evidence. The Court held that the defendant could not reasonably rely upon the trial court's ruling, and that the prosecution was entitled to obtain reciprocal discovery from the defendant of any evidence obtained by the defendant after the passage of Proposition 115. 43 Cal.4th at 997–1000.

PART III.   SCOPE OF CRIMINAL DISCOVERY STATUTE

A.   Scope of Criminal Discovery Statute—in general

§ 2:8   Parties affected

California's criminal discovery statutes do not violate the Due Process Clause by failing to require the prosecutor to disclose all exculpatory evidence as mandated by the U.S. Supreme Court in *Brady v. Maryland*. The criminal discovery statutes cannot not violate due process because the new statutes do not affect the defendant's constitutional rights under *Brady*. The prosecutor's duties of disclosure under the Due Process Clause are wholly independent of any statutory scheme of reciprocal discovery. The due process requirements are self-executing and need no statutory support to be effective. The prosecutor is obligated to disclose such evidence voluntarily. No statute can limit the foregoing due process rights of criminal defendants, and the criminal discovery statutes do not attempt to do so. On the contrary, the criminal discovery statutes contemplates disclosure outside the statutory scheme pursuant to constitutional requirements as enunciated in *Brady*. *People v. Gutierrez* (2013) 214 Cal. App. 4th 343, 153 Cal. Rptr. 3d 832.

The provisions of the Criminal Discovery Statute contained in Penal Code sections 1054 through 1054.7 "do not regulate discovery concerning uninvolved third parties.' [citations omitted]" *Kling v. Superior Court* (2010) 50 Cal.4th 1068, 1077, 116 Cal.Rptr.3d 217, 239 P.3d 670. Thus, the Criminal Discovery Statute does not apply to subpoenas issued by the prosecution or the defendant to third parties.

§ 2:8.1   Private third parties

The provisions of the Criminal Discovery Statute contained in Penal Code sections 1054 through 1054.7 "do not regulate discovery concerning uninvolved third parties.' [citations omitted]" *Kling v. Superior Court* (2010) 50 Cal.4th 1068, 1077, 116 Cal.Rptr.3d 217, 239 P.3d 670. Thus, the Criminal Discovery Statute does not apply to subpoenas issued by the prosecution or the defendant to third parties.

§ 2:8.4   Corporate defendants

California's appellate courts have now spoken on the question of the prosecutor's right to obtain corporate records of a corporate defendant in a criminal prosecution following the adoption of the Criminal Discovery Statute in 1990.

In *People v. Appellate Division of Superior Court* (2011) 197 Cal.App.4th 985, 130 Cal.Rptr.3d 116, several business entities were charged criminally by the public prosecutor of Los Angeles County with violations of the Los Angeles Municipal Code. The prosecutor filed a motion for corporate discovery from the defendant businesses. The corporate defendants opposed the discovery motion on the grounds that the discovery sought was outside the scope of the Criminal Discovery Statute. The municipal court denied the prosecutor's motion. The appellate division of the Superior Court summarily denied the prosecutor's petition for writ of mandate. The municipal court then denied the prosecutor's motion for leave to serve subpoenas duces tecum on the corporate defendants, holding that Penal Code section 1326 does not apply to a party and that the motion asked for discovery beyond the discovery permitted by the Criminal Discovery Statute. The prosecutor petitioned the Court of Appeal for writ of mandate.

The Court of Appeal granted a writ of mandate, holding that "the criminal discovery statutes do not bar production of the records, which constitute a category of nontestimonial evidence that Penal Code section 1054.4 and established precedent permit the prosecutor to obtain." 197 Cal.App.4th at 989.

In reaching this result the Court of Appeal reaffirmed the applicability of the holding in *People v. Superior Court (Keuffel & Esser Co.)* (1986) 181 Cal.App.3d 785, 227 Cal.Rptr. 13. The Court concluded that "voluntarily created [corporate records] do not involve compelled testimony and fall within the category of materials discoverable under section 1054.4." 197 Cal.App.4th at 991. The Court rejected the defendants' attempts to construe Penal Code section 1054.4 to apply only to "forensic evidence," saying that Section 1054.4 "preserves the prosecutor's right to obtain 'nontestimonial evidence.' " 197 Cal.App.4th at 992.

The Court rejected the defendants' argument that Penal Code section 1054.4 applies only to corporations, and they are not corporations. The Court stated that "all references to 'corporate' documents or records and 'corporate defendants' are fully applicable to real parties in interest, whatever their organizational structure may be." 197 Cal.App.4th at 994.

Accordingly, the Court concluded that Penal Code section 1054.3's "expansion of information that the defense must disclose in no way suggests abrogation of *Keuffel's* ruling permitting the prosecutor to obtain corporate documents from a corporate defendant as a type of nontestimonial evidence" 197 Cal.App.4th at 994. The Court determined that Penal Code section 1054.3 "imposes upon a defendant a duty to disclose, but does not purport to limit the prosecutor's ability to obtain 'real evidence' authorized by other statutes, such as section 1054.4." 197 Cal.App.4th at 994.

§ 2:9 Proceedings affected—generally

Questions have arisen whether the discovery provisions of the Criminal Discovery Statute apply to proceedings which charge a violation of public offenses classified as *infractions*.

§ 2:9.1 Proceedings affected—infraction proceedings

Prior to 1969 there were no infractions in California. In 1968 the California State Legislature amended Section 16 of the Penal Code to provide that "[c]rimes and public offenses include: 1. Felonies; 2. Misdemeanors; and 3. Infractions." By this amendment to Section 16 infractions were recognized in California law. *People v. Shults* (1978) 87 Cal.App.3d 101, 104, 150 Cal.Rptr. 747. An *infraction* is thus a *public offense. People v. Hamilton* (1986) 191 Cal.App.3d Supp. 13, 18, 236 Cal.Rptr. 894 ["The court, therefore, finds that an infraction constitutes a public offense within the meaning of section 830.1."].

The punishments for infractions differ significantly from those of misdemeanors and felonies. There can be no imprisonment for an infraction. Penal Code section 19.6. The Legislature has "generally limited the classification of infractions to minor traffic violations." *Tracy v. Municipal Court for Glendale Judicial Dist.* (1978) 22 Cal.3d 760, 765, n.4, 150 Cal.Rptr. 785, 587 P.2d 227. The punishments for Vehicle Code infractions are (1) a $100.00 fine for the first offense; (2) a $200.00 fine for an infraction resulting in a second conviction within one year; and (3) a $250.00 fine for an infraction resulting in a third or more conviction within one year. Vehicle Code section 42001. However, an infraction occurring within 12 months of three other infractions that have resulted in convictions may be charged as a misdemeanor. Vehicle Code section 42001.28.

The enforcement of traffic laws whose violation is punishable as an infraction "is 'criminal' only in a limited procedural sense." *People v. Lucas* (1978) 82 Cal.App.3d 47, 52, 147 Cal.Rptr. 235. "[A]lthough traffic violations are classified as criminal offenses, they call for a different approach in processing from that in other criminal cases." *The California Municipal and Justice Courts Manual*, California Center for Judicial Education and Research (1974), quoted with approval, *People v. Lucas*, *supra*, 82 Cal.App.3d at 51, n.1. The traffic violator is only "technically a criminal," and in traffic cases a "much more rapid adjudication of cases is possible than in any other criminal field." 82 Cal.App.3d at 51, n.1.

Thus, minor motor vehicle violation proceedings are summary in nature, and are "unconstrained by the more stringent procedural requirements of a major criminal trial . . . ." For this reason, "municipal courts and prosecutors are free to develop innovative procedures to expedite traffic cases." *In re Dennis B.* (1976) 18 Cal.3d 687, 695, 696, 135 Cal.Rptr. 82, 557 P.2d 514.

A defendant charged with the commission of an infraction is not entitled to a trial by jury. Penal Code section 19.6. Moreover, such a defendant is not entitled to the appointment of a public defender or other counsel at public expense, unless the defendant is arrested and not released on a written promise to appear, own recognizance, or by a deposit of bail. Penal Code section 19.6. The filing of a public offense as an infraction does not bar a later criminal prosecution as a misdemeanor or felony for the same act. *In re Dennis B.* (1976) 18 Cal.3d 687, 695, 135 Cal.Rptr. 82, 557 P.2d 514.

To be sure, some procedures applicable to misdemeanors and felonies are required in infraction cases. Penal Code section 19.7 provides that "all laws relating to misdemeanors shall apply to infractions unless otherwise stated." One significant common procedure is that *Boykin-Tahl-Mills* advisements of rights required for misdemeanor and felony guilty pleas also apply to infractions. *People v. Matthews* (1983) 139 Cal.App.3d 537, 188 Cal.Rptr. 796.

There is no specific language in the Criminal Discovery Statute that specifies whether its provisions apply to infractions. However, the Discovery Statute rests upon a clear presumption that a prosecutor is personally and actively involved in the discovery process. Penal Code section 1054.1 requires the *prosecuting attorney* to make disclosures to the defendant of information and evidence "in the possession of the *prosecuting attorney.*" [italics added] The *prosecuting attorney* must disclose the names and addresses of persons the *prosecutor* intends to call as witnesses at trial. Section 1054.1(a). The *prosecuting attorney* must disclose the statements and reports of statements "whom the *prosecutor* intends to call at the trial." Section 1054.1(f) [italics added]. The *prosecuting attorney* must disclose the "results of physical or mental examinations, scientific tests, or comparisons which the *prosecutor* intends to offer at the trial." Section 1054.1(f) [italics added].

The defendant's disclosure duties in criminal cases require the defendant to make disclosures of specified items and evidence "to the *prosecuting attorney.*" Penal Code section 1054.3 [italics added].

And the work product and privilege exceptions to disclosure by the prosecution are held by the *prosecuting attorney.* Penal Code section 1054.6.

Thus, the Criminal Discovery Statute as a whole requires that a *prosecuting attorney* represent the People of the State of California in order for the discovery provisions of that statute to function. Without a participating prosecutor, the Criminal Discovery Statute cannot operate.

This means that in almost all infraction cases the Criminal Discovery Statute is inoperative, because prosecuting attorneys almost never make appearances in infraction cases. "The People are not required to provide a prosecutor for every infraction trial." *People v. Marcroft* (1992) 6 Cal.App.4th Supp. 1, 4, 8 Cal.Rptr.2d 544; *People v. Carlucci* (1979) 23 Cal.3d 249, 255, 152 Cal.Rptr. 439, 590 P.2d 15.

The absence of a prosecuting attorney at the trial of an infraction does not mean that some other participant takes up the prosecutor's role. The court may not do so, because the court must conduct itself in a proper judicial manner and not assume the role of an advocate. *People v. Carlucci, supra,* 23 Cal.3d at 255. The investigating officer who testifies for the People in an infraction trial may not become the prosecutor, for that would constitute the unlawful practice of law. What it does mean is that in the absence of a prosecutor, the court must act as a neutral arbiter who facilitates the testimony of all of the witnesses and then resolves the infraction charges.

The absence of a prosecuting attorney from infraction trials means that the Criminal Discovery Statute does not apply to such trials. In this way the command of Penal Code section 4, that all provisions of the Penal Code "are to be construed according to the fair import of their terms, with a view to effect its objects, and to promote justice," can be achieved.

B. Preliminary Examinations.

§ 2:12   Discovery for preliminary examinations—in general

Where a mental health examination by a prosecution-retained expert was ordered under Penal Code section 1054.3, due process concerns were satisfied by reciprocal discovery under Penal Code section 1054.1. *Maldonado v. Superior Court* (2012) 53 Cal. 4th 1112, 140 Cal. Rptr. 3d 113, 274 P.3d 1110. The California Supreme Court held, *inter alia,* that, in order to afford the prosecution a fair opportunity to rebut mental-state evidence proffered by the defense, California's criminal-case reciprocal discovery statute, Penal Code section 1054.3, specifically provides that when the defendant places in issue his or her mental state at any phase of the criminal action, the prosecution may seek and obtain a court order that the defendant submit to examination by a prosecution-mental health expert. § 1054.3, subsection (b)(1).

In *Sharp v. Superior Court* (2012) 54 Cal. 4th 168, 141 Cal. Rptr. 3d 486, 277 P.3d 174, the petitioner, who was charged with several felonies, including murder with special circumstances, pleaded not guilty by reason of insanity and proposed to call a mental health expert on the issue of sanity. The court concluded that § 1054.3, subsection (b)(1), applied in this case. By its terms, § 1054.3, subsection (b)(1), authorizes an order compelling examination by a prosecution-retained expert whenever at any phase of the criminal action the defense has proposed its own expert testimony on mental state, unless otherwise specifically addressed by an existing provision of law. Had the legislature meant to exclude discovery in sanity phase proceedings from the scope of § 1054.3, subsection (b)(1), it would not have expressly stated the statute applies "at any phase of the criminal action." Even if the court agreed with petitioner as to the lack of need for the examination, it could not ignore the statute's broadly inclusive language authorizing a compelled examination whenever the defendant has put his or her mental state at issue at any phase of the criminal action through the proposed testimony of a mental health expert.

§ 2:12.1 Discovery for motion at preliminary examination

The enactment of the Criminal Discovery Statute by the electorate in 1990 did not eliminate the power of a magistrate to order discovery by the defendant from the prosecution prior to the holding of a preliminary examination for the purpose of enabling the defendant to make a motion to suppress evidence in conjunction with the preliminary examination.

In *Magallan v. Superior Court* (2011) 192 Cal.App.4th 1444, 121 Cal.Rptr.3d 841, a magistrate granted a defendant's discovery motion prior to the defendant's preliminary examination in which the defendant sought material related to his suppression motion to be made in conjunction with the defendant's preliminary examination. The prosecution had refused to provide this discovery. The Superior Court granted the prosecution's writ petition, and the magistrate set aside the discovery order. The defendant filed a petition in the Court of Appeal challenging the action of the superior court.

The Court of Appeal issued the requested writ, holding that because the defendant has a statutory right to litigate a suppression motion pursuant to Penal Code section 1538.5 in connection with his preliminary examination, the defendant is entitled to discovery in aid of that suppression motion. The Court of Appeal relied upon its own earlier opinion in *People v. Superior Court (Mouchaourab)* (2000) 78 Cal.App.4th 403, 92 Cal.Rptr.2d 829, which held that a defendant is entitled to discovery of a transcript of the nontestimonial portions of a grand jury indictment proceeding to assist the defendant in making a Penal Code section 995 motion to dismiss the indictment. The Court of Appeal rejected the prosecution's argument that the enactment of the Criminal Discovery Statute had ended the power of a magistrate to order discovery.

The Court stated: "Proposition 115 did not eliminate a criminal defendant's right to bring a suppression motion at the preliminary examination. Hence, the need for discovery in support of such a motion was left unchanged by Proposition 115's other changes to the nature of preliminary examinations." 192 Cal.App.4th at 1460. The Court concluded that Penal Code section 1538.5(f) [the statute which authorizes suppression motions to be made by the defendant in conjunction with a preliminary examination] is the " 'express' statutory provision which entitles a defendant to the discovery necessary to support the suppression motion." 192 Cal.App.4th at 1462.

Finally, the Court of Appeal concluded that a "defendant's procedural due process right under the California Constitution entitles [a defendant] to a full and fair opportunity to [demonstrate that evidence was obtained in violation of the Fourth Amendment] at the suppression hearing." 192 Cal.App.4th at 1463.

Practice Tip for Prosecution: Although the California Supreme Court denied review in *Magallan*, prosecutors should not shy away from efforts to challenge *Magallan* in petitions for review to the California Supreme Court. We question whether the Court of Appeal correctly characterized Penal Code section 1538.5(f) as the "express discovery statute" described in Penal Code section 1054(e). We submit that the Penal Code section 1054(e) reference to "other express statutory provisions" means a statute that expressly provides for discovery, not simply an "express statute." There is no such thing as a "non-express statutory provision," because all statutes are express statutes. Thus, the modifying language "express" in the phrase "express statutory provision" must of necessity refer to the requirement that the statute must expressly provide for discovery.

The inclusion of the modifier "express" reflects a legislative intent to prevent courts from doing exactly what the *Magallan* and *Mouchaourab* courts did: take a statute that on its face says nothing about discovery and treat it as a statute that implicitly provides for discovery.

Moreover, the idea that a broadly defined state constitutional due process right providing for discovery orders under the theory that discovery would be helpful to vindicate a defendant's implied *statutory* right seems to be inconsistent with the spirit, if not the substance, of the opinion of the California Supreme Court in *Verdin v. Superior Court* (2008) 43 Cal.4th 1096, 1107–1108, 77 Cal.Rptr.3d 287, 183 P.3d 1250, in which the Court expressed disapproval of the creation of new rules untethered to any statute or constitutional mandate, stating that "[o]nly when interpreting a statute or where a rule of discovery is 'mandated by the Constitution of the United States' [citation omitted] does this court have a role."

In *Bridgeforth v. Superior Court* (2013) 214 Cal. App. 4th 1074, 154 Cal. Rptr. 3d 528, the Second District held that defendants have a due process right to disclosure prior to the preliminary hearing of evidence that is both favorable and material, in that its disclosure creates a reasonable probability of a different outcome at the preliminary hearing; this right is independent of, and thus not impaired or affected by, the criminal discovery statutes. Further, pursuant to the Evidence Code sections 1043, 1045, defendant can obtain, on a showing of good cause, the statements of percipient witnesses that may have been placed in an officer's personnel file maintained pursuant to Penal Code section 832.5. His need for the statements was of constitutional dimension, and disclosure by the prosecution under Penal Code section 1054.1 was not the exclusive means to obtain discovery of the statements. *Rezek v. Superior Court* (2012) 206 Cal. App. 4th 633, 141 Cal. Rptr. 3d 891.

A defendant need not spell out his theory of the case in order to obtain discovery. Nor is the government entitled to know in advance specifically what the defense is going to be. Upon defendant's request, the government must disclose any documents or other objects within its possession, custody, or control that are material to preparing the defense. Fed. R. Crim. P. 16(a)(1)(E)(i). Unlike the preceding and subsequent subsections, which both require that the government knows—or through due diligence could know—that the item exists, Rule 16(a)(1)(D), (F), Rule 16(a)(1)(E) is unconditional. Lack of knowledge or even a showing of due diligence will not excuse non-compliance. It thus behooves the government to interpret the disclosure requirement broadly and turn over whatever evidence it has pertaining to the case. When there has been a proper Rule 16(a)(1)(E)(i) request, and the prosecution finds itself holding a document during the trial that it should have turned over, it must promptly advise opposing counsel and the court that it has not complied with its Rule 16 obligations. Rule 16(c). The district court can then take such remedial measures as it deems appropriate, including continuing the trial or declaring a mistrial. Rule 16(d)(2). *United States v. Hernandez-Meza* (2013, CA9 Cal.) 720 F.3d 760.

§ 2:13 Statutory amendments affecting discovery—Penal Code section 866

Penal Code section 866 was amended by Proposition 115 on January 5, 1990, to provide that the defendant has the "right to produce and examine defense witnesses at a preliminary hearing," *People v. Erwin* (1994) 20 Cal.App.4th 1542, 1550, 25 Cal.Rptr.2d 348, which restricts defense evidence at preliminary hearings to that which would be reasonably likely to establish an affirmative defense, negate a crime element, or impeach prosecution evidence, and which mandates the magistrate at the prosecution's request to require the defense to make an offer of proof that its proposed evidence will meet this standard.

These amendments to Section 866 did not impliedly repeal "what was, until its passage, an informal practice of granting *Pitchess* discovery motions before the holding of a preliminary hearing and permitting the fruits of such discovery to be used at the preliminary hearing." *Galindo v. Superior Court* (2010) 50 Cal.4th 1, 13, 112 Cal.Rptr.3d 673, 235 P.3d 1.

§ 2:20 Trial defined—procedural context of Criminal Discovery Statute

In the 2012 case of *People v. Valdez* (2012) 55 Cal. 4th 82, 144 Cal. Rptr. 3d 865, 281 P.3d 924, the California Supreme Court held that protective orders for pretrial nondisclosure of prosecution witnesses' identities under Penal Code section 1054.7, did not violate defendant's confrontation and due process rights because defense counsel obtained information about the witnesses, interviewed most of them, sought no continuances at trial, and effectively cross-examined the witnesses crucial to the case against defendant. The orders did not authorize permanent nondisclosure except as to witnesses whose testimony was inconsequential, and the evidence showed that a gang posed an extreme danger to the witnesses.

C. Other Proceedings

§ 2:26 Pretrial motions

In *People v. Superior Court (Humberto S.)* (2008) 43 Cal.4th 737, 750, 76 Cal.Rptr.3d 276, 182 P.3d 600, the California Supreme Court disapproved the holding of the Court of Appeal in *Smith v. Superior Court* (2007) 152 Cal.App.4th 205, 60 Cal.Rptr.3d 841, that opposition party involvement in a third-party discovery proceeding is prohibited. See the discussion of *Humberto S.* in Section 9:20 of this supplement.

§ 2:26.1 Discovery at and during trial pursuant to Criminal Discovery Statute

While the question is an open one and subject to argument, it appears that the Criminal Discovery Statute applies to criminal cases during the time of their trial.

We acknowledge that language in California Supreme Court cases could be read to support an argument that the Criminal Discovery Statute provides only for pretrial discovery and does not provide for discovery once the trial has commenced. For example, in *Barnett v. Superior Court* (2010) 50 Cal.4th 890, 114 Cal.Rptr.3d 576, 237 P.3d 980, the Supreme Court described provisions in the Criminal Discovery Statute as defining "what investigating agencies the *pretrial discovery provisions* cover." 50 Cal.4th at 902. [italics added] The Court then again described these provisions as "the pretrial discovery obligations." 50 Cal.4th at 902.

We are troubled by the loose language of *Barnett* and recommend that *Barnett* be read to hold that the Criminal Discovery Statute is a comprehensive discovery statute whose reach includes pretrial, in-trial, and even post-trial discovery duties and orders, as long as those duties and orders are attendant to the criminal case.

The Supreme Court has described the Criminal Discovery Statute as a "comprehensive statutory scheme governing discovery **at trial**." *In re Steele* (2004) 32 Cal.4th 682, 695, 10 Cal.Rptr.3d 536, 85 P.3d 444. Any judicial characterizations of the Discovery Statute as a pretrial discovery statute must be read either as passing references that do not constitute holdings or as references that distinguish pre-judgment from post-judgment discovery duties.

The closest that the Supreme Court has come to holding that the Discovery Statute is only a pretrial discovery statute was in *People v. Jones* (2003) 29 Cal.4th 1229, 131 Cal.Rptr.2d 468, 64 P.3d 762, a case that is discussed in Section 2:28.2 of the text. In *Jones* the California Supreme Court distinguished two opinions of the Courts of Appeal that held that a defendant does not waive his constitutional and evidentiary privileges under the reciprocal discovery provisions of the Criminal Discovery Statute when the defendant designates an expert witness for testimony in the penalty phase of a capital trial. The Court observed that these Court of Appeal opinions "dealt with pretrial discovery orders, whereas the order here was made in the midst of the penalty phase of the trial . . . . As the order in this case, unlike the orders in *Andrade* and *Rodriguez*, was not made prior to defendant's trial, the pretrial discovery rules set out in section 1054.3 are not implicated." 29 Cal.4th at 1264, n.10.

This statement in *People v. Jones* can be construed to hold that the Criminal Discovery Statute contains **only** pretrial discovery rules. We think that a more accurate interpretation of the language in footnote 10 of the *Jones* opinion is that because the discovery dispute in *Jones* arose in the middle of a capital trial, provisions of the Discovery Statute that apply to mandated pre-trial discovery—such as the rule requiring disclosure no later than 30 days prior to trial—were inapplicable. Perhaps in a future case the Supreme Court will provide a clarification whether its holding in *Jones* was intended to state that the Criminal Discovery Statute is only a pretrial discovery statute, or that discovery obligations under the Criminal Discovery Statute do not apply during the trial.

A more recent opinion of the California Supreme Court strongly implies, although it does not directly hold, that the Discovery Statute applies to in-trial discovery duties. In-trial court enforcement of discovery under the Discovery Statute is the clear basis for the Court's opinion in *People v. Riggs* (2008) 44 Cal.4th 248, 79 Cal.Rptr.3d 648, 187 P.3d 363.

In *Riggs* the defendant was charged with capital murder. More than one month after the guilt phase of the trial had begun, and three weeks after the prosecution had completed its case-in-chief, the defendant, who represented himself, disclosed the names and addresses of two alibi witnesses who would testify that at the time of the murder the defendant was with them far away from the scene of the murder.

The prosecution requested sanctions for a discovery violation by the defendant. The trial court found that the defendant had violated his discovery obligations under the Criminal Discovery Statute. The trial court declined to exclude the witnesses' testimony, but the court, at the prosecution's request, imposed a jury instruction as a sanction for the discovery violation. The defendant was convicted of murder and sentenced to death. On automatic appeal the defendant contended that the giving of the jury instruction was error. The Supreme Court rejected the defendant's argument.

The Court found that substantial evidence supported the trial court's decision that the defendant had committed a discovery violation—that the defendant "would reasonably anticipate that it was likely he would call as witnesses family members who purportedly knew that he was several hundred miles away from the scene of the crime when the murder was committed." 44 Cal.4th at 306. The Court then upheld the trial court's imposition of a jury instruction as a sanction for the defense discovery violation.

If the Criminal Discovery Statute were simply a pretrial discovery statute, the Supreme Court arguably would have held that the trial court lacked the power to find an in-trial discovery violation and impose sanctions therefor.

§ 2:26.1.1   Discovery at and during trial—language of Proposition 115 regarding "criminal cases"

In enacting the Criminal Discovery Statute the electorate created "a comprehensive statutory scheme governing discovery . . . ." *In re Steele* (2004) 32 Cal.4th 682, 695, 10 Cal.Rptr.3d 536, 85 P.3d 444. Penal Code section 1054, subdivision (e), provides that "no discovery shall occur in **criminal cases** except as provided by this chapter . . ." [emphasis added]. Penal Code section 1054.5, subdivision (a), provides, in pertinent part, that "[n]o order requiring discovery shall be made in **criminal cases** except as provided in this chapter." [emphasis added] The language of the Discovery Statute thus clearly applies to criminal cases.

A criminal prosecution is a "criminal case" from the filing of an accusatory pleading all the way through its trial, sentencing and judgment, post-judgment motions to vacate the judgment, and appeal. A criminal prosecution does not lose its character as a "criminal case" when it reaches the trial stage. That conclusion is made clear by an examination of the use of the term "criminal cases" or its singular tense "criminal case" in five other sections enacted by Proposition 115.

Section 1 of Proposition 115 read as follows:

> "SECTION 1. (a) We the people of the State of California hereby find that the rights of crime victims are too often ignored by our courts and by our State Legislature, that the death penalty is a deterrent to murder, and that comprehensive reforms are needed in order to restore balance and fairness to our criminal justice system.

> "(b) In order to address these concerns and to accomplish these goals, we the people further find that it is necessary to reform the law as developed in numerous California Supreme Court decisions and as set forth in the statutes of this state. These decisions and statutes have unnecessarily expanded the rights of accused criminals far beyond that which is required by the United States Constitution, thereby unnecessarily adding to the costs of **criminal cases**, and diverting the judicial process from its function as a quest for truth." [emphasis added]

Section 3 of Proposition 115 amended Section 24 of Article I of the California Constitution to read:

> "§ 24. Rights guaranteed by this Constitution are not dependent on those guaranteed by the United States Constitution."

> "In **criminal cases** the rights of a defendant to equal protection of the laws, to due process of law, to the assistance of counsel, to be

personally present with counsel, to a speedy and public trial, to compel the attendance of witnesses, to confront the witnesses against him or her, to be free from unreasonable searches and seizures, to privacy, to not be compelled to be a witness against himself or herself, to not be placed twice in jeopardy for the same offense, and to not suffer the imposition of cruel or unusual punishment, shall be construed by the courts of this state in a manner consistent with the Constitution of the United States. This Constitution shall not be construed by the courts to afford greater rights to criminal defendants than those afforded by the Constitution of the United States, nor shall it be construed to afford greater rights to minors in juvenile proceedings on criminal causes than those afforded by the Constitution of the United States." [emphasis added]

Section 4 of Proposition 115 added Section 29 to Article 1 of the California Constitution, to read:

"§ 29. In a **criminal case**, the people of the State of California have the right to due process of law and to a speedy and public trial."

Section 5 of Proposition 115 added Section 30 to Article I of the California Constitution, to read:

"§ 30. (a) This Constitution shall not be construed by the courts to prohibit the joining of **criminal cases** as prescribed by the Legislature or by the people through the initiative process." [emphasis added]

Section 7 of Proposition 115 added Section 223 to the Code of Civil Procedure, to read:

"223. In a **criminal case**, the court shall conduct the examination of prospective jurors. However, the court may permit the parties, upon a showing of good cause, to supplement the examination by such further inquiry as it deems proper, or shall itself submit to the prospective jurors upon such a showing, such additional questions by the parties as it deems proper. Voir dire of any prospective jurors shall, where practicable, occur in the presence of the other jurors in all criminal cases, including death penalty cases." [emphasis added]

When construing the language of a statute enacted by an initiative measure, courts should look to the initiative as a whole. *Professional Engineers in California Government v. Kempton* (2007) 40 Cal.4th 1016, 1039, 56 Cal.Rptr.3d 814, 155 P.3d 226. "The statutory language must also be construed in the context of the statute as a whole and the overall statutory scheme . . . ." *Robert L. v. Superior Court* (2003) 30 Cal.4th 894, 901, 135 Cal.Rptr.2d 30, 69 P.3d 951. When the statute is enacted by a ballot initiative, the court must look at the proposition as a whole. 30 Cal.4th at 903 ["Proposition 21 is read as a whole . . . ."].

When an initiative uses the same term in different statutes enacted by the same initiative, the term is deemed to have the same meaning, unless the statutes or their contexts indicate otherwise. *Bldg. Indus. Ass'n v. City of Camarillo* (1986) 41 Cal.3d 810, 819, 226 Cal.Rptr. 81, 718 P.2d 68 ["Legislative intent must be gleaned from the whole act rather than from isolated words."]; *IBM v. State Bd. of Equalization* (1980) 26 Cal.3d 923, 932, 163 Cal.Rptr. 782, 609 P.2d 1 ["When as in the present case both statutes are part of the same bill, enacted and chaptered together, the rule requiring the courts to reconcile the statutes is even more compelling, for neither can be viewed as an implied repeal of the other."]. In this respect the rules of statutory construction are the same for statutes enacted by initiative measures as for statutes enacted by the Legislature. *People v. Elliot* (2003) 37 Cal.4th 453, 478, 35 Cal.Rptr.3d 759, 122 P.3d 968.

When considered together, all of these references to "criminal cases" plainly encompass the trial. If a "criminal case" ceased to be a "criminal case" once it reached trial, there would be no purpose served in guaranteeing both the defendant's and the People's rights to a "speedy and public trial" in a "criminal case," as Sections 24 and 29 of Article 1 of the California Constitution provide. If a "criminal case" ceased to be a "criminal case" once it reached trial, there would have been no purpose served in enacting Section 223 of the Code of Civil Procedure to regulate jury selection in a "criminal case."

To address the concern expressed in subdivision (b) of Section 1 of Proposition 115 that "decisions and statutes have unnecessarily expanded the rights of accused criminals far beyond that which is required by the United States Constitution, thereby unnecessarily adding to the costs of criminal cases . . . .", statutes enacted in six sections of Proposition 115 made important changes to criminal trials: (1) Section 19, which enacted Penal Code section 954.1 to provide that charges may be "tried together before the same trier of fact;" (2) Section 20, which enacted Penal Code section 987.05 regulating the appointment of defense counsel for trials; (3) Section 21, which enacted Penal Code section 1049.5 to regulate the setting of dates for trials; (4) Section 22, which enacted Penal Code section 1050.1 governing continuances of trials; (5) Section 26, which enacted Penal Code section 1385.1 to prohibit the striking of a special circumstance finding by a jury; and (6) Section 28, which enacted Penal Code section 1511 to regulate the setting of trial dates beyond the dates prescribed in Penal Code section 1049.5.

These six provisions of Proposition 115 confirm that a major focus of that initiative was to reduce costs of criminal cases resulting from problems relating to their trials. If criminal cases ceased to be criminal cases once they reached trial, these changes made by Proposition 115 could hardly reduce the costs of "criminal cases."

§ 2:26.1.2   Discovery at and during trial—decisional authority regarding the meaning of "criminal cases"

California courts have routinely discussed and decided procedural issues relating to the trials arising from criminal prosecutions, referring to these events as occurring in "criminal cases." *See, e.g., Powell v. Phelan* (1903) 138 Cal. 271, 272, 71 P. 335 ["juror in criminal cases"; "a juror who has served in criminal cases"]; *Turner v. County of Siskiyou* (1895) 109 Cal. 332, 333, 42 P. 434 ["juries in criminal cases"]; *People v. Estorga* (1928) 206 Cal. 81, 84, 273 P. 575 ["tedious and unnecessary examination of prospective jurors in criminal cases"]; *People v. Smith* (1949) 34 Cal.2d 449, 452, 211 P.2d 561 (1949) ["defendant in criminal cases was not to bear the cost of the reporter's transcript"]; *Sprowl v. Superior Court* (1990) 219 Cal.App.3d 777, 781, 268 Cal.Rptr. 592 ["trials of criminal cases"]; *People v. Boulerice* (1992) 5 Cal.App.4th 463, 469, 471, 476, 7 Cal.Rptr.2d 279 [voir dire in "criminal cases"; "The essential elements of a jury in criminal cases are number (12), unanimity, and impartiality."; "jury selection practices available in criminal cases."].

In fact, the Supreme Court has held that a postjudgment motion to vacate the judgment is part of the proceedings in a criminal case. In *In re Paiva* (1948) 31 Cal.2d 503, 510, 190 P.2d 604, the Supreme Court stated that "a motion to vacate a judgment in a criminal case upon grounds which make such motion the equivalent of a proceeding in the nature of a writ of error *coram nobis*, must be regarded as a part of the proceedings in the criminal case . . . ."

The courts' routine use of the descriptor "criminal cases" when describing the trials in criminal prosecutions is strong evidence that a criminal prosecution remains a criminal case when it reaches the trial stage.

§ 2:26.1.3   Discovery at and during trial—decisional authority finding compliance with the Discovery Statute for in-trial disclosures

Confirming the conclusion that the Criminal Discovery Statute is not simply a pretrial discovery statute, the California Supreme Court and the Courts of Appeal have held in a number of cases that the disclosure by the prosecution of inculpatory prosecution evidence during the trial did not violate the Criminal Discovery Statute—not because the Discovery Statute did not apply to such disclosures, but because the disclosures satisfied the Discovery Statute's requirements.

In *People v. DePriest* (2007) 42 Cal.4th 1, 38, 63 Cal.Rptr.3d 896, 163 P.3d 896, a defendant charged with capital murder and other crimes filed a written offer of proof just prior to opening statements in support of his intent to introduce evidence in support of the defense theory that the crime was committed by a third person. The offer of proof referred to numerous shoe prints at the crime scene that could not be connected to the defendant or any other known person. The prosecutor, who believed that only a few unidentified shoeprints had been found at the crime scene, then arranged for the prosecution shoeprint expert to examine debris that had been taken from the floor of a dumpster located near to where the victim's body had been found. The prosecutor and the prosecution expert looked for prints that the expert might have missed when initially examining this debris.

The expert found two new partial shoe prints that appeared to be consistent with the shoes that the defendant had been wearing when arrested for the murder. The prosecution immediately informed the defense of the newly discovered evidence. The defendant claimed that the prosecution had violated the prosecution's duty to disclose its inculpatory evidence in a timely manner. The trial court accepted the prosecutor's explanation of how and when the prints had been found and rejected the defendant's argument, saying that " 'nothing in its pretrial discovery order or applicable law constituted 'an absolute bar to something new coming up **during trial**.' " 42 Cal.4th at 37–38. [emphasis added]

On automatic appeal the Supreme Court affirmed the trial court's ruling. The Supreme Court concluded that "[t]he trial court properly found that [the expert's] testimony and supporting exhibits constituted new evidence, and that disclosure timely occurred under [the exception in Penal Code section 1054.7]." The Court observed that the prosecutor informed the defendant of the new evidence immediately after the pathologist reported it to the prosecutor, and that there was no evidence that the prosecution had unreasonably delayed finding the new evidence. Accordingly, the Court held that the prosecution's conduct did not violate the trial court's pretrial discovery order or the Criminal Discovery Statute. 42 Cal.4th at 38.

In reaching this conclusion the Supreme Court held that the prosecutor's disclosure of discoverable information during the trial satisfied the requirement of Penal Code section 1054.7 that "[i]f the material and information becomes known to, or comes into the possession of, a party *within 30 days of trial, disclosure shall be made immediately.*" 42 Cal.4th at 38. [italics added]

If the scope of the Criminal Discovery Statute does not extend beyond pretrial discovery rules, the Supreme Court in *People v. DePriest* should have held that the prosecutor's conduct did not violate that statute because the Discovery Statute does not apply to in-trial disclosures. Instead, the Court held that the prosecutor's conduct satisfied the requirements of the Criminal Discovery Statute.

In *People v. Panah* (2005) 35 Cal.4th 395, 459–460, 25 Cal.Rptr.3d 672, 107 P.3d 790, the Supreme Court reached a similar conclusion regarding a new report that the prosecution pathologist prepared during the trial [the Friday prior to the pathologist's testimony on Monday], after the pathologist reexamined microscopic slides at the prosecutor's request.

The defendant contended in the Supreme Court that the prosecution had violated Section 1054.1 of the Discovery Statute. The Court rejected the defendant's argument, stating:

"Section 1054.1, subdivision (f) requires the prosecutor to disclose to the defense '[r]elevant written or recorded statements of witnesses or reports of the statements of witnesses whom the prosecutor intends to call at the trial, including any reports or statements of experts made in conjunction with the case, including the results of . . . scientific tests, experiments, or comparisons which the prosecutor intends to offer in evidence.' Such disclosure must be made at least 30 days before trial, but '[i]f the material and information becomes known to, or comes into the possession of, a party within 30 days of trial, disclosure shall be made immediately . . . .' (§ 1054.7.)" 35 Cal.4th at 459–460.

The Court concluded that "disclosure of the report was timely." 35 Cal.4th at 460. Instead of holding that the Criminal Discovery Statute does not apply to in-trial disclosures, the Court held that the prosecution had satisfied the "immediate disclosure of newly discovered evidence" provision of Section 1054.7 of the Discovery Statute.

The Courts of Appeal have also construed the Criminal Discovery Statute to apply to disclosures during trials. *See People v. Walton* (1996) 42 Cal.App.4th 1004, 1017, 49 Cal.Rptr.2d 917, *overruled on other grounds*, *People v. Cromer* (2001) 24 Cal.4th 889, 901, n.1, 103 Cal.Rptr.2d 23, 15 P.3d 243. *See also People v. Hammond* (1994) 22 Cal.App.4th 1611, 1622–1624, 28 Cal.Rptr.2d 180; and *People v. Bell* (1998) 61 Cal.App.4th 282, 71 Cal.Rptr.2d 415. *Walton, Hammond* and *Bell* are discussed in Section 5:5.1 of the text.

If the Criminal Discovery Statute were nothing more than a pretrial discovery statute, there would be no purpose served by holdings that the prosecution's in-trial disclosures satisfied the requirements of the Discovery Statute, which would not apply to the claimed discovery violation.

§ 2:26.1.4 Discovery at and during trial—necessity that the Discovery Statute apply to in-trial disclosures

Penal Code section 1054, subdivision (e), provides that "no discovery shall occur in criminal cases except as provided by this chapter, other express statutory provisions, or as mandated by the Constitution of the United States." Penal Code section 1054.5, subdivision (a), provides that "[n]o order requiring discovery shall be made in criminal cases except as provided in [the Criminal Discovery Statute]. [The Discovery Statute] shall be the only means by which the defendant may compel the disclosure or production of information" from the prosecution team.

These provisions of the Discovery Statute mean that unless discovery in a criminal case is authorized by the Discovery Statute. or by express discovery provisions of another statute, or is mandated by the Constitution of the United States, discovery shall not be authorized. The statutory exclusivity language of Section 1054, subdivision (e), means that "all court-ordered discovery is governed exclusively by—and is barred except as provided by—the discovery chapter newly enacted by Proposition 115." *In re Littlefield* (1993) 5 Cal.4th 122, 129, 19 Cal.Rptr.2d 248, 851 P.2d 42. Section 1054, subdivision (e), precludes courts "from broadening the scope of discovery beyond that provided in the [Discovery Statute] or other express statutory provisions, or as mandated by the federal Constitution." *People v. Tillis* (1998) 18 Cal.4th 284, 294, 75 Cal.Rptr.2d 447, 956 P.2d 409.

Materials not listed as discoverable in Penal Code section 1054.1 or in Section 1054.3 are discoverable "if required by some other statute or mandated by the United States Constitution." *Verdin v. Superior Court* (2008) 43 Cal.4th 1096, 1105, 77 Cal.Rptr.3d 287, 183 P.3d 1250. However, we are not aware of any statute other than the Criminal Discovery Statute that requires the prosecution to disclose its inculpatory evidence to the defendant in a criminal case. This means that unless prosecution disclosure of inculpatory evidence is mandated by the Constitution of the United States, the only requirements for disclosure of such information and evidence are found in the Criminal Discovery Statute.

"Section 1054, subdivision (e) authorizes pretrial discovery if '*mandated* by the Constitution of the United States.' (Italics added.) That such discovery may be constitutionally *permitted* is insufficient." *Verdin v. Superior Court,* 43 Cal.4th at 1115. The United States Constitution does not impose a general mandate that a defendant in a criminal case be given discovery. "There is no general constitutional right to discovery in a criminal case, and *Brady* [ ] did not create one . . . ." *Weatherford v. Bursey* (1977) 429 U.S. 545, 559, 97 S.Ct. 837, 51 L.Ed.2d 30; *Alvarado v. Superior Court* (2000) 23 Cal.4th 1121, 1135, 99 Cal.Rptr.2d 149, 5 P.3d 203.

"*Brady* exculpatory evidence is the only substantive discovery mandated by the United States Constitution." *People v. Superior Court (Barrett)* (2000) 80 Cal.App.4th 1305, 1314, 96 Cal.Rptr.2d 264; *People v. Ashraf* (2007) 151 Cal.App.4th 1205, 1211, 60 Cal.Rptr.3d 624; *Jones v. Superior Court* (2004) 115 Cal.App.4th 48, 62, 8 Cal.Rptr.3d 687.

Evidence that inculpates a defendant is not *Brady* evidence. *Gray v. Netherland* (1996) 518 U.S. 152, 167-168, 116 S.Ct. 2074, 135 L.Ed.2d 457. See the discussion regarding the *Brady* rule and inculpatory evidence in Section 1:10 of the text and this supplement. The prosecution has no federal constitutional duty to disclose to a defendant evidence that is unfavorable to him. *People v. Burgener* (2003) 29 Cal.4th 833, 875, 129 Cal.Rptr.2d 747, 62 P.3d 1.

The import of these principles is that unless the Criminal Discovery Statute applies to a criminal case once it has reached the trial stage of the prosecution, there would be statutory or constitutional authority requiring the prosecution to disclose its non-exculpatory evidence and information to the defendant.

It is no answer to say that courts always have the inherent authority to order discovery in criminal cases. In *Verdin v. Superior Court*, 43 Cal.4th 1096, 1106, the Supreme Court held that the enactment of Penal Code section 1054, subdivision (e), abrogated the inherent power of trial courts to order discovery in criminal cases that is not expressly authorized by the Criminal Discovery Statute, expressly authorized by some other statute, or mandated by the United States Constitution.

The inevitable result of the argument that the Criminal Discovery Statute is restricted to pretrial discovery would be that once a criminal prosecution reaches the trial stage, the defendant has no right to discovery of the inculpatory evidence the prosecution intends to use in the trial.

In enacting the Criminal Discovery Statute the electorate intended to "promote the ascertainment of truth in trials by requiring timely pretrial discovery." Penal Code section 1054, subdivision (a). In light of this desire to promote the ascertainment of truth in trials, it strains credulity to argue that the electorate intended to reward miscreant prosecutors by allowing them to completely escape their duty by making it to trial without complying with their mandated disclosure duties of Penal Code section 1054.1. This result cannot be what the voters intended when they enacted the Criminal Discovery Statute in Proposition 115.

For all of the reasons and decisional authorities discussed in Section 2:26.1 through this section of the supplement, we conclude that a criminal prosecution begins to be a "criminal case" from the filing of its accusatory pleading. That status as a criminal case does not end until the defendant is found not guilty on all counts, the case is dismissed, or the defendant's conviction and judgment is final on appeal following any postjudgment motions to vacate the judgment.

Thus, because "[n]o order requiring discovery shall be made in criminal cases except as provided in this chapter," Penal Code section 1054.5, subdivision (a), of the Discovery Statute necessarily applies to the trial of a criminal case, and the claim that the Criminal Discovery Statute is only a pretrial discovery statute is wrong.

In order for a defendant's right under Penal Code section 1054.1 to disclosure of the prosecution's evidence and information to have meaning, that right must exist both pretrial and during trial. It is a right that extends through the trial until judgment is pronounced.

§ 2:27 Sentencing—generally

Discovery related to federal criminal sentencing proceedings is limited by Rule 16 of the Federal Rules of Criminal Procedure. *Wade v. United States* (1992) 504 U.S. 181, 186, 112 S.Ct. 1840, 118 L.Ed.2d 524; *United States v. Neal* (2010, CA7 IL) 611 F.3d 399, 401.

§ 2:28 Penalty phase of capital case—generally

The penalty phase of a capital murder case imposes notice requirements upon the prosecution that are similar in purpose and substance to the prosecution's discovery obligations, but which are not discovery obligations.

§ 2:28.3 Notice pursuant to Penal Code section 190.3

Penal Code section 190.3 contains the notice requirements placed upon the prosecution for its intended evidence in aggravation in the penalty phase of a capital case.

§ 2:28.3.2 Penal Code section 190.3 notice by prosecution—features

The notice required by Penal Code section 190.3 applies to prosecution evidence in aggravation, not to the arguments that the prosecutor intends to make in the penalty phase of a capital murder trial.

In *People v. Salcido* (2008) 44 Cal.4th 93, 79 Cal.Rptr.3d 54, 186 P.3d 437, the prosecutor argued in his closing argument in the penalty phase of the defendant's capital murder prosecution that the fact that the defendant's lack of remorse for his crimes, and the fact that a sentence of life in prison without possibility of parole would give the defendant a "lifetime of unfettered leisurely pursuits," justified a sentence of death. A sentence of death was imposed.

The defendant argued on appeal that the prosecution failed to provide notice of this evidence in aggravation as required by Penal Code section 190.3. The Supreme Court rejected the defendant's argument, observing that the "prosecutor made both of these points in his closing *argument*, but did not offer any related *evidence* in aggravation. The statute requiring the prosecution to provide notice of aggravating evidence (sec. 190.3) does not require any notice relating to the prosecution's intended argument." 44 Cal.4th at 156, n.1. [italics in original]

§ 2:28.3.5 Timing of Penal Code section 190.3 notice

Penal Code section 190.3 requires the prosecution to give notice of its evidence in aggravation that the prosecution intends to offer in the penalty phase of a capital murder prosecution "prior to trial." The phrase "prior to trial" means that the prosecution must provide its notice "before the cause is called for trial or as soon thereafter as the prosecution learns of the existence of the evidence." *People v. Wilson* (2005) 36 Cal.4th 309, 356, 30 Cal.Rptr.3d 513, 114 P.3d 758.

In *People v. Salcido* (2008) 44 Cal.4th 93, 79 Cal.Rptr.3d 54, 186 P.3d 437, the Supreme Court construed the language "called for trial" to mean "the date on which the jury was sworn . . . ." 44 Cal.4th at 157. Thus, a Penal Code section 190.3 notice of evidence in aggravation that is filed after the jury is sworn is not timely as required by Section 190.3.

§ 2:28.4   Discovery of victim-impact statements

Consideration of both Penal Code section 190.3, factors (b) (criminal activity involving force or violence), and (c) (prior felony convictions) is permissible in the penalty phase of a capital murder trial. *People v. Tully* (2012) 54 Cal. 4th 952, 145 Cal. Rptr. 3d 146, 282 P.3d 173. However, note that prior felony convictions are not admissible under Penal Code section 190.3, factor (c), at the penalty phase of a capital trial unless the conviction preceded the commission of the capital crime. *People v. Thomas* (2012) 53 Cal. 4th 771, 137 Cal. Rptr. 3d 533, 269 P.3d 1109.

Instructions need not be given in the penalty phase of a capital murder trial that duplicate California Jury Instructions No. 8.85's explication of Penal Code section 190.3, factor (k). *People v. Gonzales* (2012) 54 Cal. 4th 1234, 144 Cal. Rptr. 3d 757, 281 P.3d 834. Further, the jury in the penalty phase of a capital murder trial need not make written findings, achieve unanimity as to specific aggravating circumstances, find beyond a reasonable doubt that an aggravating circumstance is proved (except for Penal Code section 190.3, factors (b) and (c)), find beyond a reasonable doubt that aggravating circumstances outweigh mitigating circumstances, or find beyond a reasonable doubt that death is the appropriate penalty. Moreover, the jury need not be instructed as to any burden of proof in selecting the penalty to be imposed. *People v. Williams* (2013) 56 Cal. 4th 630, 156 Cal. Rptr. 3d 214, 299 P.3d 1185.

Victim impact evidence, including photographic images of the victim while he or she was alive, may be introduced at penalty phase proceedings in capital cases under the United States Constitution and under state law. The State has a legitimate interest in counteracting the mitigating evidence which the defendant is entitled to put in, by reminding the sentencer that just as the murderer should be considered as an individual, so too the victim is an individual whose death represents a unique loss to society and in particular to the victim's family. Unless it invites a purely irrational response, evidence of the effect of a capital murder on the loved ones of the victim is relevant and admissible under Penal Code section 190.3, factor (a), as a circumstance of the crime. The United States Constitution bars victim impact evidence only if it is so unduly prejudicial as to render the trial fundamentally unfair. *People v. Linton* (2013) 56 Cal. 4th 1146, 158 Cal. Rptr. 3d 521, 302 P.3d 927.

Penal Code section 190.3, provides that except for rebuttal evidence and evidence in proof of the capital offense or special circumstances that subject the defendant to the death penalty, no evidence may be presented by the prosecution in aggravation unless notice of the evidence to be introduced has been given to the defendant within a reasonable period of time as determined by the court, prior to trial. The purpose of the notice required by § 190.3 is to advise the accused of the evidence against him or her so that the defendant may have a reasonable opportunity to prepare a defense at the penalty phase.

A capital defendant is entitled to notice of other violent crimes or prior felony convictions offered in the prosecution's penalty case-in-chief before the cause is called to trial or as soon thereafter as the prosecution learns the evidence exists. However, the prosecutor is not prevented from introducing all the circumstances of a duly noticed incident or transaction simply because each and every circumstantial fact was not recited therein. The notice is sufficient if it gives defendant a reasonable opportunity to prepare a defense to the allegations. *People v. Whalen* (2013) 56 Cal. 4th 1, 152 Cal. Rptr. 3d 673, 294 P.3d 915.

Penal Code section 190.3's use of adjectives such as "extreme" and "substantial" in describing mitigating circumstances does not impermissibly limit the jury's consideration of mitigating factors during the penalty phase of a capital trial. The trial court need not delete inapplicable sentencing factors or instruct that statutory mitigating factors are relevant solely in mitigation. *People v. Rountree* (2013) 56 Cal. 4th 823, 157 Cal. Rptr. 3d 1, 301 P.3d 150.

§ 2:28.5   Discovery for mental retardation hearing

Note the fact that the legislature did not expressly provide for an appeal in Penal Code section 1376, does not necessarily reflect the intent to preclude appeal or review by writ petition. Having covered the subject of pretrial prosecution appeals by generally applicable provisions in Penal Code section 1238, the legislature would not be expected to put appeal provisions into each statute that concerns a pretrial motion. Thus, that § 1376 does not itself authorize (or prohibit) appellate review provides little, if any, clue as to whether § 1238, subsection (a)(8), covers this situation. Allowing an appeal is consistent with the language of both statutes and would further the purpose of § 1238, subsection (a)(8). Section 1238, subsection (a)(8), expressly includes pretrial orders dismissing "or otherwise terminating" a portion of the action, suggesting that, as the term is used here, proceedings on a charge can be terminated before trial on it has begun. *People v. Superior Court (Vidal)* (2007) 40 Cal. 4th 999, 56 Cal. Rptr. 3d 851, 155 P.3d 259.

§ 2:29   Postjudgment proceedings

The prosecution's duty to provide discovery in postjudgment proceedings arises in a variety of contexts.

§ 2:29.1   State habeas corpus proceedings

Discovery in California state habeas proceedings is within the control and direction of the court issuing the order to show cause on the habeas petition and of a referee appointed by the court to conduct evidentiary hearings and make findings.

In *In re Lawley* (2008) 42 Cal.4th 1231, 74 Cal.Rptr.3d 92, 179 P.3d 891, a defendant convicted of capital murder and sentenced to death petitioned in state court for writ of habeas corpus, alleging that he was factually innocent of the murder. The California Supreme Court issued an order to show cause and appointed a referee to hear evidence and make factual findings. After the referee had conducted the hearing, the petitioner (defendant) argued in the Supreme Court that he had been denied a fair evidentiary hearing because of limitations placed on his discovery efforts by the referee. The Supreme Court rejected the petitioner's claim, observing that the petitioner's discovery efforts contravened the Supreme Court's order which gave the referee the power to ensure orderly discovery.

The Court stated that "[t]here is no federal right, constitutional or otherwise, to discovery in a habeas corpus proceeding. [citations omitted] Nor have we recognized any state right to unfettered discovery, instead allowing trial courts and referees to manage discovery on a case-by-case basis. [citations omitted]" 42 Cal.4th at 1249.

§ 2:29.2 Federal habeas corpus proceedings

In *Williams v. Beard* (2011, CA3 PA) 637 F.3d 195, 208–209, the Third Circuit Court of Appeals summarized the rule governing discovery in federal habeas corpus proceedings. The Court stated: "[H]abeas petitioners are entitled to discovery only upon a showing of 'good cause,' and even then, the scope of discovery is subject to a district court's sound discretion. [citations omitted] A habeas petitioner may satisfy the 'good cause' standard by setting forth specific factual allegations which, if fully developed, would entitle him or her to the writ. [citation omitted] The burden rests upon the petitioner to demonstrate that the sought-after information is pertinent and that there is good cause for its production."

The Court of Appeals observed that a district court's denial of a discovery request is reviewed for abuse of discretion, and that "[a] district court abuses its discretion when discovery is 'essential for the habeas petitioner to develop fully his underlying claim.' [citations omitted]" 637 F.3d at 209.

§ 2:29.3 Postjudgment discovery in capital murder cases

The California Penal Code contains special provisions for postjudgment discovery in capital murder cases. These provisions are contained in Penal Code section 1054.9.

§ 2:29.3.1 Penal Code section 1054.9 discovery

To prevail on a Penal Code section 1405, motion, the defendant must demonstrate that, had the DNA testing been available, in light of all of the evidence, there is a reasonable probability—that is, a reasonable chance and not merely an abstract possibility—that the defendant would have obtained a more favorable result. While the probability must be reasonable and not merely abstract, the court has cautioned against imposing too great a burden: In making this assessment, however, it is important for the trial court to bear in mind that the question before it is whether the defendant is entitled to develop potentially exculpatory evidence and not whether he or she is entitled to some form of ultimate relief such as the granting of a petition for habeas corpus based on that evidence. Obtaining post-conviction access to evidence is not habeas relief. Therefore, the trial court does not, and should not, decide whether, assuming a DNA test result favorable to the defendant, that evidence in and of itself would ultimately require some form of relief from the conviction. *Jointer v. Superior Court* (2013) 217 Cal. App. 4th 759, 158 Cal. Rptr. 3d 778.

Section 1054.9 has produced substantial litigation over its constitutionality and over the meaning and application of its terms.

§ 2:29.3.1.1   Constitutionality of Section 1054.9

After several years of litigation, the California Supreme Court has held that Penal Code section 1054.9 was constitutionally enacted.

In *Barnett v. Superior Court* (2010) 50 Cal.4th 890, 114 Cal.Rptr.3d 576, 237 P.3d 980, a convicted capital murderer sentenced to death filed a postjudgment discovery motion pursuant to Penal Code section 1054.9. The superior court granted many of the inmate's discovery requests and denied many others. The inmate petitioned the Court of Appeal for writ of mandate challenging the denials. The Court of Appeal issued a published opinion addressing a number of issues that had not been resolved by the Supreme Court in *In re Steele* (2004), 32 Cal.4th 682, 10 Cal.Rptr.3d 536, 85 P.3d 444. The Supreme Court granted review and transferred the case back to the Court of Appeal to resolve an issue raised by an amicus curiae—whether Penal Code section 1054.9 constituted an invalid amendment to the Criminal Discovery Statute enacted by Proposition 115 in 1990.

The Court of Appeal rejected the constitutional challenge to Section 1054.9 and reached the following holdings concerning the application of Section 1054.9: (1) a defendant making a motion for postjudgment discovery need not provide the People with an inventory of every single document or other item the defendant possesses already; (2) a defendant does not have a right under Section 1054.9 to duplicative discovery; (3) Section 1054.9 does not provide a vehicle for the defendant to force the People to disclose exculpatory evidence the People did not possess at the time of the defendant's trial; (4) a denial of the defendant's postjudgment discovery motion may not be grounded on an unsworn denial of the existence of any additional responsive documents.

Although both parties petitioned the Supreme Court for review, neither party petitioned for review on the question of whether Penal Code section 1054.9 had been constitutionally enacted. On September 17, 2008, the Supreme Court again granted review.

While awaiting oral argument in *Barnett*, the Supreme Court decided to resolve the question of the constitutionality of Penal Code section 1054.9 in a case other than *Barnett*. That determination occurred in *People v. Superior Court (Pearson)* (2010) 48 Cal.4th 564, 107 Cal.Rptr.3d 265, 227 P.3d 858.

In *Pearson* the Supreme Court held that Penal Code section 1054.9 had been constitutionally enacted, because even though Section 1054.9 was not enacted by a two-thirds vote of each house of the State Legislature, Section 1054.9 did not amend the provisions of the Criminal Discovery Statute that had been enacted by initiative in Proposition 115.

In reaching this conclusion, the Court reasoned in *Pearson* that the Criminal Discovery Statute enacted by Proposition 115 "governs only pretrial discovery and does not prohibit postconviction discovery of the kind that section 1054.9 provides." 48 Cal.4th at 567. The Court highlighted this conclusion in several places in its opinion in *Pearson*. " Proposition 115 provides only for *pretrial* discovery to aid in the trial process. The chapter's purposes make this clear . . . Most of these purposes, and particularly those stated in section 1054, subdivisions (a) and (c), relate solely to the trial phase of the case. Arguably, protecting victims and witnesses (sec. 1054, subd. (d)) might relate to postconviction proceedings, but even this purpose seems primarily directed to the trial. Moreover, the substance of the discovery requirements relates entirely to evidence that might be presented at trial (secs. 1054.1, 1054.2), and the time limits for providing the discovery require the discovery to be provided before trial (sec. 1054.7). These circumstances also show that the discovery referred to is pretrial." 48 Cal. 4th at 570. [italics in original]

The Court reasoned that in determining whether Section 1054.9 was constitutionally enacted, the Court must focus on two questions: (1) Did Section 1054.9 prohibit something that the Criminal Discovery Statute authorized, and (2) did Section 1054.9 authorize something that the Discovery Statute prohibited? ["In deciding whether this particular provision amends Proposition 115, we simply need to ask whether it prohibits what the initiative authorizes, or authorizes what the initiative prohibits."] 48 Cal.4th at 571.

The Court concluded that Section 1054.9 neither prohibited anything that the Criminal Discovery Statute authorized, 48 Cal.4th at 571, nor did it authorize anything that the Criminal Discovery Statute prohibited. ["[W]e do not believe the electorate that passed Proposition 115, in providing for pretrial discovery in a criminal case, intended either to provide for or to prohibit discovery in a separate habeas corpus matter. Section 1054.9 addresses an area that is *related* to Proposition 115's discovery provisions but, crucially, it is also a *distinct* area. (*People v. Kelley, supra,* 47 Cal.4th at p. 1025.) Proposition 115 does not prohibit section 1054.9's discovery."]. 48 Cal.4th at 572–573. [italics in original] For this reason, the Supreme Court concluded that Section 1054.9 had been constitutionally enacted.

§ 2:29.3.1.2 Time to file 1054.9 petition

There are no statutory or decisionally-imposed time limits for a defendant to file a petition for post conviction discovery pursuant to Penal Code Section 1054.9.

In *In Re Steele* (2004) 35 Cal.4th 682, 692–693, n.2, 10 Cal.Rptr.3d 536, 85 P.3d 444, the California Supreme Court stated that while " Section 1054.9 provides no time limits for making the discovery motion or complying with any discovery order. . . . the statute implies that the motion, any petition challenging the trial court's ruling, and compliance with a discovery order must all be done within a reasonable time period."

In reliance upon this language in *Steele*, a number of trial courts denied postjudgment discovery motions brought pursuant to Penal Code section 1054.9 on the grounds that these motions had not been brought within a reasonable time period. In *Catlin v. Superior Court* (2011) 51 Cal.4th 300, 120 Cal.Rptr.3d 135, 245, P.3d 860, the trial court denied a petition for postjudgment discovery pursuant to Penal Code section 1054.9, where the convicted inmate filed his habeas petition in 2000, 14 years after his 1986 conviction, and where the inmate filed his 1054.9 motion for postjudgment discovery in 2007, seven years after the filing of his habeas petition. The Court of Appeal affirmed the trial court's denial of the postjudgment discovery motion.

The Supreme Court reversed the judgment of the Court of Appeal and remanded the case to the Court of Appeal for further proceedings. The Supreme Court held that while a trial court may deny a habeas corpus petition on the grounds that the petition had not been filed in a timely manner, there is no statutory authority in Penal Code section 1054.9 to deny a postjudgment discovery motion on the grounds that the motion was brought within a reasonable time. The Court held that when a habeas petitioner files an untimely postjudgment discovery order, the court in which the habeas petition is filed based on the information obtained through that discovery should consider the delay in filing the postjudgment discovery motion as part of its determination whether the underlying habeas corpus petition is timely.

Thus, while an unreasonable delay in filing a postjudgment discovery order pursuant to Penal Code section 1054.9 may not prevent the granting of such an order, the court considering the underlying habeas petition may consider the delay in filing the discovery motion in determining whether to grant or deny the underlying habeas corpus petition.

§ 2:29.3.1.3　Persons entitled to file 1054.9 petition

A petition for postjudgment discovery pursuant to Penal Code section 1054.9 may be filed by the convicted defendant, without any requirement that the defendant be represented by an attorney. *Burton v. Superior Court* (2010) 181 Cal.App.4th 1519, 105 Cal.Rptr.3d 604. ["Nothing in the language of section 1054.9 limits the statute to defendants who are currently represented by counsel."]. 181 Cal.App.4th at 1522.

§ 2:29.3.1.4　Showing required for granting 1054.9 petition

Penal Code section 1054.9 "provides only for specific discovery and not the proverbial 'fishing expedition' for anything that might exist . . . . " *Barnett v. Superior Court* (2010) 50 Cal.4th 890, 898, 114 Cal.Rptr.3d 576, 237 P.3d 980.

This means that a defendant convicted of a capital murder who asks no more than that the prosecution assist in the reconstruction of defense trial files must show only a "legitimate reason for believing that counsel's current files are incomplete." 50 Cal.4th at 898. Once the defendant makes this showing, the defendant "need not identify all missing discovery materials that the prosecution had previously provided to the defense or show that they are still in the prosecution's possession." 50 Cal.4th at 898. The trial court may then "order the prosecution to provide any materials it still possesses that it had provided at time of trial." 50 Cal.4th at 898. It does not appear to matter that some of the prosecution's disclosures will duplicate what the defense already has. The prosecution must provide a complete set of materials that it had provided at the time of trial.

In addition to reconstruction of the defense trial file, Section 1054.9 allows discovery of materials to which defense trial counsel was legally entitled but did not receive. This discovery right is broader than file reconstruction. 50 Cal.4th at 898–899. However, unlike file reconstruction, which does not require the defendant to show that the materials are still possessed by the prosecution, "defendants who seek discovery beyond file reconstruction [must] show a reasonable basis to believe that other specific materials actually exist." 50 Cal.4th at 899. In meeting this burden, if the defendant provides "a reasonable basis to believe that the prosecution had possessed the materials in the past," this showing would be sufficient to "provide a reasonable basis to believe the prosecution still possesses the materials." 50 Cal.4th at 901.

The defendant need not show that the discovery materials to which the defendant's trial counsel was entitled constituted material evidence within the meaning of the *Brady* rule. Because every defendant is legally entitled to receive discovery pursuant to Penal Code section 1054.1, and because Section 1054.1, subdivision (e), entitles the defendant to disclosure of "exculpatory evidence," not simply "material exculpatory evidence, the defendant is entitled under Section 1054.9 to disclosure of all exculpatory evidence, whether material or not, to which his counsel was entitled at the time of trial. The defendant need not make a materiality showing as a pre-requisite to his or her right to this disclosure." 50 Cal.4th at 900–901.

§ 2:29.3.1.5   Section 1054.9 discovery and out-of-state law enforcement agencies

Penal Code section 1054.9 does not require the prosecution to disclose materials possessed by "out-of-state law enforcement agencies that merely provided the prosecution with information or assistance under the circumstances of the case." *Barnett v. Superior Court* (2010) 50 Cal.4th 890, 902, 114 Cal.Rptr.3d 576, 237 P.3d 980.

Section 1054.9 does not create a broader postconviction discovery right than a defendant has under the Criminal Discovery Statute. 50 Cal.4th at 902. Thus, in *In re Steele* (2004) 32 Cal.4th 682, 696, 10 Cal.Rptr.3d 536, 85 P.3d 444, the Supreme Court concluded that the "law enforcement authorities" to which Section 1054.9 refers are similar to the "investigating agencies" to which Section 1054.1 refers. Reading all of the provisions of Penal Code section 1054.1, Section 1054.5, and Section 1054.9 together, the Supreme Court concluded in *Steele* that the discovery rights under Section 1054.9 "do not extend to materials possessed by law enforcement agencies that were not involved in investigating or preparing the case against the defendant." 32 Cal.4th at 696.

In *Barnett v. Superior* Court, the Supreme Court broadened its holding in *Steele* to conclude that the prosecution's constitutional duties under *Brady* extend to information "possessed by others acting on the government's behalf that [was] gathered in connection with the investigation," but not to "evidence in the possession of *all* governmental agencies, including those not involved in the investigation or prosecution of the case." 50 Cal.4th at 903.

Thus, the Court held in *Barnett*, an out-of-state law enforcement agency that provides assistance and conducts a few interviews of potential witnesses acts "on behalf of the prosecution in a limited sense . . . "That "limited sense" is that the out-of-state law enforcement agency provides limited assistance on request to the prosecution.

However, an out-of-state law enforcement agency that provides limited assistance on request to a California prosecutor is not part of the "prosecution team," because the out-of-state agency is not under the control of any California authorities, which the Supreme Court found to be an important factor. 50 Cal.4th at 904. The out-of-state agency is not part of a team participating in a joint investigation or sharing resources. The out-of-state agency simply provides specific assistance to the California prosecution. 50 Cal.4th at 904. The Supreme Court stated in *Barnett:* " [W]e do not believe the Legislature intended the posttrial discovery right to extend so far as to permit a court to order discovery from 22 law enforcement officers working for six different out-of-state agencies, one outside the country." 50 Cal.4th at 906. Thus, the Court concluded, "the prosecution is not required to provide discovery of materials from the out-of-state law enforcement agencies of this case that the prosecution does not possess." 50 Cal.4th at 906.

§ 2:29.3.2　Penal Code section 1054.9 discovery of peace officer personnel records

A defendant has a limited right to discovery of a peace officer's confidential personnel records if those files contain information that is potentially relevant to the defense. To initiate discovery, a defendant must file a motion seeking such records, containing affidavits showing good cause for the discovery or disclosure sought, setting forth the materiality thereof to the subject matter involved in the pending litigation. Good cause requires the defendant to establish a logical link between a proposed defense and the pending charge and to articulate how the discovery would support such a defense or how it would impeach the officer's version of events. The threshold for establishing good cause is relatively low. The proposed defense must have a plausible factual foundation supported by the defendant's counsel's declaration and other documents supporting the motion. A plausible scenario is one that might or could have occurred. The defendant must also show how the information sought could lead to or be evidence potentially admissible at trial. Once that burden is met, the defendant has shown materiality under Evidence Code section 1043. *Sisson v. Superior Court* (2013) 216 Cal. App. 4th 24, 156 Cal. Rptr. 3d 533. *See also People v. Yearwood* (2013) 213 Cal. App. 4th 161, 151 Cal. Rptr. 3d 901.

Note that a peace officer's official service photograph is not a personnel record under Penal Code section 832.8 and therefore is not subject to the requirements of Penal Code section 832.7, and Evidence Code section 1043, when discovery or disclosure is sought. *Ibarra v. Superior Court* (2013) 217 Cal. App. 4th 695, 158 Cal. Rptr. 3d 751. The mere fact that officers' service photographs are contained in files maintained by the employing agency does not render them confidential or protected under Penal Code sections 832.7 and 832.8. Instead, such photographs constitute peace officer personnel records only if they fall within one of the types of information enumerated in § 832.8. *Id.*

§ 2:29.3.3 Postjudgment DNA testing

To prevail on a Penal Code section 1405, motion, the defendant must demonstrate that, had the DNA testing been available, in light of all of the evidence, there is a reasonable probability—that is, a reasonable chance and not merely an abstract possibility—that the defendant would have obtained a more favorable result. While the probability must be reasonable and not merely abstract, the court has cautioned against imposing too great a burden: In making this assessment, however, it is important for the trial court to bear in mind that the question before it is whether the defendant is entitled to develop potentially exculpatory evidence and not whether he or she is entitled to some form of ultimate relief such as the granting of a petition for habeas corpus based on that evidence. Obtaining post-conviction access to evidence is not habeas relief. Therefore, the trial court does not, and should not, decide whether, assuming a DNA test result favorable to the defendant, that evidence in and of itself would ultimately require some form of relief from the conviction. *Jointer v. Superior Court* (2013) 217 Cal. App. 4th 759, 158 Cal. Rptr. 3d 778.

In *Richardson v. Superior Court* (2008) 43 Cal.4th 1040, 77 Cal.Rptr.3d 226, 183 P.3d 1199, a companion case to *People v. Richardson* (2008) 43 Cal.4th 959, 1032–1033, 77 Cal.Rptr.3d 163, 183 P.3d 1146, in which the

California Supreme Court on automatic appeal affirmed the defendant's conviction of murder and judgment of death, the Supreme Court considered the defendant's petition for writ of mandamus regarding a discovery order of the Superior Court. The Superior Court had denied the petitioner's motion under Penal Code section 1405 for DNA testing of hair samples that had been admitted in evidence at his trial.

The Supreme Court denied the writ petition. In reaching its decision the Court construed two of the eight conditions established by Section 1405 that must be satisfied for a defendant to be entitled to DNA testing of physical evidence. The two conditions are set forth in subdivision (f)(4) and subdivision (f)(5) of Penal Code section 1405.

The first condition [subdivision (f)(4)] requires the defendant to make a "prima facie showing that the evidence sought to be tested is material to the issue of the defendant's identity as the perpetrator of, or accomplice to, the crime, special circumstance, or enhancement allegation that resulted in the conviction or sentence." The Court held that this "materiality" provision is the same one found in Evidence Code section 1043, subdivision (b)(3), the standard of "materiality" for *Pitchess* motions. The Court concluded that the moving defendant under Section 1405 is "required only to demonstrate that the DNA testing that he or she seeks would be relevant to the issue of identity, rather than dispositive of it . . . that the identity of the perpetrator of, or accomplice to, the crime was a controverted issue as to which the results of DNA testing would be relevant evidence." 43 Cal.4th at 1049.

The second condition [subdivision (f)(5)] requires the court to assess whether, in light of all of the evidence, the results of DNA tests would raise "a reasonable probability that . . . the convicted person's verdict or sentence would have been more favorable if the results of DNA testing had been available at the time of conviction." The Supreme Court determined that the term "reasonable probability" has the same meaning that it has in the context of claims of ineffective assistance of counsel. The Court concluded that "reasonable probability" means that a "defendant must demonstrate that, had the DNA testing been available, in light of all of the evidence, there is a reasonable probability—that is, a reasonable chance and not merely an abstract possibility—that the defendant would have obtained a more favorable result." 43 Cal.4th at 1051.

Applying these principles the Supreme Court found that the petitioner had met the requirement of establishing that DNA testing would have been relevant to the issue of the identity of the perpetrator, but that he failed to establish the reasonable probability requirement of a different and more favorable result. In reaching the latter conclusion the Court observed that the hair samples had not been important or essential evidence supporting the defendant's conviction, but had been simply one piece of evidence tending to show his guilt. The Court further concluded that the other evidence introduced in the trial was strong. Finally, the Court concluded that DNA testing of the hair samples would not have produced a reasonable probability of a more favorable sentence. 43 Cal.4th at 1051–1054.

In June of 2009 the United States Supreme Court resolved the question whether a criminal defendant has a *Brady*–based due process right to postjudgment access to prosecution evidence for the purpose of conducting DNA testing on that evidence.

In *District Attorney's Office for Third Judicial Dist. v. Osborne* (2009) 557 U.S. 52, 129 S.Ct. 2308, 174 L.Ed.2d 38, a state prisoner in Alaska brought a civil rights action in federal court pursuant to 42 U.S. Code section 1983 in which he sought to compel the defendants to allow him postjudgment access to biological evidence that had been used to convict him of kidnapping and sexual assault. The plaintiff wanted to subject that evidence to DNA testing methodology that had been unavailable at the time of his trial and conviction. The district court granted his request and ordered that the habeas defendants provide the petitioner with access to the evidence he sought.

The Ninth Circuit Court of Appeals affirmed the judgment of the district court, holding that the prisoner was entitled to assert in his action the due process right to postjudgment access to potentially exculpatory DNA evidence. The Court of Appeals relied upon the prosecutorial duty to disclose exculpatory evidence recognized in *Pennsylvania v. Ritchie* (1987) 480 U.S. 39, 107 S.Ct. 989, 94 L.Ed.2d 40, and *Brady v. Maryland* (1963) 373 U.S. 83, 83 S.Ct. 1194, 10 L.Ed.2d 215. Based on that authority the Court of Appeals concluded that " 'the Due Process Clause also 'extends the government's duty to disclose (or the defendant's right of access) to *post-conviction* proceedings.' " 129 S.Ct. at 2315 [italics in original]. "The court held that these potential claims extended some of the State's *Brady* obligations to the postconviction context." 129 S.Ct. at 2315.

The government petitioned the United States Supreme Court for writ of certiorari. The United States Supreme Court issued a writ of certiorari, reversed the judgment of the Court of Appeals, and remanded the case for further proceedings. In reaching its decision the Supreme Court majority observed that " '[a] criminal defendant proved guilty after a fair trial does not have the same liberty interests as a free man.' [citation omitted]" 129 S.Ct. at 2320. After a conviction the defendant's presumption of innocence disappears. *Id.* A convicted defendant has only a limited interest in post-conviction relief, and that limited interest is not parallel to a trial right. *Brady*, therefore, is the "wrong framework" with which to review a case of the defendant seeking postconviction relief. *Id.*

The Supreme Court's opinion in *Osborne* resolves the question whether the *Brady* rule applies to postjudgment proceedings—it does not. Prior authority that is contrary to the Supreme Court's opinion in *Osborne* is no longer good law and should be disregarded. The *Osborne* opinion casts doubt upon recent Court of Appeals holdings that the *Brady* rule applies to new-trial and post-conviction proceedings. *See Tennison v. City and County of San Francisco* (2009, CA9 CA) 570 F.3d 1078, 1094, an opinion filed just five days after the *Osborne* opinion was filed. In light of the Supreme Court's decision in *Osborne*, the parameters of a defendant's post-conviction *Brady* rights will have to be determined by the federal and state courts.

In *Bradley v. King* (2009, CA11 AL) 556 F.3d 1225, an opinion that predated the Supreme Court's opinion in *Osborne* by four months, the Eleventh Circuit Court of Appeals affirmed the district court's denial of a request by a death-row inmate for a stay of execution to allow him access to physical evidence for DNA testing. The Court of Appeals reasoned that the non-biological evidence of the defendant's guilt was substantial, the items he wished to test had been available prior to his trial, and his claim of actual innocence was undermined by DNA tests that showed that his and the victim's DNA had been found commingled on a blanket taken from the defendant's home. The Court concluded that there were no extraordinary circumstances entitling the defendant to further post-conviction access to DNA evidence. 556 F.3d at 1230.

In the wake of *Osborne*, convicted defendants in other jurisdictions have filed civil actions pursuant to 42 U.S. Code section 1983 seeking orders that would require state authorities to send evidence from their cases to laboratories for DNA testing. Postconviction procedures that are similar to the procedures in Alaska that the Supreme Court in *Osborne* held were adequate to satisfy due process requirements are generally held to be constitutionally adequate. *See, e.g., Cunningham v. District Attorney's Office for Escambia County* (2010, CA11 FL) 592 F.3d 1237; and *McKithen v. Brown* (2010, CA2 NY) 626 F.3d 143, 150–155.

The United States Supreme Court has affirmed the use of a civil action filed by a convicted defendant pursuant to 42 U.S.C. § 1983 to require authorities to send evidence to laboratories for DNA testing. In *Skinner v. Switzer* (2011) __ U.S. __, 131 S.Ct. 1289, 179 L.Ed.2d 233, a Texas prisoner convicted of a triple murder and sentenced to death filed a civil action in federal district court under 42 U.S.C. § 1983 seeking injunctive relief against the district attorney who had prosecuted him. The civil action sought DNA testing of evidence in the custody of the office of the district attorney.

The federal district court dismissed the action, the Fifth Circuit Court of Appeals affirmed the dismissal, and the defendant petitioned the United States Supreme Court for writ of certiorari. The United States Supreme Court reversed the judgment of dismissal, holding that a convicted defendant may bring a civil action under 42 U.S.C. § 1983 to require authorities to submit physical evidence seized by authorities to a laboratory for DNA testing of that evidence. Because DNA testing could yield results that could be exculpatory, incriminating, or inconclusive, such an action under 42 U.S.C. § 1983 does not constitute an action that by its nature calls into question the validity of the defendant's conviction. 131 S.Ct. at 1300.

§ 2:29.3.3.1   Postjudgment DNA testing—the Innocence Protection Act of 2004

The enactment of the Innocence Protection Act of 2004 (IPA) as 18 U.S. Code section 3600 has spawned a series of requests in federal court for postjudgment DNA testing. The Innocence Protection Act was passed by Congress in 2004 to provide defendants in federal and state courts who have been convicted of a crime through mostly circumstantial evidence with a mechanism to petition for DNA testing in cases where DNA testing had not been previously performed or where the DNA procedures have been improved over time. The Innocence Protection Act gives a defendant in the right circumstances a means to initiate tests which might prove that he or she is *factually innocent* of the crime for which he or she has been convicted. The scope of the Innocence Protection Act is very narrow. A defendant seeking to use the statute must meet *all* of its requirements.

A defendant who is granted DNA testing under the Innocence Protection Act risks exposure to criminal liability, because his or her DNA profile is entered in the National DNA Index System ("NDIS"). Should the defendant's DNA profile match a DNA profile connected with an unsolved crime in the NDIS system, the government is required to "notify the appropriate agency and preserve the DNA sample of the applicant." 18 U.S.C. sec. 3600(e)(2)(e)(3)(B). Defendants who know they have committed crimes for which they have not been charged—and for which DNA evidence could shed some light—should think twice before availing themselves of this statute. New DNA testing can not only confirm his or her guilt of the crime of conviction, but the test can also lead to a prosecution of the defendant for *other* crimes in the NDIS database.

In order to qualify for DNA testing under the Innocence Protection Act, the defendant must meet all ten criteria set forth in 18 U.S. Code section 3600. Much of the litigation over the Innocence Protection Act has centered around the question whether the defendant has satisfied all ten of the criteria in the Act. *See, e.g., United States v. Fasono* (2009, CA5 MS) 577 F.3d 572.

For example, in *United States v. Jordan* (2010, CA10 CO) 594 F.3d 1265, 1268, the defendant's request for DNA testing under the Act was denied, because the inmate failed to satisfy the eighth requirement of Section 3600(a)—that "[t]he proposed DNA testing of the specific evidence may produce new material evidence that would . . . raise a reasonable probability that the applicant did not commit the offense."

PART IV.   LIMITATIONS ON DISCOVERY OUTSIDE CRIMINAL DISCOVERY STATUTE

§ 2:32   Exclusive discovery procedures

The enactment of the Criminal Discovery Statute by Proposition 115 in

1990 "establish[ed] the procedures for, and limitations on, discovery in criminal cases. Section 1054 sets forth the purposes of this new chapter, including that 'no discovery shall occur in criminal cases except as provided by this chapter, other express statutory provisions, or as mandated by the Constitution of the United States.' (*Id.*, subd. (e).) We have emphasized this statutory exclusivity, noting that 'all court-ordered discovery is governed exclusively by—and is barred except as provided by—the discovery chapter newly enacted by Proposition 115.' (*In re Littlefield* (1993) 5 Cal.4th 122, 129 [19 Cal.Rptr.2d 248, 851 P.2d 42].)" *Verdin v. Superior Court* (2008) 43 Cal.4th 1096, 1102–1103, 77 Cal.Rptr.3d 287, 183 P.3d 1250.

Some have argued that even after the enactment of the Criminal Discovery Statute with its discovery exclusivity provision in subdivision (e) of Penal Code section 1054, trial courts retain "wide discretion" to control the discovery process, citing cases such as *Joe Z. v. Superior Court* (1970) 3 Cal.3d 797, 804–805, 91 Cal.Rptr. 594, 478 P.2d 26, and other opinions that predate the enactment of the Criminal Discovery Statute. The proponents of this position cite the preamble to Proposition 115 and the goals of the Criminal Discovery Statute listed in Section 1054, arguing that the inherent power of a trial court to manage trial proceedings empowers the trial court to make discovery orders that "save court time in trial and avoid the necessity for frequent interruptions and postponements." Penal Code section 1054, subdivision (c).

This position is no longer tenable in the wake of *Verdin v. Superior Court*. In *Verdin* the People argued that a trial court has the power to authorize a prosecution expert to conduct a mental examination of a defendant who announces an intention to mount a diminished actuality defense. The People argued that the purposes of Proposition 115—to make "comprehensive reforms . . . in order to restore *balance and fairness* to our criminal justice system" authorized the trial court's discovery order.

The California Supreme Court rejected the People's argument that the purposes of Proposition 115 authorize a discovery order that goes beyond the express discovery provisions of the Criminal Discovery Statute. The Court stated:

> "In order to effectuate the goals set forth in the preamble to Proposition 115, however, the framers of that initiative did not authorize the judiciary generally to create appropriate rules governing discovery in criminal cases. Although we must interpret the statutes governing discovery in criminal cases, we are not at liberty to create new rules, untethered to any statute or constitutional mandate. Instead, the framers of Proposition 115, by including the exclusivity provision of section 1054, subdivision (e), authorized *the Legislature* to create the applicable rules in the first instance. Only when interpreting a statute or where a rule of discovery is "mandated by the Constitution of the United States" (§ 1054, subd. (e))

does this court have a role. (See discussion, *post.*) We thus conclude that nothing in the preamble to Proposition 115 authorizes or justifies the judicial creation of a rule that a criminal defendant who places his mental state in issue may be ordered by the court to grant the prosecution access for purposes of a mental examination by a prosecution expert." 43 Cal.4th at 1107–1108. [italics in original]

Therefore, a trial court's authority to manage trials does not extend to making discovery orders that are not expressly authorized by the Criminal Discovery Statute, even though those non-statutory discovery orders would save court time and avoid trial interruptions and postponements. The preamble to Proposition 115 and the expressed purposes and goals of the Criminal Discovery Statute found in Penal Code section 1054 do not override the restriction of Section 1054, subdivision (e), that "no discovery shall occur in criminal cases" that is not statutorily authorized or constitutionally mandated.

Nor do the purposes and goals of the Discovery Statute override its restriction expressed in Section 1054.5, subdivision (a), that "[n]o order requiring discovery shall be made in criminal cases" unless the Discovery Statute authorizes it. Nor do the purposes and goals of the Discovery Statute allow a defendant to compel discovery from any member of the prosecution team by any means other than the methods provided in the Discovery Statute.

§ 2:33 Other statutory discovery procedures

Because the Criminal Discovery Statute expressly allows the Legislature and the People by initiative to enact statutory discovery procedures that are outside the procedures specified in the Criminal Discovery Statute, criminal prosecutions are impacted by several other discovery statutes.

§ 2:33.2 Peace officer personnel records discovery

The *Pitchess* discovery statutes (discussed in depth in Chapter 10 of the text and this supplement) "are within [Penal Code section 1054] subdivision (e)'s category of 'other express statutory provisions' that survived the voters' June 1990 passage of Proposition 115." *Galindo v. Superior Court* (2010) 50 Cal.4th 1, 11, 112 Cal.Rptr.3d 673, 235 P.3d 1.

However, the *Pitchess* discovery statutes have not remained unaffected by the enactment of the Criminal Discovery Statute in Proposition 115. The California Supreme Court has indicated that the pre-Proposition 115 practice of routinely and repeatedly granting continuances in preliminary examinations "to accommodate a criminal defendant's request for 'pretrial discovery to prepare for a preliminary examination' [citation omitted]" should no longer be countenanced. *Galindo v. Superior Court*, 50 Cal.4th at 11. The delays produced by such continuances would frustrate the goal expressed in Penal Code section 1054(d) of avoiding undue delay in criminal proceedings, and would deny the People's constitutional right to a speedy trial. 50 Cal.4th at 11–12.

Thus, in *Galindo* the California Supreme Court held that "although a defendant may file a *Pitchess* motion before a preliminary hearing, the pendency of that motion will not necessarily or invariably constitute good cause for postponing the preliminary hearing over the prosecution's objection." 50 Cal.4th at 5–6.

§ 2:33.3   Grand jury proceedings discovery

In *United States v. Caruto* (2010, CA9 CA) 627 F.3d 759, a criminal defendant prosecuted in federal district court petitioned the district court to disclose transcripts of grand jury voir dire and an instructional video that the grand jury watched before the grand jury was given its charge by the district court. The district court denied the defendant's request, and the defendant appealed her conviction to the Ninth Circuit Court of Appeals. On appeal the defendant challenged the district court's ruling denying her discovery request. The Court of Appeals rejected the defendant's argument. The Court reviewed the district court's decision not to release grand jury transcripts for abuse of discretion and concluded that the district court had not abused its discretion.

Quoting from the opinion of the United States Supreme Court in *Douglas Oil Co. v. Petrol Stops Northwest* (1979) 441 U.S. 211, 222, 99 S.Ct. 1667, 60 L.Ed.2d 156, the Court of Appeals stated: " 'Parties seeking grand jury transcripts under Rule 6(e) [of the Federal Rules of Criminal Procedure] must show that the material they seek is needed to avoid a possible injustice in another judicial proceeding, that the need for disclosure is greater than the need for continued secrecy, and that their request is structured to cover only material so needed.' " 627 F.3d 759. The Court of Appeals concluded that the defendant failed to make any of the three required showings either in the district court or in her briefs on appeal.

§ 2:33.5   Postjudgment discovery

One of the most significant forms of discovery that is outside the procedures specified in the Criminal Discovery Statute is postjudgment discovery.

§ 2:33.5.1   Postjudgment discovery in capital cases

The California Penal Code contains special provisions for postjudgment discovery in capital murder cases. These provisions are contained in Penal Code section 1054.9. Section 1054.9 has produced substantial litigation over its constitutionality and over the meaning and application of its terms.

§ 2:33.5.1.1   Constitutionality of Section 1054.9

After several years of litigation, the California Supreme Court has held that Penal Code section 1054.9 was constitutionally enacted.

In *Barnett v. Superior Court* (2010) 50 Cal.4th 890, 114 Cal.Rptr.3d 576,

237 P.3d 980, a convicted capital murderer sentenced to death filed a postjudgment discovery motion pursuant to Penal Code section 1054.9. The superior court granted many of the inmate's discovery requests and denied many others. The inmate petitioned the Court of Appeal for writ of mandate challenging the denials. The Court of Appeal issued a published opinion addressing a number of issues that had not been resolved by the Supreme Court in *In re Steele* (2004), 32 Cal.4th 682, 10 Cal.Rptr.3d 536, 85 P.3d 444. The Supreme Court granted review and transferred the case back to the Court of Appeal to resolve an issue raised by an amicus curiae—whether Penal Code section 1054.9 constituted an invalid amendment to the Criminal Discovery Statute enacted by Proposition 115 in 1990.

The Court of Appeal rejected the constitutional challenge to Section 1054.9 and reached the following holdings concerning the application of Section 1054.9: (1) a defendant making a motion for postjudgment discovery need not provide the People with an inventory of every single document or other item the defendant possesses already; (2) a defendant does not have a right under Section 1054.9 to duplicative discovery; (3) Section 1054.9 does not provide a vehicle for the defendant to force the People to disclose exculpatory evidence the People did not possess at the time of the defendant's trial; and (4) a denial of the defendant's postjudgment discovery motion may not be grounded on an unsworn denial of the existence of any additional responsive documents.

Although both parties petitioned the Supreme Court for review, neither party petitioned for review on the question of whether Penal Code section 1054.9 had been constitutionally enacted. On September 17, 2008, the Supreme Court again granted review.

While awaiting oral argument in *Barnett*, the Supreme Court decided to resolve the question of the constitutionality of Penal Code section 1054.9 in a case other than *Barnett*. That determination occurred in *People v. Superior Court (Pearson)* (2010) 48 Cal.4th 564, 107 Cal.Rptr.3d 265, 227 P.3d 858.

In *Pearson* the Supreme Court held that Penal Code section 1054.9 had been constitutionally enacted, because even though Section 1054.9 was not enacted by a two-thirds vote of each house of the State Legislature, Section 1054.9 did not amend the provisions of the Criminal Discovery Statute that had been enacted by initiative in Proposition 115.

In reaching this conclusion, the Court reasoned in *Pearson* that the Criminal Discovery Statute enacted by Proposition 115 "governs only pretrial discovery and does not prohibit postconviction discovery of the kind that section 1054.9 provides." 48 Cal.4th at 567. The Court highlighted this conclusion in several places in its opinion in *Pearson.* " Proposition 115 provides only for *pretrial* discovery to aid in the trial process. The chapter's purposes make this clear . . . Most of these purposes, and particularly those stated in section 1054, subdivisions (a) and (c), relate solely to the trial phase of the case. Arguably, protecting victims and witnesses (sec. 1054, subd. (d)) might relate to postconviction proceedings, but even this purpose seems primarily directed to the trial. Moreover, the substance of the discovery requirements relates entirely to evidence that might be presented at trial (secs. 1054.1, 1054.2), and the time limits for providing the discovery require the discovery to be provided before trial (sec. 1054.7). These circumstances also show that the discovery referred to is pretrial." 48 Cal.4th at 570. [italics in original]

The Court reasoned that in determining whether Section 1054.9 was constitutionally enacted, the Court must focus on two questions: (1) Did Section 1054.9 prohibit something that the Criminal Discovery Statute authorized, and (2) did Section 1054.9 authorize something that the Discovery Statute prohibited? ["In deciding whether this particular provision amends Proposition 115, we simply need to ask whether it prohibits what the initiative authorizes, or authorizes what the initiative prohibits."] 48 Cal.4th at 571.

The Court concluded that Section 1054.9 neither prohibited anything that the Criminal Discovery Statute authorized, 48 Cal.4th at 571, nor did it authorize anything that the Criminal Discovery Statute prohibited. ["[W]e do not believe the electorate that passed Proposition 115, in providing for pretrial discovery in a criminal case, intended either to provide for or to prohibit discovery in a separate habeas corpus matter. Section 1054.9 addresses an area that is *related* to Proposition 115's discovery provisions but, crucially, it is also a *distinct* area. (*People v. Kelly, supra*, 47 Cal.4th at p. 1025.) Proposition 115 does not prohibit section 1054.9's discovery."] 48 Cal.4th at 572–573. [italics in original] For this reason, the Supreme Court concluded that Section 1054.9 had been constitutionally enacted.

§ 2:33.5.1.2　Time to file 1054.9 petition

There are no statutory or decisionally-imposed time limits for a defendant to file a petition for post conviction discovery pursuant to Penal Code Section 1054.9.

In *In Re Steele* (2004) 35 Cal.4th 682, 692–693, n.2, 10 Cal.Rptr.3d 536, 85 P.3d 444, the California Supreme Court stated that while " Section 1054.9 provides no time limits for making the discovery motion or complying with any discovery order. . . . the statute implies that the motion, any petition challenging the trial court's ruling, and compliance with a discovery order must all be done within a reasonable time period."

In reliance upon this language in Steele, a number of trial courts denied postjudgment discovery motions brought pursuant to Penal Code section 1054.9 on the grounds that these motions had not been brought within a reasonable time period. In *Catlin v. Superior Court* (2011) 51 Cal.4th 300, 120 Cal.Rptr.3d 135, 245 P.3d 860, the trial court denied a petition for postjudgment discovery pursuant to Penal Code section 1054.9, where the convicted inmate filed his habeas petition in 2000, 14 years after his 1986 conviction, and where the inmate filed his 1054.9 motion for postjudgment discovery in 2007, seven years after the filing of his habeas petition. The Court of Appeal affirmed the trial court's denial of the postjudgment discovery motion.

The Supreme Court reversed the judgment of the Court of Appeal and remanded the case to the Court of Appeal for further proceedings. The Supreme Court held that while a trial court may deny a habeas corpus petition on the grounds that the petition had not been filed in a timely manner, there is no statutory authority in Penal Code section 1054.9 to deny a postjudgment discovery motion on the grounds that the motion was brought within a reasonable time. The Court held that when a habeas petitioner files an untimely postjudgment discovery order, the court in which the habeas petition is filed based on the information obtained through that discovery should consider the delay in filing the postjudgment discovery motion as part of its determination whether the underlying habeas corpus petition is timely.

Thus, while an unreasonable delay in filing a postjudgment discovery order pursuant to Penal Code section 1054.9 may not prevent the granting of such an order, the court considering the underlying habeas petition may consider the delay in filing the discovery motion in determining whether to grant or deny the underlying habeas corpus petition.

§ 2:33.5.1.3   Persons entitled to file 1054.9 petition

A petition for postjudgment discovery pursuant to Penal Code section 1054.9 may be filed by the convicted defendant, without any requirement that the defendant be represented by an attorney. *Burton v. Superior Court* (2010) 181 Cal.App.4th 1519, 105 Cal.Rptr.3d 604. ["Nothing in the language of section 1054.9 limits the statute to defendants who are currently represented by counsel."] 181 Cal.App.4th at 1522.

§ 2:33.5.1.4   Showing required for granting 1054.9 petition

Penal Code section 1054.9 "provides only for specific discovery and not the proverbial 'fishing expedition' for anything that might exist . . . ." *Barnett v. Superior Court* (2010) 50 Cal.4th 890, 898, 114 Cal.Rptr.3d 576, 237 P.3d 980.

This means that a defendant convicted of a capital murder who asks no more than that the prosecution assist in the reconstruction of defense trial files must show only a "legitimate reason for believing that counsel's current files are incomplete." 50 Cal.4th at 898. Once the defendant makes this showing, the defendant "need not identify all missing discovery materials that the prosecution had previously provided to the defense or show that they are still in the prosecution's possession." 50 Cal.4th at 898. The trial court may then "order the prosecution to provide any materials it still possesses that it had provided at time of trial." 50 Cal.4th at 898. It does not appear to matter that some of the prosecution's disclosures will duplicate what the defense already has. The prosecution must provide a complete set of materials that it had provided at the time of trial.

In addition to reconstruction of the defense trial file, Section 1054.9 allows discovery of materials to which defense trial counsel was legally entitled, but did not receive. This discovery right is broader than file reconstruction. 50 Cal.4th at 898–899. However, unlike file reconstruction, which does not require the defendant to show that the materials are still possessed by the prosecution, "defendants who seek discovery beyond file reconstruction [must] show a reasonable basis to believe that other specific materials actually exist." 50 Cal.4th at 899. In meeting this burden, if the defendant provides "a reasonable basis to believe that the prosecution had possessed the materials in the past," this showing would be sufficient to "provide a reasonable basis to believe the prosecution still possesses the materials." 50 Cal.4th at 901.

The defendant need not show that the discovery materials to which the defendant's trial counsel was entitled constituted material evidence within the meaning of the *Brady* rule. Because every defendant is legally entitled to receive discovery pursuant to Penal Code section 1054.1, and because Section 1054.1, subdivision (e), entitles the defendant to disclosure of "exculpatory evidence," not simply "material exculpatory evidence, the defendant is entitled under Section 1054.9 to disclosure of all exculpatory evidence, whether material or not, to which his counsel was entitled at the time of trial. The defendant need not make a materiality showing as a pre-requisite to his or her right to this disclosure. 50 Cal.4th at 900–901.

§ 2:33.5.1.5   Section 1054.9 discovery and out-of-state law enforcement agencies

Penal Code section 1054.9 does not require the prosecution to disclose materials possessed by "out-of-state law enforcement agencies that merely provided the prosecution with information or assistance under the circumstances of the case." *Barnett v. Superior Court* (2010) 50 Cal.4th 890, 902, 114 Cal.Rptr.3d 576, 237 P.3d 980.

Section 1054.9 does not create a broader postconviction discovery right than a defendant has under the Criminal Discovery Statute. 50 Cal.4th at 902. Thus, in *In re Steele* (2004) 32 Cal.4th 682, 696, 10 Cal.Rptr.3d 536, 85 P.3d 444, the Supreme Court concluded that the "law enforcement authorities" to which Section 1054.9 refers are similar to the "investigating agencies" to which Section 1054.1 refers. Reading all of the provisions of Penal Code section 1054.1, Section 1054.5, and Section 1054.9 together, the Supreme Court concluded in *Steele* that the discovery rights under Section 1054.9 "do not extend to materials possessed by law enforcement agencies that were not involved in investigating or preparing the case against the defendant." 32 Cal.4th at 696.

In *Barnett v. Superior* Court, the Supreme Court broadened its holding in

Steele to conclude that the prosecution's constitutional duties under *Brady* extend to information "possessed by others acting on the government's behalf that [was] gathered in connection with the investigation," but not to "evidence in the possession of *all* governmental agencies, including those not involved in the investigation or prosecution of the case." 50 Cal.4th at 903.

Thus, the Court held in *Barnett,* an out-of-state law enforcement agency that provides assistance and conducts a few interviews of potential witnesses acts "on behalf of the prosecution in a limited sense . . ." That "limited sense" is that the out-of-state law enforcement agency provides limited assistance on request to the prosecution.

However, an out-of-state law enforcement agency that provides limited assistance on request to a California prosecutor is not part of the "prosecution team," because the out-of-state agency is not under the control of any California authorities, which the Supreme Court found to be an important factor. 50 Cal.4th at 904. The out-of-state agency is not part of a team participating in a joint investigation or sharing resources. The out-of-state agency simply provides specific assistance to the California prosecution. 50 Cal.4th at 904. The Supreme Court stated in *Barnett:* " [W]e do not believe the Legislature intended the posttrial discovery right to extend so far as to permit a court to order discovery from 22 law enforcement officers working for six different out-of-state agencies, one outside the country." 50 Cal.4th at 906. Thus, the Court concluded, "the prosecution is not required to provide discovery of materials from the out-of-state law enforcement agencies of this case that the prosecution does not possess." 50 Cal.4th at 906.

§ 2:33.5.2   Postjudgment discovery in capital cases of peace officer personnel records

A defendant has a limited right to discovery of a peace officer's confidential personnel records if those files contain information that is potentially relevant to the defense. To initiate discovery, a defendant must file a motion seeking such records, containing affidavits showing good cause for the discovery or disclosure sought, setting forth the materiality thereof to the subject matter involved in the pending litigation. Good cause requires the defendant to establish a logical link between a proposed defense and the pending charge and to articulate how the discovery would support such a defense or how it would impeach the officer's version of events. The threshold for establishing good cause is relatively low. The proposed defense must have a plausible factual foundation supported by the defendant's counsel's declaration and other documents supporting the motion. A plausible scenario is one that might or could have occurred. The defendant must also show how the information sought could lead to or be evidence potentially admissible at trial. Once that burden is met, the defendant has shown materiality under Evidence Code section 1043. *Sisson v. Superior Court* (2013) 216 Cal. App. 4th 24, 156 Cal. Rptr. 3d 533. *See also People v. Yearwood* (2013) 213 Cal. App. 4th 161, 151 Cal. Rptr. 3d 901.

Note that a peace officer's official service photograph is not a personnel record under Penal Code section 832.8 and therefore is not subject to the requirements of Penal Code section 832.7, and Evidence Code section 1043, when discovery or disclosure is sought. *Ibarra v. Superior Court* (2013) 217 Cal. App. 4th 695, 158 Cal. Rptr. 3d 751. The mere fact that officers' service photographs are contained in files maintained by the employing agency does not render them confidential or protected under Penal Code sections 832.7 and 832.8. Instead, such photographs constitute peace officer personnel records only if they fall within one of the types of information enumerated in § 832.8. *Id.*

§ 2:33.5.3   Postjudgment DNA testing

In June of 2009 the United States Supreme Court resolved the question whether a criminal defendant has a *Brady*–based due process right to postjudgment access to prosecution evidence for the purpose of conducting DNA testing on that evidence.

In *District Attorney's Office for Third Judicial Dist. v. Osborne* (2009) 557 U.S. 52, 129 S.Ct. 2308, 174 L.Ed.2d 38, a state prisoner in Alaska brought a civil rights action in federal court pursuant to 42 U.S. Code section 1983 in which he sought to compel the defendants to allow him postjudgment access to biological evidence that had been used to convict him of kidnapping and sexual assault. The plaintiff wanted to subject that evidence to DNA testing methodology that had been unavailable at the time of his trial and conviction. The district court granted his request and ordered that the defendants provide the plaintiff with access to the evidence he sought.

The Ninth Circuit Court of Appeals affirmed the judgment of the district court, holding that the prisoner was entitled to assert in his action the due process right to postjudgment access to potentially exculpatory DNA evidence. The Court of Appeals relied upon the prosecutorial duty to disclose exculpatory evidence recognized in *Pennsylvania v. Ritchie* (1987) 480 U.S. 39, 107 S.Ct. 989, 94 L.Ed.2d 40, and *Brady v. Maryland* (1963) 373 U.S. 83, 83 S.Ct. 1194, 10 L.Ed.2d 215. Based on that authority the Court of Appeals concluded that " 'the Due Process Clause also 'extends the government's duty to disclose (or the defendant's right of access) to *post-conviction* proceedings.' " 129 S.Ct. at 2315 [italics in original]. "The court held that these potential claims extended some of the State's *Brady* obligations to the postconviction context." 129 S.Ct. at 2315.

The government petitioned the United States Supreme Court for writ of certiorari. The United States Supreme Court issued a writ of certiorari, reversed the judgment of the Court of Appeals, and remanded the case for further proceedings. In reaching its decision the Supreme Court majority observed that " '[a] criminal defendant proved guilty after a fair trial does not have the same liberty interests as a free man.' [citation omitted]" 129

S.Ct. at 2320. After a conviction the defendant's presumption of innocence disappears. *Id.* A convicted defendant has only a limited interest in postconviction relief, and that limited interest is not parallel to a trial right. *Brady*, therefore is the "wrong framework" with which to review a case of the defendant seeking post-conviction relief. *Id.*

The Supreme Court's opinion in *Osborne* resolves the question whether the *Brady* rule applies to postjudgment proceedings—it does not. Prior authority that is contrary to the Supreme Court's opinion in *Osborne* is no longer good law and should be disregarded. The *Osborne* opinion casts doubt upon recent Court of Appeals holdings that the *Brady* rule applies to new-trial and post-conviction proceedings. *See Tennison v. City and County of San Francisco* (2009, CA9 CA) 570 F.3d 1078, 1094, an opinion filed just five days after the *Osborne* opinion was filed. In light of the Supreme Court's decision in *Osborne*, the parameters of a defendant's post-conviction *Brady* rights will have to be determined by the federal and state courts.

In *Bradley v. King* (2009, CA11 AL) 556 F.3d 1225, an opinion that predated the Supreme Court's opinion in *Osborne* by four months, the Eleventh Circuit Court of Appeals affirmed the district court's denial of a request by a death-row inmate for a stay of execution to allow him access to physical evidence for DNA testing. The Court of Appeals reasoned that the non-biological evidence of the defendant's guilt was substantial; the items he wished to test had been available prior to his trial; and his claim of actual innocence was undermined by DNA tests that showed that his and the victim's DNA had been found commingled on a blanket taken from the defendant's home. The Court concluded that there were no extraordinary circumstances entitling the defendant to further post-conviction access to DNA evidence. 556 F.3d at 1230.

In the wake of *Osborne*, convicted defendants in other jurisdictions have filed civil actions pursuant to 42 U.S. Code section 1983 seeking orders that would require state authorities to send evidence from their cases to laboratories for DNA testing. Postconviction procedures that are similar to the procedures in Alaska that the Supreme Court in *Osborne* held were adequate to satisfy due process requirements are generally held to be constitutionally adequate. *See, e.g., Cunningham v. District Attorney's Office for Escambia County* (2010, CA11 FL) 592 F.3d 1237, and *McKithen v. Brown* (2010, CA2 NY) 626 F.3d 143, 150–155.

§ 2:33.5.3.1 Postjudgment DNA testing—the Innocence Protection Act of 2004

The enactment of the Innocence Protection Act of 2004 (IPA) as 18 U.S. Code section 3600 has spawned a series of requests in federal court for postjudgment DNA testing. The Innocence Protection Act was passed by Congress in 2004 to provide defendants in federal and state courts who have been convicted of a crime through mostly circumstantial evidence with a mechanism to petition for DNA testing in cases where DNA testing had not been previously performed or where the DNA procedures have been improved over time. The Innocence Protection Act gives a defendant in the right circumstances a means to initiate tests which might prove that he or she is *factually innocent* of the crime for which he or she has been convicted. The scope of the Innocence Protection Act is very narrow. A defendant seeking to use the statute must meet *all* of its requirements.

A defendant who is granted DNA testing under the Innocence Protection Act risks exposure to criminal liability, because his or her DNA profile is entered in the National DNA Index System ("NDIS"). Should the defendant's DNA profile match a DNA profile connected with an unsolved crime in the NDIS system, the government is required to "notify the appropriate agency and preserve the DNA sample of the applicant." 18 U.S.C. sec. 3600(e)(2)–(e)(3)(B). Defendants who know they have committed crimes for which they have not been charged—and for which DNA evidence could shed some light—should think twice before availing themselves of this statute. New DNA testing can not only confirm his or her guilt of the crime of conviction, but the test can also lead to a prosecution of the defendant for *other* crimes in the NDIS database.

In order to qualify for DNA testing under the Innocence Protection Act, the defendant must meet all ten criteria set forth in 18 U.S. Code section 3600. Much of the litigation over the Innocence Protection Act has centered around the question whether the defendant has satisfied all ten of the criteria in the Act. *See, e.g., United States v. Fasono* (2009, CA5 MS) 577 F.3d 572.

For example, in *United States v. Jordan* (2010, CA10 CO) 594 F.3d 1265, 1268, the defendant's request for DNA testing under the Act was denied, because the inmate failed to satisfy the eighth requirement of Sect. 3600(a)—that "[t]he proposed DNA testing of the specific evidence may produce new material evidence that would . . . raise a reasonable probability that the applicant did not commit the offense."

§ 2:33.7   California Public Records Act discovery

While mindful of the right of individuals to privacy, Government Code section 6250, the Legislature has declared access to information concerning the conduct of the People's business is a fundamental and necessary right of every person in California. Thus, the California Public Records Act (CPRA), Government Code section 6250 *et seq.*, generally provides every person has a right to inspect any public record, Government Code section 6253, subsection (a), except with respect to records exempt from disclosure by express provisions of law, § 6253, subsection (b). Government Code section 6254, in turn, lists 29 categories of documents exempt from the requirement of public disclosure, many of which are designed to protect individual privacy, including, personnel, medical, or similar files, the disclosure of which would constitute an unwarranted invasion of personal privacy. § 6254, subsection (c). Government Code section 6255, subsection (a), also permits a public agency to withhold other records if it can demonstrate on the facts of the particular case the public interest served by not disclosing the record clearly outweighs the public interest served by disclosure of the record. *Marken v. Santa Monica-Malibu Unified School Dist.* (2012) 202 Cal. App. 4th 1250, 136 Cal. Rptr. 3d 395.

The statement in the text (pages 401–402) that "it is not clear whether an attorney for a criminal defendant is entitled to use the Public Records Act to request disclosures from a public agency," because the public defender's office is not a "person" entitled to make a public records request, appears to not be a correct statement of law. In *Los Angeles Unified School Dist. v. Superior Court* (2007) 151 Cal.App.4th 759, 60 Cal.Rptr.3d 445, the Court of Appeal held that the City Attorney of Los Angeles was entitled to utilize the Public Records Act to obtain public records of the Los Angeles Unified School District. In reaching this conclusion the Court of Appeal rejected the argument that the City Attorney's Office is not a "person" within the meaning of Government Code section 6252, subdivision (c). 151 Cal.App.4th at 769.

Moreover, Government Code section 6252.5, enacted in 1999, provides that "[n]otwithstanding the definition of 'member of the public' in Section 6252, an elected member or officer of any state or local agency is entitled to access to public records of that agency on the same basis as any other person."

A defendant in a criminal case may not utilize the California Public Records Act to obtain discovery of peace officer personnel records that are part of a public agency's civil service system appeal of a disciplinary action against an officer, *Copley Press, Inc. v. Superior Court* (2006) 39 Cal.4th 1272, 48 Cal.Rptr.3d 183, 141 P.3d 288, or that are contained in the records and proceedings of a police review commission that investigates citizen complaints against the public agency's peace officers. *Berkeley Police Assn. v. City of Berkeley* (2008) 167 Cal.App.4th 385, 84 Cal.Rptr.3d 130.

The question whether a law enforcement agency may block use of a public records act to gain access to law enforcement records is one that has been raised in other jurisdictions. For an interesting discussion of the use of the "law enforcement privilege" to prevent disclosure of law enforcement techniques and procedures, to preserve the confidentiality of sources, to protect witness and law enforcement personnel, to safeguard the privacy of persons involved in a criminal investigation, and to otherwise prevent interference with a criminal investigation, see *Dinler v. City of New York (In re City of New York)* (2010, CA2 NY) 607 F.3d 923, 940–945.

§ 2:33.8 Federal Freedom of Information Act discovery

There is federal decisional authority that upholds allowing an attorney representing a convicted death row inmate to bring a request for disclosure of public records under the federal Freedom of Information Act to assist the inmate in establishing that someone else committed the homicides for which the inmate was convicted.

In *Roth v. United States DOJ* (2011, CA DC) 642 F.3d 1161, the attorney representing a convicted Texas death-row inmate sought information under the federal Freedom of Information Act from the Federal Bureau of Investigation that he asserted might corroborate the inmate's claim that four other men were the actual perpetrators of the quadruple homicide for which the inmate had been convicted. The attorney made two requests. In the first request the attorney requested records relating to the inmate's trial attorney and the four men whom the inmate alleges were the real killers. In the second request the attorney requested documents from FBI files containing information regarding its investigation of the murders.

In response to the first FOIA request, the FBI gave a "Glomar response" to the defendant's Freedom of Information Act requests, a response in which the FBI neither confirmed nor denied the existence of the requested records. In response to the second FOIA request, the FBI declined to release some of the records and also redacted other of those records. The defendant's attorney then petitioned the federal district court for the District of Columbia for an order requiring the FBI to disclose the requested documents. After reviewing *in camera* the documents which the FBI refused to disclose and which had been redacted, the district court declined to order disclosure of most of the requested documents. The Court further found that the FBI's *Glomar* response was proper. The inmate's attorney appealed to the Circuit Court for the District of Columbia.

On appeal the United States Department of Justice did not dispute the inmate attorney's argument that the Assistant United States Attorney who participated in the inmate's homicide trial had a duty to learn of any *Brady* material possessed by the FBI and to disclose that information to the inmate's trial counsel. 642 F.3d at 1175.

The Court of Appeals concluded that the FOIA requests implicated substantial privacy interests. The attorney for the inmate then asserted that disclosure would further the public interest in two ways: (1) "it [would] advance the public's interest in knowing whether the federal government complied with its *Brady* obligation to disclose material, exculpatory information to [the inmate's] trial counsel," and (2) it would "further the public's interest in knowing whether the FBI is withholding information that could corroborate a death-row inmate's claim of innocence." 642 F.3d at 1175. The Court of Appeals determined that because information is "material" for *Brady* purposes as it relates to other information known at the time of trial, that inquiry is "narrower than and does not fully encompass the public's more general interest in knowing whether the FBI is withholding information that could corroborate [the inmate's] claim of innocence." 642 F.3d at 1176.

The Court concluded that although the non-*Brady*-related public interest is substantial, the Court found from its *in camera* review of the withheld documents that the privacy interests of other persons implicated by the withheld documents in the homicide outweigh the public interest in disclosure. Even though the Court of Appeals acknowledged that "the public might well have a significant interest in knowing whether the federal government engaged in blatant *Brady* violations in a capital case," the Court expressed confidence that none of the documents the Court reviewed *in camera* revealed any such egregious governmental misconduct. 642 F.3d at 1177.

The Court then determined that its *in camera* review showed no information withheld by the FBI would substantially corroborate the inmate's contention that four other men were the true killers. 642 F.3d at 1178. The Court of Appeals thus upheld the FBI's redaction of information from disclosed documents.

The Court of Appeals then evaluated the propriety of the FBI's *Glomar* response. When evaluating the propriety of the FBI's *Glomar* response, the District of Columbia Circuit Court of Appeals deferred to the decision of the Fifth Circuit Court of Appeals, which decided the inmate's habeas petition, that the information withheld by the FBI was not "material" for *Brady* purposes. Therefore, the District of Columbia Court of Appeals concluded that the public interest in knowing whether the federal government violated its *Brady* obligations at the time of the inmate's trial had been satisfied by the Fifth Circuit's resolution of that issue. 642 F.3d at 1178–1180.

However, the Court reached a different conclusion when considering whether the attorney for the inmate could overcome the FBI's *Glomar* response "based on the public's more general interest in knowing whether the FBI is withholding information that could corroborate [the inmate's] claim of innocence." 642 F.3d at 1180. The Court ultimately concluded that the public "has a compelling interest in knowing whether the FBI is refusing to disclose information that could help exonerate [the inmate]." The Court decided that the balance of the competing interests "tilts decidedly in favor of disclosing whether the FBI's files contain information linking [three other men] to the FBI's investigation of the killings." 642 F.3d at 1181.

In reaching these conclusions the Court of Appeals explicitly held that the inmate's "personal stake in the release of the requested information is 'irrelevant' to the balancing of public and third-party privacy interests . . . . [citation omitted] FOIA is not a substitute for discovery in criminal cases or in habeas proceedings. Instead, its purpose is to protect the citizens' right to be informed about 'what their government is up to.' [citation omitted]" 642 F.3d at 1177.

Finally, the Court of Appeals concluded that "the potential availability of criminal and civil discovery in no way bars an individual from obtaining information through FOIA where no exemption otherwise applies." 642 F.3d at 1183.

The upshot of *Roth v. Bower* is that a criminal defendant who can meet the requirements of justifying disclosure under the federal Freedom of Information Act (FOIA) is not precluded from using that Act to gain disclosure of documents held by a federal agency, despite the pendency of a criminal prosecution of the defendant and the availability of criminal discovery mechanisms.

Whether and how the opinion of the Court of Appeals in *Roth v. United States* can be reconciled with Penal Code section 1054(e) ["no discovery shall occur in criminal cases except as provided by this chapter, other express statutory provisions, or as mandated by the Constitution of the United States"] awaits further judicial determination.

§ 2:34   Exclusive substantive discovery provisions

If there were any question whether trial court's inherent powers to order discovery in criminal cases had survived the enactment of Proposition 115 in 1990, those doubts were put to rest by the opinion of the California Supreme Court in *Verdin v. Superior Court* (2008) 43 Cal.4th 1096, 1106, 77 Cal.Rptr.3d 287, 183 P.3d 1250.

In *Verdin* the Supreme Court held that the enactment of Penal Code section 1054, subdivision (e), abrogated the inherent power of trial courts to order discovery in criminal cases that is not expressly authorized by the Criminal Discovery Statute, expressly authorized by some other statute, or mandated by the United States Constitution. The Court explicitly rejected the argument made by the prosecution that two of the Supreme Court's own prior opinions and a Court of Appeal opinion supported the inherent power of a trial court to order a defendant who had announced a defense of diminished actuality to submit to a psychiatric or mental examination by a prosecution psychiatrist.

In *People v. McPeters* (1992) 2 Cal.4th 1148, 9 Cal.Rptr.2d 834, 832 P.2d 146, and *People v. Carpenter* (1997) 15 Cal.4th 312, 63 Cal.Rptr.2d 1, 939 P.2d 708, the Supreme Court upheld trial court authority to order a defendant to undergo a mental examination by a prosecution psychiatrist. In *People v. Danis* (1973) 31 Cal.App.3d 782, 107 Cal.Rptr. 675, the Court of Appeal likewise upheld trial court authority to order such a mental examination of a defendant. In rejecting the prosecution's argument that the Court should follow *McPeters, Carpenter,* and *Danis,* because of court's inherent power to order such discovery, the Court stated:

> "*Danis, McPeters,* and *Carpenter* have not survived the passage of Proposition 115. *Danis* [citation omitted] opined that prosecutorial discovery from a criminal defendant, in the form of a court-ordered mental examination, was permissible even absent an 'authorizing statute,' because the trial court possessed inherent power to order such discovery. This reasoning is unsupportable following the 1990 enactment of section 1054, subdivision (e), which insists that rules permitting prosecutorial discovery be authorized by the criminal

discovery statutes or some other statute, or mandated by the United States Constitution. Although *Danis's result* may have been supportable when decided more than 30 years ago . . . no part of its *reasoning* can have survived the enactment of section 1054, subdivision (e)."

"Similarly, the rule announced in *McPeters* [citation omitted] and followed in *Carpenter* [citation omitted] did not survive Proposition 115. Neither decision explained the basis—statutory or otherwise—of their assertion that a criminal defendant who places his mental state in issue thereby creates in the prosecution the right to discovery in the form of a mental examination by a prosecution expert. Because neither *McPeters* nor *Carpenter* rests on a statutory or constitutional basis, both are inconsistent with section 1054, subdivision (e)." 43 Cal.4th at 1106–1107. [italics in original]

This holding in *Verdin* makes it unmistakably clear that following the enactment of Section 1054, subdivision (e), as part of the Criminal Discovery Statute, trial courts do not have inherent power to order discovery in criminal cases. Courts' powers to order discovery are conferred by statute and by the United States Constitution. Beyond those explicitly granted powers, courts may not order discovery.

§ 2:34.1   Discovery expressly authorized by another statute

Where discovery in a criminal case is expressly authorized by a statute other than the Criminal Discovery Statute, subdivision (e) of Penal Code section 1054 does not prohibit or limit that discovery. Subdivision (e) of Section 1054, which provides that "no discovery shall occur in criminal cases except as provided by this chapter, **other express statutory provisions,** or as mandated by the Constitution of the United States" [emphasis added], explicitly allows discovery authorized by another statute.

Thus, a defendant in a capital murder prosecution who seeks to avoid imposition of a death sentence by virtue of a mental retardation defense may be ordered to submit to a mental examination conducted by a prosecution expert. *Centeno v. Superior Court* (2004) 117 Cal.App.4th 30, 11 Cal.Rptr.3d 533. The authority for a trial court to enter such an order is Penal Code section 1376, subdivision (b)(2), which satisfies the requirement of subdivision (e) of Section 1054 that a discovery order which is outside the scope of the Criminal Discovery Statute must be expressly authorized by some other statute. *Verdin v. Superior Court* (2008) 43 Cal.4th 1096, 1104–1105, 77 Cal.Rptr.3d 287, 183 P.3d 1250.

Likewise, the *Pitchess* statutes that regulate discovery of the personnel records of peace officers constitute statutes that expressly provide for discovery in criminal cases outside the parameters of the Criminal Discovery Statute, and discovery pursuant to the *Pitchess* statutes is thereby authorized by the Criminal Discovery Statute. *Galindo v. Superior Court* (2010) 50

Cal.4th 1, 10–11, 112 Cal.Rptr.3d 673, 235 P.3d 1.

§ 2:39.5   Juvenile records in SVP proceedings

A court may not order disclosure of juvenile records that have been previously sealed pursuant to Welfare and Institutions Code section 781 for use by the Board of Parole Hearings to declare that a prisoner is a sexually violent predator (SVP) under Section 6600 et seq. of the Welfare and Institutions Code.

A court may not normally order disclosure of juvenile records that have been previously sealed pursuant to Welfare and Institutions Code section 781. Welfare and Institutions Code section 781 provides the authority for the juvenile court to order that upon satisfying the conditions established in that section, juvenile records shall be sealed. Section 781 provides that "[o]nce the court has ordered the person's records sealed, the proceedings in the case shall be deemed never to have occurred . . . except as provided in subdivision (b), the records shall not be open to inspection." The narrow exceptions allowed by subdivision (b) are the use of those records in a defamation action, and provision to an authorized vehicle insurer for determining insurance eligibility and rates.

Otherwise, unless the person to whom the sealed records relates agrees to the unsealing of the records [the subject of the sealed records may request the superior court to permit inspection of the records], the courts may not unseal them.

In *In re James H.* (2007) 154 Cal.App.4th 1078, 65 Cal.Rptr.3d 410, the Board of Parole Hearings requested the juvenile court to provide the Board with copies of records of a juvenile inmate that the court had previously ordered to be sealed, so that the Board could use those records to determine whether to declare the inmate a sexually violent predator. The superior court granted the request without affording the inmate a hearing on the request. The district attorney filed a petition to declare the inmate a sexually violent predator. The inmate sent the court two letters objecting to the release of his records and asking the court to appoint counsel to represent him. The Court of Appeal construed the second letter as a notice of appeal of the order releasing the records.

The Court of Appeal reversed the superior court's order granting the Board of Parole Hearings disclosure of the inmate's records and ordered the Board to return to the juvenile court the records that had been provided to the Board. The Court remanded the case to the superior court for further proceedings to determine the disposition of the sealed records.

In reaching this decision the Court of Appeal concluded that because of the clear and unequivocal language of Section 781, "juvenile court records may not be released for use in an SVP proceeding when those records have been sealed by court order under section 781." 154 Cal.App.4th at 1088.

Law enforcement officers looking to uncover undetected crimes of an alleged sexually violent predator know that should the evidence be obtained in violation of the Fourth Amendment, the evidence and its fruits will be excluded in a criminal trial. That deterrent being present, the social cost of excluding the same evidence in a proceeding under the Sexually Violent Predators Act (SVPA), Welfare & Institutions Code section 6600 *et seq.*,—exclusion of reliable evidence and exposure of the public to the acts of individuals who suffer from a mental disability, the existence of which adversely affects the person's volitional ability and predisposes the person to committing sexual acts against others, making him or her a danger to the health and safety of others—is not outweighed by the minimal beneficial effect that would result from excluding evidence in an SVPA proceeding. Accordingly, a superior court does to err in failing to exclude evidence claimed to have been obtained in violation of an alleged sexually violent predator's Fourth Amendment rights. *People v. Landau* (2013) 214 Cal. App. 4th 1, 154 Cal. Rptr. 3d 1.

CHAPTER 3

CRIMINAL DISCOVERY STATUTE—DISCLOSURE BY PROSECUTOR

PART I.   DUTIES AND OBLIGATIONS

§ 3:2   "Duty to disclose" defined

Under the United States Constitution's Due Process Clause, as interpreted by the United States Supreme Court in *Brady v. Maryland*, the prosecution has a duty to disclose to a criminal defendant evidence that is both favorable to the defendant and material on either guilt or punishment. The prosecution's withholding of favorable and material evidence violates due process irrespective of the good faith or bad faith of the prosecution. *In re Bacigalupo* (2012) 55 Cal. 4th 312, 145 Cal. Rptr. 3d 832, 283 P.3d 613. *See also Bridgeforth v. Superior Court* (2013) 214 Cal. App. 4th 1074, 154 Cal. Rptr. 3d 528.

Almost every section of the Criminal Discovery Statute uses the words "disclose" or "disclosure" to describe the duties of the prosecution and the defense under that statute. The statute also uses two other operative words to describe these duties. Section 1054.5, subdivision (a), provides, in pertinent part, that "[t]his chapter shall be the only means by which the defendant may compel the disclosure or **production of information** . . . ." [emphasis added] Subdivision (b) of Section 1054.5 contains the language that "[i]f within 15 days the opposing counsel fails to **provide** the materials and information requested, the party may seek a court order." [emphasis added]

The Criminal Discovery Statute does not define the term "disclose." However, the terms "production of information" and "provide" appear to be synonyms for the term "disclose." Thus, it seems that the obvious meaning of the term "disclose" is to "provide or produce information."

In *Schaffer v. Superior Court* (2010) 185 Cal.App.4th 1235, 111 Cal.Rptr.3d 245, the Court of Appeal considered a defendant's petition for writ of mandate to set aside an order of the superior court denying the defendant's motion to compel the prosecution to provide copies of discovery mandated by Penal Code section 1054.1 free of charge. In reaching this decision the Court of Appeal held that the prosecution's duty under Section 1054.1 is to "disclose" the discoverable material listed in that statute. The court observed that although the Criminal Discovery Statute does not "specify the means by which the parties must 'disclose' discoverable information to each other, neither does the Statute "specify that the party making the disclosure must produce a copy of the discoverable item for the benefit of the opposing counsel." 185 Cal.App.4th at 1242.

The Court of Appeal opined that "[t]he ordinary meaning of the word 'disclose' is to 'divulge,' 'open up,' 'expose to view,' or to 'make known.' [citing Webster's New International Dictionary]" 185 Cal.App.4th at 1242. In support of its opinion, the Court of Appeal observed that prior to enactment of the Criminal Discovery Statute, numerous judicial decisions regarding the prosecution's duty to disclose "under former sections 859 and 1102.5 referred only to the duty to allow defendants to view, inspect, and copy the materials." 185 Cal.App.4th at 1243. The Court observed that the enactment of the Criminal Discovery Statute "did not alter the prosecution's duty to make discovery available." 185 Cal.App.4th at 1243.

Finally, the Court of Appeal pointed to the fact that the courts have routinely approved prosecutors' "open files" discovery policies as a means of satisfying their constitutional disclosure obligations under *Brady* and their statutory disclosure obligations under the Criminal Discovery Statute. Thus, the Court concluded that since an "open files" disclosure policy provides access to discoverable evidence, but not copies of that evidence, "disclosure" must mean divulging, opening up, exposing to view, or making known, as opposed to the provision of copies, of evidence. 185 Cal.App.4th at 1243.

The term "disclose" [as used in the Criminal Discovery Statute] mirrors the duty of the prosecution to "disclose" material exculpatory evidence under the *Brady* rule. 185 Cal.App.4th at 1243–1244. This conclusion is in line with decisions of the federal courts.

In *Youngblood v. West Virginia* (2006) 547 U.S. 867, 869, 126 S.Ct. 2188, 165 L.Ed.2d 269, the United States Supreme Court in a *per curiam* opinion described the *Brady* rule in these terms: "A *Brady* violation occurs when the government fails to disclose evidence materially favorable to the accused."

In *United States v. Rodriguez* (2007, CA2 NY) 496 F.3d 221, the defendant was convicted of drug dealing in a multi-defendant trial. The prosecution's case rested upon the testimony of two cooperating witnesses. At trial one of these witnesses testified that the witness had lied "about everything" in her initial interviews with investigators. After the prosecution stated that no notes had been made of the false statements, the trial court declined to order the prosecution to disclose the oral false statements that had been made by the witness. The trial court did not explain its reason for denying the defense request for disclosure.

The Second Circuit Court of Appeals remanded the case to the district court to determine whether the prosecution's failure to disclose the oral false statements constituted a *Brady* violation. The Court of Appeals, however, opined that "[i]f the district court's reason for declining to compel disclosure was that the statements were not recorded, we do not agree. When the Government is in possession of material information that impeaches its witness or exculpates the defendant, it does not avoid the obligation under *Brady/Giglio* to disclose the information by not writing it down." 496 F.3d at 222.

In *United States v. Serfling* (2007, CA7 IL) 504 F.3d 672, a defendant convicted of wire fraud and mail fraud arising out of a scheme to defraud an insurance company appealed his convictions, arguing on appeal that the prosecution had withheld material exculpatory evidence from him in violation of the *Brady* rule.

Prior to trial the defendant requested prosecution disclosure of any evidence that the Fifth Third Bank, which owned the property that was the subject of the charged fraud, wanted to sell that property. The defendant sought to prove that the bank wanted to shed the property from its portfolio and had conspired with the co-defendant to perpetrate the fraud.

The prosecution informed the defendant that it had obtained 10,000 pages of documents that had been produced during civil litigation involving the bank. The prosecution told the defendant that it had not photocopied the documents, but that the prosecution would make the documents available for inspection at any time. The defendant never inspected the documents, which included a document that the defendant claimed on appeal was material exculpatory evidence.

The Seventh Circuit Court of Appeals rejected the defendant's *Brady* argument, concluding that the government had not suppressed the document. The Court stated: "The government 'suppresses' evidence for purposes of *Brady* if it fails to **disclose** the evidence in time for the defendant to use it in his defense, and the evidence was not otherwise available to the defendant through the exercise of reasonable diligence. [citation omitted] In this case, the government made the memorandum available for inspection—a fact inconsistent with suppression." 504 F.3d at 678–679. [emphasis added]

We conclude that the term "disclose" under the Criminal Discovery Statute has the same meaning as it has under the *Brady* rule. Since the prosecution's making material exculpatory evidence available to the defendant for inspection complies with the prosecutor's *Brady* duty to disclose material exculpatory evidence, it necessarily follows that when the prosecution or the defendant makes evidence or information that must be "disclosed" under the Criminal Discovery Statute available for inspection by the opposing party, the prosecution or defendant has complied with its statutory duty to "disclose" that evidence.

§ 3:2.1 Duty to disclose—place and means of disclosure

Some prosecutor's offices have elected to delegate the responsibility to actually make the prosecution's mandated disclosures to the investigating agency or to the assisting agency which has actual possession of real evidence and actual possession of discoverable items. In these jurisdictions, when the defendant requests an opportunity to examine, photocopy, or make duplicate tape or video recordings of physical evidence possessed by the investigating agency, the prosecutor's office offers to provide to the defendant's attorney a letter authorizing the investigating agency to provide the defendant's attorney with access to that physical evidence.

Criminal defense attorneys have questioned this practice, and some judges have made discovery orders requiring the prosecution to provide such access at the prosecutor's office, rather than to require the defendant's attorney to travel to the investigating agency to obtain the disclosures. As a general rule we question the authority of courts to regulate the time and place of prosecution disclosures or to regulate the identity of prosecution team personnel who actually perform the team's disclosure duties.

The issue as we see it is not whether the prosecution's delegation of the duty to provide disclosures to personnel in the investigating agency or in an assisting agency is a good or a bad idea. From a policy perspective there are substantial problems attendant to the prosecution's delegating the duty to the investigating agency to make the actual disclosures required by Section 1054.1. The issue, however, is whether this practice fails to constitute "disclosure" as mandated by the Criminal Discovery Statute. If the practice constitutes "disclosure" within the meaning of the Discovery Statute, then there has been no violation of the prosecution's duty to disclose, and there is no basis for intervention by the court.

The critical question is whether the prosecution's delegating to the investigating or assisting agency the power to make actual disclosures satisfies the prosecution's duty to "disclose" within the meaning of the Discovery Statute.

As we have observed elsewhere in the text and this supplement, the prosecution's duty to "disclose" does not constitute a duty to "deliver" discoverable items and evidence to the defense. See Sec. 3:4 of the text and this supplement, and *People v. Garner* (1961) 57 Cal.2d 135, 142, 18 Cal.Rptr. 40, 367 P.2d 680. Providing the defendant with an opportunity to examine the prosecution's evidence [such as an "open files" policy] constitutes "disclosure" within the meaning of the *Brady* rule and within the meaning of the Criminal Discovery Statute. *People v. Zambrano* (2007) 41 Cal.4th 1082, 1134, 1135, 63 Cal.Rptr.3d 297, 163 P.3d 4.

The real question is whether offering the defendant an opportunity to examine the prosecution's evidence at a place other than the prosecutor's office, supervised by personnel of the investigating or assisting agency, satisfies the prosecution's disclosure duty. Since the prosecution is not required to deliver discoverable items to the defendant, and since providing the defense with an opportunity to examine the prosecution's evidence does constitute disclosure, the question is presented where and under what conditions must this process take place to satisfy the prosecution's duty to "disclose" its evidence and information.

The easier of the two questions is where the prosecution's process of disclosing its evidence may take place to constitute "disclosure" within the meaning of the Discovery Statute. While there is no decisional authority addressing this question, we suggest a sensible answer that finds decisional support in cases construing the prosecutor's *Brady* duty and in the duties of the defendant's attorney in representing the defendant. Here is the standard we suggest: **the prosecution may offer the defendant access to the prosecution's evidence in the location where that evidence is normally kept by the prosecution team, as long as that location is not made unreasonably inaccessible to the defense.**

In order to "disclose" the prosecution's evidence, the prosecution must provide the defendant access to that evidence in the place where that evidence is normally kept. When access is sought to the records of a criminal investigation—such as police or investigative reports—or documents collected by the prosecutor's office as evidence—such as certified copies of prior convictions etc.—those records (or at least copies of those records) are normally kept in the prosecutor's trial files in the prosecutor's office. As long as the prosecutor takes steps to ensure that the prosecutor's files contain all of the police or investigative reports, it is reasonable for the prosecutor to offer the defense access to that evidence at the prosecutor's office.

Problems arise, however, when the defendant wants access to evidence that is normally retained in the investigating agency or in an agency assisting the prosecution, such as a crime laboratory. The investigating agency is not normally located in or proximate to the prosecutor's office. Some defense attorneys contend that they should not be required to travel to the investigating agency to examine the evidence held by that agency. Rather, these attorneys contend, the prosecutor must arrange for the evidence to be transported to the prosecutor's office for examination there by the defense. As a general principle, we question whether the prosecution's duty to "disclose" its evidence requires the prosecution to make disclosures at the prosecutor's office.

Requiring the investigating agency to transport its evidence to the prosecutor's office for defense inspection and copying would produce unknown but potentially substantial cost increases for the agency. Such a practice would also increase the agency's problems in keeping a proper chain of custody of its evidence. We have concluded that as long as the prosecution makes its evidence readily or reasonably accessible to the defendant's attorney at the investigating agency, the prosecution has satisfied its disclosure duty under *Brady* and under the Criminal Discovery Statute.

Although there is no decisional authority directly on point, it appears that a standard which requires the prosecution to make its evidence reasonably or readily accessible to the defense finds a parallel in the prosecutor's *Brady* duty to disclose material exculpatory evidence to a defendant.

The federal courts and California state courts have repeatedly articulated the rule that a prosecutor is obligated to locate material exculpatory evidence that is possessed by a member of the prosecution team and that is reasonably or readily available to the prosecutor. *See, e.g., In re Brown* (1998) 17 Cal.4th 873, 883, 72 Cal.Rptr.2d 698, 952 P.2d 715 [evidence "readily accessible" to the prosecution]; *In re Littlefield* (1993) 5 Cal.4th 122, 135, 19 Cal.Rptr.2d 248, 851 P.2d 42 ["information that is reasonably accessible"]; *Pitchess v. Superior Court* (1974) 11 Cal.3d 531, 535, 113 Cal.Rptr. 897, 522 P.2d 305 ["information reasonably accessible"]; *People v. Superior Court (Barrett)* (2000) 80 Cal.App.4th 1305, 1316, 96 Cal.Rptr.2d 264 ["reasonably accessible"]; *Abatti v. Superior Court* (2003) 112 Cal.App.4th 39, 51, 4 Cal.Rptr.3d 767 ["reasonably accessible"]; *People v. Little* (1997) 59 Cal.App.4th 426, 431, 68 Cal.Rptr.2d 907 ["information reasonably accessible to the prosecution"].

A defendant is entitled to discover from the prosecution the relevant statements of witnesses. Penal Code section 1054.1. The discovery provided in § 1054.1, however, is not exclusive. The reciprocal discovery chapter places no restriction on discovery provided by other express statutory provisions, or as mandated by the Constitution of the United States. Penal Code section 1054, subsection (e). Evidence Code section 1043, is one such express statutory provision. Just as the discovery procedure set forth in § 1043 *et seq.* operates in tandem with the prosecution's duty to disclose favorable information pursuant to the *Brady* rule, so too does the California Evidence Code discovery procedure work in tandem with the prosecution's duty to disclose relevant statements of witnesses under Penal Code section 1054.1, subsection (f). Except with regard to one exception, the prosecutor, as well as the defendant, must comply with the statutory *Pitchess* [see: *Pitchess v. Superior Court of Los Angeles County* (1974) 11 Cal. 3d 531, 113

Cal. Rptr. 897, 522 P.2d 305] requirements for disclosure of information contained in confidential peace officer records. There is no reason why the defense—when it has good reason to believe an officer's personnel file contains relevant statements from material witnesses to the charged incident—should be precluded from obtaining the statements because the district attorney may have the right to obtain the same information by filing a motion for discovery pursuant to § 1043. *Rezek v. Superior Court* (2012) 206 Cal. App. 4th 633, 141 Cal. Rptr. 3d 891.

The parallel which we find in these cases is that a prosecutor is required to conduct a search in reasonably accessible places within the prosecution team other than the prosecutor's own office to ensure that discoverable information and evidence possessed by the team is disclosed to the defendant.

The prosecutor's duty to access reasonably accessible sources within the prosecution team for discoverable information and evidence has a concomitant application to the defense attorney. The defendant's attorney has a due diligence, self-help duty to exercise "reasonable diligence" in searching for material exculpatory evidence. *People v. Salazar* (2005) 35 Cal.4th 1031, 1049, 29 Cal.Rptr.3d 16, 112 P.3d 14. See the discussion of the defendant's due diligence self-help duty in Sections 1:78, 1:78.1, and 1:78.2 of the text.

These two discovery principles which impose standards of reasonable diligence and conduct upon prosecutors and defense attorneys combine to support a standard in which the prosecutor must provide "reasonable access" to the prosecution's evidence and the defense attorney must exercise "reasonable diligence" in taking advantage of the access provided by the prosecution. The prosecution's duty to provide "reasonable access" means that the prosecution team can normally make its evidence available for inspection and copying at the location where that evidence is normally kept. The defendant's duty to exercise "reasonable diligence" means that the defense attorney must normally take advantage of the prosecution's offer to provide access to that evidence in the location where the evidence is normally kept. Under normal circumstances such a procedure should satisfy the prosecution's duty to "disclose" that evidence.

We caution, however, that if the investigating agencies choose to store their evidence at a facility that is a substantial distance from the population center of the criminal defense bar, or which is otherwise inaccessible to the defense bar, the prosecution team might well lose its ability to conduct defense discovery inspections and copying of that evidence at the location where that evidence is stored, because the defendant would no longer have reasonable access to the prosecution's evidence. *See People v. Zambrano* (2007) 41 Cal.4th 1082, 1134, 63 Cal.Rptr.3d 297, 163 P.3d 4, *overruled on other grounds, People v. Doolin* (2009) 45 Cal.4th 390, 421, n.22, 87 Cal.Rptr.3d 209, 198 P.3d 11 ["Concerns [about an 'open files' policy] might also arise if the prosecutor used the policy to impose impracticable or unduly oppressive self-discovery burdens on the defense."]; *Schaffer v. Superior Court* (2010) 185 Cal.App.4th 1235, 1244, 111 Cal.Rptr.3d 245.

Thus, our answer to the question, where may the prosecution make its evidence and information available to the defendant in order to constitute "disclosure" of that evidence, is this: **the prosecution may offer the defendant access to the prosecution's evidence in the location where that evidence is normally kept by the prosecution team, as long as that location is not made unreasonably inaccessible to the defense.**

§ 3:2.2   Duty to disclose—prosecution delegation of discovery duty to investigating agency

The question "under what conditions must the process of making the prosecution's evidence available to inspection and copying by the defendant take place in order to satisfy the prosecution's duty to disclose" is a trickier question. The conclusion we have reached in answering this question is that the prosecution team may not impose conditions upon the process at the investigating agency that interfere with the ability of the defendant's attorney to inspect the prosecution's evidence in a reasonably timely and speedy manner.

Some defense attorneys have reported that they have been kept waiting for long periods of time at the investigating agency, and that they have been informed that no one at the agency knew about the discovery request or was prepared to take the time to provide the defense attorney with access to the evidence. If that scenario is anything more than an occasional occurrence, the procedure of providing access to discovery at the investigating agency does not constitute making prosecution evidence "reasonably accessible" to the defendant and does not satisfy the prosecution's duty to "disclose" its evidence to the defendant.

If the prosecutor makes the policy decision to provide letters of authorization to a defendant's attorney which give that attorney the authority to inspect and copy the prosecution team's physical evidence at the investigating agency, the prosecutor must establish workable procedures whereby the defendant's attorney is able to make arrangements to inspect and copy that evidence in a reasonably efficient manner.

Some trial courts have issued discovery orders that require the prosecutor to be an integral on-the-scene participant in open files discovery, on the theory that the prosecutor must remain involved in the discovery process to ensure that the prosecution team makes proper disclosures of its evidence. Under this point of view, the prosecutor may not delegate the prosecutor's duty to disclose prosecution evidence. This position is questionable.

The statement of the Supreme Court in *In re Brown* (1998), 17 Cal.4th 873, 881, 72 Cal.Rptr.2d 698, 952 P.2d 715, that the prosecution's duty to disclose material exculpatory evidence "is nondelegable," means only that "the prosecution remains responsible for any lapse in compliance. Since the prosecution must bear the consequences of its own failure to disclose [citations omitted], a fortiori, it must be charged with any negligence on the part of other agencies acting in its behalf [citations omitted]."

Again, the question is not whether a prosecutor's decision to delegate the responsibility for making discovery disclosures to an officer of the investigating agency is a wise policy decision. It probably is not generally a wise move for the prosecutor to delegate that power, because the prosecutor is in the best position to make decisions about discovery duties that require the exercise of legal judgment.

But the question is whether the prosecutor has the right to delegate to officers of the investigating agency the work of making discovery disclosures. As long as there is no evidence that utilizing non-attorney investigators or law enforcement officers to make the prosecution's evidence available for inspection and/or copying results in failure to disclose as required by the Criminal Discovery Statute, such a practice should not offend statutory or constitutional standards. Absent such evidence, the business of designating the prosecution team's discovery representatives belongs to the prosecutor. See United States v. Quinn (1998, CA11 FL) 123 F.3d 1415, 1422, n.6; United States v. Herring (1996, CA9 CA) 83 F.3d 1120, 1121; United States v. Jennings (1992, CA9 CA) 960 F.2d 1488, 1491, 1492; United States v. Dominguez-Villa (1992, CA9 AZ) 954 F.2d 562–565; and United States v. Smith (1977, CA8 MO) 552 F.2d 257.

Officers of the agency which has investigated the underlying crimes with which the defendant is charged are members of the prosecution team, "which includes both investigative and prosecutorial personnel." In re Brown, 17 Cal.4th at 881. See also Mills v. Cal. Dep't of Corr. (D. Cal. Mar. 5, 2012) 2012 U.S. Dist. LEXIS 28887, holding, inter alia, evidence cannot be kept out of the hands of the defense just because the prosecutor does not have it, where an investigating agency does.

The investigating agency becomes part of the prosecution team because its role in investigating the criminal charges causes it to be "acting on the government's behalf," Kyles v. Whitley (1996) 514 U.S. 419, 437, 115 S.Ct. 1555, 131 L.Ed.2d 490; People v. Superior Court (Meraz) (2008) 163 Cal.App.4th 28, 47, 77 Cal.Rptr.3d 352, and "assisting the government's case . . . ." In re Brown, 17 Cal.4th 873, 881.

The Criminal Discovery Statute expressly recognizes that the prosecutor may utilize the investigating agency "to assist [the prosecutor] in performing [his] duties." Penal Code section 1054.5, subdivision (a). As part of the prosecution team, the investigating agency and its officers are under the authority of the prosecutor, who is the attorney for the prosecution team. "Brady, then, applies only to information possessed by the prosecutor or anyone over whom he has authority." United States v. Meros (1989, CA11 FL) 866 F.2d 1304, 1309; Moon v. Head (2005, CA11 GA) 285 F.3d 1301, 1309. As part of the prosecution team, information possessed by the investigating agency is considered to be "within [the government's] control." *United States v. Pelullo* (2005, CA3 NJ) 399 F.3d 197, 212.

Officers of the investigating agency are the agents of the prosecutor's office when they assist the prosecutor's work in prosecuting the case. The California Supreme Court in *In re Brown*, 17 Cal.4th 873, 881, described the role of agencies that assist the prosecution in these terms: "those assisting the government's case are no more than its agents." In *United States v. Antone* (1979, CA5 FL) 603 F.2d 566, 570, the Fifth Circuit Court of Appeals concluded that state investigators "functioned as agents of the federal government under the principles of agency law" when they assisted in an investigation of crimes that resulted in a federal prosecution.

If the prosecutor's use of the investigating agency to carry out the prosecuting attorney's discovery duties creates an agency relationship with the prosecutor's office as the principal and the investigating agency as the agent, then accepted principles of agency come into play. A principal may appoint an agent. Civil Code section 2296. An agent may represent the principal in dealing with third parties. Civil Code section 2295. A principal may authorize the agent to perform any acts which the principal might perform, except those acts to which the principal must give his or her personal attention. Civil Code section 2304.

While the Criminal Discovery Statute provides that the "prosecuting attorney" must make the disclosures required by Penal Code section 1054.1, the Discovery Statute also recognizes that the prosecuting attorney may employ other persons or agencies to assist in the performance of his or her duties. Penal Code section 1054.5, subdivision (a). There does not appear to be anything in the Criminal Discovery Statute that requires the prosecuting attorney's personal attention in the process of disclosing the prosecution's evidence or information.

The conclusion we reach is that the **prosecution may delegate to officers of the investigating agency the duty to make the disclosures required by the Criminal Discovery Statute.**

§ 3:2.3   Duty to disclose—court regulation of the process

Absent a violation of the prosecution's duty to disclose the items listed in Penal Code section 1054.1, a court does not have the authority to regulate the discovery process. Penal Code section 1054.5, subdivision (b), grants courts the authority to issue orders to regulate the discovery process only when certain conditions have been met. One of those conditions is that either the prosecution or the defendant has failed to comply with its discovery duties under the statute. That subdivision provides, in pertinent part: "Upon a showing that a party has not complied with Section 1054.1 or 1054.3 and upon a showing that the moving party complied with the informal discovery procedure provided in this subdivision, a court may make any order necessary to enforce the provisions of this chapter . . . ."

When the discovery process utilized by the prosecution does not meet the constitutional and statutory requirement that the prosecution "disclose" its evidence, and the defendant has complied with the mandatory informal discovery procedures of the Criminal Discovery Statute, the court then has the authority under the Discovery Statute to enter orders regulating the prosecution's discovery process. Penal Code section 1054.5, subdivision (b).

When faced with a failure of discovery compliance, the court's authority extends to issuing "any order necessary to enforce the provisions" of the Discovery Statute. We believe that this express language of subdivision (b) would authorize the court to regulate the time and place and process of the prosecution's disclosure to the defendant of its evidence. If the investigating agency's discovery practices do not comport with the standards necessary to constitute "disclosure," the court also has the power to issue a discovery order that regulates the persons named by the prosecuting attorney to make the mandated disclosures to the defendant.

§ 3:2.4   Duty to disclose—not duty to ensure defense use

In *United States v. King* (2011, CA4 NC) 628 F.3d 693, 702, the Fourth Circuit Court of Appeals held, in a *Brady* context, that the prosecutor's duty to disclose exculpatory evidence is met when the prosecution discloses that evidence. The prosecutor's duty to disclose evidence does not require that the prosecutor "ensure that the defense further develop and utilize that evidence."

§ 3:4   Duty to deliver discovery

The conclusion articulated in the text that the prosecutor does not have a duty to deliver discoverable items and evidence to the defendant finds support in the legislative history of Proposition 115, which enacted the Criminal Discovery Statute.

In addition to enacting the Criminal Discovery Statute as Penal Code sections 1054 through 1054.7, Proposition 115 repealed two longstanding California statutes that had required the prosecution to "deliver to, or make accessible for inspection and copying by, the defendant or counsel, copies of the police, arrest, and crime reports . . . ." in misdemeanor cases (former Penal Code section 1430) and in felony cases (former Penal Code section 859). Proposition 115, sections 15, 27, approved June 5, 1990.

"Proposition 115 also repealed several discovery provisions, including . . . Penal Code former section 1430 (requiring prosecutor to furnish defendant with police and arrest reports). Furthermore, Proposition 115 repealed the provisions in Penal Code section 859 requiring prosecutors to furnish defendants with police and arrest reports." *Izazaga v. Superior Court* (1991) 54 Cal.3d 356, 365, 285 Cal.Rptr. 231, 815 P.2d 304.

Proposition 115 thus replaced all statutory provisions requiring the prosecution to "deliver" discovery with statutes that require the prosecution to "disclose" discoverable items and evidence to the defendant.

The Legislature's enactment of Penal Code section 1054.9 in 2002 did not resurrect the discarded "deliver to" language that had been deleted from the Penal Code discovery statutes in 1990. Instead, Section 1054.9 directed that "the defendant be provided reasonable access" to enumerated post-judgment discovery.

This legislative history of the Criminal Discovery Statute supports the conclusion that the prosecution is not required by that statute to "deliver" discoverable items and evidence directly to the defendant's attorney.

The conclusion articulated in the text that the prosecutor does not have a duty to deliver discoverable items and evidence to the defendant finds additional support in the articulation of the *Brady* rule by the United States Supreme Court and the federal circuit courts of appeals. As discussed in Section 3:2 of this supplement, the requirement that the prosecution "disclose" discoverable items and evidence pursuant to Penal Code section 1054.1 mirrors the duty of the prosecution to **"disclose"** material exculpatory evidence under the *Brady* rule.

See Youngblood v. West Virginia (2006) 547 U.S. 867, 869, 126 S.Ct. 2188, 165 L.Ed.2d 269 ["A *Brady* violation occurs when the government fails to **disclose** evidence materially favorable to the accused." [emphasis added]]; *United States v. Rodriguez* (2007, CA2 NY) 496 F.3d 221, 222 ["When the Government is in possession of material information that impeaches its witness or exculpates the defendant, it does not avoid the obligation under *Brady/Giglio* to **disclose** the information by not writing it down." [emphasis added]]; *United States v. Serfling* (2007, CA7 IL) 504 F.3d 672, 678–679 ["The government 'suppresses' evidence for purposes of *Brady* if it fails to **disclose** the evidence in time for the defendant to use it in his defense . . . ." [emphasis added]]

Accordingly, the prosecutor's duty under the Criminal Discovery Statute is the same duty that the prosecutor has under the *Brady* rule—it is a duty to "disclose."

The United States Supreme Court and at least one federal circuit court have appeared to distinguish the prosecutor's duty to **disclose** from a duty to **deliver** material exculpatory evidence to the defendant. In *United States v. Bagley* (1985) 473 U.S. 667, 675, 105 S.Ct. 3375, 87 L.Ed.2d 481, the United States Supreme Court held: "Thus, the prosecutor is **not required to deliver** his entire file to defense counsel, but **only to disclose** evidence favorable to the accused that, if suppressed, would deprive the defendant of a fair trial." [emphasis added] In *Stephens v. Hall* (2005, CA11 FL) 407 F.3d 1195, 1203, the Eleventh Circuit Court of Appeals construed this quoted statement from *Bagley* to mean that "*Brady* does not require that the prosecution 'deliver [its] entire file to defense counsel, but only [that it] disclose' material evidence. [citation omitted]"

It is possible that the distinction which the Supreme Court was drawing in

Bagley was between delivering the prosecutor's entire file as opposed to delivering only the material exculpatory evidence from that file. However, if the distinction which the Supreme Court drew involved only the quantity and types of evidence that the *Brady* rule requires the prosecutor to disclose, rather than the means by which that disclosure must be made, the change in the operative verb from "deliver" to "disclose" makes no sense; it would have been much simpler for the Court to use the same operative verb. The change in the operative verb indicates to us that, whatever else the Court was saying, the Supreme Court was drawing a distinction between the prosecutor's duty to **deliver** discovery to the defendant and the prosecutor's duty to **disclose** material exculpatory evidence.

§ 3:4.1 "Disclosure" by means of "open files" policy—procedures

If the prosecution chooses to satisfy its duty to "disclose" discoverable evidence and information by following an "open files" policy, by which the prosecution allows the defendant's attorney to conduct an open examination of the trial files of the prosecution, the prosecution must enable the defendant to conduct this examination in a setting that protects the defendant's attorney-client privilege and his or her attorney's work product privilege, while at the same time protecting the integrity of the prosecution's files and evidence. *Schaffer v. Superior Court* (2010) 185 Cal.App.4th 1235, 1245, 111 Cal.Rptr.3d 245.

In *Schaffer v. Superior Court*, the Court of Appeal suggested possible procedures to protect these interests of both parties to a criminal prosecution. "[T]he district attorney could allow the defendant and his counsel to view the items in private or in a discreet location where their conversation not be overheard by the district attorney's staff but precautions could be made to protect against theft or destruction." 185 Cal.App.4th at 1245.

§ 3:5 Real evidence—generally

§ 3:5.1 Trial exhibits

The prosecution must comply with its duty under Penal Code section 1054.1(c) to disclose to the defendant all relevant real evidence seized or obtained as part of the investigation of the charged offenses, and for the reasons discussed in the main text must disclose its trial exhibits, whether or not those exhibits were seized or obtained as part of the investigation of the charged offenses.

However, it is not at all clear that the prosecution must disclose to the defendant which of its real evidence it intends to introduce as exhibits at trial—whether it must provide the defendant with a list of trial exhibits. The distinction was made by the Sixth Circuit Court of Appeals in *United States v. Prince* (2010, CA6 TN) 618 F.3d 551. In *Prince* the defendant argued on appeal that the district court erred in refusing to order the government to specifically identify the exhibits it intended to introduce at trial from among an estimated 70,000 pages of discovery material that had been disclosed to the defense. The defendant had asked the trial court to order the government to identify its trial exhibits by CD number, volume, folder, and scan image number, from scanned images of documents provided to the defense on CD-ROM. The government opposed the defense request and the district court denied the defense motion.

The defendant contended on appeal that the district court's refusal to order the government to identify its trial exhibits was error. The Court of Appeals rejected the defense argument, observing that "[d]efendant's true complaint is not a failure to make the documents available, however, and Rule 16 [of the Federal Rules of Criminal Procedure] does not entitle a defendant to pretrial disclosure of the government's exhibit list." 618 F.3d at 562.

It appears that under the Criminal Discovery Statute, as long as the prosecution discloses all of its real evidence, including its trial exhibits, to the defendant, the prosecution is not required by the Statute to disclose which of those exhibits the prosecution intends to use at trial, or the sequence in which the prosecution intends to present that real evidence at trial.

§ 3:5.3 Duplicating obscene photographs

Federal courts continue to be more restrictive than California State courts in preventing child pornography images to be duplicated for the use of a criminal defendant who is charged with child pornography offenses.

In 2006, Congress enacted and the President signed into law the Adam Walsh Child Protection and Safety Act, which is codified at 18 U.S.C. section 3509(m). This Act provides that "a court shall deny, in any criminal proceeding, any request by the defendant to copy, photograph, duplicate, or otherwise reproduce any property or material that constitutes child pornography . . . , so long as the Government makes the property or material reasonably available to the defendant." 18 U.S.C. section 3509(m)(2)(A). This Act, which governs criminal prosecutions in federal courts, is the basis for a number of opinions of the federal Circuit Courts of Appeal that uphold the refusal of federal district courts to allow child pornography evidence to be duplicated for the use of a criminal defendant in prosecutions for possession of child pornography. *See, e.g.*, *United States v. McNealy* (2010, CA5 MS) 625 F.3d 858, 868; *United States v. Wright* (2010, CA9 AZ) 625 F.3d 583, 613–617.

As defined by the Act, material is deemed to be "reasonably available" if the government "provides ample opportunity for inspection, viewing, and examination at a Government facility of the property or material by the defendant, his or her attorney, and any individual the defendant may seek to qualify to furnish expert testimony at trial." 18 U.S.C. section 3509(m)(2)(B).

An expert witness who produces pornographic images as part of his work as a defense expert witness, thereby exposes himself to criminal prosecution and civil suit for violation of federal criminal child pornography laws. *See, e.g., Doe v. Boland* (2011, CA6 OH) 630 F.3d 491 [parents of minor children whose photographs were morphed into pornographic images by a defense expert as part of preparation of expert testimony and exhibits for a criminal trial could bring a civil action against the expert witness for violation of federal child pornography laws].

§ 3:5.4 Public records

A defendant is entitled to discover from the prosecution the relevant statements of witnesses. Penal Code section 1054.1. The discovery provided in § 1054.1, however, is not exclusive. The reciprocal discovery chapter places no restriction on discovery provided by other express statutory provisions, or as mandated by the Constitution of the United States. Penal Code section 1054, subsection (e). Evidence Code section 1043, is one such express statutory provision. Just as the discovery procedure set forth in § 1043 *et seq.* operates in tandem with the prosecution's duty to disclose favorable information pursuant to the *Brady* rule, so too does the California Evidence Code discovery procedure work in tandem with the prosecution's duty to disclose relevant statements of witnesses under Penal Code section 1054.1, subsection (f). Except with regard to one exception, the prosecutor, as well as the defendant, must comply with the statutory *Pitchess* (supra) requirements for disclosure of information contained in confidential peace officer records. There is no reason why the defense—when it has good reason to believe an officer's personnel file contains relevant statements from material witnesses to the charged incident—should be precluded from obtaining the statements because the district attorney may have the right to obtain the same information by filing a motion for discovery pursuant to § 1043. *Rezek v. Superior Court* (2012) 206 Cal. App. 4th 633, 141 Cal. Rptr. 3d 891.

§ 3.5.5 Public records containing impeachment evidence on prosecution witnesses

The government has a *Brady* obligation to produce any favorable evidence in the personnel records of an officer. A defendant doesn't have to make a request for exculpatory or impeachment evidence. The duty to disclose exculpatory evidence is applicable even though there has been no request by the accused, and the duty encompasses impeachment evidence as well as exculpatory evidence. The government has a duty to examine personnel files upon a defendant's request for their production. If the prosecution isn't sure whether material in a personnel file rises to the *Brady* threshold, it may submit the information to the trial court for an in camera inspection. A prosecutor anxious about tacking too close to the wind will disclose a favorable piece of evidence. *Milke v. Ryan* (2013, CA9 Ariz.) 711 F.3d 998.

An allegation that the prosecution failed to disclose material evidence is governed by *Brady*. Under *Brady*, the government violates its constitutional duty to disclose material exculpatory evidence where (1) the evidence in question is favorable to the accused in that it is exculpatory or impeachment evidence, (2) the government willfully or inadvertently suppresses this evidence, and (3) prejudice ensues from the suppression (i.e., the evidence is material). *Jones v. Ryan* (2012, CA9 Ariz.) 691 F.3d 1093.

§ 3:6   Evidence and information about defendant—generally

The prosecution's duty to disclose information about the defendant and co-defendants includes statements made by all defendants and criminal history information about all defendants.

§ 3:6.1   Evidence and information about defendant—statements by defendants

Note that once a defendant's Sixth Amendment right to counsel attaches, the government is forbidden from deliberately eliciting incriminating statements about the crimes charged from the defendant. These Sixth Amendment protections apply to conversations between confidential informants (CIs) and defendants where the CIs relay incriminating statements from the defendant to the government, just as they do to formal questioning. *United States v. Smith* (Jan. 28, 2013, CA9 Alaska) 2013 U.S. App. LEXIS 1896.

For a discussion of the conditions under which the prosecuting attorney may withhold disclosure of the statements of a defendant, see Sections 3:22.2.8, 7:35.2, and 8:2.5 of this supplement.

§ 3:7   Trial witnesses—generally

The prosecution's duty to disclose its trial witnesses includes the names and addresses of those witnesses that the prosecution intends to call in its case-in-chief and in rebuttal.

The Criminal Discovery Statute's mandated disclosure of the names and addresses of prosecution witnesses has a counterpart in Rule 16 of the Federal Rules of Criminal Procedure, whereby federal trial courts have discretion to order the government in a federal criminal matter to provide pretrial disclosure of its witness list. *See United States v. Caro* (2010, CA4 VA) 597 F.3d 608, 616; *United States v. Fletcher* (1996, CA4 WV) 74 F.3d 49, 54.

It is unclear whether a California state trial court has the discretionary power to order the prosecution to disclose the *order* in which the prosecution intends to call its witnesses in its case-in-chief. The power to enter such an order is not expressly granted by the Criminal Discovery Statute, but might be provided by Code of Civil Procedure section 128(a)(3), which grants every court the power to "provide for the orderly conduct of proceedings before it, or its officers."

§ 3:7.1   Definition of "trial witness"

The prosecutor's duty to disclose evidence favorable to the accused extends to information known only to the police. The U.S. Constitution compels prosecutors to disclose evidence favorable to the accused, even when that evidence was known only to the police and not to the prosecutor. *Phillips v. Ornoski* (May 25, 2012, CA9 Cal.) 2012 U.S. App. LEXIS 10808.

§ 3:7.3 Required disclosures

Although the Criminal Discovery Statute's required disclosures regarding the names and addresses of prosecution trial witnesses might appear to be relatively clear-cut, the question whether the court has the power to compel the disclosure of prosecution witnesses' contact information is looming as a renewed controversial issue.

§ 3:7.3.1 Names and addresses

On November 4, 2008, the California electorate passed Proposition 9, the "Victim's Bill of Rights Act of 2008: Marsy's Law," which is commonly known by its shortened name, "Marsy's Law." "Marsy's Law" was named after Marsalee (Marsy) Nicholas, a 21-year-old college student who was murdered in 1983.

"Marsy's Law" amended Section 28 of Article I of the California Constitution, to provide:

> "(b) In order to preserve and protect a victim's rights to justice and due process, a victim shall be entitled to the following rights:
>
> . . .
>
> (4) To prevent the disclosure of confidential information or records to the defendant, the defendant's attorney, or any other person acting on behalf of the defendant, which could be used to locate or harass the victim or the victim's family."

As a provision of the California Constitution, Article I, Section 28(b)(4) could be construed to entitle the victim of a crime prosecuted in a California state criminal court who is also a prosecution trial witness to override the prosecution's statutory duty under Penal Code section 1054.1(a) to disclose the name and address of the victim or any other prosecution witness that could be used to locate or harass the victim or the family of the victim. A state constitutional provision that conflicts with a provision of a state statute takes precedence over that state statute. *Lockyer v. City and County of San Francisco* (2004) 33 Cal.4th 1055, 1092–1093, 17 Cal.Rptr.3d 225, 95 P.3d 459.

Another provision of Marsy's Law provides that upon the request of the victim, the prosecutor has the power to enforce a victim's right to prevent the disclosure of information that could be used to locate or harass the victim or the victim's family. California Constitution, Art. I, Sec. 28(c)(1).

These provisions of the California Constitution would appear to excuse the prosecutor, upon the request of the victim of the alleged crime, from being required to disclose to the defendant the names and addresses of the crime victim and the crime victim's family.

However, to the extent that the disclosure of the name and address of the victim or a member of the victim's family is compelled by either the Due Process Clause or the Confrontation Clause of the United States Constitution, the federal constitutional provision would take precedence over a conflicting provision in the California Constitution. A right that is protected even by the California Constitution cannot negate a right protected by the United States Constitution. Although the California Constitution is the supreme law of the State of California, *Sands v. Morongo Unified School Dist.* (1991) 53 Cal.3d 863, 902–903, 281 Cal.Rptr. 34, 809 P.2d 809, the United States Constitution is the supreme law of the land. U.S. Const., art. VI, cl. 2. The California Constitution likewise declares in Art. III, Sec. 1 that "the United States Constitution is the supreme law of the land." The California Constitution is thus subject to the supremacy of the United States Constitution. *California Logistics, Inc. v. State of California* (2008) 161 Cal.App.4th 242, 250, 73 Cal.Rptr.3d 825; Cal. Const., art. III, Sec. 1.

Thus, if a provision of the United States Constitution requires that the name of a prosecution witness be disclosed to the defendant, no contrary provision of the California Constitution can have any force and effect.

The Confrontation Clause of the Sixth Amendment to the United States Constitution requires that the prosecution disclose the identity of any person the prosecution calls to testify against the defendant. *Alvarado v. Superior Court* (2000) 23 Cal.4th 1121, 1125, 99 Cal.Rptr.2d 149, 5 P.3d 203. Thus, despite the language of Article I, Section 28(a)(4) of the California Constitution, the United States Constitution precludes the prosecution from calling a witness to testify whose name is permanently withheld from the defendant. It would appear that the most that a court may constitutionally order is that the disclosure of the name of the victim or another prosecution witness be delayed until shortly before the witness testifies in order to minimize the opportunities for harassment or threatening of the victim or the victim's family.

The same kind of analysis applies to the question whether the victim of the alleged crime prosecution, acting as an individual or through the prosecutor, may invoke Marsy's Law to prevent the disclosure of the victim's address or the address of a member of the victim's family. See the discussion in Section 3:7.3.4 of the text.

§ 3:7.3.3 Delayed disclosure of prosecution witness's name

There are occasions when the prosecution believes that to disclose the name of a prosecution witness will jeopardize that witness's safety and thus the integrity of the prosecution's evidence against the defendant. This scenario is not uncommon in prosecutions of defendants who are believed to be involved in drug cartels and criminal street gangs.

In *United States v. Celis* (2010, CA DC) 608 F.3d 818, several defendants convicted of conspiring to import cocaine and to manufacture and distribute cocaine for import appealed their convictions, arguing that the government had unconstitutionally obtained a protective order from the district court allowing government witnesses from Columbia to testify using pseudonyms. The protective order was issued based on evidence that a criminal organization in Columbia had issued death threats against witnesses who cooperated with the prosecution. The protective order provided that the government must disclose the true identity of these witnesses to the defendants' attorneys, and the attorneys could disclose the witnesses' true identities to their clients and to one member of the defense team located in the United States. The protective order provided that the true identities of the witnesses, however, could not be shared with anyone in Columbia.

The defendants contended on appeal that the use of pseudonyms for government witnesses prevented proper defense investigation of those witnesses and thus violated the defendants' confrontation rights under the Sixth Amendment. The Court of Appeals, citing and quoting from the Supreme Court opinion in *Weatherford v. Bursey* (1977) 429 U.S. 545, 559, 97 S.Ct. 837, 51 L.Ed.2d 30, rejected the defendants' argument, observing that there is no constitutional requirement that the prosecution must reveal the names of all government witnesses prior to trial. 608 F.3d at 831. "It does not follow from the prohibition against concealing evidence favorable to the accused that the prosecution must reveal before trial the names of all witnesses who will testify unfavorably." *Weatherford v. Bursey, supra*, 429 U.S. at 545.

The Court of Appeals in *Celis* relied upon the fact that the defendants gained access to the true identities of government witnesses days prior to their testimony, and when shown to be necessary were allowed to investigate these witnesses using their true identities in both the United States and Columbia. By delaying disclosure of the witnesses' true identities, but allowing the defense time to investigate those witnesses using their true names, the district court protected the defendants' constitutional rights while also protecting the witnesses. 608 F.3d at 834.

§ 3:7.3.6   Telephone numbers

Although the telephone numbers of a prosecution witness need not be disclosed pursuant to the Criminal Discovery Statute, the telephone number of a material exculpatory witness might be a constitutionally mandated disclosure. When exculpatory evidence involves an eyewitness to the crime, what must be disclosed is not just the witness's identity, " 'but all pertinent information which might assist the defense to locate him' [citing *Eleazer v. Superior Court of Los Angeles County* (1970) 1 Cal.3d 847, 851, 83 Cal.Rptr. 586, 464 P.3d 42]." *People v. Robinson* (1995) 31 Cal.App.4th 494, 499, 37 Cal.Rptr.2d 183.

§ 3:8   Felony convictions—generally

§ 3:8.1   "Material witness" defined

Note: The purpose of a preliminary hearing is to establish whether there is probable cause to believe the defendant has committed a felony. Penal Code section 866, subsection (b). Probable cause is shown if a person of ordinary caution or prudence would be led to believe and conscientiously entertain a strong suspicion of the guilt of the accused. That is the sole inquiry. Guilt or innocence is not determined. It is not a vehicle for discovery. § 866, subsection (b). *Curry v. Superior Court* (2013) 217 Cal. App. 4th 580, 158 Cal. Rptr. 3d 707.

§ 3:10   Juvenile records

Questions concerning access to a prosecution witness's or victim's juvenile records constitute among the most difficult discovery issues which trial courts have to confront.

§ 3:10.3   Sealing of juvenile records

A court may not normally order disclosure of juvenile records that have been previously sealed pursuant to Welfare and Institutions Code section 781. Welfare and Institutions Code section 781 provides the authority for the juvenile court to order that upon satisfying the conditions established in that section, juvenile records shall be sealed. Section 781 provides that "[o]nce the court has ordered the person's records sealed, the proceedings in the case shall be deemed never to have occurred . . . except as provided in subdivision (b), the records shall not be open to inspection." The narrow exceptions allowed by subdivision (b) are the use of those records in a defamation action, and provision to an authorized vehicle insurer for determining insurance eligibility and rates.

Otherwise, unless the person to whom the sealed records relates agrees to the unsealing of the records [the subject of the sealed records may request the superior court to permit inspection of the records], the courts may not unseal them.

In *In re James H.* (2007) 154 Cal.App.4th 1078, 65 Cal.Rptr.3d 410, the Board of Parole Hearings requested the juvenile court to provide the Board with copies of records of a juvenile inmate that the court had previously ordered to be sealed, so that the Board could use those records to determine whether to declare the inmate a sexually violent predator. The superior court granted the request without affording the inmate a hearing on the request. The district attorney filed a petition to declare the inmate a sexually violent predator. The inmate sent the court two letters objecting to the release of his records and asking the court to appoint counsel to represent him. The Court of Appeal construed the second letter as a notice of appeal of the order releasing the records.

The Court of Appeal reversed the superior court's order granting the

Board of Parole Hearings disclosure of the inmate's records and ordered BPH to return to the juvenile court the records that had been provided to the Board. The Court remanded the case to the superior court for further proceedings to determine the disposition of the sealed records.

In reaching this decision the Court of Appeal concluded that because of the clear and unequivocal language of Section 781, "juvenile court records may not be released for use in an SVP proceeding when those records have been sealed by court order under section 781." 154 Cal.App.4th at 1088.

§ 3:10.4   Defense access to juvenile records

In *People v. Martinez* (2009) 47 Cal.4th 399, 97 Cal.Rptr.3d 732, 213 P.3d 77, the California Supreme Court clarified California law concerning the right of a criminal defendant to gain access to the juvenile records of a juvenile murder victim.

In *Martinez* the defendant was convicted of first-degree murder and premeditated, attempted murder, and sentenced to death. The special circumstance allegation that resulted in the death sentence alleged that the murder occurred while the defendant was engaged in the commission or attempted commission of, or flight after the performance of, a lewd act upon a child under the age of 14 years. The victim of the defendant's attempted murder charge was a juvenile and the murder victim was her mother. The crimes occurred on the same occasion and at the same location.

Six years prior to trial the defendant requested the juvenile court to allow him to inspect the juvenile dependency case file of the minor victim of the attempted murder charge, who was under the supervision of the juvenile court because of sexual abuse by several men. The juvenile court conducted an *in camera* review of the juvenile's file. The juvenile court ordered that psychological assessments of the victim that had been performed within a two-year period prior to the murder and attempted murder be disclosed. The juvenile court also disclosed recommendations prepared for a detention hearing in the juvenile court shortly before the crimes, and a jurisdictional report dated about one month after the crimes. The juvenile court declined to release any other information from the juvenile victim's juvenile dependency case file.

On automatic appeal of his conviction to the California Supreme Court, the defendant requested full access to the juvenile dependency case file. The defendant argued that if his request were denied, the Supreme Court must review the file to determine whether the trial court erred to failing to allow him to access material information contained in that file.

In an order dated six years prior to the Court's opinion on appeal, the Supreme Court denied the defendant's request for an order that his appellate counsel be provided access to the undisclosed portion of the juvenile case file. The Court's order cited as authority for its decision denying access to the juvenile file the opinion of the United States Supreme Court in

Pennsylvania v. Ritchie (1987) 480 U.S. 39, 59–61, 107 S.Ct. 989, 94 L.Ed.2d 40. *People v. Martinez, supra*, 47 Cal.4th at 451–452.

In its opinion affirming the judgment in its entirety, the Supreme Court held that the juvenile court had followed the rule established in *Pennsylvania v. Ritchie* and had appropriately exercised its power under the authority of Welfare and Institutions Code section 827 to conduct an *in camera* review of the juvenile file. 47 Cal.4th at 452.

The Court rejected the defendant's argument that the rule of *Pennsylvania v. Ritchie* is inapposite to a defendant's request to review a confidential juvenile file on appeal. The Court held that "even at trial the defense is not entitled to review confidential documents to determine which are material for its purposes; rather, as occurred in the present case, it is the trial court's duty to review the documents and to determine which, if any, are material and should be disclosed." 47 Cal.4th at 453.

The Supreme Court reviewed the confidential juvenile court and superior court files and concluded that the undisclosed information was not material to the defense. The Court held that the contents of the juvenile files "do not support any claim that further disclosure is required to protect defendant's right to a fair appeal." 47 Cal.4th at 454.

§ 3:11 Written or recorded trial witness statements

A defendant is entitled to discover from the prosecution the relevant statements of witnesses. Penal Code section 1054.1. The discovery provided in § 1054.1, however, is not exclusive. The reciprocal discovery chapter places no restriction on discovery provided by other express statutory provisions, or as mandated by the Constitution of the United States. Penal Code section 1054, subsection (e). Evidence Code section 1043, is one such express statutory provision. Just as the discovery procedure set forth in § 1043 *et seq.* operates in tandem with the prosecution's duty to disclose favorable information pursuant to the *Brady* rule, so too does the California Evidence Code discovery procedure work in tandem with the prosecution's duty to disclose relevant statements of witnesses under Penal Code section 1054.1, subsection (f). Except with regard to one exception, the prosecutor, as well as the defendant, must comply with the statutory *Pitchess* requirements for disclosure of information contained in confidential peace officer records. There is no reason why the defense—when it has good reason to believe an officer's personnel file contains relevant statements from material witnesses to the charged incident—should be precluded from obtaining the statements because the district attorney may have the right to obtain the same information by filing a motion for discovery pursuant to § 1043. *Rezek v. Superior Court* (2012) 206 Cal. App. 4th 633, 141 Cal. Rptr. 3d 891.

The provision of the Criminal Discovery Statute, Penal Code section 1054.1(f), that requires the prosecution to disclose the written or recorded statements of prosecution trial witnesses has not been the subject of much discussion by California judicial authority. In *People v. Verdugo* (2010) 50 Cal.4th 263, 283, 113 Cal.Rptr.3d 803, 236 P.3d 1035, the California Supreme Court declined to decide "whether oral statements that are neither made by a defendant nor exculpatory must be disclosed under section 1054.1, subdivision (f) . . . ."

Many attorneys and courts appear to assume that Penal Code section 1054.1(f) requires the prosecution to disclose recordings in which prosecution witnesses speak, such as tape recordings of conversations at a crime scene (such as the scene of a traffic stop) or recordings of dispatches and records of e-mails involving officer witnesses. This assumption might be correct.

However, at least one ederal circuit Court of Appeals has construed the definition of a witness statement contained in the Jencks Act in a manner that calls the above assumption into question. We discuss this federal opinion and its possible significance for California criminal discovery in Section 3:11.1 of this supplement.

§ 3:11.1   E-mails and other recorded communications as statements within meaning of Jencks Act

In *United States v. Kimoto* (2009, CA7 IL) 588 F.3d 464, the defendant, the president of a telemarketing firm, was convicted of conspiracy, mail fraud, and wire fraud based upon evidence that the defendant had defrauded consumers with poor credit histories by charging processing fees by debit transfer for the issuance of credit cards.

On appeal the defendant argued that the government violated the Jencks Act by failing to turn over e-mails to which a government witness had been a party. The Jencks Act was enacted by the United States Congress in response to *Jencks v. United States* (1957) 353 U.S. 657, 77 S.Ct. 1007, 1 L.Ed.2d 1103, in which the Supreme Court established rules for the availability and production of statements of prosecution witnesses in federal criminal trials. 18 U.S.C. sec 3500 requires the government to produce a verbatim statement or report made by a government witness or prospective government witness, other than the defendant, after the witness has testified.

The Seventh Circuit Court of Appeals rejected the defendant's argument, holding that the e-mails were not statements within the meaning of the Jencks Act. The Court held that the term "statement" as used in the Jencks Act "refers to a recorded recital of past occurrences made by a prospective prosecution witness. From its very nature, necessarily it is made after those events have taken place." 588 F.3d at 491. Citing its opinion in *United States v. Sopher* (1966, CA7 IL) 362 F.2d 523, the Court of Appeals held that a recording of an event made concurrently to the happening of the event, such as a tape recording of a bribe as it was being offered and accepted, is not a recital of a past occurrence by a prospective witness and is not a statement within the meaning of the Jencks Act.

Whether the opinion of the Court of Appeals in *Kimoto* that an e-mail is not a "statement" within the meaning of the Jencks Act will find a receptive ear in California state court opinions construing Penal Code section 1054.1(f) of the Criminal Discovery Statute is difficult to predict. The definition of a statement contained in the Jencks Act does not differ materially from the definition of a witness statement under the California Criminal Discovery Statute.

The holding in *Kimoto* should not be construed to mean that e-mails, recorded dispatch calls, recorded transmissions of law enforcement officers, and other kinds of contemporaneously recorded words and voices would not be discoverable under the Criminal Discovery Statute. However, *Kimoto* might require a defendant seeking disclosure of such recordings and records to establish that these items are covered by a provision of Penal Code section 1054.1 other than as written or recorded statements of prosecution witnesses.

§ 3:12   "Reports of trial witness statements"—generally

In contrast to the provision requiring the prosecution to disclose written or recorded statements of prosecution trial witnesses, the provision requiring disclosure of reports of prosecution trial witness statements has been the subject of significant judicial construction.

§ 3:12.3   Oral reports of witness statements under Criminal Discovery Statute—generally

Oral reports of witness statements that contain material exculpatory evidence must be disclosed by the prosecution to the defendant.

In *United States v. Duval* (2007, CA1 MA) 496 F.3d 64, 73, the First Circuit Court of Appeals described the investigating officers' practice of keeping scant notes of conversations with a witness that tended to exculpate the prime suspects as "a practice whose propriety is questionable." In *United States v. Houlihan* (1996, CA1 MA) 92 F.3d 1271, 1289, the First Circuit opined: "Eschewing tape recordings and ordering law enforcement agents not to take notes during pretrial interviews is risky business—and not guaranteed to redound either to the sovereign's credit or to its benefit. By adopting a 'what we don't create can't come back to haunt us' approach, prosecutors demean their primary mission: to see that justice is done."

See also, United States v. Rodriguez (2007, CA2 NY) 496 F.3d 221, 222 ["If the district court's reason for declining to compel disclosure was that the statements were not recorded, we do not agree. When the Government is in possession of material information that impeaches its witness or exculpates the defendant, it does not avoid the obligation under *Brady/Giglio* to disclose the information by not writing it down."]

§ 3:12.4   Oral reports under Criminal Discovery Statute—statements made directly to counsel

Brady v. Maryland and its progeny recognize the constitutional duty of the government to disclose exculpatory evidence to a defendant if it is "material" to guilt or punishment. To establish a *Brady* violation, three elements must be satisfied: (1) the evidence must be favorable to the accused; (2) the evidence must have been suppressed by the State, either willfully or inadvertently; and (3) there must be prejudice as a result of the suppression. Suppressed evidence is considered prejudicial (or material) if there is a reasonable probability that, had the evidence been disclosed to the defense, the result of the proceeding would have been different. A "reasonable probability" exists when confidence in the outcome is undermined. Material evidence includes exculpatory evidence and impeachment evidence. *United States v. Doe* (2013, CA9 Cal.) 705 F.3d 1134.

To be considered material under *Brady*, the undisclosed, favorable evidence must either be admissible exculpatory evidence or be impeachment evidence, which need not have been independently admissible to have been material. Impeachment evidence is material because if disclosed and used effectively, it may make the difference between conviction and acquittal. Evidence can be used to impeach a witness even if the evidence is not itself admissible, even to impeach—a written statement, for instance, that contradicts a witness's testimony but is inadmissible as hearsay could still be used as a prior inconsistent statement to cross-examine the witness. Inadmissible evidence that could have led to the discovery of admissible evidence also may qualify as material under *Brady*, although the United States Court of Appeals for the Ninth Circuit has not conclusively resolved the issue. *United States v. Olsen* (2013, CA9 Wash.) 704 F.3d 1172.

§ 3:12.5 Oral reports under Criminal Discovery Statute—statutory construction

§ 3:12.5.3 Disjunctive sentence construction

The continuing viability of the rule of statutory construction announced in *White v. County of Sacramento* (1982) 31 Cal.3d 676, 680, 183 Cal.Rptr. 520, 646 P.2d 191, was affirmed in *People v. Lewis* (2008) 43 Cal.4th 415, 492, 75 Cal.Rptr.3d 588, 181 P.3d 947, in which the Supreme Court quoted from *White* that " '[e]vidence that a qualifying phrase is supposed to apply to all antecedents instead of only to the immediately preceding one may be found in the fact that it is separated from the antecedents by a comma.' [citation omitted] If a comma is enough to make the last antecedent rule inapplicable, then surely a period, which signifies a complete sentence break, is enough also."

§ 3:12.7 Draft reports of witness statements

A defendant is entitled to discover from the prosecution the relevant statements of witnesses. Penal Code section 1054.1. The discovery provided in § 1054.1, however, is not exclusive. The reciprocal discovery chapter places no restriction on discovery provided by other express statutory provisions, or as mandated by the Constitution of the United States. Penal

Code section 1054, subsection (e). Evidence Code section 1043, is one such express statutory provision. Just as the discovery procedure set forth in § 1043 *et seq.* operates in tandem with the prosecution's duty to disclose favorable information pursuant to the *Brady* rule, so too does the California Evidence Code discovery procedure work in tandem with the prosecution's duty to disclose relevant statements of witnesses under Penal Code section 1054.1, subsection (f). Except with regard to one exception, the prosecutor, as well as the defendant, must comply with the statutory *Pitchess* requirements for disclosure of information contained in confidential peace officer records. There is no reason why the defense—when it has good reason to believe an officer's personnel file contains relevant statements from material witnesses to the charged incident—should be precluded from obtaining the statements because the district attorney may have the right to obtain the same information by filing a motion for discovery pursuant to § 1043. *Rezek v. Superior Court* (2012) 206 Cal. App. 4th 633, 141 Cal. Rptr. 3d 891.

As long as the prosecution discloses the final report of a witness's statement and any existing interview notes from which the final report was prepared, the prosecution is not required to disclose a draft of the final report of the witness's statement.

In *United States v. Skilling* (2009, CA5 TX) 554 F.3d 529, the defendant, the former CEO of Enron Corporation, was prosecuted for and convicted of conspiracy, securities fraud, making false representations to auditors, and insider trading arising from the failure of that corporation. During its investigation leading to the charges against the defendant, the government conducted hundreds of hours of interviews with Andrew Fastow, the former CFO of Enron who then became a government witness against Skilling. The interviewing agents took hundreds of pages of interview notes, which were ultimately compiled into two FBI Form 302s, which are forms that summarized the substance of the interview notes.

The government provided the 302s of the Fastow interviews to the defendant. The defendant demanded that the government disclose the draft 302s that had been prepared from the interview notes and which preceded the final versions of the 302s provided to Skilling. The government refused to provide draft versions of the Fastow 302s, claiming that the draft 302s had been destroyed. The government ultimately disclosed all of the interview notes to the defendant, in compliance with an order to do so from the Fifth Circuit Court of Appeals.

Skilling argued on appeal from his judgment of conviction that the destruction of the draft 302s violated *Brady*. The Fifth Circuit Court of Appeals rejected Skilling's argument, holding that "the draft 302s are merely an intermediary step between what Fastow said—recorded in the raw notes—and what the government reported Fastow as saying—recorded in the 302s," and held that "any destruction of the draft 302s is immaterial for purposes of Brady." 554 F.3d at 577.

§ 3:13   Expert witnesses—generally

Under the California law of reciprocal discovery in criminal cases, the defense must disclose before trial the witnesses it intends to call, including expert witnesses, as well as reports of experts, including the results of mental health examinations. Penal Code section 1054.3, subsection (a)(1). *Sharp v. Superior Court* (2012) 54 Cal. 4th 168, 141 Cal. Rptr. 3d 486, 277 P.3d 174.

The provision in the Criminal Discovery Statute that requires disclosure by the prosecution regarding its expert witnesses has generated substantial appellate discussion.

§ 3:13.1   Statements and reports

In order to afford the prosecution a fair opportunity to rebut mental-state evidence proffered by the defense, California's criminal-case reciprocal discovery statute, Penal Code section 1054.3, specifically provides that when the defendant places in issue his or her mental state at any phase of the criminal action, the prosecution may seek and obtain a court order that the defendant submit to examination by a prosecution-retained mental health expert. § 1054.3, subsection (b)(1). *Maldonado v. Superior Court* (2012) 53 Cal. 4th 1112, 140 Cal. Rptr. 3d 113, 274 P.3d 1110.

§ 3:13.2   Expert's resource materials

For a discussion of the pretrial disclosure of a defense expert's resource materials, see Section 4:12.9 of this supplement.

§ 3:13.4   Expert witness and intelligence databanks

The Omnibus Crime Control and Safe Streets Act of 1968 enacted by the United States Congress authorized the creation of, and provided funding for, criminal intelligence databases created by state and local law enforcement agencies. The intelligence databases created pursuant to this authority are controlled by guidelines set forth in 28 Code of Federal Regulations Part 23 that regulate the submission, entry, and security of criminal intelligence information, the inquiries to obtain and the dissemination of that information, and the review and purging of criminal intelligence information. These regulations have two governing principles: (1) Limited Use—identifying information may not be used in and of itself to establish an independent basis for a criminal predicate; and (2) Restricted Disclosure—information from these databases is disclosed only on a need-to-know basis.

One of the criminal intelligence databases established pursuant to this federal statute is CALGANGS, a statewide computerized database managed by the Sheriff of Los Angeles County that was established around 1990. CALGANGS contains information on criminal gangs and their members that operate in California. The database contains gang cards, computer data, and police reports on identified gang members, and is designed for the use of law enforcement gang experts or gang detectives. Information is added to the CALGANGS database only after it is investigated and verified. The database can be accessed only by law enforcement officers who have special training by gang unit members.

It is common when a prosecution is conducted against a defendant who is suspected of gang-related activities, or identified as a gang member, or charged with the commission of gang-related crimes, that the defense requests the court to order the prosecution to disclose information from CALGANGS or other criminal intelligence databases about the defendant, the charged crimes, and the gang of which the defendant is allegedly a member or an associate. The law enforcement agencies which have access to this criminal intelligence information invariably make claims of privilege regarding that information pursuant to the Official Information Privilege of Evidence Code section 1040. The subject of the discovery of evidence about which a claim of privilege is made is discussed in Chapter 8 of the text.

As long as a criminal intelligence database does not contain material exculpatory evidence regarding the defendant, there is no constitutional or statutory authority that requires a criminal defendant be provided pretrial discovery of information and evidence contained in such a database, even if a prosecution witness has read, considered, or relied upon that information or evidence in forming opinions which the prosecution expert witness has reached.

Several provisions of the California Evidence Code can impact whether a criminal defendant can gain access to information contained in a criminal intelligence database. The first of these provisions is Evidence Code section 721. If a prosecution witness testifies that he or she has referred to, considered, or relied upon any information or evidence contained in the intelligence database, a different result occurs.

Evidence Code section 721, subdivision (a), provides that an expert witness "may be cross-examined to the same extent as any other witness and, in addition, may be fully cross-examined as to . . . (3) the matter upon which his or her opinion is based and the reasons for his or her opinion." Evidence Code section 721, subdivision (b), provides that if an expert witness testifies in the form of an opinion, he or she may be cross-examined regarding the content or tenor of any scientific, technical, or professional text, treatise, journal, or similar publication if the witness "referred to, considered, or relied upon such publication in arriving at or forming his or her opinion."

A series of opinions of the California Supreme Court have applied the principle that a cross-examining party has the right to see any matter which the opposing party's expert witness has considered, read, or relied upon in forming his or her opinion. This is a rule of cross-examination, not a rule of discovery. Once the prosecution witness has offered opinion testimony on direct examination, the defendant's attorney is entitled to ask the expert to identify the materials or information the expert has read, considered, or relied upon. Any such materials or information identified by the prosecution expert witness would then be subject to a discovery order.

In *People v. Combs* (2004) 34 Cal.4th 821, 862, 22 Cal.Rptr.3d 61, 101 P.3d 1007, the Court observed that the defendant's attorney had disclosed the report of a non-testifying defense expert that had been considered by a testifying defense expert, "because he knew that the prosecutor was entitled to cross-examine Dr. Crinella about its contents. [citing Evidence Code section 721]."

In *People v. Ledesma* (2006) 39 Cal.4th 641, 695, 47 Cal.Rptr.3d 326, 140 P.3d 657, the Court held that the prosecution could question testifying defense experts regarding the report of a non-testifying defense expert which was otherwise privileged in the criminal case, because the defense experts had considered the non-testifying expert's report.

In *People v. Coleman* (1989) 48 Cal.3d 112, 151–152, 255 Cal.Rptr. 813, 768 P.2d 32, the Court held that an expert who relies upon the report of another expert in forming an opinion regarding the defendant may be cross-examined by the prosecutor on the contents of that report.

In *People v. Caro* (1988) 46 Cal.3d 1035, 1060, 251 Cal.Rptr. 757, 761 P.2d 680, the Court determined that "[i]f Dr. Benson [the defense expert] had testified and had asserted that his opinion was based in no part on statements by defendant about the events surrounding the crimes, the prosecution might have been foreclosed from cross-examining him about such statements."

In *People v. Price* (1991) 1 Cal.4th 324, 420–421, 3 Cal.Rptr.2d 106, 821 P.2d 610, superceded by statute on other grounds, *People v. Hinks* (1997) 58 Cal.App.4th 1157, 1161, 68 Cal.Rptr.2d 440, the Court held that a defendant is entitled to cross-examine a prosecution expert witness regarding the witness's source and basis of his or her opinions.

In *People v. Reyes* (1974) 12 Cal.3d 486, 503–504, 116 Cal.Rptr. 217, 526 P.2d 225, the Court held that a defendant was not entitled to cross-examine a prosecution expert about a 20-year-old psychiatric report regarding the victim on which the prosecution expert did not base his opinion regarding the defendant.

The second Evidence Code provision that can impact whether a criminal defendant can gain access to information contained in a criminal intelligence database is Evidence Code section 771. Evidence Code section 771, subdivision (a), provides that "if a witness, either while testifying or prior thereto, uses a writing to refresh his memory with respect to any matter about which he testifies, such writing must be produced at the hearing at the request of an adverse party and, unless the writing is so produced, the testimony of the witness concerning such matter shall be stricken." Section 771, subdivision (b), provides that "[i]f the writing is produced at the hearing, the adverse party may, if he chooses, inspect the writing, cross-examine the witness concerning it, and introduce in evidence such portion of it as may be pertinent to the testimony of the witness."

In *People v. Smith* (2007) 40 Cal.4th 483, 54 Cal.Rptr.3d 245, 150 P.3d 1224, a defense expert witness testified regarding tests he had administered to the defendant to refresh his recollection before the defendant testified at the hearing. The expert also admitted that he had relied upon certain aspects of the testing to formulate his opinions about the defendant's anxiety condition.

The prosecution moved for disclosure of the expert's notes, tests, and test results. The trial court ordered disclosure. The defendant was convicted of two counts of first degree murder and sentenced to death. On his automatic appeal, the defendant argued that the trial court erred in requiring disclosure of the expert's notes, test data, and test materials. The California Supreme Court rejected the defendant's argument.

The Court held that by virtue of Evidence Code section 771, subdivisions (a) and (b), when a witness uses a writing to refresh his or her memory, the writing must be produced at the hearing if the adverse party requests an opportunity to examine it. The adverse party may cross-examine the witness about the writing and may introduce in evidence any portion of the writing that is pertinent to the testimony of the witness.

The Court further held that by virtue of Evidence Code section 721, subdivision (a), the adverse party is entitled to fully cross-examine a witness about the matter on which the witness's opinion is based and the reasons for that opinion. "Such cross-examination properly includes documents and records examined by an expert witness in preparing his or her testimony." *People v. Smith*, 40 Cal.4th at 509.

Thus, if a witness has used a writing or document to refresh his or her recollection or memory in preparing to testify, the opposition party is entitled to in-trial production of that writing or document.

In *People v. Goff* (1981) 127 Cal.App.3d 1039, 1045, 179 Cal.Rptr. 190, the Court of Appeal held that the defendant was entitled under Evidence Code section 771 to examine the original state hospital records which the witness and other hospital staff members had prepared several months prior to trial, even though the witness claimed that he only used the summary to refresh his recollection. The Court stated: "To the extent Dr. Bitter's personal recollection was refreshed by the summary, it was really what he recalled from his April 1980 examination of the records. This, therefore, was a use of a writing *prior to trial* by the witness and the plain import of Evidence Code section 771 is that under such circumstances it is mandatory to produce the writing or strike the testimony." 127 Cal.App.3d at 1045. [italics in original]

If a prosecution gang expert has read, considered, or relied upon CALGANGS intelligence information in forming an opinion, or if the expert has used that information to refresh his or her recollection in preparing to testify, the defendant is entitled under these provisions of the Evidence Code to disclosure of that information.

§ 3:14 Investigatory notes—historical development

Litigation over the question whether and to what extent the prosecution must disclose investigatory notes made by prosecution trial witnesses has spawned a long history of appellate opinions in California state courts.

§ 3:14.2 Under Criminal Discovery Statute

In *People v. Verdugo* (2010) 50 Cal.4th 263, 281, 113 Cal.Rptr.3d 803, 236 P.3d 1035, the California Supreme Court rejected the defendant's argument that the prosecution engaged in prejudicial misconduct in violation of Penal Code section 1054.1 by failing to disclose notes made by the prosecutor during his pretrial talk with a prosecution witness. In concluding that the prosecutor had violated Section 1054.1 by failing to disclose to the defendant the notes of that interview, but that the violation did not prejudice the defendant, the Court cited with approval the holding of the Court of Appeal in *Thompson v. Superior Court* (1997) 53 Cal.App.4th 480, 61 Cal.Rptr.2d 785, that written notes of an interview with an intended trial witness are discoverable as "witness statements" within the meaning of Penal Code sections 1054.1(f), 1054.3(a), and 1054.7.

§ 3:14.3 Bases for disclosure

Although investigatory notes are not mentioned by name in the Criminal Discovery Statute, it is clear that such notes are discoverable under that statute.

§ 3:14.3.3 Investigatory notes as statement of witness under Criminal Discovery Statute

In *People v. Verdugo* (2010) 50 Cal.4th 263, 281, 113 Cal.Rptr.3d 803, 236 P.3d 1035, the California Supreme Court rejected the defendant's argument that the prosecution engaged in prejudicial misconduct in violation of Penal Code section 1054.1 by failing to disclose notes made by the prosecutor during his pretrial talk with a prosecution witness. In concluding that the prosecutor had violated Section 1054.1 by failing to disclose to the defendant the notes of that interview, but that the violation did not prejudice the defendant, the Court cited with approval the holding of the Court of Appeal in *Thompson v. Superior Court* (1997) 53 Cal.App.4th 480, 61 Cal.Rptr.2d 785, that written notes of an interview with an intended trial witness are discoverable as "witness statements" within the meaning of Penal Code sections 1054.1(f), 1054.3(a), and 1054.7.

The Supreme Court also held that the prosecutor's in-trial one week delay in providing the prosecutor's notes of an interview of another prosecution witness was "a violation of the reciprocal-discovery statute, under which the prosecutor was required to immediately disclose his notes regarding [the witness's] statement." 50 Cal.4th at 284.

§ 3:14.3.5   Investigatory notes considered or relied upon by witness in testimony

When a prosecution witness relies upon the witness's notes or claims that those notes support the witness's testimony, the defendant is entitled to examine those notes. *United States v. Wright* (2007, CA10 KS) 506 F.3d 1293, 1299–1300.

§ 3:15   Exculpatory evidence—generally

A very strong judicial focus on the prosecutor's disclosure duties under the *Brady* rule has tended to overshadow the provision of Penal Code section 1054.1 that requires the prosecution to disclose exculpatory evidence to the defendant. There is reason to believe that this lack of emphasis on the statutory command that the prosecution disclose exculpatory evidence is in the process of changing.

§ 3:15.1   Exculpatory evidence defined—distinguished from impeachment evidence

Although we continue to believe that the term "exculpatory evidence" as used in subdivision (e) of Penal Code section 1054.1 is not a term of art and does include impeachment evidence, our view expressed in the text that the phrase "exculpatory evidence" is a shorthand way of describing *Brady* evidence has not been confirmed by the California Supreme Court.

In *Barnett v. Superior Court* (2010) 50 Cal.4th 890, 901, 114 Cal.Rptr.3d 576, 237 P.3d 980, the California Supreme Court stated that " Penal Code section 1054.1, subdivision (e), requires the prosecution to disclose '[a]ny exculpatory evidence,' not just material exculpatory evidence." While a defendant who claims that the prosecution violated this statutory duty in support of a challenge to a conviction must show the materiality of the exculpatory evidence, the defendant need not establish that exculpatory evidence is material to be entitled to receive that evidence. 50 Cal.4th at 901. Penal Code section 1054.1 "illustrates the difference between being entitled to relief for a *Brady* violation and being entitled merely to receive the evidence. If petitioner can show he has a reasonable basis for believing a specific item of exculpatory evidence exists, he is entitled to receive that evidence without additionally having to show its materiality." 50 Cal.4th at 901.

In *United States v. Smith* (2008, CA10 KS) 534 F.3d 1211, the Tenth Circuit, in considering whether the suppression of favorable evidence entitled a defendant, who had been convicted of 17 charges related to a drug conspiracy, to a new trial, the Court of Appeals, citing *United States v. Bagley* (1985) 473 U.S. 667, 676, 105 S.Ct. 3375, 87 L.Ed.2d 481, stated: "Impeachment evidence is exculpatory for *Brady* purposes." 534 F.3d at 1222.

And in *Holland v. City of Chicago* (2011, CA7 IL) 643 F.3d 248, 255, the

Seventh Circuit Court of Appeals stated: "It is well established that *Brady* requires that material exculpatory evidence, unavailable to the defense but known to the prosecution, must be disclosed. The duty to disclose includes exculpatory evidence *in the form of impeachment evidence*." [italics added].

§ 3:15.4 Exculpatory investigatory notes

Investigatory notes that contain material exculpatory evidence are subject to disclosure even when the notes have formed the basis of a final report that the prosecution has disclosed to the defendant. "[T]he 'possible importance of the rough notes' for the purpose of providing leads or of impeaching a witness for discrepancies between the notes and the witness' testimony 'is not diminished in cases where' the notes form the basis of a final report that the prosecution turns over to the defense." *United States v. Andrews* (2008, CA DC) 532 F.3d 900, 906.

Investigatory notes taken from statements made by the attorney for a potential government witness in a witness proffer session are subject to disclosure when those notes contain material exculpatory evidence.

In *United States v. Triumph Capital Group, Inc.* (2008, CA2 CT) 544 F.3d 149, the attorney for a suspect in a racketeering case charging a variety of federal offenses approached the investigating officer on behalf of the suspect. The attorney provided the officer with the client's account of his criminal activity in an effort to convince the government to offer the client a cooperation agreement. The proffer implicated some of the suspects and was exculpatory of one of the suspects, Charles Spadoni. The statements of the witness contained in the proffer were directly relevant to the intent element of the consulting contract bribe charges.

The proffer was memorialized in notes of the meeting taken by one of the government investigators. The proffered statement of the witness conflicted with later statements made by that witness and the witness's trial testimony. The proffer notes were not disclosed to the defendants, who were convicted after a trial at which the witness whose attorney had provided the proffer testified. The Second Circuit Court of Appeals reversed the conviction of the defendant Spadoni, concluding that the suppression of the proffer notes "deprived Spadoni of exculpatory evidence going to the core of [the government's] case against him," and that Spadoni "could have used the proffer notes . . . also to impeach [the witness's] credibility." 544 F.3d at 162.

§ 3:15.6 Exculpatory evidence not included in investigatory notes

An investigating officer is not bound by a duty to make investigatory notes. "We reject Rodriguez's contention that *Brady* or the Confrontation Clause requires the Government to take notes during witness interviews . . . [*Brady* and *Giglio*] have not been generally construed to require the Government to make written notes for the defendant's benefit. This is in part because the Government's representative may have no way of knowing, upon hearing a witness's statement, that the statement is inconsistent with what the witness will say at a later time . . . *Brady, Giglio*, and the Confrontation Clause have not been construed to impose this obligation, and we decline to extend them in this manner." *United States v. Rodriguez* (2007, CA2 NY) 496 F.3d 221, 224–225.

However, an investigating officer does not avoid the duty to disclose material exculpatory evidence by failing to reduce oral information to writing. "When the Government is in possession of material information that impeaches its witness or exculpates the defendant, it does not avoid the obligation under *Brady/Giglio* to disclose the information by not writing it down." 496 F.3d at 222. *Accord, United States v. Duval* (2007, CA1 MA) 496 F.3d 64, 73.

PART II.   LIMITATIONS ON DISCLOSURE

§ 3:19   Items not possessed by prosecution—duty to search for information

It is a common occurrence that the prosecuting attorney does not initially have in his or her possession all of the reports and other documents generated in the course of a criminal investigation. Whether and where the prosecutor is required to search for these missing documents has been a subject of considerable litigation and judicial opinion.

§ 3:19.4   Constructive knowledge of prosecution

§ 3:19.4.1   Constructive knowledge of prosecution—under Criminal Discovery Statute generally

Penal Code section 1054.1 provides that the "prosecuting attorney shall disclose all of the information and materials listed in that section that are "in the possession of the prosecuting attorney or if the prosecuting attorney knows it to be in the possession of the investigating agencies. . . ." The literal language of Section 1054.1 appears to limit the prosecution's disclosure duties under the Criminal Discovery Statute to those discoverable items actually possessed by the prosecutor and those discoverable items that the prosecuting attorney knows are possessed by the investigating agency. Thus, a literal reading of Section 1054.1 means that the prosecuting attorney is not required to disclose discoverable items possessed by the investigating agency about which the prosecuting attorney does not know.

Some prosecutors believe that this literal construction of Section 1054.1 means that the Criminal Discovery Statute does not impute constructive knowledge or constructive possession of discoverable items to the prosecuting attorney. Because the United States Constitution does not require disclosure of prosecution evidence that would tend to convict the defendant (inculpatory evidence), *People v. Burgener* (2003) 29 Cal.4th 833, 875–876, 129 Cal.Rptr.2d 747, 62 P.3d 1; *People v. Jenkins* (2000) 22 Cal.4th 900,

951, 95 Cal.Rptr.2d 377, 997 P.2d 1044, a construction of the Discovery Statute that does not impute constructive knowledge or possession to the prosecution of inculpatory evidence possessed by or known to only the investigating agency would be constitutional.

However, as explained in the following sections of this supplement, we question whether the Criminal Discovery Statute can or should be construed to exclude a constructive knowledge or possession component from the prosecution's disclosure duties under that statute.

§ 3:19.4.2   Constructive knowledge of prosecution under Criminal Discovery Statute—importance of the issue

Resolution of the question whether the prosecution is chargeable under the Criminal Discovery Statute with constructive possession and constructive knowledge of discoverable evidence of which the prosecution does not have actual possession and actual knowledge is important in two respects.

First, a constructive knowledge or possession component would affect the prosecutor's ability to use inculpatory evidence at trial that is possessed by the investigating agency where the prosecutor does not learn of that evidence and disclose it to the defendant until after 30 days prior to trial or even during trial.

Second, a constructive knowledge or possession component would affect the defendant's right to use the statutory enforcement procedures of the Criminal Discovery Statute regarding material exculpatory evidence possessed by the investigating agency.

A constructive knowledge or possession component impacts the prosecutor's ability to use inculpatory evidence at trial that is possessed by the investigating agency, but the prosecutor does not learn of that evidence and disclose it to the defendant until within 30 days prior to trial or even during trial.

It is not uncommon for prosecutors to learn within 30 days of trial that the investigating agency has collected inculpatory evidence (witness statements, physical evidence, etc.) that the prosecution could put to good use in trial. The most common reason that the prosecuting attorney had not known about the evidence is that the investigating agency failed to forward that evidence or investigative report to the prosecutor's office. When the prosecuting attorney learns of the evidence and notifies the defendant of the prosecution's intention to use that evidence, the defense invariably claims that the prosecution has committed a discovery violation and requests sanctions for the violation.

If there is no prosecution team under the Criminal Discovery Statute, the prosecutor is not charged with constructive possession and constructive knowledge of inculpatory evidence which is held by the investigating agency but is actually unknown to the prosecutor. The prosecutor could then claim that he or she had no duty to search for that evidence in the investigating agency, and the late discovery of the evidence does not constitute a statutory discovery violation.

However, if the Discovery Statute has a prosecution team component, the prosecutor is charged with constructive possession and constructive knowledge of inculpatory evidence which is held by the investigating agency, even if the prosecutor has no actual knowledge of that evidence. The failure to conduct an earlier search for the evidence, with its attendant late disclosure of the evidence to the defense, could constitute a statutory discovery violation.

The second reason why the question of a statutory prosecution team is important is this: Even though the *Brady* rule entitles the defendant to disclosure of material exculpatory evidence, and the constitutional right that *Brady* states is self-executing, *Izazaga v. Superior Court* (1991) 54 Cal.3d 356, 382, 285 Cal.Rptr. 231, 815 P.2d 304, the Discovery Statute contains enforcement mechanisms that can be helpful to the defendant in enforcing his or her right to disclosure of material exculpatory evidence.

The Discovery Statute entitles the defendant to statutory disclosure of exculpatory evidence within 15 calendar days of the making of an informal request therefor, Penal Code section 1054.5, subdivision (b), and no later than 30 days prior to trial. Penal Code section 1054.7. The defendant's constitutional right to disclosure of material exculpatory evidence under the *Brady* rule is satisfied by disclosure in time for the defendant to make effective use of the evidence at trial. The courts frequently hold that disclosures of such evidence made on the eve of trial satisfy that requirement. See discussion in Section 1:84.1 of the text and this supplement.

Moreover, it is arguable, even though we disagree, that the prosecutor's statutory duty under Section 1054.1 to disclose "any exculpatory evidence" does not have a materiality component, thus entitling the defendant to statutory disclosure of exculpatory evidence that is not material. See the discussion in Section 3:15.2 of the text on whether subdivision (e) of Section 1054.1 contains a materiality element.

If the courts were to hold that the defendant is entitled under the Discovery Statute to disclosure of all exculpatory evidence, material and immaterial, the existence of a statutory prosecution team would entitle the defendant to immaterial exculpatory evidence held by, and known only to, the investigating agency, and the prosecution's failure to disclose could constitute a discovery violation.

For these reasons the question whether there is a prosecution team in the Criminal Discovery Statute has real significance.

§ 3:19.4.3 Constructive knowledge of prosecution under Criminal Discovery Statute—operative language of the Discovery Statute

There are three factors that cause us concern in limiting the prosecution's statutory disclosure duties to evidence and information of which the prosecuting attorney has actual possession and actual knowledge of possession by the investigating agency.

The first factor that causes concern over limiting the prosecution's statutory disclosure duties to evidence and information of which the prosecuting attorney has actual possession and actual knowledge of possession by the investigating agency, is that the language of Section 1054.1 does not read that the prosecutor must disclose evidence possessed by the investigating agency "ONLY if the prosecuting attorney knows it to be in the possession of the investigating agencies." To read Section 1054.1 to require prosecution disclosure of discoverable evidence and information only when the prosecuting attorney has actual possession or actual knowledge of possession by the investigating agency of that evidence and information requires the insertion of the word "only" into the statutory language. The inserted word was not part of the statutory language approved by the electorate.

§ 3:19.4.4 Constructive knowledge of prosecution under Criminal Discovery Statute—operative language of the Discovery Statute

The second factor that causes concern in limiting the prosecution's statutory disclosure duties to evidence and information of which the prosecuting attorney has actual possession and actual knowledge of the investigating agency's possession is that reading the Discovery Statute as a whole shows that the prosecution's disclosure duties under the statute apply to the prosecution team as a whole, not simply to the prosecuting attorney.

The Criminal Discovery Statute must be read as a whole. *In re Littlefield* (1993) 5 Cal.4th 122, 133, 19 Cal.Rptr.2d 248, 851 P.2d 42 ["[S]ection 1054.3 is part of a general statutory discovery scheme . . . and therefore must be considered in the context of, and with reference to, the entire scheme."].

Penal Code section 1054.7, subdivision (a), provides that "[i]f the material and information becomes known to, or comes into the possession of, a **party** within 30 days of trial, disclosure shall be made immediately." [emphasis added] Section 1054.7 does not limit the duty to provide immediate disclosure to the "prosecuting attorney," but applies the duty to the **party**. The **party plaintiff** in a criminal prosecution is the People of the State of California. The **party plaintiff**, People of the State of California, includes the agency which investigated the underlying charges against the defendant. *People v. Superior Court (Barrett)* (2000) 80 Cal.App.4th 1305, 1313, 96

Cal.Rptr.2d 264 ["[I]nvestigatory agencies that work on the case are considered part of the prosecution team and a defendant must use the discovery procedures set forth in chapter 10 to obtain discovery from such agencies. (§ 1054.5, subd. (a).)]"

§ 3:19.4.5   Constructive knowledge of prosecution under Criminal Discovery Statute—judicial construction of the Discovery Statute

The third factor that causes concern over limiting the prosecution's statutory disclosure duties to evidence and information of which the prosecuting attorney has actual possession and actual knowledge is that several Court of Appeal opinions have discussed the prosecution team as if it were a feature of the Criminal Discovery Statute. *See People v. Superior Court (Barrett)* (2000) 80 Cal.App.4th 1305, 1313, 96 Cal.Rptr.2d 264 ["[I]nvestigatory agencies that work on the case are considered part of the prosecution team and a defendant must use the discovery procedures set forth in chapter 10 to obtain discovery from such agencies. (§ 1054.5, subd. (a).)"]; *County of Placer v. Superior Court* (2005) 130 Cal.App.4th 807, 814, 30 Cal.Rptr.3d 617 ["[T]he probation department is certainly not a part of a 'prosecution team' [citation omitted] It is a third party to whom the Penal Code discovery provisions do not apply . . . ."].

The California Supreme Court has referred to the "prosecution team" as including an agency that has a connection to the investigation of the criminal charge. *See In re Steele* (2004) 32 Cal.4th 682, 697, 10 Cal.Rptr.3d 536, 85 P.3d 444 [" 'Thus, information possessed by an agency that has no connection to the investigation or prosecution of the criminal charge against the defendant is not possessed by the prosecution team, and the prosecutor does not have the duty to search for or to disclose such material.' [citation omitted]"] The California Supreme Court reaffirmed its analysis in *Steele* in *Barnett v. Superior Court* (2010) 50 Cal.4th 890, 902, 114 Cal.Rptr.3d 576, 237 P.3d 980.

Perhaps the most explicit opinion of a California appellate court holding that there is a prosecution team under the Criminal Discovery Statute is *People v. Little* (1997) 59 Cal.App.4th 426, 68 Cal.Rptr.2d 907. In *Little* a defendant charged with evading an officer and resisting, delaying, or obstructing a peace officer made an informal request for "standard reciprocal discovery." After his conviction the trial court granted a new trial, because the prosecution had failed to disclose a felony conviction of one of its witnesses as required by *Brady v. Maryland* and Penal Code section 1054.1. The People appealed the granting of the new-trial motion, arguing that since the prosecution did not "possess" the felony conviction, the prosecution had not violated its disclosure duties under the Criminal Discovery Statute.

The Court of Appeal rejected the People's argument and affirmed the trial court's order granting the defendant a new trial. The Court held that "an informal request for standard reciprocal discovery is sufficient to create a prosecution duty to disclose the felony convictions of all material prosecution witnesses if the record of conviction is 'reasonably accessible' to the prosecutor." 59 Cal.App.4th at 428. In response to the People's argument that the People "had no duty to disclose Wright's felony conviction because they did not know about the conviction," the Court of Appeal stated that "even if the prosecution did not have *actual* knowledge of the witness's prior conviction . . . section 1054.1 creates a prosecution duty to inquire and disclose." 59 Cal.App.4th at 430.

The Court of Appeal then explained its reasoning that led it to its conclusion. Relying upon the holding of the Supreme Court in *In re Littlefield* (1993) 5 Cal.4th 122, 135, 19 Cal.Rptr.2d 248, 851 P.2d 42, the Court of Appeal reasoned:

> "Section 1054.1 requires disclosure of specified information 'if it is in the *possession* of the prosecuting attorney or if the *prosecuting* attorney knows it to be in the *possession* of the investigating agencies . . . .' (Italics added.) The People contend they had no actual knowledge of Wright's felony conviction; therefore, it was not in their possession. *Littlefield*, though, held that 'possession' includes information the prosecution possesses or controls, and encompasses information reasonably accessible to the prosecution. [citation omitted] Furthermore, 'materials discoverable by the defense include information in the possession of all agencies (to which the prosecution has access) that are part of the criminal justice system, and not solely information 'in the hands of the prosecutor.' (*Ibid.*)

> "The court held the likely purpose of including the words 'in the possession' in section 1054.1 'was simply to clarify and confirm that the prosecution has no *general duty* to seek out, obtain, and disclose all evidence that might be beneficial to the defense.' (*In re Littlefield*, *supra*, 5 Cal.4th at p. 135, original italics.)." 59 Cal.App.4th at 431. [italics in original]

The Court of Appeal in *Little* and the Supreme Court in *In re Littlefield* did not employ the term "prosecution team." The term used by the *Little* Court of Appeal and the Supreme Court in *In re Littlefield* is "agencies that are part of the criminal justice system." But, although the terms used in *Little* and *In re Littlefield* are different than the more common term "prosecution team," the *Little* and *In re Littlefield* analysis is precisely the same analysis used by courts that call the group of prosecutors and investigators the "prosecution team." The conclusion that the *Little* and *In re Littlefield* courts reached was that the prosecuting attorney **possesses** discoverable information and evidence within the meaning of Penal Code section 1054.1 when the prosecuting attorney **controls** or **has reasonable access** to that evidence. This standard is a classic definition of constructive possession and constructive knowledge.

Several other Court of Appeal opinions have reached the same conclusion that Section 1054.1 contains a constructive possession and constructive knowledge component, seemingly untroubled by the language that appears to require that the prosecuting attorney must know that the evidence is possessed by the investigating agency.

In *Teal v. Superior Court* (2004) 117 Cal.App.4th 488, 491, 11 Cal.Rptr.3d 784, the Court stated: "The prosecution is required to disclose a matter only if it is 'in the possession of the prosecuting attorney' or 'the prosecuting attorney knows it to be in the possession of the investigating agencies.' (§ 1054.1.) Thus, materials discoverable by the defense include information in the possession of law enforcement agencies that investigated or prepared the case against the defendant."

In *People v. Robinson* (1995) 31 Cal.App.4th 494, 498–499, 37 Cal.Rptr.2d 183, the Court stated that "[t]he prosecutor has a constitutional [citation omitted] and statutory (§ 1054.1, subd. (e)) duty to disclose to the defense any exculpatory evidence. . . . The scope of a prosecutor's disclosure duty includes not just exculpatory evidence in *his* possession but that possessed by investigative agencies to which he has reasonable access." [italics in original]

See also, Walters v. Superior Court (2000) 80 Cal.App.4th 1074, 1077, 95 Cal.Rptr.2d 880 ["The contents of a police evidence locker are the responsibility of the district attorney, not property in possession of some third party. This stringent and salutary rule is designed to protect defendants' rights. How can the prosecutor's obligation to protect the integrity of the evidence, the inculpatory on behalf of the People, the exculpatory on behalf of the defense, be reconciled with defense ex parte access to it? The short answer is, it cannot. The Santa Ana Police Department is not the detached third party the alternate defender imagines *for his present purpose* . . . ." [italics in original]]

The conclusion we reach from this analysis is that there is a prosecution team component of the Criminal Discovery Statute that is the same as or equivalent to the prosecution team component that is integral to the *Brady* rule. If we are correct in this conclusion, that component necessarily means that the prosecuting attorney has constructive possession and constructive knowledge of all of the evidence and information possessed by and known to the investigating agency.

§ 3:19.5   Information unknown to prosecutor and to investigating agency

Where neither the prosecuting attorney nor the investigating agency knows of potentially discoverable information that is known only by an officer of the investigating agency, the failure of the prosecution to disclose that information to the defendant does not constitute a violation of the Criminal Discovery Statute. *People v. Verdugo* (2010) 50 Cal.4th 263,

288–289, 113 Cal.Rptr.3d 803, 236 P.3d 1035.

§ 3:19.6 Administrative records of investigating or assisting agency

Prosecutors and defense attorneys have engaged in considerable litigation over the question whether trial courts have the authority to order the prosecution to disclose or produce administrative records of the investigating agency or of an agency assisting the prosecution, when these administrative records have an arguable connection to the criminal prosecution of the defendant. These records include maintenance and calibration logs and records of equipment used by the investigating or assisting agency, training manuals, policy manuals, pursuit policies, and jailhouse tape recordings.

Some trial courts have issued discovery orders requiring the prosecution to produce these records for examination by the defense. We question the authority of a trial court to issue such orders in light of the provisions of the Criminal Discovery Statute.

All court-ordered discovery "is governed exclusively by—and is barred except as provided by" the Criminal Discovery Statute. *In re Littlefield* (1993) 5 Cal.4th 122, 129, 19 Cal.Rptr.2d 248, 851 P.2d 42; *Verdin v. Superior Court* (2008) 43 Cal.4th 1096, 1102–1103, 77 Cal.Rptr.3d 287, 183 P.3d 1250. Thus, if neither the Criminal Discovery Statute nor another California statute expressly authorizes discovery in a criminal case, and if that discovery is not mandated by the United States Constitution, no trial court has the authority to order the prosecution to produce that discovery. Penal Code section 1054, subdivision (e); Penal Code section 1054.5, subdivision (a).

The California Supreme Court has repeatedly emphasized this limitation upon the power of trial courts to make discovery orders. In *People v. Tillis* (1998) 18 Cal.4th 284, 294, 75 Cal.Rptr.2d 447, 956 P.2d 409, the Supreme Court held that Section 1054, subdivision (e), precludes that court "from broadening the scope of discovery beyond that provided in the [Discovery Statute] or other express statutory provisions, or as mandated by the federal Constitution." The Court acknowledged in *Tillis* that "if none of those authorities requires disclosure of a particular item of evidence, we are not at liberty to create a rule imposing such a duty." 18 Cal.4th at 294.

The Court reiterated this principle in *Verdin v. Superior Court* (2008) 43 Cal.4th 1096, 1107–1108:

> "[T]he framers of [Proposition 115] did not authorize the judiciary generally to create appropriate rules governing discovery in criminal cases . . . we are not at liberty to create new rules, untethered to any statute or constitutional mandate. Instead, the framers of Proposition 115, by including the exclusivity provision of section 1054, subdivision (e), authorized *the Legislature* to create the applicable rules in the first instance. Only when interpreting a statute or where a rule of

discovery is 'mandated by the Constitution of the United State's . . . does this court have a role . . . nothing in the preamble to Proposition 115 authorizes or justifies the judicial creation of a rule that a criminal defendant who places his mental state in issue may be ordered by the court to grant the prosecution access for purposes of a mental examination by a prosecution expert." [italics in original]

If the California Supreme Court may not require discovery that is not authorized by the Discovery Statute or the express language of another statute, or that is not mandated by the federal Constitution, a trial judge may not do so.

No provision of the Criminal Discovery Statute requires the prosecution to disclose administrative records of the investigating agency or of any other agency assisting the prosecution. Nor is there any other California statute that expressly requires the prosecution to disclose such administrative records.

Only if administrative records constitute or contain material exculpatory evidence possessed by a member of the prosecution team is their disclosure constitutionally required. However, a trial court must have some evidence that administrative records constitute or contain material exculpatory evidence before the trial court may order their disclosure to the defendant. Guessing or speculating that administrative records might contain material exculpatory evidence does not suffice.

In order to justify a *Brady* disclosure order, the defendant must offer more than a plausible justification for disclosure of information he has described with some specificity. *Kennedy v. Superior Court* (2006) 145 Cal.App.4th 359, 371, 51 Cal.Rptr.3d 637. "[M]ere speculation that there might [be] something useful for impeachment purposes in . . . reports is not sufficient to demonstrate a *Brady* violation." *People v. Ashraf* (2007) 151 Cal.App.4th 1205, 1214, 60 Cal.Rptr.3d 624. "*Brady* . . . does not require the disclosure of information that is of mere speculative value." *People v. Gutierrez* (2003) 112 Cal.App.4th 1463, 1472, 6 Cal.Rptr.3d 138.

In *United States v. Olofson* (2009, CA7 WI) 563 F.3d 652, a defendant charged in federal court with illegal possession of a machine gun made a motion to compel the disclosure of four items of administrative records of the Bureau of Alcohol, Tobacco, Firearms and Explosives of the United States Department of the Treasury (commonly called "ATF"), the investigating agency in the case against Olofson. These four items were: (1) documentation of the procedures used by the ATF in testing the AR-15; (2) correspondence between the ATF and the manufacturer of the defendant's AR-15 concerning the use of M-16 parts in early models of the AR-15 rifle; (3) information about changes in the ATF's refusal to register AR-15 rifles with M-16 parts; and (4) documents pertaining to the ATF's refusal to register AR-15 rifles with M-16 parts. The district court denied the motion, concluding that the information the defendant wanted was not exculpatory.

The Seventh Circuit Court of Appeals upheld the district court, concluding that none of the requested items was relevant or germane to the charges against the defendant; none of these four items could have exonerated the defendant on the charges. Accordingly, the trial court properly refused to order disclosure of the four items of administrative records of the investigating agency.

Therefore, a trial court generally does not have the authority to issue a discovery order requiring the prosecution to disclose administrative records of the investigating agency or of an assisting agency.

§ 3:19.6.1   Administrative records of investigating or assisting agency—not possessed by prosecution team

Even if the trial court is presented with evidence that the administrative records of the investigating agency or an assisting agency constitute or contain material exculpatory evidence, a discovery order directed to the prosecution is almost certainly an unauthorized order. Administrative records of the investigating agency (at least to the extent that they are not directly connected to or a part of its investigative function) are third-party records that are not possessed by the "prosecution team."

To the extent that the investigating agency or an assisting agency performs administrative functions that are separate from its investigatory function, the agency is only a partial member of the prosecution team, and its administrative function is outside the scope of the prosecution team. Records relating to that administrative function are not possessed by the prosecution team, and the court lacks authority to order the prosecution to obtain and disclose those records.

In this respect the prosecution team, within the meaning and for purposes of the Criminal Discovery Statute, is identical to the prosecution team under the *Brady* rule for disclosure of material exculpatory evidence. In *People v. Zambrano* (2007) 41 Cal.4th 1082, 1133–1134, 63 Cal.Rptr.3d 297, 163 P.3d 4, the California Supreme Court observed that "the reciprocal discovery statute refers only to evidence possessed by the prosecutor's office and 'the investigating agencies.' (§ 1054.1.) There is no reason to assume the quoted statutory phrase assigns the prosecutor a broader duty to discover and disclose evidence in the hands of other agencies than do *Brady* and its progeny."

For a complete discussion of the concept of a partial membership in the prosecution team under the *Brady* rule, see Section 1:68 of the text and *People v. Superior Court (Barrett)* (2000) 80 Cal.App.4th 1305, 96 Cal.Rptr.2d 264 [administrative manuals and other written records generated by the Department of Corrections in its administration of the state prison system deemed to be third-party records not possessed by the prosecution team.].

This does not mean that the defendant is bereft of a means to compel the disclosure of administrative records of the investigating agency or an assisting agency. Administrative records that are not part and parcel of the agency's investigation records that have caused the agency to be a part of the prosecution team in a criminal case are in the nature of third-party records. The defendant may compel the production of those records utilizing third-party discovery mechanisms, such as a subpoena duces tecum. See Chapter 9 of the text and this supplement for a complete discussion of third-party discovery procedures.

However, if the prosecutor obtains copies of these administrative records, or takes actions to ensure that these records are preserved for possible use in the criminal prosecution, the records are no longer in the sole possession of the investigating agency, and the prosecution is not able to decline disclosure on the grounds that the records are possessed by a third party. *See People v. Jordan* (2003) 108 Cal.App.4th 349, 358, 133 Cal.Rptr.2d 434 ["The prosecution must disclose evidence that is actually or constructively in its possession or accessible to it."].

Practice Tip for Prosecution: Even though you might not be in physical or legal possession of administrative records of the investigating agency, you should consider obtaining relevant administrative records from an investigating or assisting agency, in order to make the decision for the prosecution team whether those records should be disclosed to the defendant.

A defendant denied administrative records on the grounds that the prosecution team does not possess them is likely to seek to obtain those records using third-party discovery tools, such as subpoenas duces tecum. If the defendant uses third-party discovery tools to obtain these administrative records, the fruits of those procedures will be limited to the defendant as the party issuing the subpoenas, and you will not know what those records contain until the defense determines to use them in trial against you.

If there is a legal basis to deny those records to the defendant, you as the prosecutor are far more likely to be in a position to make an effective argument against disclosure than will the city attorney or county counsel, whose office does not normally have as much at stake in the outcome of third-party discovery matters as you do as a party to the criminal action.

§ 3:19.6.2　Administrative records of investigating or assisting agency—training manuals and pursuit policies

It is not an unusual occurrence for the defendant to request that the prosecution disclose training manuals used by the investigating agency and written materials describing policies to be followed by officers in that agency. Prosecutors most commonly receive these discovery requests in cases where the defendant is charged with resisting arrest or battery upon a peace officer, and the defense is that the officers used excessive force against the defendant. Sometimes these discovery requests come in cases in which the defendant claims the police obtained an involuntary confession. In those cases the defendant requests training manuals to determine whether the manuals encourage (or discourage) conduct that the defendant claims bears on the voluntary nature of his or her statements.

Whether or not the prosecution is determined to be in possession of these records [see discussion in Section 3:19.6.1 of this supplement], the law enforcement agency whose manuals or policies are sought might interpose a claim of official information privilege. Official information, as defined in Evidence Code section 1040, is "information acquired in confidence by a public employee in the course of his or her duty and not open, or officially disclosed, to the public prior to the time the claim of privilege is made."

In *Suarez v. Office of Administrative Hearings* (2004) 123 Cal.App.4th 1191, 20 Cal.Rptr.3d 618, the Department of Real Estate (DRE) audited a real estate broker. Based on that audit the Department brought proceedings to revoke the broker's real estate license. The broker requested disclosure of the DRE Audit Manual and Enforcement Deputy Manual under which the audit had been conducted. The administrative law judge ordered most of the manual to be disclosed, and the DRE petitioned the superior court for writ of mandate/prohibition. The superior court reviewed the manuals *in camera* and concluded that the manuals were privileged, confidential, and not subject to discovery.

The broker appealed the grant of the writ. The Court of Appeal upheld the order of the superior court, finding that the information in the audit manuals constituted official information, and under the balancing test of Evidence Code section 1040, subdivision (b), should not have been ordered disclosed. 123 Cal.App.4th at 1195.

In *People v. Schmies* (1996) 44 Cal.App.4th 38, 51 Cal.Rptr.2d 185, a defendant was convicted of vehicular manslaughter with gross negligence and reckless driving causing great bodily injury following a high-speed vehicle chase in which a pursuing CHP patrol car struck another car and killed its driver. The defendant requested disclosure of the CHP pursuit policies, claiming that these policies would help him prove that the actions taken by the officer had been so inappropriate that they had become a superseding and sole proximate cause of the citizen's death by breaking the chain of proximate cause. The trial court denied the discovery request.

On appeal the Court of Appeal upheld the trial court's denial of discovery of the CHP pursuit policy, finding that whether the officers violated the CHP pursuit guidelines was immaterial to the question of the defendant's guilt. 44 Cal.App.4th at 55–56.

§ 3:19.6.3   Administrative records of investigating or assisting agency—tape recordings of jail telephone calls

Many custodial institutions, such as county jails, utilize monitoring systems that tape-record telephone calls made by inmates. This technology has provided investigatory benefits to the prosecution, because these recorded conversations can supply evidence of a defendant's guilt and can also be used to impeach the testimony of defense witnesses.

The existence of these tapes has discovery importance, raising at least five discovery questions: (1) if these tapes remain in the possession of the custodial institution, are they possessed by the prosecution team? (2) If the tapes are delivered to the prosecution, must they be disclosed without regard to their contents? (3) Must the tapes be disclosed even if the prosecution has not yet listened to them? (4) Must the tapes be disclosed even if they would be used only to impeach a potential defense witness? (5) Must the tapes be disclosed if they contain evidence favorable to the defendant?

The answer to the first question—If these tapes remain in the possession of the custodial institution, are they possessed by the prosecution team—is that if the tapes were made in the normal course of protecting the security of the custodial facility, and these tapes remain in the possession of the custodial institution, they are generally not possessed by the prosecution team.

In *People v. Zambrano* (2007) 41 Cal.4th 1082, 1133–1134, 63 Cal.Rptr.3d 297, 163 P.3d 4, the California Supreme Court held that a letter written to the jailor who held the defendant was not possessed by the prosecution team. Although the prosecutor's duty under *Brady* "extends to evidence 'known to the others acting on the government's behalf' [citation omitted] . . . the prosecution cannot reasonably be held responsible for evidence in the possession of *all* government agencies, including those not involved in the investigation or prosecution of the case . . . '[I]nformation possessed by an agency that has no connection to the investigation or prosecution of the criminal charge against the defendant is not possessed by the prosecution team, and the prosecutor does not have the duty to search for or to disclose such material.' [citation omitted]." 41 Cal.4th at 1133–1134. [italics in original]

In *In re Steele* (2004) 32 Cal.4th 682, 697, 10 Cal.Rptr.3d 536, 85 P.3d 444, the Supreme Court concluded: " 'Thus, information possessed by an agency that has no connection to the investigation or prosecution of the criminal charge against the defendant is not possessed by the prosecution team, and the prosecutor does not have the duty to search for or to disclose such material.' [citation omitted]"

An agency charged with the responsibility for keeping custody of the defendant does not thereby become part of the prosecution team for purposes of imputing possession of its jail tapes to the prosecution. Custodial institutions record telephone conversations of inmates for the purpose of preserving the security and orderly management of the facility. This tape recording is not normally done at the behest or request of the prosecution or for investigatory purposes. Even if the custodial officer (the sheriff) is also the investigating agency, the investigatory function of the sheriff does not convert the sheriff's administrative function of housing and keeping custody of the defendant into a function of the prosecution team. *People v. Superior Court (Barrett)* (2000) 80 Cal.App.4th 1305, 96 Cal.Rptr.2d 264 [Administrative prison records of Department of Corrections not possessed by prosecution team, even though Department of Corrections was investigating agency on Barrett's homicide investigation.].

However, if the prosecutor obtains a copy of the tape recording, the tape recording is no longer in the sole possession of the investigating agency, and the prosecution is not able to decline disclosure on the grounds that the tape recording is possessed by a third party. *See People v. Jordan* (2003) 108 Cal.App.4th 349, 358, 133 Cal.Rptr.2d 434 ["The prosecution must disclose evidence that is actually or constructively in its possession or accessible to it."].

Likewise, if recording of inmate calls is not standard administrative operating procedure, and the prosecution takes actions to request that the recordings be made, or if the prosecution requests the jail to preserve the recording for possible use in the criminal prosecution, the prosecution is not able to decline disclosure on the grounds that the tape recording is possessed by a third party. In this situation the custodial facility becomes an agency that is assisting in the investigation or prosecution of the defendant, and thereby becomes part of the prosecution team. *See People v. Kelley* (2002) 103 Cal.App.4th 853, 856, 127 Cal.Rptr.2d 203, and *People v. Loyd* (2002) 27 Cal.4th 997, 119 Cal.Rptr.2d 360, 45 P.3d 296. Once the prosecution requests the custodial facility to tape-record a defendant's telephone conversations or to retain tape-recorded conversations for possible use in a criminal investigation or prosecution, the making or retaining of such tapes is done on the prosecution's behalf. By "acting on the government's behalf" or "assisting the government's case," the custodial facility thereby becomes part of the prosecution team, and the prosecution has constructive custody of the jail's or prison's tape recordings.

The answer to the second question—If the tapes are delivered to the prosecution, must they be disclosed without regard to their contents—is not clear-cut. On the one hand, if the tapes contain statements by the defendant, their disclosure might be mandated by Penal Code section 1054.1, subdivision (b) [Statements of all defendants], without regard to the substance of the statements. On the other hand, even the defendant's statements might be nondiscoverable if those statements have no relevance to the crimes with which the defendant is charged. See the discussion regarding mandated disclosure of a defendant's statements in Section 3:6.1 of the text.

The answer to the third question—Must the tapes be disclosed even if the prosecution has not yet listened to them—is probably no, although there is no decisional authority on this question. Since the duty to disclose the tapes to a defendant arises out of the contents of the tapes and the prosecution's intended use of the tapes, it seems obvious that the duty to disclose them does not arise until the prosecution has listened to them and determined their contents.

The answer to the fourth question—Must the tapes be disclosed even if they would be used only to impeach a potential defense witness—is yes, once the defendant has disclosed his or her intention to call that defense witness and the prosecution has determined to use the tape to impeach the defense witness, or the prosecutor has determined to call a witness to testify to the taped telephone conversation.

However, if the prosecutor does not intend to use a rebuttal witness or to use the tape recording as real evidence in rebuttal, but intends only to question the defendant or a defense witness based on information available to the prosecutor from listening to the tape recording, the prosecutor's failure to disclose the tape recording does not violate the Criminal Discovery Statute. *People v. Tillis* (1998) 18 Cal.4th 284, 292–293, 75 Cal.Rptr.2d 447, 956 P.2d 409. *See also, Izazaga v. Superior Court* (1991) 54 Cal.3d 356, 367, 377, n.14, 285 Cal.Rtpr. 231, 815 P.2d 304 ["[T]he defense is not required to disclose any statements it obtains from prosecution witnesses that it may use to refute the prosecution's case during cross-examination."].

For a more complete discussion of the prosecution's duty to disclose its rebuttal witnesses or its impeachment evidence on defense witnesses, see Sections 3:7.4–3:7.4.4 of the text.

The answer to the fifth question—Must the tapes be disclosed if they contain evidence favorable to the defendant—might seem like an obvious answer, since the prosecution is constitutionally and statutorily obligated to disclose all material exculpatory evidence to the defendant. But the answer is not so obvious. If the defendant is a party to the telephone conversation which is recorded, the defendant already knows all exculpatory evidence that was conveyed or contained as part of that conversation. The prosecution is not constitutionally mandated to disclose to the defendant exculpatory evidence which the defendant already knows, because the defendant was a party to the conversation in which that exculpatory evidence was discussed or disclosed.

See the discussion in Section 1:77.2 of the text and this supplement concerning the prosecution's duty under *Brady* to disclose material exculpatory evidence already known to the defendant.

Practice Tip for Prosecution: Tape recordings of a defendant's telephone calls made from a custodial facility can provide a rich trove of evidence against the defendant. However, once those tape recordings come into the actual or constructive possession of the prosecution team, you must be careful to comply with all statutory and constitutional disclosure obligations attendant to those tapes. If you intend in any way to utilize the tape recordings to prove your case against the defendant or to impeach the defendant's testimony or the testimony of a defense witness, you must disclose those tape recordings in compliance with the time frames established by the Criminal Discovery Statute.

You must, therefore, listen to those tape recordings well in advance of trial so as to determine if they contain inculpatory or impeachment evidence that you can use in trial. Waiting until the last minute prior to trial to listen to the tapes puts you at serious risk of having the tapes excluded by the trial court for the violation of your disclosure obligations under the Criminal Discovery Statute.

Do not play games with tapes that contain self-serving declarations of innocence by the defendant or other statements that might seem exculpatory. Even though the *Brady* rule does not require disclosure of exculpatory evidence already known to the defendant, you should disclose such tapes in time for the defendant to make effective use of them at trial. By so doing, you will avoid defense charges of *Brady* violations and unnecessary discovery squabbles.

§ 3:19.6.4   Administrative records and *Brady* claims

Although administrative records of agencies in the prosecution team are not subject to mandated disclosure by the prosecution under the Criminal Discovery Statute, such records might be discoverable if they are materially favorable evidence to the defendant under the *Brady* rule.

In *United States v. Guzman-Padilla* (2009, CA9 CA) 573 F.3d 865, the defendants were charged with possession with intent to distribute more than 100 kilograms of marijuana following the stop of their vehicle after it had crossed the United States' border with Mexico. Agents of the United States Border Patrol used a controlled tire deflation device (CTDD) to stop the vehicle, rather than make an effort to effect a traffic stop of the vehicle. The defendants alleged that the stop of their vehicle was unlawful, arguing that the agents' use of the CTDD violated the Border Patrol's written policy on the use of CTDDs. The defendants moved for an order compelling the Border Patrol to produce the written Border Patrol policy on the use of CTDDs, claiming that this policy would show that the actions of the Border Patrol officers conflicted with the written policy. The defendants' motion for discovery was denied by the district court and their motion to suppress the evidence seized from their vehicle was denied.

The defendants pled guilty, but reserved the right to appeal the denial of their motion to suppress. In their appeal to the Ninth Circuit Court of Appeals, the defendants argued that the district court's denial of their motion to compel disclosure of the Border Patrol's written policy on the use of

CTDDs constituted a violation of due process under *Brady*. The Court of Appeals rejected the defendant's argument, concluding that the defendants failed to identify any basis for their suggestion that the actions of the Border Patrol officers were inconsistent with a written Border Patrol policy on the use of CTDDs. 573 F.3d at 890.

The defendants' motion for disclosure of the Border Patrol policy was denied only because the defendants' showing that the policy contained evidence materially favorable to them was based on speculation as to the contents of that policy, 573 F.3d at 890, and because even had the policy shown that the agent's actions violated the policy, the "government's violation of its own rules does not provide a basis for the suppression of evidence in a criminal action." 573 F.3d at 890.

Had the Border Patrol's written policy on the use of CTDDs contained evidence that was materially favorable to the defendants, the fact that the written policy constituted administrative records of the Border Patrol would not have been a basis for denial of the motion to disclose the policy.

§ 3:19.7   Information possessed by law enforcement agency not acting on government's behalf in the case

In the same way that a law enforcement agency that has not acted on the government's behalf in the case does not become a member of the prosecution team for purposes of the *Brady* rule, see Sections 1:70.5-1:70.5.5 in the text and in this supplement, a law enforcement agency that has not participated in the investigation or prosecution of the charges against the defendant has not acted on the government's behalf in the case for purposes of the Criminal Discovery Statute. Accordingly, that agency is not a member of the prosecution team for purposes of the Criminal Discovery Statute. *Barnett v. Superior Court* (2010) 50 Cal.4th 890, 902, 114 Cal.Rptr.3d 576, 237 P.3d 980; *In re Steele* (2004) 32 Cal.4th 682, 696, 10 Cal.Rptr.3d 536, 85 P.3d 444.

And since "law enforcement authorities" to which Section 1054.9 refers are similar to the "investigating agencies" to which Section 1054.1 refers, a law enforcement agency which has not participated in the investigation or prosecution of the criminal charges against the defendant is not a member of the prosecution team for purposes of the posttrial discovery statute of Penal Code section 1054.9. *Barnett v. Superior Court, supra*, 50 Cal.4th at 902.

Thus, for all three purposes—the *Brady* rule, the Criminal Discovery Statute, and the posttrial discovery statute—a noninvestigating law enforcement agency is not a member of the prosecution team, and information possessed by that agency is not constructively attributed to the prosecution.

§ 3:19.8   Information possessed by out-of-state law enforcement agency

It is not uncommon for a California law enforcement agency or a California prosecutor's office to request assistance from a law enforcement agency in another state. The question has arisen whether an out-of-state law enforcement agency that provides such assistance in a specific case thereby becomes a member of the California prosecution team in that case.

In *Barnett v. Superior Court* (2010) 50 Cal.4th 890, 114 Cal.Rptr.3d 576, 237 P.3d 980, the defendant was prosecuted and convicted of capital murder and other crimes occurring in California. In preparing the case against the defendant, the prosecuting attorney obtained copies of investigative reports from six out-of-state law enforcement agencies in five other states and in Canada. The prosecution used these reports to obtain witnesses who were used to provide aggravating evidence against the defendant at the penalty phase of the trial.

Following imposition of a sentence of death, the defendant filed a postjudgment discovery motion pursuant to Penal Code section 1054.9. The superior court granted many of the defendant's discovery requests, but denied 24 of the defendant's discovery requests. The defendant petitioned the Court of Appeal for writ of mandate challenging the denials. The Court of Appeal issued a published opinion ordering the prosecution to disclose to the defendant original notes written by 22 out-of-state law enforcement officers, who worked for six different out-of-state law enforcement agencies, and who had been involved in investigating the prior crimes that the prosecution used as aggravating evidence at the penalty phase of the trial.

The People petitioned the California Supreme Court for review of the Court of Appeal's holding regarding the notes from the out-of-state law enforcement officers. The Supreme Court ultimately reversed the decision of the Court of Appeal. The Supreme Court held that Penal Code section 1054.9 does not require the prosecution to provide to the defendant materials possessed by out-of-state law enforcement agencies that merely provided the prosecution with information or assistance in preparing the penalty phase case against the defendant, as long as the California prosecutor does not possess those materials.

In reaching this decision the Supreme Court observed that in *In re Steele* (2004) 32 Cal.4th 682, 10 Cal.Rptr.3d 536, 85 P.3d 444, the Court had previously held that the prosecution's Penal Code section 1054.1 pretrial discovery obligations and the defendant's Penal Code section 1054.9 posttrial discovery rights "do not extend to materials possessed by law enforcement agencies that were not involved in investigating or preparing the case against the defendant." 32 Cal.4th at 696. The Court further observed that the scope of the prosecutor's statutory disclosure obligations is consistent with the scope of the prosecutor's constitutional disclosure obligations under *Brady*.

The Court reaffirmed its holding in *Steele* that " 'a prosecutor does not have a duty to disclose exculpatory evidence or information to a defendant unless the prosecution team actually or constructively possessed that evidence or information. Thus, information possessed by an agency that has no connection to the investigation or prosecution of the criminal charge against the defendant is not possessed by the prosecution team, and the prosecutor does not have the duty to search for or to disclose such material.' [citations omitted]" 50 Cal.4th at 903.

The Court then applied these principles to out-of-state law enforcement agencies. The Court observed that out-of-state law enforcement agencies "provided assistance and perhaps conducted a few interviews of potential witnesses" on behalf of the California prosecutors. 50 Cal.4th at 903. The Court concluded that "the out-of-state agencies acted on the prosecution's behalf in the sense that they provided certain limited assistance on request." 50 Cal.4th at 904. But in spite of that limited assistance, the Court concluded that "they are not part of the 'prosecution team' as discussed in *Steele* . . . ." 50 Cal.4th at 903.

The Court based its conclusion that the out-of-state agencies were not part of the California prosecution team on two factors: First, "none of them were or are under the control of any California authorities—an important factor." 50 Cal.4th at 904. Second, none of these out-of-state agencies were "part of a team participating in a joint investigation or sharing resources;" these agencies "merely provided specific assistance." 50 Cal.4th at 904.

The Supreme Court rejected the opinion of the Court of Appeal that the prosecution's disclosure duties are greater than evidence in the actual possession of the prosecution team, and, therefore, require the prosecution to disclose exculpatory information possessed by outside agencies that the prosecution used to assist in the prosecution of the capital case against Barnett.

Because the out-of-state agencies were not a part of the California prosecution team, the prosecutor had no duty to obtain and disclose evidence from the out-of-state agencies that the prosecution did not already possess. The Court observed that the prosecutor's *Brady* duties, the prosecutor's statutory pretrial disclosure duties [Penal Code section 1054.1], and the prosecutor's statutory posttrial disclosure duties [Penal Code section 1054.9] impose upon the prosecutor the same duty to discover and disclose evidence in the hands of other agencies—a duty that is limited to members of the prosecution team. 50 Cal.4th at 905; *People v. Zambrano* (2007) 41 Cal.4th 1082, 1133–1134, 63 Cal.Rptr.3d 297, 163 P.3d 4. The Court concluded:

> "[W]e do not believe the Legislature intended the posttrial discovery right to extend so far as to permit a court to order discovery from 22 law enforcement officers working for six different out-of-state agencies, one outside the country, regarding crimes committed between 1965 and 1968 . . . Accordingly, we conclude the prosecution is not required to provide discovery of materials from the out-of-state law enforcement agencies of this case that the prosecution does not itself possess." 50 Cal.4th at 906.

While curiously the Supreme Court declined to "decide definitively whether the out-of-state agencies would have been considered part of the prosecution team under *pretrial* discovery rules," 50 Cal.4th at 906, the Court's opinion equating the scope of the prosecution team as being the same for *Brady* purposes, pretrial statutory discovery purposes, and posttrial statutory discovery purposes, effectively makes inevitable the conclusion that the out-of-state law enforcement agencies in this case were not part of the prosecution team for any discovery purpose under California law.

§ 3:20 Work product—generally

The United States Supreme Court developed the work product doctrine to shield counsel's private memoranda from the liberal discovery permitted by the Federal Rules of Civil Procedure. The Court grounded the doctrine not in the Constitution, but on the assumption that the drafters of the Federal Rules of Civil Procedure did not seek to alter the historical and the necessary way in which lawyers act within the framework of our system of jurisprudence to promote justice and to protect their clients' interests. The doctrine governs discovery and disclosure in federal cases, both civil and criminal, and it cannot support a state prisoner's habeas claim any more than a violation of the Federal Rules of Evidence could. *Varghese v. Uribe* (2013, CA9 Cal.) 720 F.3d 1100.

The work product privilege applies only to the written impressions, opinions, legal research or theories of the defendant's attorney. It does not apply to statements made by the defendant to another jail inmate, even if those statements are construed to declare the intentions of the defendant's attorney. *People v. Smith* (2007) 40 Cal.4th 483, 515, 54 Cal.Rptr.3d 245, 150 P.3d 1224.

§ 3:20.2 Work product—under Criminal Discovery Statute

The work product privilege is explicitly recognized in criminal cases by the Criminal Discovery Statute.

§ 3:20.2.1 Work product protection under Criminal Discovery Statute

In order for evidence to be protected by the work product privilege, that evidence must be a *writing* that reflects the attorney's impressions, conclusions, opinions, or legal research or theories.

In *People v. Bennett* (2009) 45 Cal.4th 577, 88 Cal.Rptr.3d 131, 199 P.3d 535, the California Supreme Court considered an argument on appeal by a criminal defendant convicted of murder and sentenced to death that the prosecution violated his attorney's work product privilege by eliciting evidence in trial that, contrary to defense counsel's implication, DNA samples were available for independent testing. The Supreme Court rejected this argument, concluding that the questions asked by the prosecutor in trial "did not elicit or attempt to elicit evidence of a 'writing' reflecting defense counsel's 'impressions, conclusions, opinions, or legal research or theories' and therefore did not violate the work product privilege." 45 Cal.4th at 595.

§ 3:20.2.2   Work product protection from non-statutory discovery

We predicted in the text that it appeared unlikely the present Supreme Court would reconsider its holding in *People v. Coddington* (2000) 23 Cal.4th 529, 97 Cal.Rptr.2d 528, 2 P.3d 1081, that the work product privilege extends beyond the writings listed in subdivision (a) of Code of Civil Procedure section 2018.030. Our prediction was wrong. The Supreme Court has essentially reconsidered *Coddington* in such a way that the *Coddington* holding regarding the work product privilege has been severely limited.

In *People v. Zamudio* (2008) 43 Cal.4th 327, 75 Cal.Rptr.3d 289, 181 P.3d 105, the defendant was charged with capital murder arising out of the stabbing deaths of two of his neighbors. Prior to trial the prosecution criminalist examined a ring upon which there was an apparent small spot of blood and clothing taken from the defendant at the time of his arrest. The prosecution had not tested the blood spot on the ring. The ring and the clothing were delivered to a laboratory designated by the defense under a confidential appointment.

At trial the prosecution introduced evidence that these items had been delivered to the defense laboratory. The defendant objected to this evidence, but the objection was overruled. The defendant was convicted of murder and sentenced to death.

The defendant contended on appeal that allowing this evidence violated the work product privilege, citing *Coddington*. The Supreme Court rejected the defendant's argument, holding that *Coddington* applied only to trials that took place prior to the enactment of Penal Code section 1054.6 by Proposition 115 in 1990. The Court stated:

> "Defendant's reliance on *Coddington* is misplaced. Although we decided *Coddington* after section 1054.6's enactment, our opinion did not mention that statute, and properly so. Because the trial in *Coddington* ended in 1989 [citation omitted], before section 1054.6's enactment, the statute was inapplicable in the case and irrelevant to our work product analysis . . . because defendant's crimes and his trial occurred well after 1990, Penal Code section 1054.6 applies and strictly limits the scope of the work product privilege only to 'writing[s] that reflect[] an attorney's impressions, conclusions, opinions, or legal research or theories . . . .' Code Civ. Proc., sec. 2018.030, subd. (a).) As explained above, defendant's work product claim falls under this restricted definition." 43 Cal.4th at 356.

The Court then concluded that the defendant's work product objection was without merit. Because Penal Code section 1054.6 explicitly limits the work product definition in criminal cases to the core work product of subdivision (a) of Code of Civil Procedure section 2018.030, the testimony of the prosecution's actions in sending the tested items and test results to a defense laboratory does not meet the definition of work product contained in that provision of the Code of Civil Procedure. Thus, "[t]he admission of this evidence therefore did not contravene the work product privilege as it applies in criminal cases." 43 Cal.4th at 355.

Coddington had spawned a series of defense motions requesting that trial courts forbid prosecutors and their investigating officers from monitoring jail records to determine the identity of visitors to incarcerated defendants prior to trial. *Coddington* held that such monitoring violated non-statutory work product protected by *Coddington*. In the wake of *Zamudio*, such *Coddington*-based motions would appear to be without merit.

In *Kling v. Superior* Court (2010) 50 Cal.4th 1068, 116 Cal.Rptr.3d 217, 239 P.3d 670, the California Supreme Court continued its restrictive construction of the meaning of the "work product" protection of Code of Civil Procedure section 2018.030(a) that is applicable to criminal cases.

In *Kling* the Supreme Court held that the prosecution is typically entitled to know the identity of a party served with a defense-issued subpoena *duces tecum*, the nature of the documents subpoenaed, and the identity of the person to whom the subpoenaed records relate. The Court reached this conclusion in the face of the defendant's argument that allowing the prosecution to know this information would violate the right of the defendant and the defendant's attorney to protection of defense work product. Quoting from the opinion of the Court of Appeal in *Department of Corrections v. Superior Court* (1988) 199 Cal.App.3d 1087, 1097, 245 Cal.Rptr. 293, the Court stated: " 'In essence it is [the defense] position that the prosecution, by . . . knowing [the records] have been subpoenaed by the defense, will have access to his attorneys' work product because the prosecutor will be able to 'glean' the attorneys' thought processes and determine defense strategy. There is no basis in law for interpreting attorneys' work product so broadly.' " 50 Cal.4th at 1077–1078.

§ 3:20.2.4 Work product—the *Brady* rule

When evidence otherwise protected by the work product privilege is disclosed to a governmental agency that has a *Brady* duty to disclose material exculpatory evidence to a criminal defendant, the *Brady* duty "trumps" the work product privilege.

In *United States v. Thompson* (2009, CA DC) 562 F.3d 387, the Williams Power Company (WPC), which was a non-party to the government's prosecution of Mr. Thompson, turned over records to the government while the government was investigating the trading activities of WPC in connection with the California energy crisis in 2002. The defendant, a former employee of WPC, obtained an order from the district court requiring the government to disclose those records to him. The district court implicitly held that the documents were material to Thompson's defense and therefore discoverable under *Brady* and Rule 16 of the Federal Rules of Criminal Procedure.

WPC filed a third-party appeal of the disclosure order, arguing that disclosure of the records violated its work product privilege. The Ninth Circuit Court of Appeals rejected WPC's work product privilege argument, concluding, *inter alia*, that "WPC's expectation of privacy cannot reach the disclosures grounded in the government's *Brady* obligations, which are constitutionally based . . . ." 562 F.3d at 395. Since the work product protection is only a "qualified privilege," 562 F.3d at 397, the Court concluded that WPC's standing to protect its interest in the confidentiality of its records must be "consistent with Thompson's right to a fair trial and the government's *Brady* and Rule 16 obligations to Thompson." 562 F.3d at 396.

When a document contains both protected work product and exculpatory evidence, the prosecution has a duty to disclose the non-cumulative underlying exculpatory facts contained in the document, while protecting from disclosure opinion work product contained therein. *United States v. Kohring* (2011, CA9 AK) 637 F.3d 895, 908.

A document which contains legal opinions does not constitute discoverable *Brady* evidence unless the legal opinions themselves contain exculpatory facts. Legal opinions are otherwise protected from disclosure by the work product privilege. *Lopez v. Ryan* (2011, CA9 AZ) 630 F.3d 1198, 1210.

§ 3:20.2.6   Work product and witness preparation sessions

Although California courts have repeatedly held that notes taken by an attorney in interviewing a witness are not work product to the extent that these notes simply recount the statements of that witness, this analysis could be open to question in light of the opinion of the Eighth Circuit Court of Appeals in *In re Green Grand Jury Proceedings* (2007, CA8 MN) 492 F.3d 976. In *In re Green Grand Jury Proceedings* the Government moved for a court order to require an attorney to produce documents and to testify before a federal grand jury. The district court granted the motion in part and denied it in part. Both sides appealed.

The Eighth Circuit Court of Appeals held that except for documents resulting from an effort by a client to perpetrate a fraud, the documents the government sought to obtain were protected by the work product privilege. In reaching this conclusion the Court stated that " '[n]otes and memoranda of an attorney, or an attorney's agent, from a witness interview are opinion work product entitled to almost absolute immunity.' [citation omitted] An attorney's notes of a witness interview are opinion work product because 'when taking notes, an attorney often focuses on those facts that she deems legally significant.' Id. Accordingly, the district court correctly determined that the attorney's notes were protectable as opinion work product." 492 F.3d at 982.

See also, Baker v. General Motors Corp. (In re GMC) (2000, CA8 MO) 209 F.3d 1051, 1054.

Whether California courts will adopt this reasoning of the Eighth Circuit Court of Appeals when dealing with work product claims arising out of an attorney's interview of a witness in a criminal case remains to be seen.

§ 3:20.2.8   Work product crime or fraud exception

Under the crime/fraud exception, neither the work product privilege nor the attorney-client privilege extends to "communications made for the purpose of getting advice for the commission of a fraud or a crime." *United States v. Zolin* (1989) 491 U.S. 554, 563, 109 S.Ct. 2619, 105 L.Ed.2d 469. Thus, a client "who has used his attorney's assistance to perpetrate a crime or fraud cannot assert the work product privilege as to any documents generated in furtherance of his misconduct." *In re Green Grand Jury Proceedings* (2007, CA8 MO) 492 F.3d 976, 980.

However, if the attorney does not knowingly participate in the client's fraud or crime, the attorney is entitled to assert the work product privilege as to his or her opinion work product. *In re Green Grand Jury Proceedings*, 492 F.3d at 980.

§ 3:20.2.9   Work product and *Batson* claims

Although the work product privilege protects a prosecutor's handwritten voir dire notes from forced disclosure to a defendant who is making a *Batson* motion [*Batson v. Kentucky* (1986) 476 U.S. 79, 106 S.Ct. 1712, 90 L.Ed.2d 69], one federal district court ruled that the work product privilege does not prevent the defendant from questioning the prosecutor under oath about the prosecutor's writings in her voir dire notes. *See Williams v. Beard* (2011, CA3 PA) 637 F.3d 195, 210.

§ 3:20.2.10   Work product and attorney-client privilege [NEW]

The scope of the waiver of the attorney-client and work product privileges is delineated when a federal habeas petitioner raises a claim of ineffective assistance of counsel. Although that petitioner impliedly waives his attorney-client privilege, such waiver is narrow and does not extend beyond the adjudication of the ineffectiveness claim in the federal habeas proceeding. In order to protect that limited waiver, district courts have the obligation, whenever they permit discovery of attorney-client materials as relevant to the defense of ineffective assistance of counsel claims in habeas cases, to ensure that the party given such access does not disclose these materials, except to the extent necessary in the habeas proceeding. Parties in habeas cases, unlike those in ordinary civil cases, have no right to discovery, and that discovery is available if, and only to the extent that, the judge in the exercise of his discretion and for good cause shown grants leave to do so. If a district court exercises its discretion to allow such discovery, it must ensure compliance with the fairness principle. To that end, it must enter appropriate orders clearly delineating the contours of the limited waiver before the commencement of discovery, and strictly police those limits thereafter. *Lambright v. Ryan* (2012, CA9 Ariz.) 698 F.3d 808. A waiver of the attorney-client and **work product** privileges is implied out of fairness to the State, in that a habeas petitioner could not use the privilege as both a shield and a sword. The court thus gives the holder of the privilege a choice: If you want to litigate this claim, then you must waive your privilege to the extent necessary to give your opponent a fair opportunity to defend against it. Similarly, a waiver of the Fifth Amendment privilege is implied out of fairness to the State, and the petitioner is given a choice: If you want to litigate this claim, which puts your mental health and state of mind at the time of the crime at issue, you must waive your privilege to the extent necessary to allow the State a fair opportunity to defend against such claim. This justification means that the court must impose a waiver no broader than needed to ensure the fairness of the proceedings before it. Most important, failure to impose a narrow waiver would force the petitioner to the painful choice of, on the one hand, asserting his ineffective assistance claim and risking a trial where the prosecution can use against him any statements he may have made during the habeas proceeding and, on the other hand, retaining the privilege but abandoning his claim. *Id.*

The joint defense privilege is an extension of the attorney-client privilege and does establish a duty of confidentiality on the part of the additional attorney and party to the agreement. Privilege cannot be overcome by a showing of need, whereas a showing of need may justify discovery of an attorney's work product. *United States v. Gonzalez* (2012, CA9 Cal.) 669 F.3d 974. One party to a joint defense agreement cannot unilaterally waive the privilege for other holders. The privileged status of communications falling within the common interest doctrine cannot be waived without the consent of all of the parties. One party to a common-interest arrangement lacks the ability to waive the privilege as to other members. Any member of a common-interest arrangement may invoke the privilege against third persons, even if the communication in question was not originally made by or addressed to the objecting member. Any member may waive the privilege with respect to that person's own communications. Correlatively, a member is not authorized to waive the privilege for another member's communication. *Id.*

§ 3:22 Good cause excusing or delaying disclosure

Good cause has constituted a basis for excusing or delaying a prosecution disclosure both prior to and following the adoption of the Criminal Discovery Statute.

§ 3:22.2 Withholding disclosure pursuant to Criminal Discovery Statute

A good cause showing can empower the court to authorize a number of different kinds of protective orders under Penal Code section 1054.7 that delay or excuse the prosecution or the defendant from complying with their duties under Penal Code sections 1054.1 and 1054.3 to disclose evidence or information to each other.

§ 3:22.2.3 Permanent withholding of name of prosecution witness

While a defendant's right to due process of law and the right of confrontation prevents a trial court from making a protective order that permanently withholds the names of prosecution witnesses from the defense, a trial court may craft a protective order that permanently withholds the names of those witnesses from public disclosure and transmission to others who are not part of the defense team, and that delays disclosure of that information to the defendant.

There are occasions when the prosecution believes that to disclose the name of a prosecution witness will jeopardize that witness's safety and thus the integrity of the prosecution's evidence against the defendant. This scenario is not uncommon in prosecutions of defendants who are believed to be involved in drug cartels and criminal street gangs.

In *United States v. Celis* (2010, CA DC) 608 F.3d 818, several defendants convicted of conspiring to import cocaine and to manufacture and distribute cocaine for import appealed their convictions, arguing that the government had unconstitutionally obtained a protective order from the district court allowing witnesses from Columbia to testify using pseudonyms. The protective order was issued based on evidence that a criminal organization in Columbia had issued death threats against witnesses who cooperated with the prosecution. The protective order provided that the government must disclose the true identity of these witnesses to the defendants' attorneys, and the attorneys could disclose the witnesses' true identities to their clients and to one member of the defense team located in the United States. The protective order provided that the true identities of the witnesses, however, could not be shared with anyone in Columbia.

The defendants contended on appeal that the use of pseudonyms for government witnesses prevented proper defense investigation of those witnesses and thus violated the defendants' confrontation rights under the Sixth Amendment. The Court of Appeals, citing and quoting from the Supreme Court opinion in *Weatherford v. Bursey* (1977) 429 U.S. 545, 559, 97 S.Ct. 837, 51 L.Ed.2d 30, rejected the defendants' argument, observing that there is no constitutional requirement that the prosecution must reveal the names of all government witnesses prior to trial. 608 F.3d at 831. "It does not follow from the prohibition against concealing evidence favorable to the accused that the prosecution must reveal before trial the names of all witnesses who will testify unfavorably." *Weatherford v. Bursey, supra*, 429 U.S. at 545.

The Court of Appeals in *Celis* relied upon the fact that the defendants gained access to the true identities of government witnesses days prior to their testimony, and when shown to be necessary, were allowed to investigate these witnesses using their true identities in both the United States and Columbia. By delaying disclosure of the witnesses' true identities, but allowing the defense time to investigate those witnesses using their true names, the district court protected the defendants' constitutional rights while also protecting the witnesses. 608 F.3d at 834.

§ 3:22.2.5   Protective order

Trial courts have discretionary power to impose and then modify a protective order to enable the parties to fairly prepare for and to litigate their cases.

In *People v. Loker* (2008) 44 Cal.4th 691, 80 Cal.Rptr.3d 630, 188 P.3d 580, the attorney for a defendant charged with capital murder agreed, because of reciprocal discovery statutes and to assist in settlement negotiations, to pretrial disclosure to the prosecution of notes and tapes of defense interviews with numerous potential defense witnesses. Attendant to these disclosures, the prosecution and the defense agreed upon a protective order that temporarily precluded the prosecution from disclosing discovery information or contacting defense penalty phase witnesses.

After the defendant had been convicted, the prosecution asked the trial court to lift the protective order so that the prosecution could contact defense penalty phase witnesses. The defendant opposed the prosecution's request, claiming that allowing the prosecution to discuss proposed defense testify with these witnesses would impede the defendant's ability to persuade these witnesses to testify. The trial court lifted the protective order, ruling that because the penalty phase of the trial was set to begin in only three weeks, the prosecutor was entitled at that point to investigate the proposed defense penalty phase evidence. The defense then requested that the trial court preclude the prosecution from discussing certain sensitive topics with potential defense witnesses that were expected to be the subject of defense penalty phase evidence. The court declined to regulate or restrict the prosecution's ability to discuss these subjects with the defense witnesses.

Following the penalty phase trial, the defendant was sentenced to death. On automatic appeal to the California Supreme Court of the judgment of conviction and death, the defendant argued that the court erred in lifting the protective order, because the prosecution was then allowed to abuse discovery procedures by intimidating defense witnesses and limiting defense mitigating evidence. The Supreme Court rejected the defendant's arguments.

The Court stated that the defendant "fails to explain how the prosecutor's legitimate questioning of defense witnesses about the very matters defendant intended to explore at trial would lead to the loss or destruction of evidence. Witnesses might be reluctant to discuss sensitive issues, or might deny they happened. However, such reluctance flows from the nature of the evidence itself and its public discussion, not from the trial court's refusal to issue a protective order." 44 Cal.4th at 734.

§ 3:22.2.7   Withholding discoverable information without court order

It appears that a party who wishes to take advantage of the right to withhold disclosure or to delay disclosure of information or evidence that the Criminal Discovery Statute requires the party to disclose must first obtain court approval of that withholding under Penal Section 1054.7.

In *People v. Riggs* (2008) 44 Cal.4th 248, 79 Cal.Rptr.3d 648, 187 P.3d 363, the defendant was charged with capital murder. More than one month after the guilt phase of the trial had begun, and three weeks after the prosecution had completed its case-in-chief, the defendant, who represented himself, disclosed the names and addresses of two alibi witnesses who would testify that at the time of the murder the defendant was with them far away from the scene of the murder.

The prosecution requested sanctions for a discovery violation by the defendant. The trial court declined to exclude the witnesses' testimony, but the court, at the prosecution's request, imposed a jury instruction as a sanction for the discovery violation. The defendant was convicted of murder and sentenced to death. On automatic appeal the defendant contended that the giving of the jury instruction was error. The Supreme Court rejected the defendant's argument.

The Court found that substantial evidence supported the trial court's decision that the defendant had committed a discovery violation. The Court rejected the argument made at trial by defendant's advisory counsel that the defendant might have withheld the witnesse's names to protect them from harassment and threats by the prosecution's investigator. The Court concluded that the Criminal Discovery Statute "seems to contemplate that the parties would not engage in self-help in this manner, but rather would timely seek permission from the trial court to defer disclosure. [citing Penal Code section 1054.7]" 44 Cal.4th at 310.

§ 3:22.2.8   Withholding defendant's statements

The Criminal Discovery Statute requires the prosecuting attorney to disclose to the defendant all statements made by the defendant. See Section 3:6.1 of the text. The prosecution does not ordinarily have any legitimate reason for withholding disclosure of a defendant's statements.

However, when statements have been obtained from a defendant who was not aware that the statements were being heard or recorded by law enforcement, the prosecution might have a need to protect the fact that law enforcement overheard and recorded the defendant's statements. This situation arises when the defendant's voice has been heard and recorded because of a wiretap on a land wire telephone, a digital pager, or a cell phone. The prosecution's duty to disclose a defendant's statements recorded in a wiretap, and the statutory authority excusing or delaying such disclosure, are found in both the Criminal Discovery Statute and the wiretapping statutes.

Federal Wiretapping Statute

In *Katz v. United States* (1967) 389 U.S. 347, 88 S.Ct. 507, 19 L.Ed.2d 576, the United States Supreme Court held that, absent prior authorization by a court, wiretapping violates the Fourth Amendment prohibition of unreasonable search and seizure.

In response to the holding in *Katz,* Congress enacted a federal wiretapping statute as Title III of the Omnibus Crime Control and Safe Streets Act of 1968, 18 U.S.C. sections 2510 to 2520. The heart of that statute is found in 18 U.S.C. section 2518. The federal wiretapping statute "provides a comprehensive scheme for the regulation of wiretapping and electronic surveillance," *People v. Otto* (1992) 2 Cal.4th 1088, 1097, 9 Cal.Rptr.2d 596, 831 P.2d 1178, and "in effect establishes minimum standards for the admissibility of evidence procured through electronic surveillance; state law cannot be less protective of privacy than the federal Act." 2 Cal.4th at 1098.

In addition to establishing minimum standards for state wiretap laws, the federal wiretap statute is the standard for analyzing the suppression of evidence obtained by a wiretap authorization issued by a federal court. *People v. Reyes* (2009) 172 Cal.App.4th 671, 683, 91 Cal.Rptr.3d 415.

Accordingly, because the federal wiretap statute "authorizes the states to enact their own wiretap laws only if the provisions of those laws are at least as restrictive as the federal requirements for a wiretap set out in Title III," *People v. Jackson* (2005) 129 Cal.App.4th 129, 146, 28 Cal.Rptr.3d 136, "state law cannot be less protective of privacy than the federal act. Thus, we look to federal and California statutes, legislative history and case law in applying the California wiretap statute." *People v. Jackson, supra,* 129 Cal.App.4th at 146. *See People v. Zepeda* (2001) 87 Cal.App.4th 1183, 105 Cal.Rptr.2d 187, in which the Court of Appeal construed California's requirement of a showing of necessity for a wiretap in light of federal cases construing a similar requirement in Title III.

For this reason an analysis of the California wiretap statute "is necessarily informed by title III of the Omnibus Crime Control and Safe Streets Act of 1968 . . . ." *People v. Leon* (2007) 40 Cal.4th 376, 384, 53 Cal.Rptr.3d 524, 150 P.3d 207.

California Wiretapping Statutes

California law prohibits wiretapping, except as provided by statute. Because the federal wiretap act establishes minimum standards for the admissibility of evidence procured through electronic surveillance, and state law cannot be less protective of privacy than the federal wiretap act, California courts may look for guidance to cases under title III of the

Omnibus Crime Control and Safe Streets Act of 1968, 18 U.S.C. § 2510 *et seq.*, which provides a comprehensive scheme for the regulation of wiretapping and electronic surveillance. In applying the California wiretap statute, the court therefore looks to both federal and California law. *People v. Acevedo* (2012) 209 Cal. App. 4th 1040, 147 Cal. Rptr. 3d 467.

Wiretaps have generally been prohibited and even made criminal conduct by California law. See Penal Code section 630 *et seq. People v. Zepeda* (2001) 87 Cal.App.4th 1183, 1195, 105 Cal.Rptr.2d 187. The California Legislature enacted a limited wiretapping statute called The Presley-Felando-Eaves Wiretap Act of 1988 that authorized issuance of a court order to intercept wire communications in specific types of illegal drug investigations. See former Penal Code section 629.02 *et seq.*

In 1995 the Legislature replaced the Wiretap Act of 1988 with a more expansive wiretapping statute that was intended " 'to expand California wiretap law to conform to the federal law.' [citation omitted]." *People v. Leon* (2007) 40 Cal.4th 376, 383, 53 Cal.Rptr.3d 524, 150 P.3d 207.

The existing California wiretap statute, which has been amended by subsequent initiative and legislative enactments, is found in Penal Code section 629.50 *et seq.* The wiretapping statute authorizes issuance of a wiretap order only on the application of a specified prosecuting attorney. "Under Title III [and under the California wiretap statute as well] a police officer cannot go directly to a magistrate and ask for a wiretap. Rather, the person seeking the order, usually an assistant United States attorney, must first obtain the personal approval for the wiretap from the United States Attorney General or a statutorily authorized designee." *People v. Jackson* (2005) 129 Cal.App.4th 129, 159, 28 Cal.Rptr.3d 136.

The court may issue a wiretap authorization order when four conditions are met: (1) there is probable cause to believe that a person has committed, is committing, or is about to commit one or more of the crimes listed in Penal Code section 629.52, subdivision (a); (2) there is probable cause to believe that communications concerning the illegal activities will be obtained through the interception; (3) there is probable cause to believe that a communications device, which includes wire communications, electronic digital pagers, and electronic cellular telephones, will be used by the person whose communications are to be intercepted; and (4) normal investigative procedures have been tried and have failed or reasonably appear either to be unlikely to succeed or to be too dangerous. Penal Code section 629.52, subdivisions (a)–(d).

The wiretap statutes apply to interception of land wire telephones, electronic digital pagers, and electronic cellular telephones. The statutes apply to prisons and jails and monitoring of telephone calls to and from such institutions. *People v. Kelley* (2002) 103 Cal.App.4th 853, 857, 127 Cal.Rptr.2d 203.

However, an inmate who uses a jail phone system to engage in conversations has impliedly consented to monitoring of that phone without the necessity of a court order when a warning sign has been posted above the telephones stating that calls may be monitored or when the jail phone system contains a warning at the beginning of each call stating that all calls are subject to monitoring or recording. The implied consent takes any wiretap outside the prohibitions of the federal wiretapping statute. "So long as a prisoner is given meaningful notice that his telephone calls over prison phones are subject to monitoring, his decision to engage in conversations over those phones constitutes implied consent to that monitoring and takes any wiretap outside the prohibitions of Title III." *People v. Kelley, supra,* 103 Cal.App.4th at 858. *Accord, People v. Windham* (2006) 145 Cal.App.4th 881, 887, 51 Cal.Rptr.3d 884. *See People v. Loyd* (2002) 27 Cal.4th 997, 1010, 119 Cal.Rptr.2d 360, 45 P.3d 296 [Penal Code section 2600 permits law enforcement officers to monitor and record nonprivileged communications between inmates and their visitors.].

The wiretap application and order must be sealed by the judge issuing the order. Penal Code sections 629.50, subdivision (c), and 629.66. As soon as the wiretap order or extensions of that order have expired, the recordings must be provided to the issuing judge and sealed by the court. Penal Code section 629.64. The sealing requirement is designed to combat claims that any of the recordings have been subject to tampering. *People v. Davis* (2008) 168 Cal.App.4th 617, 631, 86 Cal.Rptr.3d 55.

Unless it is extended by the California Legislature or the electorate, the California wiretap statute will expire on January 1, 2012. Penal Code section 629.98.

Thus, "[t]he collection and use of wiretap evidence is regulated by federal law . . . and analogous California law . . . ." *People v. Davis* (2008) 168 Cal.App.4th 617, 625, 86 Cal.Rptr.3d 55.

Disclosure Provisions of Wiretap Statutes

The California Wiretap Statute contains five disclosure requirements.

California law prohibits wiretapping, except as provided by statute. Because the federal wiretap act establishes minimum standards for the admissibility of evidence procured through electronic surveillance, and state law cannot be less protective of privacy than the federal wiretap act, California courts may look for guidance to cases under title III of the Omnibus Crime Control and Safe Streets Act of 1968, 18 U.S.C. § 2510 *et seq.*, which provides a comprehensive scheme for the regulation of wiretapping and electronic surveillance. In applying the California wiretap statute, the court therefore looks to both federal and California law. *People v. Acevedo* (2012) 209 Cal. App. 4th 1040, 147 Cal. Rptr. 3d 467.

1. Notice of wiretap identification.

The first disclosure requirement is that a defendant in a criminal case must be notified "that he or she was identified as the result of an interception that was obtained pursuant to [the wiretap statute] . . . prior to the entry of a plea of guilty or nolo contendere, or at least 10 days prior to any trial, hearing, or proceeding in the case other than an arraignment or grand jury proceeding." Penal Code section 629.70, subdivision (a).

Although the legislature in enacting the California wiretap statute stated that its intent was "to expand California wiretap law to conform to the federal law," *People v. Leon* (2007) 40 Cal.4th 376, 383, 53 Cal.Rptr.3d 524, 150 P.3d 207, the federal wiretap statute does not contain a provision that is comparable to subdivision (a) of Penal Code section 629.70. Therefore, this disclosure provision of the California wiretap statute is broader than the federal wiretap statute.

2. Disclosure of copy of recorded interceptions, court order, wiretap application, and monitoring logs.

The second disclosure requirement is that not less than 10 days before the trial, hearing, or proceeding, "the prosecution shall provide to the defendant a copy of all recorded interceptions *from which evidence against the defendant was derived*, including a copy of the court order, accompanying application, and monitoring logs." Penal Code section 629.70, subdivision (b) [italics added].

The federal wiretap statute provision that is comparable to subdivision (b) of Penal Code section 629.70 provides that the defendant is entitled to disclosure of the "court order, and accompanying application, under which the interception was authorized or approved" only when the contents of any intercepted oral or electronic communications are "received in evidence or otherwise disclosed in any trial, hearing, or other proceeding in a Federal or State court." 18 U.S.C. sec. 2518, subsection (9).

Thus, this disclosure provision of the California wiretap statute is broader in scope than its federal wiretap statute counterpart.

3. Disclosure of transcript of contents of interception.

The third disclosure requirement applies when the prosecution introduces into evidence or otherwise discloses the contents of an intercepted wire, pager, or cell telephone, or evidence derived from those contents, in a trial, hearing, or other proceeding. This disclosure requirement is that not less than 10 days before the trial, hearing, or proceeding the prosecution must furnish the defendant "with a transcript of the contents of the interception and with the materials specified in subdivision (b)." Penal Code section 629.70, subdivision (c).

This disclosure provision of the California wiretap statute mirrors the federal wiretap statute. 18 U.S.C. sec. 2518, subsection (9).

4. Disclosure of interception relating to other crimes and copy of contents used in subsequent application to obtain additional intercept warrant.

The fourth disclosure requirement applies when an intercepted wire, pager, or cell telephone contains communications relating to crimes other than the crimes specified in the interception authorization order. This disclosure requirement is that in order to use the contents of an "other crimes interception" for which an additional intercept warrant was obtained, the person named in the additional warrant must be provided "notice of the intercepted wire, electronic pager, or electronic cellular telephone communication and a copy of the contents thereof that were used to obtain the warrant." Penal Code section 629.82, subdivision (c).

Although the language is different, this disclosure provision of the California statute is comparable to the federal wiretap statute. 18 U.S.C. sec. 2518, subsection 9, applies to the "contents of any wire, oral, or electronic communication intercepted pursuant to this chapter . . . or evidence derived therefrom," and requires disclosure of "a copy of the court order, and accompanying application, under which the interception was authorized or approved." The federal and state statutory language appears substantively identical.

5. Disclosure of interception 90 days after termination of order.

The fifth disclosure requirement requires the agency that requested the wiretap order to serve an inventory upon any person named in the wiretap order or application, and upon any known parties to intercepted communications. The inventory must include three items of information: (1) the fact of the entry of the wiretap order; (2) the date of the entry of the wiretap order and the period of authorized interception; and (3) the fact that during the period wire, electronic pager, or electronic cellular telephone communications were or were not intercepted. Penal Code section 629.68.

This disclosure provision of the California statute is substantively identical to its counterpart in the federal wiretap statute. See 18 U.S.C. sec. 2518, subsection (8)(d).

While not a mandated disclosure, the court may grant a motion making available for inspection to the person or his or her counsel "the portions of the intercepted communications, applications, and orders that the court determines are in the interest of justice." Penal Code section 629.68.

Orders Limiting, Excusing, or Delaying Wiretap Disclosures

1. Order limiting disclosures

The trial court may, upon a showing of good cause, limit the requirement that the defendant be notified that he or she was identified as the result of a wiretap interception. And the trial court may, also upon a showing of good cause, limit the requirement that the prosecution disclose a copy of recorded interceptions, the wiretap authorization order, the wiretap application, and the wiretap monitoring logs. Penal Code section 629.70, subdivision (d), provides that "[a] court may issue an order limiting disclosures pursuant to subdivisions (a) and (b) upon a showing of good cause."

The federal wiretap statute does not contain a similar provision.

Unlike Section 1054.7 of the Criminal Discovery Statute, the California wiretap statute does not define "good cause," and there is no California appellate authority defining good cause for purposes of limiting or excusing disclosures under the wiretap statutes.

Moreover, there is no definition of "good cause" in the federal wiretap statute. *In re N.Y. Times Co.* (2009, CA2 NY) 577 F.3d 401, 406 [In enacting the federal wiretap statute, "Congress did not define the term, and we are aware of no Supreme Court case that has done so."].

However, in *In re Applications of Kansas City Star* (1981, CA8 MO) 666 F.2d 1168, the Eighth Circuit Court of Appeals defined the term "good cause" in the context of disclosure of wiretap information in these terms:

"[T]he decisive question then, as we see it, remains as to whether there was good cause to disclose the documents. Good cause to us means that, at least minimally, there must be a need for disclosure." The Court of Appeals continued, "It is our view that the good cause requirement of the [wiretap] statute calls for at least some consideration by courts of the privacy of other people which might be affected by disclosure. Until the government has some need to disclose intercepted conversations and the orders and applications under which they were intercepted, Title III would seem to insure that those conversations would not be made public." 666 F.2d at 1176.

Although the Eighth Circuit's definition of "good cause" was related to cause for disclosure, as opposed to cause for nondisclosure, the working definition appears equally appropriate: a need for nondisclosure.

2. Order excusing timely disclosures.

The 10-day notice period required by subdivisions (b) and (c) of Penal Code section 629.70 to disclose the transcript of the intercepted communications may be excused. The notice period requirement "may be waived by the judge . . . if he or she finds that it was not possible to furnish the party with the transcript 10 days before the trial, hearing, or proceeding, and that the party will not be prejudiced by the delay in receiving that transcript." Penal Code section 629.70, subdivision (c).

The federal wiretap statute contains a similar provision. See 18 U.S.C. sec. 2518, subsection (9).

3. Order postponing service of inventory.

The court may grant an ex parte request, based on good cause from the agency that requested the intercept order, to postpone the serving of the inventory for a period no longer than is deemed necessary to achieve the purposes for which the postponement is granted. Penal Code section 629.68.

The federal wiretap statute contains a similar provision. See 18 U.S.C. sec. 2518, subsection (8)(d).

One important caveat about obtaining orders that limit, excuse, or delay disclosure of wiretap information must be remembered: Even though contained in wiretap information, any exculpatory information or evidence must be disclosed to the defendant pursuant to the constitutional command of *Brady v. Maryland* (1963) 373 U.S. 83, 83 S.Ct. 1194, 10 L.Ed.2d 215. *People v. Jackson* (2005) 129 Cal.App.4th 129, 170, n.135, 28 Cal.Rptr.3d 136.

Criminal Discovery Statute and Wiretap Information

The wiretap statutes are not the only California statutes that require disclosure of information about wiretaps. The California Criminal Discovery Statute, although not containing any direct reference to wiretaps, requires the prosecution to disclose to the defendant all statements of the defendant. This disclosure requirement includes statements captured in wiretap recordings.

In *People v. Jackson* (2005) 129 Cal.App.4th 129, 28 Cal.Rptr.3d 136, the defendant was in jail pending trial on murder and attempted murder charges arising out of a street gang war. The investigating agency, under the authority of a court order, tape recorded numerous telephone calls in which Jackson participated. The prosecution later disclosed 14 of these tape-recorded conversations to the defendant, but declined to disclose to the defense the remaining tape-recorded conversations.

The defendant was convicted and appealed. On appeal the defendant argued that the prosecution had violated its disclosure duty under subdivision (b) of Section 1054.1 by failing to disclose all of the tape-recorded conversations that the investigating officers had made of Jackson's telephone conversations.

In resolving this contention, the Second District Court of Appeal addressed an apparent conflict between the Criminal Discovery Statute (Penal Code section 1054.1, subdivision (b)), which requires the prosecution to disclose all statements of all defendants, and the wiretap statute (Penal Code section 629.70), which provides that the prosecution must disclose the statements of a defendant "from which evidence against the defendant was derived." The Court concluded that "all statements by the defendant captured on a wiretap must be disclosed to the defense whether they are inculpatory, exculpatory or neither." 129 Cal.App.4th at 170. The Court reasoned that where both the Criminal Discovery Statute and the California wiretap statute require the disclosure of recorded statements of a criminal defendant, the narrower scope of disclosures required under the wiretap statute "do not supersede the scope of discovery under section 1054.1, subdivision (b)," which provides a very broad disclosure requirement. 129 Cal.App.4th at 171. The Court held that the prosecution is required to disclose all of the statements of the defendant as provided by the Criminal Discovery Statute, not simply those statements of the defendant "from which evidence against the defendant was derived." *Id.*

The Court concluded that the Criminal Discovery Statute and the wiretap statute can be reconciled by an interpretation which holds that an "item is discoverable if discovery is authorized *either* under section 1054.1 or some other statutory provision." *Id.*, at 171. And the wiretap statute should be construed to hold that the prosecution must furnish the defense with copies of all recorded interceptions which resulted in inculpatory evidence against the defendant, "but it does not specifically *limit* the right to discovery to interceptions which led to inculpatory evidence." *Id.* [italics in original]

Protective Order

The prosecution might be able to avoid mandatory disclosure of wiretapped statements of a defendant under the Criminal Discovery Statute by applying for and obtaining a protective order under Penal Code section 1054.7. See the discussion of protective orders pursuant to Penal Code section 1054.7 in Sections 3:22–3:22.2.6 of the text.

Together with the provisions in the wiretap statutes that allow the prosecution to establish good cause for the issuance of a court order limiting the disclosure of wiretap information, Penal Code section 629.70, subdivision (d), the prosecution might be able to shield a wiretap and its non-exculpatory fruits from defense discovery by use of a protective order under Penal Code section 1054.7. See Form 7 in the Forms Appendix of the text.

The California wiretap statutes require the state to provide timely reports to the court. When those reports are inadequate or untimely, the evidence obtained by a wiretap might be suppressed. For an extensive discussion of the reporting requirements of the California wiretap statutes, see *People v. Roberts* (2010) 184 Cal.App.4th 1149, 109 Cal.Rptr.3d 736.

§ 3:22.2.9   Withholding disclosures from defendant but providing disclosure to defendant's counsel

Although this question is not likely to often arise in a California state court criminal prosecution, if the disclosure of sensitive *Brady* evidence to the defendant personally would constitute a danger to national security, a court has the power to order that the *Brady* disclosure be made to the defendant's attorney, but withheld from being disclosed to the defendant. The authority for such a protective order is the federal Classified Information Procedures Act (CIPA), which was enacted by Congress on October 15, 1980, as 18 U.S.C. App. III. Sections 1-16.

The primary purpose of CIPA was to limit the practice of "graymail" by criminal defendants who possess sensitive government secrets. "Graymail" refers to the threat by a criminal defendant to disclose classified information during the course of a trial. A gray mailing defendant essentially presents the government with a "Hobson's choice:" to either allow disclosure of classified information or dismiss the indictment. The procedural protections of CIPA prevent unnecessary disclosure of classified information without requiring dismissal of the criminal charges. *United States v. Moussaoui* (2010, CA4 VA) 591 F.3d 263, 281.

Thus in criminal prosecutions such as those involving defendants who are accused or suspected of being involved in terrorist activities against the United States, a court may order that the disclosure of evidence or information that is materially favorable to the defendant under *Brady* may be restricted to the defendant's attorney, but withheld from the defendant. *See, e.g., United States v. Moussaoui* (2010, CA4 VA) 591 F.3d 263 [Zacarias Moussaoui has often been called "the 20th hijacker" who at the time of the September 11, 2001 attacks on the United States had already been arrested.].

CHAPTER 4

CRIMINAL DISCOVERY STATUTE — RECIPROCAL DISCLOSURE BY DEFENDANT

PART I.   RECIPROCAL DISCOVERY BACKGROUND AND SCOPE

§ 4:2   Constitutionality of reciprocal discovery under Criminal Discovery Statute

Further, Penal Code sections 1027 and 1054.3, subsection (b)(1), are in no way inconsistent; indeed, when a defendant pleads not guilty by reason of insanity, the two statutes appear to operate in a complementary manner. Under § 1027, court appointment of experts to evaluate the defendant is mandatory. Under § 1054.3, subsection (b)(1), the court may grant the People's motion to compel a further examination by a prosecution-retained expert. In deciding how to exercise its discretion under § 1054.3, subsection (b)(1), the trial court may consider the extent to which such an additional examination is needed, in light of any existing court appointments, to rebut the defense's proposed expert testimony. That appointments have already been made under § 1027 thus may influence, but does not preclude, the decision to order an examination under § 1054.3, subsection (b)(1). *Sharp v. Superior Court* (2012) 54 Cal. 4th 168, 141 Cal. Rptr. 3d 486, 277 P.3d 174.

PART II. DEFENDANT'S DISCLOSURE DUTIES AND OBLIGATIONS

§ 4:5 Defense trial witnesses — generally

The duty of the defendant to disclose the names and addresses of his or her trial witnesses is not excused simply because the defendant does not know the addresses of those witnesses.

In *People v. Riggs* (2008) 44 Cal.4th 248, 79 Cal.Rptr.3d 648, 187 P.3d 363, the defendant was charged with capital murder. More than one month after the guilt phase of the trial had begun, and three weeks after the prosecution had completed its case-in-chief, the defendant, who represented himself, disclosed the names and addresses of two alibi witnesses who would testify that at the time of the murder the defendant was with them far away from the scene of the murder.

The prosecution requested sanctions for a discovery violation by the defendant. The defendant argued that he had not committed a discovery violation, because he did not know the addresses of these witnesses until shortly before he disclosed them to the prosecution. Therefore, the defendant argued, since he could not reasonably anticipate calling them as witnesses until he knew their location, he had not violated his discovery duties. The trial court rejected the defendant's argument and found a discovery violation. The court imposed a jury instruction as a sanction for the violation.

The defendant was convicted of murder and sentenced to death. On automatic appeal the defendant contended that the giving of the jury instruction was error. The Supreme Court rejected the defendant's argument.

The Court found that substantial evidence supported the trial court's decision that the defendant had committed a discovery violation—that the defendant "would reasonably anticipate that it was likely he would call as witnesses family members who purportedly knew that he was several hundred miles away from the scene of the crime when the murder was committed." 44 Cal.4th at 306.

To the defendant's argument presented to the trial court that he had not violated his discovery obligations because he had not known the *addresses* of these two witnesses until shortly before he disclosed their names, the Supreme Court held that the defendant "should have disclosed their names at least 30 days before the trial began." The Court thus held that disclosure of the *names* was not excused simply because the defendant did not know their *addresses*. 44 Cal.4th at 306. The Court further held that "[d]elayed disclosure of *both* the name and address of a witness due to an inability to locate him or her is not good cause as defined in section 1054.7." 44 Cal.4th at 309, n.29. [italics in original]

The Supreme Court also rejected the defendant's argument in the trial court that he had not *intended* to call the witnesses until he had located them.

The Court stated that the "notion that defendant did not *intend* for purposes of discovery to call these critical witnesses, who might have established his absolute innocence, because defendant was not sure that he would be *able* to call them at trial, arguably conflicts with our prior interpretations of the statute . . . ." 44 Cal.4th at 310. [italics in original]

§ 4:5.4 Objective component of definition

The objective component of the definition of a trial witness was utilized by the California Supreme Court in *People v. Riggs* (2008) 44 Cal.4th 248, 79 Cal.Rptr.3d 648, 187 P.3d 363.

In *Riggs* the defendant was charged with capital murder. More than one month after the guilt phase of the trial had begun, and three weeks after the prosecution had completed its case-in-chief, the defendant, who represented himself, disclosed the names and addresses of two alibi witnesses who would testify that at the time of the murder the defendant was with them far away from the scene of the murder.

The prosecution requested sanctions for a discovery violation by the defendant. The defendant argued that he had not committed a discovery violation, because he did not know the addresses of these witnesses until shortly before he disclosed them to the prosecution. Therefore, the defendant argued, since he could not reasonably anticipate calling them as witnesses until he knew their location, he had not violated his discovery duties. The trial court rejected the defendant's argument and found a discovery violation. The court imposed a jury instruction as a sanction for the violation.

The defendant was convicted of murder and sentenced to death. On automatic appeal the defendant contended that the giving of the jury instruction was error. The Supreme Court rejected the defendant's argument.

The Court found that substantial evidence supported the trial court's decision that the defendant had committed a discovery violation—that the defendant "would reasonably anticipate that it was likely he would call as witnesses family members who purportedly knew that he was several hundred miles away from the scene of the crime when the murder was committed." 44 Cal.4th at 306.

To the defendant's argument presented to the trial court that he had not violated his discovery obligations because he had not known the *addresses* of these two witnesses until shortly before he disclosed their names, the Supreme Court that the defendant "should have disclosed their names at least 30 days before the trial began." The Court thus held that disclosure of the *names* was not excused simply because he did not know their *addresses*. 44 Cal.4th at 306. The Court further held that "[d]elayed disclosure of *both* the name and address of a witness due to an inability to locate him or her is not good cause as defined in section 1054.7." 44 Cal.4th at 309, n.29. [italics in original]

The Supreme Court also rejected the defendant's argument in the trial court that he had not *intended* to call the witnesses until he had located them. The Court stated that the "notion that defendant did not *intend* for purposes of discovery to call these critical witnesses, who might have established his absolute innocence, because defendant was not sure that he would be *able* to call them at trial, arguably conflicts with our prior interpretations of the statute . . . ." 44 Cal.4th at 310. [italics in original]

The holding and reasoning of the Court in *Riggs* appears to support the conclusion that the definition of a trial witness has an objective as well as a subjective component.

§ 4:11   Defense trial witness statements or reports — generally

§ 4:11.3   Redacting/editing discoverable material

If potentially discoverable material does not contain *Brady* evidence, a trial court may allow the prosecutor to redact sensitive information from that material without the courts also reviewing the prosecutor's redactions.

In *United States v. Stinson* (2011, CA9 CA) 647 F.3d 1196, two defendants were charged in federal district court with conspiracy under the Racketeer Influenced and Corrupt Organizations (RICO) Act. One of the defendants served a subpoena duces tecum on the California Department of Corrections to obtain the confidential file that CDC maintained on him. The district court ordered CDC to produce the confidential file in unredacted form to the government. The Court then ordered the government to redact sensitive information from that file in order to protect the safety and security of witnesses.

The defendant filed a motion for an order that the government produce an unredacted version of his confidential file, or in the alternative, to require the trial court to review the redacted material *in camera* to determine what materials should remain redacted. The district court denied the defendant's motion. Following their convictions the defendants appealed, arguing, *inter alia*, that the trial court erred in denying his discovery motion. The Ninth Circuit Court of Appeals rejected the defendants' argument.

The Court observed that the defendant did not show that the redacted documents constituted *Brady* evidence. The documents contained in Stinson's confidential file consisted of debriefing interviews of inmates who did not testify in Stinson's trial, "so the redacted identities of the debriefers were not material, let alone exculpatory or impeaching." 647 F.3d at 1208. The court held that "[a] district court need not make such documents available based on 'mere speculation about materials in the government's files.' [citations omitted]" 647 F.3d at 1208.

The Court of Appeals then held that the trial court had not erred in denying the defendant's motion that the court review the unredacted version of the documents *in camera*. The Court distinguished *United States v. Alvarez* (1996, CA9 CA) 86 F.3d 901, a case in which the Court of Appeals held that when the government claims that a statement ordered to be produced does not relate to the testimony of a witness, "the court shall order the United States to deliver such statement for the inspection of the court in camera," and "the court shall excise the portions of such statement which do not relate." 86 F.3d at 906–907. The Court of Appeals held that the redaction procedure approved in *Alvarez* did not apply, because "none of the redactions at issue concerned statements of testifying witnesses. We therefore conclude that the district court did not err in supervising discovery because the government did not redact *Brady* material and the court was not required to review unredacted documents *in camera*." 647 F.3d at 1208.

§ 4:12   Defense-retained trial expert witnesses — generally

While the names and addresses of defense-retained trial expert witnesses are not protected from mandatory disclosure to the prosecution, almost all communications from the defendant to such experts are privileged, unless and until that privilege is waived by the defense.

§ 4:12.4   Defendant's statements to defense expert witnesses

The most important privilege relating to defense-retained trial expert witnesses is the attorney-client privilege, which along with the defendant's privilege against self-incrimination shields from disclosure statements made to the expert by the defendant. These statements are absolutely privileged unless and until the defense announces an intention to call the expert as a defense trial witness or otherwise reveals a substantial portion of the privileged communication.

§ 4:12.4.1   Pretrial protection of defendant's statements to expert witness

In the 2012 case of *Maldonado v. Superior Court* (2012) 53 Cal. 4th 1112, 140 Cal. Rptr. 3d 113, 274 P.3d 1110, the California Supreme Court held, *inter alia*, that, by presenting, at trial, a mental-state defense to criminal charges or penalties, a defendant waives his or her Fifth Amendment privilege to the limited extent necessary to allow the prosecution a fair opportunity to rebut the defense evidence. Under such circumstances, the Constitution allows the prosecution to receive unredacted reports of the defendant's examinations by defense mental experts, including any statements by the defendant to the examiners and any conclusions they have drawn therefrom. The prosecution is also constitutionally permitted to obtain its own examination of the accused, and to use the results, including the accused's statements to the prosecution examiners, as is required to negate the asserted defense. If the defendant refuses to cooperate with the prosecution examiners, the court may impose sanctions, such as advising the jury that it may consider such noncooperation when weighing the opinions of the defense experts. On the other hand, except for appropriate rebuttal, the defendant's statements to the prosecution experts may not be used, either directly or as a lead to other evidence, to bolster the prosecution's case against the defendant.

§4:12.4.2 In-trial protection of defendant's statements to expert witness

In *People v. Smith* (2007) 40 Cal.4th 483, 54 Cal.Rptr.3d 245, 150 P.3d 1224, a defense expert witness testified regarding tests he had administered to the defendant to refresh his recollection before the witness testified at the hearing. The expert also admitted that he had relied upon certain aspects of the testing to formulate his opinions about the defendant's anxiety condition.

The prosecution moved for disclosure of the expert's notes, tests, and test results. The trial court ordered disclosure. The defendant was convicted of two counts of first degree murder and sentenced to death. On his automatic appeal, the defendant argued that the trial court erred in requiring disclosure of the expert's notes, test data, and test materials. The California Supreme Court rejected the defendant's argument.

The Court held that by virtue of Evidence Code section 771, subdivisions (a) and (b), when a witness uses a writing to refresh his or her memory, the writing must be produced at the hearing if the adverse party requests an opportunity to examine it. The adverse party may cross-examine the witness about the writing and may introduce in evidence any portion of the writing that is pertinent to the testimony of the witness.

The Court further held that by virtue of Evidence Code section 721, subdivision (a), the adverse party is entitled to fully cross-examine a witness about the matter on which the witness's opinion is based and the reasons for that opinion. "Such cross-examination properly includes documents and records examined by an expert witness in preparing his or her testimony." *People v. Smith*, 40 Cal.4th at 509.

Thus, if a witness has used a writing or document to refresh his or her recollection or memory in preparing to testify, the opposing party is entitled to in-trial production of that writing or document.

§4:12.5 Reports of non-testifying defense experts

Reports of non-testifying defense experts are privileged from disclosure unless the defense announces an intention to call the expert as a witness or otherwise waives the attorney-client privilege as to that expert.

§4:12.5.1 Pretrial protection of non-testifying defense expert's statements and reports

The prosecution does not have the right to disclosure of defense experts' statements and reports prior to trial until the defendant makes the decision to call those experts to testify in the trial.

In *Wellons v. Hall* (2009, CA11 GA) 554 F.3d 923, the prosecution, citing a state case as authority, moved the trial court for an order to require the defendant, who was charged with murder and rape, to disclose the identities, addresses, and written reports of any experts whom the defense had consulted in preparation for trial. The trial court granted the prosecution's motion. The defendant ultimately disclosed the identities of defense expert witnesses who had been consulted, but his counsel refrained from having the experts prepare any written reports. In light of the trial court's rulings, the defendant's attorney decided not to present any mental health expert testimony in the guilt phase of trial. The defendant was convicted and sentenced to death.

Ultimately the defendant filed a habeas corpus petition in the federal courts. In support of this petition the defendant-petitioner argued, *inter alia*, that the trial court's ruling requiring the disclosure of the identities and reports of defense experts consulted violated his due process right to present insanity and mentally ill defenses, and constituted constitutional error under *Wardius v. Oregon* (1973) 412 U.S. 470, 93 S.Ct. 2208, 37 L.Ed.2d 82, because full disclosure of this information to the prosecution "chilled his investigation and consultation with mental health experts, which were critical to his defense." 554 F.3d at 938.

Although ultimately concluding that the trial court's order was harmless error, the Eleventh Circuit Court of Appeals held that the trial court's ruling "violated the Due Process Clause of [the] Fourteenth Amendment because it granted the prosecution greater discovery rights than Wellons possessed in preparing for trial." 554 F.3d 939.

§ 4:12.5.3   In-trial protection of non-testifying defense expert's identity

In *People v. Coddington* (2000) 23 Cal.4th 529, 97 Cal.Rptr.2d 528, 2 P.3d 1081, the California Supreme Court held that the work product privilege in criminal cases extends beyond the writings listed in subdivision (a) of Code of Civil Procedure section 2018.030 and bars the use of non-statutory discovery mechanisms to obtain writings that reflect an attorney's impressions, conclusions, opinions, or legal research or theories.

The Supreme Court has essentially reconsidered the more expansive definition of work product in criminal cases that it announced in *Coddington* in light of the enactment of Penal Code section 1054.6 in 1990. The Court's reconsideration of its holding in *Coddington* has substantially limited the scope of that privilege in criminal cases.

In *People v. Zamudio* (2008) 43 Cal.4th 327, 75 Cal.Rptr.3d 289, 181 P.3d 105, the defendant was charged with capital murder arising out of the stabbing deaths of two of his neighbors. Prior to trial the prosecution criminalist examined a ring upon which there was an apparent small spot of blood and clothing taken from the defendant at the time of his arrest. The prosecution did not test the blood spot on the ring. The ring and the clothing were delivered to a laboratory designated by the defense under a confidential appointment.

At trial the prosecution introduced evidence that these items had been delivered to the defense laboratory. The defendant objected to this evidence, but the objection was overruled. The defendant was convicted of murder and sentenced to death.

The defendant contended on appeal that allowing this evidence violated the work product privilege, citing *Coddington*. The Supreme Court rejected the defendant's argument, holding that *Coddington* applied only to trials that took place prior to the enactment of Penal Code section 1054.6 by Proposition 115 in 1990. The Court stated:

> "Defendant's reliance on *Coddington* is misplaced. Although we decided *Coddington* after section 1054.6's enactment, our opinion did not mention that statute, and properly so. Because the trial in *Coddington* ended in 1989 [citation omitted], before section 1054.6's enactment, the statute was inapplicable in the case and irrelevant to our work product analysis . . . because defendant's crimes and his trial occurred well after 1990, Penal Code section 1054.6 applies and strictly limits the scope of the work product privilege only to 'writing[s] that reflect[] an attorney's impressions, conclusions, opinions, or legal research or theories . . . .' Code Civ. Proc., sec. 2018.030, subd. (a).) As explained above, defendant's work product claim falls under this restricted definition." 43 Cal.4th at 356.

The Court then concluded that the defendant's work product objection was without merit. Because Penal Code section 1054.6 explicitly limits the work product definition in criminal cases to the core work product of subdivision (a) of Code of Civil Procedure section 2018.030, the testimony of the prosecution's actions in sending the tested items and test results to a defense laboratory does not meet the definition of work product contained in that provision of the Code of Civil Procedure. Thus, "[t]he admission of this evidence therefore did not contravene the work product privilege as it applies in criminal cases." 43 Cal.4th at 355.

Coddington had spawned a series of defense motions requesting trial courts to forbid prosecutors and their investigating officers from monitoring jail records to determine the identity of visitors to incarcerated defendants prior to trial. *Coddington* held that such monitoring violated protected non-statutory work product. In the wake of *Zamudio*, such *Coddington*-based motions would appear to be without merit.

The conclusion we reached in the text in reliance on *Coddington*—that it is improper for a prosecutor to utilize discovery to determine the identity of defense-retained experts that the defendant does not intend to call to testify as defense witnesses at the trial—does not appear to have continuing viability in the wake of *People v. Zamudio.*

§ 4:12.7   Test results of defense experts on prosecution evidence

When defense testing of prosecution evidence would consume all of that evidence, a trial court may order that the defendant share the results of the defense tests with the prosecution.

In *People v. Varghese* (2009) 162 Cal.App.4th 1084, 76 Cal.Rptr.3d 449, the defendant was charged with murder. A portion of a small bloodstain found at the murder scene was tested by a police criminalist. The police criminalist's DNA testing showed that the blood was the defendant's. The defendant moved for an order allowing a defense expert to test the remaining portion of the bloodstain. The defendant's test would have destroyed the remaining part of the bloodstain. The defense opposed any order that the defense expert be required to share the results of the defense testing with the prosecution. The prosecution opposed the defense motion, claiming that the prosecution wanted to conduct further testing on the sample to corroborate the DNA results obtained by the police criminalist.

The trial court found that the prosecution was entitled to corroborate the findings of the police criminalist and concluded that further testing of the bloodstain would likely consume the remaining sample. The court offered to allow the defense expert or any independent laboratory agreeable to the defense to test the remaining sample, but only if the results were made available to both parties. The defense declined the court's offer. The defendant was convicted of murder and appealed.

On appeal the Court of Appeal concluded that neither *Prince v. Superior Court* (1992) 8 Cal.App.4th 1176, 10 Cal.Rptr.2d 855, nor *People v. Cooper* (1991) 53 Cal.3d 771, 281 Cal.Rptr. 90, 809 P.2d 865, was controlling authority governing the defendant's claim that the trial court erred in its ruling. The Court concluded that "where there are multiple pieces of evidence sufficient enough to allow multiple testing by each of the parties . . . the findings and investigation of a defense expert may not be subject to prosecution discovery." 76 Cal.Rptr.3d at 457. But when defense testing of prosecution evidence would destroy the remaining prosecution evidence, depriving the prosecution of an opportunity to corroborate prosecution test results, and the defense could challenge the prosecution's expert or the prosecution's test results, the prosecution must be allowed to corroborate its test by calling the defense expert as a prosecution witness. Thus, the court may order that the defense share the results of its testing with the prosecution as a condition of allowing defense testing that would consume all of a piece of prosecution evidence.

The Court of Appeal stated:

> "The opportunity for the prosecution to adequately meet a defen-
> dant's challenge to its expert and the expert's findings is an
> important component of the choice to be made . . . the function of

the second sample becomes important because it must protect and serve the needs of both the prosecution and defense . . . its use must not subvert the truth-finding role of the criminal justice process . . . the second test should permit the defense to scrutinize the evidence to assure the prosecution test is proper and correct. At the same time, it cannot be given over to the defense, destroyed through its testing procedures, thereby leaving it unusable as corroboration if at trial the defense challenges the prosecution's testing." 76 Cal.Rptr.3d at 458.

§ 4:12.8   Designating defense expert trial witnesses

Note, that if a defense expert gives at trial what is represented to be his or her valid, soundly based opinion, and if something in the defendant's previous testimony at the suppression hearing is inconsistent with a material aspect of that opinion, there should be no constitutional or policy bar to admitting the defendant's own suppression hearing testimony into evidence to contradict the opinions of his own expert, at least in cases where the expert has interviewed the defendant and relies in part on the defendant's statements. *People v. Spence* (2012) 212 Cal. App. 4th 478, 151 Cal. Rptr. 3d 374.

Whether an appellate court applies the federal standard requiring reversal unless the error is harmless beyond a reasonable doubt, or the California standard requiring reversal only if it is reasonably probable the defendant would have obtained a better outcome in the absence of the error, if the appellate court is confident a defendant would not have obtained a more favorable result had a defense expert testified as defense counsel represented he or she would, reversal of a trial court's order denying a defense motion for mistrial is not required. *People v. Dunn* (2012) 205 Cal. App. 4th 1086, 141 Cal. Rptr. 3d 193.

§ 4:12.9   Defense expert's resource materials

An expert witness for the defendant is not required by the Criminal Discovery Statute to disclose his or her resource materials in advance of trial. In this respect the defense expert is treated in the same way that the prosecution expert is treated. See Section 3:13.3 of the text and this supplement.

However, once a defense (or prosecution) expert testifies on direct examination, the expert may be required to answer questions on cross-examination that ask the expert to disclose the expert's sources of information upon which the expert bases his or her opinions. If the expert declines to identify his or her sources, including a refusal to disclose the identities of persons interviewed by the expert, the trial court may decline to admit the testimony of the expert. *People v. Price* (1991) 1 Cal.4th 324, 420–421, 3 Cal.Rptr.2d 106, 821 P.2d 610, superceded by statute on other grounds, *People v. Hinks* (1997) 58 Cal.App.4th 1157, 1161, 68 Cal.Rptr.2d 440.

The California Supreme Court reaffirmed its holding in *Price* in *People v. Prince* (2007) 40 Cal.4th 1179, 1233, 57 Cal.Rptr.3d 543, 156 P.3d 1015.

Whether an appellate court applies the federal standard requiring reversal unless the error is harmless beyond a reasonable doubt, or the California standard requiring reversal only if it is reasonably probable the defendant would have obtained a better outcome in the absence of the error, if the appellate court is confident a defendant would not have obtained a more favorable result had a defense expert testified as defense counsel represented he or she would, reversal of a trial court's order denying a defense motion for mistrial is not required. *People v. Dunn* (2012) 205 Cal. App. 4th 1086, 141 Cal. Rptr. 3d 193.

PART III.   LIMITATIONS ON DEFENDANT'S DISCLOSURE OBLIGATIONS

§ 4:14   Exempted disclosures — generally

A number of constitutional and statutory privileges protect the defendant from always being forced to comply with every disclosure requirement included in Penal Code section 1054.3.

§ 4:14.2   Attorney-client privilege

Standing alone, the attorney-client privilege is merely a rule of evidence; it has not been held to encompass a constitutional right. In some situations, however, government interference with the confidential relationship between a defendant and his counsel may implicate Sixth Amendment rights. A petitioner must show, at a minimum, that the intrusion was purposeful, that there had been communication of defense strategy to the prosecution, and that the intrusion resulted in tainted evidence. Further, the intrusion violates the Sixth Amendment only when it substantially prejudiced the defendant, in that the prosecutor actually used or otherwise gained an unfair advantage from the confidential information. *Peyton v. Lopez* (C.D. Cal. Feb. 22, 2012) 2012 U.S. Dist. LEXIS 50350.

A defendant who alleges ineffective assistance of counsel waives attorney-client privilege as to matters he or she challenges. *United States v. Joseph* (Jan. 12, 2012, CA9 Haw.) 2012 U.S. App. LEXIS 527. However, where a movant impliedly waives the attorney-client privilege by asserting an ineffective assistance of counsel claim, the privilege is waived only to the extent necessary to allow the opposing party to rebut the claim. Furthermore, the privileged material disclosed may only be used to respond to movant's motion and cannot be used in other proceedings. *United States v. Sewell* (E.D. Cal. Nov. 14, 2012) 2012 U.S. Dist. LEXIS 162986.

Further, the important right to attorney-client confidentiality is sufficiently protected by post-judgment appeals: appellate courts can remedy the improper disclosure of privileged material in the same way they remedy a host of other erroneous evidentiary rulings: by vacating an adverse judgment and remanding for a new trial in which the protected material and its fruits are excluded from evidence. Deferring review until final judgment will not chill attorney communications because clients and counsel are unlikely to focus on the remote prospect of an erroneous disclosure order, let alone on the timing of a possible appeal. Moreover, parties must already account for the real possibility of disclosure due to a misapprehension of the privilege's scope, waiver, or the crime-fraud exception. *United States v. Guerrero* (2012, CA9 Cal.) 693 F.3d 990.

Although the Criminal Discovery Statute protects against disclosures which violate statutory and constitutional privileges, such as the attorney-client privilege, those privileges are not protected if the party or attorney holding the attorney-client privilege takes actions that waive the privilege.

In *In re: Grand Jury (Attorney-Client Privilege)* (2008, CA DC) 527 F.3d 200, a physician suspected of defrauding the federal government in billing Medicaid for services that he did not provide delivered his patient records to his attorney. The attorney showed those records to the Assistant United States Attorney in an effort to exonerate the doctor. The government copied those records and kept the copies. The government then served the physician with a subpoena duces tecum to obtain the originals of the records in order to conduct forensic ink analysis on them. The physician and his attorney moved to quash the subpoena duces tecum as violating the attorney-client privilege. The district court denied the motion.

The District of Columbia Court of Appeals affirmed the district court's holding. In reaching this decision the Court of Appeals concluded that "[s]haring the doctor's records with the government destroyed whatever attorney-client privilege might have attached to them. [citations omitted] There is no argument that the documents were shown to the government without the doctor's approval. It is of no consequence that the doctor might have initially given the documents to his attorney for the purpose of obtaining legal advice." 527 F.3d at 201.

It is significant that the Court held that the attorney-client privilege had been waived by the actions of the attorney in disclosing writings to the government without the approval or consent of the physician.

Moreover, the attorney-client privilege protects confidential communications between a client and his or her attorney. This privilege does not protect against disclosure of the actions or inaction of the defendant's attorney regarding prosecution evidence.

In *People v. Bennett* (2009) 45 Cal.4th 577, 88 Cal.Rptr.3d 131, 199 P.3d 535, the California Supreme Court considered an argument on appeal by a defendant convicted of murder and sentenced to death that the prosecution violated his attorney-client privilege by introducing evidence that prosecution evidence was available for retesting by the defense and the defense had not sought to conduct such retesting. The Court rejected this argument, concluding that "[a]sking whether was evidence available for retesting, and even whether the defense sought a split of the sample [for retesting] did not violate the privilege." 45 Cal.4th at 596.

The attorney-client privilege protects a criminal defendant from being forced to disclose reports prepared by a defense-retained expert consultant and witness statements obtained by that consultant. Factual investigations performed by attorneys in their capacity as attorneys "fall comfortably within the protection of the attorney-client privilege." *Sandra T.E. v. S. Berwin Sch. Dist. 100* (2010, CA7 IL) 600 F.3d 612, 619; *Upjohn Co. v. United States* (1981) 449 U.S. 383, 101 S.Ct. 677, 66 L.Ed.2d 584. When an attorney is retained to provide legal assistance to a criminal defendant, any fact finding which that attorney performs pertaining to legal advice or legal assistance constitutes protected attorney-client communications.

Thus, in *Sandra T.E. v. S. Berwin Sch. Dist. 100*, in which the defendant school district retained an attorney to interview potential witnesses, perform a factual investigation, and to provide legal services to the school district, the Court of Appeals held that communications made and documents generated during that investigation were protected by the attorney-client privilege.

An attorney's duty of confidentiality is broader than the lawyer-client privilege and protects virtually everything the lawyer knows about the client's matter regardless of the source of the information. *Elijah W. v. Superior Court* (2013) 216 Cal. App. 4th 140, 156 Cal. Rptr. 3d 592.

Practice Tip for Defendant: You should never disclose to the prosecution evidence provided to you by your client without first consulting and obtaining the approval of the defendant. You must advise the defendant that disclosure of such evidence will waive the attorney-client privilege, and the prosecution will be free to utilize that evidence against your client.

§ 4:14.3   Attorney client privilege in habeas proceedings

The scope of the waiver of the attorney-client and work product privileges is delineated when a federal habeas petitioner raises a claim of ineffective assistance of counsel. Although that petitioner impliedly waives his attorney-client privilege, such waiver is narrow and does not extend beyond the adjudication of the ineffectiveness claim in the federal habeas proceeding. In order to protect that limited waiver, district courts have the obligation, whenever they permit discovery of attorney-client materials as relevant to the defense of ineffective assistance of counsel claims in habeas cases, to ensure that the party given such access does not disclose these materials, except to the extent necessary in the habeas proceeding. Parties in habeas cases, unlike those in ordinary civil cases, have no right to discovery, and that discovery is available if, and only to the extent that, the judge in the exercise of his discretion and for good cause shown grants leave to do so. If a district court exercises its discretion to allow such discovery, it must ensure compliance with the fairness principle. To that end, it must enter appropriate orders clearly delineating the contours of the limited waiver before the commencement of discovery, and strictly police those limits thereafter. *Lambright v. Ryan* (2012, CA9 Ariz.) 698 F.3d 808.

§ 4:14.7   Work product

Where a plea agreement obligates a defendant to make full and truthful disclosures, partial disclosure by a defendant may constitute a material and substantial breach, such that the prosecution is released from its obligations. The fact that the prosecution may have benefitted from a defendant's partial performance under the plea agreement does not bar the prosecution from moving to vacate the plea agreement based on a material and substantial breach of it. *People v. Peterson* (2012) 211 Cal. App. 4th 1072, 150 Cal. Rptr. 3d 340.

In order for evidence to be protected by the work product privilege, that evidence must be a *writing* that reflects the attorney's impressions, conclusions, opinions, or legal research or theories.

In *People v. Bennett* (2009) 45 Cal.4th 577, 88 Cal.Rptr.3d 131, 199 P.3d 535, the California Supreme Court considered an argument on appeal by a criminal defendant convicted of murder and sentenced to death that the prosecution violated his attorney's work product privilege by eliciting evidence in trial that contrary to defense counsel's implication, DNA samples were available for independent testing. The Supreme Court rejected this argument, concluding that the questions asked by the prosecutor in trial "did not elicit or attempt to elicit evidence of a 'writing' reflecting defense counsel's 'impressions, conclusions, opinions, or legal research or theories' and therefore did not violate the work product privilege." 45 Cal.4th at 595.

The work-product privilege protects against the forced disclosure of reports prepared by a defense-retained attorney consultant and witness statements obtained by that attorney. Factual investigations performed by attorneys in their capacity as attorneys are protected by the work-product privilege. This privilege "applies to attorney-led investigations when the documents at issue 'can fairly be said to have been prepared or obtained because of the prospect of litigation.' [citation omitted]." *Sandra T.E. v. S. Berwin Sch. Dist 100* (2010, CA7 IL) 600 F.3d 612, 622. When an attorney is retained to provide legal assistance to a criminal defendant, any statements obtained or documents created by that attorney pertaining to legal advice or legal assistance constitute work-product protected communications.

Thus, in *Sandra T.E. v. S. Berwin Sch. Dist. 100*, in which the defendant school district retained an attorney to interview potential witnesses, perform a factual investigation, and to provide legal services to the school district, the Court of Appeals held that communications made and documents generated during that investigation were protected by the work-product privilege. 600 F.3d at 622–623.

Although the work-product privilege protects a prosecutor's handwritten voir dire notes from forced disclosure to a defendant who is making a *Batson* motion [*Batson v. Kentucky* (1986) 476 U.S. 79, 106 S.Ct. 1712, 90 L.Ed.2d 69], one federal district court ruled that the work-product privilege does not prevent the defendant from questioning the prosecutor under oath about the prosecutor's writings in her voir dire notes. *See Williams v. Beard* (2011, CA3 PA) 637 F.3d 195, 210.

When a document contains both protected work product and exculpatory evidence, the prosecution has a duty to disclose the non-cumulative underlying exculpatory facts contained in the document, while protecting from disclosure opinion work product contained therein. *United States v. Kohring* (2011, CA9 AK) 637 F.3d 895, 908.

A document which contains legal opinions does not constitute discoverable *Brady* evidence unless the legal opinions themselves contain exculpatory facts. Legal opinions are otherwise protected from disclosure by the work-product privilege. *Lopez v. Ryan* (2011, CA9 AZ) 630 F.3d 1198, 1210.

§ 4:14.8   Marital communications privilege—waivers

Confidential marital communications that are otherwise protected by the marital communications privilege lose that protection when the holder of the privilege makes repeated selective disclosures of those communications. *Edwards v. Ayers* (2008, CA9 CA) 542 F.3d 759, 771.

§ 4:16   Restricted disclosures — defense reciprocal disclosures in habeas corpus proceeding

§ 4:16.1   Reciprocal discovery in habeas corpus proceeding

The scope of the waiver of the attorney-client and work product privileges is delineated when a federal habeas petitioner raises a claim of ineffective assistance of counsel. Although that petitioner impliedly waives his attorney-client privilege, such waiver is narrow and does not extend beyond the adjudication of the ineffectiveness claim in the federal habeas proceeding. In order to protect that limited waiver, district courts have the obligation, whenever they permit discovery of attorney-client materials as relevant to the defense of ineffective assistance of counsel claims in habeas cases, to ensure that the party given such access does not disclose these materials, except to the extent necessary in the habeas proceeding. Parties in habeas cases, unlike those in ordinary civil cases, have no right to discovery, and that discovery is available if, and only to the extent that, the judge in the exercise of his discretion and for good cause shown grants leave to do so. If a district court exercises its discretion to allow such discovery, it must ensure compliance with the fairness principle. To that end, it must enter appropriate orders clearly delineating the contours of the limited waiver before the commencement of discovery, and strictly police those limits thereafter. *Lambright v. Ryan* (2012, CA9 Ariz.) 698 F.3d 808.

§ 4:17 Exempted disclosures — mental examination of defendant

Disclosures of mental examinations of any defendant must be evaluated. In order to properly distinguish the federal constitutional issue from the state law issue, it is necessary, in determining whether the disclosure of a defendant's therapy records and the admission of the therapist's testimony violates a federal constitutional right of privacy, to look to the specific nature and extent of the federal constitutional privacy interests that are actually implicated in the particular setting and to the permissible state law interests that would support the disclosure and admission of testimony in question in such a setting. *People v. Gonzales* (2013) 56 Cal. 4th 353, 154 Cal. Rptr. 3d 38, 296 P.3d 945.

Since the publication of the Fourth Edition text in 2007, the California Supreme Court has filed its opinion in *Verdin v. Superior Court* (2008) 43 Cal.4th 1096, 1106, 77 Cal.Rptr.3d 287, 183 P.3d 1250. In *Verdin* the California Supreme Court held that the enactment of Penal Code section 1054, subdivision (e), abrogated the inherent power of trial courts to order discovery in criminal cases that is not expressly authorized by the Criminal Discovery Statute, expressly authorized by some other statute, or mandated by the United States Constitution.

In response to the *Verdin* holding, the California Legislature amended Penal Code section 1054.3 to explicitly authorize trial courts under certain circumstances to order a defendant in a criminal case and a minor in a juvenile proceeding to submit to a mental examination by an expert retained by the prosecution.

Accordingly, a trial court may exercise its discretion to order a criminal defendant who has raised a battered woman syndrome to submit to an examination by a prosecution expert and to give an instruction to the jury if the defendant refuses to submit to such an examination. *See People v. Gonzales* (2011) 51 Cal.4th 894, 925–930, 126 Cal.Rptr.3d 1, 253 P.3d 185.

For a more complete discussion of *Verdin*, the amendments to the Criminal Discovery Statute in response to *Verdin*, and the subject of the prosecution's right to conduct a mental examination of the defendant, see Section 5:8.2.4 of Chapter 5 of this Supplement.

CHAPTER 5

DISCOVERY PROCEDURES, COSTS AND SANCTIONS

PART I. DISCOVERY PROCEDURES

§ 5:1   Disclosure generally—without request or preconditions

While the requirements of timely reciprocal pretrial discovery, as set forth in Penal Code section 1054.3, apply to the penalty phase of a capital case, the trial court has discretion to delay prosecution discovery of defense penalty evidence until after conclusion of the guilt trial. *Maldonado v. Superior Court* (2012) 53 Cal. 4th 1112, 140 Cal. Rptr. 3d 113, 274 P.3d 1110.

§ 5:4   Compliance dates

A working knowledge of the compliance dates established by the Criminal Discovery Statute is critical to a successful implementation of that Statute. When properly enforced and followed, these compliance dates, although serving different immediate purposes, appear to mesh together to form a workable scheme of reciprocal discovery compliance.

§ 5:4.2   Immediate disclosure rule

Several examples of the kind of discovery compliance that satisfies the immediate disclosure rule of the Criminal Discovery Statute have received the approval of the California Supreme Court.

In *People v. Verdugo* (2010) 50 Cal.4th 263, 113 Cal.Rptr.3d 803, 236 P.3d 1035, a law enforcement investigator for the prosecution conducted measurements of the vehicle of the murder victim on a Saturday in the middle of Verdugo's trial. The following Tuesday morning the investigator provided the notes of his measurements to the prosecutor, who produced them to the defense the same morning he received them from the investigator. In the face of a defense allegation that the prosecution had violated the Criminal Discovery Statute, the Supreme Court held: "Nor was there any violation of the reciprocal-discovery statute. The prosecutor produced the notes to the defense the same morning that he received them, which satisfies the statutory requirement of immediate disclosure of materials that became known during trial." 50 Cal.4th at 287.

In *People v. DePriest* (2007) 42 Cal.4th 1, 63 Cal.Rptr.3d 896, 163 P.3d 896, during an evening in the middle of the defendant's trial, a prosecution expert accompanied the prosecutor for a re-examination of physical evidence taken from a dumpster alcove at the scene of the charged murder. The expert found two new partial shoe prints which he had not found in the initial examination of the debris taken from the crime scene. The new partial shoe prints were consistent with the defendant's shoes. The prosecutor informed the defendant's attorney of these two new partial shoeprints the morning after they were discovered.

The defendant's attorney moved to exclude the evidence of the two new shoeprints, claiming that the prosecution had violated the Discovery Statute. The trial court denied the motion, finding that the prosecution complied with its immediate disclosure duty under Penal Code section 1054.7.

The California Supreme Court affirmed the trial court's ruling. The Court stated: "The trial court properly found that [the expert's] testimony and supporting exhibits constituted new evidence, and that disclosure timely occurred under the latter provision. The prosecutor informed both the court and counsel of such evidence immediately after he acquired it. Nothing in the record suggests such acquisition was unreasonably delayed." 42 Cal.4th at 38.

See also People v. Panah (2005) 35 Cal.4th 395, 459–460, 25 Cal.Rptr.3d 672, 107 P.3d 790, which reached a similar conclusion regarding a new report that the prosecution pathologist prepared on the eve of the pathologist's testimony after reexamining microscopic slides at the prosecutor's request.

The continuing investigations which produced the new prosecution evidence during the defendants' trials do not necessarily constitute untoward prosecution conduct. "Some degree of investigation undoubtedly continues after the complaint is filed; indeed it may go on until the parties rest their cases at trial, and sometimes beyond." *People v. Viray* (2005) 134 Cal.App.4th 1186, 1197, 36 Cal.Rptr.3d 693.

§ 5:4.3 Thirty-day rule

The thirty-day rule of Penal Code section 1054.7 does not preclude entry of a discovery order requiring disclosure more than 30 days prior to trial.

In *Magallan v. Superior Court* (2011) 192 Cal.App.4th 1444, 121 Cal.Rptr.3d 841, a magistrate granted a defendant's discovery motion prior to the defendant's preliminary examination. The defendant's motion sought material related to his suppression motion to be made in conjunction with the defendant's preliminary examination. The prosecution had refused to provide this discovery and petitioned the superior court for a writ to overturn the magistrate's ruling. The superior court granted the prosecution's writ petition, and the magistrate set aside the discovery order. The defendant filed a writ petition in the Court of Appeal challenging the action of the superior court.

The Court of Appeal issued the requested writ, holding that because the defendant has a statutory right to litigate a suppression motion pursuant to Penal Code section 1538.5 in connection with his preliminary examination, the defendant is entitled to discovery in aid of that suppression motion. Relying upon its own earlier opinion in *People v. Superior Court (Mouchaourab)* (2000) 78 Cal.App.4th 403, 92 Cal.Rptr.2d 829, which held that a defendant is entitled to discovery of a transcript of the nontestimonial portions of a grand jury indictment proceeding to assist the defendant in making a Penal Code section 995 motion to dismiss the indictment, the Court of Appeal rejected the prosecution's argument that the enactment of the Criminal Discovery Statute had ended the power of a magistrate to order discovery.

The People argued in opposition to the writ petition that the Criminal Discovery Statute in Chapter 10 of the Penal Code cannot apply to a discovery motion made prior to a preliminary examination, because the parties cannot know whether there will even be a trial, and that would make Penal Code section 1054.7's timing requirements ineffectual. The Court of Appeal rejected the People's argument, saying that " Penal Code section 1054.7 requires the prosecution to provide the required information to the defense '*at least* 30 days before trial.' (italics added) It does not preclude a defendant from making an earlier discovery motion under Penal Code section 1054.5, nor does it preclude such a motion from being granted more than 30 days in advance of trial.

If the Attorney General's interpretation were correct, the prosecutor's discovery obligations would suddenly take effect 30 days before trial, and the defense would be deprived of the opportunity to prepare for trial before that time. Such an interpretation would be completely at odds with the express statutory purposes of Chapter 10, which are to promote 'timely pretrial discovery,' avoid the necessity for postponements, and avoid 'undue delay of the proceedings.' Precluding the granting of discovery motions until 30 days before trial would work against the goal of 'timely pretrial discovery' and would inevitably result in postponements and delays in the proceedings. In this case, delaying the discovery of this information material to a suppression motion until just 30 days before trial would result in the delay of the suppression hearing, which would hamper the goals that Chapter 10 was intended to serve." 192 Cal.App.4th at 1460.

§ 5:4.5   Disclosure within 30 days prior to trial

The requirement of Penal Code section 1054.7 that disclosures under the Criminal Discovery Statute must be made no later than 30 days prior to trial is the general rule. However, "[i]f the material and information becomes known to, or comes into the possession of, a party within 30 days of trial, disclosure shall be made immediately . . . ." Penal Code section 1054.7. The California Supreme Court has described this latter provision as an exception to the general rule. *People v. DePriest* (2007) 42 Cal.4th 1, 38, 63 Cal.Rptr.3d 896, 163 P.3d 896.

In *DePriest* the defendant, who was charged with and ultimately convicted of capital murder and other crimes, filed a written offer of proof just prior to opening statements in support of his intent to introduce evidence to bolster the defense theory that the crime was committed by a third person. The offer of proof referred to numerous shoe prints at the crime scene that could not be connected to the defendant or any other known person. The prosecutor, who believed that only a few unidentified shoeprints had been found at the crime scene, arranged for the prosecution shoeprint expert to examine debris that had been taken from the floor of a dumpster located near to where the victim's body had been found. The prosecutor and the prosecution expert looked for prints that the expert might have missed when initially examining this debris.

The expert found two new partial shoe prints that appeared to be consistent with the shoes that the defendant had been wearing when arrested for the murder. The prosecution immediately informed the defense of the newly discovered evidence. The defendant claimed that the prosecution had violated the prosecution's duty to disclose its inculpatory evidence in a timely manner. The trial court accepted the prosecutor's explanation of how and when the prints had been found and rejected the defendant's argument.

On automatic appeal the Supreme Court affirmed the trial court's ruling. The Supreme Court concluded that "[t]he trial court properly found that [the expert's] testimony and supporting exhibits constituted new evidence, and that disclosure timely occurred under [the exception in Penal Code section 1054.7]." The Court observed that the prosecutor informed the defendant immediately after finding the new evidence, and that there was no evidence that the prosecution had unreasonably delayed finding the new evidence. Accordingly, the Court held that the prosecution's conduct did not violate the trial court's pretrial discovery order or the Criminal Discovery Statute. 42 Cal.4th at 38.

In *People v. Panah* (2005) 35 Cal.4th 395, 459–460, 25 Cal.Rptr.3d 672, 107 P.3d 790, which is discussed in the text, the Supreme Court had reached a similar conclusion regarding a report that the prosecution pathologist prepared on the eve of trial after the pathologist reexamined microscopic slides at the request of the prosecution.

The exception to the 30-day cut-off rule for prosecution disclosure prior to trial appears to be satisfied when three conditions are met: (1) the prosecution has not unreasonably delayed its searching for or obtaining evidence; (2) the prosecution comes upon or generates new incriminating evidence within 30 days prior to trial; and (3) the prosecution immediately notifies the defendant of the finding or generation of that evidence.

In *People v. Rutter* (2006) 143 Cal.App.4th 1349, 49 Cal.Rptr.3d 925, the defendant offered to sell a Hollywood actress pictures from a photoshoot the defendant had taken of the actress 11 years before, when she was only 19 years of age. The actress filed a civil suit to enjoin the defendant from selling the photographs. The defendant produced a release form which he claimed contained the actress's signature, and he submitted a declaration under penalty of perjury stating that the actress's signature on the release form was genuine.

The actress contacted the police and pretended to negotiate with the defendant to purchase the photographs. The police obtained a warrant to search the defendant's residence and recovered computers and CD-ROMS, which contained numerous copies of the photo shoot release form. The defendant was charged with attempted grand theft, forgery, and perjury.

Five days before trial the prosecution computer consultant provided the prosecutor with a long report that summarized the computer evidence that supported the charge that the defendant had forged the actress's name on the photo shoot release form. The prosecutor, who was newly assigned to the case, had requested that the expert prepare the report so that he (the prosecutor) would have a summary of the computer-related evidence for trial. The prosecutor provided the report to the defendant the next day after receiving it from the consultant.

Even though the defense team had been given "unfettered access" to the defendant's computers for two years prior to trial, defense counsel claimed that it was only when he read the new report of the prosecution's computer consultant that he learned the expert would testify that the defendant's laptop computer showed that the release had been forged. The defendant moved to exclude the expert's testimony, claiming that the late disclosure prior to trial violated the prosecution's duty to timely disclose the expert's opinions. The trial court denied the motion to exclude the expert's testimony. The defendant was convicted and appealed.

The Court of Appeal rejected the defendant's argument that the trial court erred in refusing to exclude the opinion of the prosecution expert, because the prosecution did not disclose the expert's report of his examination of the computer until a few days before trial. The Court concluded that there was no evidence the prosecutor knew of the expert's opinion prior to receiving the expert's report, and the prosecution immediately disclosed the report to the defendant. The Court concluded that the prosecution's evidence in question was covered by the "within 30 days of trial" exception of Penal Code section 1054.7, and that the prosecution "satisfied section 1054.7 as to the computer expert's report." 143 Cal.App.4th at 1353–1354.

Although it involved a federal capital trial statute and not the application of the 30-day disclosure rule of California Penal Code section 1054.7, the opinion of the Sixth Circuit Court of Appeals in *United States v. Young* (2008, CA6 TN) 533 F.3d 453, contains some helpful analysis on the question of the impact of a "close-to-trial" disclosure of prosecution inculpatory evidence.

There is a discovery or notice rule that applies to a capital trial in federal courts. That rule, found in 18 U.S.C. section 3432, requires the prosecution to furnish the capital defendant with a list of the witnesses to be produced at the trial no later than three entire days before the commencement of the trial. In *United States v. Young* (2008, CA6 TN) 533 F.3d 453, the government in a federal capital trial found 19 new witnesses after voir dire had begun in the defendant's trial. The defendant moved to exclude the 19 new witnesses. The trial court granted the defendant's motion under the authority of 18 U.S.C. sec. 3432, and the government sought interlocutory review of the district court's ruling.

The Sixth Circuit Court of Appeals vacated the district court order, finding that although the government's notification to the defense of the 19 newly found witnesses violated the capital case witness notice statute, the district court abused its discretion in excluding the witnesses without evidence of a discovery abuse or bad faith by the government. The Court concluded that the "government acted in good faith and conducted a reasonably diligent investigation . . . ." The Court remanded the case for the district court to determine whether the defendant would suffer irreparable harm from the late disclosure of the witnesses. 533 F.3d at 466.

The dangers to the prosecution of providing discovery to the defendant close in time to the beginning of trial were emphasized by the Second Circuit Court of Appeals in *United States v. Gil* (2002, CA2 NY) 297 F.3d 93, as follows:

"[D]isclosure of critical information on the eve of trial is unsafe for the prosecution: When such a disclosure is first made on the eve of trial, or when trial is under way, the opportunity to use it may be impaired . . . [Disclosures made just prior to the start of trial would be] "at a time presumably when a conscientious defense lawyer would be preoccupied working on an opening statement and witness cross-examinations, and all else. Moreover, disclosure on the eve of trial 'may be insufficient unless it is fuller and more thorough than may have been required if the disclosure had been made at an earlier stage.' [citation omitted]." 297 F.3d at 106.

However, when the prosecution first learns of inculpatory evidence close in time to the trial and then discloses that evidence quickly to the defendant, the prosecution does not commit a discovery violation. In *United States v. Lofton* (2009, CA8 IA) 557 F.3d 594, the prosecution first interviewed a jail inmate days before the trial of a defendant charged with being a felon in possession of a firearm. The inmate stated that the defendant confessed to him that he had possessed the firearm. The inmate negotiated a deal with the prosecution to testify against the defendant, and the prosecution immediately notified the defense of the witness, the deal, and the witness's expected testimony.

The defendant's motion to exclude the inmate's testimony on the basis of late disclosure of that evidence was denied by the district court, and the defendant was convicted. On appeal the defendant argued that the trial court erred in denying his motion to exclude the witness's testimony. The Eighth Circuit Court of Appeals rejected the defendant's argument. The Court noted that the government disclosed the witness's identity and the details of his plea agreement more than one week before defendant's trial. The Court further observed that the government disclosed the witness's testimony immediately after the witness was interviewed. The Court found that there was no evidence that the government attempted to gain a tactical advantage in its timing of the disclosures to the defendant. 557 F.3d at 596.

In *United States v. Stenger* (2010, CA8 IA) 605 F.3d 492, the prosecutor learned shortly before the defendant's trial that a cooperating government witness had heard the defendant make inculpatory statements while both men were in jail. The prosecutor informed the defense on the last day before the defendant's trial of the government's intention to call the witness to testify. The defendant's motion to exclude the prosecution witness's testimony was denied, and the defendant was convicted.

On appeal the defendant renewed his argument, claiming that the district court abused its discretion by allowing the cooperating witness to testify. The Eighth Circuit Court of Appeals rejected the defendant's argument, observing that "the prosecutor did not know that [the cooperating witness] had information about [the defendant] until shortly before the trial commenced." 605 F.3d at 501. There was no evidence that the government "purposely withheld information about [the cooperating witness] in order to create an unfair advantage at trial." 605 F.3d at 501. And the government took steps to provide the defense with copies of the witness's plea agreement and presentence investigation report.

Continuing investigations which produce new prosecution evidence even during a defendant's trial do not necessarily constitute untoward prosecution conduct. "Some degree of investigation undoubtedly continues after the complaint is filed; indeed it may go on until the parties rest their cases at trial, and sometimes beyond." *People v. Viray* (2005) 134 Cal.App.4th 1186, 1197, 36 Cal.Rptr.3d 693.

In *People v. Blacksher* (2011) 52 Cal.4th 769, 837–838, 130 Cal.Rptr.3d 191, 259 P.3d 370, the California Supreme Court observed: "[A]lthough the prosecution was late in disclosing a tape recording of defendant's statements to police, the recording was turned over before trial began. As a result, defense counsel had nearly three months to allow Dr. Pierce to listen to that tape before his appearance at the sanity phase. The doctor did not do so. Under the circumstances, there was nothing unfair in allowing the prosecutor to ask Dr. Pierce whether he had listened to that tape."

§ 5:6　Asserting disclosure exceptions—procedures

Penal Code section 1054.6, merely protects those privileges the Constitution or statutes themselves afford, and thus imposes no broader restrictions on pretrial discovery than the Constitution, or the statutes defining privileges, otherwise require. U.S. Const., 5th Amend., does not provide a privilege against the compelled disclosure of self-incriminating materials or information, but only precludes the use of such evidence in a criminal prosecution against the person from whom it was compelled. Accordingly, nothing in § 1054.6 exempts the results of the prosecution examinations from pretrial discovery. *Maldonado v. Superior Court* (2012) 53 Cal. 4th 1112, 140 Cal. Rptr. 3d 113, 274 P.3d 1110.

PART II. PRESERVING AND PRODUCING EVIDENCE

§ 5:8   In general

There are numerous pretrial investigatory and discovery processes that existed prior to the Criminal Discovery Statute and that are not regulated by or subject to the rules of the Criminal Discovery Statute.

§ 5:8.1   Non-testimonial evidence

The relevant question under the confrontation clause, when considering the admissibility of a statement, is whether an individual statement is testimonial, not whether an entire document is testimonial. But when an immigration record is prepared under circumstances objectively indicating that the primary purpose of the record is non-testimonial, the ordinary contents of the record are likewise non-testimonial. Business and public records are generally admissible absent confrontation because, having been created for the administration of an entity's affairs and not for the purpose of establishing or proving some fact at trial, they are not testimonial. *United States v. Rojas-Pedroza* (2013, CA9 Cal.) 716 F.3d 1253.

Statements unwittingly made to an informant are not "testimonial" within the meaning of the Confrontation Clause of the Sixth Amendment. *People v. Arauz* (2012) 210 Cal. App. 4th 1394, 149 Cal. Rptr. 3d 211.

A failure to preserve evidence violates a defendant's right to due process if the unavailable evidence possessed exculpatory value that was apparent before the evidence was destroyed, and is of such a nature that the defendant would be unable to obtain comparable evidence by other reasonably available means. A defendant must also demonstrate that the police acted in bad faith in failing to preserve the potentially useful evidence. The presence or absence of bad faith turns on the government's knowledge of the apparent exculpatory value of the evidence at the time it was lost or destroyed. The mere failure to preserve evidence which could have been subjected to tests which might have exonerated the defendant does not constitute a due process violation. *Jensen v. Hernandez* (E.D. Cal. 2012) 864 F. Supp. 2d 869.

In the context of preserving evidence, bad faith requires more than mere negligence or recklessness. *United States v. Toro-Barboza* (2012, CA9 Cal.) 673 F.3d 1136.

- **The defendant's blood and buccal swab samples for DNA testing.**

The constitutionality of the federal DNA collection statute, which requires the Director of the Bureau of Prisons to collect DNA samples from federal prisoners, parolees, and probationers, has been upheld by every federal Circuit Court of Appeals which has considered the issue. See *United States v. Stewart* (2008, CA1 MA) 532 F.3d 32, 33–34; *United States v. Amerson* (2007, CA2 NY) 483 F.3d 73, 79; *United States v. Sczubelek* (2005, CA3 DE) 402 F.3d 175, 184; *Groceman v. United States Department of Justice* (2004, CA5 TX) 354 F.3d 411, 413-414; *United States v. Conley* (2006, CA6 TN) 453 F.3d 674, 679–681 [described in the text]; *United States v. Hook* (2006, CA7 IL) 471 F.3d 766, 773; *United States v. Kraklio* (2006, CA8 IA) 451 F.3d 922, 924; *United States v. Kriesel* (2007, CA9 WA) 508 F.3d 941; *Banks v. United States* (2007, CA10 OK) 490 F.3d 1178; and *Johnson v. Quander* (2006, CA DC) 440 F.3d 489, 496.

The remaining three Circuit Courts have upheld state statutes authorizing the collection of DNA samples from convicted prisoners. See *Hamilton v. Brown* (2010, CA9 CA) 630 F.3d 889 [California statute]; *Jones v. Murray* (1992, CA4 VA) 962 F.2d 302, 306-307 [Virginia statute]; and *Padgett v. Donald* (2005, CA11 GA) 401 F.3d 1273, 1280 [Georgia statute].

California's DNA statute, the Forensic Identification Data Base and Data Bank Act of 1998, which is codified as Penal Code section 295 et seq., also authorizes collection of DNA samples from persons arrested for a felony, even though not yet convicted. Whether it is constitutional to forcibly collect a blood or buccal swab sample from a felony arrestee who has not been convicted is the subject of pending litigation in California. In *People v. Buza* (2010) 197 Cal.App.4th 1424, 129 Cal.Rptr.3d 753, the First District Court of Appeal held that the forcible collection of bodily samples for DNA purposes from a person who has been arrested for a felony, but whose guilt has not been adjudicated, without independent suspicion, without a warrant, or without a judicial or grand jury determination of probable cause, violates an arrestee's expectation of privacy and is constitutionally invalid under the Fourth Amendment to the United States Constitution. On October 19, 2011, the California Supreme Court granted review in *Buza*. *People v. Buza*, S196200.

In *United States v. Pool* (2010, CA9 CA) 621 F.3d 1213, the Ninth Circuit Court of Appeals upheld a district court order that a defendant who wanted to be released on pretrial bail must provide a DNA sample. The Court held that the government had a legitimate interest in definitively determining the defendant's identity, and that this governmental interest outweighed the defendant's privacy interest.

- **Photographs of the defendant's body.**

An arrested person may be subjected to photographs taken of portions of the arrestee's body for identification purposes, as long as those photographs do not constitute an unconstitutional intrusion of the arrestee's body.

In *Schmidt v. Magyari* (2009, CA8 MO) 557 F.3d 564, a young adult woman was arrested after she provided false personal information after a car in which she was a passenger was stopped. At the police station the police chief took a photograph of a tattoo that was located two inches from her hipbone on her abdomen for identification purposes. The woman filed a federal civil rights action against the chief and the city alleging that the taking of the photograph violated her right against unlawful search and seizure and violated Missouri's strip search law.

The district court rejected the woman's claims and she appealed. The Eighth Circuit Court of Appeals affirmed the district court, holding that "[t]here are legitimate law-enforcement purposes served by photographing the tattoos of an arrestee for use in identification." 557 F.3d at 572. The Court also held that the manner in which the photograph was taken did not violate the plaintiff's privacy rights. "Given the location of the tattoo, [the male police chief] required Schmidt to be no more exposed than necessary to permit photographing the tattoo, which minimized the invasion of Schmidt's privacy." 557 F.3d at 572. The photograph was taken in private, Ms. Schmidt was not required to disrobe, and the police chief did not touch the woman. The Court found that the photograph was necessary to establish the woman's identity.

The Court found that enlisting a female officer to take the photograph would have been required only if Ms. Schmidt had been subjected to a strip search.

- **Corporate business records.**

Nontestimonial evidence subject to discovery by the prosecution under the authority of Penal Code section 1054.4 is not limited to samples or depictions of the defendant's body. Such evidence also includes business or corporate records kept by the defendant.

In *People v. Appellate Division of Superior Court* (2011) 197 Cal.App.4th 985, 130 Cal.Rptr.3d 116, several business entities were charged criminally by the public prosecutor of Los Angeles County with violations of the Los Angeles Municipal Code. The prosecutor filed a motion for corporate discovery from the defendant businesses. The corporate defendants opposed the discovery motion on the grounds that the discovery sought was outside the scope of the Criminal Discovery Statute. The municipal court denied the prosecutor's motion. The appellate division of the Superior Court summarily denied the prosecutor's petition for writ of mandate. The municipal court then denied the prosecutor's motion for leave to serve subpoenas duces tecum on the corporate defendants, holding that Penal Code section 1326 does not apply to a party and that the motion asked for discovery beyond the discovery permitted by the Criminal Discovery Statute. The prosecutor petitioned the Court of Appeal for writ of mandate.

The Court of Appeal granted a writ of mandate, holding that "the criminal discovery statutes do not bar production of the records, which constitute a category of nontestimonial evidence that Penal Code section 1054.4 and established precedent permit the prosecutor to obtain." 197 Cal.App.4th at 989.

In reaching this result the Court of Appeal reaffirmed the applicability of the holding in *People v. Superior Court (Keuffel & Esser Co.)* (1986) 181 Cal.App.3d 785, 227 Cal.Rptr. 13. The Court concluded that "voluntarily created [corporate records] do not involve compelled testimony and fall within the category of materials discoverable under section 1054.4." 197 Cal.App.4th at 991. The Court rejected the defendants' attempts to construe Penal Code section 1054.4 to apply only to "forensic evidence," saying that Section 1054.4 "preserves the prosecutor's right to obtain 'nontestimonial evidence.' " 197 Cal.App.4th at 992.

The Court rejected the defendants' argument that Penal Code section 1054.4 applies only to corporations, and they are not corporations. The Court stated that "all references to 'corporate' documents or records and 'corporate defendants' are fully applicable to real parties in interest, whatever their organizational structure may be." 197 Cal.App.4th at 994.

Accordingly, the Court concluded that Penal Code section 1054.3's "expansion of information that the defense must disclose in no way suggests abrogation of *Keuffel*'s ruling permitting the prosecutor to obtain corporate documents from a corporate defendant as a type of nontestimonial evidence." 197 Cal.App.4th at 994. The Court determined that Penal Code section 1054.3 "imposes upon a defendant a duty to disclose, but does not purport to limit the prosecutor's ability to obtain 'real evidence' authorized by other statutes, such as section 1054.4." 197 Cal.App.4th at 994.

§ 5:8.2   Nontestimonial evidence—mental examination of defendant

The prosecution's power to obtain evidence against the defendant through a mental examination of the defendant has produced considerable litigation. Much of that litigation has now been resolved.

§ 5:8.2.4   Psychological examination of defendant's mental state at time of alleged crime

The question whether a trial court may order a defendant to submit to a examination of his or her mental state at the time of the alleged crime has been a contentious one.

1.   *Verdin v. Superior Court.*

In *Verdin v. Superior Court* (2008) 43 Cal.4th 1096, 1106, 77 Cal.Rptr.3d 287, 183 P.3d 1250, the California Supreme Court held that the enactment of Penal Code section 1054, subdivision (e), abrogated the inherent power of trial courts to order discovery in criminal cases that is not expressly authorized by the Criminal Discovery Statute, expressly authorized by some other statute, or mandated by the United States Constitution. The Court explicitly rejected the argument made by the prosecution that two of the Supreme Court's own prior opinions and a Court of Appeal opinion supported the inherent power of a trial court to order the defendant, who had announced a defense of diminished actuality, to submit to a psychiatric or mental examination by a prosecution psychiatrist.

In *People v. McPeters* (1992) 2 Cal.4th 1148, 9 Cal.Rptr.2d 834, 832 P.2d 146, and *People v. Carpenter* (1997) 15 Cal.4th 312, 63 Cal.Rptr.2d 1, 935 P.2d 708, the Supreme Court upheld trial court authority to order a defendant to undergo a mental examination by a prosecution psychiatrist. In *People v. Danis* (1973) 31 Cal.App.3d 782, 107 Cal.Rptr. 675, the Court of Appeal likewise upheld trial court authority to order such a mental examination of a defendant. In rejecting the prosecution's argument that the Court should follow *McPeters, Carpenter*, and *Danis*, because of courts' inherent power to order such discovery, the *Verdin* Court stated:

> "*Danis, McPeters*, and *Carpenter* have not survived the passage of Proposition 115. *Danis* [citation omitted] opined that prosecutorial discovery from a criminal defendant, in the form of a court-ordered mental examination, was permissible even absent an 'authorizing statute,' because the trial court possessed inherent power to order such discovery. This reasoning is unsupportable following the 1990 enactment of section 1054, subdivision (e), which insists that rules permitting prosecutorial discovery be authorized by the criminal discovery statutes or some other statute, or mandated by the United States Constitution. Although *Danis's result* may have been supportable when decided more than 30 years ago . . . no part of its *reasoning* can have survived the enactment of section 1054, subdivision (e).
>
> "Similarly, the rule announced in *McPeters* [citation omitted] and followed in *Carpenter* [citation omitted] did not survive Proposition 115. Neither decision explained the basis—statutory or otherwise—of their assertion that a criminal defendant who places his mental state in issue thereby creates in the prosecution the right to discovery in the form of a mental examination by a prosecution expert. Because neither *McPeters* nor *Carpenter* rests on a statutory or constitutional basis, both are inconsistent with section 1054, subdivision (e)." 43 Cal.4th at 1106–1107. [italics in original]

The Supreme Court explicitly rejected the prosecution's argument that the Criminal Discovery Statute does not apply to a mental examination of a defendant by a prosecution expert, because such an examination is nontestimonial evidence allowed by Penal Code section 1054.4. The Court concluded that because such an examination would not be limited to observation by the expert of the defendant's demeanor or gestures, any statements made by the defendant would be testimonial in nature. Thus, the mental examination would not be permissible under the authority of Section 1054.5. 43 Cal.4th at 1110–1114.

2.   2009 Amendment of Criminal Discovery Statute.

In response to the decision of the Supreme Court in *Verdin*, the California Legislature amended the Criminal Discovery Statute to explicitly authorize trial courts under certain circumstances to order a defendant in a criminal case and a minor in a juvenile proceeding to submit to a mental examination by an expert retained by the prosecution.

Assembly Bill 1516, which was passed by the Legislature in 2009 and signed into law by the governor on October 11, 2009, has amended Penal Code section 1054.3. In addition to renumbering the existing provisions of Section 1054.3 so that both existing provisions are paragraphs in subdivision (a), AB 1516 added the following new substantive language as subdivision (b) of Section 1054.3:

"(b) (1) Unless otherwise specifically addressed by an existing provision of law, whenever a defendant in a criminal action or a minor in a juvenile proceeding brought pursuant to a petition alleging the juvenile to be within Section 602 of the Welfare and Institutions Code places in issue his or her mental state at any phase of the criminal action or juvenile proceeding through the proposed testimony of any mental health expert, upon timely request by the prosecution, the court may order that the defendant or juvenile submit to examination by a prosecution-retained mental health expert.

(A) The prosecution shall bear the cost of any such mental health expert's fees for examination and testimony at a criminal trial or juvenile court proceeding.

(B) The prosecuting attorney shall submit a list of tests proposed to be administered by the prosecution expert to the defendant in a criminal action or a minor in a juvenile proceeding. At the request of the defendant in a criminal action or a minor in a juvenile proceeding, a hearing shall be held to consider any objections raised to the proposed tests before any test is administered. Before ordering that the defendant submit to the examination, the trial court must make a threshold determination that the proposed tests bear some reasonable relation to the mental state placed in issue by the defendant in a criminal action or a minor in a juvenile proceeding. For the purposes of this subdivision, the term 'tests' shall include any and all assessment techniques such as a clinical interview or a mental status examination."

In order to afford the prosecution a fair opportunity to rebut mental-state evidence proffered by the defense, California's criminal-case reciprocal discovery statute, Penal Code section 1054.3, specifically provides that when the defendant places in issue his or her mental state at any phase of the criminal action, the prosecution may seek and obtain a court order that the defendant submit to examination by a prosecution-retained mental health expert. § 1054.3, subsection (b)(1). *Maldonado v. Superior Court* (2012) 53 Cal. 4th 1112, 140 Cal. Rptr. 3d 113, 274 P.3d 1110.

The stated legislative purpose in amending Penal Code section 1054.3 was "to respond to Verdin v. Superior Court 43 Cal.4th 1096, which held that only the Legislature may authorize a court to order the appointment of a prosecution mental health expert when a defendant has placed his or her mental state at issue in a criminal case or juvenile proceeding pursuant to Section 602 of the Welfare and Institutions Code." Penal Code section 1054.3, subdivision (b)(2). The amendments were not intended to impact "the remaining body of case law governing the procedural or substantive law that controls the administration of these tests or the admission of the results of these tests into evidence." *Id.*

There are six important features of these amendments to Penal Code section 1054.3 that deserve comment.

First, the amendments confer statutory authorization for a trial court in a criminal case and a juvenile court in a juvenile proceeding to order the defendant to submit to a mental examination conducted by a prosecution expert. This explicit reference to juvenile proceedings is unlike any other provision of the Criminal Discovery Statute; none of the remaining provisions of the Criminal Discovery Statute contain an explicit statutory application to juvenile cases. See Section 2:11 *et seq.* of the text.

Second, the amendments do not grant an open-ended authorization for a trial court to order the defendant to submit to such an examination. The authority to order the examination does not arise until the defendant "places in issue his or her mental state . . . through the proposed testimony of any mental health expert . . . ." The trigger point is proposed testimony of a defense mental health expert. Thus, if the defendant places in issue his or her mental state utilizing evidence other than the testimony of a mental health expert, a trial court would not have authority under this statute to order the defendant to submit to a mental health examination by a prosecution expert.

Moreover, this language strongly suggests that the defendant must first disclose the identity of a defense mental health expert whom the defendant intends to call as a witness "at some phase of the criminal action or juvenile proceeding." Until the defendant makes this disclosure, the prosecution does not have the right to request the trial court to order a prosecution-conducted mental health examination of the defendant.

The statutory language implies that the prosecution need not wait until the defense mental health expert actually testifies before requesting the court to order the defendant to submit to a mental health examination conducted by a prosecution-retained expert. In fact, the statutory language clearly anticipates that the mental health examination of the defendant by a prosecution expert should take place before trial, because the prosecution's right to conduct an examination is triggered by the defendant's placing his or her mental state in issue "through the *proposed* testimony of any mental health expert." Penal Code section 1054.3, subdivision (b)(1) [italics added].

The third significant feature is that the amendments appear to require the defendant to disclose the substance of the defense expert witness's expected testimony. Were the defendant not required to disclose that substance, the defendant could defeat a prosecution request for a mental health examination of the defendant by simply not disclosing the expected testimony. The statute requires the prosecuting attorney who requests a prosecution mental health examination of the defendant to "submit a list of tests proposed to be administered by the prosecution expert." Penal Code section 1054.3(b)(1)(B). If the defendant objects to any of the proposed prosecution expert's tests, the trial court must "make a threshold determination that the proposed tests bear some reasonable relation to the mental state placed in issue by the defendant . . . ." Penal Code section 1054.3(b)(1)(B).

There is no way that the prosecution could construct a list of tests to be administered that bears "a reasonable relation to the mental state placed in issue by the defendant" unless the defendant first discloses the substance of the defense expert's expected testimony. And there would be no way for the trial court to make the threshold ruling required by the statute. *See Centeno v. Superior Court* (2004) 117 Cal.App.4th 30, 45, 11 Cal.Rptr.3d 533 [prosecution mental "examinations [of the defendant] are permissible only to the extent they are reasonably related to the determination of the existence of the mental condition raised."].

The fourth significant feature of the amendments to Section 1054.3 is that the prosecution must make a "timely request" for a prosecution-conducted mental health examination. The statute does not define what would constitute a "timely request." We suspect that since the right of the prosecution to request a prosecution mental health examination of the defendant does not arise until the defendant has disclosed the identity and substance of the *proposed* defense expert testimony, the prosecution would have a very short window of time to make the request in order for that request to be considered timely.

In determining what constitutes a timely request, courts are likely to look at related areas of the criminal law which impose a timely request obligation. One such area is defense requests for lineups under the authority of *Evans v. Superior Court* (1974) 11 Cal.3d 617, 114 Cal.Rptr. 121, 522 P.2d 681. One prerequisite for obtaining an *Evans* lineup is that the defendant make a timely request for the lineup. *People v. Farnam* (2002) 28 Cal.4th 107, 183, 121 Cal.Rptr.2d 106, 47 P.3d 988.

In *People v. Baines* (1981) 30 Cal.3d 143, 177 Cal.Rptr. 861, 635 P.2d

455, the California Supreme Court held that a defendant's motion for a pretrial lineup 60 days after his preliminary hearing was untimely because the defendant did not explain why he did not make the motion to a magistrate prior to his arraignment. In *People v. Vallez* (1978) 80 Cal.App.3d 46, 55–56, 143 Cal.Rptr. 914, the Court of Appeal upheld a trial court's ruling denying a defense request for a voice lineup on the ground the motion, filed one week before trial, was untimely.

The determination whether a request is timely made is fact specific. We anticipate that the courts will construe the language *timely request* sensibly, so that a request will be considered timely when it is made within a time frame that is reasonable under all of the facts and circumstances of the case.

The fifth significant feature of the amendments to Section 1054.3 is that they authorize the trial court to grant a prosecution request for a mental examination of the defendant by a prosecution expert whenever the defense expert witness's testimony is proposed for "any phase of the criminal action or juvenile proceeding . . . ." Penal Code section 1054.3(b)(1). This means that if the defendant proposes to introduce expert mental health testimony in the sanity phase of a criminal trial, or in the sentencing phase of a capital trial, the trial court will have authority to grant a prosecution request for a prosecution-conducted mental health examination.

The sixth significant feature of the amendments to Section 1054.3 is that they require the prosecution to pay the prosecution expert's examination and testimonial fees. This feature would be unremarkable except for the fact that it does not limit the prosecution's obligation to pay the witness's testimonial fees to situations in which the prosecution calls the expert to testify. It is conceivable that the prosecution might decide to not call its own expert to testify, but the defendant would call the prosecution expert to testify, because that expert reached a conclusion favorable to the defendant. The statutory language appears to require the prosecution to pay the expert witness's testimonial fees even if the defendant calls that witness to testify. If the courts give this language a literal interpretation, that feature would put this statute at odds with the accepted practice for paying expert witness testimonial fees.

3. Constitutional Issues Regarding Penal Code Section 1054.3 Amendments.

It is very likely that the amendments to Penal Code section 1054.3 will trigger substantial litigation. One area of litigation left unresolved by *Verdin v. Superior Court, supra,* and by the enactment of Penal Code section 1054.3 is the question whether a court may constitutionally order a defendant to submit to a prosecution mental health examination when the defendant places his or her mental state in issue through the proposed testimony of a defense mental health expert as provided in Section 1054.3.

While the requirements of timely reciprocal pretrial discovery, as set forth in Penal Code section 1054.3, apply to the penalty phase of a capital case, the trial court has discretion to delay prosecution discovery of defense penalty evidence until after conclusion of the guilt trial. *Maldonado v. Superior Court* (2012) 53 Cal. 4th 1112, 140 Cal. Rptr. 3d 113, 274 P.3d 1110.

In *Verdin* the California Supreme Court explicitly left open the constitutional question. The Court stated that in light of its holding that there was no statutory authority for a trial court to order a defendant to submit to a mental examination by a prosecution expert, the Court found it "unnecessary to decide whether the trial court's order violates petitioner's constitutional rights." *Verdin v. Superior Court, supra*, 43 Cal.4th at 1116.

The California Supreme Court, however, has previously rejected the argument that ordering a criminal defendant who has placed his mental condition in issue to submit to a mental examination by a prosecution expert violates the defendant's constitutional rights.

In *People v. McPeters* (1992) 2 Cal.4th 1148, 9 Cal.Rptr.2d 834, 832 P.2d 146, a defendant convicted of murder in the guilt phase of a capital murder case called two expert psychiatrists to testify about his mental condition in the penalty phase of the trial. At the request of the prosecutor, the court ordered the defendant to submit to an examination by a prosecution expert. The defendant refused to talk to the prosecution psychiatrist. The trial court then allowed the prosecution psychiatrist to testify about the defendant's refusal to participate in the examination.

On appeal the defendant argued that the trial court violated his Fifth and Sixth Amendment rights. The Supreme Court rejected his argument, stating that "[b]y tendering his mental condition as an issue in the penalty phase, defendant waived his Fifth and Sixth Amendment rights to the extent necessary to permit a proper examination of that condition. Therefore, those rights were not violated when the examining psychiatrist testified to defendant's refusal to cooperate. [citations omitted] Any other result would give an unfair tactical advantage to defendants, who could, with impunity, present mental defenses at the penalty phase, secure in the assurance they could not be rebutted by expert testimony based on an actual psychiatric examination. Obviously, this would permit and, indeed, encourage spurious mental illness defenses." 2 Cal.4th at 1190.

In *People v. Carpenter* (1997) 15 Cal.4th 312, 63 Cal.Rptr.2d 1, 935 P.2d 708, a defendant convicted of multiple murders presented expert testimony about the defendant's mental condition in the penalty phase of a capital trial. The prosecution then moved for and obtained a court order ordering the defendant to submit to a psychiatric examination by a psychiatrist hired by the prosecution. The defendant refused to talk to the prosecution expert, although he voluntarily talked to defense experts. The trial court informed the jury of the defendant's refusal and instructed the jury that it could take the defendant's refusal into consideration when weighing the opinions of the defense experts. The defendant was convicted and sentenced to death. The defendant appealed the convictions and judgment, arguing, *inter alia*, that the trial court's ruling, the prosecution expert's testimony, and the jury instruction had violated his federal constitutional rights.

The California Supreme Court rejected the defendant's argument, quoting from its prior opinion in *McPeters. People v. Carpenter, supra,* 15 Cal.4th at 412–413. The holding in *Carpenter* that by tendering his mental condition as an issue in the penalty phase, the defendant had waived his Fifth and Sixth Amendment rights was cited with approval by the California Supreme Court in *In re Hawthorne* (2005) 35 Cal.4th 40, 45, 24 Cal.Rptr.3d 189, 105 P.3d 552.

The *McPeters* and *Carpenter* holdings appear to have support in decisions of the United States Supreme Court. *See Buchanan v. Kentucky* (1987) 483 U.S. 402, 422, 107 S.Ct. 2906, 97 L.Ed.2d 336; and *Estelle v. Smith* (1981) 451 U.S. 454, 465, 101 S.Ct. 1866, 68 L.Ed.2d 359.

Since the court may constitutionally order a defendant to submit to a mental examination conducted by a prosecution psychiatrist when the defendant places in issue his mental state through the proposed testimony of a mental health expert, it naturally follows that the prosecution expert is not required to first advise the defendant of his rights pursuant to *Miranda v. Arizona* (1966) 384 U.S. 436, 478–479, 86 S.Ct. 1602, 16 L.Ed.2d 694. While "[a]n examination of a criminal defendant by a psychiatrist or psychologist retained by the prosecution constitutes a custodial interrogation, for Fifth Amendment purposes and must be preceded by *Miranda* warnings," *People v. San Nicolas* (2004) 34 Cal.4th 614, 640, 21 Cal.Rptr.3d 612, 101 P.3d 509, the requirement of a *Miranda* warning does not apply when the defendant has placed his mental state at issue. *People v. Williams* (1988) 44 Cal.3d 883, 961, 245 Cal.Rptr. 336, 751 P.2d 395 ["The appointment of a psychiatrist pursuant to sections 1026 and 1027 is made only in response to the defendant's entry of a plea of not guilty by reason of insanity. The examination, initiated at the behest of the defendant, is not 'compelled' and *Miranda* warnings are not required."]. More recently, in *Maldonado v. Superior Court* (2012) 53 Cal. 4th 1112, 140 Cal. Rptr. 3d 113, 274 P.3d 1110, the California Supreme Court held that Penal Code section 1054.3, subdivision (b)(1), specifically provides that when a criminal defendant places his or her mental state in issue, the prosecution may obtain a court order that the defendant submit to examination by a prosecution-retained mental health expert.

To require a prosecution psychiatrist to deliver a *Miranda* warning before conducting a Penal Code section 1054.3 mental examination would make no sense. It would be anomalous for the court to order the defendant to submit to the mental examination, but then to hold that the prosecution expert must inform the defendant that he has the right to remain silent and to not speak to the prosecution expert.

The California Supreme Court resolved the constitutionality of the amendments to Penal Code section 1054.3 in *People v. Clark* (2011) 52 Cal.4th 856, 131 Cal.Rptr.3d 225, 261 P.3d 243. In *Clark* a defendant convicted of capital murder and numerous other crimes and sentenced to death contended on appeal that the trial court erred in ordering him to submit to mental examination by prosecution experts. The defendant had raised guilt phase defenses of unconsciousness and diminished actuality. Although the trial court's order occurred in 1993, prior to the decision of the California Supreme Court in *Verdin v. Superior Court* (2008) 43 Cal.4th 1096, 1106, 77 Cal.Rptr.3d 287, 183 P.3d 1250, the *Verdin* opinion has been applied retroactively. *People v. Wallace* (2008) 44 Cal.4th 1032, 1087–1088, 81 Cal.Rptr.3d 651, 189 P.3d 911; and *People v. Gonzales* (2011) 51 Cal.4th 894, 927, 126 Cal.Rptr.3d 1, 253 P.3d 185.

The Supreme Court thus agreed with the defendant that "the court was not authorized under [Penal Code] section 1054 to order him to submit to mental examination by the prosecutor's three experts." 52 Cal.4th at 940. The Court, however, concluded that the trial court's error was harmless.

Relying upon *Estelle v. Smith* (1981) 451 U.S. 454, 101 S.Ct. 1866, 68 L.Ed.2d 359, the defendant contended that it was constitutional error for the trial court to allow evidence from a compelled mental examination by a prosecution expert to be used against him in trial. The Supreme Court rejected the defendant's argument, holding that "[d]efendant cites no decision, and we are aware of none, holding that the Fifth Amendment or any other *federal constitutional* provision prohibits a court from ordering a defendant who has placed his or her mental state in issue to submit to a mental examination by a prosecution expert." 52 Cal.4th at 940.

4. Sanctions for Defendant's Refusal to Speak to Prosecution Expert.

If the defendant may be ordered to submit to a mental examination by a prosecution expert when the defendant has placed his or her mental state in issue, and the defendant does not have the right to refuse to speak to the expert, the question arises what actions are available to the trial court to deal with a defendant who declines to speak with the expert and/or to submit to any tests. Several sanctions have been approved by California courts.

The trial court may allow the prosecution expert to testify to the jury about the defendant's refusal to participate in the examination. *People v. McPeters, supra,* 2 Cal.4th 1148, 1190; *People v. Carpenter, supra,* 15 Cal.4th at 412.

The court may also instruct the jury that the court had ordered the defendant to submit to a mental examination by the prosecution expert, and the defendant's refusal to be examined may be considered by the jury. *People v. Carpenter, supra,* 15 Cal.4th at 413 ["Defendant had no right to refuse to cooperate with the psychologist, so the jury could properly consider his refusal. [citation omitted] The jury could properly infer that defendant wanted only his self-chosen experts, not others, to evaluate him, an inference relevant to its consideration of all the evidence of his mental condition."].

And the court may impose an "issue sanction," which is an order that the issues to which the examination related be taken as established in favor of the prosecution. "In the event the . . . petitioner refuses to submit, the court, on motion of the prosecution, may make those orders that are just, including imposition of the issue and evidence sanctions specified in [former] subdivision (f) of Code of Civil Procedure section 2032 . . . ." *Baqleh v. Superior Court* (2002) 100 Cal.App.4th 478, 122 Cal.Rptr.2d 673. Section 2032 was repealed effective January 1, 2005, and replaced by Section 2032.410 [court on motion of the party entitled to a physical or mental examination may make "those orders that are just, including the imposition of an issue sanction, an evidence sanction . . . ."].

The court might also impose an "evidence sanction," in which the court precludes testimony of the defendant's experts on the mental state placed in issue by the defendant's proposed testimony of those experts.

5. Defendant's Right To Presence of Counsel at Examination.

Penal Code section 1054.3 does not contain any provisions that specify whether the defendant has a right to the presence of counsel at the mental examination conducted by the prosecution expert. The question whether a defendant has a Sixth Amendment right to the presence of his counsel at the mental examination is certain to provoke litigation.

However, case law in California is fairly well settled that as long as the defendant has tendered his or her mental state as an issue in the case, the prosecution expert confines the mental examination and testimony to the mental state placed in issue, and the jury is appropriately instructed to limit the prosecution expert's testimony to that mental issue, the defendant does not have a constitutional right to the presence of counsel at the prosecution mental examination. See the discussion of this subject in *In re Spencer* (1965) 63 Cal.2d 400, 403, 46 Cal.Rptr. 753, 406 P.2d 33; *People v. Jantz* (2006) 137 Cal.App.4th 1283, 1294, 40 Cal.Rptr.3d 875; *Baqleh v. Superior Court* (2002) 100 Cal.App.4th 478, 503–505, 122 Cal.Rptr.2d 673; and *Tarantino v. Superior Court* (1975) 48 Cal.App.3d 465, 469, 122 Cal.Rptr. 61.

Practice Tips for Prosecution: When prosecuting a criminal case in which you suspect that the defendant will raise a mental health defense, and you anticipate that you will request a prosecution mental health examination of the defendant, you should take a number of preliminary steps to enable you to obtain such an examination. First, you should retain the services of a mental health expert and provide that expert with enough case information to educate the expert about the case. That will enable you to move quickly with a *timely request* for a prosecution mental health examination that contains an informed list of proposed tests to be administered by the expert.

Second, you should make a written informal reciprocal discovery request followed by a formal discovery motion as early as possible after the defendant's arraignment on an information or indictment in which you request disclosure of the identity of the defense expert, any written, recorded, or oral reports of the expert, the results of mental examinations, scientific tests, or experiments conducted on the defendant, and the proposed testimony of the defense expert. Even if your request does not produce early disclosure of that information, you will have alerted the court that the defendant should not be allowed to wait until just before trial to make those disclosures in order to prevent the prosecution from being able to conduct a prosecution mental health examination of the defendant. If you have not already received the information, you should almost always make a second formal request or discovery motion for this information 30 days prior to trial.

Third, when the defendant identifies a defense mental health expert and discloses that expert's proposed testimony, you should *immediately* file a written request for a prosecution mental health examination of the defendant. Do not delay making such a request beyond any time necessary to refine the list of the proposed mental health tests that the expert proposes to conduct. Any delay on your part will allow the defendant to defeat your request on the grounds that the request was not *timely*.

Fourth, you should request that the defense's disclosure be in writing and specifically identify the mental state which the defense is placing in issue through its expert's proposed testimony. Normally, a written report from the defense expert should suffice. However, if the expert has not prepared a written report, you should consider requesting the court to order the expert to prepare a written report which includes an identification of the defendant's mental state being placed in issue. An oral statement of that mental state will assuredly lead to confusion and disputes over the proposed prosecution tests.

Fifth, you should ensure that the prosecution expert crafts the list of proposed tests narrowly, so that you can preclude a judicial denial of your request on the grounds that the proposed tests do not bear a reasonable relation to the mental state placed in issue by the defendant.

Finally, if your prosecution expert is comfortable with the idea, you should consider requesting the defense to allow your expert to speak to the defense expert regarding that expert's tests, findings, and proposed testimony.

Practice Tips for Defendant: You should not disclose the identity of a defense-retained mental health expert or the subject of the expert's proposed testimony until your expert has had a sufficient time to evaluate the defendant and advise you about the possible mental health defense. While your disclosures will not commit you to making that defense at trial, a premature disclosure of your proposed mental health defense is not normally in your client's best interests.

You should prepare the defendant for the prosecution mental health examination, so that the defendant is not surprised by the examination and knows that the examiner is a mental health expert who is working for the prosecution. The defendant must clearly understand that his or her statements to the prosecution examiner are not privileged and could be used against him or her in trial. You should also ensure that the defendant understands that a refusal to talk to the prosecution expert will be used against the defendant in trial.

You should demand that the prosecution make quick disclosure of the prosecution expert's findings and proposed testimony following the expert's mental health examination of your client. You must provide your defense expert with sufficient time to consider and study the prosecution expert's findings. If the prosecution expert reaches conclusions that are opposed to the findings of your expert, you should consider retaining an additional mental health expert to evaluate the defendant. If you decide to call more than one mental health expert to testify, you will be required to disclose that additional witness and the witness's proposed testimony. Whether the disclosure of an additional mental health expert would entitle the prosecution to conduct a *second* mental health examination of the defendant is not addressed by the statute.

You should be alert in trial to ensure that the prosecution mental expert testifies only to the mental state which your client has placed in issue and does not testify to the defendant's statements that are outside the scope of the mental state placed in issue, and that the court issues an appropriate limiting instruction on the jury's use of statements made by the defendant purposes other than resolving the defendant's mental state placed in issue.

6. Evidence Code section 730 Mental Examination.

In *Verdin v. Superior Court* (2008) 43 Cal.4th 1096, 1106, 77 Cal.Rptr.3d 287, 183 P.3d 1250, the California Supreme Court declined to decide whether a mental examination of the defendant could be performed by a prosecution expert under the authority of Evidence Code section 730.

Evidence Code section 730 authorizes a trial court on its own motion or on the motion of any party to appoint an expert to investigate, render a report, and testify at the trial to any fact or matter about which expert evidence might be required. Although the People contended in the Supreme Court that the trial court's order in *Verdin* was authorized by Evidence Code section 730, the People's motion in the trial court was not made pursuant to Section 730, and the trial court's appointment of the prosecution expert was not made pursuant to that section. Accordingly, the Supreme Court held that the prosecution had not preserved for appeal the question of the application of Evidence Code section 730.

Whether Evidence Code section 730 would authorize a trial court to appoint a prosecution expert to conduct a mental examination of a defendant under Section 730 is an unresolved question. The language of Section 730 does not restrict the court from appointing either a prosecution or a defense expert, and Section 730 allows the court to appoint more than one such expert. However, once appointed under Section 730 the expert becomes the trial court's expert.

In order to afford the prosecution a fair opportunity to rebut mental-state evidence proffered by the defense, California's criminal-case reciprocal discovery statute, Penal Code section 1054.3, specifically provides that when the defendant places in issue his or her mental state at any phase of the criminal action, the prosecution may seek and obtain a court order that the defendant submit to examination by a prosecution-retained mental health expert. § 1054.3, subsection (b)(1). *Maldonado v. Superior Court* (2012) 53 Cal. 4th 1112, 140 Cal. Rptr. 3d 113, 274 P.3d 1110.

The Supreme Court has perhaps signaled its resolution of the question whether a trial court may utilize Evidence Code section 730 as an additional basis for an order that the defendant submit to a compelled mental examination conducted by a prosecution expert. See the discussion in *People v. Gonzales* (2011) 51 Cal.4th 894, 927–928, 126 Cal.Rptr.3d 1; 253 P.3d 185.

Practice Tip for Prosecution: If the defendant announces an intention to present a mental defense to a charge and you wish to obtain a mental examination of the defendant by a prosecution expert, you should base your request not only on Penal Code section 1054.3, but you should also request the examination under the authority of Evidence Code section 730. If the trial court grants your request, you should ensure that the court's order cites both statutory provisions as the authority for the order.

Practice Tip for Defendant: If the trial court seems inclined to appoint a prosecution expert under Evidence Code section 730, you should give serious consideration to requesting that the trial court also appoint a defense expert whose reputation and expertise you trust.

§ 5:8.2.6   Prosecution mental examination of defendant regarding battered woman syndrome defense [NEW]

A trial court may order a defendant who raises a battered woman syndrome defense to submit to a mental examination conducted by a prosecution expert.

In *People v. Gonzales* (2011) 51 Cal.4th 894, 126 Cal.Rptr.3d 1, 253 P.3d 185, a woman was charged with murdering her four-year-old niece with special circumstances of torture and murder committed while committing mayhem. Prior to trial the prosecutor moved for an order directing the defendant to submit to a psychiatric examination conducted by a prosecution expert, if the defendant produced expert testimony about her own mental condition. The defendant opposed the motion, contending that she was not presenting a defense based on her mental condition, but that she would instead offer battered woman syndrome as an explanation for her actions. The Court ultimately ruled that it would allow two prosecution experts to examine the defendant—one with regard to battered woman syndrome and one to determine more generally whether other mental conditions might explain her behavior. 51 Cal.4th at 925–926. The defendant refused to be examined by one of the prosecution's experts.

On appeal of her conviction and sentence of death, the defendant argued that the trial court had erred in ordering her to submit to the prosecution mental examinations. The Supreme Court acknowledged that in light of its opinion in *Verdin v. Superior Court* (2008) 43 Cal.4th 1096, 1106, 77 Cal.Rptr.3d 287, 183 P.3d 1250, the trial court had been deprived by the Criminal Discovery Statute of its inherent authority at the time of the defendant's trial to order a prosecution mental examination of the defendant. The defendant, however, had not contended that the prosecutor's request for a prosecution mental examination of the defendant was precluded by the Criminal Discovery Statute. The Supreme Court concluded that the defendant's failure to raise this argument deprived the prosecution and the trial court from basing the request and the discovery order on Evidence Code section 730. In telling language, the Supreme Court stated that had the defendant made the Criminal Discovery Statute argument, "the [trial] court could and likely would have resorted to its power to appoint experts under Evidence Code section 730, which was invoked in the prosecutor's motion." The Court concluded that the trial court's "mistaken reliance on [prior decisional authority] was not prejudicial, given the alternate source of authority provided by Evidence Code section 730." 51 Cal.4th at 928.

The Court concluded that the defendant had raised her mental condition as a defense. The Court determined that "[t]he centerpiece of the defense was defendant's assertion that her actions were explained by battered woman syndrome. Defendant squarely placed her mental state at issue, claiming she was a victim unable to overcome her fear of [her husband] and protect the child she had taken into her care. . . . [S]ince the defense did present expert testimony based on interviews with defendant, the court properly found that fairness required giving the prosecution the opportunity to counter that testimony." 51 Cal.4th at 928–929.

The Court concluded by holding that "[i]t is settled that a defendant who makes an affirmative showing of his or her mental condition by way of expert testimony waives his or her Fifth and Sixth Amendment rights to object to examination by a prosecution expert. [citations omitted]" 51 Cal.4th at 929.

§ 5:9　Depositions

A failure to preserve evidence violates a defendant's right to due process if the unavailable evidence possessed exculpatory value that was apparent before the evidence was destroyed, and is of such a nature that the defendant would be unable to obtain comparable evidence by other reasonably available means. A defendant must also demonstrate that the police acted in bad faith in failing to preserve the potentially useful evidence. The presence or absence of bad faith turns on the government's knowledge of the apparent exculpatory value of the evidence at the time it was lost or destroyed. The mere failure to preserve evidence which could have been subjected to tests which might have exonerated the defendant does not constitute a due process violation. *Jensen v. Hernandez* (E.D. Cal. 2012) 864 F. Supp. 2d 869.

In the context of preserving evidence, bad faith requires more than mere negligence or recklessness. *United States v. Toro-Barboza* (2012, CA9 Cal.) 673 F.3d 1136.

§ 5:10　Conditional examinations

A conditional examination is a deposition in a criminal case. "A conditional examination is not part of the trial; rather, it is a deposition taken in cases where a material witness is unavailable to testify in person at trial. [citations omitted]." *People v. Mays* (2009) 174 Cal.App.4th 156, 173, 95 Cal.Rptr.3d 219.

§ 5:10.1　Conditional examinations—capital cases

Although subdivision (a) of Penal Code section 1335 provides that the defendant, but not the prosecution, may conduct a conditional examination of a witness in a case in which the punishment may be death, that limitation does not apply when the prosecution seeks to conduct a conditional examination in a capital case because the People have evidence that the life of the witness is in jeopardy.

In *People v. Jurado* (2006) 38 Cal.4th 72, 41 Cal.Rptr.3d 319, 131 P.3d 400, the prosecution conducted a conditional examination of a critical prosecution witness in a capital murder case. The defendant objected to the examination, citing Section 1335, subdivision (a), which provides:

> "When a defendant has been charged with a public offense triable in any court, he or she in all cases, and the people in cases other than those for which the punishment may be death, may, if the defendant has been fully informed of his or her right to counsel as provided by law, have witnesses examined conditionally in his or her or their behalf, as prescribed in this chapter." [emphasis added]

The trial court overruled the defendant's objection. When the witness was unavailable to testify at trial, the transcript of the conditional examination was read into evidence. The defendant was convicted of first degree murder and sentenced to death.

On automatic appeal the defendant argued that the trial court erred in allowing the conditional examination in a capital case, again citing subdivision (a) of Section 1335. The California Supreme Court rejected the defendant's argument, holding that subdivision (b) of Penal Code section 1335 constitutes an exception to the general ban on the prosecution's right to conduct a conditional examination in a capital case.

Subdivision (b) of Section 1335, which at the time of Jurado's trial applied only to the prosecution and which has since been amended to allow the defendant to utilize its provisions, provides as follows:

> "When a defendant has been charged with a serious felony, the people or the defendant may, if the defendant has been fully informed of his or her right to counsel as provided by law, have a witness examined conditionally as prescribed in this chapter, if there is evidence that the life of the witness is in jeopardy."

After an examination of the legislative history of the Conditional Witness Statute, the Supreme Court held that subdivision (b) constitutes an exception to the general prohibition against conditional examinations conducted by the prosecution in capital cases. The Court held that allowing the prosecution to conduct a conditional examination in a capital case when a witness's life is in danger, but not allowing such a prosecution examination when the witness is likely to be unavailable to testify at trial for reasons other than danger to the witness's life, such as the witness's age or infirmity, makes rational sense.

The Court reasoned that a common problem to which subdivision (b) was the legislative response was "criminal violence against prospective prosecution witnesses to prevent their testimony. The risk that this will occur likely increases in proportion to the potential punishment for the charged offense, and thus it is greatest in capital cases. Absent language expressly barring application of these provisions to capital cases, therefore, it is reasonable to infer that the Legislature intended to permit the prosecution to conditionally examine witnesses in capital cases when there is evidence that their lives are in serious danger." 38 Cal.4th at 113.

The Court concluded that "under subdivision (b) of section 1335, conditional examination of a prosecution witness is permitted in a capital case when the witness's life is in jeopardy." 38 Cal.4th at 113.

The Supreme Court then held that the prosecution satisfied its burden of proving that the witness's life was in jeopardy by submitting a declaration of a deputy prosecutor stating that the witness's life was in danger from the defendant and his associates, and that it was "not necessary, under the circumstances of this case, for the prosecution to present evidence that anyone had expressly threatened [the witness] or conspired to harm him." 38 Cal.4th at 114.

Finally, the Court rejected the defendant's constitutional challenges to allowing the conditional examination testimony to be introduced in evidence at the trial.

The prohibition against the use of a conditional examination in a capital case is limited to cases in which the prosecution actually seeks the death penalty. It does not prohibit the use of a conditional examination in a murder case in which the prosecution does not seek, and may not lawfully seek, a death sentence.

In *People v. Mays* (2009) 174 Cal.App.4th 156, 95 Cal.Rptr.3d 219, the defendant, who was under the age of 18 years, was prosecuted for murder with a lying-in-wait special circumstance. The murder was the result of a shooting that occurred at a fast-food restaurant. The police obtained photographs from a surveillance camera at a neighboring gasoline station mini market and showed the photographs to a woman who identified the defendant in the photos.

The prosecution moved to conduct a conditional examination of the woman, arguing that she would be unavailable to testify at the trial, because she suffered from panic disorder and agoraphobia that caused sudden onsets of shortness of breath, chest pain, dizziness, and extreme fear. Over defense objection the trial court ordered a videotaped conditional examination of the woman witness in a courtroom in the presence of the defendant, counsel, and the judge. The defense was allowed to cross-examine the witness, but the public and jurors were excluded from the courtroom.

After the conditional examination had been conducted, the trial court found that the witness was unavailable to testify at trial and allowed the prosecution to play the videotaped testimony of the witness for the jury in open court. The defendant was convicted of first-degree murder with a lying-in-wait special circumstance and appealed.

On appeal the defendant argued that the trial court had erred in allowing the videotaped testimony to be introduced in evidence at the trial. The defendant argued that the conditional witness statute prohibits conditional examinations in death penalty cases. The defendant contended that even though the prosecution did not seek the death penalty against him, the special allegation of lying in wait made his case a death penalty case. The defendant also argued that a conditional examination was not necessary, because the witness would have been able to testify in the trial. The Court of Appeals rejected both of the defendant's arguments.

The Court of Appeal observed that although the crime of murder may be punished by death, the prosecution was statutorily prohibited from seeking the death penalty against the defendant because he was a minor; Penal Code section 190.5, subdivision (a), prohibits the death penalty for persons under age 18 at the time of the crime. 174 Cal.App.4th at 170. The Court rejected the defendant's argument that the lying-in-wait special allegation made the case a death penalty case, because the defendant himself was not subject to a penalty of death. The Court stated: "[W]e see no reason, as to why a conditional examination should be barred where the individual defendant is not subject to the death penalty." 174 Cal.App.4th at 171.

The Court then found that the defendant had forfeited the argument that the trial court erred in granting a conditional examination under Penal Code section 1336, which allows conditional examinations when a People's witness is so infirm as to cause apprehension that the witness will be unable to attend the trial. The defendant argued that Penal Code section 1335, subdivision (b), limits conditional examinations in serious felony cases to situations in which the witness's life is in jeopardy. Because the defendant had not made this argument to the trial court, the Court of Appeal held that he had forfeited the argument. The Court reasoned that the opinion of the Supreme Court in *People v. Jurado, supra,* 38 Cal.4th 72, 110–113, could be read as construing Penal Code section 1335, subdivision (b) "as a release from the historical prohibition against conditional examinations of prosecution witnesses in capital cases." 174 Cal.App.4th at 171. Because the defendant's case was not a capital case, Section 1335, subdivision (b), did not make the defendant's case statutorily ineligible for a conditional examination.

The Court of Appeal held that the trial court did not abuse its discretion in finding that the conditional examination was necessary under the facts of the case. The Court stated that a trial court has discretion whether to grant a conditional examination, and its determination whether a witness is "unavailable to testify at trial due to mental illness or infirmity that would cause substantial trauma, is a mixed question of law and fact . . . ." 174 Cal.App.4th at 172. The standard for making that finding is that the "infirmity must be sufficiently problematic that it makes live testimony at trial 'relatively impossible,' not merely inconvenient. 'Relatively impossible' includes 'the relative impossibility of eliciting testimony without risk of inflicting substantial trauma on the witness.' [citation omitted]." 174 Cal.App.4th at 172.

Finally, the Court of Appeal rejected the defendant's contention that by allowing the witness to testify in a conditional examination outside the presence of the jury and the public violated his right to a public trial. The Court stated that a "conditional examination is not part of the trial; rather, it is a deposition taken in cases where a material witness is unavailable to testify in person at trial. [citations omitted]." 174 Cal.App.4th at 173.

Practice Tip for Prosecution and Defendant. Counsel should be careful in citing or relying upon *People v. Mays, supra,* for the proposition that a conditional examination may be held in a serious felony case when a prosecution witness is so infirm as to cause apprehension that the witness will be unable to attend the trial. The Court of Appeal in *People v. Mays, supra,* held that the defendant forfeited his objection to a conditional examination of an infirm prosecution witness by not making the objection in the trial court. *Mays* might not stand as authority for the underlying proposition of law that a conditional examination of a prosecution witness in a serious felony case is not limited to situations in which the witness's life is in jeopardy. We consider this issue as an open one ripe for further litigation.

§ 5:10.2 Conditional examinations—criminal proceedings suspended

A trial court may conduct a conditional examination in a criminal case in which proceedings have been suspended pursuant to Penal Code section 1368, and the testimony taken at such an examination is admissible at trial, unless the defendant has subsequently been found to have been incompetent at the time of the conditional examination.

In *People v. Cadogan* (2009) 173 Cal.App.4th 1502, 93 Cal.Rptr.3d 881, the defendant was charged with a variety of sexual assault crimes and first-degree residential burglary. Based on his counsel's representation that he believed the defendant might be incompetent to stand trial, the trial court suspended proceedings pursuant to Penal Code section 1368 and ordered that he undergo a mental competence examination pursuant to that section. While proceedings were suspended the prosecution applied for a court order authorizing a conditional examination of the defendant's wife, on the grounds that she was terminally ill and would not live to testify at the defendant's trial.

The defendant objected to the holding of the conditional examination, arguing that a conditional examination could not be held while criminal proceedings were suspended. The defendant's argument was rejected by the trial court and the conditional examination took place. A subsequent trial on the defendant's competency to stand trial resulted in a jury verdict that the defendant was competent to stand trial. By the time of the criminal trial the defendant's wife had died, and her testimony from the conditional examination was introduced in evidence by the prosecution at the trial. The defendant was convicted and appealed.

On appeal the defendant contended that the trial court had erred in conducting the conditional examination while criminal proceedings were suspended and had then erred in allowing that testimony to be introduced in his trial. The Court of Appeal rejected the defendant's argument. The Court concluded:

> "Trial courts have discretion to allow conditional examinations of dying witnesses to go forward, notwithstanding the suspension of criminal proceedings mandated by section 1368, subdivision (c). The testimony taken at a conditional examination should be excluded from trial only if the defendant is subsequently found to have been incompetent at the time of the conditional examination." 173 Cal.App.4th at 1506–1507.

The Court of Appeal agreed with the defendant that "a conditional examination, like a trial on the merits or a sentencing hearing, is a "proceeding" subject to the suspension requirement set forth in section 1368, subdivision (c). When possible, a conditional examination should be suspended until the defendant has been found to be competent." 173 Cal.App.4th at 1512. However, because of the danger that the defendant's wife would soon die, and because the defendant's intransigence was a primary cause of the delay in holding a competency hearing, the Court of Appeal held that in order to not lose testimony forever, a trial court has the discretion to hold a conditional examination under such circumstances. 173 Cal.App.4th at 1512–1513.

§ 5:11 Examination of witness on commission

An examination of a witness on commission under Penal Code sections 1349 through 1362 is authorized when the witness is a material witness who is residing outside the state of California or the United States, "the examination of the witness is necessary to the attainment of justice," and the witness is willing to consent to the giving of testimony. *People v. Salcido* (2008) 44 Cal.4th 93, 131–132, 79 Cal.Rptr.3d 54, 186 P.3d 437. Only the defendant may apply for a commission to depose such a witness. "The commission itself is a process issued under seal of the court, authorizing a designated individual to take the deposition of the named foreign witness and return it to the court. [citations omitted] Depositions taken under the commission may be read into evidence by either party at trial on a finding the witness is unavailable under Evidence Code section 240." *People v. Salcido*, 44 Cal.4th at 131.

If the trial court is satisfied that examining a witness on commission is not necessary to the attainment of justice, the trial court has the discretion to deny the defendant's request. *See, e.g., People v. Salcido*, 44 Cal.4th at 132.

PART III. DISCOVERY COSTS

§ 5:12 Costs of discovery—in general

The subject of responsibility for paying the costs for the prosecution's providing copies of written and recorded discovery materials to the defendant has been a contentious one. The appellate courts are beginning to address this subject.

§ 5:12.3 Due process basis for discovery without cost

In *Schaffer v. Superior Court* (2010) 185 Cal.App.4th 1235, 1244, 111 Cal.Rptr.3d 245, the Court of Appeal agreed that the cost of providing discovery to an indigent must be borne by the county. "The responsibility for bearing the costs of providing legal services to indigent criminal defendants rests upon the county, either through the public defender, through its conflicts panel, or through its general fund." 185 Cal.App.4th at 1244.

§ 5:12.5　Prosecutor provides access and defendant wants copies

The question whether a trial court may assess the office of the prosecuting attorney to pay for the costs of providing copies of discoverable documents to criminal defendants has produced a variety of trial court rulings. Because the subject of who pays for the costs of providing copies of discoverable materials is not addressed in the Criminal Discovery Statute, there have been no direct and easy answers for courts to adopt. Some courts have made discovery orders requiring the costs to be absorbed by the prosecutor's office. Other courts have declined to enter orders requiring that the prosecution "foot the bill" for the cost of providing discovery copies. The question of who pays the cost of providing discovery to criminal defendants depends upon whether the defendant has retained counsel or is otherwise capable of paying for retained counsel, or whether the defendant is indigent and has appointed counsel at public expense.

§ 5:12.5.1　Paying the costs of discovery for indigent defendants

Because we believe that there is no statutory authority that would require the prosecution to absorb the cost of providing discovery to criminal defendants, we question the authority of a court to enter such an order.

Penal Code section 987.2 authorizes appointment of counsel for indigents in criminal proceedings. The cost of indigent defense in criminal cases is a charge against the county. "In any case in which a person . . . desires but is unable to employ counsel, and . . . counsel is assigned in the superior court to represent the person in a criminal trial, proceeding, or appeal . . . counsel shall receive a reasonable sum for compensation **and for necessary expenses**, the amount of which shall be determined by the court, **to be paid out of the general fund of the county**." Penal Code section 987.2, subdivision (a). [emphasis added]

A criminal defendant who has "established his indigent status . . . is constitutionally entitled to those defense services for which he demonstrates a need." *People v. Worthy* (1980) 109 Cal.App.3d 514, 520, 167 Cal.Rptr. 402. However, "[t]he test of entitlement to **county assistance** in defense preparation must be indigency." [emphasis added] The duty to provide this assistance is upon the **government**, *Tran v. Superior Court* (2001) 92 Cal.App.4th 1149, 1154, 112 Cal.Rptr.2d 506, or upon the **county**. *Taylor v. Superior Court* (1985) 168 Cal.App.3d 1217, 1220, 215 Cal.Rptr. 73. [emphasis added] The cost of appointed counsel in a habeas corpus proceeding challenging the underlying conviction is a **county charge**. *Charlton v. Superior Court* (1979) 93 Cal.App.3d 858, 862, 156 Cal.Rptr. 107. [emphasis added]

The responsibility for bearing the burden of providing legal services to indigent criminal defendants rests upon the county, either through the Public Defender, through its conflicts panel, or through its general fund. It is the county, not the district attorney, who is entitled to recoup those costs from indigent defendants who are later determined to have the ability to pay some or all of the costs of their defense. Penal Code section 987.8 reflects a strong legislative policy of preserving scarce financial resources by shifting the costs of trial from the county taxpayers to the defendant when the defendant has the financial ability to pay some or all of those costs. *People v. Smith* (2000) 81 Cal.App.4th 630, 641, 96 Cal.Rptr.2d 856. Section 987.8, subdivision (b), reflects a legislative concern for "replenishing a county treasury from the pockets of those who have directly benefited from county expenditures." *People v. Flores* (2003) 30 Cal.4th 1059, 1063, 135 Cal.Rptr.2d 63, 69 P.3d 979.

Although an indigent criminal defendant has the right to appointment of counsel at public expense, *Gideon v. Wainwright* (1963) 372 U.S. 335, 83 S.Ct. 792, 9 L.Ed.2d 799, and has constitutional and statutory discovery rights without charge, there is no authority of which we are aware that makes the public prosecutor responsible for paying the costs of defending against the criminal prosecutions which the district attorney has initiated. It is the county, not the district attorney, which is obligated to fund the costs of indigent criminal defense.

In *Schaffer v. Superior Court* (2010) 185 Cal.App.4th 1235, 111 Cal.Rptr.3d 245, the Court of Appeal agreed that the cost of providing discovery to an indigent must be borne by the county. "The responsibility for bearing the costs of providing legal services to indigent criminal defendants rests upon the county, either through the public defender, through its conflicts panel, or through its general fund." 185 Cal.App.4th at 1244.

§ 5:12.5.2 Paying the costs of discovery for non-indigent defendants

The prosecution has no duty under the Criminal Discovery Statute to pay for the costs of providing copies of discoverable materials to a defendant who is not indigent and who either has retained counsel or who represents himself.

In *Schaffer v. Superior Court* (2010) 185 Cal.App.4th 1235, 111 Cal.Rptr.3d 245, a defendant charged with felony offenses and represented by retained counsel filed a motion to abate discovery costs, which consisted of photocopying fees that the prosecutor's office charges for making copies of discoverable documents. The defendant argued that a defendant should not be required to pay for duplication of discovery items. The trial court denied the defendant's motion. The defendant sought a petition for writ of mandate to overturn the trial court's order, but the defendant was found not guilty in a jury trial while his writ petition was pending.

The Court of Appeal chose to resolve the question, even though the defendant's acquittal had made the case moot. The Court of Appeal rejected the defendant's argument that he had a right to free provision of discovery materials and denied the writ petition. The Court concluded that "[Penal

Code] section 1054.1 imposes no [ ] duty on the prosecution" to furnish copies of discoverable items free of charge to a defendant who is represented by retained counsel. The Court held that the People "comply with section 1054.1 by affording the defendant an opportunity to examine, inspect, or copy the discoverable items. A nonindigent defendant may receive at his or her own expense copies of discovery made available by the People." 185 Cal.App.4th at 1237–1238,

The Court of Appeal reasoned that because "a nonindigent criminal defendant can be required to pay for the costs associated with his defense, including attorney's fees, we conclude it does not offend the Constitution to require a nonindigent defendant to pay reasonable fees or duplicating discovery materials disclosed by the district attorney pursuant to section 1054.1." 185 Cal.App.4th at 1245.

The Court observed that prosecutors in most counties in California charge nominal fees for duplication charges of discovery materials, and that prosecutors in other states and in the federal courts do the same. 185 Cal.App.4th at 1241–1242. The Court found that the fees charged by the district attorney in Ventura County, where the *Schaffer* case originated, were reasonable and in line with normal governmental duplication charges. 185 Cal.App.4th at 1241.

Finally, the Court found that the Criminal Discovery Statute does not contain any provision requiring the party which provides mandated discovery to pay the costs of that discovery. Since the prosecution's duty under the Criminal Discovery Statute is to "disclose" discoverable items, there is no requirement that the prosecution provide copies of any discoverable material. The prosecution's disclosure duty can be satisfied by making discoverable items available through an "open files" policy for the defendant to inspect and copy, if the defendant wishes to do so. 185 Cal.App.4th at 1242.

PART IV.　SANCTIONS FOR NONCOMPLIANCE

§ 5:14　Available sanctions—in general

The sanctions for a discovery violation provided in the Criminal Discovery Statute are not available post-trial. *People v. Bowles* (2011) 198 Cal.App.4th 318, 129 Cal.Rptr.3d 290. In *People v. Bowles, supra*, the defendant was convicted of burglary, grand theft, and receiving stolen property by jury verdict. After the verdict had been returned, the defendant filed a motion for dismissal for alleged prosecution failure to comply with the prosecutor's *Brady* duties and with discovery rules. The trial court conducted a hearing and issued a written order denying the motion to dismiss or to strike the prior conviction allegations. The court instead imposed a sanction for which the defendant had not asked—a new trial on two counts—and ruled that evidence which had not been timely disclosed could not be used in the People's case-in-chief on retrial. The People filed an appeal from the order granting a new trial.

The Fourth District Court of Appeal reversed the order granting a new trial. The Court of Appeal held that the trial court erred in granting a new trial as a discovery violation sanction under Penal Code section 1054.5, because sanctions under the Criminal Discovery Statute are not available post-trial. The Court reasoned that "the purposes of the discovery statutes cannot be furthered where, as here, a jury has already rendered its verdict on the substantive charges against the defendant and the trial court has decided the remaining prior conviction allegations . . . . [I]n this situation any violation of a defendant's pretrial right to discovery is appropriately addressed by available posttrial remedies such as an appeal from the judgment [citation omitted], a motion for new trial [citation omitted], or a petition for habeas corpus [citation omitted]." 198 Cal.App.4th at 327.

The Court reasoned that "where a jury has already rendered its verdict on the substantive charges against a defendant and the trial court has decided any remaining allegations, the mere fact that the trial court has jurisdiction over the matter does not render sanctions under section 1054.5 appropriate. Once the trier of fact has rendered a verdict it is no longer possible to remedy a discovery violation by the sanctions outlined in section 1054.5; rather, the issue turns from remediation to an examination of whether the discovery violation prevented the defendant from obtaining a fair trial. Accordingly, the trial court erred by granting a new trial as a sanction under section 1054.5 as sanctions under this statute were no longer available." 198 Cal.App.4th at 327.

§ 5:15   Discretionary nature of sanctions

A trial court has discretion whether to impose sanctions for a discovery violation, and what kinds of sanctions should be imposed. *United States v. Brown* (2009, CA10 OK) 592 F.3d 1088, 1090. However, a court's power to impose sanctions for a discovery violation is not an unfettered discretion. The discretion whether to impose a sanction or what kind of sanction to impose is subject to statutory restrictions. *People v. Superior Court (Mitchell)* (2010) 184 Cal.App.4th 451, 459, 109 Cal.Rptr.3d 207.

§ 5:15.1   Exhaustion of other sanctions

The Criminal Discovery Statute provides that a trial court may prohibit the testimony of a witness only if " 'all other sanctions have been exhausted.' [citation omitted]" *People v. Superior Court (Mitchell)* (2010) 184 Cal.App.4th 451, 459, 109 Cal.Rptr.3d 207. Thus, where a trial court precludes the testimony of a witness as a sanction for a discovery violation, without first considering or exhausting other sanctions, the court exceeds its jurisdiction. 184 Cal.App.4th at 459.

The requirement of the Criminal Discovery Statute that other sanctions have been considered or exhausted before the court may preclude the testimony of a witness applies to exclusion of non-testimonial evidence.

Thus, a court may not preclude evidence, such as dog scent and gunshot residue evidence, for a discovery violation without first considering and exhausting other possible sanctions. The reason is that excluding the evidence itself would then preclude the party from calling a witness to testify as an expert on the subjects of that physical evidence. "A trial court must not be allowed to indirectly do what it is barred from directly doing." 184 Cal.App.4th at 459.

Federal courts are under similar restrictions upon the imposition of sanctions for discovery violations. "The court should impose the least severe sanction that will accomplish prompt and full compliance with the discovery order." *United States v. Ivy* (1996, CA10 OK) 83 F.3d 1266, 1280; *accord, United States v. Brown* (2009, CA10 OK) 592 F.3d 1088, 1090.

§ 5:16   Preconditions to sanctions—in general

§ 5:16.2   Request or motion for sanctions

When necessary, a district court may hold an evidentiary hearing on a motion for sanctions. Hence, the district court has the discretion, but is not required, to hold an evidentiary hearing prior to imposing sanctions on a party. Indeed, in cases in which the sanctioned party argues that it was deprived of due process because the district court failed to conduct an evidentiary hearing, the opportunity to brief the issue fully satisfies due process requirements. *Lambright v. Ryan* (2012, CA9 Ariz.) 698 F.3d 808.

§ 5:17   Types of allowable sanctions

A trial court which finds that a party has committed a discovery violation has a wide range of possible sanctions from which to choose to deal with that violation. When making a choice of sanctions to impose for a discovery violation, a trial court should consider three factors: (1) the reason for the delayed production of the discoverable evidence; (2) the extent of the prejudice to the aggrieved party as a result of the discovery violation; and (3) the feasibility of curing prejudice to the aggrieved party by granting a continuance. *United States v. Brown* (2009, CA10 OK) 592 F.3d 1088, 1090.

§ 5:17.2   Continuance, postponement, adjournment

Granting a continuance to the aggrieved party can often be more than adequate to remedy a statutory discovery violation. *People v. Verdugo* (2010) 50 Cal.4th 263, 281, 113 Cal.Rptr.3d 803, 236 P.3d 1035.

Even without a continuance, postponement, or adjournment, undisclosed evidence that upsets a party's trial strategy might be admissible if the aggrieved party has an opportunity to adjust its trial strategy and to respond to the undisclosed evidence. *United States v. Lee* (2009, CA3 PA) 573 F.3d 155, 164.

§ 5:17.4.   Altering order of trial

A trial court may change the normal order of trial in order to rectify any harm done to an aggrieved party by a discovery violation. The changes in the order of trial can take many forms.

§ 5:17.4.1 Deferring cross-examination of a witness

In order to rectify a discovery violation relating to a particular witness who has not completed his or her testimony when the discovery violation is uncovered, a trial court may defer the cross-examination of the witness to allow the opposing, aggrieved party to prepare for the withheld evidence. *People v. Verdugo* (2010) 50 Cal.4th 263, 289, 113 Cal.Rptr.3d 803, 236 P.3d 1035.

§ 5:17.4.2 Recalling witness for further cross-examination

In order to rectify a discovery violation relating to a particular witness, a trial court may allow the opposing, aggrieved party to recall the witness for further cross-examination. *People v. Verdugo* (2010) 50 Cal.4th 263, 282–283, 286, 113 Cal.Rptr.3d 803, 236 P.3d 1035.

§ 5:17.5 Advising and instructing jury

What had seemed to be a significant obstacle to the use of a jury instruction as a sanction for a discovery violation appears to have been circumvented by the holding of the California Supreme Court in *People v. Riggs* (2008) 44 Cal.4th 248, 79 Cal.Rptr.3d 648, 187 P.3d 363.

In *Riggs* the defendant was charged with capital murder. More than one month after the guilt phase of the trial had begun, and three weeks after the prosecution had completed its case-in-chief, the defendant, who represented himself, disclosed the names and addresses of two alibi witnesses who would testify that at the time of the murder the defendant was with them far away from the scene of the murder.

The prosecution requested sanctions for a discovery violation by the defendant. The trial court declined to exclude the witnesse's testimony, but the court, at the prosecution's request, gave a jury instruction as a sanction for the discovery violation. The jury instruction read:

"California Penal Code Section 1054.7 requires that each side in a criminal action provide names and addresses of witnesses that it expects to call at trial at least 30 days prior to the trial unless good cause is shown for this not to be done. [¶] There has been evidence presented to you from which you may find that there was a failure by the defense to provide timely notice to the prosecution of the names and addresses of witnesses Ina Ross and Minny [*sic*] Jean Hill. [¶] You may consider such failure, if any, in determining the weight to be given to the testimony of such witnesses. The weight to be given such failure is entirely a matter for the jury's determination."

The defendant was convicted of murder and sentenced to death. On automatic appeal the defendant contended that the giving of the jury instruction was error. The Supreme Court rejected the defendant's argument.

The Court found that substantial evidence supported the trial court's decision that the defendant had committed a discovery violation—that the defendant "would reasonably anticipate that it was likely he would call as witnesses family members who purportedly knew that he was several hundred miles away from the scene of the crime when the murder was committed." 44 Cal.4th at 306.

The Supreme Court held that the giving of the jury instruction was not error. The Court found that the jury instruction did not suffer from the problems with jury instructions for discovery violations that had been criticized in prior Court of Appeal opinions. The Court focused on several factors in reaching this decision. First, the defendant represented himself, so "any discovery violation therefore was his responsibility, not an error of counsel." 44 Cal.4th at 307.

Second, the Court concluded that the instruction limited the inferences that the jury could draw from the nondisclosure of the defense witnesses, by "expressly directing the jury that it could consider a discovery violation in assessing the weight of the alibi testimony." 44 Cal.4th at 307. The Court reasoned that the jury "could reasonably infer from the fact that the defendant thereby violated his or her duty under the discovery statutes that even the defense did not have much confidence in the ability of its own evidence to withstand full adversarial testing." 44 Cal.4th at 308. The Court held that the discovery violation "might properly be viewed by the jury as evidence of the defendant's consciousness of the lack of credibility of the evidence that has been presented on his or her behalf." 44 Cal.4th at 307.

The Court inferred, though it did not hold, that a jury instruction for a discovery violation may direct the jury that a discovery violation has taken place, without giving the jury the power to determine whether that violation had occurred. 44 Cal.4th at 309.

Because the jury instruction in *Riggs* was directed at advising the jury that it could consider the discovery violation in assessing the credibility of the defense testimony, and not that it could use that violation to draw an inference of the defendant's guilt, the jury instruction was not error.

Practice Tip for Prosecution and Defense: While the facts of the case you are trying must dictate whether a jury instruction should be given by the court for a discovery violation by the opposing party, the jury instruction crafted by the trial court in *Riggs* offers a model that appears to pass constitutional muster. Before requesting a jury instruction for a discovery violation by the opposing party, counsel should carefully read *Riggs* to ensure that any such instruction complies with the requisites of *Riggs*.

§ 5:17.5.3 Jury instruction for prosecution discovery violation

A failure to preserve evidence violates a defendant's right to due process if the unavailable evidence possessed exculpatory value that was apparent before the evidence was destroyed, and is of such a nature that the defendant would be unable to obtain comparable evidence by other reasonably available means. A defendant must also demonstrate that the police acted in bad faith in failing to preserve the potentially useful evidence. The presence or absence of bad faith turns on the government's knowledge of the apparent exculpatory value of the evidence at the time it was lost or destroyed. The mere failure to preserve evidence which could have been subjected to tests which might have exonerated the defendant does not constitute a due process violation. *Jensen v. Hernandez* (E.D. Cal. 2012) 864 F. Supp. 2d 869.

In the context of preserving evidence, bad faith requires more than mere negligence or recklessness. *United States v. Toro-Barboza* (2012, CA9 Cal.) 673 F.3d 1136.

§ 5:17.5.4   Jury instruction for defense violation

The giving of a jury instruction as a sanction for a defense discovery violation has appeared to be a risky proposition for the prosecution. Several opinions by the Courts of Appeal have criticized the use of a jury instruction for a defense discovery violation. See Section 5:17.5.3 of the text for a discussion of these criticisms.

However, the obstacles to a jury instruction as a sanction for a defense discovery violation seem to have been overcome or averted by the holding of the California Supreme Court in *People v. Riggs* (2008) 44 Cal.4th 248, 79 Cal.Rptr.3d 648, 187 P.3d 363.

In *Riggs* the defendant was charged with capital murder. More than one month after the guilt phase of the trial had begun, and three weeks after the prosecution had completed its case-in-chief, the defendant, who represented himself, disclosed the names and addresses of two alibi witnesses who would testify that at the time of the murder the defendant was with them far away from the scene of the murder.

The prosecution requested sanctions for a discovery violation by the defendant. The trial court declined to exclude the witnesses' testimony, but the court, at the prosecution's request, gave a jury instruction as a sanction for the discovery violation. The jury instruction read:

"California Penal Code Section 1054.7 requires that each side in a criminal action provide names and addresses of witnesses that it expects to call at trial at least 30 days prior to the trial unless good cause is shown for this not to be done. [¶] There has been evidence presented to you from which you may find that there was a failure by the defense to provide timely notice to the prosecution of the names and addresses of witnesses Ina Ross and Minny [*sic*] Jean Hill. [¶] You may consider such failure, if any, in determining the weight to be given to the testimony of such witnesses. The weight to be given such failure is entirely a matter for the jury's determination."

The defendant was convicted of murder and sentenced to death. On automatic appeal the defendant contended that the giving of the jury instruction was error. The Supreme Court rejected the defendant's argument.

The Court found that substantial evidence supported the trial court's decision that the defendant had committed a discovery violation—that the defendant "would reasonably anticipate that it was likely he would call as witnesses family members who purportedly knew that he was several hundred miles away from the scene of the crime when the murder was committed." 44 Cal.4th at 306.

The Supreme Court held that the giving of the jury instruction was not error. The Court found that the jury instruction did not suffer from the problems with jury instructions for discovery violations that had been criticized in prior Court of Appeal opinions. The Court focused on several factors in reaching this decision. First, the defendant represented himself, so "any discovery violation therefore was his responsibility, not an error of counsel." 44 Cal.4th at 307.

Second, the Court concluded that the instruction limited the inferences that the jury could draw from the nondisclosure of the defense witnesses, by "expressly directing the jury that it could consider a discovery violation in assessing the weight of the alibi testimony." 44 Cal.4th at 307. The Court reasoned that the jury "could reasonably infer from the fact that the defendant thereby violated his or her duty under the discovery statutes that even the defense did not have much confidence in the ability of its own evidence to withstand full adversarial testing." 44 Cal.4th at 308. The Court held that the discovery violation "might properly be viewed by the jury as evidence of the defendant's consciousness of the lack of credibility of the evidence that has been presented on his or her behalf." 44 Cal.4th at 307.

The Court inferred, though it did not hold, that a jury instruction for a discovery violation may direct the jury that a discovery violation has taken place, without giving the jury the power to determine whether that violation had occurred. 44 Cal.4th at 309.

Because the jury instruction in *Riggs* was directed at advising the jury that it could consider the discovery violation in assessing the credibility of the defense testimony, and not that it could use that violation to draw an inference of the defendant's guilt, the jury instruction was not error.

Practice Tip for Prosecution: While the dangers of giving a jury instruction for a defense discovery violation have not been eliminated, and while the facts of the case you are trying must dictate whether a jury instruction should be given by the court for a discovery violation by the opposing party, the opinion of the Supreme Court in *Riggs* makes the giving of a jury instruction for a defense discovery violation a viable option. The jury instruction crafted by the trial court in *Riggs* offers a model that appears to pass constitutional muster. Before requesting a jury instruction for a discovery violation by the opposing party, you should carefully read *Riggs* to ensure that any such instruction complies with the requisites of *Riggs*.

§ 5:17.5.5 Spoilation instruction

If there is evidence from which a jury might conclude that a party has not only committed a discovery violation, but has committed a bad faith destruction of that evidence, and the destroyed evidence would have been favorable to the opposing party, a trial court may give a "spoilation" jury instruction. A spoilation jury instruction allows the trier of fact to draw an adverse inference that the evidence would have been unfavorable to the party which has destroyed the evidence. *United States v. Laurent* (2010, CA1 NH) 607 F.3d 895, 901–903.

§ 5:17.8 Contempt

§ 5:17.8.1 Contempt—in general

Whether a contempt sanction is civil or criminal is determined by examining the character of the relief itself. A sanction generally is civil if it coerces compliance with a court order or is a remedial sanction meant to compensate the complainant for actual losses. A criminal sanction, in contrast, generally seeks to punish a completed act of disobedience. The line between civil and criminal contempt is blurred where contempts involving out-of-court disobedience to complex injunctions are at issue. As a result, non-compensatory sanctions for violations of complex injunctions required heightened procedural protections including a jury trial and a beyond reasonable doubt burden of proof. *Ahearn v. Int'l Longshore & Warehouse Union, Local 21* (2013, CA9 Wash.) 721 F.3d 1122.

§ 5:17.9 State Bar report

To escape the *Brady* sanction, disclosure must be made at a time when disclosure would be of value to the accused. *United States v. Villa* (Oct. 31, 2012, CA9 Or.) 2012 U.S. App. LEXIS 22516.

§ 5:17.10 Exclusion of prosecution evidence

Appellate courts appear to be increasingly averse to preclusion of prosecution evidence as a sanction for a prosecution discovery violation, particularly if the prosecutor's conduct in committing the violation is not repeated or egregious.

§ 5:17.10.2 Exclusion of prosecution evidence after Criminal Discovery Statute

The Criminal Discovery Statute provides that a trial court may prohibit the testimony of a witness only if " 'all other sanctions have been exhausted.' [citation omitted]" *People v. Superior Court (Mitchell)* (2010)

184 Cal.App.4th 451, 459, 109 Cal.Rptr.3d 207. Thus, where a trial court precluded the testimony of a prosecution witness as a sanction for a discovery violation, without first considering or exhausting other sanctions, the Court of Appeal reversed the trial court's order as an order in excess of the court's jurisdiction. 184 Cal.App.4th at 459.

The requirement of the Criminal Discovery Statute that other sanctions have been considered or exhausted before the court may preclude the testimony of a witness applies to exclusion of non-testimonial evidence. Thus, a court may not preclude evidence, such as dog scent and gunshot residue evidence, as a sanction for a discovery violation without first considering and exhausting other possible sanctions. The reason is that excluding the evidence itself would then preclude the party from calling a witness to testify as an expert on the subjects of that physical evidence. "A trial court must not be allowed to indirectly do what it is barred from directly doing." 184 Cal.App.4th at 459.

Exclusion of prosecution evidence as a sanction for a discovery violation should not be imposed in the absence of evidence that the discovery violation has caused prejudice to the defendant that could not be cured by a continuance. In *People v. McKinnon* (2011) 52 Cal.4th 610, 130 Cal.Rptr.3d 590, 259 P.3d 1186, the prosecutor failed to make timely disclosure of a threat made by the defendant's sister against a prosecution witness. The defendant requested that the trial court exclude the evidence of the sister's threat, but the defendant did not seek a continuance or make a showing that the untimely disclosure of the threat caused his defense to be different than it would have been had he been provided timely discovery of that evidence. The trial court allowed the prosecution to introduce the evidence of the threat.

On appeal the defendant, who had been convicted of capital murder and sentenced to death, argued that the trial court's ruling was error. The Supreme Court rejected the defendant's argument, holding that the defendant had the burden to show that any prejudice caused by the prosecution's untimely disclosure would not have been cured by a continuance. The Court noted that the defendant had not asked for a continuance and had not shown that his defense would have been different had the prosecutor provided him with timely discovery of the evidence of the sister's threat. The Court found no abuse of discretion by the trial court in declining to exclude the prosecution evidence of the threat. 52 Cal.4th at 668–669.

§ 5:17.10.3   Exclusion of prosecution evidence in federal courts

If the prosecution has not committed a discovery violation, even though disclosure of a prosecution witness's identity and statement is given close in time to the start of the trial, and there is no evidence that the government attempted to gain a tactical advantage by the late disclosure, excluding the prosecution's evidence is not warranted.

In *United States v. Lofton* (2009, CA8 IA) 557 F.3d 594, the prosecution first interviewed a jail inmate days before the trial of a defendant charged with being a felon in possession of a firearm. The inmate stated that the defendant confessed to him that he had possessed the firearm. The inmate negotiated a deal with the prosecution to testify against the defendant, and the prosecution immediately notified the defense of the witness, the deal, and the witness's expected testimony.

The defendant's motion to exclude the inmate's testimony on the basis of late disclosure of that evidence was denied by the district court, and the defendant was convicted. On appeal the defendant argued that the trial court erred in denying his motion to exclude the witness's testimony. The Eighth Circuit Court of Appeals rejected the defendant's argument. The Court noted that the government disclosed the witness's identity and the details of his plea agreement more than one week before defendant's trial. The Court further observed that the government disclosed the witness's testimony immediately after the witness was interviewed. The Court found that there was no evidence that the government attempted to gain a tactical advantage in its timing of the disclosures to the defendant. 557 F.3d at 596.

In *United States v. Brown* (2009, CA10 OK) 592 F.3d 1088, the government provided a summary of its expert witness's expected testimony that did not completely comply with Rule 16 of the Federal Rules of Criminal Procedure, because the report failed to state the "bases and reasons" for the expert's opinions. The defendant failed to complain about the inadequate disclosure of the expert's expected testimony until cross-examination of the witness. The trial court declined to preclude the prosecution expert witness from testifying, finding that the government substantially complied with the requirements of Rule 16.

The Court of Appeals affirmed the trial court's ruling, observing that exclusion of evidence "is extreme," and, citing its opinion in *United States v. Charley* (1999, CA10 NM) 189 F.3d 1251, 1262, stated that exclusion of evidence " 'is almost never imposed 'in the absence of a constitutional violation or statutory authority for such exclusion.' [citations omitted]" 592 F.3d at 1090.

§ 5:17.11 Exclusion of defense evidence

When the defendant intentionally withholds mandated reciprocal discovery from the prosecution, and it appears that the withholding was motivated by a desire to gain an advantage at trial, a proper sanction might be to exclude the defense evidence.

§ 5:17.11.1 Authority supporting exclusion of defense evidence for discovery violation

In *United States v. Hardy* (2009, CA6 TN) 586 F.3d 1040, a defendant charged with embezzling money from her employer claimed in her defense that she had loaned money to the company, and that she was simply transferring money from a company bank account to repay her loans. After the company responded to a subpoena *duces tecum* that the company did not have any documentation of defendant's claims, the defense produced at trial copies of check stubs that the defendant claimed proved the existence of the loan.

The government objected to the admission into evidence of the copies of the check stubs, because the defendant had not complied with her duty to disclose the copies of the check stubs to the government prior to trial. The defendant had given the copies to her attorney one week before trial, but the defense waited until the trial to disclose them to the prosecution.

The trial court ruled that the defense had intentionally withheld mandated reciprocal discovery in an apparent effort to gain a tactical advantage over the government. The trial court accordingly excluded the copies of the check stubs from being admitted in evidence. The defendant was convicted and appealed, arguing, *inter alia*, that the trial court had violated her Sixth Amendment Right to Compulsory Process by the exclusion of the evidence.

The Sixth Circuit Court of Appeals rejected the defendant's argument, finding that the defendant and her attorney had access to the copies of the check stubs at least one week prior to trial, and could offer no satisfactory explanation as to why they had waited until the day of trial to disclose them to the government. 586 F.3d at 1044. The Court determined that the defendant had attempted to "gain an advantage at trial by not allowing the government access to evidence tending to prove its case and later springing that same evidence on the government when it was advantageous for Defendant." 586 F.3d at 1045.

The Court of Appeals concluded a "proper sanction for failure to disclose, under Rule 16, is exclusion of the evidence." 586 F.3d at 1044.

§ 5:17.11.3　Standards for determining whether to exclude defense evidence for discovery violation

Before dismissing a case on the ground that a defendant attorney's due process right to present a defense would be violated by the defendant's inability to disclose a client's confidential information, a court must consider at least four factors: The evidence at issue must be the client's confidential information, which the client insists on keeping confidential; the evidence must be highly material to the defendant's defenses; the trial court must determine whether it could effectively use ad hoc measures from its equitable arsenal, including techniques such as sealing and protective orders, limited admissibility of evidence, orders restricting the use of testimony in successive proceedings, and, where appropriate, in camera proceedings, so as to permit the action to proceed; and the court should consider whether it would be fundamentally unfair to allow the action to proceed. The last of these considerations is an extension of the principle that the privilege which protects attorney-client communications may not be used both as a sword and a shield. It would be unfair to allow a plaintiff to bring a claim necessitating a defense based on confidential information where the plaintiff has either directly supplied such confidential information to the defendant, or where the plaintiff seeks to derivatively represent a third party who has supplied such information to the defendant. *People ex rel. Herrera v. Stender* (2012) 212 Cal. App. 4th 614, 152 Cal. Rptr. 3d 16.

§ 5:17.13 Striking testimony

A decision to grant or deny a motion to strike as a sanction is vested in the trial judge's sound discretion. Courts generally disfavor motions to strike, however, because they propose a drastic remedy and are typically a delay tactic. *United States v. Baisden* (E.D. Cal. Mar. 25, 2013) 2013 U.S. Dist. LEXIS 41787.

The Federal Circuit applies the law of the regional circuit in reviewing sanctions orders. *Apple Inc. v. Samsung Elecs. Co.* (N.D. Cal. 2012) 888 F. Supp. 2d 976. The appellate court reviews sanctions and the terms of a disciplinary order for abuse of discretion. *Chandler v. Hopper (In re Nieto)* (Dec. 6, 2012, B.A.P. CA9) 2012 Bankr. LEXIS 5667. A bankruptcy appellate panel reviews all aspects of an award of sanctions for an abuse of discretion. The bankruptcy court's choice of sanction is also reviewed for abuse of discretion. A bankruptcy court abuses its discretion if it bases a decision on an incorrect legal rule, or if its application of the law was illogical, implausible, or without support in inferences that may be drawn from the facts in the record. *Guerra v. Dumas (In re Avon Townhomes Venture)* (Mar. 29, 2012, B.A.P. CA9) 2012 Bankr. LEXIS 1410.

§ 5:17.14 Dismissal of charges

A dismissal of charges for a prosecution discovery violation is a substantial sanction that should not be imposed unless dismissal is required by the United States Constitution.

§ 5:17.14.2 Dismissal under Criminal Discovery Statute

In *People v. Superior Court (Meraz)* (2008) 163 Cal.App.4th 28, 77 Cal.Rptr.3d 352, a defendant in a capital murder case requested discovery of information about a vehicle stop and an in-field showup that had been made in the vicinity of and shortly after the alleged homicide. The prosecutor believed that no reports concerning the traffic stop existed and repeatedly stated that fact to counsel and the trial court.

During jury selection, the prosecutor learned that field interview cards and photographs from the vehicle stop were possessed by the agency that had investigated the homicide. The prosecutor immediately disclosed the FI cards and the photographs to the defendant. The trial court dismissed the special circumstance allegation "to ensure that such untimely disclosure by law enforcement will not happen again." 163 Cal.App.4th at 33. The prosecution petitioned the Court of Appeal for writ of prohibition and/or mandate to overturn the trial court's dismissal of the special circumstance allegation.

The trial court granted the prosecution's petition and issued a writ of mandate directing the superior court to set aside its dismissal of the special circumstance allegation and to enter an order denying the defense motion to dismiss. In reaching this decision, the Court of Appeal held that the trial court's power to dismiss the allegation was subject to subdivision (c) of Penal Code section 1054.5, which provides that "[t]he court shall not dismiss a charge pursuant to subdivision (b) unless required to do so by the Constitution of the United States."

The initial question presented in *Meraz* was whether the restriction on dismissal as a discovery violation sanction applies to a special allegation that goes beyond the underlying substantive offense. The Court of Appeal concluded that it is "highly doubtful the electorate intended to permit dismissal of a charging allegation—particularly a special circumstance—if not required by the federal Constitution." 163 Cal.App.4th at 50.

The Court of Appeal observed that since a "criminal defendant has no general constitutional right to discovery," the " 'only substantive discovery mandated by the United States Constitution' " is *Brady* material exculpatory evidence. 163 Cal.App.4th at 50. The Court then determined whether a *Brady* violation had occurred, opining that " 'if there was no *Brady* violation, then there was no conceivable basis for concluding the federal Constitution required dismissal.' [citation omitted]" 163 Cal.App.4th at 50.

After analyzing the evidence and the case against the defendant, the Court of Appeal concluded that the record did not support a conclusion that the prosecution had committed a *Brady* violation. Accordingly, the Court concluded that dismissal of the special circumstance allegation was not mandated by the United States Constitution. The Court further rejected the idea that the trial court's dismissal of the allegation was justified as a punitive sanction against the investigating agency and as a deterrent to future police misconduct in withholding discoverable evidence. 163 Cal.App.4th at 53, n.13.

Finally, the Court of Appeal rejected the defendant's argument that dismissal of the special circumstance allegation was justified by the trial court's discretionary power to dismiss provided by Penal Code section 1385. The Court determined that even if the procedural hurdles to exercise of the trial court's power to dismiss under Section 1385 had been overcome, "because dismissal occurred in the context of a discovery violation, we believe the situation would still be covered by section 1054.5, subdivision (c), and that section 1385 could not be used to circumvent the limitation on dismissal contained therein." 163 Cal.App.4th at 54.

The trial court does not have the lawful power to dismiss a charge as a post-trial sanction for a discovery violation. *People v. Bowles* (2011) 198

Cal.App.4th 318, 129 Cal.Rptr.3d 290. In *People v. Bowles, supra*, the defendant was convicted of burglary, grand theft, and receiving stolen property by jury verdict. After the verdict had been returned, the defendant filed a motion for dismissal for alleged prosecution failure to comply with the prosecutor's *Brady* duties and with discovery rules. The trial court conducted a hearing and issued a written order denying the motion to dismiss or to strike the prior conviction allegations. The court instead imposed a sanction for which the defendant had not asked—a new trial on two counts—and ruled that evidence which had not been timely disclosed could not be used in the People's case-in-chief on retrial. The People filed an appeal from the order granting a new trial.

The Fourth District Court of Appeal reversed the order granting a new trial. The Court of Appeal held that the trial court erred in granting a new trial as a discovery violation sanction under Penal Code section 1054.5, because sanctions under the Criminal Discovery Statute are not available post-trial. The Court reasoned that "the purposes of the discovery statutes cannot be furthered where, as here, a jury has already rendered its verdict on the substantive charges against the defendant and the trial court has decided the remaining prior conviction allegations. . . . [I]n this situation any violation of a defendant's pretrial right to discovery is appropriately addressed by available posttrial remedies such as an appeal from the judgment [citation omitted], a motion for new trial [citation omitted], or a petition for habeas corpus [citation omitted]." 198 Cal.App.4th at 327.

The Court reasoned that "where a jury has already rendered its verdict on the substantive charges against a defendant and the trial court has decided any remaining allegations, the mere fact that the trial court has jurisdiction over the matter does not render sanctions under section 1054.5 appropriate. Once the trier of fact has rendered a verdict it is no longer possible to remedy a discovery violation by the sanctions outlined in section 1054.5; rather, the issue turns from remediation to an examination of whether the discovery violation prevented the defendant from obtaining a fair trial. Accordingly, the trial court erred by granting a new trial as a sanction under section 1054.5 as sanctions under this statute were no longer available." 198 Cal.App.4th at 327.

§ 5:17.14.4 Dismissal of special circumstance allegation

A special allegation, such as a special circumstance allegation, is considered to be a "charge" that is not subject to dismissal for a discovery violation under the authority of subdivision (c) of Penal Code section 1054.5, which provides that "[t]he court shall not dismiss a charge pursuant to subdivision (b) unless required to do so by the Constitution of the United States." *See People v. Superior Court (Meraz)* (2008) 163 Cal.App.4th 28, 77 Cal.Rptr.3d 352, discussed in Section 5:17.14.2 of this supplement, in which the Court of Appeal held that the restriction on dismissal as a discovery violation sanction applies to a special allegation that goes beyond the underlying substantive offense. The Court of Appeal concluded that it is "highly doubtful the electorate intended to permit dismissal of a charging allegation—particularly a special circumstance—if not required by the federal Constitution." 163 Cal.App.4th at 50.

§ 5:17.16   Monetary sanctions

The imposition of monetary sanctions pursuant to Section 177.5 of the Code of Civil Procedure is within the discretion of the trial court. *People v. Ward* (2009) 173 Cal.App.4th 1518, 1527, 93 Cal.Rptr.3d 871.

A trial court which wishes to utilize monetary sanctions as allowed by Code of Civil Procedure section 177.5 for a discovery violation must comply with the statutory requirements of that section.

Imposition of monetary sanctions is not allowed under Section 177.5 unless the attorney upon whom sanctions are to be imposed has violated a court order. The existence of a discovery order by the court and a violation of that order by the party or attorney to be disciplined is essential to the use of that sanction for a discovery violation. *People v. Hundal* (2008) 168 Cal.App.4th 965, 969–970, 86 Cal.Rptr.3d 166.

When a court proposes to use the monetary sanctions of Section 177.5 for a discovery violation, the court must provide the attorney to be sanctioned "with a written statement of reasons for the sanction." *People v. Hundal, supra,* 168 Cal.App.4th at 970. The trial court must "prepare a written order explaining its issuance of sanctions . . . ." *People v. Ward, supra,* 173 Cal.App.4th at 1531. The order imposing sanctions must be in writing and must "recite in detail the conduct or circumstances justifying the order." *People v. Ward, supra.*

The court must also provide an attorney to be sanctioned under Section 177.5 with an opportunity to be heard on the proposed sanction. *People v. Hundal, supra,* 168 Cal.App.4th at 970. This is a due process protection to which the attorney is entitled.

§ 5:17.19   Mistrial and new trial

A court which finds that the defendant committed a reciprocal discovery violation may, under appropriate conditions, declare a mistrial and order a new trial as a sanction for the discovery violation. However, a mistrial/new trial sanction for a discovery violation should be ordered by the court only if less drastic alternatives would not be a satisfactory solution to cure the discovery violation. *Gouleed v. Wengler* (2009, CA8 MN) 589 F.3d 976, 981.

A "less drastic alternative" does not mean "any conceivable option available to the trial judge. It means a reasonable and satisfactory alternative—a solution to a trial problem which strikes a better balance between 'the defendant's interest in proceeding to verdict' and the 'competing and equally legitimate demand for public justice' than would a mistrial."

589 F.3d at 983. A mistrial must be justified by a "manifest necessity" or a "high degree of necessity." 589 F.3d at 984.

When the discovery violation has been committed by the prosecution, the court must consider whether the prejudice resulting from the violation is serious enough to adversely affect a court's ability to reach a just conclusion. *United States v. Lee* (2009, CA3 PA) 573 F.3d 155, 164. "One way a discovery violation may do this is by interfering with the defendant's ability to prepare for trial and develop an intelligent defense strategy." 573 F.3d at 164.

§ 5:18   Posttrial sanctions

The trial court does not have the lawful post-trial power to impose sanctions for a discovery violation. In *People v. Bowles* (2011) 198 Cal.App.4th 318, 129 Cal.Rptr.3d 290, the Fourth District Court of Appeal agreed with the holding of the Second District Court of Appeal in *People v. Bohannon* (2000) 82 Cal.App.4th 798, 806, 98 Cal.Rptr.2d 488, that a trial court lacks the power under the Criminal Discovery Statute to impose such sanctions.

In *People v. Bowles, supra*, the defendant was convicted of burglary, grand theft, and receiving stolen property by jury verdict. After the verdict had been returned, the defendant filed a motion for dismissal for alleged prosecution failure to comply with the prosecutor's *Brady* duties and with discovery rules. The trial court conducted a hearing and issued a written order denying the motion to dismiss or to strike the prior conviction allegations. The court instead imposed a sanction for which the defendant had not asked—a new trial on two counts—and ruled that evidence which had not been timely disclosed could not be used in the People's case-in-chief on retrial. The People filed an appeal from the order granting a new trial.

The Fourth District Court of Appeal reversed the order granting a new trial. The Court of Appeal held that the trial court erred in granting a new trial as a discovery violation sanction under Penal Code section 1054.5, because sanctions under the Criminal Discovery Statute are not available post-trial. The Court reasoned that "the purposes of the discovery statutes cannot be furthered where, as here, a jury has already rendered its verdict on the substantive charges against the defendant and the trial court has decided the remaining prior conviction allegations. . . . [I]n this situation any violation of a defendant's pretrial right to discovery is appropriately addressed by available posttrial remedies such as an appeal from the judgment [citation omitted], a motion for new trial [citation omitted], or a petition for habeas corpus [citation omitted]." 198 Cal.App.4th at 327.

The Court reasoned that "where a jury has already rendered its verdict on the substantive charges against a defendant and the trial court has decided any remaining allegations, the mere fact that the trial court has jurisdiction over the matter does not render sanctions under section 1054.5 appropriate.

Once the trier of fact has rendered a verdict it is no longer possible to remedy a discovery violation by the sanctions outlined in section 1054.5; rather, the issue turns from remediation to an examination of whether the discovery violation prevented the defendant from obtaining a fair trial. Accordingly, the trial court erred by granting a new trial as a sanction under section 1054.5 as sanctions under this statute were no longer available." 198 Cal.App.4th at 327.

CHAPTER 6

DISCOVERY OUTSIDE CRIMINAL DISCOVERY STATUTE

PART I.   DISCLOSING EXCULPATORY EVIDENCE TO GRAND JURY

§ 6:1   Disclosing exculpatory evidence to grand jury — in general

The duty of California prosecutors to disclose exculpatory evidence to a grand jury continues to be a statutory, not a constitutional, duty. "[T]he grand jury is an accusatory, rather than an adjudicatory, body, and so the disclosure of exculpatory evidence is not required. [citations omitted]" *United States v. Mahalick* (2007, CA7 IL) 498 F.3d 475, 479.

PART II.   DISCLOSURE MANDATED BY PROCEDURAL DUE PROCESS

§ 6:3   Procedural due process discovery requirements — in general

Nothing in the discovery statutes alters the obligation imposed upon the prosecutor by due process. The prosecutor's duties of disclosure under the Due Process Clause are wholly independent of any statutory scheme of reciprocal discovery. The due process requirements are self-executing and need no statutory support to be effective. Such obligations exist whether or not the state has adopted a reciprocal discovery statute. Furthermore, if a statutory discovery scheme exists, these due process requirements operate outside such a scheme. The prosecutor is obligated to disclose such evidence voluntarily, whether or not the defendant makes a request for discovery. No statute can limit the foregoing due process rights of criminal defendants. *Bridgeforth v. Superior Court* (2013) 214 Cal. App. 4th 1074, 154 Cal. Rptr. 3d 528. Likewise, California's criminal discovery statutes do not violate the Due Process Clause by failing to require the prosecutor to disclose all exculpatory evidence as mandated by the U.S. Supreme Court in *Brady v. Maryland*. The criminal discovery statutes cannot not violate due process because the new statutes do not affect the defendant's constitutional rights under *Brady*. The prosecutor's duties of disclosure under the Due Process Clause are wholly independent of any statutory scheme of reciprocal discovery. The due process requirements are self-executing and need no statutory support to be effective. The prosecutor is obligated to disclose such evidence voluntarily. No statute can limit the foregoing due process rights of criminal defendants, and the criminal discovery statutes do not attempt to do so. On the contrary, the criminal discovery statutes contemplates disclosure outside the statutory scheme pursuant to constitutional requirements as enunciated in *Brady*. *People v. Gutierrez* (2013) 214 Cal. App. 4th 343, 153 Cal. Rptr. 3d 832.

§ 6:4 Defendant's right to lineup

A defendant who makes a motion for a court-ordered lineup pursuant to *Evans v. Superior Court* (1974) 11 Cal.3d 617, 114 Cal.Rptr. 121, 522 P.2d 681, must meet two conditions or requirements in order to be entitled to such a lineup.

First, the defendant must establish that there is a reasonable likelihood of mistaken identification. In *People v. Redd* (2010) 48 Cal.4th 691, 108 Cal.Rptr.3d 192, 229 P.3d 101, a defendant charged with first degree murder, attempted murder, second degree robbery, and second degree burglary moved for an *Evans* lineup involving the victim of the second degree robbery. The trial court denied the motion, and the defendant was convicted and sentenced to death for the first-degree murder.

On automatic appeal to the California Supreme Court the defendant argued that the trial court had erred in denying his motion for an *Evans* lineup. The Supreme Court rejected the defendant's argument. The Court based its opinion on two factors, one of which was that there was an absence of a reasonable likelihood of a mistaken identification, and the other was that the defendant's motion for the lineup was not timely.

The Court observed that the defendant did not even address the trial court's conclusion that there was no reasonable likelihood of mistaken identification. The Court then listed all of the circumstances surrounding the victim's identification of the defendant from a photo lineup, and the Court concluded that the trial court did not err in concluding that there was no reasonable likelihood of mistaken identification. The Court held that in the absence of a reasonable likelihood of a mistaken identification, the defendant did not have a right to an *Evans* lineup. 48 Cal.4th at 724–725.

In addition, the Supreme Court affirmed the trial court's denial of the defendant's request for an *Evans* lineup, because the defendant's request for such a lineup was not made in a timely fashion. The Court noted that the defendant had waited more than a year after his arrest to move for the lineup, and that the defendant's motion was made less than two months before the trial date. The Court stated that because "the motion was made shortly before trial, and defendant did not clearly demonstrate good cause for the delay," the trial court did not abuse its discretion in denying the defendant's motion for an *Evans* lineup. 48 Cal.4th at 725.

PART III. DISCOVERY TO ESTABLISH DISCRIMINATORY PROSECUTION DEFENSE

§ 6:5   Discriminatory prosecution discovery — in general

The fact that prosecutorial decisions are sometimes made to charge or accept a plea to a lesser offense than one which the evidence would support does not mean that another person who has not received that leniency has been deprived of equal protection, absent a showing of discriminatory prosecution. *People v. Tuck* (2012) 204 Cal. App. 4th 724, 139 Cal. Rptr. 3d 407.

§ 6:8   Required showing for discriminatory prosecution discovery

§ 6:8.2   *Armstrong* constitutional standard

§ 6:8.2.1   "Similarly situated" defendant defined [NEW]

Because the standard for obtaining a court order for discovery in support of a claim of selective or discriminatory prosecution is that a defendant must provide evidence showing that "similarly situated individuals were not prosecuted," *United States v. Smith* (2000, CA11 AL) 231 F.3d 800, 809, it is important to understand the definition of "similarly situated individuals." A "similarly situated" person for selective prosecution purposes is "one who engaged in the same type of conduct, which means that the comparator committed the same basic crime in substantially the same manner as the defendant—so that any prosecution of that individual would have the same deterrence value and would be related in the same way to the Government's enforcement priorities and enforcement plan—and against whom the evidence was as strong or stronger than that against the defendant." 231 F.3d at 810. A "comparison of the criminal histories of defendants is essential when conducting a 'similarly situated' inquiry." *United States v. Jordan* (2011, CA11 GA) 635 F.3d 1181, 1188. A comparison that does not include the criminal histories of other defendants is "not probative of the 'similarly situated' inquiry of the discriminatory effect test." 635 F.3d at 1189.

In general terms, "defendants are similarly situated when their circumstances present no distinguishable legitimate prosecutorial factors that might justify making different prosecutorial decisions with respect to them." *United States v. Olvis* (1996, CA4 VA) 97 F.3d 739, 744; *United States v. Lighty* (2010, CA4 MD) 616 F.3d 321, 370.

PART IV.   DISCOVERY TO ESTABLISH VINDICTIVE PROSECUTION

§ 6:11   Vindictive prosecution discovery—in general

A defendant who claims that the filing of criminal charges against him or her violates due process of law because it constitutes vindictive prosecution can obtain a discovery order in support of a vindictive-prosecution defense. However, before courts enter a discovery order at the defendant's request to enable the defendant to unearth evidence supporting that defense, the defendant is required to produce "objective evidence tending to show the existence of prosecutorial vindictiveness." *United States v. Bucci* (2009, CA1 MA) 582 F.3d 108, 113, and cases cited therein.

This standard which the defendant must meet in order to be entitled to discovery in support of a vindictive prosecution defense is "derived from the opinion of the United States Supreme Court in *United States v. Armstrong* (1996) 517 U.S. 456, 468, 116 S.Ct. 1480, 134 L.Ed.2d 687, a case in which the Supreme Court established the standard for discovery sought by a defendant to support a selective-prosecution claim. The trial court applied this standard in the *Bucci* case, and the First Circuit Court of Appeals adopted that standard. 582 F.3d at 113.

Thus, a defendant must "do more than simply 'identify a potential motive for prosecutorial animus.' [citation omitted] He must connect any vindictive animus to those making the challenged charging decisions in his case." 582 F.3d at 114.

In *Bucci* the Court of Appeals rejected the defendant's showing that law enforcement officers resented the defendant's establishment of a web site entitled "whosarat.com," which allowed people to post information about government informants, out of serious concern that these postings on the defendant's web site posed serious dangers to government informants. The Court observed that the decision to increase charges against the defendant prior to the defendant's trial was made by the prosecuting attorney, not by the law enforcement officers whose opposition to the defendant's web site formed the basis of the defendant's vindictive prosecution defense. 582 F.3d at 114.

The Court of Appeals rejected the defendant's argument that the government's opposition to the motion of a co-defendant for early disclosure of statements made by prosecution witnesses, in which the government expressed concern that the defendants were trying to intimidate government witnesses through their web site, established that the refiled charges constituted vindictive prosecution. The Court concluded that the defendant "set forth no evidence suggesting that this concern ever affected the prosecutors making the specific charging decisions in his case." 582 F.3d at 113.

Finally, the Court of Appeals rejected the "suspicious timing" argument of the defendant—that the refiling of increased charges was suspiciously close in time to the defendant's establishment of the "whosarat.com" web site. The filing of the first superseding indictment occurred six months after the defendant's web site was first operated, and the second superseding indictment occurred another six months later. "These superseding indictments were not so close in time to Bucci's starting the whosarat.com website to provide strong evidence that the prosecutor acted vindictively." 582 F.3d at 114.

CHAPTER 7

DISCOVERY REGARDING INFORMANTS

PART I. DISCOVERY OF INFORMANT IDENTITY

A. Discovering Informant Identity-In general

§ 7:1   Overview

Brady v. Maryland does not impose an obligation to necessarily produce the entire file of a confidential informant. *United States v. Bermudez-Chavez* (Apr. 4, 2012, CA9 Ariz.) 2012 U.S. App. LEXIS 6739).

Once a defendant's Sixth Amendment right to counsel attaches, the government is forbidden from deliberately eliciting incriminating statements about the crimes charged from the defendant. These Sixth Amendment protections apply to conversations between confidential informants (CIs) and defendants where the CIs relay incriminating statements from the defendant to the government, just as they do to formal questioning. *United States v. Smith* (Jan. 28, 2013, CA9 Alaska) 2013 U.S. App. LEXIS 1896. In *Randolph v. California* (2004, CA9 Cal.) 380 F.3d 1133, 1144, the United States Court of Appeals for the Ninth Circuit laid out the test for determining whether an individual acting as a confidential informant (CI) violates a defendant's Sixth Amendment right to counsel. This test requires a showing that (1) the CI was acting as an agent of the State when he obtained the information from him, and that (2) the CI made some effort to stimulate conversations about the crime charged. Stimulation of conversation falls far short of interrogation. Although a confidential informant (CI) need not formally interrogate the defendant to violate his rights, where an informant is placed in close proximity to the defendant, but makes no effort to stimulate conversations about the crime charged, there is no violation of the defendant's Sixth Amendment rights. *Id.* A defendant does not make out a violation of his Sixth Amendment right simply by showing that an informant, either through prior arrangement or voluntarily, reported his incriminating statements to the police. Rather, the defendant must demonstrate that the police and their informant took some action, beyond merely listening, that was designed deliberately to elicit incriminating remarks. *Id.*

Statements unwittingly made to an informant are not "testimonial" within the meaning of the Confrontation Clause of the Sixth Amendment. *People v. Arauz* (2012) 210 Cal. App. 4th 1394, 149 Cal. Rptr. 3d 211.

§ 7:3 Persons protected by privilege

Evidence Code sections 1040 and 1041 codify the privileges to refuse disclosure of confidential official information and the identity of confidential informants, and Evidence Code section 1042, provides the procedures used to determine whether these privileges may be invoked to prevent disclosures in any particular case. Evidence Code section 1040, subsection (b)(2), provides governmental entities with a privilege to refuse to disclose confidential official information when the public interest in preserving the confidentiality of the information outweighs the necessity for disclosure in the interest of justice. Section 1041 provides that a public entity is privileged to refuse to disclose the identity of a person who has furnished information in confidence concerning a violation of law if disclosure of the identity of the informer is against the public interest because there is a necessity for preserving the confidentiality of the informer's identity that outweighs the necessity for disclosure in the interest of justice. *People v. Acevedo* (2012) 209 Cal. App. 4th 1040, 147 Cal. Rptr. 3d 467.

B. *Prima Facie* Showing of Materiality

§ 7:5 Defendant's burden of proof

A defendant seeking an order that the prosecution disclose the identity of a confidential informant has the burden of producing some evidence that there is a reasonable possibility that the informant could give evidence on the issue of guilt that might exonerate the defendant. *People v. Lawley* (2002) 27 Cal.4th 102, 159, 115 Cal.Rptr.2d 614, 38 P.3d 461; *Davis v. Superior Court* (2010) 186 Cal.App.4th 1272, 1276, 113 Cal.Rptr.3d 365.

§ 7:6 Informant's physical proximity to crime as basis

A showing that the informant was in a position to observe the commission of the alleged crime is sufficient to establish that the informant could give evidence on the issue of guilt that might exonerate the defendant. *Davis v. Superior Court* (2010) 186 Cal.App.4th 1272, 1276, 113 Cal.Rptr.3d 365.

§ 7:8 Informant eyewitness as basis

A showing that the informant was an eyewitness to the charged crime is sufficient to establish that the informant could give evidence on the issue of guilt that might exonerate the defendant. *Davis v. Superior Court* (2010) 186 Cal.App.4th 1272, 1276. 113 Cal.Rptr.3d 365. However, the fact that a confidential informant was a percipient witness to the crime does not mean that disclosure of that informant is required. "[D]isclosure occurs only if the defendant makes an adequate showing that the informant can give exculpatory evidence . . . [The defendant] thus may be entitled to the opportunity to make such a showing at an in camera hearing, but he is not, at this stage in the proceedings, entitled to automatic disclosure." 186 Cal.App.4th at 1277.

§ 7:9   Informant witness to circumstances immediately preceding crime as basis

A showing that the informant was in a position to observe the commission of the immediate antecedents of the alleged crime is sufficient to establish that the informant could give evidence on the issue of guilt that might exonerate the defendant. *Davis v. Superior Court* (2010) 186 Cal.App.4th 1272, 1276, 113 Cal.Rptr.3d 365.

§ 7:10   Informant witness to remote circumstances preceding crime as basis

Where an informant's controlled drug buy from the defendant that was used as probable cause for the issuance of a search warrant for the defendant's residence occurred remotely in time from the seizure of drugs pursuant to the search warrant that formed the basis of the charges against the defendant, the informant was not a material witness—someone who could give evidence on the issue of guilt that might exonerate the defendant. *United States v. El-Alamin* (2009, CA8 MN) 574 F.3d 915, 926–927.

§ 7:12   Informant non-exculpatory witness as basis

A showing that the informant was an eyewitness, but without any showing that the informant could give evidence that might exonerate the defendant, is not sufficient for a court to determine that the informant is a material witness. *Davis v. Superior Court* (2010) 186 Cal.App.4th 1272, 1276, 113 Cal.Rptr.3d 365. "[D]isclosure occurs only if the defendant makes an adequate showing that the informant can give exculpatory evidence." 186 Cal.App.4th at 1277.

C.   *In Camera* Hearing

§ 7:25   Court *sua sponte* order for hearing

Note: It is not constitutionally relevant whether an informant utilizes an audio-video device, rather than merely an audio recording device, to record activities occurring inside a home, into which the informer has been invited. *United States v. Wahchumwah* (2013, CA9 Wash.) 710 F.3d 862.

§ 7:26   Informant participation in hearing

Note that when parties dispute the factual foundation for a defendant's requested informant credibility instruction, an appellate court reviews a district court's refusal to give the requested jury instruction for an abuse of discretion. *United States v. Anekwu* (2012, CA9 Cal.).

The presence of the confidential informant at an *in camera* hearing to determine whether the identity of the informant should be ordered to be disclosed is not required. *Davis v. Superior Court* (2010) 186 Cal.App.4th 1272, 1277–1278, 113 Cal.Rptr.3d 365.

§ 7:27 Defense participation in hearing

Although the Court of Appeal in *Davis v. Superior Court* (2010) 186 Cal.App.4th 1272, 1277, 113 Cal.Rptr.3d 365, opined that a defendant moving for an order that the identity of a confidential informant be disclosed "may be entitled to the opportunity to make" a showing at an *in camera* hearing, this statement should not be construed to mean that the defendant and/or the defendant's attorney should be allowed to be present at or participate in the *in* camera hearing.

§ 7:31 Denying disclosure—informant's incriminating evidence

§ 7:31.1 Denying disclosure—affirmative defense

A defendant who produces some evidence of entrapment as a defense might be entitled to disclosure of an informant who could produce exculpatory evidence in support of that defense. However, where the defendant fails to adduce some evidence of entrapment, the defendant does not adequately raise an entrapment defense, and a trial court does not abuse its discretion in refusing to order disclosure of the identity of a confidential informant. *United States v. Vincent* (2010, CA10 UT) 611 F.3d 1246, 1251–1252.

PART II. DISCOVERY OF INFORMANT COMMUNICATION

§ 7:34 Protecting informant communication—search warrant affidavit

In *People v. Galland* (2008) 45 Cal.4th 354, 86 Cal.Rptr.3d 841, 197 P.3d 736, the California Supreme Court reaffirmed its holding in *People v. Hobbs* (1994) 7 Cal.4th 948, 30 Cal.Rptr.2d 651, 873 P.2d 1246, that a judge may seal a portion of the affidavit or statement of probable cause in support of a search warrant in order to protect the identity of a confidential informant whose information is included in that affidavit or statement of probable cause. The judge may then consider the sealed information when determining whether to grant or deny a defendant's motion to suppress evidence seized pursuant to that search warrant or whether to quash the search warrant. 45 Cal.4th at 363–365.

Citing its opinion in *Hobbs*, the Supreme Court explained the procedures to be followed in the following language:

"When a defendant seeks to quash or traverse a warrant where a portion of the supporting affidavit has been sealed, the relevant materials are to be made available for in camera review by the trial court. [citations omitted] The court should determine first whether there are sufficient grounds for maintaining the confidentiality of the informant's identity. If so, the court should then determine whether the sealing of the affidavit (or any portion thereof) 'is necessary to avoid revealing the informant's identity.' [citation omitted] Once the affidavit is found to have been properly sealed, the court should proceed to determine "whether, under the 'totality of the circumstances' presented in the search warrant affidavit and the oral testimony, if any, presented to the magistrate, there was 'a fair probability' that contraband or evidence of a crime would be found in the place searched pursuant to the warrant' (if the defendant has moved to quash the warrant) or 'whether the defendant's general allegations of material misrepresentations or omissions are supported by the public and sealed portions of the search warrant affidavit, including any testimony offered at the in camera hearing' (if the defendant has moved to traverse the warrant). [citation omitted] The prosecutor may be present at the in camera hearing; the defendant and defense counsel are to be excluded unless the prosecutor elects to waive any objection to their presence. However, defense counsel should be afforded the opportunity to submit written questions, reasonable in length, which shall be asked by the trial judge of any witness called to testify at the proceeding." 45 Cal.4th at 364.

The procedure outlined in *Hobbs* does not authorize a court which has ordered the partial unsealing of a search warrant affidavit as step one of the *Hobbs* procedure to then order the remaining portions of the affidavit disclosed.

In *People v. Heslington* (2011) 195 Cal.App.4th 947, 125 Cal.Rptr.3d 740, the defendant's residence was searched pursuant to a warrant obtained following a gang fight at a bar. The magistrate who issued the warrant ordered 19 pages of the affidavit to be sealed in order to protect the identity of informants and the confidentiality of official information. The defendant was charged with possession of illegal drugs with firearm arming enhancements. The defendant filed a motion to suppress the evidence seized pursuant to the warrant, and requested that the court unseal the sealed portions of the affidavit. The issuing magistrate reviewed the sealed portions of the affidavit and ordered a substantial amount of the sealed portions to be unsealed and disclosed to the defendant. The prosecution complied with the order to disclose the unsealed portions to the defense.

Applying the *Hobbs* standard the magistrate found a reasonable "probability" that the defendant would prevail on his motion to quash the warrant and a reasonable "possibility" he would prevail on his motion to traverse it. The magistrate then ordered the prosecution to disclose the entire sealed affidavit to the defense. The prosecution refused to consent to the disclosure of the remaining sealed portions of the affidavit. The magistrate granted the defendant's suppression motions *not* on the merits but rather pursuant to *Hobbs*. The People advised that they were unable to proceed to trial because of the court's suppression of the evidence, and the trial court dismissed the case.

The People argued on appeal that the trial court misapplied Step 2 of the *Hobbs* procedure by ordering disclosure of the remaining sealed portions of the affidavit. The Court of Appeal agreed with the People's contention and reversed the dismissal of the charges against the defendant. The Court reasoned: "When the critical parts of the sealed affidavit have been disclosed to the defense, there is no need for further unsealing of confidential material or for the court to act on the defendant's behalf. At that point, a court should *not* proceed to the second stage of the *Hobbs* procedure. Instead, the suppression motion should proceed to decision with a further evidentiary hearing if necessary." 195 Cal.App.4th at 958–959.

The Court of Appeal then recapped the *Hobbs* procedure as follows: "[T]he first stage of the *Hobbs* procedure requires the court to determine (1) whether any or all of the warrant is properly sealed, i.e., whether any further disclosures must be made to the defendant, and (2) whether any of the remaining confidential information is significant to defendant's cause. Only if the answer to this second question is yes does the court proceed to the next stage of *Hobbs* and decide whether there is a reasonable probability the defendant will prevail on the suppression motion." 195 Cal.App.4th at 959.

The trial court's decision to proceed to the next step under *Hobbs* was erroneous, "because the disclosures ordered by the court were so substantial that the affidavit's remaining sealed material was insignificant to defendant's cause." 195 Cal.App.4th at 959. "In sum, after the court ordered the People to divulge the final redacted affidavit to defendant, no further need existed for the court to continue with the *Hobbs* procedure. Instead, the court should have allowed defendant to amend or renew his suppression motions in light of the further disclosures. The court should then have conducted an evidentiary hearing, if necessary." 195 Cal.App.4th at 960.

§ 7:35   Protecting informant communication—warrantless arrests and searches

Informant communications that are used to make warrantless arrests and searches have been the subject of numerous motions by defendants who want to be able to attack the probable cause to effect those arrests and execute those searches.

§ 7:35.1   Protecting informant communication—"walls" and confidential information

Law enforcement agencies investigating criminal activities have developed techniques that enable them to utilize confidential information while protecting that information and/or its sources from disclosure. One of these lawful techniques shields confidential information or the identities of persons supplying that confidential information from disclosure. This mechanism is sometimes colloquially called a "wall."

A "wall" is an investigative and prosecutorial technique in which non-exculpatory information is legally and ethically blocked ("walled off") from the defendant. In "wall" cases officers and prosecutors work together as a team to utilize existing statutory privileges, such as Evidence Code sections 915(b) and 1040–1042, and Penal Code sections 1054.6 and 1054.7, to build and maintain a barrier ("wall") to prevent the disclosure of confidential information possessed by the prosecution team. See Chapter 8 of the text regarding the discovery of official information.

For example, if an officer has confidential information that a vehicle contains, or one of its occupants possesses, contraband, but the officer cannot reveal the confidential information without destroying its confidentiality, the officer must develop an additional lawful reason to stop the vehicle and detain its occupants that is independent of the confidential information.

The "wall" investigative technique provides that an officer follow the vehicle until the driver commits a traffic violation, or some other situation develops that gives probable cause or reasonable suspicion necessary to lawfully stop the vehicle and detain its occupants that is independent of the confidential information. The resulting traffic stop and detention of the occupants is justified by a reasonable suspicion to believe that an offense has been committed, is being committed, or is about to be committed—the standard of an investigative detention. A search of the vehicle and its occupants, and the seizure of the contraband, are then made lawful by probable cause that is independent of the original confidential information.

In this manner the confidential information can be protected from disclosure. This investigative technique is sometimes referred to as a "wall stop," because the confidential information is kept behind a "disclosure wall," and the law enforcement action is justified only by the independent information that is disclosed to the defendant.

Whether the existence of a "wall" and the confidential information behind that "wall" are subject to disclosure have been contentious subjects. After years of litigation in which defense attorneys argued that such law enforcement actions were nothing more than pretext stops, and that pretext stops were unconstitutional, the United States Supreme Court issued definitive rulings that have ended the debate over the lawfulness of such stops. In a nutshell, the Court held that as long as a law enforcement officer has a lawful basis to stop, detain, and search a suspect and/or the suspect's vehicle, the fact that the officer was originally impelled to act by some other motivation is not relevant. Therefore, the existence of a "wall" that protects confidential evidence or information related to a traffic stop is not favorable evidence that would support a defendant's motion to suppress the fruits of that stop.

As long as an officer has objective probable cause or a reasonable suspicion to stop a vehicle, the fact that the officer wanted to search the vehicle for contraband because of additional confidential information is irrelevant. The ulterior motives of the officer making the traffic stop or of another officer who has requested the traffic stop do not render unlawful a stop that is otherwise justified by reasonable suspicion or probable cause known to the stopping or authorizing officer. *Arkansas v. Sullivan* (2001) 532 U.S. 769, 121 S.Ct. 1876, 149 L.Ed.2d 994; *Whren v. United States* (1996) 517 U.S. 806, 116 S.Ct. 1769, 135 L.Ed.2d 89. The California Supreme Court has reached the same holdings. *See People v. Sanders* (2003) 31 Cal.4th 318, 334, 2 Cal.Rptr.3d 630, 73 P.3d 496; and *People v. Woods* (1999) 21 Cal.4th 668, 678–679, 88 Cal.Rptr.2d 88, 981 P.2d 1019.

In *United States v. Pulliam* (2009, CA8 MO) 566 F.3d 784, the Eighth Circuit Court of Appeals held that undisclosed evidence that would have supported a defense that the traffic stop of the defendant had been pretextual was not material evidence, because "[t]he subjective intent of an officer is rarely relevant to the propriety of a traffic stop." 566 F.3d at 787. Because the officer had an objectively lawful reason for stopping the defendant's vehicle, the Court concluded that disclosure of the suppressed impeachment evidence of the officer's intent "would have had little or no impact." *Id.*

Therefore, evidence of the existence of a "wall" and the confidential information behind that "wall" is not normally favorable evidence supporting a defense motion to suppress the evidentiary fruits of a traffic stop. Because evidence of a confidential additional reason for the traffic stop is not evidence that supports the defendant's motion to suppress the fruits of the stop, the confidential information may be protected from disclosure by a "wall."

However, the fact that a "wall" is a lawful mechanism to protect confidential information from forced disclosure to justify a detention, an arrest, or a search, does not exhaust the prosecution's duty to determine whether a particular "wall" is constitutionally lawful. The prosecutor must also determine whether the confidential information behind the "wall" is itself evidence favorable to the defendant. To do this the prosecutor must know the substance of the confidential information behind the "wall," so that the prosecutor can determine whether that information or evidence is exculpatory for a defendant as to any charge being prosecuted.

If, for example, there is more than one person in the vehicle at the time it is stopped, or the vehicle does not belong to the person driving it at the time of the stop, the confidential information behind the "wall" might consist of incriminating probable cause information about just one person, thus potentially exculpating other persons who are riding in the vehicle. Or the confidential information might be directed toward the owner of the vehicle, thus potentially exculpating non-owners who are driving or riding in the vehicle at the time of the traffic stop. Or the confidential information might show that the driver of the vehicle was simply a "blind mule" who had no knowledge that the vehicle contained contraband.

In these scenarios, although the confidential information would be irrelevant for purposes of a suppression motion, it could constitute evidence tending to exculpate the driver or a passenger from criminal responsibility for contraband found in that vehicle.

Practice Tip for Prosecution: You must learn as early as possible if a "wall" has been employed in a case in which you are requested to issue a criminal complaint, so that you may legally and ethically work with the investigating officer to protect confidential information behind that "wall." The best way to learn this information is to ask an officer submitting a case for filing, and to ask prior to the testimony of any officer, whether there is confidential information that needs to be protected from disclosure.

If you learn that the case might involve confidential information protected behind a "wall," you must speak privately with the officer who is most knowledgeable about the case. By learning the nature and substance of the confidential information, you can evaluate potential discovery issues regarding that information. Since you as the prosecutor are legally responsible for *Brady* evidence that is part of confidential information behind a "wall," you must effectively inquire about the confidential information of any officer who knows about it. It is legally and ethically unacceptable for you to remain intentionally ignorant about the confidential information behind the "wall." " '[A] prosecutor cannot adopt a practice of 'see no evil or hear no evil.' " *People v. Kasim* (1997) 56 Cal.App.4th 1360, 1386, 66 Cal.Rptr.2d 494.

To learn the complete substance of confidential information behind a "wall," you must earn and maintain the trust of the officer who knows the information. You must advise the officer that you will not unilaterally disclose confidential information without the officer's consent. You must also agree that if the officer agrees to the disclosure of any confidential information, you will ensure that advance notice is given to any officer, informant, or anyone else who would potentially be compromised by the disclosure of confidential information.

Once you determine that confidential information behind a "wall" does contain *Brady* evidence, but the officer informs you that this confidential information may not be disclosed, your only ethical recourse is to either decline to file a complaint against any defendant who would be entitled to disclosure of the confidential information. Early teamwork communication about these matters between you and the officer will facilitate appropriate case charging.

If your case has already been filed when you first learn of *Brady* evidence contained in confidential information behind a "wall," and that information may not be disclosed, you must dismiss the prosecution against any defendant entitled to that *Brady* evidence. You must not disclose confidential information protected by privilege over the objection of the officer who shared it with you. Nor may you continue with a prosecution knowing that *Brady* evidence is being withheld from the defendant. Ultimately, your professional reputation and ethical standards will be at stake.

If your case contains confidential information behind a "wall" that does not contain exculpatory evidence, but that evidence may not be disclosed, you must prepare in advance of any court hearing with your testifying officers to protect against inadvertent disclosure of the information in their testimony. That preparation should include instructing testifying officers on the procedures they should follow to assert appropriate privileges in a court proceeding. See Evidence Code sections 915, 1040, 1041, and 1042(b), and Penal Code section 1054.7. You must also prepare appropriate objections to and tactics to prevent defense questions that call for your officer witness to disclose the confidential information. These objections might include, but not be limited to, (1) relevance objections to the use of a preliminary examination to obtain discovery, and (2) relevance objections to questions that ask for the officer's justification for a stop or search if the defendant has not filed a motion to suppress evidence in connection with a preliminary examination. You should also consider filing a request under Penal Code section 1054.7 to obtain a protective order against the disclosure of non-exculpatory confidential information. See *California Criminal Discovery* Form 7 in the text.

§ 7:35.2 Protecting informant communication—"walls" and wiretaps

"Walls" are occasionally used to prevent the disclosure of a wiretap in which the voice of the defendant is recorded. When a wiretap has recorded the voice of the defendant, and the investigating agency wants or needs to prevent the disclosure of that wiretap, the prosecutor is faced with a discovery problem that does not apply in the other situations described in Section 1:21.1 of this supplement in which "walls" are used to protect against the disclosure of confidential information, informants, or cooperating individuals. Not all "walls" involve wiretaps, and not all wiretaps involve "walls."

The discovery problem facing the prosecutor handling a case in which a wiretap is protected behind a "wall" is that Section 1054.1 of the Criminal Discovery Statute requires the prosecution to disclose all statements made by the defendant, and the wiretap statute, Penal Code section 629.70, subdivision (b), requires the prosecution to "provide to the defendant a copy of all recorded interceptions from which *evidence against the defendant was derived* . . . ." [italics added] These two statutes operate to entitle a defendant whose voice has been recorded in a wiretap to obtain a copy of all statements made by the defendant on the wiretap recording, *People v. Jackson* (2005) 129 Cal.App.4th 129, 28 Cal.Rptr.3d 136, unless disclosure of that information has been limited by court order under Penal Code section 629.70, subdivision (d), and the court has also entered a protective order under Penal Code section 1054.7. See the detailed discussion of *People v. Jackson, supra*, found in Section 3:6.1 of the text and Sections 3:22.2.8 and 8:2.5 of this supplement.

Using a "wall" to prevent disclosure of a wiretapped conversation in which statements of the defendant have been recorded would be lawful only if nothing in or about the defendant's wiretapped statements themselves constitutes materially exculpatory evidence. The defendant is constitutionally entitled by *Brady* to the disclosure of materially exculpatory evidence, notwithstanding the desire by the law enforcement investigating agency or by the prosecutor that a "wall" be erected to prevent that disclosure.

The conditions that would justify the use of a "wall" to protect against the disclosure of wiretap evidence consisting of statements made by the defendant, and the procedures that should be followed by the prosecution and by the court in that situation, have not been the subject of any reported California opinion.

A wiretap's supporting documentation may validly be withheld from disclosure only to the extent necessary to protect official information or an informant's identity. Where disclosure of an informant's identity, or the contents of his or her communication, is relevant and helpful to the defense of an accused, or is essential to the fair determination of a cause, the privilege must give way. *People v. Acevedo* (2012) 209 Cal. App. 4th 1040, 147 Cal. Rptr. 3d 467.

§ 7:36   Controverting search warrant affidavit (*Luttenberger* discovery)—generally

When necessary to protect a confidential informant's identity, major portions (or even all) of a search warrant's supporting affidavit may validly be sealed and withheld from disclosure to the defendant. *People v. Acevedo* (2012) 209 Cal. App. 4th 1040, 147 Cal. Rptr. 3d 467.

Based analysis of the relevant California constitutional and statutory provisions, the United States Court of Appeals for the Ninth Circuit has concluded that California district attorneys act as local policymakers when adopting and implementing internal policies and procedures related to the use of jailhouse informants. *Goldstein v. City of Long Beach* (2013, CA9 Cal.) 715 F.3d 750.

Regarding an accomplice's statements to a jailhouse informant, the informant's level of preparedness prior to questioning the intended target is not controlling. It is in the final analysis the declarant's statements, not the interrogator's questions, that the Confrontation Clause of the Sixth Amendment requires a court to evaluate. An interrogator's questions, unlike a declarant's answers, do not assert the truth of any matter. *People v. Arauz* (2012) 210 Cal. App. 4th 1394, 149 Cal. Rptr. 3d 211.

A defense motion for an order that the identity of a confidential informant whose information has been used to establish probable cause for the issuance of a search warrant be revealed raises thorny questions for courts to resolve.

§ 7:36.2 *Prima facie* showing

A defendant who requests the court to order the disclosure of the identity of a confidential informant whose information has been used to establish probable cause for the issuance of a search warrant may attack the probable cause for the issuance of the warrant on the grounds that the affiant omitted materially important facts from the affidavit in support of the issuance of the warrant. When this situation occurs, the court must determine whether the informant was a percipient witness to the alleged crime or merely a "tipster" who provided information by which a search warrant was obtained.

In *United States v. Wilburn* (2009, CA7 IL) 581 F.3d 618, an officer obtained a search warrant for the defendant's residence based upon a controlled drug buy by a confidential informant, and also based upon information from a citizen "tipster." After illegal drugs and a firearm were found in the defendant's residence, the defendant was charged with possession with intent to distribute crack cocaine and possession of a firearm by a felon.

The defendant moved for an order suppressing the fruits of the search pursuant to the warrant. In support of his motion the defendant conducted an evidentiary hearing in which he questioned the warrant affiant. The defendant alleged that the affiant recklessly omitted three facts from the warrant the inclusion of which would have caused the magistrate to not issue the warrant. The magistrate precluded the defendant from asking questions of the detective on four subjects: (1) the exact date of the controlled buy; (2) the exact amount of buy money used; (3) whether the detective had previously worked with the informant; and (4) whether the tipster citizen had stated that he or she personally witnessed drug transactions inside the house. 581 F.3d at 622. The trial judge held that the questions would tend to reveal the identity of the informant or were otherwise irrelevant to the question whether the warrant had material omissions.

The suppression motion was denied, and the defendant entered a conditional guilty plea, allowing him to appeal the denial of his motion.

The Seventh Circuit Court of Appeals upheld the district court's decision. The Court of Appeals concluded the confidential informant was only a "tipster," not a percipient witness to the crime; that questions regarding the date and amount of the drug sale would tend to reveal the informant's identity; and that questions regarding the informant's prior relationship with the detective were irrelevant to the issue whether the search warrant affidavit contained material omissions.

The Court further held that questions about the citizen "tipster" were of little importance to the actual charges against the defendant. The Court stated that the lack of information about the informant's personal observation of the defendant's drug transactions "does not amount to a material omission from the warrant affidavit because the affidavit assumes no personal knowledge on the part of the tipster . . . ." 581 F.3d at 625.

The Court found that nothing omitted from the warrant affidavit would have affected the magistrate's finding of probable cause to issue the search warrant.

CHAPTER 8

DISCOVERY OF OFFICIAL INFORMATION

PART I.   SCOPE OF OFFICIAL INFORMATION PRIVILEGE

§ 8:1   Overview — definitions

The official information privilege protects information *acquired in confidence* by a public employee in the course of duty and not openly or officially disclosed to the public prior to the assertion of privilege. Evidence Code section 1040, subsection (a), (b). A service photograph does not contain information acquired in confidence by a public employee in the course of duty. *Ibarra v. Superior Court* (2013) 217 Cal. App. 4th 695, 158 Cal. Rptr. 3d 751.

A defendant's right to challenge a search warrant's supporting affidavit does not automatically negate or overcome the privileges that protect official information and the identity of confidential informants. The right to disclosure is not absolute, even when nondisclosure might impair the defendant's ability to challenge the accuracy and sufficiency of an affidavit that establishes probable cause or necessity for an investigatory wiretap. No fixed rule with respect to disclosure is justifiable. The problem is one that calls for balancing the public interest in protecting the flow of information against the individual's right to prepare a defense, taking into consideration the crime charged, the possible defenses, the possible significance of the informer's testimony, and other relevant factors. The trial court retains wide discretion to protect against the disclosure of information which might unduly hamper the prosecution or violate some other legitimate governmental interest. It is, however, the defendant's burden to establish the need for the information. A defendant must show more than a mere suspicion that the information sought will prove relevant and helpful to the defense, or that it will be essential to a fair determination. The defendant must make a minimal threshold showing that the disclosure would be relevant and helpful to at least one asserted defense. *People v. Acevedo* (2012) 209 Cal. App. 4th 1040, 147 Cal. Rptr. 3d 467.

In *Dinler v. City of New York (In re City of New York)* (2010, CA2 NY) 607 F.3d 923, the Second Circuit Court of Appeals denominated the subject of official information privilege as a "law enforcement privilege," which the Court viewed as an umbrella under which a number of specific privileges, including the "informer's privilege," a privilege to protect sensitive law enforcement techniques and procedures, undercover operations, and other such information are subsumed. 607 F.3d at 940–945.

§ 8:1.2 Meaning of term "in confidence"

Evidence Code sections 1040 and 1041 codify the privileges to refuse disclosure of confidential official information and the identity of confidential informants, and Evidence Code section 1042 provides the procedures used to determine whether these privileges may be invoked to prevent disclosures in any particular case. Evidence Code section 1040, subsection (b)(2), provides governmental entities with a privilege to refuse to disclose confidential official information when the public interest in preserving the confidentiality of the information outweighs the necessity for disclosure in the interest of justice. Section 1041 provides that a public entity is privileged to refuse to disclose the identity of a person who has furnished information in confidence concerning a violation of law if disclosure of the identity of the informer is against the public interest because there is a necessity for preserving the confidentiality of the informer's identity that outweighs the necessity for disclosure in the interest of justice. *People v. Acevedo* (2012) 209 Cal. App. 4th 1040, 147 Cal. Rptr. 3d 467.

§ 8:2 Information from informants

Information provided by confidential informants has been an important source of investigative leads for law enforcement agencies. Consequently, the protection of such information is vitally important to these agencies.

§ 8:3 Police surveillance locations

In some circumstances disclosure of neither confidential official information nor the identity of an undisclosed informant is required in order to establish the existence of reasonable cause for an arrest or search or the admissibility of evidence obtained as a result of it. Evidence Code section 1042, subsections (b), (d). Under that procedure, when the prosecution refuses to disclose information pursuant to such a privilege, the trial court must hear the evidence in camera, if necessary. The court must not order disclosure unless it then concludes from the evidence—including the evidence presented to it in camera—that there is a reasonable possibility that nondisclosure might deprive the defendant of a fair trial. § 1042, subsection (d). *People v. Acevedo* (2012) 209 Cal. App. 4th 1040, 147 Cal. Rptr. 3d 467.

§ 8:5 Criminal investigation records

Criminal investigation records consists of a variety of records, including records created as the result of wiretaps.

§ 8:5.1 Wiretaps

The official information privilege may be invoked to prevent the disclosure of the existence of a wiretap and the substance of statements and conversations recorded by the wiretap.

Federal Wiretapping Statute

In *Katz v. United States* (1967) 389 U.S. 347, 88 S.Ct. 507, 19 L.Ed.2d 576, the United States Supreme Court held that, absent prior authorization by a court, wiretapping violates the Fourth Amendment prohibition of unreasonable search and seizure.

In response to the holding in *Katz*, Congress enacted a federal wiretapping statute as Title III of the Omnibus Crime Control and Safe Streets Act of 1968, 18 U.S.C. sections 2510 to 2520. The heart of that statute is found in 18 U.S.C. section 2518. The federal wiretapping statute "provides a comprehensive scheme for the regulation of wiretapping and electronic surveillance," *People v. Otto* (1992) 2 Cal.4th 1088, 1097, 9 Cal.Rptr.2d 596, 831 P.2d 1178, and "in effect establishes minimum standards for the admissibility of evidence procured through electronic surveillance; state law cannot be less protective of privacy than the federal Act." 2 Cal.4th at 1098.

In addition to establishing minimum standards for state wiretap laws, the federal wiretap statute is the standard for analyzing the suppression of evidence obtained by a wiretap authorization issued by a federal court. *People v. Reyes* (2009) 172 Cal.App.4th 671, 683, 91 Cal.Rptr.3d 415.

Accordingly, because the federal wiretap statute "authorizes the states to enact their own wiretap laws only if the provisions of those laws are at least as restrictive as the federal requirements for a wiretap set out in Title III," *People v. Jackson* (2005) 129 Cal.App.4th 129, 146, 28 Cal.Rptr.3d 136, "state law cannot be less protective of privacy than the federal act. Thus, we look to federal and California statutes, legislative history and case law in applying the California wiretap statute." *People v. Jackson, supra,* 129 Cal.App.4th at 146. *See People v. Zepeda* (2001) 87 Cal.App.4th 1183, 105 Cal.Rptr.2d 187, in which the Court of Appeal construed California's requirement of a showing of necessity for a wiretap in light of federal cases construing a similar requirement in Title III.

For this reason an analysis of the California wiretap statute "is necessarily informed by title III of the Omnibus Crime Control and Safe Streets Act of 1968 . . . ." *People v. Leon* (2007) 40 Cal.4th 376, 384, 53 Cal.Rptr.3d 524, 150 P.3d 207.

California Wiretapping Statutes

Wiretaps have generally been prohibited and even made criminal conduct by California law. See Penal Code section 630 *et seq. People v. Zepeda* (2001) 87 Cal.App.4th 1183, 1195, 105 Cal.Rptr.2d 187. The California Legislature enacted a limited wiretapping statute called The Presley-Felando-Eaves Wiretap Act of 1988 that authorized issuance of a court order to intercept wire communications in specific types of illegal drug investigations. See former Penal Code section 629.02 *et seq.*

In 1995 the Legislature replaced the Wiretap Act of 1988 with a more expansive wiretapping statute that was intended " 'to expand California wiretap law to conform to the federal law.' [citation omitted]." *People v. Leon* (2007) 40 Cal.4th 376, 383, 53 Cal.Rptr.3d 524, 150 P.3d 207.

The existing California wiretap statute, which has been amended by subsequent initiative and legislative enactments, is found in Penal Code section 629.50 *et seq.* The wiretapping statute authorizes issuance of a wiretap order only on the application of a specified prosecuting attorney. "Under Title III [and under the California wiretap statute as well] a police officer cannot go directly to a magistrate and ask for a wiretap. Rather, the person seeking the order, usually an assistant United States attorney, must first obtain the personal approval for the wiretap from the United States Attorney General or a statutorily authorized designee." *People v. Jackson* (2005) 129 Cal.App.4th 129, 159, 28 Cal.Rptr.3d 136.

The court may issue a wiretap authorization order when four conditions are met: (1) there is probable cause to believe that a person has committed, is committing, or is about to commit one or more of the crimes listed in Penal Code section 629.52, subdivision (a); (2) there is probable cause to believe that communications concerning the illegal activities will be obtained through the interception; (3) there is probable cause to believe that a communications device, which includes wire communications, electronic digital pagers, and electronic cellular telephones, will be used by the person whose communications are to be intercepted; and (4) normal investigative procedures have been tried and have failed or reasonably appear either to be unlikely to succeed or to be too dangerous. Penal Code section 629.52, subdivisions (a)–(d).

The wiretap statutes apply to interception of land wire telephones, electronic digital pagers, and electronic cellular telephones. The statutes apply to prisons and jails and monitoring of telephone calls to and from such institutions. *People v. Kelley* (2002) 103 Cal.App.4th 853, 857, 127 Cal.Rptr.2d 203.

However, an inmate who uses a jail phone system to engage in conversations has impliedly consented to monitoring of that phone without the necessity of a court order when a warning sign has been posted above the telephones stating that calls may be monitored or when the jail phone system contains a warning at the beginning of each call stating that all calls are subject to monitoring or recording. The implied consent takes any wiretap outside the prohibitions of the federal wiretapping statute. "So long as a prisoner is given meaningful notice that his telephone calls over prison phones are subject to monitoring, his decision to engage in conversations over those phones constitutes implied consent to that monitoring and takes any wiretap outside the prohibitions of Title III." *People v. Kelly, supra,* 103 Cal.App.4th at 858. *Accord, People v. Windham* (2006) 145 Cal.App.4th 881, 887, 51 Cal.Rptr.3d 884. *See People v. Loyd* (2002) 27 Cal.4th 997, 1010, 119 Cal.Rptr.2d 360, 45 P.3d 296 [Penal Code section 2600 permits law enforcement officers to monitor and record nonprivileged communications between inmates and their visitors.].

The wiretap application and order must be sealed by the judge issuing the order. Penal Code sections 629.50, subdivision (c), and 629.66. As soon as the wiretap order or extensions of that order have expired, the recordings must be provided to the issuing judge and sealed by the court. Penal Code section 629.64. The sealing requirement is designed to combat claims that any of the recordings have been subject to tampering. *People v. Davis* (2008) 168 Cal.App.4th 617, 631, 86 Cal.Rptr.3d 55.

A wiretap's supporting documentation may validly be withheld from disclosure only to the extent necessary to protect official information or an informant's identity. Where disclosure of an informant's identity, or the contents of his or her communication, is relevant and helpful to the defense of an accused, or is essential to the fair determination of a cause, the privilege must give way. *People v. Acevedo* (2012) 209 Cal. App. 4th 1040, 147 Cal. Rptr. 3d 467.

Unless other action is taken by the California Legislature or the electorate, the California wiretap statute will remain in effect only until January 1, 2015, and as of that date is repealed. Penal Code section 629.98.

Thus, "[t]he collection and use of wiretap evidence is regulated by federal law . . . . and analogous California law . . . ." *People v. Davis* (2008) 168 Cal.App.4th 617, 625, 86 Cal.Rptr.3d 55.

Disclosure Provisions of Wiretap Statutes

The California Wiretap Statute contains five disclosure requirements.

1. Notice of wiretap Identification.

The first disclosure requirement is that a defendant in a criminal case must be notified "that he or she was identified as the result of an interception that was obtained pursuant to [the wiretap statute] . . . prior to the entry of a plea of guilty or nolo contendere, or at least 10 days prior to any trial, hearing, or proceeding in the case other than an arraignment or grand jury proceeding." Penal Code section 629.70, subdivision (a).

Although the legislature in enacting the California wiretap statute stated that its intent was "to expand California wiretap law to conform to the federal law," *People v. Leon* (2007) 40 Cal.4th 376, 383, 53 Cal.Rptr.3d 524, 150 P.3d 207, the federal wiretap statute does not contain a provision that is comparable to subdivision (a) of Penal Code section 629.70. Therefore, this disclosure provision of the California wiretap statute is broader than the federal wiretap statute.

Although defendants challenged the trial court's refusal to compel discovery of redacted and sealed portions of the documentation supporting the wiretap authorization orders, and its refusal to suppress the resulting wiretap and other evidence that led to their arrest, defendants failed to demonstrate that the trial court abused its discretion by ruling that the procedures set forth in *People v. Hobbs* adequately protected their rights with respect to their requests for disclosure of privileged documentation, and to their challenges to the sufficiency of the wiretap authorization orders. *People v. Acevedo* (2012) 209 Cal. App. 4th 1040, 147 Cal. Rptr. 3d 467.

2. Disclosure of copy of recorded interceptions, court order, wiretap application, and monitoring logs.

The second disclosure requirement is that not less than 10 days before the trial, hearing, or proceeding, "the prosecution shall provide to the defendant a copy of all recorded interceptions *from which evidence against the defendant was derived*, including a copy of the court order, accompanying application, and monitoring logs." Penal Code section 629.70, subdivision (b) [italics added].

The federal wiretap statute provision that is comparable to subdivision (b) of Penal Code section 629.70 provides that the defendant is entitled to disclosure of the "court order, and accompanying application, under which the interception was authorized or approved" only when the contents of any intercepted oral or electronic communications are "received in evidence or otherwise disclosed in any trial, hearing, or other proceeding in a Federal or State court." 18 U.S.C. sec. 2518, subsection (9).

Thus, this disclosure provision of the California wiretap statute is broader in scope than its federal wiretap statute counterpart.

3. Disclosure of transcript of contents of interception.

The third disclosure requirement applies when the prosecution introduces into evidence or otherwise discloses the contents of an intercepted wire, pager, or cell telephone, or evidence derived from those contents, in a trial, hearing, or other proceeding. This disclosure requirement is that not less than 10 days before the trial, hearing, or proceeding the prosecution must furnish the defendant "with a transcript of the contents of the interception and with the materials specified in subdivision (b)." Penal Code section 629.70, subdivision (c).

This disclosure provision of the California wiretap statute mirrors the federal wiretap statute. 18 U.S.C. sec. 2518, subsection (9).

4. Disclosure of interception relating to other crimes and copy of contents used in subsequent application to obtain additional intercept warrant.

The fourth disclosure requirement applies when an intercepted wire, pager, or cell telephone contains communications relating to crimes other than the crimes specified in the interception authorization order. This disclosure requirement is that in order to use the contents of an "other crimes interception" for which an additional intercept warrant was obtained, the person named in the additional warrant must be provided "notice of the intercepted wire, electronic pager, or electronic cellular telephone communication and a copy of the contents thereof that were used to obtain the warrant." Penal Code section 629.82, subdivision (c).

Although the language is different, this disclosure provision of the California statute is comparable to the federal wiretap statute. 18 U.S.C. sec. 2518, subsection 9, applies to the "contents of any wire, oral, or electronic communication intercepted pursuant to this chapter . . . or evidence derived therefrom," and requires disclosure of "a copy of the court order, and accompanying application, under which the interception was authorized or approved." The federal and state statutory language appears substantively identical.

5. Disclosure of interception 90 days after termination of order.

The fifth disclosure requirement requires the agency that requested the wiretap order to serve an inventory upon any person named in the wiretap order or application, and upon any known parties to intercepted communications. The inventory must include three items of information: (1) the fact of the entry of the wiretap order; (2) the date of the entry of the wiretap order and the period of authorized interception; and (3) the fact that during the period wire, electronic pager, or electronic cellular telephone communications were or were not intercepted. Penal Code section 629.68.

This disclosure provision of the California statute is substantively identical to its counterpart in the federal wiretap statute. See 18 U.S.C. sec. 2518, subsection (8)(d).

While not a mandated disclosure, the court may grant a motion making available for inspection to the person or his or her counsel "the portions of the intercepted communications, applications, and orders that the court determines are in the interest of justice." Penal Code section 629.68.

Orders Limiting, Excusing, or Delaying Wiretap Disclosures

1. Order limiting disclosures.

The trial court may, upon a showing of good cause, limit the requirement that the defendant be notified that he or she was identified as the result of a wiretap interception. And the trial court may, also upon a showing of good cause, limit the requirement that the prosecution disclose a copy of recorded interceptions, the wiretap authorization order, the wiretap application, and the wiretap monitoring logs. Penal Code section 629.70, subdivision (d), provides that "[a] court may issue an order limiting disclosures pursuant to subdivisions (a) and (b) upon a showing of good cause."

The federal wiretap statute does not contain a similar provision.

Unlike Section 1054.7 of the Criminal Discovery Statute, the California wiretap statute does not define "good cause," and there is no California appellate authority defining good cause for purposes of limiting or excusing disclosures under the wiretap statutes.

Moreover, there is no definition of "good cause" in the federal wiretap statute. *In re N.Y. Times Co.* (2009, CA2 NY) 577 F.3d 401, 406 [In enacting the federal wiretap statute, "Congress did not define the term, and we are aware of no Supreme Court case that has done so."].

However, in *In re Applications of Kansas City Star* (1981, CA8 MO) 666 F.2d 1168, the Eighth Circuit Court of Appeals defined the term "good cause" in the context of disclosure of wiretap information in these terms:

"[T]he decisive question then, as we see it, remains as to whether there was good cause to disclose the documents. Good cause to us means that, at least minimally, there must be a need for disclosure."
The Court of Appeals continued, "It is our view that the good cause requirement of the [wiretap] statute calls for at least some consideration by courts of the privacy of other people which might be affected by disclosure. Until the government has some need to disclose intercepted conversations and the orders and applications under which they were intercepted, Title III would seem to insure that those conversations would not be made public." 666 F.3d at 1176.

Although the Eighth Circuit's definition of "good cause" was related to cause for disclosure, as opposed to cause for nondisclosure, the working definition appears equally appropriate: a need for nondisclosure.

2. Order excusing timely disclosures.

The 10-day notice period required by subdivisions (b) and (c) of Penal Code section 629.70 to disclose the transcript of the intercepted communications may be excused. The notice period requirement "may be waived by the judge . . . if he or she finds that it was not possible to furnish the party with the transcript 10 days before the trial, hearing, or proceeding, and that the party will not be prejudiced by the delay in receiving that transcript." Penal Code section 629.70, subdivision (c).

The federal wiretap statute contains a similar provision. See 18 U.S.C. sec. 2518, subsection (9).

3. Order postponing service of inventory.

The court may grant an ex parte request, based on good cause from the agency that requested the intercept order, to postpone the serving of the inventory for a period no longer than is deemed necessary to achieve the purposes for which the postponement is granted. Penal Code section 629.68.

The federal wiretap statute contains a similar provision. See 18 U.S.C. sec. 2518, subsection (8)(d).

One important caveat about obtaining orders that limit, excuse, or delay disclosure of wiretap information must be remembered: Even though contained in wiretap information, any exculpatory information or evidence must be disclosed to the defendant pursuant to the constitutional command of *Brady v. Maryland* (1963) 373 U.S. 83, 83 S.Ct. 1194, 10 L.Ed.2d 215. *People v. Jackson* (2005) 129 Cal.App.4th 129, 170, n.135, 28 Cal.Rptr.3d 136.

Criminal Discovery Statute and Wiretap Information

The wiretap statutes are not the only California statutes that require disclosure of information about wiretaps. The California Criminal Discovery Statute, although not containing any direct reference to wiretaps, requires the prosecution to disclose to the defendant all statements of the defendant. This disclosure requirement includes statements captured in wiretap recordings.

In *People v. Jackson* (2005) 129 Cal.App.4th 129, 28 Cal.Rptr.3d 136, the defendant was in jail pending trial on murder and attempted murder charges arising out of a street gang war. The investigating agency, under the authority of a court order, tape recorded numerous telephone calls in which Jackson participated. The prosecution later disclosed 14 of these tape-recorded conversations to the defendant, but declined to disclose to the defense the remaining tape-recorded conversations.

The defendant was convicted and appealed. On appeal the defendant argued that the prosecution had violated its disclosure duty under subdivision (b) of Section 1054.1 by failing to disclose all of the tape-recorded conversations that the investigating officers had made of Jackson's telephone conversations.

In resolving this contention, the Second District Court of Appeal addressed an apparent conflict between the Criminal Discovery Statute (Penal Code section 1054.1, subdivision (b)), which requires the prosecution to disclose all statements of all defendants, and the wiretap statute (Penal Code section 629.70), which provides that the prosecution must disclose the statements of a defendant "from which evidence against the defendant was derived." The Court concluded that "all statements by the defendant captured on a wiretap must be disclosed to the defense whether they are inculpatory, exculpatory or neither." 129 Cal.App.4th at 170. The Court reasoned that where both the Criminal Discovery Statute and the California wiretap statute require the disclosure of recorded statements of a criminal defendant, the narrower scope of disclosures required under the wiretap statute "do not supersede the scope of discovery under section 1054.1, subdivision (b)," which provides a very broad disclosure requirement. 129 Cal.App.4th at 171. The Court held that the prosecution is required to disclose all of the statements of the defendant as provided by the Criminal Discovery Statute, not simply those statements of the defendant "from which evidence against the defendant was derived." *Id.*

The Court concluded that the Criminal Discovery Statute and the wiretap statute can be reconciled by an interpretation which holds that an "item is discoverable if discovery is authorized *either* under section 1054.1 or some other statutory provision." *Id.*, at 171. And the wiretap statute should be construed to hold that the prosecution must furnish the defense with copies of all recorded interceptions which resulted in inculpatory evidence against the defendant, "but it does not specifically *limit* the right to discovery to interceptions which led to inculpatory evidence." *Id.* [italics in original]

Protective Order

The prosecution might be able to avoid mandatory disclosure of wire-tapped statements of a defendant under the Criminal Discovery Statute by applying for and obtaining a protective order under Penal Code section 1054.7. See the discussion of protective orders pursuant to Penal Code section 1054.7 in Sections 3:22–3:22.2.6 of the text.

Together with the provisions in the wiretap statutes that allow the prosecution to establish good cause for the issuance of a court order limiting the disclosure of wiretap information, Penal Code section 629.70, subdivision (d), the prosecution might be able to shield a wiretap and its non-exculpatory fruits from defense discovery by use of a protective order under Penal Code section 1054.7. See Form 7 in the Forms Appendix of the text.

Reports to the Court

The California wiretap statutes require the state to provide timely reports to the court. When those reports are inadequate or untimely, the evidence obtained by a wiretap might be suppressed. For an extensive discussion of the reporting requirements of the California wiretap statutes, see *People v. Roberts* (2010) 184 Cal.App.4th 1149, 109 Cal.Rptr.3d 736.

PART II. PROCEDURES FOR RULING ON CLAIM OF PRIVILEGE

§ 8:10   *In camera* hearing — reported proceeding

In some circumstances, disclosure of confidential official information and/or the identity of an undisclosed informant is not required in order to establish the existence of reasonable cause for an arrest or search or the admissibility of evidence obtained as a result of it. Evidence Code section 1042, subsections (b), (d). Under that procedure, when the prosecution refuses to disclose information pursuant to such a privilege, the trial court must hear the evidence in camera, if necessary. The court must not order disclosure unless it then concludes from the evidence—including the evidence presented to it in camera—that there is a reasonable possibility that nondisclosure might deprive the defendant of a fair trial. § 1042, subsection (d). *People v. Acevedo* (2012) 209 Cal. App. 4th 1040, 147 Cal. Rptr. 3d 467. The privileges of Evidence Code sections 1040 and 1041 apply, by their terms, whenever the need for confidentiality outweighs the necessity for disclosure; their application is not confined to proceedings involving search warrants or any other particular circumstance. Although Evidence Code section 1042, expressly references its applicability in proceedings to establish the existence of reasonable cause for an arrest or search, it does not limit its application to those proceedings. Nothing in Evidence Code sections 1040 through 1042, precludes the application of these privileges and procedures in proceedings to establish the sufficiency and legality of wiretap authorization orders. *Id.*

§ 8:13 Resolving materiality — generally

As to Fed. R. Crim. P. 16(a)(1)(E)(i), materiality is a low threshold; it is satisfied so long as the information would have helped the defendant prepare a defense. Information is material even if it simply causes a defendant to completely abandon a planned defense and take an entirely different path. *United States v. Hernandez-Meza* (2013, CA9 Cal.) 720 F.3d 760. A defendant must make a threshold showing of materiality, which requires a presentation of facts which would tend to show that the government is in possession of information helpful to the defense. Fed. R. Crim. P. 16 permits discovery that is relevant to the development of a possible defense. General descriptions of the information sought or conclusory allegations of materiality are insufficient. *United States v. Muniz-Jaquez* (2013, CA9 Cal.) 718 F.3d 1180.

See also United States v. Doe (2013, CA9 Cal.) 705 F.3d 1134, holding, *inter alia*, that Fed. R. Civ. P. 16 grants defendants a broad right to discovery, providing that upon a defendant's request, the government must permit the defendant to inspect and to copy or photograph documents within the government's possession, custody, or control that are material to preparing the defense. Fed. R. Crim. P. 16(a)(1)(E)(i). To receive discovery under this Rule, the defendant must make a threshold showing of materiality, which requires a presentation of facts which would tend to show that the Government is in possession of information helpful to the defense. Assuming a discovery violation occurred, reversal is only appropriate if the defendant shows a likelihood that the verdict would have been different had the government complied with the discovery rules. The mere possibility that an item of undisclosed information might have helped the defense, or might have affected the outcome of the trial, does not establish materiality in the constitutional sense. For purposes of determining prejudice, therefore, the withheld evidence must be analyzed in the context of the entire record. The terms "material" and "prejudicial" are used interchangeably in *Brady* cases. Evidence is not "material" unless it is "prejudicial," and not "prejudicial" unless it is "material." Thus, for *Brady* purposes, the two terms have come to have the same meaning. *United States v. Olsen* (2013, CA9 Wash.) 704 F.3d 1172.

CHAPTER 9

THIRD-PARTY DISCOVERY

PART I. VOLUNTARY DISCOVERY FROM THIRD PARTIES

§ 9:2 Orders mandating pretrial witness interviews

In *United States v. Heppner* (2008, CA8 MN) 519 F.3d 744, defendants convicted of mail fraud offenses arising out of misrepresentations made to investors in an investment club alleged on appeal that their ability to cross-examine an important government witness had been impeded by the refusal of that witness to talk with them prior to trial and the witness's failure to keep records. The Eighth Circuit Court of Appeals summarily rejected this argument, stating that " 'no constitutional violation occurs when a witness chooses of her own volition not to be interviewed by the defense,' [citation omitted], and nonexistent records cannot be disclosed." 519 F.3d at 750.

In *United States v. Skilling* (2009, CA5 TX) 554 F.3d 529, the Fifth Circuit Court of Appeals was presented with an argument by the defendant on appeal of his convictions in federal district court that the government had intimidated and dissuaded witnesses from talking to his attorneys and from testifying on his behalf. The Court reviewed the basic principles governing the manner in which attorneys to a case must deal with potential witnesses, saying:

."[A]s a general rule, '[w]itnesses . . . to a crime are the property of neither the prosecution nor the defense. Both sides have an equal right, and should have an equal opportunity, to interview them.' [citations omitted] Of course, [n]o right of a defendant is violated when a potential witness freely chooses not to talk [to defense counsel].' [citation omitted]." 554 F.3d at 567.

Witnesses have the free choice to speak or to decline to speak to any or all of the attorneys in a criminal prosecution.

§ 9:2.1 Marsy's Law protections and defense interviews and depositions

The right of a witness to choose or to decline to speak to any attorney in a criminal case is now recognized in the California Constitution.

On November 4, 2008, the California electorate passed Proposition 9, the "Victims' Bill of Rights Act of 2008: Marsy's Law," which is commonly known by its shortened name, "Marsy's Law." "Marsy's Law" was named after Marsalee (Marsy) Nicholas, a 21-year-old college student who was murdered in 1983.

"Marsy's Law" amended Section 28 of Article I of the California Constitution, to provide:

"(b) In order to preserve and protect a victim's rights to justice and due process, a victim shall be entitled to the following rights:

. . .

(5) To refuse an interview, deposition, or discovery request by the defendant, the defendant's attorney, or any other person acting on behalf of the defendant, and to set reasonable conditions on the conduct of any such interview to which the victim consents."

Another provision of Marsy's Law provides that upon the request of the victim, the prosecutor has the power to enforce a victim's right to refuse an interview, deposition or discovery request by the defendant . . . ." California Constitution, Art. I, Sec. 28(c)(1).

Certainly this provision of Section 28 of Article I of the California Constitution would guarantee that a crime victim may refuse to speak to the defendant, the defendant's attorney, and any other person acting for the defendant, including a defense investigator.

It would appear that this same provision of Section 28 would also guarantee that a crime victim may refuse to submit to a defense-conducted deposition. Because depositions are not authorized in California criminal prosecutions, see Section 5:9 of the text, if California enacted a statute authorizing depositions in criminal prosecutions, Section 28(b)(5)'s constitutional protection for crime victims would give a crime victim the right to refuse to participate in a defense-noticed deposition, despite any statutory authorization for depositions.

There is no federal constitutional authority that would override a crime victim's right to refuse a defense deposition as guaranteed by the California Constitution, because "[t]here is no general constitutional right to discovery in a criminal case . . . ." *Weatherford v. Bursey* (1976) 429 U.S. 545, 559, 97 S.Ct. 837, 51 L.Ed.2d 30.

Marsy's Law further amends California Penal Code section 3041.5(b)(2) to impose a minimum deferral period for subsequent parole suitability hearings of three years, and to authorize the deferral of the California Board of Parole Hearings of a subsequent parole hearing for up to seven, ten, or fifteen years. California Penal Code section 3041.5(b)(3) (2010). *Walker v. Swarthout* (E.D. Cal. Oct. 3, 2012) 2012 U.S. Dist. LEXIS 149763. *See also In re Vicks* (2013) 56 Cal. 4th 274, 153 Cal. Rptr. 3d 471, 295 P.3d 863, holding, *inter alia*, that, as amended in 2008 by Marsy's Law, Penal Code section 3041.5, establishes longer deferral periods following the denial of parole than did the statute in 1983. The deferral periods range from a default period of 15 years to a minimum of three years. More specifically, the next hearing is to occur in 15 years, unless the Board of Parole Hearings finds by clear and convincing evidence that the criteria relevant to the setting of parole release dates are such that consideration of the public and victim's safety does not require a more lengthy period of incarceration for the prisoner than 10 additional years. Penal Code section 3041.5, subsection (b)(3)(A). If the board makes such a finding, the next hearing shall be in 10 years, unless the board finds, again by clear and convincing evidence and considering the same criteria and considerations, that a period of more than seven years is not required. § 3041.5, subsection (b)(3)(B). In that event, the next hearing shall be in three, five, or seven years. § 3041.5, subsection (b)(3)(C). The board is required to consider the views and interests of the victim before selecting the appropriate deferral period. § 3041.5, subsection (b)(3).

§ 9:2.2 Marsy's Law protections and defense subpoenas *duces tecum*

On November 4, 2008, the California electorate passed Proposition 9, the "Victims' Bill of Rights Act of 2008: Marsy's Law," which is commonly known by its shortened name, "Marsy's Law." "Marsy's Law" was named after Marsalee (Marsy) Nicholas, a 21 year old college student who was murdered in 1983.

"Marsy's Law" amended Section 28 of Article I of the California Constitution, to provide:

> "(b) In order to preserve and protect a victim's rights to justice and due process, a victim shall be entitled to the following rights:
>
> . . .
>
> (5) To refuse an interview, deposition, or discovery request by the defendant, the defendant's attorney, or any other person acting on behalf of the defendant, and to set reasonable conditions on the conduct of any such interview to which the victim consents."

The phrase "discovery request" in paragraph (5) of subdivision (b) of Section 28 of Article I of the California Constitution could be construed to apply to defense-issued subpoenas duces tecum. A subpoena duces tecum is a form of defense discovery, although a subpoena is more a court order than a "request."

Whether the language of Article I, Section 28(b)(5)—that provides that a crime victim has the right to refuse a discovery request by the defendant, the defendant's attorney, or someone else acting for the defendant—would allow a crime victim to refuse to comply with a defense subpoena *duces tecum* poses a thorny potential problem. There is little question that a provision of

461

the California State Constitution would override California Penal Code provisions [Sections 1326 and 1327] relating to subpoenas duces tecum in criminal cases. However, allowing a crime victim to refuse to comply with a defense-issued subpoena *duces tecum* in a criminal case could violate the Confrontation Clause of the Sixth Amendment to the United States Constitution (if the evidence possessed by the victim were inculpatory), or the Due Process Clause of the Fifth Amendment to the United States Constitution (if the evidence possessed by the victim were exculpatory).

The constitutionality of the provision of Marsy's Law immunizing crime victims from defense "discovery requests" would be particularly doubtful if the language were to be construed to create a crime victim's privilege that would deprive a defendant of the right to obtain materially exculpatory evidence. Conflicts between this language in Marsy's Law and defendants' constitutional right to due process of law are virtually certain to erupt in the next several years. We suspect that instead of attempting to resolve this conundrum, trial courts are more likely to construe the term "discovery requests" in Marsy's Law to mean informal requests by the defense for a crime victim to provide discovery to the defendant, and that this term does not include court orders such as subpoenas *duces tecum*.

It is difficult to conceive that the courts would uphold the constitutionality under the United States Constitution of a state constitutional provision that would allow a crime victim to refuse to comply with a court order such as a subpoena *duces tecum*.

§ 9:4   Legislative regulation of opposing party witness interviews

Penal Code section 1054, subsection (e), has no power to preclude discovery where it is required to vindicate rights guaranteed by the California Constitution. *Bridgeforth v. Superior Court* (2013) 214 Cal. App. 4th 1074, 154 Cal. Rptr. 3d 528.

§ 9:5   Orders prohibiting in-trial witness interviews

Because a trial court "retains authority to regulate discovery to protect a defendant's constitutional rights," *People v. Loker* (2008) 44 Cal.4th 691, 733–734, 80 Cal.Rptr.3d 630, 188 P.3d 580, it would appear that a trial court has the authority to order that the parties not conduct in-trial interviews of witnesses disclosed by the opposing party.

Whether a trial court exercises its power to enter an order prohibiting in-trial interviews of the opposing party's witnesses is a matter within the court's discretion. If the court were to conclude that a protective order were necessary to avoid a possible loss or destruction of evidence, the court might well enter such an order. However, in the absence of any real indicated danger of loss or destruction of evidence, a court should not limit "legitimate questioning of [opposing party] witnesses about the very matters [the opposing party] intend[s] to explore at trial . . . ." *People v. Loker*, 44 Cal.4th at 734.

§ 9:6   Orders prohibiting defendant's contact with witnesses or alleged victim

Penal Code section 136.2, otherwise known as Kathy's Law, has been amended effective January 1, 2013 and provides as follows:

---

§ 136.2. Kathy's Law; Electronic Monitoring of defendants accused of domestic violence; Payment for electronic monitoring

(a) Except as provided in subdivision (c), upon a good cause belief that harm to, or intimidation or dissuasion of, a victim or witness has occurred or is reasonably likely to occur, a court with jurisdiction over a criminal matter may issue orders including, but not limited to, the following:

(1) An order issued pursuant to Section 6320 of the Family Code.

(2) An order that a defendant shall not violate any provision of Section 136.1.

(3) An order that a person before the court other than a defendant, including, but not limited to, a subpoenaed witness or other person entering the courtroom of the court, shall not violate any provisions of Section 136.1.

(4) An order that a person described in this section shall have no communication whatsoever with a specified witness or a victim, except through an attorney under reasonable restrictions that the court may impose.

(5) An order calling for a hearing to determine if an order as described in paragraphs (1) to (4), inclusive, should be issued.

(6) (A) An order that a particular law enforcement agency within the jurisdiction of the court provide protection for a victim or a witness, or both, or for immediate family members of a victim or a witness who reside in the same household as the victim or witness or within reasonable proximity of the victim's or witness' household, as determined by the court. The order shall not be made without the consent of the law enforcement agency except for limited and specified periods of time and upon an express finding by the court of a clear and present danger of harm to the victim or witness or immediate family members of the victim or witness.

(B) For purposes of this paragraph, "immediate family members" include the spouse, children, or parents of the victim or witness.

(7) (A) An order protecting victims of violent crime from all contact by the defendant, or contact, with the intent to annoy,

---

harass, threaten, or commit acts of violence, by the defendant. The court or its designee shall transmit orders made under this paragraph to law enforcement personnel within one business day of the issuance, modification, extension, or termination of the order, pursuant to subdivision (a) of Section 6380 of the Family Code. It is the responsibility of the court to transmit the modification, extension, or termination orders made under this paragraph to the same agency that entered the original protective order into the Domestic Violence Restraining Order System.

(B) (i) If a court does not issue an order pursuant to subparagraph (A) in a case in which the defendant is charged with a crime of domestic violence as defined in Section 13700, the court on its own motion shall consider issuing a protective order upon a good cause belief that harm to, or intimidation or dissuasion of, a victim or witness has occurred or is reasonably likely to occur, that provides as follows:

(I) The defendant shall not own, possess, purchase, receive, or attempt to purchase or receive, a firearm while the protective order is in effect.

(II) The defendant shall relinquish any firearms that he or she owns or possesses pursuant to Section 527.9 of the Code of Civil Procedure.

(ii) Every person who owns, possesses, purchases, or receives, or attempts to purchase or receive, a firearm while this protective order is in effect is punishable pursuant to Section 29825.

(C) An order issued, modified, extended, or terminated by a court pursuant to this paragraph shall be issued on forms adopted by the Judicial Council of California and that have been approved by the Department of Justice pursuant to subdivision (i) of Section 6380 of the Family Code. However, the fact that an order issued by a court pursuant to this section was not issued on forms adopted by the Judicial Council and approved by the Department of Justice shall not, in and of itself, make the order unenforceable.

(D) A protective order under this paragraph may require the defendant to be placed on electronic monitoring if the local government, with the concurrence of the county sheriff or the chief probation officer with jurisdiction, adopts a policy to authorize electronic monitoring of defendants and specifies the agency with jurisdiction for this purpose. If the court determines that the defendant has the ability to pay for the monitoring program, the court shall order the defendant to pay for the monitoring. If the court determines that the defendant does not have the ability to pay for the electronic monitoring, the court may order electronic monitoring to be paid for by the local government that adopted the policy to authorize electronic monitoring. The duration of electronic monitoring shall not exceed one year from the date the order is issued. At no time shall the electronic monitoring be in place if the protective order is not in place.

(b) A person violating an order made pursuant to paragraphs (1) to (7), inclusive, of subdivision (a) may be punished for any substantive offense described in Section 136.1, or for a contempt of the court making the order. A finding of contempt shall not be a bar to prosecution for a violation of Section 136.1. However, a person so held in contempt shall be entitled to credit for punishment imposed therein against a sentence imposed upon conviction of an offense described in Section 136.1. A conviction or acquittal for a substantive offense under Section 136.1 shall be a bar to a subsequent punishment for contempt arising out of the same act.

(c) (1) Notwithstanding subdivisions (a) and (e), an emergency protective order issued pursuant to Chapter 2 (commencing with Section 6250) of Part 3 of Division 10 of the Family Code or Section 646.91 of the Penal Code shall have precedence in enforcement over any other restraining or protective order, provided the emergency protective order meets all of the following requirements:

(A) The emergency protective order is issued to protect one or more individuals who are already protected persons under another restraining or protective order.

(B) The emergency protective order restrains the individual who is the restrained person in the other restraining or protective order specified in subparagraph (A).

(C) The provisions of the emergency protective order are more restrictive in relation to the restrained person than are the provisions of the other restraining or protective order specified in subparagraph (A).

(2) An emergency protective order that meets the requirements of paragraph (1) shall have precedence in enforcement over the provisions of any other restraining or protective order only with respect to those provisions of the emergency protective order that are more restrictive in relation to the restrained person.

(d) (1) A person subject to a protective order issued under this section shall not own, possess, purchase, receive, or attempt to purchase or receive a firearm while the protective order is in effect.

(2) The court shall order a person subject to a protective order

issued under this section to relinquish any firearms he or she owns or possesses pursuant to Section 527.9 of the Code of Civil Procedure.

(3) A person who owns, possesses, purchases or receives, or attempts to purchase or receive a firearm while the protective order is in effect is punishable pursuant to Section 29825.

(e) (1) In all cases where the defendant is charged with a crime of domestic violence, as defined in Section 13700, the court shall consider issuing the above-described orders on its own motion. All interested parties shall receive a copy of those orders. In order to facilitate this, the court's records of all criminal cases involving domestic violence shall be marked to clearly alert the court to this issue.

(2) In those cases in which a complaint, information, or indictment charging a crime of domestic violence, as defined in Section 13700, has been issued, a restraining order or protective order against the defendant issued by the criminal court in that case has precedence in enforcement over a civil court order against the defendant, unless a court issues an emergency protective order pursuant to Chapter 2 (commencing with Section 6250) of Part 3 of Division 10 of the Family Code or Section 646.91 of the Penal Code, in which case the emergency protective order shall have precedence in enforcement over any other restraining or protective order, provided the emergency protective order meets the following requirements:

(A) The emergency protective order is issued to protect one or more individuals who are already protected persons under another restraining or protective order.

(B) The emergency protective order restrains the individual who is the restrained person in the other restraining or protective order specified in subparagraph (A).

(C) The provisions of the emergency protective order are more restrictive in relation to the restrained person than are the provisions of the other restraining or protective order specified in subparagraph (A).

(3) Custody and visitation with respect to the defendant and his or her minor children may be ordered by a family or juvenile court consistent with the protocol established pursuant to subdivision (f), but if ordered after a criminal protective order has been issued pursuant to this section, the custody and visitation order shall make reference to, and acknowledge the precedence of enforcement of, an appropriate criminal protective order. On or before July 1, 2006, the Judicial Council shall modify the criminal and civil court forms consistent with this subdivision.

(f) On or before January 1, 2003, the Judicial Council shall promulgate a protocol, for adoption by each local court in substantially similar terms, to provide for the timely coordination of all orders against the same defendant and in favor of the same named victim or victims. The protocol shall include, but shall not be limited to, mechanisms for assuring appropriate communication and information sharing between criminal, family, and juvenile courts concerning orders and cases that involve the same parties, and shall permit a family or juvenile court order to coexist with a criminal court protective order subject to the following conditions:

(1) An order that permits contact between the restrained person and his or her children shall provide for the safe exchange of the children and shall not contain language either printed or handwritten that violates a "no contact order" issued by a criminal court.

(2) Safety of all parties shall be the courts' paramount concern. The family or juvenile court shall specify the time, day, place, and manner of transfer of the child, as provided in Section 3100 of the Family Code.

(g) On or before January 1, 2003, the Judicial Council shall modify the criminal and civil court protective order forms consistent with this section.

(h) In any case in which a complaint, information, or indictment charging a crime of domestic violence, as defined in Section 13700, has been filed, the court may consider, in determining whether good cause exists to issue an order under paragraph (1) of subdivision (a), the underlying nature of the offense charged, and the information provided to the court pursuant to Section 273.75.

(i) (1) In all cases in which a criminal defendant has been convicted of a crime of domestic violence as defined in Section 13700, the court, at the time of sentencing, shall consider issuing an order restraining the defendant from any contact with the victim. The order may be valid for up to 10 years, as determined by the court. This protective order may be issued by the court regardless of whether the defendant is sentenced to the state prison or a county jail, or whether imposition of sentence is suspended and the defendant is placed on probation. It is the intent of the Legislature in enacting this subdivision that the duration of any restraining order issued by the court be based upon the seriousness of the facts before the court, the probability of future violations, and the safety of the victim and his or her immediate family.

(2) An order under this subdivision may include provisions for electronic monitoring if the local government, upon receiving the concurrence of the county sheriff or the chief probation officer with jurisdiction, adopts a policy authorizing electronic monitor-

ing of defendants and specifies the agency with jurisdiction for this purpose. If the court determines that the defendant has the ability to pay for the monitoring program, the court shall order the defendant to pay for the monitoring. If the court determines that the defendant does not have the ability to pay for the electronic monitoring, the court may order the electronic monitoring to be paid for by the local government that adopted the policy authorizing electronic monitoring. The duration of the electronic monitoring shall not exceed one year from the date the order is issued.

(j) For purposes of this section, "local government" means the county that has jurisdiction over the protective order.

History:

Added Stats 1980 ch 686 § 2.2. Amended Stats 1988 ch 182 § 1, effective June 15, 1988; Stats 1989 ch 1378 § 1; Stats 1990 ch 935 § 6 (AB 3593); Stats 1996 ch 904 § 2 (AB 2224); Stats 1997 ch 48 § 1 (AB 340), ch 847 § 1.5 (AB 45); Stats 1998 ch 187 § 2 (AB 1531); Stats 1999 ch 83 § 136 (SB 966), ch 661 § 9 (AB 825) (ch 661 prevails); Stats 2001 ch 698 § 4 (AB 160); Stats 2003 ch 498 § 6 (SB 226); Stats 2005 ch 132 § 1 (AB 112), ch 465 § 2 (AB 118), ch 631 § 3 (SB 720), ch 702 § 1.7 (AB 1288), effective January 1, 2006; Stats 2008 ch 86 § 1 (AB 1771), effective January 1, 2009; Stats 2010 ch 178 § 42 (SB 1115), effective January 1, 2011, operative January 1, 2012; Stats 2011 ch 155 § 1 (SB 723), effective January 1, 2012; Stats 2012 ch 162 § 121 (SB 1171), effective January 1, 2013, ch 513 § 2 (AB 2467), effective January 1, 2013 (ch 513 prevails).

Kathy's Law give the courts authority to issue a protective order on its own motion (and presumably also on the motion of the prosecutor) to a defendant who is charged with a crime of domestic violence as defined in Penal Code section 13700, whereby the defendant is prohibited from communicating with a specified witness or an alleged victim, except through an attorney under reasonable restrictions ordered by the court. The trial court's authority to issue such an order extends through the pendency of the criminal proceedings and terminates when the case has ended. *People v. Stone* (2004) 123 Cal.App.4th 153, 19 Cal.Rptr.3d 771.

§ 9:7 Prosecutor interference with defense interviews of prosecution witnesses

However, note that a juvenile witness' own decision (through his guardian ad litem, his appointed counsel, and his social workers) to refuse to be interviewed by defense counsel is no different from a concerned parent refusing to allow a child to be interviewed by defense counsel. *Fenenbock v. Dir. of Corr. for Cal.* (2012, CA9 Cal.) 681 F.3d 968.

In *United States v. Skilling* (2009, CA5 TX) 554 F.3d 529, the defendant argued in the trial court that the government had made plea agreements with potential witnesses that forbade those witnesses from cooperating with Skilling's defense, that prohibited those witnesses from testifying in any manner that contradicted the terms of the plea agreements, that prohibited meetings between the defense and those witnesses unless the prosecutors were present, and prevented information sharing between the defense and employees of several investment firms. The defendant argued that these provisos imposed by the government upon potential witnesses in their plea agreements "improperly forbade witnesses from cooperating with his defense," 554 F.3d at 569, by intimidating and dissuading witnesses from talking to his attorneys and from testifying on his behalf.

When presented with these claims, the district court sent a letter to the witnesses which was intended to clarify the government's position regarding the witnesses' conduct and testimony in the case. The court's letter stated that the witnesses, even those subject to a plea agreement, were free to testify on the defendant's behalf in trial. The letter told witnesses that they did not need to seek the government's permission for or tell the government about meetings they had with the defense. The district court's letter stated that witnesses were not limited in the information they could share with the defense.

Following the defendant's conviction of the charges, he argued on appeal that the government by its plea agreements with witnesses had interfered with his ability to interview those witnesses. The Fifth Circuit Court of Appeals rejected the defendant's argument, concluding that "the district court's letter mitigated any misunderstanding regarding the contours of the plea agreements. The district court's action was sufficient to allay any concern, especially given that the most natural reading of the agreements is that they restricted only divulging information learned from the government and did not ban talking with Skilling altogether." 554 F.3d at 570.

The defendant further contended that the government's agents extended or enlarged its ongoing investigation to intimidate witnesses. In rejecting this argument, because there was no evidence that the defendant did not receive a fair trial, the Court of Appeals emphasized that "[t]he government obviously could not use its prosecutorial power to intimidate potential witnesses into refusing to consult with Skilling [citation omitted], or to badger them into silence by meritless perjury threats [citation omitted] . . . ." 554 F.3d at 571.

Finally, the Court of Appeals rejected the defendant's contention that the fact that a large number of potential witnesses chose not to cooperate with the defense was evidence that the government engaged in the nefarious conduct of witness intimidation. The Court found there was no direct evidence of witness intimidation, and "the mere fact that many witnesses chose not to cooperate with Skilling does not prove substantial interference with the witnesses' free and unhampered choice to testify." 554 F.3d at 571.

When the defendant requests an opportunity to interview government witnesses prior to trial, those witnesses have the right to decline such a request. When prosecution witnesses decline to be interviewed by the defense, without some evidence that the prosecution has engineered those decisions, the refusal of prosecution witnesses to submit to a defense interview does not constitute government interference with a defendant's access to witnesses. *United States v. Celis* (2010, CA DC) 608 F.3d 818, 841. It is when "witnesses are made unavailable through the suggestion, procurement, or negligence of the government," that a criminal defendant's right to due process of law might be violated. *United States v. Bohn* (2010, CA9 WA) 622 F.3d 1129, 1138.

§ 9:7.1   Prosecution interference with presentation of defense witness

The prosecution may not "block or hinder a criminal defendant's access to witnesses whose testimony would be material and favorable to the defense." *People v. Treadway* (2010) 182 Cal.App.4th 562, 567, 106 Cal.Rptr.3d 99.

In *People v. Treadway* the defendant was charged with attempted robbery, assault with a firearm, use of a firearm in the commission of the offenses, and infliction of great bodily injury. The prosecution entered into plea agreements with two co-defendants that required the co-defendants to agree not to testify at the defendant's trial. The defendant was convicted and appealed.

On appeal the defendant argued that the prosecution's plea bargains with his co-defendants violated his constitutional rights to compulsory process and due process of law. The Court of Appeal agreed with the defendant and reversed his convictions. The Court concluded that requiring the co-defendants to agree not to testify in the defendant's trial in order to secure a specific term of imprisonment constituted a form of coercion that could hardly be more explicit. 182 Cal.App.4th at 569.

The Court concluded that the prosecution's plea agreements with the co-defendants deprived the defendant of exculpatory evidence to support his defense that he was unable to form the requisite intent to murder or to discharge a firearm. 182 Cal.App.4th at 571. The Court held that the prosecution thereby "made a material witness unavailable and, in so doing, violated defendant's right to due process." 182 Cal.App.4th at 571.

The prosecution may not interfere in a defense witness's decision whether to testify. "Undue prosecutorial interference in a defense witness's decision to testify arises when the prosecution intimidates or harasses the witness to discourage the witness from testifying." *Williams v. Woodford* (2004, CA9 CA) 384 F.3d 567, 601. However, a prosecutor's improper actions in interfering with a defense witness's decision to testify violate a defendant's right to due process of law only when the testimony of that witness would have been material. *United States v. Bohn* (2010, CA9 WA) 622 F.3d 1129, 1138.

PART II. COMPELLING THIRD-PARTY DISCOVERY

§ 9:9 Discovery from third parties—in general

The provisions of the Criminal Discovery Statute contained in Penal Code sections 1054 through 1054.7 "do not regulate discovery concerning uninvolved third parties.' [citations omitted]" *Kling v. Superior Court* (2010) 50 Cal.4th 1068, 1077, 116 Cal.Rptr.3d 217, 239 P.3d 670. Thus, the Criminal Discovery Statute does not apply to subpoenas issued by the prosecution or the defendant to third parties.

Discovery from third parties is governed by the rules and procedures specified in Penal Code sections 1326 and 1327, and Evidence Code section 1560. Those sections are set forth as follows:

---

§ 1326. Subpoena; Signing and issuance; Business records; Non-parties

(a) The process by which the attendance of a witness before a court or magistrate is required is a subpoena. It may be signed and issued by any of the following:

(1) A magistrate before whom a complaint is laid or his or her clerk, the district attorney or his or her investigator, or the public defender or his or her investigator, for witnesses in the state.

(2) The district attorney, his or her investigator, or, upon request of the grand jury, any judge of the superior court, for witnesses in the state, in support of an indictment or information, to appear before the court in which it is to be tried.

(3) The district attorney or his or her investigator, the public defender or his or her investigator, or the clerk of the court in which a criminal action is to be tried. The clerk shall, at any time, upon application of the defendant, and without charge, issue as many blank subpoenas, subscribed by him or her, for witnesses in the state, as the defendant may require.

(4) The attorney of record for the defendant.

(b) A subpoena issued in a criminal action that commands the custodian of records or other qualified witness of a business to produce books, papers, documents, or records shall direct that those items be delivered by the custodian or qualified witness in the manner specified in subdivision (b) of Section 1560 of the Evidence Code. Subdivision (e) of Section 1560 of the Evidence Code shall not apply to criminal cases.

(c) In a criminal action, no party, or attorney or representative of a party, may issue a subpoena commanding the custodian of records or other qualified witness of a business to provide books, papers, documents, or records, or copies thereof, relating to a person or entity other than the subpoenaed person or entity in any manner other than that specified in subdivision (b) of Section 1560 of the Evidence Code. When a defendant has issued a subpoena to a person or entity that is not a party for the production of books, papers, documents, or records, or copies thereof, the court may order an in camera hearing to determine whether or not the defense is entitled to receive the documents. The court may not order the documents disclosed to the prosecution except as required by Section 1054.3.

(d) This section shall not be construed to prohibit obtaining books, papers, documents, or records with the consent of the person to whom the books, papers, documents, or records relate.

History:

Enacted 1872. Amended Code Amdts 1880 ch 47 § 97; Stats 1937 ch 215 § 1; Stats 1939 ch 1015 § 1; Stats 1951 ch 1674 § 138; Stats 1953 ch 613 § 4; Stats 1959 ch 501 § 19, ch 1058 § 1; Stats 1971 ch 1196 § 3; Stats 1972 ch 543 § 1; Stats 2004 ch 162 § 2 (AB 1249); Stats 2007 ch 263 § 30 (AB 310), effective January 1, 2008.

§ 1327. Form of subpoena

A subpoena authorized by Section 1326 shall be substantially in the following form:

The people of the State of California to A.B.:

You are commanded to appear before C.D., a judge of the _____ Court of _____ County, at (naming the place), on (stating the day and hour), as a witness in a criminal action prosecuted by the people of the State of California against E.F.

Given under my hand this _____ day of _____, A.D. 19 _____. G.H., Judge of the _____ Court (or "J.K., District Attorney," or "J.K., District Attorney Investigator," or "D.E., Public Defender," or "D.E., Public Defender Investigator," or "F.G., Defense Counsel," or "By order of the court, L.M., Clerk," or as the case may be).

If books, papers, or documents are required, a direction to the following effect must be contained in the subpoena: "And you are required, also, to bring with you the following" (describing intelligibly the books, papers, or documents required).

History:

Enacted 1872. Amended Stats 1951 ch 1608 § 20, operative

January 1, 1952; Stats 1971 ch 1196 § 2; Stats 1972 ch 543 § 1; Stats 1998 ch 931 § 403 (SB 2139), effective September 28, 1998.

§ 1560. Compliance with subpoena duces tecum for business records; Alternative procedure in civil actions

(a) As used in this article:

(1) "Business" includes every kind of business described in Section 1270.

(2) "Record" includes every kind of record maintained by a business.

(b) Except as provided in Section 1564, when a subpoena duces tecum is served upon the custodian of records or other qualified witness of a business in an action in which the business is neither a party nor the place where any cause of action is alleged to have arisen, and the subpoena requires the production of all or any part of the records of the business, it is sufficient compliance therewith if the custodian or other qualified witness delivers by mail or otherwise a true, legible, and durable copy of all of the records described in the subpoena to the clerk of the court or to another person described in subdivision (d) of Section 2026.010 of the Code of Civil Procedure, together with the affidavit described in Section 1561, within one of the following time periods:

(1) In any criminal action, five days after the receipt of the subpoena.

(2) In any civil action, within 15 days after the receipt of the subpoena.

(3) Within the time agreed upon by the party who served the subpoena and the custodian or other qualified witness.

(c) The copy of the records shall be separately enclosed in an inner envelope or wrapper, sealed, with the title and number of the action, name of witness, and date of subpoena clearly inscribed thereon; the sealed envelope or wrapper shall then be enclosed in an outer envelope or wrapper, sealed, and directed as follows:

(1) If the subpoena directs attendance in court, to the clerk of the court.

(2) If the subpoena directs attendance at a deposition, to the officer before whom the deposition is to be taken, at the place designated in the subpoena for the taking of the deposition or at the officer's place of business.

(3) In other cases, to the officer, body, or tribunal conducting the hearing, at a like address.

(d) Unless the parties to the proceeding otherwise agree, or unless the sealed envelope or wrapper is returned to a witness who is to appear personally, the copy of the records shall remain sealed and shall be opened only at the time of trial, deposition, or other hearing, upon the direction of the judge, officer, body, or tribunal conducting the proceeding, in the presence of all parties who have appeared in person or by counsel at the trial, deposition, or hearing. Records that are original documents and that are not introduced in evidence or required as part of the record shall be returned to the person or entity from whom received. Records that are copies may be destroyed.

(e) As an alternative to the procedures described in subdivisions (b), (c), and (d), the subpoenaing party in a civil action may direct the witness to make the records available for inspection or copying by the party's attorney, the attorney's representative, or deposition officer as described in Section 2020.420 of the Code of Civil Procedure, at the witness' business address under reasonable conditions during normal business hours. Normal business hours, as used in this subdivision, means those hours that the business of the witness is normally open for business to the public. When provided with at least five business days' advance notice by the party's attorney, attorney's representative, or deposition officer, the witness shall designate a time period of not less than six continuous hours on a date certain for copying of records subject to the subpoena by the party's attorney, attorney's representative, or deposition officer. It shall be the responsibility of the attorney's representative to deliver any copy of the records as directed in the subpoena. Disobedience to the deposition subpoena issued pursuant to this subdivision is punishable as provided in Section 2020.240 of the Code of Civil Procedure.

History:

Enacted Stats 1965 ch 299 § 2, operative January 1, 1967. Amended Stats 1969 ch 199 § 2; Stats 1982 ch 452 § 2.5; Stats 1984 ch 481 § 2; Stats 1986 ch 603 § 6; Stats 1991 ch 1090 § 14 (AB 1484); Stats 1997 ch 442 § 16 (AB 758); Stats 1999 ch 444 § 4 (AB 794); Stats 2000 ch 287 § 1 (SB 1955); Stats 2004 ch 162 § 1 (AB 1249) (ch 162 prevails), ch 182 § 32 (AB 3081), operative July 1, 2005, ch 294 § 18 (AB 333), effective January 1, 2006; Stats 2006 ch 538 § 155 (SB 1852), effective January 1, 2007.

§ 9:13   Subpoena *duces tecum*—good cause showing for issuance

ERRATA: The following paragraph should be omitted from page 837 of the text:

There is no statutory requirement that a good cause affidavit be filed as a pre-requisite to the issuance of a subpoena *duces tecum* in a criminal case. *M.B. v. Superior Court* (2002) 103 Cal.App.4th 1384, 1391–1396, 127 Cal.Rptr.2d 454.

§ 9:19 Subpoena *duces tecum*—prosecution access to defense-subpoenaed materials

The prosecution typically has the right to know the identity of any party served with a defense-issued subpoena *duces tecum* and the right to know the nature of the documents sought by that subpoena, including the identity of the person to whom the subpoenaed documents pertain.

In *Kling v. Superior Court* (2010) 50 Cal.4th 1068, 116 Cal.Rptr.3d 217, 239 P.3d 670, a defendant charged by indictment with two counts of murder with special circumstances, issued several subpoenas *duces tecum* upon third parties. The subpoenaed records were delivered to the clerk of the trial court and examined by the court *in camera*. Defense counsel was present for the *in camera* proceedings, but some of those hearings occurred without notice to the People.

The defense requested that the court withhold from the prosecution information regarding the subpoenas, saying that informing the prosecution of the records subpoenaed would reveal defense strategies and work product. The prosecution opposed the defense request, arguing that the People had a right to know the identity of the items subpoenaed in order for the prosecution to determine whether the People had standing to object to the subpoenas or whether the prosecution should alert third parties who had standing to object to the subpoenas.

The trial court ordered that all documents received in response to the subpoenas be logged in the court's docket, noting the date received and the party supplying the documents. The trial court found that no privilege applies to the identity of the party responding to a subpoena or the identity of the documents received. The court conducted a series of *in camera* hearings at which the defense was present to determine which documents should be released to the defense. The court then released subpoenaed documents to the defense. Transcripts of these hearings were prepared and sealed.

In reliance upon *People v. Superior Court (Humberto S.)* (2008) 43 Cal.4th 737, 76 Cal.Rptr.3d 276, 182 P.3d 600, the prosecution requested that the trial court unseal any transcripts of *in camera* hearings that did not contain defense theories of relevance. The trial court granted the People's request and ordered that some transcripts be unsealed. The court stayed its unsealing order to allow the defendant to seek writ relief.

The Court of Appeal granted a peremptory writ directing the superior court to vacate its order unsealing the *in camera* hearing transcripts and to enter a new order denying the People's motion. The Court held that "[a]bsent unusual circumstances, the prosecution may not know who the defense has subpoenaed or what documents were subpoenaed unless the defense decides to use them at trial . . . The prosecution's compelled silence may be broken when the court calls upon it to 'address any questions the trial court has.'

[citation omitted] This is likely to occur when the subpoena concerns privacy rights of third parties." *Kling v. Superior Court* (2008) 177 Cal.App.4th 223, 227.

The Court reasoned in support of its holding that "[n]o statutory or constitutional authority permits disclosure to the prosecution of the names of the third parties to whom defense subpoenas have been issued or the nature of the records produced. Unsealing transcripts of any in camera hearing could result in disclosure of information the defense may not use at trial, and, in turn, inhibit defense counsel's investigation." 177 Cal.App.4th at 231–232.

Finally, the Court of Appeal rejected the People's argument that recent amendments to the California Constitution made by Proposition 9, the "Victim's Bill of Rights Act of 2008: Marsy's Law," provided authority for the trial court's order. The Court determined that the *in camera* hearings in the case pre-dated the passage of Proposition 9. The Court further concluded that a prosecutor is not statutorily authorized to argue or otherwise participate in an *in camera* hearing on a defense-issued subpoena *duces tecum*, unless the prosecutor has been requested by a victim to enforce rights guaranteed by Proposition 9. 177 Cal.App.4th at 232–233.

Upon the People's petition the California Supreme Court granted review of the case. The Supreme Court reversed the decision of the Court of Appeal, holding that when a defendant issues a subpoena duces tecum in a criminal case the prosecution typically has the right to know: (1) the identity of the subpoenaed party, (2) the nature of the documents sought by the third-party subpoena, and (3) the identity of the person to whom the documents pertain. 50 Cal.4th at 1072.

In reaching these conclusions the Supreme Court reiterated and clarified the rules and procedures governing subpoenas *duces tecum* in criminal cases.

The issuance of a subpoena *duces tecum* under Penal Code section 1326 " 'is purely a ministerial act and does not constitute legal process in the sense that it entitles the person on whose behalf it is issued to obtain access to the records described therein until a judicial determination has been made that the person is legally entitled to receive them.' [citations omitted]" 50 Cal.4th at 1074.

The statutory restriction that directs a subpoenaing party to follow the procedures of Evidence Code section 1560 that require subpoenaed materials to be delivered to the clerk of the court "maintains the court's control over the discovery process . . . ." 50 Cal.4th at 1074.

If the third party objects to disclosure of the information sought by the subpoena, the party issuing the subpoena "must make a plausible justification or a good cause showing of the need [for those materials]." 50 Cal.4th at 1074–1075.

These same procedures apply to subpoenas *duces tecum* issued by the prosecution and the defense. 50 Cal.4th at 1075.

If the defendant has issued the subpoena *duces tecum*, the court may order an *in camera* hearing to determine whether the defendant is entitled to receive the subpoenaed documents. The court may not order documents subpoenaed by the defendant disclosed to the prosecution except as required by Penal Code section 1054.3. 50 Cal.4th at 1075.

The Supreme Court concluded that these holdings are consistent with the language and legislative history of Penal Code section 1326 and are necessary to "effectuate the People's right to due process under the California Constitution." 50 Cal.4th at 1078. The Court stated: "It is difficult to see how the People can have a meaningful opportunity to be heard if they are categorically barred from learning the identity of the subpoenaed party or the nature of the documents requested." 50 Cal.4th at 1078.

Finally, the Court held that when considering a defendant's claim of a need for confidentiality, the trial court "is not bound by defendant's naked claim of confidentiality," and should "make such orders as are appropriate to ensure that the maximum amount of information, consistent with protection of the defendant's constitutional rights, is made available to the party opposing the motion for discovery." 50 Cal.4th at 1080. The Court emphasized that the use of "extraordinary procedures" such as *in camera* review and *ex parte* proceedings from which the prosecution is excluded "should be limited to that which is necessary to safeguard the rights of the defendant or of a third party, inasmuch as ex parte proceedings are generally disfavored because of their inherent deficiencies." 50 Cal.4th at 1080.

The Supreme Court concluded its analysis by observing that its determinations are consistent with the "Victims' Bill of Rights Act of 2008: Marsy's Law," which "evidently contemplates that the victim and the prosecuting attorney would be aware that the defense had subpoenaed confidential records regarding the victim from third parties . . . we do agree with the People that a victim's right to notice of a third party subpoena would be consistent with the presumption that court proceedings are open and with the prosecution's right to due process." 50 Cal.4th at 1080.

Practice Tips for Prosecution: The California Supreme Court opinion in *Kling* represents a significant victory for prosecutors who have been frustrated by courts that have ruled that prosecutors have no role to play in court proceedings involving defense-issued subpoenas *duces tecum*. Now, prosecutors should typically or usually, although not always, be able to learn the identity of the recipient of any defense-issued subpoena *duces tecum*, the nature of the documents and writings subpoenaed by the defense, and the identity of the person about whom the subpoena was issued.

Whether *Kling* will produce any advantage to the prosecution will largely depend upon what actions the prosecution takes with the information the prosecution receives from the court. We recommend a number of possible prosecution actions.

The prosecutor's first action should be to request that a copy of the affidavit in support of the subpoena *duces tecum* be provided to the prosecution, and that the determination whether the documents and writings should be provided to the defendant should follow a hearing in open court. In support of this request, the prosecutor should remind the court that withholding information is to be the exception, and not the rule; that *in camera* and *ex parte* proceedings from which the prosecution is excluded are extraordinary, not ordinary, circumstances; and that the court is commanded by *Kling* to ensure that the maximum amount of information, consistent with protecting a defendant's legitimate privileges, is shared with the prosecution.

An early action that the prosecutor should take is to notify the person about whom a defense subpoena *duces tecum* has been issued, so to enable that person to either request the prosecution to take action to quash or limit the subpoena or to retain private counsel to represent the person. If the defense subpoena relates to a named victim of the charged crimes, the prosecutor should advise the victim of his or her right to request the prosecution to take action to enforce the victim's rights pursuant to Marsy's Law. We recommend that any authorization from the victim for the prosecution to enforce the victim's Marsy's Law rights be in writing and signed by the victim, so there is no question about the prosecutor's authority to enforce those rights.

Since the Supreme Court declined in *Kling* to prohibit prosecutors from using the information they receive about a defense subpoena *duces tecum* to gain insight into the defendant's trial preparation, another recommended prosecution action is to contact the person who has been served with the subpoena to determine if that person is legally able and willing to share with the prosecution copies or the substance of the documents and writings supplied to the court in compliance with the subpoena.

Of course, if the prosecution obtains its own copies of these documents and writings, the prosecution would be hard pressed to persuade the court that the defense subpoena should be quashed. Moreover, if the prosecution obtains copies of privileged documents with the consent of the holder of the privilege, the privilege would probably be deemed waived, and the prosecution could well be required to disclose the documents and writings to the defendant pursuant to the Criminal Discovery Statute and/or the *Brady* rule. Before a prosecutor obtains any documents and writings to which a privilege would attach, the prosecutor should discuss these concerns carefully with the holders of the privilege.

An additional action for the prosecutor would be to consider issuing a prosecution subpoena for the documents and writings that had been subpoenaed by the defendant. There is nothing in the *Kling* opinion that precludes the prosecutor from "piggybacking" upon the defense subpoena, although the prosecutor issuing the subpoena should be certain to submit an affidavit in support of the subpoena that supplies good cause for its issuance beyond a simple "me too" claim that "if it's good cause for the defendant, it's good cause for the prosecution."

One benefit of this approach is that production of the documents and writings to the court in compliance with a prosecution subpoena does not waive any privileges adhering to these documents and writings. Another benefit of this approach is that the prosecution can avoid the restriction of Penal Code section 1326, subdivision (c), that precludes the trial court from sharing the fruits of a defense subpoena *duces tecum* with the prosecution.

Practice Tips for Defendant: The opinion of the Supreme Court in *Kling* poses problems for the conscientious defense attorney. On the one hand, counsel's professional duties require that he or she take all necessary actions to ensure production of writings and documents that could be used in the defense of the case. An attorney should not refrain from aggressively engaging in third-party discovery simply because use of the court's subpoena powers might enable the prosecutor to divine the tactics and thinking of the defense. On the other hand, defense-issued subpoenas *duces tecum* now cannot be issued without the defense's running the risk that the prosecution will know a lot about those subpoenas, allowing the prosecution to peer into the workings of the defense strategies.

There will be some third-party discovery subpoenas *duces tecum* about which the defense does not care if the prosecution learns what the defense has subpoenaed, from whom it has been subpoenaed, and about whom it has been subpoenaed. The defense attorney should not take the position that every defense subpoena *duces tecum* requires maximum judicial protection. If it truly doesn't matter if the prosecutor learns all about a defense subpoena and the fruits of that subpoena, the attorney should not attempt to preclude prosecution access.

However, there will be defense subpoenas that seek documents and materials the confidentiality of which really matters to an effective preparation of a defense. As to these matters, the defense attorney should carefully issue the subpoena, carefully craft the affidavit in support of that subpoena, and prepare a written motion and supporting memorandum to be filed under seal to justify a request that no information regarding the identity of the documents subpoenaed, the identity of the person or entity from which the documents have been subpoenaed, the identity of the person about whom the documents have been subpoenaed, and/or the good cause for disclosing the documents and writings to the defense, be given in open court—that all such discussions with the court occur *ex parte* and *in camera*.

It is significant that the holding in *Kling* is that the People's due process rights *typically require* that the prosecution be informed of the identity of the subpoenaed party, the nature of the documents subpoenaed, and the identity of the person to whom the documents pertain. 50 Cal.4th at 1072. The Court in *Kling* did not hold that the prosecution has an absolute right to these three pieces of information.

Very importantly, the defense attorney should remember that the protections provided to the defense by Penal Code section 1326(c), as set forth, *supra*, apply only to defense-issued subpoenas, and not to prosecution-issued subpoenas. The defense should insist on full open-court participation in litigating whether materials subpoenaed by the prosecution should be given to the prosecution. And if the court rules that the prosecution is entitled to the fruits of a prosecution-issued subpoena *duces tecum*, the defense is entitled to those same fruits as a matter of law.

Finally, *Kling* does not represent a change in the holding of the California Supreme Court in *Alford v. Superior Court* (2003) 29 Cal.4th 1033, 130 Cal.Rptr.2d 672, 63 P.3d 228, that the prosecution is not entitled to the fruits of a defense subpoena duces tecum unless and until the defense intends to offer that evidence at trial. *Kling v. Superior Court*, 50 Cal.4th at 1077 ["the records will not be disclosed to the prosecution unless or until the defendant intends to offer them as evidence at trial," citing Penal Code sections 1054.3, subdivision (a), and 1326, subdivision (c).].

If the defendant is compelled to disclose defense-subpoenaed records to the prosecution, and thereafter the defense opts not to introduce that evidence at trial, the prosecution should be precluded from using those records in the prosecution's case-in-chief. *See Kastigar v. United States* (1972) 406 U.S. 441, 92 S.Ct. 1653, 32 L.Ed.2d 212; and *Izazaga v. Superior Court* (1991) 54 Cal.3d 356, 386, 285 Cal.Rptr. 231, 815 P.2d 304 (Kennard, J. concurring). Under these circumstances, the defendant should consider bringing a *Kastigar* motion to exclude that evidence as the fruit of compelled disclosures of privileged information or attorney work product.

If there is no statutory prohibition against disclosure of the identity of a subpoenaed witness or documents produced pursuant to that subpoena, disclosure of that information is prohibited only if there is a constitutional prohibition against the disclosure. We wonder what constitutional provision entitles a defendant to utilize the process of the court in secret in order to hide the defendant's preparation for trial. If there were any such constitutional provision, that provision would prohibit noticed motions in federal court that are required before a third-party subpoena may issue in a federal case.

The subject of the right of the prosecution to learn the identity of persons to whom the defense has issued a subpoena duces tecum and the identity of documents produced in response to such subpoenas is ripe for continued litigation.

§ 9:20   Counsel for third parties

A party to a criminal prosecution, including the prosecutor, may actively oppose third-party discovery by the opposing party, when the party's interests align with those of the third party from whom discovery is sought, without becoming the attorney for that third party.

For many years, going back to *Bullen v. Superior Court* (1988) 204 Cal.App.3d 22, 251 Cal.Rptr. 32 [discussed in the text], prosecutors have been wary of taking actions to oppose defense-initiated third-party discovery out of concern that such efforts would cause them to become the attorneys for the third party and thus subject them to recusal. These fears have been significantly eased in light of the decision of the California Supreme Court in *In re Humberto S.* (2008) 43 Cal.4th 737, 76 Cal.Rptr.3d 276, 182 P.3d 600.

In *Humberto S.* a minor was charged in a wardship petition with the continuous sexual abuse of a child under the age of 14 years, in violation of Penal Code section 288.5. The alleged victim of the sexual abuse was the daughter of the minor's brother—his eight-year old niece. Prior to trial the attorney for Humberto issued third-party subpoenas for the victim's medical and psychotherapy records. The custodian of the child's medical records disclosed those records directly to Humberto's counsel, who opened them. The custodian of the psychotherapy records delivered them to the trial court. The court delivered the already opened psychotherapy records to Humberto's counsel in an ex parte proceeding at which the prosecutor did not appear.

When Humberto's counsel provided copies of both sets of records to the People, who were represented by the district attorney, the prosecutor objected to the defendant's possession of the records on the grounds that proper subpoena procedure had not been followed and that *People v. Hammon* (1997) 15 Cal.4th 1117, 65 Cal.Rptr.2d 1, 938 P.2d 986, restricts the right of a defendant to pretrial access to the minor victim's records. The juvenile court ordered the defendant to return all records to the court, and a series of hearings ensued. The district attorney filed several motions to quash the defense subpoenas and repeatedly argued against the juvenile court's releasing the records to the defendant. The district attorney also requested that the juvenile court appoint a guardian ad litem to assert the minor victim's privileges regarding her records.

The juvenile court denied the People's motions to quash the subpoenas and to appoint a guardian ad litem for the minor victim, and the court ordered that the records be delivered to Humberto's attorneys. The disclosure order was stayed pending a writ petition by the People in the Court of Appeal. When the Court of Appeal denied the People's writ petition, the records were released to Humberto's counsel.

Humberto then filed a motion to recuse the district attorney pursuant to Penal Code section 1434, arguing that when the district attorney had opposed the defense third-party discovery, the district attorney had represented three separate third parties: the minor victim, the mother of the victim, and the custodian of the minor's psychotherapy records. The trial court partially granted the motion, saying that the prosecution attempted to represent third-party interests and had thereby compromised the prosecutor's ability to provide Humberto with a fair trial.

The People sought writ review and a stay in the Court of Appeal, which ultimately denied the petition and lifted the stay. The Court of Appeal concluded that the conduct of the district attorney in opposing defense third-party discovery "demonstrated a one-sided perspective on the role of the prosecution and an apparent attempt to represent the victim's interest in protecting her privacy that exceeded the exercise of balanced discretion necessary to ensure a just and fair trial." 43 Cal.4th at 745.

After granting the People's petition for review "to consider the application of the recusal statute to situations involving the alleged advocacy of third party interests," 43 Cal.4th at 746, the Supreme Court held that the trial court's decision to recuse numerous prosecutors was based on an error of law and an abuse of discretion.

In reaching its decision the Supreme Court held that "the good faith assertion of legal argument, without more, does not establish a conflict [of interest by the prosecutor]." The Court opined that a prosecutor is entitled to be zealous in the prosecutor's enforcement of discovery law, as long as the prosecutor's zeal remains within legal limits. The Court upheld the trial court's finding that the prosecution's objections to the defense third-party discovery efforts were motivated by a desire to ensure that the law regulating third-party discovery was followed, not by a desire to obstruct that discovery. 43 Cal.4th at 747.

The Supreme Court concluded that "the People were allowed to participate in the third party discovery hearings, that in doing so they did not represent third party interests . . . ." 43 Cal.4th at 748. The Court determined that trial courts have the power to permit or solicit prosecutorial participation in third-party discovery litigation to assist the courts in performing their duty to "regulate the use of subpoenas to obtain privileged third party discovery." 43 Cal.4th at 750.

The Court then rejected Humberto's argument that a prosecutor's providing argument at a third-party discovery hearing constitutes the representation of third-party interests. The Court concluded that in participating in litigation over a defendant's third-party discovery actions, "the prosecution's interests and arguments may *align* with those of one or more third parties, but the prosecution does not thereby assume representation of those parties any more than an amicus curiae whose interests align with a party represents that party by submitting arguments that support its position." 43 Cal.4th at 752. [italics in original]

The Court distinguished *Bullen v. Superior Court* (1988) 204 Cal.App.3d 22, 251 Cal.Rptr. 32, from the prosecution's actions in *Humberto S.* Unlike the scenario in *Bullen*, the prosecution did not formally represent any third party, did not have a corresponding duty of loyalty to a third party, and did not have a divided loyalty or a structural incentive that was potentially contrary to the prosecutor's duty to handle the prosecution of Humberto S. in a fair and impartial manner. The Court found that "the prosecution vigorously advocated a legal position that happened to align with the interests of various third parties at one moment in time. In doing so, it was representing not the third party, but its own interest in promoting victim cooperation." 43 Cal.4th at 754. The Court concluded that "[t]he prosecutors' advocacy in these hearings of positions in line with the interests of third parties did not involve actual representation of those parties' interests and thus created no ongoing conflict or divided loyalty that might jeopardize Humberto S.'s right to a fair trial." 43 Cal.4th at 755.

The Court also observed that its prior decision in *Alford v. Superior Court* (2003) 29 Cal.4th 1033, 130 Cal.Rptr.2d 672, 63 P.3d 228, is not inconsistent with allowing the prosecution to participate in third-party subpoena hearings. The Court further observed that to the extent that the Court of Appeal in *Smith v. Superior Court* (2007) 152 Cal.App.4th 205, 60 Cal.Rptr.3d 841, construed *Alford* as holding that opposition party involvement in a third-party discovery proceeding is prohibited, the *Smith* Court misread *Alford*. 43 Cal.4th at 748–750.

The decision of the Supreme Court in *Humberto S.* constitutes an important clarification of the appropriate and lawful role of the prosecution in third-party discovery initiated by the defendant in criminal cases.

In 2008 the California electorate granted constitutional authority to prosecutors to take actions to enforce the rights of victims of crime.

On November 4, 2008, the California electorate passed Proposition 9, the "Victims' Bill of Rights Act of 2008: Marsy's Law:" which is commonly known as "Marsy's Law." "Marsy's Law" was named after Marsalee (Marsy) Nicholas, a 21-year-old-college student who was murdered in 1983.

"Marsy's Law" amended Section 28 of Article I of the California Constitution, to provide a long list of rights for victims of crimes that had not previously been included in the California Constitution. These rights are found in subdivision (b) of Section 28 of Article I of the California Constitution.

Marsy's Law also added language found in paragraph (1) of subdivision (c) of Section 28 that provides that upon the request of the victim, the prosecutor has the power to enforce a victim's right to refuse an interview, deposition or discovery request by the defendant . . . ." California Constitution, Art. 28(c)(1). This language added to the California Constitution provides prosecutors with constitutional authority to take actions to protect the rights of victims enumerated in Section 28 of Article 1 of the California Constitution.

Practice Tip for Prosecution: The opinion in *Humberto S.* frees you to participate in litigation over third-party discovery actions by the defendant, as long as the trial court does not preclude or restrict your participation. If you are allowed to participate in such litigation, you should be careful to restrict your actions to those that are intended to advance a societal or public interest, such as enforcing those laws that regulate third-party discovery or protect minor victims and witnesses. You should be prepared to articulate how your conduct advances a public interest that you are allowed to enforce.

As we advise in the text, prosecutors should never purport to represent a third party in their actions. As long as your conduct does not constitute actual or legal representation of a third party, the fact that your actions align with the interests of the third party does not make you subject to recusal for representing a third-party interest. And although you may be zealous in your advocacy in third-party discovery litigation, you must be careful to avoid "persistent, bad faith use of litigation tactics lawful in and of themselves . . . ." *In re Humberto S.*, 43 Cal.4th at 747.

§ 9:22 Third-party privileges and privacy rights

It is common for the defendant in a criminal prosecution to seek discovery from or regarding the victim named in the charging allegations. The most frequently-used vehicle for this third-party discovery is the subpoena *duces tecum*. Quite frequently these defense discovery mechanisms seek information from or about the victim that is confidential or otherwise privileged. The defense discovery procedures thus come into conflict with victims' desires to keep that information confidential or to protect its privileged status.

The California Constitution now recognizes the right of a crime victim to have his or her confidential information or records protected from disclosure.

This right of crime victims was added to the California Constitution on November 4, 2008, when the California electorate passed Proposition 9, the "Victims' Bill of Rights Act of 2008: Marsy's Law." This Act, which is commonly known by its shortened name "Marsy's Law," was named after Marsalee (Marsy) Nicholas, a 21-year-old college student who was murdered in 1983.

"Marsy's Law" amended Section 28 of Article I of the California Constitution, to provide:

"(b) In order to preserve and protect a victim's rights to justice and due process, a victim shall be entitled to the following rights:

. . .

(4) To prevent the disclosure of confidential information or records to the defendant, the defendant's attorney, or any other person acting on behalf of the defendant, which could be used to locate or harass the victim or the victim's family or which disclose confidential communications made in the course of medical or counseling treatment, or which are otherwise privileged or confidential by law."

Marsy's Law also added language found in paragraph (1) of subdivision (c) of Section 28 that provides that upon the request of the victim, the prosecutor has the power to enforce a victim's right to prevent the disclosure of confidential information or records as outlined in paragraph (4) of subdivision (b) of Section 28. This language provides prosecutors with constitutional authority to take actions to protect the rights of victims enumerated in Section 28 of Article 1 of the California Constitution.

Paragraph (4) of subdivision (b) of Section 28 appears to elevate the legal protection of a victim's confidential and privileged records from a statutory to a constitutional status. This heightened level of protection might prevent the disclosure of a victim's privileged medical, psychological, and counseling records in criminal cases, except for disclosures made necessary by the defendant's right to due process of law pursuant to the *Brady* rule.

A right that is protected even by the California Constitution cannot negate a right protected by the United States Constitution. Although the California Constitution is the supreme law of the State of California, *Sands v. Morongo Unified School Dist.* (1991) 53 Cal.3d 863, 902–903, 281 Cal.Rptr. 34, 809 P.2d 809, the United States Constitution is the supreme law of the land. U.S. Const., art. VI, cl. 2; California Constitution, art. III, Sec. 1. The California Constitution is thus subject to the supremacy of the United States Constitution. *California Logistics, Inc. v. State of California* (2008) 161 Cal.App.4th 242, 250, 73 Cal.Rptr.3d 825; Cal. Const., art. III, Sec. 1.

§ 9:23 Defense discovery—victim's psychiatric records

In *People v. Martinez* (2009) 47 Cal.4th 399, 97 Cal.Rptr.3d 732, 213 P.3d 77, the California Supreme Court clarified California law concerning the right of a criminal defendant to gain access to the psychiatric or psychological records of a juvenile murder victim.

In *Martinez* the defendant was convicted of first-degree murder and premeditated, attempted murder, and was sentenced to death. The special circumstance allegation that resulted in the death sentence alleged that the murder occurred while the defendant was engaged in the commission, or attempted commission of, or flight after the performance of, a lewd act upon a child under the age of 14 years. The victim of the defendant's attempted murder charge was a juvenile and the murder victim was her mother. The crimes occurred on the same occasion at the same location.

Six years prior to trial the defendant requested the juvenile court to allow him to inspect the juvenile dependency case file of the minor victim of the attempted murder charge, who was under the supervision of the juvenile court because of sexual abuse by several men. The juvenile court conducted an *in camera* review of the juvenile's file. The juvenile court ordered that psychological assessments of the victim that had been performed within a two-year period prior to the murder and attempted murder be disclosed. The juvenile court also disclosed recommendations prepared for a detention hearing in the juvenile court shortly before the crimes, and a jurisdictional report dated about one month after the crimes. The juvenile court declined to release any other information from the juvenile victim's juvenile dependency case file.

On automatic appeal of his conviction to the California Supreme Court, the defendant requested full access to the juvenile dependency case file. The defendant argued that if his request were denied, the Supreme Court must review the file to determine whether the trial court erred to failing to allow him to access material information contained in that file.

In an order dated six years prior to the Court's opinion on appeal, the Supreme Court denied the defendant's request for an order that his appellate counsel be provided access to the undisclosed portion of the juvenile case file. The Court's order cited as authority for its decision denying access to the juvenile file the opinion of the United States Supreme Court in *Pennsylvania v. Ritchie* (1987) 480 U.S. 39, 59–61, 107 S.Ct. 989, 94 L.Ed.2d 40. 47 Cal.4th at 451–452.

In its opinion affirming the judgment in its entirety, the Supreme Court held that the juvenile court had followed the rule established in *Pennsylvania v. Ritchie* and had appropriately exercised its power under the authority of Welfare and Institutions Code section 827 to conduct an *in camera* review of the juvenile file. *People v. Martinez, supra*, 47 Cal.4th at 452.

The Court rejected the defendant's argument that the rule of *Pennsylvania v. Ritchie* is inapposite to a defendant's request to review a confidential juvenile file on appeal. The Court held that "even at trial the defense is not entitled to review confidential documents to determine which are material for its purposes; rather, as occurred in the present case, it is the trial court's duty to review the documents and to determine which, if any, are material and should be disclosed." 47 Cal.4th at 453.

The Supreme Court reviewed the confidential juvenile court and superior court files and concluded that the undisclosed information was not material to the defense. The Court held that the contents of the juvenile files "do not support any claim that further disclosure is required to protect defendant's right to a fair appeal." 47 Cal.4th at 454.

§ 9:24 Defense discovery—witness's psychiatric records

The pretrial discovery of a witness's psychiatric records continues to produce litigation in the federal and state courts.

§ 9:24.1 Pretrial disclosure of witness's psychiatric records

In *Rizzo v. Smith* (2008, CA7 WI) 528 F.3d 501, a defendant convicted in state court of sexually assaulting a child engaged in protracted post-trial litigation over requests that he had made to the trial court that he be given access to psychiatric treatment records of the child and that the child be subjected to an independent psychological examination. He ultimately did not prevail in this post-trial litigation and brought a federal habeas petition challenging the state court denials. The federal district court denied his petition, but the district court certified both issues for review by the Seventh Circuit Court of Appeals.

The Court of Appeals affirmed the judgment of the district court denying the habeas petition. The Court based its denial on the fact that the trial court, in compliance with *Pennsylvania v. Ritchie* (1987) 480 U.S. 39, 107 S.Ct. 989, 94 L.Ed.2d 40, had conducted an *in camera* review of the child's treatment records and had found nothing in those records that was not contained in a six-page summary which had been prepared by the child's treating psychologist and disclosed to the defendant. "Ritchie says that due process requires confidential information that is potentially exculpatory to be submitted to the trial court for an *in camera* review. That's exactly what Rizzo got." 528 F.3d at 506.

The Court further found that the defendant had not presented a compelling need or reason to subject the victim to a psychological examination, as required by *Chambers v. Mississippi* (1973) 410 U.S. 284, 93 S.Ct. 1038, 35 L.Ed.2d 297, and *Ake v. Oklahoma* (1985) 470 U.S. 68, 105 S.Ct. 1087, 84 L.Ed.2d 53. 528 F.3d at 506–507.

§ 9:24.4 Witness's psychiatric records and psychotherapist-patient privilege

The defendant might have a due-process right to access the psychiatric records of a material prosecution witness. The defendant's right to due process of law and to present a defense might override the witness's statutory psychotherapist-patient privilege.

In *Johnson v. Norris* (2008, CA8 AR) 537 F.3d 840, a defendant charged with capital murder requested the court to allow him access to the psychotherapy records of the principal witness against him, a young girl eyewitness to the murder who had undergone psychotherapy after the defendant's first trial, which had resulted in a conviction and death sentence that was reversed on appeal. The trial court rejected the defendant's request, and he was again convicted and sentenced to death. The second judgment was affirmed on appeal, and the defendant exhausted his state court habeas remedies.

The defendant then filed a federal habeas petition in which he argued that denial of access to the young child's psychotherapy records denied him due process of law and a chance to present a defense. The district court denied the habeas petition, and the defendant appealed. The Eighth Circuit Court of Appeals affirmed the denial of the habeas petition, but did so only on the grounds that the district court's decision under the Antiterrorism and Effective Death Penalty Act of 1996 (AEDPA) was not contrary to or an unreasonable application of clearly established law.

The Court of Appeals acknowledged cases such as *Davis v. Alaska* (1974) 415 U.S. 308, 94 S.Ct. 1105, 39 L.Ed.2d 347, which held that a defendant's right to cross-examine a key witness prevailed over a state policy of protecting the anonymity of juvenile offender records. But the Court observed that the law concerning the relationship between a defendant's rights of confrontation, cross-examination, and due process and state-protected privileged records of a witness is unsettled. *See Swidler & Berlin v. United States* (1998) 524 U.S. 399, 408, n.3, 118 S.Ct. 2081, 141 L.Ed.2d 379, and *Pennsylvania v. Ritchie* (1987) 480 U.S. 39, 107 S.Ct. 989, 94 L.Ed.2d 40. But the Court concluded that "[a]lthough *Davis* and *Ritchie* establish that in at least some circumstances, an accused's constitutional rights are paramount to a State's interest in protecting confidential information, those decisions do not establish a specific legal rule that answers whether a State's psychotherapist-patient privilege must yield to an accused's desire to use confidential information in defense of a criminal case." 537 F.3d at 846.

In spite of the ultimate holding of *Johnson v. Norris, supra,* we believe that it is probable that California appellate courts will hold, when presented with the issue, that a defendant's constitutional due-process right to a fair trial overrides the statutory psychotherapist-patient privilege of Evidence Code sections 1010 *et seq.*

§ 9:25   Defense discovery—physical examination of victim

In *People v. Landau* (2013) 214 Cal. App. 4th 1, 154 Cal. Rptr. 3d 1, in a proceeding under the Sexually Violent Predators Act (SVPA) (more analogous to conservatorship proceedings than criminal proceedings), the California Fourth District Appellate Court held, *inter alia,* that, subject to certain restrictions, any party may obtain a mental or physical examination of another party to the action. Code Civ. Proc. § 2032.020, subsection (a). This section does not require a party to put his or her mental state into controversy. It merely requires the mental condition of that party or other person is in controversy in the action. Code Civ. Proc. § 2019.010, subsection (d), also authorizes discovery via mental examinations. Although repetitive mental or physical examinations of a party may become unduly burdensome in any case, they are permissible if there is a showing of good cause.

§ 9:26 Defense discovery—psychiatric examination of victim

In *Rizzo v. Smith* (2008, CA7 WI) 528 F.3d 501, a defendant convicted in state court of sexually assaulting a child engaged in protracted post-trial litigation over requests that had made to the trial court that he be given access to psychiatric treatment records of the child and that the child be subjected to an independent psychological examination. He ultimately did not prevail in this post-trial litigation and brought a federal habeas petition challenging the state court denials. The federal district court denied his petition, but the district court certified both issues for review by the Seventh Circuit Court of Appeals.

The Court of Appeals affirmed the judgment of the district court denying the habeas petition. The Court based its denial on the fact that the trial court, in compliance with *Pennsylvania v. Ritchie* (1987) 480 U.S. 39, 107 S.Ct. 989, 94 L.Ed.2d 40, had conducted an *in camera* review of the child's treatment records and had found nothing in those records that was not contained in a six-page summary which had been prepared by the child's treating psychologist and disclosed to the defendant. "Ritchie says that due process requires confidential information that is potentially exculpatory to be submitted to the trial court for an *in camera* review. That's exactly what Rizzo got." 528 F.3d at 506.

The Court further found that the defendant had not presented a compelling need or reason to subject the victim to a psychological examination, as required by *Chambers v. Mississippi* (1973) 410 U.S. 284, 93 S.Ct. 1038, 35 L.Ed.2d 297, and *Ake v. Oklahoma* (1985) 470 U.S. 68, 105 S.Ct. 1087, 84 L.Ed.2d 53. *Rizzo v. Smith*, 528 F.3d at 506–507.

§ 9:27 Defense discovery—psychiatric examination of witness

In *United States v. Sabhnani* (2010, CA2 NY) 599 F.3d 215, two defendants charged with forced labor, harboring aliens, holding a person in peonage, document servitude, and conspiracy, arising out their employment of two maids from a third-world country, requested the trial court to order that one of the victims be required to undergo a psychiatric examination. The district court denied the motion.

On appeal following their convictions, the Second Circuit Court of Appeals held that the district court had not abused its discretion in denying the motion. The Court of Appeals observed that " '[o]rdering a witness to undergo a psychological examination is a drastic measure.' [citations omitted]; that a "court should exercise its discretion to require such examinations only sparingly;" that a psychiatric examination would not have added measurably to the jury's ability to assess the witness's credibility; and that the evidence offered in support of the motion was insufficient to show the need for a psychiatric exam. 599 F.3d at 234–236.

§ 9:28   Defense discovery—other third-party privacy rights

In addition to the privacy rights attendant to a victim's or witness's medical or psychiatric records, defense discovery efforts can conflict with other privacy rights held by third parties.

§ 9:28.1   Defense discovery—third-party attorney-client privilege

A defendant's efforts to obtain discovery from a third party to the criminal prosecution can conflict with the attorney-client privilege of that third party. Such a conflict requires the trial court to resolve the question whether the attorney-client privilege precludes the defendant's access to the records and documents in question.

In *Murdoch v. Castro* (2010, CA9 CA) 609 F.3d 983, a prosecution witness and participant in a murder apparently wrote a letter to his attorney in which he claimed that the defendant was not involved in the murder and that he (the witness) had been coerced into implicating the defendant. The prosecutor informed the court and the defendant of this information when the prosecutor learned of it. The defendant's efforts to gain access to the letter in state court were rejected by the trial judge, who ruled in the face of an assertion by the witness's attorney of the attorney-client privilege that the letter was a protected attorney-client communication. The defendant was convicted of murder and sentenced to life in prison without the possibility of parole.

After exhausting his appellate remedies and state court habeas proceedings, the defendant filed a habeas petition in the federal courts in which he argued, *inter alia*, that the trial court had erred in ruling on his discovery request. Following the district court's denial of his habeas petition, the defendant appealed to the Court of Appeals. The Ninth Circuit Court of Appeals *en banc* rejected the defendant's argument regarding his denied access to the witness's letter, holding that since the attorney-client privilege protects only the communications between the attorney and the client, and not the subject matter of those communications, the defendant remained free to question the witness at trial regarding the matters contained in the letter. The Court of Appeals did not address the question whether its ruling would have been different had the letter been possessed by the prosecution team, as opposed to its possession by the attorney for a witness, a third party to the criminal prosecution.

§ 9:29   Records protected by constitutional right to privacy

§ 9:29.2   Utility and escrow records

Penal Code section 1326 reads as follows:

---

§ 1326. Subpoena; Signing and issuance; Business records; Non-parties

(a) The process by which the attendance of a witness before a court or magistrate is required is a subpoena. It may be signed and issued by any of the following:

(1) A magistrate before whom a complaint is laid or his or her clerk, the district attorney or his or her investigator, or the public defender or his or her investigator, for witnesses in the state.

(2) The district attorney, his or her investigator, or, upon request of the grand jury, any judge of the superior court, for witnesses in the state, in support of an indictment or information, to appear before the court in which it is to be tried.

(3) The district attorney or his or her investigator, the public defender or his or her investigator, or the clerk of the court in which a criminal action is to be tried. The clerk shall, at any time, upon application of the defendant, and without charge, issue as many blank subpoenas, subscribed by him or her, for witnesses in the state, as the defendant may require.

(4) The attorney of record for the defendant.

(b) A subpoena issued in a criminal action that commands the custodian of records or other qualified witness of a business to produce books, papers, documents, or records shall direct that those items be delivered by the custodian or qualified witness in the manner specified in subdivision (b) of Section 1560 of the Evidence Code. Subdivision (e) of Section 1560 of the Evidence Code shall not apply to criminal cases.

(c) In a criminal action, no party, or attorney or representative of a party, may issue a subpoena commanding the custodian of records or other qualified witness of a business to provide books, papers, documents, or records, or copies thereof, relating to a person or entity other than the subpoenaed person or entity in any manner other than that specified in subdivision (b) of Section 1560 of the Evidence Code. When a defendant has issued a subpoena to a person or entity that is not a party for the production of books, papers, documents, or records, or copies thereof, the court may order an in camera hearing to determine whether or not the defense is entitled to receive the documents. The court may not order the documents disclosed to the prosecution except as required by Section 1054.3.

(d) This section shall not be construed to prohibit obtaining books, papers, documents, or records with the consent of the person to whom the books, papers, documents, or records relate.

History:

Enacted 1872. Amended Code Amdts 1880 ch 47 § 97; Stats 1937 ch 215 § 1; Stats 1939 ch 1015 § 1; Stats 1951 ch 1674 § 138; Stats 1953 ch 613 § 4; Stats 1959 ch 501 § 19, ch 1058 § 1; Stats 1971 ch 1196 § 3; Stats 1972 ch 543 § 1; Stats 2004 ch 162 § 2 (AB 1249);

Stats 2007 ch 263 § 30 (AB 310), effective January 1, 2008.).

§ 9:29.4   Medical records

Medical records are presumptively private, such that a plaintiff is not required to state the obvious in a declaration, that she would be personally embarrassed to have her medical records copied into court records. The public, through its courts and legislatures, has recognized that medical records are constitutionally private and statutorily confidential. While privacy concerns are not absolute and must be balanced against other important interests, the public's general right of access to court records recognized in California Rules of Court, rule 2.550, must give way to the public's concern about the privacy of medical information when the information appears tangentially related to the litigation. *Oiye v. Fox* (2012) 211 Cal. App. 4th 1036, 151 Cal. Rptr. 3d 65.

§ 9:30   Jurors' personal data

In *People v. Carrasco* (2008) 163 Cal.App.4th 978, 77 Cal.Rptr.3d 912, a defendant convicted of attempted arson and resisting an executive officer brought a post-trial motion under Code of Civil Procedure section 206, subdivision (a), to obtain contact information of one of the jurors.

The juror in question, when polled along with the other jurors collectively by the clerk as to whether the verdict was their verdict, answered in the affirmative. Then when questioned individually by the court as to whether the verdict was that juror's verdict, the juror did not answer. When asked a second time by the court the juror replied yes. The trial judge then directed the jurors to leave the courtroom so the court could question the juror individually. The juror then told the judge that the verdict was not her verdict, because she had reasonable doubt that the charge was a felony. The juror further informed the court that she was convinced of the defendant's guilt beyond a reasonable doubt, but she had reservations about the verdict because she did not think it should be a felony conviction. The trial court then entered the verdict.

The defendant's petition asked the court to release contact information on the juror so that the defense could question her about her reluctance to find the defendant guilty of a felony. The defendant wanted to question the juror to determine whether to make a new-trial motion. The trial court denied the defendant's request.

On appeal the defendant argued that the trial court had erred in denying release of the juror's contact information. The Court of Appeal rejected the defense claim of error. The Court observed that the trial court had made an express finding that the juror's hesitation and "reasonable doubt" were "based on her concern about the felony nature of the charged offenses and finality of the decision, and not the lack of proof." 163 Cal.App.4th at 991. The Court further observed that the juror stated that she was satisfied that the defendant was guilty beyond a reasonable doubt, putting to one side whether the conviction should be a felony. Finally, the Court concluded that there was no evidence of misconduct by any other juror in producing the juror's decisions. Based on these findings the Court of Appeal upheld the decision of the trial court that the defendant had failed to present a prima facie showing of good cause to justify release of the juror's contact information. The Court of Appeal concluded that in light of the trial court's clarification of the juror's feelings and actions, "there was no need for juror information to conduct such questioning after the court discharged the jury." 163 Cal.App.4th at 991.

§ 9:32 Jury lists and selection procedures

It is not uncommon for a defendant who has been convicted at a jury trial to request that the trial court release confidential information about the jurors who rendered the verdict of conviction, so that the defense can contact those jurors in the hopes of developing grounds for a new-trial motion. These requests present difficult issues for trial courts to resolve.

§ 9:32.1 Prosecution participation in defense motion for disclosure of personal juror data

In *People v. Superior Court (Humberto S.)* (2008) 43 Cal.4th 737, 750, 76 Cal.Rptr.3d 276, 182 P.3d 600, the California Supreme Court disapproved the holding in *Smith v. Superior Court* (2007) 152 Cal.App.4th 205, 60 Cal.Rptr.3d 841, that opposition party involvement in a third-party discovery proceeding is prohibited. See the discussion of *Humberto S.* in Section 9:20 of this supplement.

§ 9:35 Prosecution discovery of defendant's psychiatric records—generally

§ 9:35.1 Psychotherapist—patient privilege

In a dependency proceeding, the Fourth District held that a mother did not tender the issue of her psychiatric condition, thus waiving the privilege attached to her confidential psychiatric records, merely by contesting the allegations against her. She also did not waive the privilege by disclosing to the agency that she had been diagnosed with a mental condition, had received psychiatric treatment, and was taking medication because there was not a broad disclosure of confidential communications to the therapist. *In re M.L.* (2012) 210 Cal. App. 4th 1457, 148 Cal. Rptr. 3d 911.

§ 9:35.2 Dangerous patient exception

In *People v. Gonzales* (2013) 56 Cal. 4th 353, 154 Cal. Rptr. 3d 38, 296 P.3d 945, the Supreme Court of California held that the trial court erred in permitting disclosure of a defendant's psychological records and in admitting his former therapist's testimony in reliance on the dangerous patient exception to the psychotherapist-patient privilege. The Court held that neither Evidence Code section 1024, nor any other provision renders the psychotherapist-patient privilege inapplicable in a sexually violent predator (SVP) proceeding. Further, in the case at bar, the Court found that there was no evidence that the therapist herein ever considered it necessary to disclose particular confidential communications in order to prevent a defendant from harming someone. However, the Court also held that, contrary to the decision of the Court of Appeal, disclosure and use of defendant's statements did not violate his federal constitutional right of privacy. The state had a particularly strong and legitimate interest in authorizing the disclosure and use of a parolee's prior statements in parole-mandated therapy in a subsequent SVP proceeding, especially when the therapy was occasioned by the parolee's prior conviction of a sex offense.

In a case in which a wardship petition under Penal Code section 602 was filed against a minor, the Second District held that the trial court erred in denying the minor's motion to have a psychotherapist appointed as a defense expert because, to the extent that the minor was only seeking the appointment for assistance in the defense and not to evaluate his competence to stand trial, he was entitled to the appointment of the psychotherapist and was not limited to a psychotherapist from the panel of psychologists or psychiatrists selected for the Juvenile Competency Pilot Program in the Pasadena, California, juvenile courts. To the extent that the minor was making a request for a competency to stand trial evaluation, the attorney-client privilege applied to any disclosure made in conjunction with that evaluation because the psychotherapist he sought to hire would be assisting defense counsel, not unlike a translator or other expert witness, and the psychotherapist only needed to report information about child abuse or neglect or threats of violence to the minor's attorney. *Elijah W. v. Superior Court* (2013) 213 Cal. App. 4th 1343, 153 Cal. Rptr. 3d 606.

§ 9:35.3   Patient-litigant exception

The patient-litigant exception compels disclosure of only those matters that the patient himself or herself has chosen to reveal by tendering them in litigation. A court must look to what issues have been raised by the litigant who seeks to assert the privilege, including potential defenses to the litigant's cause of action. The most frequent application of this exception is in a case where the patient files an action seeking damages for personal injuries. *Karen P. v. Superior Court* (2011) 200 Cal. App. 4th 908, 133 Cal. Rptr. 3d 67.

§ 9:35.5   Court-appointed psychotherapist exception

ERRATA: The following paragraph should be omitted from page 876 of the text:

"The psychotherapist privilege does not apply if the court appoints the psychotherapist to examine the patient." *People v. Perry* (1972) 7 Cal.3d 756, 782, 103 Cal.Rptr. 161, 499 P.2d 129.

Communications between a psychotherapist and a patient are generally confidential. Evidence Code section 1014. Specifically, when a psychotherapist is appointed by the court in a criminal proceeding at the request of defense counsel in order to provide the lawyer with information needed so that he or she may advise the defendant whether to enter or withdraw a plea based on insanity or to present a defense based on his or her mental or emotional condition, the psychotherapist-patient privilege applies to communications between the defendant and the court-appointed psychotherapist. Evidence Code section 1017, subsection (a). There is no privilege, however, if the psychotherapist is appointed by the court to examine the patient for any other purpose than to assist the defense. Evidence Code section 1017, subsection (a). *Elijah W. v. Superior Court* (2013) 216 Cal. App. 4th 140, 156 Cal. Rptr. 3d 592.

In re Eduardo A. was cited most recently in *In re M.L.* (2012) 210 Cal. App. 4th 1457, 1468, 148 Cal. Rptr. 3d 911, in which the Fourth District held, *inter alia*, that "[i]n post-jurisdictional proceedings, a juvenile court may order psychiatric evaluations of parents, the substance of which is both disclosable and admissible in subsequent proceedings." (*In re Eduardo A.* (1989) 209 Cal. App. 3d 1038, 1041–1042, 261 Cal. Rptr. 68.) However, "at the pre-jurisdictional stage, an allegation by the Department that a parent is mentally ill or the fact of mental illness alone does not justify a psychological examination of that parent." (*Laurie S. v. Superior Court* (1994) 26 Cal. App. 4th 195, 202, 31 Cal. Rptr. 2d 506.) However, this barrier should not, in and of itself, permit wholesale discovery and admissibility of a parent's previous psychological records, which have no relation to any dependency proceeding.

§ 9:36   Prosecution discovery of defendant's psychiatric records—psychotherapy as condition of probation

Story v. Superior Court, supra, was cited most recently in *People v. Gonzales* (2013) 56 Cal. 4th 353, 361, 154 Cal. Rptr. 3d 38, 296 P.3d 945 wherein, at a hearing on a motion to quash, the defense maintained that the records sought by the prosecution were protected by the psychotherapist-patient privilege and could not be disclosed over the defendant's objection. Defense counsel relied heavily upon the Court of Appeal opinion in Story. At the conclusion of the hearing, the trial court determined that although the psychotherapist-patient privilege applied to the records in question, the prosecution was entitled to obtain access to the records under the dangerous patient exception to the privilege. Accordingly, the court denied the defense motion to quash the subpoena. Because the trial court relied upon the dangerous patient exception, it did not reach or resolve the district attorney's alternative theory that defendant had consented to the disclosure of such materials as part of the standard parole outpatient therapy procedure. The Supreme Court of California held that the trial court erred in permitting disclosure of defendant's psychological records and in admitting his former therapist's testimony in reliance on the dangerous patient exception to the psychotherapist-patient privilege. Neither Evidence Code section 1024, nor any other provision renders the psychotherapist-patient privilege inapplicable in a sexually violent predators (SVP) proceeding.

§ 9:37　Prosecution discovery of defendant's psychiatric records—attorney-client privilege

Rodriguez, supra, was cited most recently in *Maldonado v. Superior Court* (2012) 53 Cal. 4th 1112, 1134, 140 Cal. Rptr. 3d 113, 274 P.3d 1110, in a footnote:

> Two Court of Appeal decisions, *Rodriguez v. Superior Court* (1993) 14 Cal.App.4th 1260 [18 Cal. Rptr. 2d 120] and *Andrade v. Superior Court* (1996) 46 Cal.App.4th 1609 [54 Cal. Rptr. 2d 504], have held that section 1054.6 absolves the defendant from disclosing, prior to trial, the otherwise discoverable written or recorded statement of an expert witness he or she intends to call (§ 1054.3, subd. (a)(1)) if the statement includes or discusses communications from the defendant to the expert that are protected by the statutory attorney-client privilege. This privilege, unlike that provided by the Fifth Amendment, is one of true confidentiality. Unless and until waived, it protects against any and all disclosure of most communications from a client to his or her lawyer, or to a third person to whom the communication is necessary for "accomplishment of the purpose for which the lawyer is consulted." (Evid. Code, § 952; see also Cal. Law Revision Com. com., 29B pt. 3A West's Ann. Evid. Code (2009 ed.) foll. § 952, p. 307 [privilege covers client's disclosures to expert consultant, such as physician, for purposes of assisting counsel in advising client].) But neither the attorney-client privilege, nor any other privilege of true confidentiality, is at issue here. Petitioner has never claimed that his examination by prosecution experts might involve the disclosure of private communications to his counsel, as to which confidentiality has not been waived, or of attorney work product, and the Court of Appeal majority did not devise its prophylactic measures with those issues in mind.

§ 9:38　Prosecution discovery of defendant's psychiatric records—waiver of attorney-client privilege on retained expert

Cited most recently in *Maldonado v. Superior Court* (2012) 53 Cal. 4th 1112, 140 Cal. Rptr. 3d 113, 274 P.3d 1110, in which the California Supreme Court held that neither the Fifth Amendment right against self-incrimination, nor prophylactic concerns about the protection of that right, justify precluding the prosecution from full pretrial access to the results of mental examinations by prosecution experts conducted, pursuant to Penal Code section 1054.3, subsection (b)(1), for the purpose of obtaining evidence to rebut a mental-state defense the defendant has indicated he or she intends to present on the issue of guilt. The Court of Appeal majority in the current case erred in ordering that prosecutors could not observe the examinations and could obtain access to the examination materials only under a procedure whereby the trial court would consider defendant's privilege objections pretrial, and would inspect and redact the examination materials in camera, before allowing the prosecution any access to them. Forcing the trial court to resolve defense claims of privilege prior to trial, without prosecutorial access to the evidence in dispute, imposed procedures that were neither required nor justified by U.S. Constitution, 5th & 6th Amendments and that were manifestly unfair to the prosecution.

§ 9:39   Expert witness/hospital staff committee records

A hospital's institutional review board is a committee of hospital medical staff whose proceedings and records are exempt from discovery under Evidence Code section 1157. *Pomona Valley Hospital Medical Center v. Superior Court* (2012) 209 Cal. App. 4th 687, 147 Cal. Rptr. 3d 376.

PART III.   COMBATING THIRD-PARTY DISCOVERY

§ 9:42   Quashing subpoenas *duces tecum*

The primary tool available to the prosecution and the defense to combat subpoenas *duces tecum* issued by the opposing party is a motion to quash the subpoena.

§ 9:42.1   Prosecutor's power re defense third-party subpoena *duces tecum*

The question whether the prosecution may move to quash a defense-issued subpoena has largely been resolved by the California Supreme Court in *In re Humberto S.* (2008) 43 Cal.4th 737, 76 Cal.Rptr.3d 276, 182 P.3d 600. The answer to the question is that "[t]he People, even if not the target of the discovery, also generally have the right to file a motion to quash [a defense-issued subpoena for a third party] 'so that evidentiary privileges are not sacrificed just because the subpoena recipient lacks sufficient self-interest to object [citation omitted] or is otherwise unable to do so.' [citation omitted]" *Kling v. Superior Court* (2010) 50 Cal.4th 1068, 1078, 116 Cal.Rptr.3d 217, 239 P.3d 670.

§ 9:42.1.2   Prosecution motion to quash defense subpoena as representing third-party interest

It now appears clear that a prosecutor may make a motion to quash a defense subpoena for third-party discovery in a criminal prosecution without running afoul of the principle that the prosecutor may not represent third-party interests in a criminal prosecution.

For many years, going back to *Bullen v. Superior Court* (1988) 204 Cal.App.3d 22, 251 Cal.Rptr. 32 [discussed in the text], prosecutors have been wary of taking actions to oppose defense-initiated third-party discovery out of concern that such efforts would cause them to become the attorneys for the third party and thus subject them to recusal. These fears have been significantly eased because of the decision of the California Supreme Court in *In re Humberto S.* (2008) 43 Cal.4th 737, 76 Cal.Rptr.3d 276, 182 P.3d 600.

In *Humberto S.* a minor was charged in a wardship petition with the continuous sexual abuse of a child under the age of 14 years, in violation of Penal Code section 288.5. The alleged victim of the sexual abuse was the daughter of the minor's brother—his eight-year old niece. Prior to trial the attorney for Humberto issued third-party subpoenas for the victim's medical and psychotherapy records. The custodian of the child's medical records disclosed those records directly to Humberto's counsel, who opened them. The custodian of the psychotherapy records delivered them to the trial court. The court delivered the already opened psychotherapy records to Humberto's counsel in an ex parte proceeding at which the prosecutor did not appear.

When Humberto's counsel provided copies of both sets of records to the People, who were represented by the district attorney, the prosecutor objected to the defendant's possession of the records on the grounds that proper subpoena procedure had not been followed and that *People v. Hammon* (1997) 15 Cal.4th 1117, 65 Cal.Rptr.2d 1, 938 P.2d 986, restricted the right of a defendant to pretrial access to the minor victim's records. The juvenile court ordered the defendant to return all records to the court, and a series of hearings ensued. The district attorney filed several motions to quash the defense subpoenas and repeatedly argued against the juvenile court's releasing the records to the defendant. The district attorney also requested that the juvenile court appoint a guardian ad litem to assert the minor victim's privileges regarding her records.

The juvenile court denied the People's motions to quash the subpoenas and to appoint a guardian ad litem for the minor victim, and the court ordered that the records be delivered to Humberto's attorneys. The disclosure order was stayed pending a writ petition by the People in the Court of Appeal. When the Court of Appeal denied the People's writ petition, the records were released to Humberto's counsel.

Humberto then filed a motion to recuse the district attorney pursuant to Penal Code section 1434, arguing that when the district attorney had opposed the defense third-party discovery, the district attorney had represented three separate third parties: the minor victim, the mother of the victim, and the custodian of the minor's psychotherapy records. The trial court partially granted the motion, saying that the prosecution attempted to represent third-party interests and had thereby compromised the prosecutor's ability to provide Humberto with a fair trial.

The People sought writ review and a stay in the Court of Appeal, which ultimately denied the petition and lifted the stay. The Court of Appeal concluded that the conduct of the district attorney in opposing defense third-party discovery "demonstrated a one-sided perspective on the role of the prosecution and an apparent attempt to represent the victim's interest in protecting her privacy that exceeded the exercise of balanced discretion necessary to ensure a just and fair trial." 43 Cal.4th at 745.

The California Supreme Court granted the People's petition for review "to consider the application of the recusal statute to situations involving the alleged advocacy of third party interests." 43 Cal.4th at 746. The Court held that the trial court's decision to recuse numerous prosecutors was based on an error of law and an abuse of discretion.

In reaching its decision the Supreme Court held that "the good faith assertion of legal argument, without more, does not establish a conflict [of interest by the prosecutor]." The Court opined that a prosecutor is entitled to be zealous in the prosecutor's enforcement of discovery law, as long as the prosecutor's zeal remains within legal limits. The Court upheld the trial court's finding that the prosecution's objections to the defense third-party discovery efforts were motivated by a desire to ensure that the law regulating third-party discovery was followed, not by a desire to obstruct that discovery. 43 Cal.4th at 747.

The Supreme Court concluded that "the People were allowed to participate in the third party discovery hearings, that in doing so they did not represent third party interests . . . ." 43 Cal.4th at 748. The Court determined that trial courts have the power to permit or solicit prosecutorial participation in third-party discovery litigation to assist the courts in performing their duty to "regulate the use of subpoenas to obtain privileged third party discovery." 43 Cal.4th at 750.

The Court then rejected Humberto's argument that a prosecutor's providing argument at a third-party discovery hearing constitutes the representation of third-party interests. The Court concluded that in participating in litigation over a defendant's third-party discovery actions, "the prosecution's interests and arguments may *align* with those of one or more third parties, but the prosecution does not thereby assume representation of those parties any more than an amicus curiae whose interests align with a party represents that party by submitting arguments that support its position." 43 Cal.4th at 752. [italics in original].

The Court distinguished *Bullen v. Superior Court* (1988) 204 Cal.App.3d 22, 251 Cal.Rptr. 32, from the prosecution's actions in *Humberto S.* Unlike the scenario in *Bullen*, the prosecution did not formally represent any third party, did not have a corresponding duty of loyalty to a third party, and did not have a divided loyalty or a structural incentive that was potentially contrary to the prosecutor's duty to handle the prosecution of Humberto S. in a fair and impartial manner. The Court found that "the prosecution vigorously advocated a legal position that happened to align with the interests of various third parties at one moment in time. In doing so, it was representing not the third party, but its own interest in promoting victim cooperation." 43 Cal.4th at 754. The Court concluded that "[t]he prosecutors' advocacy in these hearings of positions in line with the interests of third parties did not involve actual representation of those parties' interests and thus created no ongoing conflict or divided loyalty that might jeopardize Humberto S' right to a fair trial." 43 Cal.4th at 755.

The Court also observed that its prior decision in *Alford v. Superior Court* (2003) 29 Cal.4th 1033, 130 Cal.Rptr.2d 672, 63 P.3d 228, is not inconsistent with allowing the prosecution to participate in third-party subpoena hearings. The Court further observed that to the extent that the Court of Appeal in *Smith v. Superior Court* (2007) 152 Cal.App.4th 205, 60 Cal.Rptr.3d 841, construed *Alford* as holding that opposition party involvement in a third party discovery proceeding is prohibited, the *Smith* Court misread *Alford*. 43 Cal.4th at 748–750.

The decision of the Supreme Court in *Humberto S.* constitutes an important clarification of the appropriate and lawful role of the prosecution in third-party discovery initiated by the defendant in criminal cases. The Court's decision affirms that prosecutors may move to quash defense-issued third-party subpoenas in criminal cases without necessarily becoming the attorney for a third party.

§ 9:42.1.3　Prosecution's legitimate interests in defense third-party subpoena *duces tecum*

The public prosecutor might have a legitimate interest in third-party discovery actions by the defendant in a criminal case. The prosecutor's possible legitimate interest was described by the California Supreme Court in *In re Humberto S.* (2008) 43 Cal.4th 737, 76 Cal.Rptr.3d 276, 182 P.3d 600. *Humberto S.* is discussed in greater detail in Sections 9:20 and 9.42.1.2 of this supplement.

The nature of the public prosecutor's lawful interest in combating defense third-party discovery actions can take many potential forms. In *Humberto S.* the prosecutor had a legitimate interest in ensuring that the law governing subpoenas to third parties be followed, 43 Cal.4th at 747, that the statutory and constitutional rights of the alleged minor victim in the privacy of her communications with her therapist be protected, 43 Cal.4th at 752–753, and that victim cooperation with a criminal prosecution be promoted. 43 Cal.4th at 754, n.13.

When the prosecution litigates defense-initiated third-party discovery actions that appear to the prosecution to infringe upon these legitimate public policy concerns, the prosecutor is acting as the representative of the public to enforce accepted public policy.

PART IV. DISCOVERY BY THIRD PARTIES IN CRIMINAL PROSECUTIONS

§ 9:44 Third party subpoena for prosecution's records

The emergence of victims' rights movements in recent years has spawned efforts by victims and their families for discovery of prosecution records relating to the cases in which they are victims.

§ 9:44.1 Discovery by crime victims

The victims in crimes do not have the right to intervene in a criminal prosecution in order to obtain discovery from the prosecution to be used in a civil action.

In *United States v. Moussaoui* (2007, CA4 VA) 483 F.3d 220, a federal district court allowed survivors of victims of the September 11, 2001, terrorist attacks on the United States to intervene in the criminal prosecution of one of those alleged terrorists for the purpose of obtaining nonpublic discovery materials for their use in civil litigation against third parties in a different jurisdiction. The government appealed the district court orders requiring the government to provide the survivors with the nonpublic discovery materials that the government had provided to the defendant in his criminal case.

The Fourth Circuit Court of Appeals reversed the district court's orders, holding that the trial court lacked authority, inherent or otherwise, to enter the discovery orders which it had made, and the Court articulated four cogent policy reasons—efficiency, competency, fairness, and slippery slope concerns—for denying the district court the general power to allow victims to intervene in a criminal process in order to obtain discovery from the government to be used in civil litigation. 483 F.3d at 237–238.

§ 9:44.2 Discovery by parents of juvenile crime victim

Whether a parent of a juvenile who was alleged to be the victim of a molestation has the right to be informed of the molestation investigation, or of attempts to change the testimony of the juvenile, are unresolved questions.

In *James v. Rowlands* (2010, CA9 CA) 606 F.3d 646, the father of a juvenile molestation victim sued county officials under the federal civil rights act, 42 U.S.C. Sec. 1983, alleging that the officials violated his due process rights by failing to inform him of allegations that his daughter had been molested and that she was coerced to change her trial testimony. The district court granted summary judgment to the defendants, and declined to decide if the father had a constitutional right to be informed of his daughter's molestation or attempts to coerce her to change her testimony.

§ 9:45 Discovery by witness of witness's own statement

Whether a witness has a right to access and inspect a transcript of the witness's own prior testimony is a question that has divided the federal courts.

The most recent exposition of a federal circuit court on this subject came in *In re: Grand Jury* (2007, CA DC) 490 F.3d 978. In *In re: Grand Jury* the government conducted a grand jury investigation of a company and its employees. Two employees testified before the grand jury under compulsion of grand jury subpoenas. After each of these employees had testified, they were subpoenaed to again appear to testify before the same grand jury. Each employee asked to be able to review transcripts of their prior testimony which the government possessed. The government denied the requests, and the employees filed motions in the district court for orders to compel the government to allow the witnesses to read the transcripts of their own testimony. The district court denied the motions, and the employees appealed.

The Court of Appeals for the District of Columbia Circuit reversed the orders denying the motions for disclosure of the witnesses' prior grand jury testimony to the extent that the orders denied the witnesses access to their own testimony. The Court concluded that "[w]eighing the interests of witnesses and the Government, we therefore hold that the grand jury witnesses are entitled under Rule 6(e)(3)(E)(i) [of the Federal Rules of Criminal Procedure] to review transcripts of their own grand jury testimony in private at the U.S. Attorney's Office or a place agreed to by the parties or designated by the district court." 490 F.3d at 990.

Because the witnesses sought only access to, and not copies of, the transcripts of their own testimony, the Court declined to decide whether a witness has a right to obtain a copy of the transcript of the witness's testimony. Prior decisions of the federal circuit courts have reached differing results on the question whether a witness has a right to obtain a transcript of the witness's testimony. The Ninth Circuit Court of Appeals and the former Special Division for the Purpose of Appointing Independent Counsels held that grand jury witnesses are entitled in certain circumstances to obtain a copy of their grand jury transcripts. *See In re Sealed Motion* (1989, CA DC) 880 F.2d 1367, 1368, 1370–71; *Bursey v. United States* (1972, CA9 CA) 466 F.2d 1059, 1080; *see also, United States v. Rose* (1954, CA3 PA) 215 F.2d 617, 628–630.

Reaching the opposite result were the Fourth, First, Second, and the Fifth Circuit Courts of Appeals, which held that grand jury witnesses are not entitled to obtain copies of the transcripts of their testimony. *Bast v. United States* (1976, CA4 VA) 542 F.2d 893, 894, 896; *In re Bianchi* (1976, CA1 MA) 542 F.2d 98, 100; *In re Grand Jury Subpoena* (1995, CA2 NY) 72 F.3d 271, 273–75; *United States v. Scrimgeour* (1981, CA5 FL) 636 F.2d 1019, 1025.

PART V. DISCOVERY OF INDEPENDENT GOVERNMENT RECORDS

§ 9:46 Indian reservation records

Indian nations were "separate sovereigns pre-existing the Constitution . . . ." *Santa Clara Pueblo v. Martinez* (1978) 436 U.S. 49, 56, 98 S.Ct. 1670, 56 L.Ed.2d 106. Accordingly, Indian tribes "have historically been regarded as unconstrained by those constitutional provisions framed specifically as limitations on federal or state authority." *Santa Clara Pueblo v. Martinez, supra,* 436 U.S. at 56.

Although the United States Constitution is the supreme law of the land, it is part of the laws of the United States, and binds Indian nations "only where it expressly binds them, or is made binding by treaty or some act of Congress." *Native American Church v. Navajo Tribal Council* (1969, CA10 NM) 272 F.2d 131, 134–135. Indian nations are "domestic dependent nations," *Cherokee Nation v. Georgia* (1831) 30 U.S. (5 Pet.) 1, 17, 8 L.Ed. 25, and are under the protection of the United States government. An Indian tribe is much like a state or political entity within the United States.

The United States Congress "has plenary authority to limit, modify or eliminate the powers of local self-government which the tribes otherwise possess." *Santa Clara Pueblo v. Martinez, supra,* 436 U.S. at 56. Article I, section 8 of the United States Constitution gives Congress the power to regulate commerce with Indian tribes. *United States v. Antelope* (1977) 430 U.S. 641, 97 S.Ct. 1395, 51 L.Ed.2d 701. *See generally, People v. Ramirez* (2007) 148 Cal.App.4th 1464, 1469–1470, 56 Cal.Rptr.3d 631.

Indian reservations are treated as independent territory to the extent that Congress has not granted state jurisdiction over offenses committed by or against Indians in "Indian country."

In 1953 Congress enacted Public Law 280. Public Law 280 gave six states—Alaska, California, Minnesota, Nebraska, Oregon and Wisconsin—criminal jurisdiction over tribal members and other people on Indian reservations. The heart of Public Law 280 is found in 18 U.S.C. sec. 1162. Subdivision (a) of Section 1162 provides that

> "[e]ach of the States or Territories listed in the following table shall have jurisdiction over offenses committed by or against Indians in the areas of Indian country listed opposite the name of the State or Territory to the same extent that such State or Territory has jurisdiction over offenses committed elsewhere within the State or Territory, and the criminal laws of such State or Territory shall have the same force and effect within such Indian country as they have elsewhere within the State or Territory."

Section 1162 granted state jurisdiction over criminal offenses to Alaska, California, Minnesota, Nebraska, Oregon, and Wisconsin. Three of these states, California, Nebraska, and Wisconsin, have jurisdiction over criminal offenses in all Indian country within their state. The other three have jurisdiction over all Indian country, except for named reservations for which federal jurisdiction is reserved. *Anderson v. Gladden* (1961, CA9 OR) 293 F.2d 463.

The grant of state jurisdiction extends to and includes Indian reservations which were created after Section 1162 was enacted in 1953. *United States v. Hoodie* (1978, CA9 OR) 588 F.2d 292. The grant of state jurisdiction does not give these six states exclusive jurisdiction over offenses that arise under federal laws having general application. *United States v. Anderson* (2004, CA9 CA) 391 F.3d 1083.

The Ninth Circuit Court of Appeals held in *Bishop Paiute Tribe v. County of Inyo* (2002, CA9 CA) 291 F.3d 549, *vacated on other grounds and remanded, Inyo County v. Paiute-Shoshone Indians of the Bishop Cmty. Of the Bishop Colony* (2003) 538 U.S. 701, 123 S.Ct. 1887, 155 L.Ed.2d 933, that Section 1162 granted jurisdiction to the State of California over criminal *offenses* committed by or against Indians in Indian country in California, but did not confer state jurisdiction over the Indian *tribes* themselves. 291 F.3d at 556–557. Thus, concluded the Ninth Circuit, the tribes themselves retained their sovereign immunity, which includes immunity from the processes of California state courts. 291 F.3d at 557. Therefore, held the Ninth Circuit, California state courts may not issue a search warrant to search and seize the records and property of an Indian tribe in California. 291 F.3d at 557–560.

Indian tribes retain attributes of sovereignty over their members and their land, and that sovereignty is dependent upon and subordinate to only the United States Government, not a state government. *California v. Cabazon Band of Mission Indians* (1987) 480 U.S. 202, 207, 107 S.Ct. 1083, 94 L.Ed.2d 244. Indian tribes retain their sovereign power to operate a tribal law enforcement agency on and within an Indian reservation to enforce laws for crimes committed on that reservation. *Cabazon Band of Mission Indians v. Smith* (1998, C.D. CA) 34 F.Supp.2d 1195; *reversed on other grounds, Cabazon Band of Mission Indians v. Smith* (2004, CA9 CA) 388 F.3d 691.

Indian tribes in California are treated as independent sovereign powers, except when an Indian tribe participates in the investigation of a criminal act prosecuted in state court, and parties must utilize third-party discovery tools that recognize that the Indian tribes and reservations are independent sovereigns.

For a discussion of the discovery obligations of the prosecution when an Indian tribe has participated in the investigation of a criminal act prosecuted in state court, see Section 1:70.17.1 of this supplement.

CHAPTER 10

PEACE OFFICER PERSONNEL RECORDS

PART I. *PITCHESS* MOTIONS FOR PERSONNEL RECORDS DISCLOSURE

§ 10:1 *Pitchess* motions—overview

Motions filed by criminal defendants to obtain access to or information from the personnel records of peace officers have generated substantial trial and appellate litigation.

§ 10:1.2 *Pitchess* statutes as exclusive procedural framework

A party who wishes to access the personnel records of a peace officer must utilize the *Pitchess* statutes when the records are contained in proceedings related to the officer's employment, even though the records of those proceedings are not held by the officer's employing law enforcement agency.

Thus, in *Copley Press, Inc. v. Superior Court* (2006) 39 Cal.4th 1272, 48 Cal.Rptr.3d 183, 141 P.3d 288, the California Supreme Court held that a newspaper which petitioned for disclosure of the records of the County of San Diego Civil Service Commission that related to a peace officer's administrative appeal of a disciplinary matter was required to request access to those records using the procedures and standards provided by the *Pitchess* statutes of Penal Code section 832.7 *et seq.* and Evidence Code section 1043 *et seq.*, and that the newspaper could not substitute the provisions of the California Public Records Act, Government Code section 6250 *et seq.*, for the *Pitchess* statutes. The Court held that the *Pitchess* statutes govern disclosure of peace officer personnel records even in a context other than civil or criminal proceedings, and that no person or entity may circumvent the privacy protections of Penal Code section 832.7 *et seq.* by attempting to gain access to peace officer personnel records using the California Public Records Act.

Likewise, in *Berkeley Police Assn. v. City of Berkeley* (2008) 167 Cal.App.4th 385, 84 Cal.Rptr.3d 130, the Court of Appeal, relying upon the Supreme Court's opinion in *Copley Press, supra,* held that the City of Berkeley may not hold public hearings of its police review commission (PRC), because a public hearing would constitute disclosure of peace officer personnel records in violation of Penal Code section 832.7, and that peace officer personnel records may not be disclosed "except in accordance with a special discovery procedure set forth in . . . Evidence Code section 1043." 167 Cal.App.4th at 391.

Therefore, any disclosure of peace officer personnel records must comply with the *Pitchess* statutes provisions found in Penal Code section 832.7 and Evidence Code section 1043 *et seq.* Such statutes are the exclusive procedural framework for access to and the disclosure of such records.

Traditionally, *Pitchess* motions seek information about past complaints by third parties of excessive force, violence, dishonesty, or the filing of false police reports contained in the officer's personnel file. Thus, once a defendant has made the relatively low threshold showing of good cause and the court has reviewed the pertinent documents in camera, the court releases the contact information of the third party complainant and potential witnesses to the past alleged misconduct. On those occasions when that information proves insufficient, either because a witness does not remember the earlier events or the witness cannot be located, a supplemental *Pitchess* motion may be filed and the statements of the witnesses may be disclosed to the defendant. *Rezek v. Superior Court* (2012) 206 Cal. App. 4th 633, 141 Cal. Rptr. 3d 891.

An appellate court reviews the denial of a *Pitchess* motion for abuse of discretion. When a trial court finds a defendant has shown good cause for discovery of peace officer personnel information, the custodian of records is obligated to bring to the trial court all potentially relevant documents to permit the trial court to examine them for itself. A custodian need not produce any documents clearly irrelevant to the defendant's *Pitchess* request; however, if a custodian is uncertain whether a document is relevant, the custodian should present it to the trial court. Such practice is consistent with the premise of Evidence Code sections 1043 and 1045, that the locus of decision-making is to be the trial court, not the prosecution or the custodian of records. The custodian must also be prepared to state during the in-camera review and for the record what documents or category of documents the custodian did not produce and why. A court reporter should document the custodian's statements and any questions from the trial court regarding the completeness of the record. A trial court is not permitted to abdicate to a custodian its responsibility to examine the produced documents and assess the discoverability of the information contained in them. To the contrary, it is the trial court's active involvement in the *Pitchess* process that allows the process to work as intended. Both *Pitchess* and the statutory scheme codifying *Pitchess* require the intervention of a neutral trial judge, who examines the personnel records in camera, away from the eyes of either party, and orders disclosed to the defendant only those records that are found both relevant and otherwise in compliance with statutory limitations. In this manner, the Legislature has attempted to protect the defendant's right to a fair trial and the officer's interest in privacy to the fullest extent possible. *Sisson v. Superior Court* (2013) 216 Cal. App. 4th 24, 156 Cal. Rptr. 3d 533.

§ 10:1.4   Exception to exclusive *Pitchess* procedures

A defendant is entitled to discover from the prosecution the relevant statements of witnesses. Penal Code section 1054.1. The discovery provided in § 1054.1, however, is not exclusive. The reciprocal discovery chapter places no restriction on discovery provided by other express statutory provisions, or as mandated by the Constitution of the United States. Penal Code section 1054, subsection (e). Evidence Code section 1043 is one such express statutory provision. Just as the discovery procedure set forth in § 1043 *et seq.* operates in tandem with the prosecution's duty to disclose favorable information pursuant to the *Brady* rule, so too does the California Evidence Code discovery procedure work in tandem with the prosecution's duty to disclose relevant statements of witnesses under Penal Code section 1054.1, subsection (f). Except with regard to one exception, the prosecutor, as well as the defendant, must comply with the statutory *Pitchess* requirements for disclosure of information contained in confidential peace officer records. There is no reason why the defense—when it has good reason to believe an officer's personnel file contains relevant statements from material witnesses to the charged incident—should be precluded from obtaining the statements because the district attorney may have the right to obtain the same information by filing a motion for discovery pursuant to § 1043. *Rezek v. Superior Court* (2012) 206 Cal. App. 4th 633, 141 Cal. Rptr. 3d 891.

§ 10.4   Motion to disclose records—parties affected

A defendant has a limited right to discovery of a peace officer's confidential personnel records if those files contain information that is potentially relevant to the defense. To initiate discovery, a defendant must file a motion seeking such records, containing affidavits showing good cause for the discovery or disclosure sought, setting forth the materiality thereof to the subject matter involved in the pending litigation. Good cause requires the defendant to establish a logical link between a proposed defense and the pending charge and to articulate how the discovery would support such a defense or how it would impeach the officer's version of events. The threshold for establishing good cause is relatively low. The proposed defense must have a plausible factual foundation supported by the defendant's counsel's declaration and other documents supporting the motion. A plausible scenario is one that might or could have occurred. The defendant must also show how the information sought could lead to or be evidence potentially admissible at trial. Once that burden is met, the defendant has shown materiality under Evidence Code section 1043. *Sisson v. Superior Court* (2013) 216 Cal. App. 4th 24, 156 Cal. Rptr. 3d 533.

The persons who are the subjects of a motion to disclose records under the *Pitchess* statutes are peace officers, whether these officers are employed by the prosecuting or investigating agency.

§ 10:4.1 District Attorney Investigator personnel records

An interesting problem is presented when a district attorney investigator is a material witness in a criminal prosecution conducted by that office.

Many prosecutors' offices have hired peace officers to serve as investigators. These investigators retain their peace officer status when they serve as district attorney investigators, but unlike police or other law enforcement officers, district attorney investigators are employed by and work for the elected prosecutor. These DA investigators work criminal cases in an investigative capacity, and they sometimes become material witnesses in their cases. The employing District Attorney commonly keeps personnel records on these investigators. These personnel records can contain derogatory or other information that could be used to impeach the investigators when they testify in criminal cases.

Difficult questions are presented when a defendant's attorney seeks disclosure of unfavorable information from the personnel records of a DA investigator who is a material witness in a criminal case. On the one hand, the employing District Attorney is in actual and legal possession of these personnel records, in the same manner that the chief of police or sheriff is in actual and legal possession of personnel records of officers employed by investigative agencies other than the prosecutor's office. Thus, the District Attorney has lawful access to these personnel records and the right to review those records as the investigator's employer.

On the other hand, the DA investigator as a peace officer has the right to confidentiality in his or her personnel records, and part of that confidentiality protects the right of privacy in those personnel records as against the prosecutor. See Chapter 10 of the text for a discussion of the confidential nature of peace officer personnel records. Thus, the District Attorney faces a conflict between the role as the investigating officer's employer and the role as the prosecuting attorney in a criminal case. So the question is clearly presented: Is the District Attorney deemed to possess and know the contents of the personnel records of DA criminal investigators within the meaning of both the *Brady* rule and the the *Pitchess* statutes and the body of cases developed under those statutes?

A criminal defendant has a limited right to discovery of a peace officer's personnel records. Peace officer personnel records are confidential and can only be discovered pursuant to Evidence Code sections 1043 and 1045. A defendant is entitled to discovery of relevant information from the confidential records upon a showing of good cause, which exists when the defendant shows both materiality to the subject matter of the pending litigation and a reasonable belief that the agency has the type of information sought. If the trial court concludes the defendant has fulfilled these prerequisites and made a showing of good cause, the custodian of records should bring to court all documents potentially relevant to the defendant's motion. The trial court reviews the records in camera to determine what information, if any, should be disclosed. Subject to the exceptions and limitations contained in § 1045, subdivisions (b)–(e), the court must disclose to the defendant such information as is relevant to the subject matter involved in the litigation. *People v. Yearwood* (2013) 213 Cal. App. 4th 161, 151 Cal. Rptr. 3d 901.

The District Attorney is the public prosecutor charged with the duty of initiating and conducting all prosecutions of public offenses on behalf of the People of the State of California. Government Code section 26500. The District Attorney's duty to prosecute includes the duty to investigate and gather evidence relating to criminal offenses, since investigation of crimes is inseparable from prosecution. Government Code section 25303; *Hicks v. Board of Supervisors* (1977) 69 Cal.App.3d 228, 241, 138 Cal.Rptr. 101; *Los Angeles City Ethics Com. v. Superior Court* (1992) 8 Cal.App.4th 1287, 1302, 11 Cal.Rptr.2d 150.

The District Attorney thus has statutory authority to investigate crime occurring in his or her jurisdiction. Government Code section 26500. Investigators employed by the District Attorney to perform that investigative function have the status of peace officers. Penal Code section 830.1, subdivision (a). Thus, the personnel records of these investigators are protected by the statutes which generally protect peace officer personnel records.

As an employer of peace officers, the District Attorney is charged with the statutory responsibility of protecting the confidentiality of those personnel records. As the employer, the District Attorney has the right to review and inspect those records. As a practical matter, the District Attorney will know the unfavorable information and evidence in the personnel records of his or her employees. As the employer, the District Attorney has the duty to protect these personnel records from unauthorized disclosure.

However, as the public prosecutor, the District Attorney has a constitutionally based duty to disclose material exculpatory evidence possessed by any member of the prosecution team, which includes the prosecutor's office. This conundrum presents the District Attorney with a dilemma—which of these duties must he or she follow? If the District Attorney unlawfully discloses evidence and information from the personnel record of a district attorney investigator, the District Attorney and the County are exposed to potential civil liability for that disclosure. On the other hand, if the District Attorney fails to disclose *Brady* evidence contained in the personnel record, the District Attorney endangers the integrity of his or her office's prosecutions and convictions.

There are no reported California opinions on this subject. The best analysis we can provide is that when the District Attorney is a member of the prosecution team as both the public prosecutor and as an investigating agency, the office of the District Attorney is a partial member of the prosecution team. To the extent that the office of the District Attorney is the public prosecutor, all of the records and personnel of the prosecution component of the District Attorney's office are part of the prosecution team. To the extent that the office of the District Attorney is an investigating agency, the investigating personnel and the records of their investigative work are also part of the prosecution team. But to the extent that the District Attorney performs an administrative function of keeping personnel records, those records of a DA investigator who is a prosecution witness, like the personnel records of a peace officer employed by a separate investigative agency, are not possessed by or part of the prosecution team.

For a more complete discussion of the partial prosecution team membership concept, see Section 1:68 through Section 1:68.3 of the text. For practical suggestions on how the District Attorney should attempt to reconcile these apparently conflicting duties, see the Practice Tip for Prosecution at the end of this section, and see Sections 10:19 through Section 10:30 of Chapter 10 of the text.

> **Practice Tip for Prosecution:** When you are aware that your office has or might have *Brady* evidence in the personnel records of a district attorney investigator who is a prosecution witness in a case you are handling, we recommend that you bring a prosecutor's *Pitchess* motion in which you request the court to conduct an *in camera* inspection of those personnel records to determine if they contain exculpatory or impeaching evidence that should be disclosed to the defendant. You should request that the elected District Attorney, or someone delegated by the District Attorney to perform this task, file a declaration with the court under seal. This declaration, which should set forth the good-cause justification for an *in camera* inspection by the court of the personnel records in question, should not be shared with or disclosed to the defendant and the prosecutor assigned to the case. The prosecutor assigned to the case should file an unsealed declaration with the *Pitchess* motion that establishes the materiality of the investigator's testimony, so that the court in conducting an *in camera* inspection of the investigator's personnel records will be able to determine whether exculpatory or impeaching information in those records is relevant to an issue in the case and should be disclosed to the defendant.

If a defendant establishes good cause for discovery of a peace officer's confidential personnel records, the court must review the requested records in camera to determine what information, if any, should be disclosed. Subject to certain statutory exceptions and limitations, the trial court should then disclose to the defendant such information that is relevant to the subject matter involved in the pending litigation. *Sisson v. Superior Court* (2013) 216 Cal. App. 4th 24, 156 Cal. Rptr. 3d 533.

§ 10:4.2   Probation officer personnel records

A probation officer is a "peace officer" whose personnel records are subject to disclosure under the *Pitchess* statutes if they contain information that is potentially relevant to a defendant's defense. *People v. Moreno* (2011)

192 Cal.App.4th 692, 700–701, 121 Cal.Rptr.3d 669. This is true even though the probation officer is no longer working as a probation officer. 192 Cal.App.4th at 702–703.

Thus, in *People v. Moreno, supra,* the personnel records of a homicide victim who had previously worked as a probation officer, but who was no longer working as a probation officer at the time of her killing, were subject to an *in camera* review to determine whether they contained information that might support the defendant's proposed defense that he acted in self-defense or in response to the victim's aggressive behavior.

§ 10:4.3 Retired peace officer personnel records

The discovery procedures prescribed by the *Pitchess* statutes do not apply only to peace officers who are employed as peace officers at the time of the crime. "Although cases involving the discovery of peace officer personnel records will usually involve alleged 'misconduct' of officers *qua* [in the capacity of] officers, there is nothing in Evidence Code section 1043 or case law that limits the procedure in this way. [citation to *Gremminger* omitted] Nor would such a limitation make sense. Material in a peace officer's personnel file that is relevant and potentially exculpatory does not become less so merely because the officer is no longer in the employ of a law enforcement agency." *People v. Moreno* (2011) 192 Cal.App.4th 692, 702–703, 121 Cal.Rptr.3d 669.

See also People v. Superior (McKunes) (1976) 62 Cal.App.3d 853–857, 133 Cal.Rptr. 440 [personnel records of police officer who was off duty at the time of the assault on that officer are discoverable].

§ 10:5 Motion to disclose records—proceedings covered

Penal Code section 832.7 provides that peace officer and custodial officer personnel records are confidential. Government Code section 6254, subsection (f), while not making such records confidential, partially exempts from disclosure under the Public Records Act certain police investigative files. Penal Code section 832.7, expressly provides that its designation of confidentiality of peace officer personnel records shall not apply to investigations or proceedings concerning the conduct of peace officers conducted by a grand jury. Additionally, the grand jury does not seek records pursuant to the authority of the Public Records Act, that is, as a member of the general public; instead, it acts pursuant to the express statutory authority afforded to grand juries by Penal Code sections 925 and 925a. *City of Woodlake v. Tulare County Grand Jury* (2011) 197 Cal. App. 4th 1293, 129 Cal. Rptr. 3d 241.

The *Pitchess* statutes apply to more than criminal proceedings in the court of trial jurisdiction. The statutes also apply to proceedings before a magistrate on a felony complaint.

§ 10:5.4 Preliminary examinations

A defendant charged by felony complaint may file a *Pitchess* motion prior to the time of the preliminary examination. However, the making of a *Pitchess* motion does not necessarily constitute good cause to justify a continuance of the preliminary examination, if the prosecution objects to a continuance.

In *Galindo v. Superior Court* (2010) 50 Cal.4th 1, 112 Cal.Rptr.3d 673, 235 P.3d 1, a defendant charged by felony complaint with threatening and resisting an arresting officer in the performance of his duties filed a *Pitchess* motion as to the personnel records of five police officers who had been present at his arrest. The magistrate denied the motion on the grounds that *Pitchess* discovery was not as a matter of course available for use at a preliminary hearing, and because the defendant had not shown that obtaining the discovery would yield anything that would change the outcome of the preliminary examination.

The defendant's petition for writ of mandate was denied by the superior court and the Court of Appeal. The Supreme Court granted the defendant's petition for review.

The Supreme Court affirmed the denial by the Court of Appeal of the defendant's petition for writ of mandate. The Court held that "although a defendant may file a *Pitchess* motion before a preliminary hearing, the pendency of that motion will not necessarily or invariably constitute good cause for postponing the preliminary hearing over the prosecution's objection." 50 Cal.4th at 5–6.

In reaching this decision the Supreme Court concluded that "[i]t is highly unlikely that the testimony of *Pitchess* witnesses at the preliminary hearing would defeat a finding that there was probable cause to believe that the defendant 'committed a felony and should be held for trial.' [citations omitted]" 50 Cal.4th at 10. The Court further held that denial of the defendant's *Pitchess* motion would not prevent the defendant from receiving effective assistance of counsel at the preliminary hearing. 50 Cal.4th at 10.

Thus, while a defendant may make a *Pitchess* motion prior to a preliminary examination, and if the defendant's motion is granted and he or she obtains information that leads to evidence favorable to the defendant, the defendant may use that evidence at the preliminary examination, the defendant is not necessarily entitled to a continuance or a postponement of the preliminary hearing in order for the defense to gather evidence arising out of the fruits of a successful *Pitchess* motion.

§ 10:6   Motion to disclose records—personnel records defined and covered

One common mistake made by litigants is the assumption that the location of a document, rather than its content or nature, determines whether the document is a personnel record. It is the nature or content of a document, not the place that it is kept, that determines whether it is a personnel record of a peace officer.

Thus, peace officer personnel records include only the types of information that are enumerated in Penal Code section 832.8. *Commission on Peace Officer Standards & Training v. Superior Court* (2007) 42 Cal.4th 278, 293, 64 Cal.Rptr.3d 661, 165 P.3d 462; *Zanone v. City of Whittier* (2008) 162 Cal.App.4th 174, 187–188, 75 Cal.Rptr.3d 439. Information or a document that is physically located in a peace officer's personnel file is not a personnel record protected by the *Pitchess* statutes if that information or document is not one of the items enumerated in Penal Code section 832.8. *Commission on Peace Officer Standards & Training v. Superior Court, supra,* 42 Cal.4th at 293; *Zanone v. City of Whittier, supra,* 162 Cal.App.4th at 188.

Likewise, documents and information enumerated in Section 832.8 as personnel records retain that status even though they are found in the records of proceedings related to an officer's employment, such as proceedings of a civil service commission and a police review commission. *See Copley Press, Inc. v. Superior Court* (2006) 39 Cal.4th 1272, 48 Cal.Rptr.3d 183, 141 P.3d 288; and *Berkeley Police Assn. v. City of Berkeley* (2008) 167 Cal.App.4th 385, 84 Cal.Rptr.3d 130.

Moreover, although personnel records include information relating to the investigation of a complaint, only those complaints or investigations of complaints that also pertain to the manner in which the officer performed his or her duties are included as personnel records in Penal Code section 832.8. *Zanone v. City of Whittier, supra,* 162 Cal.App.4th at 188–189.

§ 10:6.1 Internal affairs investigation files

Internal affairs investigations are "investigations of complaints" covered by California Evidence Code section 1045. *Doyle v. Gonzales* (E.D. Cal. Sept. 6, 2011) 2011 U.S. Dist. LEXIS 100639.

§ 10:6.2 Information obtained from personnel records

A defendant has a limited right to discovery of a peace officer's confidential personnel records if those files contain information that is potentially relevant to the defense. To initiate discovery, a defendant must file a motion seeking such records, containing affidavits showing good cause for the discovery or disclosure sought, setting forth the materiality thereof to the subject matter involved in the pending litigation. Good cause requires the defendant to establish a logical link between a proposed defense and the pending charge and to articulate how the discovery would support such a defense or how it would impeach the officer's version of events. The threshold for establishing good cause is relatively low. The proposed defense must have a plausible factual foundation supported by the defendant's counsel's declaration and other documents supporting the motion. A plausible scenario is one that might or could have occurred. The defendant must also show how the information sought could lead to or be evidence potentially admissible at trial. Once that burden is met, the defendant has shown materiality under Evidence Code section 1043. *Sisson v. Superior*

Court (2013) 216 Cal. App. 4th 24, 156 Cal. Rptr. 3d 533.

§ 10:6.3   Misconduct impeaching peace officer witness

Reliable evidence of a law enforcement officer's misconduct in unrelated cases is admissible to impeach that officer's credibility, particularly where credibility is the central issue in the case and the evidence presented at trial consists of opposing stories presented by the defendant and government agents. *Milke v. Ryan* (2013, CA9 Ariz.) 711 F.3d 998.

§ 10:7   Motion procedures—notice of motion requirements

On a showing of good cause, a criminal defendant is entitled to discovery of relevant documents or information in the confidential personnel records of a peace officer accused of misconduct against the defendant. Evidence Code section 1043, subsection (b). The good cause requirement embodies a relatively low threshold for discovery, under which a defendant need demonstrate only a logical link between the defense proposed and the pending charge and describe with some specificity how the discovery being sought would support such a defense or how it would impeach the officer's version of events. Once good cause is established, the trial court conducts an in camera review to determine which, if any, pieces of information contained in the personal records of the officer are relevant and, therefore, subject to disclosure to the defense. Evidence Code section 1045, subsection (b). *Blumberg v. Superior Court* (2011) 197 Cal. App. 4th 1245, 129 Cal. Rptr. 3d 716.

A showing of good cause for discovery of an officer's personnel file under Evidence Code section 1043, subsection (b), exists if the defendant demonstrates both (1) a specific factual scenario that establishes a plausible factual foundation for the allegations of officer misconduct; and (2) that the misconduct would (if credited) be material to the defense. Accordingly, defense counsel's supporting declaration must propose a defense and articulate how the requested discovery may be admissible as direct or impeachment evidence in support of the proposed defense, or how the requested discovery may lead to such evidence. Thus, a defendant meets the materiality element by showing (1) a logical connection between the charges and the proposed defense; (2) the requested discovery is factually specific and tailored to support the claim of officer misconduct; (3) the requested discovery supports the proposed defense or is likely to lead to information that will do so; and (4) the requested discovery is potentially admissible at trial. *Rezek v. Superior Court* (2012) 206 Cal. App. 4th 633, 141 Cal. Rptr. 3d 891.

Because intrusion into a peace officer's personnel records constitutes an invasion of the officer's privacy, courts have tended to require strict compliance with the mandatory procedures established by the *Pitchess* statutes as a precondition to granting access to those records.

§ 10:7.1 Notice requirements for supplemental *Pitchess* motion

A defendant who has made a successful *Pitchess* motion and has received information from a peace officer's personnel records pursuant to that motion, and who then seeks a supplemental hearing to receive additional information from the officer's personnel records, must comply with the same notice requirements of Evidence Code section 1043 and Code of Civil Procedure section 1005 that apply to all *Pitchess* motions. *City of Tulare v. Superior Court* (2008) 169 Cal.App.4th 373, 86 Cal.Rptr.3d 707. In *City of Tulare v. Superior Court*, the Court of Appeal stated: "We fail to see how the second disclosure should not be subject to the safeguards of a properly noticed motion . . . A properly noticed motion . . . allows a sufficient time for the law enforcement agency and its officers to challenge and scrutinize the adequacy of the motion in question." 169 Cal.App.4th at 383.

See also Rezek v. Superior Court (2012) 206 Cal. App. 4th 633, 141 Cal. Rptr. 3d 891, holding, *inter alia*, that *Pitchess* motions traditionally seek information about past complaints by third parties of excessive force, violence, dishonesty, or the filing of false police reports contained in the officer's personnel file. Thus, once a defendant has made the relatively low threshold showing of good cause and the court has reviewed the pertinent documents in camera, the court releases the contact information of the third party complainant and potential witnesses to the past alleged misconduct. On those occasions when that information proves insufficient, either because a witness does not remember the earlier events or the witness cannot be located, a supplemental *Pitchess* motion may be filed and the statements of the witnesses may be disclosed to the defendant. *Id.*

§ 10:7.2 Motion procedures—police report attached to motion

Evidence Code section 1043 does not explicitly provide that the police report must be attached to a *Pitchess* motion. However, one Court of Appeal has observed that "in our review of the *Pitchess* case law, which has been substantial, we have found no published case where it was not attached." *People v. Sanderson* (2010) 181 Cal.App.4th 1334, 1338, n.5, 105 Cal.Rptr.3d 326. In Sanderson, the Court of Appeal commented that the defendant's failure to attach a copy of the police report to the motion had been cured by the trial court's judicial notice of the officer's testimony at the preliminary examination. 181 Cal.App.4th at 1339, n.6.

Thus, even though the *Pitchess* statutes do not expressly require that the police report be attached to the *Pitchess* motion, in order to obviate one possible ground for denial of the motion, counsel should always attach a copy of the police report to the motion.

§ 10:8 Sealed *Pitchess* motion or declaration

Under certain circumstances, the district court may conduct an in camera inspection of alleged confidential communications to determine whether the attorney-client privilege applies to specific documents. The privilege extends to cover the substance of the client's confidential communications and the attorney's advice in response thereto. Because the attorney-client privilege has the effect of withholding relevant information from the factfinder, it is applied only when necessary to achieve its limited purpose of encouraging full and frank disclosure by the client to his or her attorney. The court has said repeatedly that fee information generally is not privileged. Payment of fees is incidental to the attorney-client relationship, and does not usually involve disclosure of confidential communications arising from the professional relationship. *Gjerde v. United States* (E.D. Cal. Aug. 13, 2012) 2012 U.S. Dist. LEXIS 114689.

§ 10:8.2 Agency attorney access to sealed *Pitchess* motion/declaration

Under certain circumstances, the district court may conduct an in camera inspection of alleged confidential communications to determine whether the attorney-client privilege applies to specific documents. The privilege extends to cover the substance of the client's confidential communications and the attorney's advice in response thereto. Because the attorney-client privilege has the effect of withholding relevant information from the factfinder, it is applied only when necessary to achieve its limited purpose of encouraging full and frank disclosure by the client to his or her attorney. The court has said repeatedly that fee information generally is not privileged. Payment of fees is incidental to the attorney-client relationship, and does not usually involve disclosure of confidential communications arising from the professional relationship. *Gjerde v. United States* (E.D. Cal. Aug. 13, 2012) 2012 U.S. Dist. LEXIS 114689.

§ 10:9. Good cause showing by moving party—components

In order for a party to gain access to information in the personnel records of a peace officer, the party must prove that there is good cause for that access. If the moving party fails to establish good cause, the court's inquiry need go no further.

In a case of assault and provocative act murder, specific factual assertions that police officers had lied about whether other officers identified themselves while trying to apprehend defendant provided good cause supporting defense motions under Evidence Code section 1043 and Penal Code section 832.5 for discovery of complaints in peace officer personnel files about dishonesty or false reporting. Excessive force complaints were irrelevant, however, because the provocative act murder doctrine does not require that the use of force be reasonable; moreover, as to the assault charges, defendant provided no supporting authority. *Sisson v. Superior Court* (2013) 216 Cal. App. 4th 24, 156 Cal. Rptr. 3d 533.

§ 10:9.1 Evidentiary "materiality"

In *United States v. Williams* (2009, CA10 OK) 576 F.3d 1149, a defendant who sought access to Internal Affairs files pertaining to the police officer who had obtained a warrant to search his home, who had recovered drugs from his home, and who had obtained his confession to selling drugs from his home. The defendant alleged that the requested internal affairs files would show that the officer had been disciplined by his police agency. One of the files involved the officer's purported violation of a police department regulation against making an arrest in the officer's own personal quarrel with another person. The second file involved an alleged failure to include information in a search warrant affidavit. 576 F.3d at 1154–1155.

After his motion for access to the Internal Affairs files was denied, the defendant was convicted. On appeal he argued that the failure to produce the officer's Internal Affairs files constituted a *Brady* violation. The Court of Appeals rejected the defendant's argument, holding that the defendant failed to make a plausible showing that any information contained in the officer's Internal Affairs files related to the defendant's case. 576 F.3d at 1163.

§ 10:9.2 Specific factual scenario

A showing of good cause for discovery of an officer's personnel file under Evidence Code section 1043, subsection (b), exists if the defendant demonstrates both (1) a specific factual scenario that establishes a plausible factual foundation for the allegations of officer misconduct; and (2) that the misconduct would (if credited) be material to the defense. *Rezek v. Superior Court* (2012) 206 Cal. App. 4th 633, 141 Cal. Rptr. 3d 891.

A defendant who seeks access to information from the personnel records of a California peace officer is entitled to have the court conduct an *in camera* review of those records when the defendant presents a specific factual scenario of officer misconduct that is plausible when read in light of pertinent documents, and "the defendant need not point to any corroboration for the defendant's account" of that specific factual scenario. *Uybungco v. Superior Court* (2008) 163 Cal.App.4th 1043, 1049, 78 Cal.Rptr.3d 30.

In *Uybungco v. Superior Court* a defendant charged with resisting a peace officer and vandalism made a *Pitchess* motion seeking information from the personnel records of the officers who had arrested him. The defendant's motion sought access to obtain evidence that the officers had written dishonest police reports. In support of this motion, the defendant submitted a sworn declaration that he did not resist the police and that the statements in the police reports about his conduct were false. The trial court agreed to conduct an *in camera* review of two of the four officers' personnel records for evidence of dishonesty in their report writing.

The defendant petitioned a series of courts for writ of mandate. Ultimately, the Supreme Court granted the petition and transferred the petition to the Court of Appeal with directions to issue a show-cause order on the petition. The Court of Appeal concluded that the trial court had erred in failing to conduct an *in camera* examination of all four officers' personnel records for evidence of dishonest report-writing. The Court held that the defendant's sworn declaration "was sufficient to compel the trial court to conduct an *in camera* review of each of the four officers' personnel files for information that they previously had included false information in a police report." 163 Cal.App.4th at 1050.

The Court concluded that a fair comparison of the defendant's declaration with the police reports revealed "a clear allegation of police misconduct and false accusation which, if believed, would strongly support a defense to the charged offenses—in short, the very essence of the 'low threshold' showing required to trigger in camera *Pitchess* review." 163 Cal.App.4th at 1050.

In order for the defendant to meet the "specific factual scenario" requirement, the defendant must make a greater showing than simply denying the truth of an officer's report. The defendant must also present an "alternative, specific factual scenario" that is plausible.

In *People v. Sanderson* (2010) 181 Cal.App.4th 1334, 105 Cal.Rptr.3d 326, a defendant charged with making criminal threats made a *Pitchess* motion for the personnel records of two peace officers. The charges arose out of a domestic dispute in which the two officers had been called to the victims' home, and while there heard on a loudspeaker attached to the victims' telephone the defendant threaten to kill the victims. In his *Pitchess* motion the defendant denied making the threatening statements to which the officers had testified. The motion averred that the officers falsified information in their police report and requested that the court order disclosure of records of dishonesty and fabrication by the officers in order to enable the defendant to disprove that the defendant made the statements on the telephone which formed the basis of the charges against him.

The trial court denied the *Pitchess* motion without conducting an *in camera* review of the officers' personnel records. The defendant was convicted of the charges at jury trial and appealed his conviction. On appeal the defendant argued that the trial court erred in failing to grant his *Pitchess* motion. The Court of Appeal rejected the defendant's argument, concluding that the trial court "could reasonably conclude that defendant failed to demonstrate sufficient good cause" by not presenting 'a specific factual scenario that is plausible when read in light of the . . . undisputed circumstances.' [citation omitted]" 181 Cal.App.4th at 1340.

The Court of Appeal concluded that the defendant's shortcoming was that he did not present an "alternative, specific factual scenario" to the story about which the officer wrote in his report and to which he testified. 181 Cal.App.4th at 1342. Thus, held the Court of Appeal, a defendant who does nothing more than "merely denying the elements of the charge against him," does not establish a specific factual scenario. 181 Cal.App.4th at 1342. Accordingly, the defendant failed to establish good cause for the court to conduct an *in camera* review of the officer's personnel records or to order any information from those records to be disclosed.

In *Eulloqui v. Superior Court* (2010) 181 Cal.App.4th 1055, 105

Cal.Rptr.3d 248, a habeas petitioner filed a discovery motion seeking access to the personnel records of the police detective who had testified as a prosecution witness at the defendant's trial. The habeas petitioner's motion was made under authority of both *Brady v. Maryland* and *Pitchess*. The court hearing the habeas petition denied the motion without reviewing the officer's personnel records in an *in camera* proceeding.

The habeas petitioner petitioned the Court of Appeal for writ of mandate challenging the denial of his discovery motion. The Court of Appeal issued a peremptory writ commanding the trial court to issue an order granting the motion with respect to one subject—whether the officer failed to report to his supervisor payments or other incentives given to informants. The Court of Appeal's order was based on the Court's determination that failure to disclose that information violated *Brady*. The Court otherwise affirmed the trial court's denial of the discovery motion.

In reaching this decision the Court affirmed a number of principles relating to discovery of peace officer personnel records. First, corroboration of officer misconduct is not required to satisfy the requirements of a *Pitchess* motion. 181 Cal.App.4th at 1064. Second, "[m]aterials from an officer's personnel file reflecting dishonesty or nonfelony acts of moral turpitude do not become discoverable simply because a defendant argues that the officer will testify and might testify falsely." 181 Cal.App.4th at 1064. An allegation that " 'the officer lied and will do so again' " does not constitute a plausible factual scenario of officer misconduct. If such an allegation were to constitute a plausible factual scenario of officer misconduct warranting review of confidential personnel records, that would "abrogate the strong ring of protection the Legislature and courts have erected around peace officer personnel records. [citation omitted]" 181 Cal.App.4th at 1069.

Third, if evidence from an officer's personnel records is material under *Brady,* " the statutory restrictions pertaining to the *Pitchess* procedure are inapplicable [citation omitted], but if the defendant only shows materiality under the less stringent *Pitchess* standard, the statutory limitations apply." 181 Cal.App.4th at 1065. Thus, the five-year limitation on disclosure of complaints found in Evidence Code section 1045 does not apply to disclosures of exculpatory evidence under the compulsion of the *Brady* rule.

In *People v. Moreno* (2011) 192 Cal.App.4th 692, 121 Cal.Rptr.3d 669, a defendant charged with the murder of a former probation officer at a sober living house moved for disclosure of information from the victim's personnel records from when she was a probation officer. The specific factual scenario offered by the defendant was that he defended himself against the victim officer's excessive and unwarranted force, which included the officer's acts of threatening the defendant and pushing her hand against the defendant's chest. The defendant asserted that materials in the officer's personnel records might consist of complaints against the victim for engaging in excessive and illegal force, drug abuse, and aggressive actions while under the influence of controlled substances.

The trial court denied the motion without conducting an *in camera* review of the victim's personnel records. On appeal of his conviction for murder, the defendant argued that the trial court erred in failing to conduct an *in camera* review of the personnel records. The Court of Appeal agreed with the defendant, finding that "[b]ased upon the documents submitted in support of the motion, the aggression described by counsel might have occurred. If it did, the actions could support arguments that defendant did not plan or premeditate the killing of [the victim] and that he acted in pure or imperfect self-defense. Evidence, including material in [the victim's] personnel file, indicating that [the victim] had a propensity for violence or aggressive behavior is potentially relevant to such defenses. [citation omitted] Therefore, defendant satisfied the low threshold required to obtain an in camera review of discoverable material." 192 Cal.App.4th at 702.

§ 10:9.3   Plausible factual foundation

The threshold for establishing good cause is relatively low. The proposed defense must have a plausible factual foundation supported by the defendant's counsel's declaration and other documents supporting the motion. A plausible scenario is one that might or could have occurred. The defendant must also show how the information sought could lead to or be evidence potentially admissible at trial. Once that burden is met, the defendant has shown materiality under Evidence Code section 1043. *Sisson v. Superior Court* (2013) 216 Cal. App. 4th 24, 156 Cal. Rptr. 3d 533. *See also Rezek v. Superior Court* (2012) 206 Cal. App. 4th 633, 141 Cal. Rptr. 3d 891.

A party moving for disclosure of information from the personnel records of a peace officer must establish a specific factual scenario that is plausible. Establishing a plausible specific factual scenario requires that the defendant make a greater showing in his or her *Pitchess* motion than simply denying the officer's version of events. The moving party must present a version of the events that is an alternative to the officer's version.

In *People v. Sanderson* (2010) 181 Cal.App.4th 1334, 105 Cal.Rptr.3d 326, a defendant charged with making criminal threats made a *Pitchess* motion for the personnel records of two peace officers. The charges arose out of a domestic dispute in which the two officers had been called to the victims' home, and while there heard on a loudspeaker attached to the victims' telephone the defendant threaten to kill the victims. In his *Pitchess* motion the defendant denied making the threatening statements to which the officers had testified. The motion averred that the officers falsified information in their police report and requested that the court order disclosure of records of dishonesty and fabrication by the officers in order to enable the defendant to disprove that the defendant made the statements on the telephone which formed the basis of the charges against him.

The trial court denied the *Pitchess* motion without conducting an *in camera* review of the officers' personnel records. The defendant was convicted of the charges at jury trial and appealed his conviction. On appeal the defendant argued that the trial court erred in failing to grant his *Pitchess* motion. The Court of Appeal rejected the defendant's argument, concluding that the trial court "could reasonably conclude that defendant failed to demonstrate sufficient good cause" by not presenting 'a specific factual scenario that is plausible when read in light of the . . . undisputed circumstances.' [citation omitted]" 181 Cal.App.4th at 1340.

The Court of Appeal concluded that defendant's shortcoming was that he did not present an "alternative, specific factual scenario" to the scenario about which the officer wrote in his report and to which he testified. 181 Cal.App.4th at 1342. Thus, held the Court of Appeal, a defendant who does nothing more than "merely denying the elements of the charge against him," does not establish a specific factual scenario. 181 Cal.App.4th at 1342.

Because the defendant did not present an alternative specific factual scenario, the defendant failed to establish that his version of the events was "plausible." Accordingly, the defendant failed to establish good cause for the court to conduct an *in camera* review of the officer's personnel records or to order any information from those records to be disclosed.

The *Sanderson* Court emphasized that the defendant's alternative specific factual scenario need not be corroborated for the scenario to be "plausible." Nor need the defendant's alternative specific factual scenario show a motivation for the officer's misconduct. Moreover, the Court of Appeal noted, establishing a "plausible scenario" does not require that the trial court assess or weigh the persuasive value of the evidence. 181 Cal.App.4th at 1340.

In determining whether a defendant meets the requirement of articulating a specific factual scenario that is plausible, the trial court may determine whether the defense-proposed scenario is internally consistent. A defendant who presents a proposed factual scenario that conflicts with the defendant's own description of the event to the police, a description reported by the officer in his report that the defendant does not challenge, does not meet this requirement. *People v. Galan* (2009) 178 Cal.App.4th 6, 13, 100 Cal.Rptr.3d 103.

Moreover, the defense-proposed scenario must support the defense proposed to the charges. Thus, where a defendant's proposed scenario of police misconduct does not support the defendant's defense, the court is entitled to " 'apply common sense in determining what is plausible, and to make determinations based on a reasonable and realistic assessment of the facts and allegations.' [citation omitted]" 178 Cal.App.4th at 13. In *People v. Galan*, the defendant's proposed scenario that the officers fabricated their need to take evasive action to avoid being struck by the defendant's vehicle did not comport with a reasonable and realistic assessment of the facts. "No reasonable person with this goal in mind [escaping the police] would twice stop, shift into reverse, and back his vehicle toward pursuing police officers." 178 Cal.App.4th at 13.

§ 10:9.4   Meaning of "the pending litigation" requirement

A defendant who makes a *Pitchess* motion must submit an affidavit in support of the motion that "set[s] forth the materiality [of the requested personnel records] to the subject matter involved in the pending litigation . . . ." Evidence Code section 1043, subdivision (b)(3).

It is critical to note that California Evidence Code section 1045 strikes the state balance in favor of disclosing internal investigations pertaining to the manner in which a peace officer performed his or her duties, so long as they are relevant to pending litigation. *Doyle v. Gonzales* (E.D. Cal. Sept. 6, 2011) 2011 U.S. Dist. LEXIS 100639. *See also Sisson v. Superior Court* (2013) 216 Cal. App. 4th 24, 156 Cal. Rptr. 3d 533; *Rezek v. Superior Court* (2012) 206 Cal. App. 4th 633, 141 Cal. Rptr. 3d 891.

A defendant is entitled to discovery of relevant information from the confidential records upon a showing of good cause, which exists when the defendant shows both materiality to the subject matter of the pending litigation and a reasonable belief that the agency has the type of information sought. *People v. Yearwood* (2013) 213 Cal. App. 4th 161, 151 Cal. Rptr. 3d 901.

When a defendant makes a post-trial *Pitchess* motion in support of a new-trial motion, the *pending litigation* is the new-trial motion, not the underlying criminal prosecution. *People v. Nguyen* (2007) 151 Cal.App.4th 1473, 60 Cal.Rptr.3d 773. Thus, in *People v. Nguyen* the Court of Appeal held that the trial court did not err in denying the defendant's *Pitchess* motion, because the pending litigation to which the *Pitchess* motion related was the defendant's ineffective assistance of counsel claim that formed the basis for his new-trial motion. The Court of Appeal rejected the defendant's argument that the requested personnel records should have been disclosed, because they were material to his trial defense. Because the defendant had already been convicted, the *pending litigation* was his new-trial motion, and the officers' personnel records were not material to the new-trial motion.

For a similar holding, see *Hurd v. Superior Court* (2006) 144 Cal.App.4th 1100, 50 Cal.Rptr.3d 893, discussed in Section 10:5.3 of the text, in which the Court of Appeal held that a defendant making a post-trial *Pitchess* motion in support of a habeas petition must show that the information sought by the *Pitchess* motion is material to the habeas petition.

§ 10:11   Judicial review of personnel records—generally

When a court determines that the disclosure of a peace officer's personnel records is compelled by due process of law under *Brady*, the restrictions and limitations on disclosure found in the *Pitchess* statutes do not apply. *Eulloqui v. Superior Court* (2010) 181 Cal.App.4th 1055, 1065, 105 Cal.Rptr.3d 248.

§ 10:11.1   Exclusion of old information (five year rule)

The proviso of California Evidence Code section 1045 that information will be deemed per se irrelevant if it includes complaints concerning conduct occurring more than five years before the event or transaction which is the subject of the litigation, too rigid to comport with federal law, in which "remoteness" is a matter generally weighed in determining the relevance of particular information. The overall balancing provisions contained within Fed. R. Civ. P. 26(b) dictate that the court must carefully assess the request for discovery in light of the remoteness of sought discovery to the issues in the case. *Doyle v. Gonzales* (E.D. Cal. Sept. 6, 2011) 2011 U.S. Dist. LEXIS 100639.

Although Evidence Code section 1045(b)(1) provides that a court may not order disclosure of information about complaints made more than five years prior to the event that is the subject of the criminal litigation, this limitation does not apply to citizen complaints made after the defendant's arrest. "[T]he only time-based rule of exclusion provided by the Legislature is that the court may not order disclosure of information in complaints made more than five years prior to the event that is the subject of the criminal litigation. [citation omitted] However, this limitation does not apply to complaints that postdate the arrest at issue." *Blumberg v. Superior Court* (2011) 197 Cal.App.4th 1245, 1249, 129 Cal.Rptr.3d 716.

§ 10:13   *In camera* judicial review procedures

An appellate court routinely independently examines the sealed records of in camera hearings to determine whether the trial court abused its discretion in denying a defendant's motion for disclosure of police personnel records. *People v. Myles* (2012) 53 Cal. 4th 1181, 139 Cal. Rptr. 3d 786, 274 P.3d 413.

Any witness, including a custodian of records, who testifies in an *in camera* proceeding, must be placed under oath. *People v. Mooc* (2001) 26 Cal.4th 1216, 1230 n.4, 114 Cal.Rptr.2d 482, 36 P.3d 21. The requirement that the witness be placed under oath is intended to protect the defendant's right to a fair trial. When a witness who presents personnel records in an *in camera* proceeding pursuant to the *Pitchess* statutes is not placed under oath, the records produced and the statements made by that witness relating to those records are not evidence that an appellate court may consider. The failure compels the appellate court to reverse a judgment of conviction. *People v. White* (2011) 191 Cal.App.4th 1333, 120 Cal.Rptr.3d 332.

§ 10:14   *In camera* good cause determination—five factors

If the prosecution isn't sure whether material in a personnel file rises to the *Brady* threshold, it may submit the information to the trial court for an in camera inspection. A prosecutor anxious about tacking too close to the wind will disclose a favorable piece of evidence. *Milke v. Ryan* (2013, CA9 Ariz.) 711 F.3d 998. In camera review is not necessary where the defendant fails to make the initial showing that the official information privilege applies. *Dowell v. Griffin* (S.D. Cal. 2011) 275 F.R.D. 613.

If a defendant establishes good cause for discovery of a peace officer's confidential personnel records, the court must review the requested records in camera to determine what information, if any, should be disclosed. Subject to certain statutory exceptions and limitations, the trial court should then disclose to the defendant such information that is relevant to the subject matter involved in the pending litigation. *Sisson v. Superior Court* (2013) 216 Cal. App. 4th 24, 156 Cal. Rptr. 3d 533.

See also People v. Lockwood (2013) 214 Cal. App. 4th 91, 153 Cal. Rptr. 3d 663, holding, *inter alia*, that the presumption created by Penal Code section 1202.4, subsection (f)(4)(A), affects the burden of proof. However, a defendant is entitled to release of the California Victim Compensation and Government Claims Board's records, regardless of the nature of the presumption, if (1) the defendant offers evidence to rebut the presumption and (2) the trial court determines after an in camera review of the records that the records are relevant to the dispute.

§ 10:14.1   Unavailability factor

The federal "qualified" governmental privilege is consistent with California statutes according a qualified privilege to peace officer personnel records. California Penal Code section 832.7. Disclosure requires "good cause" (California Evidence Code section 1043), relevance, and unavailability by other means (California Evidence Code section 1045). *Doyle v. Gonzales* (E.D. Cal. Sept. 6, 2011) 2011 U.S. Dist. LEXIS 100639.

§ 10:14.4   Relevance factor

Disclosure requires "good cause" (California Evidence Code section 1043), relevance, and unavailability by other means (California Evidence Code section 1045). *Doyle v. Gonzales* (E.D. Cal. Sept. 6, 2011) 2011 U.S. Dist. LEXIS 100639.

§ 10:15   Balancing good cause against other factors

An in camera review is not necessary where the defendant fails to make the initial showing that the official information privilege applies. *Dowell v. Griffin* (S.D. Cal. 2011) 275 F.R.D. 613.

If a defendant establishes good cause for discovery of a peace officer's confidential personnel records, the court must review the requested records in camera to determine what information, if any, should be disclosed. Subject to certain statutory exceptions and limitations, the trial court should then disclose to the defendant such information that is relevant to the subject matter involved in the pending litigation. *Sisson v. Superior Court* (2013) 216 Cal. App. 4th 24, 156 Cal. Rptr. 3d 533.

At the *in camera* hearing the court must consider whether disclosure of the personnel records meets the five factors discussed in Sections 10:14.1—

10:14.5.2 of this text—that is, (1) whether the information sought is unavailable from sources other than the personnel records; (2) whether the information sought is reasonably accessible from the personnel records; (3) whether the information sought is described specifically; (4) whether the information sought is relevant to the case; and (5) whether disclosure requested is limited to information that is necessary for the defendant to make legitimate use of the information.

Once a defendant has established good cause for disclosure of information from a peace officer's personnel records, the court must determine what information is to be released.

§ 10:15.1 Information subject to disclosure

After a court has determined that the defendant has established good cause for disclosure of information from an officer's personnel records, and has completed its examination of the personnel records in an *in camera* proceeding, the normal order is to disclose the "names, addresses, and telephone numbers of individuals who have in the past witnessed alleged officer misconduct or who have complained of misconduct by the officer named in the motion." *Galindo v. Superior Court* (2010) 50 Cal.4th 1, 5, 112 Cal.Rptr.3d 673, 235 P.3d 1.

§ 10:16 Protective orders

Because of the sensitive nature of peace officer personnel records, the court's determination of appropriate and reasonable protective orders accompanying the disclosure of information from the personnel records is an important component of the trial court's decision-making on a *Pitchess* discovery motion.

§ 10:16.1 Protective orders and derivative information

The court can issue all appropriate protective orders against improper use, both direct and derivative, of evidence derived from the examinations. *Maldonado v. Superior Court* (2012) 53 Cal. 4th 1112, 140 Cal. Rptr. 3d 113, 274 P.3d 1110.

Evidence Code section 1045, subdivision (e), requires a trial court granting a *Pitchess* motion to impose a protective order covering the information released to the party moving for disclosure of the personnel records information. The protective order shall provide that the "records disclosed or discovered may not be used for any purpose other than a court proceeding pursuant to applicable law." Evidence Code section 1045, subdivision (e).

When a defendant has received "complainant information" (name, address, and telephone number of any prior complainants and witnesses, and the dates of the incidents) from the personnel records of a peace officer pursuant to a *Pitchess* motion, and that information has been made subject to a statutorily required protective order, the question has arisen whether information derived from the complainant information ("derivative information") may be used in a different case without violating the protective order.

In *Chambers v. Superior Court* (2007) 42 Cal.4th 673, 68 Cal.Rptr.3d 43, 170 P.3d 617, a defendant charged with resisting an officer filed a *Pitchess* motion to discover information from his arresting officer's personnel records, claiming that the officer used unnecessary force and had lied about the event resulting in the defendant's arrest. The trial court examined the officer's personnel records and found no relevant information to disclose. Eight months later the defendant filed a supplemental *Pitchess* motion. The defendant's attorney had learned of complainant information from the officer's personnel records in her representation of another defendant and had developed independent information derived from the disclosed information. The information in the other case was covered by a protective order.

The trial court denied the supplemental *Pitchess* motion and denied the defendant's request that the court reconsider his original motion. The Court of Appeal granted writ relief to the defendant, holding that the information disclosed in the other case should be disclosed to the defendant subject to a protective order. The Court of Appeal further held that that the defendant's attorney could use the derivative information developed in the other case without violating the protective order. The officer's employing law enforcement agency petitioned the California Supreme Court for review.

The Supreme Court held that an attorney who obtains derivative information from a successful *Pitchess* motion in one case may not use that information in other cases in which that attorney is counsel. The reason for this rule is that using derivative information developed in the first case "would reveal complainant information from the officer's record that is subject to the section 1045(e) protective order under which the disclosure was made in [the first defendant's] case." 42 Cal.4th at 681.

However, the Court held that "when complainant information has been ordered disclosed to counsel who, when later representing a different defendant, succeeds under *Pitchess* in discovering the same complainant information relating to the same officer, counsel may then refer to the derivative information uncovered as part of the earlier followup investigation." 42 Cal.4th at 681.

Thus, a defense attorney may use derivative information generated in one case in a second case only when the attorney makes a successful *Pitchess* motion in the second case.

PART II. PROSECUTOR ACCESS TO PERSONNEL RECORDS

§ 10:19 Prosecutor access to California personnel records for *Brady* evidence

However, the government has a *Brady* obligation to produce any favorable evidence in the personnel records of an officer. *Milke v. Ryan* (2013, CA9 Ariz.) 711 F.3d 998.

The federal privilege applicable to the government interest in preserving confidentiality of law enforcement records has various names: (1) the "official information privilege"; (2) the "law enforcement privilege"; and (3) a type of "executive privilege." The federal privileges are based on the following rationale: The purpose of this privilege is to prevent disclosure of law enforcement techniques and procedures, to preserve the confidentiality of sources, to protect witness and law enforcement personnel, to safeguard the privacy of individuals involved in an investigation, and otherwise to prevent interference with an investigation. This federal "qualified" governmental privilege is consistent with California statutes according a qualified privilege to peace officer personnel records. California Penal Code section 832.7. Disclosure requires "good cause" (California Evidence Code section 1043), relevance, and unavailability by other means (California Evidence Code section 1045). *Doyle v. Gonzales* (E.D. Cal. Sept. 6, 2011) 2011 U.S. Dist. LEXIS 100639.

A defendant is entitled to discover from the prosecution the relevant statements of witnesses. Penal Code section 1054.1. The discovery provided in § 1054.1, however, is not exclusive. The reciprocal discovery chapter places no restriction on discovery provided by other express statutory provisions, or as mandated by the Constitution of the United States. Penal Code section 1054, subsection (e). Evidence Code section 1043, is one such express statutory provision. Just as the discovery procedure set forth in § 1043 *et seq.* operates in tandem with the prosecution's duty to disclose favorable information pursuant to the *Brady* rule, so too does the California Evidence Code discovery procedure work in tandem with the prosecution's duty to disclose relevant statements of witnesses under Penal Code section 1054.1, subsection (f). Except with regard to one exception, the prosecutor, as well as the defendant, must comply with the statutory *Pitchess* requirements for disclosure of information contained in confidential peace officer records. There is no reason why the defense—when it has good reason to believe an officer's personnel file contains relevant statements from material witnesses to the charged incident—should be precluded from obtaining the statements because the district attorney may have the right to obtain the same information by filing a motion for discovery pursuant to § 1043. *Rezek v. Superior Court* (2012) 206 Cal. App. 4th 633, 141 Cal. Rptr. 3d 891.

ERRATA: The paragraph on page 957 of the text that begins with the words "This intriguing statement" contains a typographical error in which the word "officer" is incorrectly spelled "offer." The paragraph should read as follows:

This intriguing statement, which appeared unnecessary to the court's opinion in *Brandon* because that issue was not presented in *Brandon*, was worded in a manner that implied that the prosecutor already has the right to access peace officer personnel records for *Brady* purposes. The use of the language "right of the prosecutor to obtain access to officer personnel records" suggested that the Supreme Court had already decided that this right exists, and the open question in *Brandon* was whether Section 832.7 would be constitutional if it were construed to negate the prosecutor's already established right to access those records for *Brady* purposes.

§ 10:20　Prosecutor's duty and right to search personnel records—generally

The government (i.e. prosecutor) has a *Brady* obligation to produce any favorable evidence in the personnel records of an officer. *Milke v. Ryan* (2013, CA9 Ariz.) 711 F.3d 998.

§ 10:20.1　Prosecutor-initiated *Pitchess* motion

A defendant is entitled to discover from the prosecution the relevant statements of witnesses. Penal Code section 1054.1. The discovery provided in § 1054.1, however, is not exclusive. The reciprocal discovery chapter places no restriction on discovery provided by other express statutory provisions, or as mandated by the Constitution of the United States. Penal Code section 1054, subsection (e). Evidence Code section 1043, is one such express statutory provision. Just as the discovery procedure set forth in § 1043 *et seq.* operates in tandem with the prosecution's duty to disclose favorable information pursuant to the *Brady* rule, so too does the California Evidence Code discovery procedure work in tandem with the prosecution's duty to disclose relevant statements of witnesses under Penal Code section 1054.1, subsection (f). Except with regard to one exception, the prosecutor, as well as the defendant, must comply with the statutory *Pitchess* requirements for disclosure of information contained in confidential peace officer records. There is no reason why the defense—when it has good reason to believe an officer's personnel file contains relevant statements from material witnesses to the charged incident—should be precluded from obtaining the statements because the district attorney may have the right to obtain the same information by filing a motion for discovery pursuant to § 1043. *Rezek v. Superior Court* (2012) 206 Cal. App. 4th 633, 141 Cal. Rptr. 3d 891.

§ 10:24　Prosecutor's duty to search personnel records—triggering events

§ 10:24.2　California state court decisions

Recently the Fourth District held that the defendant is entitled to discover from the prosecution the relevant statements of witnesses. Penal Code section 1054.1. The discovery provided in § 1054.1, however, is not exclusive. The reciprocal discovery chapter places no restriction on discovery provided by other express statutory provisions, or as mandated by the Constitution of the United States. Penal Code section 1054, subsection (e). Evidence Code section 1043, is one such express statutory provision. Just as the discovery procedure set forth in § 1043 *et seq.* operates in tandem with the prosecution's duty to disclose favorable information pursuant to the *Brady* rule, so too does the California Evidence Code discovery procedure work in tandem with the prosecution's duty to disclose relevant statements of witnesses under Penal Code section 1054.1, subection (f). Except with regard to one exception, the prosecutor, as well as the defendant, must comply with the statutory *Pitchess* requirements for disclosure of information contained in confidential peace officer records. There is no reason why the defense—when it has good reason to believe an officer's personnel file contains relevant statements from material witnesses to the charged incident—should be precluded from obtaining the statements because the district attorney may have the right to obtain the same information by filing a motion for discovery pursuant to § 1043. *Rezek v. Superior Court* (2012) 206 Cal. App. 4th 633, 141 Cal. Rptr. 3d 891.

§ 10:26   Required disclosures—kinds of *Brady* evidence

Whether evidence is admissible has no bearing on the prosecution's duty to disclose the evidence to the defense under *Brady*. *Mills v. Cal. Dep't of Corr.* (S.D. Cal. Mar. 5, 2012) 2012 U.S. Dist. LEXIS 28887. The government only has a *Brady* obligation to disclose exculpatory information in its "possession." *United States v. Venegas-Reynoso* (May 17, 2013, CA9 Ariz.) 2013 U.S. App. LEXIS 9954. This includes all evidence in the possession of the "prosecution team."

PART IV.   APPELLATE REVIEW OF *PITCHESS* MOTION ORDERS

§ 10:34   Appellate review of order denying *Pitchess* motion—standard of review

The remedy for an erroneous denial of a *Pitchess* motion is not an outright reversal. Instead, "a defendant who has established that the trial court erred in denying *Pitchess* discovery must also demonstrate a reasonable probability of a different outcome had the evidence been disclosed." *People v. Gaines* (2009) 46 Cal.4th 172, 182, 92 Cal.Rptr.3d 627, 205 P.3d 1074. This "reasonable probability of a different result" standard is the same one that the courts have applied generally to determinations of prejudice resulting from improper suppression of exculpatory evidence in violation of *Brady*. *People v. Gaines, supra*, 46 Cal.4th at 183. Trial courts are as well-equipped to determine the prejudicial effect of failing to disclose evidence tending to impeach an officer from confidential personnel files as they are equipped to determine the prejudicial effect of failing to disclose evidence tending to impeach the officer from other sources. 46 Cal.4th at 184.

An appellate court reviews the denial of a *Pitchess* motion for abuse of discretion. When a trial court finds a defendant has shown good cause for discovery of peace officer personnel information, the custodian of records is obligated to bring to the trial court all potentially relevant documents to permit the trial court to examine them for itself. A custodian need not produce any documents clearly irrelevant to the defendant's *Pitchess* request; however, if a custodian is uncertain whether a document is relevant, the custodian should present it to the trial court. Such practice is consistent with the premise of Evidence Code sections 1043 and 1045, that the locus of decision-making is to be the trial court, not the prosecution or the custodian of records. The custodian must also be prepared to state during the in-camera review and for the record what documents or category of documents the custodian did not produce and why. A court reporter should document the custodian's statements and any questions from the trial court regarding the completeness of the record. A trial court is not permitted to abdicate to a custodian its responsibility to examine the produced documents and assess the discoverability of the information contained in them. To the contrary, it is the trial court's active involvement in the *Pitchess* process that allows the process to work as intended. Both *Pitchess* and the statutory scheme codifying *Pitchess* require the intervention of a neutral trial judge, who examines the personnel records in camera, away from the eyes of either party, and orders disclosed to the defendant only those records that are found both relevant and otherwise in compliance with statutory limitations. In this manner, the Legislature has attempted to protect the defendant's right to a fair trial and the officer's interest in privacy to the fullest extent possible. *Sisson v. Superior Court* (2013) 216 Cal. App. 4th 24, 156 Cal. Rptr. 3d 533.

CHAPTER 11

LOST, DESTROYED, AND UNCOLLECTED EVIDENCE

PART I. PROSECUTION'S DUTY TO PRESERVE EVIDENCE

§ 11:2 Material evidence rule of *California v. Trombetta*

A party's destruction of evidence need not be in "bad faith" to warrant the imposition of evidentiary sanctions. Sanctions may be imposed on a party that merely had notice that the destroyed evidence was potentially relevant to litigation. Motive or degree of fault in destroying the evidence, however, should be considered in choosing the appropriate sanction. *In re Hitachi TV Optical Block Cases* (S.D. Cal. Aug. 12, 2011) 2011 U.S. Dist. LEXIS 90882.

The California Supreme Court held, most recently, that to establish a violation of a defendant's rights under *Trombetta*, it must be shown both that evidence with an exculpatory value apparent on its face was destroyed and that the defendant could not obtain comparable evidence by any other available means. *People v. Thomas* (2012) 54 Cal. 4th 908, 144 Cal. Rptr. 3d 366, 281 P.3d 361.

The determination whether the loss or destruction of allegedly material exculpatory evidence by the prosecution constitutes a due process violation within the meaning of *California v. Trombetta* (1984) 467 U.S. 479, 104 S.Ct. 2528, 81 L.Ed.2d 413, focuses upon the "state of mind of police or prosecutors at the time the evidence is lost or destroyed." *Richter v. Hickman* (2008, CA9 CA) 521 F.3d 1222, 1235.

In *Richter v. Hickman*, two defendants convicted of murder, attempted murder, and other crimes and sentenced to life in prison without the possibility of parole, filed a federal habeas petition in which they contended that the prosecution had destroyed or lost evidence that would have supported their trial defense. The evidence was a piece of the floorboard in the home of the victim of the attempted murder that contained what appeared to be a bullet hole. A prosecution investigator attempted to cut the floorboard out of the floor, but the piece with the hole in it fell into the crawlspace under the home. The investigator believed that the crawlspace was inaccessible and did not recover the piece of floorboard.

After the trial had been concluded, the father of defendant Richter managed to retrieve the piece of the floorboard. The piece of flooring supported the defense contention that the attempted murder victim had fired a.380 caliber weapon at the defendants on the night of the crimes, and would have contradicted the attempted murder victim's testimony that he had created the hole at an earlier date when he accidentally fired a.22 caliber handgun in his home.

At the time of apparent loss of the floorboard into the crawlspace under the victim's home, the police investigators did not know the defense contention that the victim had fired at them. Thus, the investigator and the prosecutor "did not believe that the floorboard would be exculpatory evidence at the time that it fell into the crawl space beneath the house." 521 F.3d at 1235. The district court denied the defendants' petitions for writs of habeas corpus, and the defendants appealed the denials to the Court of Appeals.

In rejecting the defendant's contention that the loss of the floorboard violated the defendant's right to due process, the Ninth Circuit Court of Appeals concluded that the police and prosecutor did not believe that the evidence had exculpatory value when it was lost. The Court concluded that the standard of *California v. Trombetta* does not change if the evidence is later recovered and determined to have exculpatory value. The Court stated:

"The Supreme Court did not approve a constitutional standard where acceptable management of evidence by law enforcement could retroactively be found unconstitutional if, after trial and conviction, a defendant shows that the evidence would have been exculpatory." 521 F.3d at 1235.

In *United States v. Ossai* (2007, CA1 NH) 485 F.3d 25, the police examined the surveillance tape of a fast food restaurant where a robbery had occurred shortly before. The police and the restaurant manager determined that the manager had forgotten to load a new tape in the camera, and the tape stopped recording some seven hours prior to the robbery. Because the tape was not operating at any time close to the time of the robbery, there was no videotape recording of the robbery, and the police did not take the tape into evidence.

The defendant's motion to dismiss the charges based on the government's claimed loss or destruction of the video surveillance tape was denied, and the defendant was convicted of robbery and conspiracy to commit robbery. On appeal the defendant renewed his argument that the failure to seize the tape from the surveillance camera violated his right to due process of law. However, the defendant did not argue that the missing tape was exculpatory in the sense that it would have established that someone else had committed the robbery. Rather, the defendant contended that the loss of the tape prevented him from establishing that one of the employees of the business who was named as a robbery victim had actually conspired with him, and that the employee's access to the camera could have enabled the employee to stop or rewind the tape in order to prevent it from recording the robbery.

The First Circuit Court of Appeals rejected the defendant's argument for a number of reasons. One of the reasons on which the Court relied was the fact that the police had no reason to know of the defense theory regarding the manner in which the robbery occurred at the time they allowed the tape to be retained by the business and subsequently re-used. The Court stated:

"[W]hile the defense subsequently developed the theory that [the victim-employee] was complicit in the offense, Ossai cannot demonstrate that the police lost or destroyed the tape at a time when they reasonably would have foreseen its relevance to the defense theory. To assume such prescience on the part of the police officers would necessitate that they had reason to suspect that [the victim-employee] was a coconspirator in the fake robbery." 485 F.3d at 30.

Thus, unless the evidence has an apparent exculpatory value *at the time the evidence is lost or destroyed*, the loss or destruction of that evidence by the police or the prosecution does not constitute a violation of the defendant's due process rights.

Where evidence that has been lost was "far from clearly exculpatory," and it is "possible that it would have further incriminated [the defendant]," and where evidence comparable to the lost evidence was available, the loss of that evidence does not constitute a due-process violation. *United States v. Drake* (2008, CA9 HI) 543 F.3d 1080, 1090. In *United States v. Drake*, *supra*, the Ninth Circuit Court of Appeals rejected a defendant's claim that the loss of a digital surveillance video of a robbery of a store violated his right to a fair trial. The Court of Appeal concluded that the digital recording of the robbery was "far from clearly exculpatory," could have possibly further incriminated the defendant, and fourteen still images of the robbery had been preserved.

In *United States v. Kimoto* (2009, CA7 IL) 588 F.3d 464, the defendant, the president of a telemarketing firm, was convicted of conspiracy, mail fraud, and wire fraud based upon evidence that the defendant had defrauded consumers with poor credit histories by charging processing fees by debit transfer for the issuance of credit cards.

On appeal the defendant argued that the government violated his right to due process by losing or destroying hundreds of thousands of customer service complaints seized by government investigators from a company to which the defendant's firm outsourced its business. The defendant claimed that these records would have helped him defend against the charges by supporting his theory that the great majority of complaints received by the outsourced company were not complaints from customers who claimed that they were misled into believing that they would receive a credit card.

The government provided to the defendant more than 6,000 records, of which only 22 identified that a caller to the company had complained that the caller believed that the product was a credit card. The defendant claimed that if he had complete access to the database of consumer contacts, his argument would have been made with considerably more force. 588 F.3d at 490.

The Court of Appeals rejected the defendant's argument. The district court had found that the defendant did not establish that the government destroyed or lost the documents, and the remaining documents constituted comparable evidence to that which the defendant claimed the government had lost or destroyed. The fact that the entire database of documents might have enabled the defendant to make his argument with more force did not constitute a denial of due process. 588 F.3d at 490–491.

Where the defendant does not know of any potentially exculpatory evidence that was destroyed by the government, the destroyed evidence "should be considered 'potentially useful evidence' rather than 'material exculpatory evidence.' " *United States v. McNealy* (2010, CA5 MS) 625 F.3d 858, 869. The destruction of potentially useful evidence is analyzed under the bad-faith standard of *Arizona v. Youngblood* (1988) 488 U.S. 51, 109 S.Ct. 333, 102 L.Ed.2d 281, not under the "material exculpatory evidence" standard of *California v. Trombetta* (1984) 467 U.S. 479, 104 S.Ct. 2528, 81 L.Ed.2d 413. A small possibility that further analysis of government evidence would have produced evidence favorable to the defendant is not sufficient to establish that destroyed evidence was "material exculpatory evidence." *United States v. Webster* (2010, CA8 IA) 625 F.3d 439, 448.

§ 11:2.1   Copying evidence as preserving that evidence

Evidence that is in electronic form may be copied into a different electronic form without destroying that evidence within the meaning of *California v. Trombetta* (1984) 467 U.S. 479, 104 S.Ct. 2528, 81 L.Ed.2d 413.

In *United States v. Lanzon* (2011, CA11 FL) 639 F.3d 1293, the defendant was convicted of attempting to persuade, entice, or coerce a minor to engage in sexual activity by conducting sexually explicit online conversations in a chat room with a man he thought was the boyfriend of a mother of a 14-year-old girl. The man was actually a police officer, and the defendant was arrested when he met the officer at an arranged location.

The officer saved his online conversations with the defendant using a standard method he had learned at the police department—by copying the instant messages into a Word document, which he then saved on a floppy disc. The instant messages were then printed in hard copy form as transcripts, which the officer compared to the actual instant message chat screens to ensure that they exactly matched and that he had accurately recorded the conversations in their entirety. The officer did not save the instant messages to his computer's hard drive in order to conserve computer memory.

In the trial court the defendant moved to exclude the transcripts, arguing that because the officer had not saved the instant messages directly to his computer's hard drive, the defense could not determine whether the officer had altered the original instant message conversations. The trial court denied the defendant's motion.

On appeal from his conviction the defendant argued that the trial court had erred in declining to exclude the transcripts of the instant messages. The Eleventh Circuit Court of Appeals rejected the defendant's contention, concluding that the defendant did not offer any evidence showing that the transcripts of the instant messages had been edited or altered. 639 F.3d at 1300–1301. The upshot of the decision of the Court of Appeals was that the instant messages had been preserved by copying them into a different electronic format.

§ 11:3   Bad faith rule of *Arizona v. Youngblood*

Under the authority of *Arizona v. Youngblood* (1988) 488 U.S. 51, 109 S.Ct. 333, 102 L.Ed.2d 281, bad-faith destruction or loss of potentially material exculpatory evidence violates a defendant's right to due process of law. The difficulty which courts face when encountering claims by defendants that law enforcement has lost or destroyed potentially material exculpatory evidence is that the task of "divining the import of materials whose contents are unknown and, very often, disputed" is a treacherous one. *United States v. Beckstead* (2007, CA10 UT) 500 F.3d 1154, 1159.

It is, therefore, useful to have some standards for making the determination whether the conduct of law enforcement resulting in loss or destruction of such evidence evidences "bad faith." In *United States v. Beckstead*, the Tenth Circuit Court of Appeals listed five factors that courts should utilize in determining whether the government acted in bad faith in its loss or destruction of potentially material exculpatory evidence. The five factors listed by the Court of Appeals, which the Court had previously explained in *United States v. Bohl* (1994, CA10 OK) 25 F.3d 904, 910–911, are these:

1. Did the government have explicit notice that the defendant believed the evidence was exculpatory?

2. Is the defendant's claim that the evidence is potentially exculpatory a conclusory claim, or is it backed up with objective, independent evidence giving the government reason to believe that the destroyed or lost evidence might lead to exculpatory evidence?

3. Did the government still have the ability to control the disposition of the evidence at the time the defendant indicated that the evidence might be exculpatory?

4. Was the lost or destroyed evidence central to the case?

5. Does the government offer an innocent explanation for its failure to preserve the evidence?

In *United States v. Beckstead*, investigating officers destroyed methamphetamine laboratory components and related chemicals found at two locations, one of which was in the defendant's vehicle. The items were destroyed in compliance with standard police department policy that had been developed to deal with dangers presented by methamphetamine labs and the chemicals associated with those labs. Before destroying these items the officers took samples of the chemicals for testing, photographed the lab pieces, documented the pieces of lab equipment, and dusted the equipment for prints.

The defendant was convicted of various drug offenses and sentenced to 20 years in federal prison. On appeal from his conviction the defendant contended that the destruction of these items constituted bad-faith destruction of potentially material exculpatory evidence. The Court of Appeals rejected the defendant's argument, holding that "destroying the evidence according to 'an established procedure,' as the Government did here, 'precludes a finding of bad faith absent other compelling evidence.' [citation omitted]" 500 F.3d at 1159. The government destroyed the evidence pursuant to an established and routinely followed department policy, and the Court found no evidence that the government had acted in bad faith when it destroyed the lab and its related chemicals.

Bad faith is not established simply because the law enforcement agency made a conscious choice to destroy evidence. The conscious choice must be accompanied by a belief that the evidence had exculpatory value. *United States v. Cody* (2007, CA6 TN) 498 F.3d 582, 589 [law enforcement failure to collect videotapes from surveillance camera at a convenience store near a bank robbery not a due process violation, because the officers did not consider that the surveillance tape had any evidentiary value. Dye-stained money deposited at another bank by the convenience store after the bank robbery was determined to not be associated with the dye-stained bait money from the bank that had been robbed.].

Although such occurrences are hopefully rare, a law enforcement officer will intentionally occasionally destroy evidence knowing that the evidence has exculpatory value. Such actions constitute bad-faith destruction of evidence and result in a due process violation. In *White v. McKinley* (2008, CA8 MO) 514 F.3d 807, an officer who was investigating an alleged sexual molestation of a minor girl developed an intimate relationship with the girl's mother. The subject of the investigation, who was charged and prosecuted, was the girl's adoptive father and the ex-husband of the girl's mother. The officer intentionally failed to preserve the diary of the minor, knowing that the diary contained evidence that could have exculpated the father, because it did not corroborate the molestation allegations.

After the father had been acquitted of the charges, he brought a civil action against the mother and the officer, alleging that the officer's destruction of the child's diary had denied him due process of law. The officer's and the mother's motion for summary judgment, which was based in part on a claim of qualified immunity, was denied by the district court. The officer and the mother filed an interlocutory appeal with the Eighth Circuit Court of Appeals. The Court of Appeals upheld the district court's denial of qualified immunity, stating:

> "[A] reasonable juror could find Richard [the officer] deprived White [the father] of a fair trial in bad faith by deliberately steering the investigation to benefit his love interest, Tina [the mother]. Richard deliberately withheld from prosecutors the full extent of his relationship with Tina and failed to preserve the alleged victim's diary which did not corroborate the molestation allegations. Failing to preserve the diary deprived White of his right to a fair trial, in part, because he could not testify about the diary without waiving his right not to testify. Whether Richard's failure to disclose the full extent of his relationship with Tina and preserve the diary were done in bad faith are disputed factual questions inappropriate for summary judgment." 514 F.3d at 815.

At the trial of the civil action, the jury found that the defendant had violated White's due process rights and assessed damages against the defendant Officer McKinley and the mother. The defendant officer appealed.

The Eighth Circuit Court of Appeals held that "a reasonable jury could have concluded that McKinley's misrepresentation of his relationship with Tina to the prosecutors and failure to preserve the diary was done in bad faith." *White v. McKinley* (2010, CA8 MO) 605 F.3d 525, 532. In what is hopefully the end of this sordid tale, the Court of Appeals upheld the judgment for the plaintiff.

The failure to preserve evidence that would have been only potentially useful to the defendant does not constitute a violation of due process of law unless the officers' destruction or failure to preserve that evidence was in bad faith. *United States v. Hood* (2010, CA10 UT) 615 F.3d 1293, 1299. Even though Justice Stevens concluded in his concurring opinion in *Arizona v. Youngblood* (1988) 488 U.S. 51, 60–61, 109 S.Ct. 333, 102 L.Ed.2d 281, that bad faith should not be an essential element of a due process violation, Justice Stevens' concurring opinion did not express a majority view of the Supreme Court, and has not been followed by at least one circuit Court of Appeals. *See United States v. Hood, supra,* 615 F.3d at 1299–1301.

While a bad faith destruction or failure of preservation of potentially useful evidence is a necessary element of a due process violation, bad faith by itself is not a sufficient basis for a finding of a due process violation.

In *United States v. Ludwig* (2011, CA10 WY) 641 F.3d 1243, Wyoming state troopers recovered illegal drugs from the defendant's vehicle after stopping that vehicle for speeding. Three troopers in separate vehicles participated in the stop and arrest, and each had a video camera which recorded the events. One of the three videos was destroyed. The defendant moved the court for an order dismissing the case against him because of the destroyed video footage. The trial court denied the motion. The defendant entered a conditional guilty plea and appealed the denial of his motion to dismiss. The defendant contended that the officers acted in bad faith in destroying the third video and that he was denied an evidentiary opportunity to prove the officers' bad faith in the trial court.

The Tenth Circuit Court of Appeals rejected the defendant's argument. The Court of Appeals concluded that "[b]ad faith is a necessary but not sufficient element of [the defendant's] *Trombetta* claim. To prevail, Mr. Ludwig must *also and separately* show the videotape in question was irreplaceable." 641 F.3d at 1254 [italics in original]. The defendant argued that even though the two videos recorded by the other troopers recorded the event, those two videos were inaudible. The Court of Appeals rejoined that even though the missing video might have provided missing dialogue, the defendant had yet another means of obtaining evidence comparable to the video that had been destroyed by calling and questioning the officers who had witnessed the event. 641 F.3d at 1254.

Thus, while bad faith in the destruction of evidence is a necessary element of a due process destruction of potentially useful evidence claim, a bad faith destruction does not constitute a due process denial unless the defendant can show that the destroyed evidence was irreplaceable.

The burden of establishing bad faith on the part of the government in destroying or losing evidence rests on the shoulders of the defendant making the bad faith claim. *United States v. Webster* (2010, CA8 IA) 625 F.3d 439, 447.

When the state suppresses or fails to disclose material exculpatory evidence, the good or bad faith of the prosecution is irrelevant: a due process violation occurs whenever such evidence is withheld. However, the United States Supreme Court applies a different test if there is a failure of the state to preserve evidentiary material of which no more can be said than that it could have been subjected to tests, the results of which might have exonerated the defendant. Instead, the failure to preserve this potentially useful evidence does not violate due process unless a criminal defendant can show bad faith on the part of the police. The applicability of the *Youngblood* bad-faith requirement depends on whether the evidence was material exculpatory evidence or simply potentially useful evidence. *United States v. Toro-Barboza* (2012, CA9 Cal.) 673 F.3d 1136.

§ 11:4   California application of *Trombetta-Youngblood* rule

People v. DePriest. In *People v. DePriest* (2007) 42 Cal.4th 1, 43–44, 63 Cal.Rptr.3d 896, 163 P.3d 896, the defendant was charged with and ultimately convicted of capital murder and other crimes that occurred in California. The defendant was arrested in possession of the victim's vehicle in Missouri several days after the murder. The investigating officers traveled to Missouri two weeks after the murder to process the vehicle for evidence. The vehicle was photographed and processed for fingerprints and other forensic evidence. The police then released the vehicle from police custody before it had been examined by anyone acting on the behalf of the defendant. The prosecution disclosed the results of its examination of the vehicle to the defense.

The defendant requested the trial court give several instructions to the jury based upon the defendant's complaint that the police had deprived him of the opportunity to examine the vehicle by releasing it. The trial court declined to give the defense-requested instructions. The defendant was convicted of capital murder and sentenced to death.

On automatic appeal to the California Supreme Court the defendant argued that the police denied him a fair trial by releasing the victim's vehicle before the defense could examine it. In particular, the defendant complained that three fingerprints had been lifted from the vehicle that could not be identified, and he contended that had the defense been given an opportunity to examine the vehicle, further testing might have found fingerprints inculpating the third party that the defendant contended had committed the murder. The defendant also argued that if a further examination of the vehicle had found no blood, hair, or other trace evidence linking him to the murder, the absence of such evidence would have been exculpatory.

The Supreme Court rejected the defendant's argument, stating:

"Defendant stipulated to being in the possession of the murder victim's car in Missouri. The evidence also disclosed that he had tried to disguise and hide the vehicle after attracting the attention of Missouri police . . . most of the fingerprints that [the print technician] found inside the car, and that the killer presumably left there, belonged to defendant . . . neither [the prosecution print technician] nor the defense counterpart, Hensgen, could say that the three unidentified fingerprints found in the driver's compartment necessarily belonged to anyone other than defendant or the victim. Thus, the trial court properly concluded that the car had no discernible value favoring the defense before it disappeared."

The Court then held that there was no evidence of bad faith in the release of the victim's vehicle.

"The record discloses that the prosecution scoured [the victim's] car for trace evidence, and provided the results of that examination to the defense. Defendant has not argued at trial or on appeal that the prosecution failed to conduct necessary tests or performed any testing in a deficient manner, Rather, he claims only that the prosecution should have preserved the car from which forensic test results were obtained. Even assuming negligence on the prosecution's part, no more can be said than that the car could have been subjected to further testing by the defense. Accordingly, no due process violation occurred . . . ." 42 Cal.4th at 42.

- *People v. Cook.* In *People v. Cook* (2007) 40 Cal.4th 1334, 58 Cal.Rptr.3d 340, 157 P.3d 950, a defendant convicted of multiple murders and sentenced to death argued on appeal that the prosecution had destroyed critical pieces of evidence that he could have used in his defense. The defendant identified three such pieces of evidence: (1) a trash bag found in his garage containing items of evidence; (2) gel plates used in testing of stains on a pair of tennis shoes; and (3) a book of pictures of parolees shown to witnesses who identified the defendant's photo.

  The Supreme Court rejected the defendant's arguments, holding that the defendant failed to show that the trash bag actually contained exculpatory evidence or that the officers destroyed the bag in bad faith, that there was no indication that preservation of the gel plates themselves would have added any additional evidence helpful to the defense, and that the defendant offered no evidence of undue suggestiveness in the photo lineup or that there was bad faith involved in its alteration. 40 Cal.4th at 1348–1351.

- *People v. Alexander.* In *People v. Alexander* (2010) 49 Cal.4th 846, 113 Cal.Rptr.3d 190, 235 P.3d 873, a defendant convicted of murder and sentenced to death argued on appeal that the prosecution had failed to preserve an audiotape of an attempted hypnosis session with an eyewitness to the murder, the original composite drawings created by a police sketch artist based on the eyewitness's description of the killer, and swabs used in a blood test on a jacket taken from the defendant's parents' home, and that the trial court erred in declining to dismiss the charges for the loss of this evidence.

The Supreme Court rejected the defendant's argument, finding that "defendant failed to sustain his burden of proving the threshold requirement that the unavailable evidence had any exculpatory value, and therefore the exculpatory value of these items could not have been apparent before they were 'destroyed.' " 49 Cal.4th at 879.

The California Supreme Court held, most recently, that to establish a violation of a defendant's rights under *Trombetta*, it must be shown both that evidence with an exculpatory value apparent on its face was destroyed and that the defendant could not obtain comparable evidence by any other available means. *People v. Thomas* (2012) 54 Cal. 4th 908, 144 Cal. Rptr. 3d 366, 281 P.3d 361.

When the state suppresses or fails to disclose material exculpatory evidence, the good or bad faith of the prosecution is irrelevant: a due process violation occurs whenever such evidence is withheld. However, the United States Supreme Court applies a different test if there is a failure of the state to preserve evidentiary material of which no more can be said than that it could have been subjected to tests, the results of which might have exonerated the defendant. Instead, the failure to preserve this potentially useful evidence does not violate due process unless a criminal defendant can show bad faith on the part of the police. The applicability of the *Youngblood* bad-faith requirement depends on whether the evidence was material exculpatory evidence or simply potentially useful evidence. *United States v. Toro-Barboza* (2012, CA9 Cal.) 673 F.3d 1136.

§ 11:4.1   California application of *Trombetta-Youngblood* rule to penalty phase of capital murder prosecution

The *Trombetta-Youngblood* standards for determining whether law enforcement destruction or loss of allegedly material exculpatory evidence constitutes a violation of a defendant's right to due process of law apply equally to evidence in the penalty phase of a capital murder prosecution.

In *People v. Tafoya* (2007) 42 Cal.4th 147, 64 Cal.Rptr.3d 163, 164 P.3d 590, the defendant was charged with and convicted of two counts of first degree murder and other crimes. At the penalty phase of the trial the prosecution presented evidence in aggravation of the penalty that 15 years prior to his capital murder trial the defendant had raped a woman by force or violence. The defendant had not been convicted of the rape, because the victim had failed to appear to testify at a preliminary examination. The defendant was sentenced to death in his capital murder case.

The defendant contended at trial and on automatic appeal in the California Supreme Court that the prosecutor in the rape case 15 years earlier had failed to preserve evidence in violation of *Youngblood.* In support of this argument the defendant speculated that the police files on the rape case contained information that would have been "potentially useful" to his defense of the rape allegations.

The Court held that the destruction of evidence that is only potentially useful to the defendant is not a due process violation, unless the prosecution acted in bad faith in destroying the evidence. The Court found that the prosecution records of the rape case were destroyed in the normal course of business, and therefore the prosecution did not act in bad faith. The Court concluded: "We agree with the Attorney General that a law enforcement agency cannot be expected to preserve criminal records for possible use at future capital trials as it has no way to foresee which arrestees or suspects will commit capital crimes in the future." 42 Cal.4th at 187.

§ 11:5 Destruction or loss as component of due process violation

When the government destroys evidence before trial, a showing of bad faith is required for dismissal but is not required for a remedial adverse-inference jury instruction. *United States v. Sivilla* (2013, CA9 Cal.) 714 F.3d 1168. In order for destruction of evidence to rise to the level of a constitutional violation, a party must make two showings. First, that the government acted in bad faith, the presence or absence of which turns on the government's knowledge of the apparent exculpatory value of the evidence at the time it was lost or destroyed. Second, that the missing evidence is of such a nature that the defendant would be unable to obtain comparable evidence by other reasonably available means. Another configuration of this test requires the showing of bad faith where the evidence is only potentially useful and not materially exculpatory. For evidence to be materially exculpatory, its exculpatory nature must be apparent. *Id.*

In order for a defendant to be entitled to dismissal of charges for destruction or loss of exculpatory evidence, the defendant must establish that the destruction or loss was the result of governmental conduct. If the defendant does "not establish that the Government destroyed or lost the documents in question," the defendant fails to establish a due process violation from the destruction or loss of evidence. *United States v. Kimoto* (2009, CA7 IL) 588 P.3d 464, 489–490.

It is not sufficient to establish a due process violation that the person or agency which destroyed or lost potentially exculpatory evidence worked as a government employee or was a governmental agency. The "government," for purposes of a due process violation, is a person or entity that is part of the prosecution team.

In *People v. Jacinto* (2010) 49 Cal. 4th 263, 109 Cal.Rptr.3d 610, 231 F.3d 341, the sheriff of Sonoma County investigated a stabbing that had occurred in a restaurant. The defendant was charged with attempted murder and assault with a deadly weapon. One of the witnesses to the stabbing was an illegal alien who was later incarcerated in the county jail on an unrelated domestic violence charge. An investigator hired by the defense interviewed the incarcerated witness and determined that he could give testimony that would be favorable to the defendant. The sheriff's jail staff later released the witness to federal authorities for deportation at the request of the Immigration and Naturalization Service. As a consequence, that witness was not available for the defense to utilize in trial.

The defendant moved to dismiss the charges on the grounds that the deportation deprived him of his rights under the Due Process Clause and the Compulsory Process Clause. The trial court granted the motion and the prosecution appealed. The Court of Appeal reversed the dismissal of the charges, and the defendant petitioned for review in the California Supreme Court.

The California Supreme Court affirmed the order of the Court of Appeal reversing the dismissal of the charges. The Supreme Court concluded that the deportation of the witness was not the result of prosecutorial misconduct. 49 Cal.4th at 270. The Court reasoned that since it was not the prosecutor who caused or facilitated the deportation of the defense witness, the deportation would be chargeable to the prosecution only if the sheriff's jail officials were part of the prosecution team.

The Court concluded that the Sheriff's jail officials were not part of the prosecution team, even though the Sheriff's criminal investigators handled the investigation of the charges against the defendant, and even though those criminal investigators were part of the prosecution team. The Court stated:

> "[F]ormal identity between sheriff's deputies operating and providing protective services in the jail and detectives in the law enforcement division investigating crimes does not automatically render the deputies assigned to the jail members of the prosecution team. Absent some additional showing of affirmative prosecutorial involvement in [the witness's] removal, we cannot hold the prosecutor legally responsible merely because a sheriff's deputy working at the jail was involved." The Supreme Court quoted with approval the words of the Court of Appeal that " '[t]he sheriff's department was no more than the custodian of witness Esparza. In this case, it was not part of the prosecutorial investigative team . . . [and] the action of the sheriff's department or county jail personnel may not be attributed to the prosecution.' " 49 Cal.4th at 270–271.

Even if the originals of important documents have been lost or destroyed, if photographs or copies of those original documents have been preserved, the destruction or loss component of a due process violation is not established. *People v. Alexander* (2010) 49 Cal.4th 846, 878, 113 Cal.Rptr.3d 190, 235 P.3d 873.

§ 11:6 Bad faith and routine administrative destruction of evidence

The routine destruction of evidence by law enforcement authorities in the ordinary course of business does not ordinarily constitute a bad-faith destruction of evidence that can violate a defendant's right to due process of law.

In *People v. Tafoya* (2007) 42 Cal.4th 147, 64 Cal.Rptr.3d 163, 164 P.3d 590, the defendant was charged with and convicted of two counts of first degree murder and other crimes. At the penalty phase of the trial the prosecution presented evidence in aggravation of the penalty that 15 years prior to his capital murder trial the defendant had raped a woman by force or violence. The defendant had not been convicted of the rape, because the victim had failed to appear to testify at a preliminary examination. The defendant was sentenced to death in his capital murder case.

The defendant contended at trial and on automatic appeal in the California Supreme Court that the prosecutor in the rape case 15 years earlier had failed to preserve evidence in violation of *Youngblood*. In support of this argument the defendant speculated that the police files on the rape case contained information that would have been "potentially useful" to his defense of the rape allegations.

The Court held that the destruction of evidence that is only potentially useful to the defendant is not a due process violation, unless the prosecution acted in bad faith in destroying the evidence. The Court found that the prosecution records of the rape case were destroyed in the normal course of business, and therefore the prosecution did not act in bad faith. The Court concluded: "We agree with the Attorney General that a law enforcement agency cannot be expected to preserve criminal records for possible use at future capital trials as it has no way to foresee which arrestees or suspects will commit capital crimes in the future." 42 Cal.4th at 187.

Similarly, in *United States v. Beckstead* (2007, CA10 UT) 500 F.3d 1154, investigating officers destroyed methamphetamine laboratory components and related chemicals found at two locations, one of which was in the defendant's vehicle. The items were destroyed in compliance with standard police department policy that had been developed to deal with dangers presented by methamphetamine labs and the chemicals associated with those labs. Before destroying these items the officers took samples of the chemicals for testing, photographed the lab pieces, documented the pieces of lab equipment, and dusted the equipment for prints.

The defendant was convicted of various drug offenses and sentenced to 20 years in federal prison. On appeal from his conviction the defendant contended that the destruction of these items constituted bad-faith destruction of potentially material exculpatory evidence. The Court of Appeals rejected the defendant's argument, holding that "destroying the evidence according to 'an established procedure,' as the Government did here, 'precludes a finding of bad faith absent other compelling evidence.' [citation omitted]" 500 F.3d at 1159. The government destroyed the evidence pursuant to an established and routinely followed department policy, and the Court found no evidence that the government had acted in bad faith when it destroyed the lab and its related chemicals.

§ 11:8   Bad faith and negligent destruction of evidence

Courts continue to hold that the negligent destruction or loss of evidence by a member of the prosecution does not constitute bad-faith destruction or loss of material exculpatory evidence.

In *Richter v. Hickman* (2008, CA9 CA) 521 F.3d 1222, two defendants convicted of murder, attempted murder, and other crimes and sentenced to life in prison without the possibility of parole filed a federal habeas petition in which they contended that the prosecution had destroyed or lost evidence that would have supported their trial defense. The evidence was a piece of the floorboard in the home of the victim of the attempted murder that contained what appeared to be a bullet hole. A prosecution investigator attempted to cut the floorboard out of the floor, but the piece with the hole in it fell into the crawlspace under the home. The investigator believed that the crawlspace was inaccessible and did not recover the piece of floorboard.

After the trial had been concluded, the father of defendant Richter managed to retrieve the piece of the floorboard. The piece of flooring supported the defense contention that the attempted murder victim had fired a .380 caliber weapon at the defendants on the night of the crimes, and would have contradicted the attempted murder victim's testimony that he had created the hole at an earlier date when he accidentally fired a .22 caliber handgun in his home.

At the time of apparent loss of the floorboard into the crawlspace under the victim's home, the police investigators did not know the defense contention that the victim had fired at them. Thus, the investigator and the prosecutor "did not believe that the floorboard would be exculpatory evidence at the time that it fell into the crawl space beneath the house." 521 F.3d at 1235. The district court denied the defendants' petitions for writs of habeas corpus, and the defendants appealed the denials to the Court of Appeals.

In rejecting the defendant's contention that the loss of the floorboard violated the defendant's right to due process, the Ninth Circuit Court of Appeals concluded that the police and prosecutor did not believe that the evidence had exculpatory value when it was lost. The Court also found no evidence of bad faith by the investigator or the prosecution.

> "[The prosecution investigator] testified that he believed the floor-board to be in an inaccessible location after he cut it out of the floor in Johnson's residence. The prosecution fully disclosed the nature and location of the evidence. At worst, [the prosecution investiga-

tor's] actions could be described as negligent. Appellants were not denied due process of law . . . ." 521 F.3d at 1235–1236.

For additional cases in which California courts and federal courts have held that negligence and even gross negligence by an officer that causes evidence to be lost or destroyed, does not constitute bad faith within the meaning of *Youngblood v. Arizona* (1988) 488 U.S. 51, 109 S.Ct. 333, 102 L.Ed.2d 281, *see People v. Cook* (2007) 40 Cal.4th 1334, 1350–1351, 58 Cal.Rptr.3d 340, 157 P.3d 950; *United States v. Branch* (2008, CA6 KY) 537 F.3d 582, 589; *United States v. Houston* (2008, CA8 NE) 548 F.3d 1151, 1155; *United States v. Laurent* (2010, CA1 NH) 607 F.3d 895, 902; *United States v. McNealy* (2010, CA5 MS) 625 F.3d 858, 869–870 [negligence by and miscommunication between government agents not bad faith]; *United States v. Fletcher* (2011, CA7 IL) 634 F.3d 395, 407–408 [careless and negligent handling of evidence that destroyed possible fingerprints on the evidence not bad faith]; *United States v. Flyer* (2011, CA9 AZ) 633 F.3d 911, 915–916 [negligent mishandling of evidence not bad faith]; and *United States v. Branch* (2008, CA6 KY) 537 F.3d 582, 590 ["Negligence, even gross negligence on the part of the government does not constitute bad faith."].

In *United States v. Webster* (2010, CA8 IA) 625 F.3d 439, the defendant was arrested and charged in state court for drug offenses following a series of controlled purchases of cocaine from the defendant. After his arrest he was later indicted in federal court, and the state court prosecution was dismissed. Thereafter, law enforcement authorities, who believed his prosecution had ended, obtained a court order authorizing destruction of the drugs. The defendant then moved for an order dismissing the federal indictment, arguing that the destruction of the physical evidence denied him due process of law. The district court found that the destruction of the evidence was due to miscommunication among law enforcement officials and denied the motion to dismiss.

The defendant pled guilty and appealed the denial of his motion to dismiss. On appeal the defendant argued that the government's conduct in destroying the evidence was reckless, and that reckless destruction of evidence should be sufficient to justify dismissal of the charges. The Court of Appeals rejected the defendant's argument that the proved governmental conduct was sufficient to constitute a due process violation, and that bad faith destruction was not required to justify a dismissal. The Court found that at most the officers' conduct amounted to negligence. The Court then concluded: "In light of *Youngblood*, we have required a showing of bad faith to sustain a due process claim based on the failure to preserve evidence." 625 F.3d at 447.

In light of *Webster*, it appears that not even a finding of reckless destruction of evidence would be sufficient to constitute a due process violation.

§ 11:9   Bad faith and incompetent destruction of evidence

The destruction or loss of exculpatory evidence that is the result of incompetent actions by a law enforcement officer does not constitute bad faith within the meaning of *Youngblood v. Arizona* (1988) 488 U.S. 51, 109 S.Ct. 333, 102 L.Ed.2d 281. *See United States v. Branch* (2008, CA6 KY) 537 F.3d 582, 590 [officer's bad judgment in recirculating videotape of traffic stop of defendant because the officer thought the tape had no evidentiary value did not constitute bad faith]; *People v. Cook* (2007) 40 Cal. 4th 1334, 1351–1352, 58 Cal.Rptr.3d 340, 157 P.3d 950 [officer's incompetent changing of photographs in photo lineup did not constitute bad faith]; and *United States v. Corsmeier* (2010, CA6 OH) 617 F.3d 417, 420, n.1 ["[T]he district court's determination that the officer whose incompetence led to the destruction of evidence did not act in bad faith is not clearly erroneous."].

§ 11:11   Destruction/loss of evidence and *Brady* rule [*Trombetta-Youngblood* and *Brady* standards compared]

It is not uncommon for counsel and courts alike to describe the loss of potentially exculpatory evidence as if the loss constituted a *Brady* violation. *See, e.g., Lewis v. Horn* (2009, CA3 PA) 581 F.3d 92, 108–109. However, "suppression" of exculpatory evidence as a component of a *Brady* violation is not established by a loss or destruction of potentially exculpatory evidence. While suppression of materially favorable evidence by the government constitutes a *Brady* violation, the failure to preserve potentially favorable evidence does not constitute a due process violation absent evidence of bad faith by the police. *United States v. Williams* (2009, CA8 MO) 577 F.3d 878, 882. Conflating these two separate standards only creates confusion.

§ 11:13   Defense witness deportation

The United States Court of Appeals for the Ninth Circuit has adopted a two-part test to evaluate whether the government's deportation of an alien-witness amounts to a constitutional violation. First, the defendant must show that the government acted in bad faith. There is no violation where the executive has made a good-faith determination that the alien-witness possesses no evidence that might exculpate the defendant. Second, a defendant must demonstrate that deportation of the witness prejudiced his case. To prevail under the prejudice prong, a defendant must at least make a plausible showing that the testimony of the deported witnesses would have been material and favorable to his defense, in ways not merely cumulative to the testimony of available witnesses. That test balances the defendant's right to present his version of events to the jury with the government's interest in enforcing the immigration laws by promptly deporting aliens who possess no material evidence relevant to a criminal trial. *United States v. Leal-Del Carmen* (2012, CA9 Cal.) 697 F.3d 964. When the government does not know what a witness will say, it does not act in bad faith by deporting him. But if the government interviews the witness or has other information suggesting that he could offer exculpatory evidence, the government may not deport him without first giving defense counsel a chance to interview him. The question of bad faith thus turns on what the government knew at the time it deported the witness. The presence or absence of bad faith by the police for purposes of the Due Process Clause must necessarily turn on the police's knowledge of the exculpatory value of the evidence at the time it was lost or destroyed. *Id.*

A due process violation arises when the government deports a potentially favorable witness, thereby denying access to that witness. But United States Supreme Court rulings have significantly narrowed this rule to require a showing that the Government acted in bad faith and that this conduct resulted in prejudice to the defendant's case. Bad faith is relevant to the inquiry in such cases because the denial of access relates to potentially exculpatory evidence, rather than evidence known to be exculpatory. *Fenenbock v. Dir. of Corr. for Cal.* (2012, CA9 Cal.) 692 F.3d 910.

Moreover, the California courts have held that, even when a witness's deportation prior to trial cannot reasonably be avoided, the government must still undertake reasonable and good faith efforts to procure his or her attendance at trial. In other words, the government cannot simply throw up its hands and do nothing when faced with the prospect of one of its witnesses being deported or leaving the country on his or her own accord. Instead, it must undertake reasonable efforts to preserve the defendant's constitutional right to be confronted with the witnesses against him or her. *People v. Roldan* (2012) 205 Cal. App. 4th 969, 141 Cal. Rptr. 3d 88.

Note: *Dring* [*United States v. Dring* (1991, CA9 Cal.) 930 F.2d 687, 693], not *Brady*, applies to access-to-evidence claims based on illegal witness deportation. *United States v. Noriega-Perez* (Feb. 1, 2012, CA9 Cal.) 2012 U.S. App. LEXIS 1918, at *2–*7, citing *United States v. Carreno* (2004, CA9 Cal.) 363 F.3d 883, 890 (citing *United States v. Velarde-Gavarrete* (1992, CA9 Cal.) 975 F.2d 672), vacated and remanded on other grounds, (2005) 543 U.S. 1099, 125 S. Ct. 1000, 160 L. Ed. 2d 1000.

While the deportation of a material defense witness can constitute a due process violation destruction of defense evidence, in order for the deportation of a witness to constitute a due process violation, the prosecution team must play a role in the deportation.

In *People v. Jacinto* (2010) 49 Cal. 4th 263, 109 Cal.Rptr.3d 610, 231 P.3d 341, the sheriff of Sonoma County investigated a stabbing that had occurred in a restaurant. The defendant was charged with attempted murder and assault with a deadly weapon. One of the witnesses to the stabbing was an illegal alien who was later incarcerated in the county jail on an unrelated domestic violence charge. An investigator hired by the defense interviewed the incarcerated witness and determined that he could give testimony that would be favorable to the defendant. The sheriff's jail staff later released the witness to federal authorities for deportation at the request of the Immigration and Naturalization Service. As a consequence, that witness was not available for the defense to utilize in trial.

The defendant moved to dismiss the charges on the grounds that the deportation deprived him of his rights under the Due Process Clause and the Compulsory Process Clause. The trial court granted the motion and the prosecution appealed. The Court of Appeal reversed the dismissal of the charges, and the defendant petitioned for review in the California Supreme Court.

The California Supreme Court affirmed the order of the Court of Appeal reversing the dismissal of the charges. The Supreme Court concluded that the deportation of the witness was not the result of prosecutorial misconduct. 49 Cal.4th at 270. The Court reasoned that since it was not the prosecutor who caused or facilitated the deportation of the defense witness, the deportation would be chargeable to the prosecution only if the sheriff's jail officials were part of the prosecution team.

The Court concluded that the sheriff's jail officials were not part of the prosecution team, even though the sheriff's criminal investigators handled the investigation of the charges against the defendant, and even though those criminal investigators were part of the prosecution team. The Court stated:

> "[F]ormal identity between sheriff's deputies operating and providing protective services in the jail and detectives in the law enforcement division investigating crimes does not automatically render the deputies assigned to the jail members of the prosecution team. Absent some additional showing of affirmative prosecutorial involvement in [the witness's] removal, we cannot hold the prosecutor legally responsible merely because a sheriff's deputy working at the jail was involved."

The Supreme Court quoted with approval the words of the Court of Appeal that " '[t]he sheriff's department was no more than the custodian of witness Esparza. In this case, it was not part of the prosecutorial investigative team . . . [and] the action of the sheriff's department or county jail personnel may not be attributed to the prosecution.' " 49 Cal.4th at 270–271.

§ 11:13.2   Repatriation of defense witnesses

To warrant an instruction that the jury could infer from the government's destruction of certain personal property that it would have yielded evidence harmful to the government, a criminal defendant must establish (1) that the evidence was destroyed in bad faith, and (2) that he was prejudiced by its destruction. *United States v. Romo-Chavez* (2012, CA9 Ariz.) 681 F.3d 955.

PART II.   PROSECUTION'S DUTY TO COLLECT EVIDENCE

§ 11:23   Failure to investigate or collect evidence—generally

In *McSherry v. City of Long Beach* (2009, CA9 CA) 560 F.3d 1125, the plaintiff had been convicted of kidnapping and forcible rape and was later exonerated by DNA evidence and a confession by the actual perpetrator. The plaintiff then filed a civil action against the city and the investigating officers alleging, *inter alia*, that the officers had ignored three items of exculpatory evidence in their investigation of the crime: (1) the arrest of the actual perpetrator in a nearby county for a similar crime one week after the crime for which the plaintiff was convicted; (2) differences between the plaintiff and witnesses' descriptions of the perpetrator; and (3) possible improper influences affecting witness identifications of the plaintiff from a newspaper photograph of the plaintiff.

The district court granted summary judgment to the defendants, and the plaintiff appealed. The Ninth Circuit Court of Appeals reversed the grant of summary judgment and remanded the case for trial. In reaching this decision, the Court of Appeals rejected the plaintiff's "failure to collect exculpatory evidence" argument. The Court found that the plaintiff had presented no evidence that the officers knew of the perpetrator's arrest in the nearby county, there was no bad faith in the officers' reliance on the photo lineup identifications of the plaintiff, and the plaintiff did not present any evidence that the victim had ever seen the newspaper photograph of the plaintiff or that she based her identification on that newspaper photograph. 560 F.3d at 1131–1132.

Because " '[a] police officer's failure to preserve or collect potential exculpatory evidence does not violate the Due Process Clause unless the officer acted in bad faith' [citation omitted]," McSherry's failure to establish bad faith by the officers was fatal to his Due Process Clause claim. 560 F.3d at 1131.

§ 11:25   Failure to test evidence

In *United States v. Jordan* (2010, CA10 CO) 594 F.3d 1265, a defendant incarcerated in a federal prison was charged with and convicted of murdering another inmate with a knife. The knife was recovered and blood was found on the knife. Numerous witnesses saw the defendant stab the victim, and these eyewitnesses testified at trial. The defendant testified at trial that another inmate had stabbed the victim and then handed the knife to him. The defendant admitted throwing the knife away in the prison yard.

The prosecution did not subject the knife to DNA tests. After his conviction the defendant moved for an order under the Innocence Protection Act of 2005 that the knife, a cloth found wrapped around the knife, and a bloody glove found next to the knife be subjected to DNA testing. The federal district court denied the defendant's motion and the defendant appealed the denial.

The Tenth Circuit Court of Appeals affirmed the district court's order denying DNA blood testing. The Court concluded that even if DNA testing were to identify the DNA of a third person on the knife, cloth, and glove, the strength of the government's case would not be undermined in any meaningful way. The presence of a third person's DNA on these items would not tend to prove that the defendant had not handled these items or that he had not used them to stab the victim. Thus, the failure of the government to test these items for the third person's DNA was not error.

For an additional discussion of DNA testing under the authority of the Innocence Protection Act, see Section 2:29.3.3.1 in this supplement.

§ 11:26   Failure to make record of witness interviews

The prosecution does not have a constitutional duty to take notes while interviewing witnesses.

In *United States v. Rodriguez* (2007, CA2 NY) 496 F.3d 221, the defendant was convicted of drug dealing in a multi-defendant trial. The prosecution's case rested upon the testimony of two cooperating witnesses. At trial one of these witnesses testified that the witness had lied "about everything" in her initial interviews with investigators. After the prosecution stated that no notes had been made of the false statements, the trial court declined to order the prosecution to disclose the oral false statements that had been made by the witness. The trial court did not explain its reason for denying the defense request for disclosure.

The defendant contended on appeal that by failing to take notes during the interviews with the cooperating witnesses the government violated his statutory and constitutional rights. The defendant equated the government's conduct with the destruction of evidence. The Second Circuit Court of Appeals rejected the defendant's argument. The Court stated:

> "We reject Rodriguez's contention that *Brady* or the Confrontation Clause requires the Government to take notes during witness interviews . . . [*Brady* and *Giglio*] have not been generally construed to require the Government to make written notes for the defendant's benefit. This is in part because the Government's representative may have no way of knowing, upon hearing a witness's statement, that the statement is inconsistent with what the witness will say at a later time . . . *Brady, Giglio*, and the Confrontation Clause have not been construed to impose this obligation, and we decline to extend them in this manner." 496 F.3d at 224–225.

In *Koubriti v. Convertino* (2010, CA6 MI) 593 F.3d 459, a defendant charged with the commission of several federal offenses, including conspiracy to provide material support or resources to terrorists, was convicted of these offenses. Then Assistant United States Attorney Richard Convertino was the prosecutor in Mr. Koubriti's prosecution.

Following his conviction, it was discovered that the government had failed to disclose numerous items of materially favorable evidence. The district court dismissed the terrorism charge without prejudice and granted a new trial on another count. A grand jury then indicted Convertino for violating several federal statutes arising out of his participation in the withholding of evidence that was materially favorable to Koubriti. That prosecution went to trial, and Convertino was acquitted of all charges.

Koubriti, who was free on bond awaiting trial on the fraud charge for which he had been granted a new trial, then filed a civil action against Convertino. In his civil action Koubriti alleged that Convertino, while acting in an investigative role, withheld exculpatory evidence or fabricated evidence against Koubriti. Koubriti alleged that Convertino had directed agents to make no notes or reports of numerous interviews they conducted with Koubriti's former housemate.

Convertino filed a motion to dismiss, arguing, *inter alia*, that he had absolute immunity from civil action arising out of his role as the prosecutor in Koubriti's criminal prosecution. The trial court denied the motion to dismiss as to alleged acts of Convertino that were investigatory in nature, as opposed to prosecutorial in nature. Convertino appealed the denial of his motion to dismiss to the Sixth Circuit Court of Appeals.

The Court of Appeals reversed the district court's denial of the motion to dismiss. The Court held that Convertino enjoyed absolute immunity from civil action for an alleged *Brady* violation. In reaching this decision the Court of Appeals concluded that "it would indeed go well beyond the reasonable limits of the *Brady* non-disclosure doctrine to say that it also requires memorialization of interviews." 593 F.3d at 471.

In an effort to avoid Convertino's absolute immunity, Koubriti argued that Convertino's conduct amounted to a general due process of law violation. The Court of Appeals noted, but declined to reach, the question whether Convertino's conduct amounted to a more general due process violation, because that question had not been briefed in the district court or in the Court of Appeals. 593 F.3d at 471. However, the Court observed that "cases analyzing sets of facts more similar to the instant case than those in *Brady* have suggested that [Convertino's directive to not make any record of interviews] is not a constitutional violation." 593 F.3d at 471.

PART III. SPOILATION OF EVIDENCE

§ 11:30   Spoilation of evidence doctrine

A doctrine developed in civil cases called the "spoilation doctrine" might apply to criminal cases. The spoilation doctrine appears to be independent from traditional concepts of unconstitutional loss or destruction of evidence as articulated in *California v. Trombetta* (1984) 467 U.S. 479, 104 S.Ct. 2528, 81 L.Ed.2d 413, and *Arizona v. Youngblood* (1988) 488 U.S. 51, 109

S.Ct. 333, 102 L.Ed.2d 281, because the spoilation doctrine cases do not cite *Trombetta* or *Youngblood* and do not appear to require state action as the cause of evidence loss or destruction.

Spoilation " 'is the destruction or significant alteration of evidence, or failure to preserve property for another's use as evidence in pending or reasonably foreseeable litigation.' [citations omitted]." *In re Terrorist Bombings of U.S. Embassies in East Africa v. Odeh* (2008, CA2 NY) 552 F.3d 93, 148.

In *In re Terrorist Bombings, supra*, the defendants were convicted of offenses arising from their involvement in an international conspiracy organized through the Al Qaeda terrorist network to kill American citizens and destroy American facilities around the world. On appeal one of the defendants argued that the government had failed to preserve tape recordings made by governmental intelligence agents, thereby depriving him of the opportunity to use those tape recordings in his defense at trial. The defendant claimed that the government's conduct constituted "spoilation of evidence."

The Second Circuit Court of Appeals rejected the defendant's argument. The Court found that the tape recordings had been made for intelligence purposes that were unconnected to any criminal investigation or prosecution; that the agents who made the recordings did not know that the recordings could be used in a criminal investigation; and therefore, the intelligence agents who destroyed the tape recordings "had no obligation to preserve the recordings at the time that they were destroyed." 552 F.3d at 148.

Moreover, the Court of Appeals concluded, there was no evidence that the tape recordings were intentionally destroyed, because "the government was itself disadvantaged by the destruction of the tapes." 552 F.3d at 148. Accordingly, the Court of Appeals held that the district court properly refused to impose sanctions on the prosecution for spoilation. 552 F.3d at 149.

In *United States v. Laurent* (2010, CA1 NH) 607 F.3d 895, local police erased prior to trial a videotape of an undercover officer's first drug buy from the defendant as a routine action pursuant to police department standard practice. The defendant was convicted of multiple counts of distributing and possession with intent to distribute crack cocaine. He appealed. The Court of Appeals held that the erasure of the tape did not constitute a due process violation, because the videotape was only potentially useful evidence, and there was no evidence that the police destruction of the video was anything other than a routine action—that it constituted a bad faith destruction. 607 F.3d at 900.

The defendant had requested that the trial court give a "spoilation" instruction. The district court declined to give the instruction, and the defendant argued on appeal that the trial court thereby erred. The Court of Appeals rejected the defendant's claim of error. The Court observed that a spoilation instruction, which allows an adverse inference, "is commonly appropriate in both civil and criminal cases where there is evidence from which a reasonable jury might conclude that evidence favorable to one side was destroyed by the other. [citation omitted] The burden is upon the party seeking the instruction to establish such evidence." 607 F.3d at 902.

The Court noted that a spoilation instruction "makes sense only where the evidence permits a finding of bad faith destruction; ordinarily, *negligent* destruction would not support the logical inference that the evidence was favorable to the defendant." 607 F.3d at 902. The Court concluded that "no adverse-inference instruction would make sense here. The routine erasure of a video surveillance . . . after much time had elapsed without an arrest creates no inference that the tape was destroyed because it contained evidence favorable to the defendant." 607 F.3d at 903.

The destruction of evidence need not be in bad faith to warrant the imposition of an adverse inference. California district courts have adopted the three-part adverse inference test from the United States Court of Appeals for the Second Circuit requiring: (1) the party having control over the evidence had an obligation to preserve it; (2) the records were destroyed with a culpable state of mind; and (3) the destroyed evidence was relevant to the party's claim or defense. Even if these three requirements are met, the court must exercise its discretion to determine if an adverse inference is appropriate. *In re Hitachi TV Optical Block Cases* (S.D. Cal. Aug. 12, 2011) 2011 U.S. Dist. LEXIS 90882.

Whether a spoilation claim can be raised in a criminal case is not universally accepted. In *United States v. Hood* (2010, CA10 UT) 615 F.3d 1293, a defendant convicted of possession of methamphetamine with intent to distribute it argued on appeal that the district court erred in failing to sanction the government by giving a spoilation instruction, because the government's destruction of evidence prevented him from proving that he possessed less than 50 grams of the drug. The Court of Appeals declined to find plain error in the district court's refusal to give such an instruction, saying that the defendant "has cited to no case applying this civil discovery doctrine to the criminal context." 615 F.3d at 1301.

CHAPTER 12

APPELLATE REVIEW OF DISCOVERY ORDER

§ 12:1 Appellate review—in general

The court reviews an order compelling discovery for abuse of discretion.

Ibarra v. Superior Court (2013) 217 Cal. App. 4th 695, 158 Cal. Rptr. 3d 751.

There is no statutory provision for appeal from an order compelling compliance with a discovery order. A party may seek extraordinary writ relief to prevent discovery of information protected by the right of privacy. An attempt to appeal from a non-appealable order does not give an appellate court jurisdiction or authority to review it. Consequently, it is the duty of the appellate court to dismiss an appeal from an order that is not appealable. *Doe v. United States Swimming, Inc.* (2011) 200 Cal. App. 4th 1424, 133 Cal. Rptr. 3d 465.

§ 12:2   Order compelling discovery—prosecution review

§ 12:2.1   Order compelling discovery—third party review

When a trial court enters a discovery order compelling a third party to a criminal prosecution to provide discovery, the third party may challenge that order by filing a petition for a writ of mandate/prohibition in the Court of Appeal. *City of Tulare v. Superior Court* (2008) 169 Cal.App.4th 373, 86 Cal.Rptr.3d 707. Writ review is appropriate to challenge a discovery order that might undermine a privilege or a right of privacy, " 'because appellate remedies are not adequate to remedy the erroneous disclosure of information.' [citation omitted]." 169 Cal.App.4th at 380. Moreover, " 'writ review of discovery orders is appropriate to establish general guidelines for the lower courts.' [citation omitted]." 169 Cal.App.4th at 380.

§ 12:6   Order excluding prosecution witness and evidence

Where an order of a trial court that excludes a prosecution witness and other prosecution evidence exceeds the statutory authority of the court, that order is an act in excess of subject matter jurisdiction of the court. *People v. Superior Court (Mitchell)* (2010) 184 Cal.App.4th 451, 458, 109 Cal.Rptr.3d 207. An act that exceeds statutory authority qualifies for writ review by an appellate court. 184 Cal.App.4th at 458.

In *People v. Superior Court (Mitchell)*, the trial court excluded prosecution witnesses and evidence because of a prosecution discovery violation regarding that evidence. The prosecution then sought writ relief in the Court of Appeal. The defendant argued that an order excluding prosecution witnesses and evidence may not be challenged by a writ petition.

The Court of Appeal rejected the defendant's argument, holding that writ relief in such a scenario is available to the prosecution, because the trial court's exclusion order exceeded its statutory jurisdiction, and hence constituted an act in excess of the court's subject-matter jurisdiction. The Criminal Discovery Statute provides that a trial court may prohibit the testimony of a witness only if " 'all other sanctions have been exhausted.' [citation omitted]" *People v. Superior Court (Mitchell)* (2010) 184 Cal.App.4th 451, 459, 109 Cal.Rptr.3d 207. Thus, where a trial court precludes the testimony of a witness as a sanction for a discovery violation, without first considering or exhausting other sanctions, the court exceeds its jurisdiction. 184 Cal.App.4th at 459.

The Court of Appeal concluded that "[a]n act that exceeds a grant of statutory power qualifies . . . for writ review." 184 Cal.App.4th at 458.

INDEX CORRECTIONS TO MAIN VOLUME

[Editor's Note: Please note the following corrections to the main volume Index]

A

ADDRESS DISCLOSURE

[Under "jurors" entry, delete 9.17.2 9:17.2 at end of reference]

ADMONITION TO JURY

[Under "sanction" for discovery violation entry, change reference to read § 5:16.3]

C

"CLEAN HANDS"

[Under "precondition to sanctions" entry, change reference to read § 5:16.5]

CONTEMPT

[Under "proceedings as discovery motion" entry, change reference to read § 5:17.8–5:17.8.2]

D

DISCLOSURE

[Under "good cause requirement" entry, change reference to read § 3:22–3:22.2.6]

DUE PROCESS

[Under "basis for prosecution's *Brady* disclosure duty" entry, delete duplicate reference to § 6:4]

E

EVIDENCE

[Under "exclusion, defendant's noncompliance" entry, change reference to read § 5:17.11–5:17.11.4]

[Under "exclusion, prosecution's noncompliance" entry, change reference to read § 5:17.10–5:17.10.3]

EXCLUSION OF EVIDENCE

[Under "sanction for defense noncompliance" entry, change reference to read § 5:17.11–5:17.12]

[Under "sanction for prosecution noncompliance" entry, change reference to read § 5:17.10–5:17.10.3]

J

JURY

[Under "admonition as discovery sanction" entry, change reference to read § 5.17.7]

[Under "instruction as discovery sanction" entry, change reference to read § 5:17.5–5:17.5.3]

K

KNOWLEDGE

[Under "investigating law enforcement agency" entry, delete 3:43 at end of reference]

M

MONETARY SANCTIONS

[Under "court's power to impose for discovery violation" entry, change reference to read § 5:17.16]

P

PRECONDITIONS

[Under "sanctions, 'clean hands' " entry, change reference to read § 5:16.5]

[Under "sanctions, exhaustion of other sanctions" entry, change reference to read § 5:16.6]

[Under "sanctions, informal request/noncompliance" entry, change reference to read § 5:16.1]

[Under "sanctions, motion/request for sanctions" entry, change reference to read § 5:16.2]

PRELIMINARY EXAMINATIONS

[Under "magistrate's power to order discovery" entry, delete duplicate reference to § 2:25]

PROTECTIVE ORDERS

[Under "regulating use of discovered materials" entry, change reference to read § 3:22–3:22.2.6]

R

REBUTTAL WITNESS

[Under "prosecution's disclosure duty" entry, delete duplicate reference to § 6:3]

REQUEST

[Under "sanctions, motion for" entry, change reference to read § 5:16.2]

S

SANCTIONS

[Under "preconditions to, 'clean hands' " entry, change reference to read § 5:16.5]

[Under "preconditions to, exhaustion of other sanctions" entry, change reference to read § 5:16.6]

[Under "preconditions to, formal discovery order" entry, change reference to read § 5:16.3]

[Under "preconditions to, motion/request for sanctions" entry, change reference to read § 5:16.2]

[Under "types of, altering order of trial" entry, change reference to read § 5:17.4]

[Under "types of, comment and argument by counsel" entry, change reference to read § 5:17.6]

[Under "types of, contempt" entry, change reference to read § 5:17.8–5:17.8.2]

[Under "types of, continuance" entry, change reference to § 5:16.2 to read § 5:17.2]

[Under "types of, dismissal of charges/allegations" entry, change reference to § 5:16.14–5:16.14.3 to read § 5:17.14–:17.14.3]

[Under "types of, exclusion of defense evidence" entry, change reference to read § 5:17.11–5:17.13]

[Under "types of, exclusion of prosecution evidence" entry, change reference to read § 5:17.10–5:17.10.3]

[Under "types of, immediate disclosure order" entry, change reference to read § 5:17.1]

[Under "types of, jury admonition" entry, change reference to read § 5:17.7]

[Under "types of, jury advice and instruction" entry, change reference to read § 5:17.5–5:17.5.3]

[Under "types of, State Bar report" entry, change reference to read § 5:17.9]

[Under "types of, striking testimony" entry, change reference to read § 5:17.13]

[Under "types of, sur-rebuttal evidence exclusion" entry, change reference to read § 5:17.12]

STATE BAR REPORT

[Under "discovery violation sanction" entry, change reference to read § 5:17.9]

SUR-REBUTTAL

[Under "as exclusion sanction" entry, change reference to read § 5:17.12]

INDEX

D